D1422716

A HISTORY OF BRITAIN THROUGH BOOKS

1900-1964

CHRISTOPHER TUGENDHAT

First published in 2019 by whitefox

ISBN 978-1-912892-34-1

Also available as an ebook
ISBN 978-1-912892-35-8

Typeset by seagulls.net
Cover design by Kid-ethic
Project management by whitefox
Printed and bound by Clays

For my grandchildren, Lily, Eva,
Christopher, Rachel and Isobel

Contents

Sex and Relationships

Race and Immigration

Diverse Perspectives

Introduction

This book has two wellsprings. The first is my collection of books by British authors, written or published between 1900 and the early 1960s, that I believe shows what it was like to live in this country during those years. The second is Neil MacGregor's great work *A History of the World in 100 Objects* in which he examines previous civilizations through the prism of objects that have come down to us from the past. This has inspired me to use my collection as a prism through which to convey the British experience during the first two-thirds of the twentieth century.

It was a tumultuous period that began with the British empire at the plenitude of its power and ended with the empire's dissolution and the reversal of a population flow that had been in place for some two centuries. Instead of people going out from these islands to settle overseas, people from the former colonies began to come here. Because of the two world wars, the build-up to them and the Cold War the nation was, for much of the time, facing an existential threat. It witnessed a transformation in the lives of the great mass of the people from poverty to relative prosperity. And it saw some traditional prejudices begin to crumble while others endured.

The books I write about, fiction and non-fiction, have been chosen for the light they cast on the period or for the influence they exercised on the minds of men and women at the time. Some occupy a permanent place in the canon of English literature or as part of the nation's intellectual heritage. Others have fallen into obscurity. Together they provide a kaleidoscope of perspectives, unencumbered by hindsight, into the way people lived, the challenges they faced and the assumptions and ideas that lay behind their actions.

Like archaeological objects the books and their contents cannot be altered. But they can be mixed and matched and read in different combinations – an exercise that both deepens understanding of the past and throws up unexpected insights that in turn stimulate a reassessment of received opinions. To give three examples:

I had always assumed that it was the suffragettes and winning the right to vote that, more than anything else, made it possible for women to engage in active politics and to influence public policy. The autobiography of Margaret Bondfield, the first woman to enter the Cabinet, overturned that view. For many years before the vote was won, she had been actively engaged as a trade unionist in bringing about change in the workplace. More than fifteen years before women cast their first vote, and even before the suffragettes had broken away from the main body of the women's suffrage movement, she was giving evidence before a parliamentary committee and helping to mould legislation. Crucial as the right to vote was to the advancement of women's aspirations, the largely middle class-led campaign to acquire it has diverted attention away from the practical work done on behalf of working-class women by women in the trade union movement.

Another surprise was to discover that perhaps the first person to call time on the British empire in Africa was that arch-reactionary Evelyn Waugh in his 1931 travel book *Remote People*. One of its sections is on Kenya where, with the active encouragement of the British government, men and women from this country were between the wars building new lives in the confident expectation that British rule would last beyond their lifetimes. He wrote with approval of their efforts to reproduce the life of the English squirearchy in Africa and with sympathy of their colour bar and discrimination against the Africans. Yet he forecast that the European colonization of Africa might not last for more than another twenty-five years, which proved to be only a few years out.

My third example is about looking back rather than forward and is drawn from John Braine's 1957 novel *Room at the Top*. The narrator, Joe Lampton, explains that his lucky break during the war was to have been shot down while on an RAF bombing raid over Germany and to have been kept safe from danger in a prison camp. Under the auspices of the International Red Cross, he used his time there to pass the accountancy exams which, after the war, enabled him to jump from his working-class background into the middle class. It is hard to imagine a wartime reminiscence more at variance with the patriotic terms in which they are conventionally expressed both in biography and in literature.

I begin my book by considering two titles that set out to debunk the Victorian era and which contain within them the seeds of the iconoclasm that became the hallmark of the first part of the twentieth century: Samuel Butler's *The Way of All Flesh* and Lytton Strachey's *Eminent Victorians*. I end with three books by George Orwell and two by John Maynard Keynes: *Homage to Catalonia*, *Animal Farm* and *Nineteen Eighty-Four* by the former and *The Economic Consequences of the Peace* and *The General Theory of Employment, Interest and Money* by the latter. To the extent that anyone could be said to have had answers to the problems of the age it was these two men.

The chapters in between range widely: from the two world wars and issues arising out of them to the rise of feminism, from working-class life in the North of England to life in the great public schools, from racism and anti-Semitism to sexual relationships, from living in the empire to medical care before the NHS and from class distinctions to cookery. The result is not so much a panorama of the age as an eclectic collage – a big picture made up of many smaller ones with a good deal of overlap between them. In more than half the chapters I cite experiences and recollections of my own and my family.

One of the strongest themes to run through the period was fear of mass destruction and the end of civilization. In 1903 Erskine Childers, in his pioneering espionage novel *The Riddle of the Sands*, had fanned the already widespread fears that Britain might be invaded with his detailed fictional account of German plans to launch an assault across the North Sea. H. G. Wells then added an altogether more frightening dimension. In his 1908 novel, *The War in the Air*, he described a war in the near future in which the aerial bombing would be so intense and so widespread that civilization would be brought to an end. In 1914 he forecast in *The World Set Free* that there would be a nuclear war by the middle of the century, as indeed there was. The fear of universal mass destruction that he conjured up, and to which subsequent technological advances gave increasing credibility, would hang over society throughout the following decades.

Between the wars Stanley Baldwin, who was Prime Minister for much of the period, was among many who forecast that in a future war bombing from the air would destroy civilization. This fear, rather than a repetition of the trenches of the First World War, was the major driver of the pacifist movement that was so strong in this country at that time, as Storm Jameson's 1934 collection of essays, *Challenge to Death*, shows. The same fear drove the Campaign for Nuclear Disarmament during the Cold War and is reflected in Nevil Shute's 1957 novel, *On the Beach*, which describes how the world ends after a nuclear exchange.

The two wars left a legacy with which Britain is still living. Though very different from each other, they involved the whole population directly and indirectly as no previous wars had ever done. The diaries and letters I write about give some idea in a highly personal way of the extent to which the ultimate victory in both was the result of a national team effort. No other European nation can look back on its wartime experiences with such unalloyed satisfaction. For their part the British people have experienced nothing so dramatic, so unifying or so unequivocally successful since 1945. The result is a national obsession with those wars, especially the second, that continues to generate endless books, television programmes and films and to influence contemporary political attitudes towards our European neighbours and our place in the world.

At the beginning of the century the British were in the peculiar position of fearing an invasion at home while ruling a vast empire overseas. This created tensions in the national psyche that are reflected in the original 1908 edition of Robert Baden-Powell's basic text for the Scout Movement, *Scouting for Boys*. It is about much more than the organized camaraderie and outdoor pursuits now normally associated with scouting. It is a call to arms. He encourages scouts to be prepared for an invasion of Britain in which eventuality their tracking and signalling skills will be of great help to the defending forces. He also preaches the pure doctrine of white racial superiority over other ethnic groups and the importance of maintaining it in order to uphold the empire. As training in how to do this, he urges scouts to stage plays as a means of learning the techniques by which white men can impose their will on subject peoples of other races and provides allegedly real-life incidents on which to base them.

The corrosive effect of the belief in racial superiority on the characters of those who ran the empire is central to E. M. Forster's classic, *A Passage to India*, published in 1924. The extent to which it prevented the white settlers in Kenya from establishing a modus vivendi with the Africans that might have enabled them to remain there on a permanent basis is explained in the autobiography of the colonial-era

Kenya politician Michael Blundell, published in 1964. Those chapters in our history are now closed. The one concerning racism in this country is still being written.

Until after 1945 there were only minuscule numbers of people of black and minority ethnic origin in Britain itself. But when immigrants from the Caribbean and the Indian subcontinent began to arrive in significant numbers in the 1950s they found themselves facing a wall of racial prejudice. Among the early arrivals was the West Indian Sam Selvon, who, based on his own experiences, describes what this meant to them and how they reacted in his remarkable 1956 novel *The Lonely Londoners*. It provides a base position against which can be judged the efforts that have since been made to break down prejudice and to achieve racial equality.

Anti-Semitism is another prejudice that recurs in several of my commentaries. Somerset Maugham's 1936 short story, *The Alien Corn*, provides a vivid example of the form in which it was widely expressed in literature and socially until the revelations about the Holocaust after the war changed attitudes or at least made the expression of old ones unacceptable. Britain avoided the anti-Semitic excesses that on the Continent led to this catastrophe. It also benefited greatly, as I explain when writing about Ernst Gombrich and Nikolaus Pevsner, from providing a safe haven for some of those fleeing from persecution. But few in this country are aware that among the basic anti-Semitic texts from which the Nazis drew their inspiration was the work of a British author, Houston Stewart Chamberlain's *The Foundations of the Nineteenth Century*, which I discuss in conjunction with *The Alien Corn*.

Prejudice against gays and lesbians was deeply felt and loudly expressed throughout the period covered by this book. Sex between men was against the law and punishable by imprisonment in Britain, unlike other European countries, and remained so until 1967. Lesbianism, though not illegal, attracted a similar degree of opprobrium.

E. M. Forster's *Maurice*, written before the First World War, and Mary Renault's *The Charioteer*, set during the Second, convey something of what it was like to have been gay. Radclyffe Hall's *The Well of Loneliness*, published and almost immediately banned for being obscene in 1928, does the same for lesbians. The agonizing of the characters in these books over their orientation, how they come to terms with it and what it means for their lives will shock readers who have grown up in a world where sexual relations between people of the same sex have long since ceased to be taboo. The contrast between then and now is an encouraging example of how, over time, even the most deep-seated national attitudes can change for the better.

During the period itself the greatest improvement was in the lives of the working class. Robert Tressall's* influential and readable socialist novel, *The Ragged-Trousered Philanthropists*, is about a group of men and their wives on the south coast in the early years of the century. In *Love on the Dole* Walter Greenwood describes the hardships of a family in the North-West during the Great Depression in the early 1930s. Fear of debt and unemployment are dominant themes in both and life a constant struggle against adversity. By 1958, when Alan Sillitoe's *Saturday Night and Sunday Morning* became a bestseller, everything had changed. The crucial leap had been made to the dawn of the consumer society underpinned by the welfare state.

Throughout the period questions of class arise, sometimes in terms that almost take one's breath away, as in the case of an entry in *The Bickersteth Diaries* recording life in the trenches during the First World War. In the summer of 1917, after serving for three years at the front as an army officer, Burgon Bickersteth records in a letter home, 'the first time I had ever sat down to eat out here in uniform with soldiers.' On other occasions it is the frame of reference within which issues are

* This is how the name is spelled on the title page of the book's first edition, which I have used. In subsequent editions it is Tressell.

discussed that is striking. Virginia Woolf's *A Room of One's Own* and her lesser known *Three Guineas* provide a case in point. The former, published in 1929, is among the most important feminist texts of the twentieth century. The latter, which followed in 1938, argues the case for equal pay and equal opportunities for women in the professions. Although of ground-breaking significance, they only address matters of concern to middle- and upper-class women, those whom Woolf describes in *Three Guineas* as 'the daughters of educated men'. They have nothing to say of relevance to the majority of women then working in shops, factories and domestic service.

Graham Greene's collection of essays entitled *The Old School*, published in 1934, casts an interesting light on the class question. The contributors argue that the schools were machines for turning out 'gentlemen'. Whether the fathers of the boys who attended them were established members of the middle and upper classes or had only recently made money didn't matter. So long as they could pay the fees the schools would ensure that their sons (daughters did not yet enter the equation) would emerge with the right credentials and consequential advantages in terms of career opportunities. The schools were thus simultaneously vehicles for validating new money and integrating the sons of those who had made it into the 'gentleman' class while acting as barriers for those who had not been educated by them.

Each of the two wars broke down barriers and opened up previously undreamed-of opportunities for those with the right attributes and lucky enough to be in the right place at the right time, regardless of where they had been educated. C. P. Snow's *Strangers and Brothers* sequence of novels charts the rise of Lewis Eliot from provincial obscurity to influence in the heart of government, an ascent that closely paralleled that of his creator. A fictional character who turned down the chance to move up in the world was Lady Chatterley's lover, the gamekeeper Mellors. During the 1914–18 war he had risen from the ranks to become an officer and could, had he so wished, have been assimilated into the 'gentleman' class after it ended rather than return to his origins. Lady Chatterley remarks when they first meet on how like a gentleman he is and I doubt that she would have wanted to marry him if he had been an ordinary working man.

In real life a far more extreme renunciation than Mellors' was that of Erskine Childers, who had inherited an established position in society and built on it with the success of *The Riddle of the Sands*. After distinguished service in the Royal Navy, he became so disgusted by what he regarded as British hypocrisy in claiming to be fighting for the rights of small nations while denying those rights to Ireland that he threw in his lot with the most extreme wing of the Irish rebels fighting for independence from Britain.

The complexities and inconsistencies in the way people behaved in the past are often hard for later generations to fathom. In the words of the novelist L. P. Hartley, 'The past is a foreign country: they do things differently there.'[1] To explain what they did and the consequences is one thing; to capture the mentality that led to their actions is quite another. To examine a period through the prism of contemporaneous books is a means of at least partially achieving that. In the case of the years from 1900 to the early 1960s that is not only interesting in itself; it also casts light on the background to some of the issues that still perplex us today.

Debunking Victorianism

The Way of All Flesh by Samuel Butler, 1903.

Eminent Victorians by Lytton Strachey, 1918.

The Way of All Flesh

by Samuel Butler (1903)

The Way of All Flesh by Samuel Butler, published in 1903, is the first great twentieth-century literary blast against Victorian values and institutions. With a title inspired by the Book of Genesis,* its enormous popularity and the influence it exercised tell us a great deal about the intellectual climate of that time. The cultural historian Richard Hoggart has described it as 'one of the intellectual watersheds between the Victorian age and the twentieth century'.[1]

Butler in fact wrote it during the 1870s and 1880s, but never sought a publisher during his lifetime – whether because he felt he could not get it quite right, as some suggest, or, as others claim, because he did not want its similarities with their own family history to cause pain to his sisters. Whatever the reason, its attack on the whole edifice of what came to be called Victorianism is so excoriating that, had it been published during the high noon of the Victorian era, its reception would have been very different from the accolades it received when it finally appeared a year after Butler's death.

The timing was ideal. With Queen Victoria's death in 1901 the intellectual revolt against the bourgeois orthodoxies of her reign,

* And God looked upon the earth and behold, it was corrupt: for all flesh had corrupted his way upon the earth. Genesis 6.12.

already simmering beneath the surface of society while she was alive, broke into the open. *The Way of All Flesh* captured and articulated the mood of the moment. Leonard Woolf, Virginia's husband and the founder of the Hogarth Press, recalls in his memoirs, 'We read it when it came out and felt at once its significance for us.'[2] The playwright George Bernard Shaw wrote to his friend Henry Salt: 'Get it instantly, it is one of the great books of the world … I do not exaggerate: it is enormous.'[3] Other young writers were similarly enthused. It always remained one of Somerset Maugham's favourite novels while E. M. Forster, in a characteristic phrase, thought that, 'If Butler had not lived, many of us would now be a little deader than we are, a little less aware of the tricks and traps in life and of our own obtuseness.'[4]

These words go to the heart of what made the book popular. It helped those wanting to rebel to think for themselves and to find words to express those thoughts. In 1928 Virginia Woolf suggested[5] that Victorian family life had been disrupted by two great forces. *The Way of All Flesh* was one, the other was Constance Garnett's translations of the great Russian authors, which first brought them to the attention of English-speaking readers during the opening decades of the century.

It is never easy to assess how much influence one writer exercises over others. All writers are open to a variety of influences of various kinds. George Bernard Shaw, however, was in no doubt about his debt to Butler. In the preface to his play *Major Barbara*, first performed in 1906, he castigates those critics who claimed that he drew inspiration from Ibsen and Nietzsche and failed to see that 'Butler's extraordinary fresh, free and future piercing suggestions have an obvious share'. The reference to 'future piercing' suggests he had in mind Butler's earlier utopian satire *Erewhon*, as well as *The Way of All Flesh*. Other notable works in which traces of the latter are clearly detectable, or for which it at least paved the way, include Arnold Bennett's *Clayhanger*, published in 1910, D. H. Lawrence's *Sons and Lovers* (1913), Somerset

Maugham's *Of Human Bondage* (1915), and, in the view of some critics, James Joyce's *A Portrait of the Artist as a Young Man* (1919).

At over four hundred pages and covering five generations of the Pontifex family, *The Way of All Flesh* looks at first sight as if it belongs with John Galsworthy's *Forsyte Saga*. But there the similarity ends. It begins with the rise of the Pontifex family from the working class to the bourgeoisie. But instead of rejoicing in this upward mobility, as Galsworthy does, Butler presents it as a downward progression in moral terms. Old Mr Pontifex, a village carpenter, who we meet aged eighty in the opening pages, is portrayed as being both a happier and a better man than his son George, a successful businessman, and his grandson, Theobald, who completes the gentrification process by moving out of trade to become a clergyman.

The hero, if such he can be called as he is far from being heroic, is Theobald's son, the naïve and well-meaning Ernest, who reverses the family's social advancement. After obediently following his father into the priesthood, he becomes a curate at a fashionable London church where he is expected to confine his ministrations to its well-to-do parishioners. Instead he tries to proselytize among the poor, with disastrous results, when he becomes involved entirely innocently with a prostitute. He is accused of an offence he didn't commit, prosecuted, found guilty and sentenced to six months in prison. His father is appalled by the disgrace and banishes Ernest from the family circle. After his release Ernest tries his hand as a tailor and as a shopkeeper but fails again, marries and fathers two children by a woman he subsequently discovers is already married. These misfortunes persuade him that the values he was brought up with are false and that the paternal tyranny of his childhood has ruined his chances of achieving happiness and fulfilment.

At this point he seems destined for a life of penury from which he is saved by a legacy from a long-forgotten aunt. He uses this to become a writer, but his most significant decision is to keep his children with the family of a bargee on the Thames to whom he had entrusted them when their mother left him. Instead of restoring them to the bourgeois fold, he wants them to grow up without the pretensions and restrictions of gentility. When, in due course, they become adults he enables his son to buy a boat of his own while his daughter marries within the river community. Thus, the wheel turns full circle. The new generation is back in more or less the same social stratum as was old Mr Pontifex. In defiance of the conventional view of how social mobility should work, this is a matter for celebration rather than regret.

Several themes relating to middle-class life and values run through the book and interact with each other – paternal tyranny, hypocrisy, the corrosive effect of money on family relationships and the absence of any real emotional commitment both within the family and in the discharge of clerical duties. The family is presented as a unit that revolves round the paterfamilias whose principal concern is to exercise power over his wife and children.

The women too are ruthless in pursuit of their own ends. Among the book's most memorable passages, so vivid one feels it must have been drawn, or at least derived, from life, is the description of how the Reverend Mr Allaby's five daughters react when, as a young curate, Theobald arrives to assist their father in his parish duties. All 'are in want of a husband', as Jane Austen would have described them. They resolve the matter by 'playing at cards with Theobald for the stakes', behaviour beyond anything one can imagine Austen's characters engaging in.

The winner is Christina, the second unmarried daughter and, at twenty-seven, four years older than Theobald. Mrs Allaby immediately packs the other girls off to stay with friends to give her a clear run. She duly catches him, but, as they drive away from the church after their marriage, remorse sets in. Theobald experiences that feeling akin to death, 'what the Italians call la figlia della Morte', that a man suffers during 'the first half-hour that he is alone with a woman who he has married but never genuinely loved'. The language of love and of the marriage service is shown up to be a sham, but Theobald and Christina have each fulfilled a social requirement. She has escaped spinsterhood while he has acquired a housekeeper and both can form a family with children.

The relationships between fathers and sons – George with Theobald and Theobald with Ernest – are bleak and violent, but in that respect, we are assured, similar to those around them. George thrashes Theobald and his brother 'two or three times a week and some weeks a good deal oftener', which 'may have been a little sterner … than some of his neighbours, but not much'. Theobald does the same to Ernest. The purpose is always for their own good: to make them work harder at their lessons, to inculcate obedience and, as Theobald and Christina say to each other in the case of Ernest, 'so that from the first he might have been kept pure from every taint of evil'. As the sons grow older the fathers threaten to withhold allowances and to alter wills to ensure that they follow the careers laid down for them. When they comply with their fathers' desires they are rewarded financially. Again, all is couched in terms of being in their own best interests. This is the cycle from which Ernest wishes to escape though it requires a series of accidents rather than deliberate action on his part to do so.

The violence adds colour to Butler's argument, but is peripheral to his central point, which is the conflict between filial obedience and free will at a time when it was taken for granted that sons should do as their fathers wished and often follow them into the same profession. It was the questioning of this assumption that many found so liberating. George Orwell, who, as a young man, followed his father into a branch of the imperial administration, in his case the Burma Police, from which, after some years' service, he resigned to become a writer, reflected that feeling in a radio broadcast many years later. He called *The Way of All Flesh*, 'A great book because it gives an honest picture of the relationship between father and son.'[6]

At a time when Darwin's theory of evolution was beginning to eat away at the foundations of Christian belief, the Church of England was vulnerable to Butler's attack upon the clergy. It went much further than portraying Theobald as violent, selfish and narrow-minded. A clergyman, Butler claimed, could never make an 'unbiased examination' of facts or issues because, in preaching the gospel, he 'is as much a paid advocate as a barrister who is trying to persuade a jury to acquit a prisoner'. Moreover, he suggests, social ambition, rather than a vocation to serve God, was often the reason why men wanted to become clergymen. Among Ernest's fellow students at Cambridge were some imbued with the missionary spirit, but for many, 'the fact of becoming clergymen would be the entrée into a social position from which they were at present kept out by barriers they well knew to be impassable; ordination, therefore, opened fields for their ambition'. In a telling passage, Christina whispers to the book's narrator as the congregation 'bobs' before Theobald as they enter his church for Sunday service, 'The people hereabouts are truly respectful, they know their betters.'

In Butler's view, both the clergy and the Church as an institution are fundamentally no different from the society of which they were a part and deserving of no special respect. This analysis had the same impact on public opinion, when *The Way of All Flesh* was published, as that of the child in Hans Christian Anderson's fairy story who dares to proclaim that the Emperor has no clothes when everybody has been pretending to admire them. As such it made a significant contribution to the decline in respect for the clergy and in religious observance that were already under way and would gather momentum as the century progressed.

Butler's relationship with his own clergyman father to some extent mirrored that of Ernest and Theobald. He too was destined to follow his father into the Church. After leaving Cambridge he served as a lay reader at St James's, Piccadilly, in London, a fashionable church similar to the one at which Ernest served as a curate in the novel. He then rebelled and announced that he wanted to become an artist. His father regarded this as ridiculous but behaved more generously than Theobald. In a grand Victorian gesture, he gave his son a substantial sum of money and told him that if he could make his fortune in the colonies, he would be free to do as he wished. In 1859 Butler sailed to New Zealand where he achieved such success as a sheep farmer that in 1864 he was able to return to London as a man of independent means.

Thereafter he embarked on an astonishingly eclectic literary career. The most successful of his books in his own lifetime was *Erewhon*, an anagram of nowhere, published in 1872, which has been compared with *Gulliver's Travels* as a satirical utopia. Others followed on Darwin and Darwinism, his travels in Italy and his rediscovery of forgotten artists and craftsmen associated with pilgrimage sites in that country. Two that appeared towards the end of his life attracted particular attention. In one he argued that Homer's *Odyssey* and *Iliad* had been written by a woman and set in Sicily, an idea later pursued by Robert Graves in his novel *Homer's Daughter*. In the other, published in 1899, Butler suggested that Shakespeare's sonnets were about homosexual love; a less original theory, but a brave one for a man, widely supposed to be gay, to propound at a time when a wave of homophobia was sweeping the country following the trial of Oscar Wilde.

Eminent Victorians

by Lytton Strachey (1918)

In *Eminent Victorians*, published in 1918, Lytton Strachey's angle of attack on the Victorians was quite different from Samuel Butler's. Whereas Butler directed his fire at institutions – the Church of England and the family – Strachey's aim in his book of four short biographical essays was the character assassination of named individuals. The only one who is still famous is Florence Nightingale. Most people today would not be able to place Cardinal Manning, Dr Arnold or General Gordon, but in Strachey's day they were household names and Victorian icons. In an age of deference, they were people his readers had been brought up to revere. His purpose in attacking them was to indict an age, one whose values he believed had helped to bring about the First World War.

He achieved his objective. After Strachey's death in 1932, the great American critic Edmund Wilson wrote, 'neither the Americans nor the English have ever, since *Eminent Victorians* appeared, been able to feel quite the same about the legends that had dominated their pasts. Something had been punctured for good.'[7] In his influential book *Enemies of Promise*, the British author and critic Cyril Connolly made the same point in more hyperbolic terms. He described *Eminent Victorians* 'as the work of a great anarch, a revolutionary textbook on bourgeois society written in the language through which the bourgeois ear could be lulled and beguiled, the Mandarin style'.[8] These judgements remain valid. Although much has since been written about the Victorian era, *Eminent Victorians* has proved to be one of the most enduring templates against which subsequent generations have formulated their own assessments of that era.

It also had a significant literary impact. On the one hand Strachey's wit and irreverence helped to create the climate in which the iconoclasm and satire of such writers as Michael Arlen, Noël Coward and Evelyn Waugh, whom I write about in later chapters, could flourish in the 1920s and 1930s. On the other Strachey contributed to the evolution of biographical writing into the literary art form that it is today. His approach represented a dramatic break from the way in which biography had up till then been written – those great ponderous volumes, often two or even three, with which the lives of the great had traditionally been commemorated. In the preface to his own book, Strachey compares them to the 'the cortège of the undertaker'.

Whereas their objective was comprehensiveness, Strachey aimed for brevity and lightness of touch. While they tended towards hagiography, he sought to unravel and expose his subject's mentality and motives. In the words of his biographer Michael Holroyd, he believed 'that history yielded up more of her secrets to the heightened intuition of the artist than to the over-diffident, over-earnest, humdrum and humourless investigations conducted by scientific minds'.[9] His technique was similar to that of those producers of films about the past who tamper with their material, rearrange events and redraw characters, often unfairly, in order to achieve a desired dramatic effect. The result frequently misrepresents what actually happened while conveying such a powerful feeling for the period as to carry complete conviction.

The extent to which Strachey achieved this may be judged by the reaction of the publisher to whom he sent his manuscript, Frank

Swinnerton of Chatto & Windus. Swinnerton replied saying that he had read it during an air raid: 'The whirring of aeroplanes overhead, the rattle of machine gun fire, and finally the frightful thunder of a gun in the field at the bottom of our garden, would all have served to distract a mind less happily engaged; but as it was, with the curtain closely drawn to prevent the escape of light, I consorted that evening with Cardinal Manning, Thomas Arnold, Florence Nightingale and General Gordon. The nineteenth century had come alive again.'[10]

Eminent Victorians was published in May 1918 just as the fighting in France began tilting in favour of the Allies, but while the outcome of the war was still in the balance. Thousands of men were being killed or wounded every day. Even so, it received long and laudatory reviews and an accolade, as important as it was unexpected, from the former Prime Minister Herbert Asquith, who praised it in the course of a prestigious lecture at Oxford.[11] There were denunciations too, but these were often of the kind that attract readers. By July it was into its third, albeit small, edition, making three thousand copies in all. In November, the month the war finally ended, an American edition was published to be followed by Swedish, German, French, Italian and Spanish translations. The proceeds and the spin-offs made Strachey financially secure as well as famous for the rest of his life.

The book's timing turned out to be impeccable. Before the outbreak of the First World War in 1914, it would not have made the same impact. Many would have been shocked by the disrespect and often contempt that characterize Strachey's portraits. By 1918 attitudes had been transformed as a result of the dreadful loss of life in the trenches. Virtually everyone had lost family members or friends, very often both, and a deep shadow had been cast over the way they regarded the past. A book about the Victorian age that sought to undermine the moral foundations on which it was built turned out to meet a deep psychological need, regardless of the misrepresentation involved.

This is most extreme in the case of Cardinal Manning. The position Manning had held in public life is perhaps best illustrated by what happened when he died in 1892. The queues to file past his body as it lay in state at Archbishop's House in Victoria blocked traffic for four days. When his coffin was carried along a four-mile route from the Brompton Oratory to Kensal Green cemetery the streets were packed with mourners all the way.[12] That the head of the Catholic Church in England, then still a minority sect and an object of suspicion, if not anathema to many, should have evoked such an outpouring of public grief was extraordinary. It arose because of the practical concern Manning had shown over many years for the poor and disadvantaged and the way he had used his office and connections on their behalf in stark contrast to the hierarchy of the Church of England.

Strachey was not interested in any of that. His focus is on how Manning advanced his career in the Church of England before his conversion to Catholicism, on how he used his influence behind the scenes in Rome to work his way up in his new Church and how, in Strachey's view, he sought to do down that other great Catholic convert from Anglicanism, Cardinal Newman. That Manning was one of nature's executives, born to command and always in search of promotion, as well as an effective political operator, is not in doubt. But that is not at all the same as being a vindictive careerist forever justifying his manoeuvres to himself as being the fulfilment of God's will, which is how Strachey portrays him. Moreover, Strachey fails to answer the crucial question of why, if Manning was so driven by worldly ambition and so skilled at presenting his machinations to himself as being divinely led, he did not stay in the established Church whose bishops at that time lived in palaces and enjoyed large incomes. Had he done so, Manning would undoubtedly have secured one of the most prestigious dioceses with the wealth and status that went with it. His life would have been much easier and he would have avoided the painful break with old friends, including Gladstone, who regarded his conversion to Catholicism as an apostasy.

The portrait of Manning stands out for its unremitting hostility. In the others the denigration is tempered with humour. This is particularly so in the case of Dr Thomas Arnold, the famous headmaster of Rugby from 1828 to 1841. The reforms he introduced there were so widely copied by other schools that he is generally credited with creating the public school ethos that was for so long afterwards such a distinguishing feature of British life. Strachey treats him as a figure of fun: a pompous little man filled with a sense of his own importance and rushing around in pursuit of petty objectives.

Strachey's mockery of Arnold's belief that the classical languages and a devotion to the Anglican religion should provide the bedrock of an educational system and that discipline should be maintained by flogging set the tone for much of the future criticism of that ethos. But *Eminent Victorians* lacks any examination of the reasons why such a system, promulgated by a man as ludicrous as Arnold is made out to be, should have been so widely adopted by his contemporaries. Nor did Strachey's criticism have any practical effect as parents continued to send their sons to the public schools. In the 1930s, as I describe in a later chapter, it was thought they might become priced out of the market, but that proved to be a false alarm.

General Gordon is portrayed as a credulous and somewhat ridiculous Christian obsessed by the Bible. His death at the hands of the Sudanese at the siege of Khartoum in 1885 was the most memorable feature of one of the greatest British imperial defeats of the nineteenth century. Strachey set out to strip it of its aura of martyrdom and to present it as typical of the type of bungling that had cost so many lives during the First World War. He glories in describing buck-passing in government circles, the obtuseness of politicians, the self-interest of high officials and the muddles that combined to leave Gordon and his troops isolated and at the mercy of the Sudanese. His readers would have drawn an immediate connection with events during the war. They would also have appreciated his cynical comment on the British victory over the Sudanese some years later: 'At any rate, it all ended very happily – in a glorious slaughter of 20,000 Arabs, a vast addition to the British Empire, and a step in the peerage for Sir Evelyn Baring.'

The essay on Florence Nightingale left me with a surprising sense of déjà vu. It reads so like the things I used to read and hear about Margaret Thatcher in her prime – the same male sense of awe tempered by outrage that a woman should be able to move such mountains and dominate the men around her mingled with mockery at the exhibition she thereby makes of herself. Strachey cannot but approve of her nursing activities during the Crimean War and of her subsequent campaign back in London to overcome official resistance to reforming the archaic army medical services. But he has to present her as a harridan until, worn down by her efforts, she loses her mind and becomes a gentle old woman, as happened to Margaret Thatcher at the end of her life.

The idea that a strong woman in the public sphere is somehow an aberration and against nature is deeply embedded in his text and it was not only in this country that it endured into the 1980s and beyond. In 1980, when I was a European Commissioner, Thatcher had a particularly bruising encounter with the German Chancellor, Helmut Schmidt, after which a German minister came to see me to convey a message. 'You must tell your Prime Minister,' he said, 'that she has hurt my Chancellor in his male pride. If things are to be put right between our two countries, she must find a way of making it up to him.' I had to explain why I thought it would not be helpful to British-German relations to pass it on.

Strachey's work strikes another chord in my memory. His portrayal and mockery of his subjects and their motives, and his use of ridicule and misrepresentation to puncture their pretensions, are reminiscent of the 'satire boom' that, in the early 1960s, first brought to prominence such varied characters as the writer and dramatist Alan Bennett, the theatre and opera director and all-round polymath Jonathan Miller, the comedian Peter Cook and the television interviewer David Frost, among others. There is the same youthful exuberance, the same delight in being irreverent and pushing back the boundaries of taste. Both Strachey and the satirists reflected and helped to mould the spirit of their age; in the case of the satirists by undermining the anachronistic pretensions of the then Conservative government and the Establishment in general, in the case of Strachey by making Victorian icons appear ridiculous.

It is not only because of its own intrinsic merits and the social and literary influence it once exercised that *Eminent Victorians* has so successfully outlived the period of its own youthful exuberance. It has benefited from Strachey having been a colourful member of the Bloomsbury Group of advanced, free-thinking intellectuals that revolved round the writer Virginia Woolf and her sister, the artist Vanessa Bell. This remarkable coterie, named after the part of London in which Woolf and Bell originally set up house together, included the great economist John Maynard Keynes, the artist Duncan Grant, the artist and critic Roger Fry and the writer E. M. Forster, to name only the best-known. Their reputations have become mutually reinforcing as, among later generations, those who become interested in the books and paintings of one member frequently then wish to know more about the work of the others.

Besides that, the Bloomsbury Group has become a sort of composite cultural celebrity. The heady mix of their unconventional sex lives – gay, straight and promiscuous – their disregard for the social mores of their time and their high intellectual and creative achievements has made them the subject of countless books and television documentaries. These tend to concentrate on their sexual activities and their flouting of convention rather than on their contribution to the nation's cultural life.

That contribution was, however, considerable. In the twentieth century there was no other group of friends whose combined influence has been remotely as great. I shall have more to say on this when writing about other members of the group in subsequent chapters.

War 1 – Warnings and Reality

The Riddle of the Sands by Erskine Childers, 1903, and *The Thirty-Nine Steps* by John Buchan, 1915.

The War in the Air by H. G. Wells, 1908,
The World Set Free by H. G. Wells, 1914,
and *The Great Illusion* by Norman Angell, 1910.

The Bickersteth Diaries, 1914–18, edited by John Bickersteth, and *Private Lord Crawford's Great War Diaries*, edited by Christopher Arnander.

The Riddle of the Sands

by Erskine Childers (1903)

The Thirty-Nine Steps

by John Buchan (1915)

As the twentieth century opened, the British empire stood at the plenitude of its power. The government in London held sway over some 24 per cent of the earth's surface and 23 per cent of its people. Yet fears about the country's vulnerability and of what the future might hold were germinating. In his famous poem 'Recessional', published for Queen Victoria's Diamond Jubilee in 1897, Rudyard Kipling had prayed to God that the British empire might not go the way of the biblical empires of Nineveh and Tyre.[1] The Boer War against the small and scattered population of Afrikaans-speaking farmers of Dutch and Huguenot origin in South Africa known as Boers, which began in 1899 and ended in 1902, had proved to be a salutary experience. At its outset the British Army had suffered defeats. In the end it emerged victorious, but victory had been hard-won. Britons had also been shocked to find how much support the underdog Boers had enjoyed in Europe and the United States. Beneath the surface of their imperial pomp and splendour they were beginning to feel isolated and insecure. So called 'invasion novels' envisaging an invasion of Britain had become a popular genre and in his maiden speech to the House of Commons in 1901 the young Winston Churchill made a passing reference to such a possibility.[2]

It was in this atmosphere that Erskine Childers, then working as a clerk in the House of Commons, captured the imagination of the nation with *The Riddle of the Sands*, published in 1903. It did so because of the detail it deployed in explaining how Germany could mount an invasion of the east coast. It was this rather than the naming of Germany as a likely invader that marked it out from other invasion novels. Germany had been named before, although at the time of *The Riddle of the Sands'* publication relations between Britain and Germany were good. The memory of how, only two years before, the Kaiser, Wilhelm II, as Queen Victoria's grandson had been present at her deathbed with his cousin, Edward VII, was still fresh in the public mind and there was, as yet, no ostensible quarrel between the two countries. By contrast, Britain was at odds with France in Africa and competing for influence with Russia in central Asia. With strategic acumen, Childers identified the North Sea as the point at which Britain would be at greatest risk in a future naval war with Germany and when war came it was indeed there that the decisive Battle of Jutland was fought.

The Riddle of the Sands tells the story of two friends, Charles Carruthers of the Foreign Office and Arthur Davies, a solicitor, on a yachting holiday cruising round the Frisian Islands off the coast of Germany. When Davies had sailed in those waters before he had become suspicious that something sinister and mysterious was afoot and, with Carruthers' help, he had set sail determined to find out what was happening. What they discover, after various adventures, is nothing less than well-advanced preparations to enable a German army to be secretly transported across the North Sea to England. At great risk to themselves, they then succeed in bringing the information back to London.

Childers' taut, straightforward prose and the professionalism of the accompanying maps, charts and technical data, drawn from his own experience as an enthusiastic yachtsman, all combine to give their account of their adventures an alarming verisimilitude; an impression enhanced by the book's subtitle, *A Record of Secret Service Recently Achieved.* The novel's patriotic tone and its tale of how a pair of British amateurs gets the better of highly professional opponents played precisely to how the British liked to think of themselves, which added to its popularity.

Eleven years were to pass before the war Davies prophesied 'was bound to come' actually broke out. During that time, while the naval arms race between Britain and Germany gathered momentum and Britain formed an alliance with France and Russia, *The Riddle of the Sands* exercised influence in two directions. In the literary sphere it became, in conjunction with John Buchan's famous book *The Thirty-Nine Steps*, published in 1915, one of the progenitors of the espionage spy thriller that has ever since been such a notable feature of British popular literature. In the government, it was credited with having been among the factors that led to the establishment of the naval bases at Scapa Flow, Invergordon and Rosyth to protect the east coast from the German fleet.

Whether, as is widely claimed, Churchill as First Lord of the Admiralty was directly influenced by *The Riddle of the Sands* I have been unable to verify. But it is certainly the case that within days of war having broken out the Director of Naval Intelligence at the Admiralty was instructed to find Childers and recruit him into the Royal Navy.[3]

Naval secrets are also at the heart of *The Thirty-Nine Steps*, but this time with the Germans trying to steal Britain's. After a thrilling chase, mostly set in the Highlands of Scotland, that, for perhaps the first time in literature, features an aeroplane, they are thwarted by the book's hero, Richard Hannay. As in *The Riddle of the Sands* the Germans are portrayed as highly professional and fiendishly clever, but somehow too clever by half, which results in them being outwitted by the brilliant improvisation of their British antagonist.

As Buchan, who already had a string of books to his credit, published *The Thirty-Nine Steps* after hostilities had begun, it has none of Childers' foresight nor did it in any way influence government policy. But it is notable for other reasons. In Hannay, Buchan created the prototype of the resourceful, intelligent and tenacious hero of so many subsequent thrillers. They include Bulldog Drummond, who remained popular from the 1920s to the 1950s, BBC Radio's Dick Barton 'special agent', to whose adventures boys of my generation, as well as adults, listened avidly in the 1940s, and above all James Bond, launched in the 1950s and still going strong, among a host of others.

Hannay has another significant characteristic. He had been brought up in Africa and felt himself to be an outsider in London among the native English. His element was the 'veldt', that great open landscape comprising mostly grass or scrub of southern Africa. There, fighting African tribesmen and hunting big game, he had learned the skills that enable him to outwit his German pursuers. In this he personified an idea, widespread in the early twentieth century, that a stronger, more resourceful breed of Briton was to be found in the wild new lands of the empire than in the urbanized mother country and that they would come to Britain's rescue if it ever found itself in danger.

Hannay fulfils that expectation. In the book's closing pages, after his adventure has been successfully concluded, war is declared between Britain and Germany. He immediately joins the army and, thanks to his African experience, is straightaway commissioned as a captain, thereby leapfrogging the junior ranks. His example, though not the leapfrogging, was followed in real life by many hundreds of thousands of other young men from the empire, as happened again in the Second World War. Paradoxically, however, far from strengthening the sense of Britishness in the countries from which they came, the experience of war fostered the evolution of distinctive Australian, Canadian and New Zealand identities.

In its admiration for Hannay's colonial background *The Thirty-Nine Steps* reflects one aspect of early twentieth-century attitudes. Another was suspicion and fear of Jews. At the outset of the novel Hannay is warned by the man whose murder precipitates him into his adventures to beware of Jews. 'The Jew is everywhere, but you have to go far down the backstairs to find him,' he is told. This is particularly so with Germany. In 'any big Teutonic business', if you get to the real boss, 'ten to one you are brought up against a little white-faced Jew in a bath-chair with an eye like a rattlesnake. Yes, sir, he is the man ruling the world just now.' Somewhat surprisingly after this warning, Jews play no further part in the story.

Childers and Buchan are remembered for their books, but their careers and the contrast between them cast an even more revealing light upon the age they lived in. That of Childers is the more astonishing. His father was English and his mother Irish and, after their deaths while he was still a child, he was brought up by her family in Co. Wicklow. His education in England at Haileybury and Cambridge provided him with an assured position in the English upper middle class and, after the success of *The Riddle of the Sands*, he had the world at his feet. His drama and his tragedy arose from the fact that his Irish identity proved to be stronger than his English, leading him to turn against Britain and to meet his death as an Irish martyr.

His first intervention in Irish affairs came in 1910 when he gave up the parliamentary seat in Plymouth where he was a Liberal candidate in protest at the Liberal government's decision to exempt the six counties of Ulster from the provisions of its bill to give Home Rule to Ireland in an attempt to buy off the Unionist opposition. This did not satisfy the Unionists and in the early months of 1914 a group of them imported guns into Ulster in preparation for taking up arms against the bill's implementation. Childers decided to respond in kind and, in an echo of his novel, used his yacht to bring guns into Howth, near Dublin, for the Nationalists supporting the bill.

The outbreak of war distracted Childers from Irish affairs. Having been invited to join the navy he served with such bravery and distinction that he was awarded a Distinguished Service Cross. But Ireland was never far from his mind. When Sinn Fein mounted the Easter Rising in 1916, he was shocked by the brutality of the government's response. In 1918, he was further outraged when conscription, which had been in operation in Britain since 1916, was extended to Ireland. A central plank of the government's wartime propaganda was that Britain was fighting for the rights of small nations and Childers believed that it was hypocritical to deny those rights to Ireland.

When the war ended and Ireland was in open revolt he joined the Sinn Fein rebels.* To those in Britain who remembered how, in his novel, a renegade British naval officer who had been working for the Germans preferred to commit suicide rather than allow Carruthers and Davies to bring him home to face justice, this was a shocking and incomprehensible betrayal. In 1922 he went a step further when a majority of the Sinn Fein leadership settled with the British government and set up the Irish Free State, owing allegiance to the King. A dissident faction led by Eamon de Valera determined to fight on until a completely independent republic could be established, and Childers joined them. During the bitter Irish civil war that followed, he fell into the hands of Free State troops and was sentenced to death by the government in Dublin.

The manner of his dying became the stuff of legend. On the night before the execution he told his sixteen-year-old son, also called Erskine, to shake the hand of each of the men who had played a role

* See the essay on *The Last September* by Elizabeth Bowen.

in sentencing him and never to use his name for political advantage. When the firing squad was drawn up, Childers shook hands with each of its members. When he was facing the guns, he called out, 'Take a step or two forwards lads. It will be easier that way.'[4] In 1973 the wheel turned full circle when the younger Erskine succeeded de Valera as the fourth President of the republic.

Buchan's career could not have been more different. The privileged position in British society that Childers threw up to join the Irish was what Buchan strove successfully to acquire. He was born in 1875 in Fife, where his father was a minister of the Free Church of Scotland. From the local board school he progressed via a grammar school to Glasgow University and thence, with a scholarship, to Oxford. While there he published his first novel. In 1901 he became Private Secretary to the British High Commissioner in South Africa, the influential Alfred Milner, which gave him his entrée into political circles. In 1907 he married a cousin of the Duke of Westminster. Poor health kept him away from the fighting during the war, which he spent working in various branches of government propaganda and as a *Times* correspondent, roles that enabled him to build up a huge network of useful friends and contacts.

Thereafter, he pursed a varied career as a successful writer, as a publisher, as an MP and as a pillar of the Church of Scotland. In 1935 he became Lord Tweedsmuir on his appointment as Governor-General of Canada, an office he filled with great distinction. When he died in 1940 he was accorded a state funeral in Canada and the British government sent a Royal Navy destroyer to bring back his ashes for burial at the estate he had acquired in Oxfordshire.

The contrasting trajectories of these two authors' lives show how much more complex issues of loyalty, identity and class sometimes were in the first part of the twentieth century than they appear in hindsight.

The War in the Air

by H. G. Wells (1908)

The World Set Free

by H. G. Wells (1914)

The Great Illusion

by Norman Angell (1910)

If these three books, all of which were bestsellers before the outbreak of the First World War in 1914, had been taken to heart by the governments of the major European powers, how different the twentieth century might have been – how much suffering and destruction might have been avoided. Someone who read them when they first appeared and then read them again in the late 1940s must surely have thought, 'we were warned'. They would have lived through and either witnessed or experienced much of what had been the stuff of fantasies and nightmares when they were young.

In *The War in the Air*, published in 1908, H. G. Wells foresaw how air power would transform the nature of war, putting the civilian populations of large cities as much at risk as front-line troops and trumping the sea power on which Britain relied. In *The World Set Free*, published in 1914, he foresaw the atomic bomb. In *The Great Illusion*, published in 1910,* Norman Angell analysed in meticulous detail how, as a result of the growth of international credit markets and of international trade based upon them, national economies had become so dependent on each other that a war between major powers would be ruinous to victor and vanquished alike. It was not until the Second World War that most of Wells' prophecies were fulfilled and then in different circumstances from those he had envisaged. Angell's warnings were vindicated almost immediately by the irreparable damage wrought by the First World War on Britain and France as well as on Germany and its allies.

Wells sets *The War in the Air* a couple of decades or so after 1908. The world has been living at peace throughout that time while Germany and the United States have become the world's leading powers with New York overtaking London as the leading financial centre. Instead of going to war with Britain and France, as happened in 1914, the German government decides to establish a colonial empire in South America. It denounces the Monroe Doctrine, on the basis of which the United States had, since 1823, proclaimed that European powers should keep out of the American continent, and launches a huge fleet of airships† to invade New York. Following a series of improbable accidents and misunderstandings, the novel's hero, Bert Smallways, a young man from south London, is a captive on the flagship. It is partly

* The book grew out of a pamphlet published the year before under the title *Europe's Optical Illusion*.

† An airship is a balloon with a rigid frame that can navigate through the air under its own power. It derives its lift from large bags filled with gas. A gondola suspended beneath houses the crew, passengers and engine. The most famous was the German Zeppelin, named after its designer, Count Ferdinand von Zeppelin, and Zeppelin became a generic term. During the 1914–18 war airships were used to bomb Britain and France. Both before and after the war they were used for commercial flights and during the 1930s for a regular transatlantic service between Germany and North and South America.

through his eyes and partly in the form of a history written after the event that the story unfolds.

Wells was writing when the naval arms race between Britain and Germany was in full swing and just as the United States too had become a great naval power. The prestige weapon on which all three, and other powers as well, were spending millions of pounds was the big battleship, or dreadnought. In *The War in the Air* he showed that the development of air power would soon render these behemoths obsolete, though he was wrong in believing that the future of air power lay with the airship rather than the aeroplane. On their way to New York the German airships destroy the United States' Atlantic Fleet with ease. They then blitz New York, much as London would be blitzed in 1940. Unlike London, New York surrenders, but, as would be demonstrated many times subsequently, the Germans find that an attacker can't take possession of enemy territory without having troops on the ground. The United States fights on and, as winter sets in, the German airships are stranded over the Atlantic seaboard at the mercy of powerful winds.

At this point the German plan falls apart as other countries enter the war. In Europe Britain, France and Italy turn on Germany, violating Swiss neutrality in the process, just as the Germans would violate Belgian neutrality in 1914. The two sides mount bombing campaigns against each other's cities as would later happen during the Second World War. But the biggest sufferer is the United States. Japan and China form an alliance and dispatch a massive air fleet across the Pacific to attack Americans and Germans alike with airships that prove superior to both. As the war rages in the air the great American cities are blown to smithereens.

To suggest, as Wells did, that Asian countries could technologically outstrip Europeans and Americans required a huge leap of the imagination in the early twentieth century. At the same time, it tapped into deep-seated fears about what might happen should the Asian giants ever find the means to hit back at the white races then riding roughshod over their continent. Some thirty-four years later, in 1942, his scenario looked very prescient after the Japanese attack on the American fleet at Pearl Harbor and their victories over the British land and sea forces in South East Asia. It does so again today as China asserts itself militarily as well as industrially on the world stage and a host of other Asian economies outperform those of the West.

The War in the Air ends with the collapse of civilization. 'As the exhaustion of the mechanical resources of civilization clears the heavens of airships at last altogether, Anarchy, Famine and Pestilence are discovered triumphant below. The great nations have become but names in the mouths of men. Everywhere there are ruins and unburied dead, and shrunken, yellow faced survivors in a mortal apathy.' In the final scene, set thirty years after the end of the war, an old man and a boy, Smallways' brother and son, wander through the ruins of south London as the old man describes what it had once been like before the war and the plague, famine and other horrors that followed it. This was the future that those who campaigned for peace between the wars feared would follow a war in the air while later, during the Cold War, it was feared that a nuclear exchange would go a step further and destroy the world itself.*

In *The World Set Free*, Wells describes a nuclear war, which he envisages taking place in the 1950s, the decade after the Americans actually dropped atomic bombs on Hiroshima and Nagasaki. The book's most remarkable feature is that in 1914, on the basis of the scientific knowledge then available, he was able to foresee the potential of nuclear power both as a limitless source of energy to the great benefit of the human race and as the ultimate weapon of mass destruction. Initially he sees it being developed for peaceful purposes with two Indian inventors producing some of the most spectacular results, an idea that would have seemed outlandish to British readers, accustomed to regarding Indians

---

* See the essays on *Challenge to Death* and *Guilty Men*, and on *Lord of the Flies* and *On the Beach*.

as a subject race. Then in 1956 comes a financial crash, even more calamitous than the one that in fact occurred in 1929, and war follows.

The war pits Britain and France against a central European alliance led by Germany. After an attack by the Germans has destroyed the Franco-British headquarters in Paris, the commander of the French special scientific corps and his lieutenant take it upon themselves to drop three atomic bombs on Berlin. These are small devices that can be dropped by hand over the side of an aeroplane, but their effects are devastating. When the pilot looks down after releasing the first, 'it was like looking down upon the crater of a small volcano'. Thereafter the war spreads. There are battles on the ground and in the air in Europe, China and Japan attack Russia and the United States attacks Japan. Atomic bombs that continue to pour out radioactive substances with diminishing force for several weeks on a seventeen-day cycle are freely used.

'By the spring of 1959 from nearly two hundred centres, and every week added to their number, roared the unquenchable crimson conflagrations of the atomic bombs, the flimsy fabric of the world's credit had vanished, industry was completely disorganized and every city, every thickly populated area was starving or trembled on the verge of starvation.' In the real world, fears of a nuclear holocaust ran particularly high in the late 1950s and early 1960s. In Britain each Easter was marked by a march of tens of thousands of people from the Atomic Weapons Research Establishment at Aldermaston to Trafalgar Square in London. Wells' scenario exemplified the fears blazoned on their banners and expressed in their chants and the speeches at their final rally.

In *The War in the Air* the world never recovers from the effects of the fighting. In *The World Set Free* the nuclear exchange ushers in an improbable utopia that reflects to an extreme degree the hopes that were to be reposed in the League of Nations after the First World War. Faced with the prospect of the collapse of civilization, the world's leaders come together at a conference at Lake Como in Italy and agree to set up a World

Republic to be based there. Monarchs give up their crowns, governments pool their sovereignty and war is outlawed. There are difficulties at the outset in bringing a recalcitrant Balkan ruler into line. A prominent role in outwitting him is played by Egbert, the idealistic former British King. The great cities remain as radioactive no-go areas while a new society, stripped of the national rivalries that lead to wars, is created around them. Towards the end of the book the situation in London has improved to the point where work can begin on repairing the ruins.

The Great Illusion has none of the leaps of the imagination that characterize Wells' books. While writing it, Norman Angell was the managing editor of the continental edition of the *Daily Mail* in Paris,* a more serious publication than today's tabloid *Daily Mail*, and it reads somewhat like an extended think piece in a good newspaper. Its central thesis is that a new form of international economy had evolved over the preceding decades with the result that military and commercial security were no longer linked as they had been in the past. British prosperity, he argued, no longer resulted from its command of the oceans and acquiring a large navy or conquering more territory would not make the German people more prosperous.

Angell argues that in the world of 1910 a country's prosperity stemmed not from military or naval might, but from the competitivity of its products on world markets and the creditworthiness of its governments on financial markets. From this it follows that the citizens of small countries, such as Holland and Belgium, could be richer than those of a large one with a large army, like Germany, let alone Russia. Likewise, their governments could raise money on better terms. Nor, he points out, does imperial power promote commercial success in a free

---

* His full name was Ralph Norman Angell Lane. He wrote the book under his two middle names to conceal his identity from the paper's proprietor, Lord Northcliffe. After leaving the *Daily Mail* and becoming a celebrity, he adopted the name of Norman Angell and that is how he has been known ever since.

trade environment. 'Although England "owns" Canada, the English merchant is driven out of the Canadian markets by the merchant of Switzerland, who does not "own" Canada.'

Because of the changes that had taken place since the Franco-Prussian war of 1870–71 a decisive victory, like Prussia's in that conflict, was, he believed, no longer possible. The cost of a war would be catastrophic, whichever side won. With considerable foresight he added that for the victor to force the loser to pay reparations, as Prussia had forced France to do in 1871, would, in the new circumstances, be self-defeating as it would hold back the recovery of world trade and so damage the victorious power as well as the defeated. His explanations and arguments on both these points were later borne out by what happened during the First World War and afterwards with the Treaty of Versailles. In many respects they are similar to those put forward after the event in 1919 by Keynes in his great polemic, *The Economic Consequences of the Peace.**

Another of the book's features is its attack both on the glorification of martial valour and on the view that expansionist foreign and colonial policies reflected a praiseworthy national spirit. Such notions were by no means confined to imperial Germany. They enjoyed widespread support in Britain and France. Among their most eloquent advocates was the former President of the United States, Theodore Roosevelt, whom Angell quotes as saying: 'We must play a great part in the world, and especially … perform those deeds of blood, of valour, which above everything else bring national renown.'

For his part Angell argued that just as duelling had fallen out of fashion in Britain as a means of settling disputes between individuals, so should war as a means of settling disputes between nations. He saw that for as long as it was widely believed 'warlike qualities alone can give the virile energy necessary for nations to win the struggle for life' and for as

* See essay on *The Economic Consequences of the Peace* and *The General Theory of Employment, Interest and Money*.

long as governments poured money into building more battleships and other armaments wars might easily break out. He sought to persuade his readers that 'human nature is not unchanging ... that the struggle between nations is no part of the evolutionary law of man's advance', and that the concept of victory had become a great illusion.

The book turned Angell into a celebrity pundit, which proved to be his undoing. He had not in its pages ruled out the possibility of war nor had he argued that war was no longer possible. It is, however, easy to draw that conclusion from a casual reading of his text and some of his own subsequent statements, after he had become a publicist for peace, encouraged that interpretation. As a result, when war broke out he found himself being pilloried for having been wrong. For the rest of his life – he lived until 1967 – he argued with only limited success to put the record straight. At the same time, he continued to campaign and in 1934 was awarded a Nobel Peace Prize.

Besides being a prolific, popular and imaginative author with a huge body of work to his credit, H. G. Wells was one of the most outspoken public intellectuals of his day and a prominent figure in left-wing political circles. There were few subjects on which he did not speak and write, from art and design to women's rights, the organization of society and world government. He was a polymath, who would like to have been remembered as a serious novelist and political thinker. Had he known that subsequent generations would think of him mainly as a founder of science fiction he would probably have been disappointed. His most famous book, and one of the most celebrated of all science fiction books, is *The War of the Worlds*. In its original form, when published in 1898, it is about a Martian invasion of England. In 1938 Orson Welles adapted it for radio in the United States and transferred the setting to that country. The result was so realistic that it was taken by many to be a genuine news broadcast and provoked a mass panic.

The Bickersteth Diaries, 1914–1918

edited by John Bickersteth and published in 1995

Private Lord Crawford's Great War Diaries

edited by Christopher Arnander and published in 2013

The First World War, or The Great War as it was always called until the Second one came along, is the greatest calamity to have befallen the British people in the twentieth century. The war memorials in every city, town and village the length and breadth of the country and the commemorative plaques in so many churches and institutional buildings show the extent to which it affected every community, urban and rural, rich and poor, alike. The names of the fallen in the First War always substantially outnumber those who gave their lives in the Second. Precise overall figures differ from one source to another, as some include men from what were then the colonies and others not. For the British Isles alone the total is something over 700,000, which is more than double the figure for the Second, even when civilian deaths from the bombing of British cities are included. In terms of deaths as a percentage of their population France, Germany and Italy lost even more men in the First War than this country. Australia, Canada, New Zealand, India and other Commonwealth countries that fought alongside Britain also suffered grievously.

It is impossible to encompass the scale of the grief that overwhelmed the nation during the four years of war from August 1914 to November 1918 – the women who lost their husbands, parents their sons and children their fathers. In many cases two or even more sons from the same family were killed and instances were recorded of as many as five. It is through what happened to named individuals that the full extent of the horror can sometimes be most graphically illustrated. The society beauty Lady Diana Cooper told her son many years later that by the end of 1916 when she was twenty-four years old, 'with the single exception of my father, every man she had ever danced with was dead'.[5] By the end of the war, Vera Brittain, famous for her autobiography, *Testament of Youth*, had lost her fiancé, her brother and her two closest men friends.

That was not all. Many hundreds and thousands of the men who returned were physically maimed and often hideously disfigured and/or mentally and psychologically damaged as well. Their lives and those of their families never recovered.

Throughout Europe, on both sides, the war inspired an outpouring of writing – poems, novels, memoirs, histories, diaries and letters – commensurate with its scale. The flood began within months of the first guns being fired and continues to this day with new books being published and old records brought to light. No other conflict involving Britain has inspired so many words. Most have not endured, but wherever English is read the most famous poems written during the war by Rupert Brooke, Wilfred Owen, Edmund Blunden and others still resonate. The prose works published in the 1920s and 1930s by Robert Graves, Siegfried Sassoon, Ford Madox Ford and others who served are also still widely read.

The Bickersteth Diaries and *Private Lord Crawford's Great War Diaries* are among those that have only relatively recently become publicly available. They were private documents not intended for publication and written as and when the opportunity arose. They are snapshots that capture the thoughts and feelings of the writers at the moment they were committed to paper. As such they provide an intimate account of how the war was seen through the eyes of the writers.

Canon Sam Bickersteth was a well-connected Anglican clergyman. He and his wife, Ella, had six sons. By the spring of 1915 four were on active service while one was in the War Office and another a rector in the Midlands. The sons wrote home regularly and Ella transcribed and circulated the letters within the family. As published the *Diaries* consist mainly of letters written by Julian, a chaplain, and Burgon, an officer in a cavalry regiment. Occasionally, the editor, a nephew of the writers, includes a contribution from one of the others or a comment by Ella herself.

The Earl of Crawford and Balcarres, to give him his full title, was a great aristocrat, Scotland's premier earl with a title dating from 1398, and a man of many parts. When the war began he was forty-three and a former Conservative Chief Whip in the House of Commons. He had written a book about the Italian Renaissance sculptor Donatello, helped to found what is now the Art Fund and was chairing a coal and iron company. In 1915, when it became apparent that the war might last a long time, and having turned down an offer to enter the government, he felt he should do something practical to help. Instead of seeking a role in keeping with his status, he joined the Royal Army Medical Corps as a hospital orderly with the rank of private, the lowest in the British Army, a crossing of the rigid class divides of the period that must have been greeted with incredulity by all who knew him.

His diary provides a unique worm's-eye view of how the war and the army appeared to a man with experience at the top of the social, political and business worlds. He served for some fourteen months, in the course of which he refused another ministerial offer, before being persuaded to return to London during a political crisis to become Minister of Agriculture. He was the only member of the government throughout the war to have served in the ranks with the ordinary soldiers, as distinct from being an officer.

When the war began it was greeted with enthusiasm all over Europe and men flocked to the colours – over one million two hundred thousand in Britain by the end of 1914 and double that number by the end of 1915. That they should have continued to do so in 1915 when the horrors had become apparent says a great deal about both the attitudes and condition of the British people at that time. Julian Bickersteth felt he owed it to the country to return from Australia, where he was working, to join up. Ford Madox Ford, who volunteered at the age of forty-one, expressed a widespread feeling when he wrote to his mother: 'If one has enjoyed the privileges of the ruling class of a country all one's life, there seems no alternative to fighting for that country if necessary.'[6]

Others who had not enjoyed such privileges felt similarly impelled. In October 1915 a private suffering from rheumatism was admitted to Crawford's Casualty Clearing Station. He turned out to be sixty-one and had misled the recruitment office about his age. As he had three sons at the front he 'thought it my duty to come out and help them'. Not many elderly men would have lied about their age to join the army, but it is estimated that some quarter of a million underage boys claimed to be nineteen in order to get accepted.

Many volunteers were swept up by the fervour and effectiveness of the recruitment campaigns, epitomized by the famous poster of the mustachioed Lord Kitchener pointing a finger above the caption

'Your Country Needs You'. Some were influenced by the intense social pressure that was put on young men to join up. Others were escaping from boring jobs and marriages. In many cases need was the motivation. Men were better clothed and better fed in the army than leading the kind of lives described in the chapter on *Anna of the Five Towns, The Condition of England* and *The Ragged-Trousered Philanthropists*. 'In my four months' training with the regiment I put on nearly a stone [fourteen pounds] in weight and got a bit taller,' remembered one survivor from a Suffolk village.[7]

Both Burgon Bickersteth and Crawford inveigh against those who don't volunteer. 'You have no conception of the contempt which men out here have for the non-combatant corps,' writes Burgon in 1915. He is strongly in favour of universal conscription while Crawford criticizes the government for its reluctance to introduce it, which it eventually did in 1916. Theirs was the majority view, but there were exceptions. One was the future Labour Prime Minister Clement Attlee, who joined up immediately while his brother Tom became a conscientious objector. Yet they remained on the closest terms of affection and mutual respect both then and for the rest of their lives.[8]

The letters Julian and Burgon sent home provide a vivid impression of the extent to which they were living in the midst of death and must have been agonizing for the parents to receive. Three are typical. In one Julian tells of how 'At least six men died in my arms at the Corps Main Dressing Station during the twenty-four hours following the opening of the battle and many more were hurried away to the Casualty Clearing Stations, only to die there.' Burgon writes in January 1916 about how his unit is to be moved 'to a pretty hot part of the line – an average of thirty yards between us and the Hun'. In another letter he describes breezily how a shell that landed twelve feet away from him turned out to be a dud and only covered him with earth instead of killing him. A letter that Julian found particularly harrowing to write describes an all-night vigil with a man who had been condemned to death for desertion and was to face a firing squad in the morning.*

In Crawford's diary the most striking passages, and those that reveal most about what it was like to be in the army at that time, are about how differently the other ranks, or ordinary soldiers, were treated by comparison with the officers. No social radical or left-wing firebrand could have been more indignant than he, who until then had enjoyed all the privileges of the aristocracy. He makes no complaint about the menial tasks he has to perform in the operating theatre, tending patients or doing manual work around the camp. It is what he signed up for. What shocks him is 'the disparity between the treatment of officers and men based on the old theory that one officer is worth twenty men'. He experiences this most vividly on landing in France with his unit to board the train to take them to the town where they are to be stationed. While the officers travel in a carriage he and thirty-one other men are crammed into a cattle truck of the sort that in the Second World War would be used for deporting Jews to the concentration camps.

One of his biggest complaints is about how much more often officers go on leave than their men, a source of bitterness, he writes, among the rank and file. He himself had to wait eight months for his first leave, during which time his Colonel had four. Whereas officers got leave every three months 'with mathematical regularity' that of the men was allocated in a very hit-and-miss manner. In his own unit it was settled by ballot, which he favoured.

---

* Execution by firing squad was the standard punishment for desertion, cowardice and mutiny in all the armies involved in the war. The Italian Chief of the General Staff when Italy entered the war, General Luigi Cadorna, took this a stage further when he revived the ancient Roman practice of decimation, that is executing one in ten men in units that mutinied, disobeyed orders or simply failed in some other way, although he did not insist on the exact ratio.

Another of his gripes was the way officers disregarded the rule that their baggage should be limited to thirty-five pounds. One of his tasks when wounded officers arrived at his Casualty Clearing Station was to unpack and disinfect their kit. Some would have several times as much as they were allowed with cases full of extra boots, overcoats and other comforts, such as primus stoves. Whatever their rank, officers and men faced the prospect of death together, but, for as long as they survived, these comforts made life somewhat less unpleasant for the officers.

The extent to which officers and men, while serving together in the mud and rat-infested squalor of the trenches and risking death and disablement together on a daily basis, remained members of different castes receives further confirmation in a letter written by Burgon in the summer of 1917. He mentions having a meal with some private soldiers and notes that it was 'the first time I had ever sat down to eat out here in uniform with soldiers'. As a chaplain with the rank of an officer and ministering to officers and men alike, his brother Julian sees the war as an opportunity to bridge this divide. In a passage that shows how far removed middle-class Anglican clergymen were from their working-class parishioners, he writes that the war 'has given parsons the opportunity which nothing else in their lifetime would have given them' to be 'in close touch with the ordinary men and opened one's eyes to their point of view'.

Much of Julian's correspondence deals with the religious services he has arranged, including – a chilling detail – the constant need to find new recruits to assist at them to replace those who have been killed or wounded. He writes about his efforts to spread the Faith through confirmation classes and describes the practical ways in which he consoles the dying, comforts the wounded and acts as an unofficial link between them and their families at home. 'Between us, my chaplains and I wrote and dispatched 3,000 to 4,000 postcards and letters to relatives,' he writes after a particularly bloody engagement in 1917. These added comfort, reassurance and further information to the official notification provided to relatives by the War Office.

Some two years earlier, in 1915, my maternal grandmother had received just such a letter from a chaplain after my grandfather, serving with the Royal Artillery, was killed at the Battle of Neuve Chapelle. The details it gave were so precise that in 1980 it enabled my brother and I to locate the field in which he most likely fell.

The Bickersteths, with four brothers at the front, were phenomenally lucky that only one was killed: Morris at the Battle of the Somme on 1 July 1916, the worst day for casualties in the history of the British Army. The depth of the family's grief is palpable and the language in which they communicate with each other about his death is deeply emotional. There is nothing of the stilted stiff upper lip that is supposed to have characterized that generation. As devout Christians, they believe he has gone straight to heaven. 'We may indeed be proud of him, and we know, don't we, darling ones that he is happy now,' Julian writes to his parents. The 'magnificence' of his death for his country is a recurring theme in the family's correspondence.

It recurs constantly on the memorials and commemorative plaques in churches and elsewhere that were erected after the war. It is part of the language by means of which society and individuals coped with the human cost of war. To this day the solemnity and the sonorous tone of the words on these plaques and memorials retain their power to evoke the grief of those whose sons, brothers and husbands are named on them.

The Bickersteths were a deeply religious family. These words had real meaning for them. But as Julian recognized, their faith was not shared by the vast majority. To most, he writes in one letter, 'religion is simply a name and has never touched heart or mind'. This applies not just to the men, but to the officers too. Despite the prominence of religious education in the curriculum of the public schools, those schools had in Julian's view 'not produced a type of man who feels any need for religion'.

Burgon confirms this analysis. On Good Friday, 1917, he writes, 'not one per cent of the Brigade are aware of the fact, certainly not the significance of the day'. A chaplain, he explains, is not valued for what he represents. He is only 'appreciated by the men in so far as he busies himself with their recreational and physical comfort and respected if he visits the front line and shares their dangers'. Far from being brought, even temporarily, to take religion seriously by their constant exposure to death and disablement, Burgon reports, 'The average British soldier is very fatalistic: "Well, Sir, yer'll be 'it when yer'll be 'it and not afore", sums up his approach.'

As the war dragged on attitudes towards it among those at the front evolved. This is reflected in the brothers' letters. When it began they, like the country at large, were confident of victory and full of animosity towards the Germans. 'As to the Germans!' writes Julian during the early months, 'May God help them! We shall win this war because God cannot allow such scum to exist.' Burgon talks of 'the hated Hun'. By 1917 Julian wonders how the war will ever end and wishes for 'a round table conference'. In 1918 he writes, 'men don't and won't hate the Germans – they only hate the war'. Burgon utters a *cri de cœur*: 'When will this grim butchery of unfledged boys, German and English end?' The trajectory of their feelings reflected that of many at the front, but by no means all, as an argument Burgon had with his Colonel shows. The Colonel intends 'to teach my children to hate the Germans, and to teach their children to hate the Germans'. Burgon replies: 'If you do that, what is to be the future of Europe?'

While those at the front were becoming disillusioned, the civilian population at home, egged on by government propaganda and the press, remained bellicose. When in 1917 the Conservative Lord Lansdowne suggested that the possibility of a negotiated peace should be explored he was howled down at home while, as Julian reports, widely supported at the front. As might be expected Crawford saw through the propaganda at an early stage, as an October 1915 diary entry about the Battle of Neuve Chapelle shows: 'a great victory as announced to the world, but in reality a costly and dangerous fiasco. Our casualties gigantic, our net gains negligible.'

Towards the end of 1916 Julian writes of how 'The country is hoodwinked. Facts are distorted or totally misrepresented by the press.' This follows a letter from Burgon about a lunch with the *Daily Mail* correspondent Philip Gibbs that casts a fascinating light on the contrast between what the troops were experiencing and how it was reported at home. 'I am not allowed to tell the truth or what is worse, I am made to tell lies,' Gibbs complained. He had received a letter from the celebrated author G. K. Chesterton, complimenting him on his articles and 'praising the great spirit of the Briton' to which he had responded with one explaining the true horrors of the war. 'Chesterton, sitting safely in England, wrote back totally unconvinced and spoke of the necessity for sacrifice.'

War 2 – Warnings and Reality

Challenge to Death edited by Storm Jameson, 1934, and *Guilty Men* by 'Cato', 1940.

My Early Life by Winston S. Churchill, 1930.

Flare Path by Terence Rattigan, 1942, *Few Eggs and No Oranges: The Diaries of Vere Hodgson, 1940–45*, and *Darling Monster: The Letters of Lady Diana Cooper to Her Son John Julius Norwich, 1939–52*.

Challenge to Death

edited by Storm Jameson (1934)

Guilty Men

by 'Cato' (1940)

So dreadful was the loss of life and suffering caused to all the combatant countries by the 1914–18 war that it was widely hoped, in a phrase originally coined by H. G. Wells, that it would prove to be, 'The war to end war'.* Only that, it was thought, could possibly, in any way, justify the sacrifice that had taken place. The yearning to ensure that there could be no repetition of what had happened was felt in all countries. Its tangible result was the formation of the League of Nations, under the terms of which the member states committed themselves to the peaceful resolution of disputes in the hope that war could be banished for ever.

This aspiration held sway in Britain to a greater extent than in the other major European countries because the nation was untroubled

* In the months following the outbreak of war Wells published a number of articles that were brought together in a book entitled *The War That Will End War*. This gave rise to the pithier 'The war to end war', which soon became a catchphrase.

by historic nightmares or grudges against its neighbours. France was haunted by the spectre of its defeat by Prussia in 1871, after which the new German empire had been proclaimed in Louis XIV's Palace of Versailles; a humiliating memory. It had also suffered more than any other country from the recent war as nearly all the fighting and destruction had taken place on its territory. Germany had not only been defeated; it also believed itself to be the victim of an unjust peace settlement in the Treaty of Versailles. Italy was one of the victorious powers, but believed it had been cheated of the fruits of victory by its allies. All three countries, like Britain, had peace movements and the League of Nations was active in promoting cooperation between them by means of conferences and other gatherings. But in each there was a significant body of opinion that believed in the need to prepare for another round of fighting and opinion was more divided than in Britain.

Challenge to Death was published in 1934 just as those preparations for another round were beginning to gather momentum on the Continent. It expressed the dreams and wishful thinking of the British peace movement based on the belief, in the words of its editor, the popular novelist (Margaret) Storm Jameson, that, 'Ours is the largest and most important political unit in the world.' She believed that, 'More than any other state, more even than those which exceed us in actual or potential wealth, we can influence world thought.' In this view she reflected the beliefs of many in this country at that time.

Guilty Men is a scream of rage and recrimination published in 1940, when all such illusions had been swept away, as the country fought for its life against the might of Nazi Germany after the evacuation of its army from Dunkirk and the defeat of its French ally. Its authors, writing under the pseudonym of Cato, the Roman statesman famous for his probity and tenacity in opposing Julius Caesar, were three left-wing journalists, one of whom, Michael Foot,* went on to become leader of the Labour Party in the 1980s.

The peace movement in Britain had reached its peak in 1931 when membership of its principal vehicle, the League of Nations Union, a sort of supporters' club for the League, rose above the million mark. Thereafter it had declined under the pressure of events. In 1932 the League failed to prevent Japan's invasion of Manchuria and in February 1933 Japan walked out of the League. In May 1933 Hitler came to power in Berlin. Germany then walked out too and embarked on a rearmament programme. In 1938, Hitler took over Austria and in March 1939 Czechoslovakia before finally triggering the Second World War with the invasion of Poland in September 1939. Italy invaded Abyssinia in 1935 and the Spanish Civil War raged from 1936 to 1939.

Despite the movement's declining membership and all that was happening abroad, anti-war feeling remained strong in Britain. In February 1933 the Oxford Union passed a resolution 'that in no circumstances will this House fight for King and Country'. It was widely reported across Europe and taken in some circles to mean that the elite of British youth had become irredeemably pacifist. In Britain too, it caused a considerable stir and led to similar votes in some other universities. In October of the same year a by-election was held in Fulham at which a Conservative pro-rearmament candidate defending a large majority was defeated by a Labour pacifist. In the winter of 1934–5 the League of Nations Union with the support of thirty-four other groups organized a ballot on the lines of a general election. A total of over eleven and a half million votes were cast of which 96 per cent were in favour of continued British membership of the League. In

---

* The other two were Frank Owen and Peter Howard. In a private letter in my possession to Donald McCormick dated 30 June 1969, Michael Foot wrote: 'We concealed our identities under the name of Cato partly for publicity purposes, and partly to hide the matter from our common employer at that time, Beaverbrook. But we did not have much success for long with the second aim.'

1936 the charismatic Canon of St Paul's Cathedral, the Reverend Dick Sheppard, founded the Peace Pledge Union that enrolled a hundred and thirty-five thousand men in favour of absolute pacifism in order to demonstrate that men were just as much against war as women.

These and other expressions of anti-war feeling led the government to play down the need for rearmament during the 1935 general election campaign and not to press ahead with it afterwards as vigorously as those, like Churchill, who were warning of impending danger, wanted.

Challenge to Death was conceived in the months after Hitler took power as a way of bringing together the various strands of the peace movement in a single propaganda exercise. It emerged from a dinner held in February 1934 at London's Wellington Club, an ironic choice of venue for an anti-war meeting, presided over by Viscount Cecil of Chelwood. As a Conservative minister in the wartime coalition, he had played a significant role in formulating the ideas on which the League of Nations covenant was based. Besides Storm Jameson, the list of contributors to the book included a number of then prominent public intellectuals, of whom only the writers J. B. Priestley, Rebecca West and Vera Brittain, the poet Edmund Blunden and the scientist Julian Huxley have any resonance today.*

When the book emerged later that year, it received widespread attention and not only in this country. The *New York Herald Tribune* hailed it as speaking for the post-war 'lost generation'.[1] Its assumptions and recommendations reveal much about the hopes and fears of the period. The authors correctly identified the link between dictatorship and nationalism on the one hand with a propensity to aggression on the other that made Germany and Italy such obvious sources of danger. They assumed, like everyone else in this country, that Britain would always be on the side of peace, although Lord Cecil made a telling point

* It is worthy of note that within only sixteen years of women gaining the vote in 1918, five of the sixteen contributors were women.

when he drew attention to the words of 'Land of Hope and Glory'. As he pointed out, a nation with a large colonial empire that sang, 'Wider still and wider may her bounds be set/God who made her mighty make her mightier yet' could hardly 'throw stones across the channel'.

Besides overestimating British power and influence, the authors' most serious geopolitical error was to take insufficient account of the United States and the Soviet Union. That it would be those two powers who, when war came, would determine its outcome simply did not occur to them. This was in part because their actual military strength, as distinct from its potential, looked modest in the 1930s. Extraordinary as it now seems, the United States' army was smaller than Portugal's. Another reason was the overwhelmingly Eurocentric focus of the authors. Unlike H. G. Wells in his novels *The War in the Air* and *The World Set Free*, they could not imagine the destiny of the world being shaped by anyone other than Western Europeans. In this they were typical of their time.

However, they shared Wells' fear that the outcome of the next war would be determined in the air rather than on the ground. It was not the prospect of a resumption of trench warfare that haunted them, it was the fear of being bombarded from the air. The essence of this fear was distilled in two oft-repeated phrases by the Conservative leader Stanley Baldwin, who was three times Prime Minister between 1923 and 1937. In 1927 he had asked, 'and who in Europe does not know that one more war in the West, and the civilization of the ages will fall with as great a crash as that of Rome?'[2] In 1932, during a House of Commons debate in which he was arguing in favour of rearmament, he warned that 'the bomber will always get through'[3] and that therefore the only defence was offence.

These fears, but not Baldwin's conclusion, lie at the heart of *Challenge to Death*. Gerald Heard, a broadcaster and writer, foresaw a situation in which, 'outside Whitehall, as soon as the attack begins,

London has ceased to function as a capital or even as a city'. He forecast that a dictatorship would follow. Philip Noel-Baker, a former Labour MP who later became a Cabinet minister in the 1945 Labour government, quoted various scenarios put forward by military experts. One suggested that within forty-eight hours of an attack 40 per cent of London's population would leave the city and within a week 80 per cent. Other forecasts were equally alarming. Noel-Baker suggested that, though these fears might turn out to be exaggerated, the question remained, 'How long will it be after war begins before London and Paris and Berlin will each be a shattered, flaming hell?' His conclusion was 'that the next war, if it should happen, will obliterate the civilization in which we live', as Wells had warned in his novels would be the case. In the event, that proved to be wrong. Civilization survived, but the fears were none the less real for that.

As Harold Macmillan recalled in 1962 when he was Prime Minister, 'We thought of warfare in 1938 rather as people think of nuclear warfare today',* a point not generally given sufficient weight when the government's efforts during the 1930s to avoid war are condemned as appeasement. Nor have subsequent generations been sufficiently understanding of how my parents' generation, which had lost husbands, fathers, sons and brothers in the previous war, dreaded the prospect of going through the same agony again. In their position I should have felt the same and, like them, wished the government to do everything it reasonably could to avoid a repetition. I only hope I would have realized in time when that policy became self-defeating.

The attempt by the British government to avoid another war by reaching an enduring settlement with Hitler failed, not least because it was based on a fundamental misjudgement of his character and capacity

* Macmillan was speaking during the Cuban Missile Crisis of that year when the United States and the Soviet Union probably came closer to a nuclear exchange than at any other time during the Cold War.

for evil, but, in the circumstances of the time, it is understandable that it should have enjoyed widespread support. Likewise, though the proposals put forward in *Challenge to Death* were misconceived and impractical, even at the moment they were launched they reflected real fears and should be seen as a constructive attempt by a group of concerned individuals to tackle the underlying problems of their age.

The contributors came up with a variety of ideas for creating an environment that would diminish the chances of war. Among the problems they identified was the relationship in all countries between arms manufacturers promoting their products and the armed forces wanting always to have the most up-to-date equipment. The novelist and journalist Winifred Holtby argued that the only way to break this link was for the arms manufacturing companies to be nationalized and subjected to international control.

The most ambitious scheme was for 'the transference of control over aviation to the League, and [the creation of] an international air force'. In a chapter headed 'The International Air Police Force', Noel-Baker developed this idea. He advocated the total abolition of all national air forces of every kind and the supervision and control of this disarmament by a permanent commission with the right 'to inspect at will all aerodromes and airports, aviation establishments of every kind and aircraft factories'.

The result would be that, 'Once it is established, the International Police will be the only armed air force in the world.' He discussed whether it should be composed of national contingents or be a homogeneous international corps and came down in favour of the latter. The commander, he suggested, should come from a small country, such as Sweden or the Netherlands, and that its working languages should be French and English. His description of how it would function and the facilities it would need went into considerable detail, but was weak on how and according to what rules and safeguards international civilian control would be exercised. Nor did he face up to the question of what to do if a non-member of the League, such as the United States, Germany or Japan, refused to sign up and created a powerful air force of its own.

The difficulties of gaining agreement to set up the force are glossed over. Noel-Baker was convinced that, if Britain would support the scheme, 'our acceptance would be decisive'. Jameson wrote, 'Of the politicians who throng that Hall of Hopes, the Assembly at Geneva [the League's headquarters], it is the English on whom all wait. It is therefore our duty, and should be our pleasure, to assume responsibility and show the bogged and strayed nations of Europe a road to follow.' This illusion that where Britain led others would follow did not end with the 1930s. Between the 1950s and 1970s the Campaign for Nuclear Disarmament, generally known as CND, argued that if Britain would unilaterally renounce its nuclear weapons, it would set an example that would influence others.

None of the contributors to *Challenge to Death* was among the twelve men the authors of *Guilty Men* held responsible for Britain's desperate plight in 1940. Their purpose was to praise the army evacuated from Dunkirk for its courage and to show how, by ignoring Churchill's warnings of German rearmament and their own ineptitude, those in power during the 1930s had been responsible for the mess the country was in. Apart from Ramsay MacDonald, who in 1931 had resigned the leadership of the Labour Party to lead the coalition National government, all those in the dock were Conservatives. The pacifist George Lansbury, who had briefly led the Labour Party, was excoriated, but not charged. Because Conservatives had dominated the National government, whose efforts to reach an accommodation with Hitler through the policy of appeasement had failed, the authors' accusations both reflected and confirmed the public mood. They also helped to form the subsequent judgement of history on the period.

Written in a matter of weeks, *Guilty Men* is a powerful and convincing narrative. The authors showed how at each step of the way, from Hitler's assumption of power in the spring of 1933 to Prime Minister Neville Chamberlain's agreement with him at Munich in the autumn of 1938, the government had misjudged both his intentions and the speed of his rearmament. Against that background, they were scornful of the government for allowing itself to be influenced by the 'Peace Vote' in the general election of 1935. Reading their denunciations alongside *Challenge to Death* is like being in two parallel universes at the same time. In one the politicians are blamed for endangering the country by not rearming enough, in the other they are condemned for not leading the way to international disarmament. In one they are condemned for not building up the strength of the Royal Air Force more quickly, in the other for not promoting an International Air Force Police. That was the political story of the 1930s.

The desire for peace was still deeply felt in 1938 when Chamberlain and the French Prime Minister signed their now notorious pact with Hitler in Munich. Chamberlain hailed it as 'peace in our time'. He returned home a hero to appear with the King and Queen on the balcony at Buckingham Palace to receive the plaudits of the crowds cheering in the Mall; an unprecedented demonstration of royal support for a government of the day, and a reflection of the widespread public support for the agreement at that time. Fortunately, the government was by then sufficiently seized of the impending danger that it pushed ahead with rearmament and, by the skin of its teeth, was able to provide the Royal Air Force with the men and machines that, in 1940, enabled it to defeat the Luftwaffe in the Battle of Britain, which followed the retreat from Dunkirk.

The Battle of Britain and Dunkirk were heroic exploits. They have become engraved on the national memory as emblematic of the British spirit. It is right that they should be remembered and commemorated.

But, as well as providing an inspiration to subsequent generations, they have given rise to a serious misreading of the national interest. Instead of being seen as an awful warning of the existential dangers of isolation, they have led some to believe that distancing ourselves from our continental neighbours, rather than joining with them in common enterprises, is inherent in our national character and destiny.

My Early Life

by Winston S. Churchill* (1930)

The one man, above all others, to whom Britain owes its salvation in 1940 is Winston Churchill, who became Prime Minister in May, the month before Dunkirk. Thanks to his leadership, this country, supported by its empire and Commonwealth, was able to hold out alone until June 1941 when Hitler invaded Russia and then in December declared war on the United States following the Japanese attack on Pearl Harbor. His role in 1940 and 1941 constitutes the hinge on which the history of this country, of Europe and, in many ways, the world turned during the twentieth century. He remained in office until victory was achieved in 1945 and was again Prime Minister from 1951 until 1955. But, to paraphrase the title of one of his own books, the period when Britain stood alone was his finest hour.

For many of the forty-three books in seventy-two volumes that he published during his lifetime he relied on teams of researchers and ghost writers whose drafts he then transformed, 'by adding insights, comparisons, metaphors and flights of fancy'.[4] *My Early Life* is all his own work, or at least very largely so. It is highly personal and

---

* His earliest books were signed Winston Churchill until in 1899 he became aware of a successful American novelist of that name and decided to add the initial S for Spencer.

self-revealing and covers the years and the experiences that moulded him between his birth in 1874 and his early years in the House of Commons after the 1900 general election. In his own words it goes a long way to explaining why he was so distrusted by the British public until the moment in 1940 when it became apparent that only under his leadership could Britain defy Hitler.

He was feeling rather out of sorts when he wrote it. He had recently lost office as a result of the 1929 general election. He had also lost a good deal of money in the financial crash of that year. At the same time the country's prospects were overshadowed by the onset of the Great Depression. His sombre mood is reflected in the preface where he compares 'these anxious and dubious times' to 'a vanished age' in the late nineteenth century, when he was young and 'the dominant forces in Great Britain were very sure of themselves and their doctrines'. His nostalgic recollections, which would have been shared by many of his fellow citizens, and not just of his class and background, cast a revealing, and, sometimes, surprising light on that vanished age.

Like almost all members of the more prosperous classes until well into the twentieth century, the most important influence on Churchill's childhood was his nurse, or nanny, a woman called Mrs Everest. His father was the charismatic politician Lord Randolph Churchill, whose rise to high office was followed by a precipitate fall and early death; his mother, Jennie, was a beautiful and promiscuous American heiress. They were distant and glamorous figures, rarely seen and to be adored from afar. It was to Mrs Everest, 'your loving old woom', as she signed her letters to him when he was away at school, that he felt closest. Although accustomed to the grandest of grand houses, including Blenheim Palace where he was born, he 'loved Ventnor' on the Isle of Wight, where Mrs Everest would take him to stay with her sister, whose husband was a retired prison warder. The bond between them remained very close. Recalling her death in *My Early Life*, he writes,

'She had been my dearest and most intimate friend during the whole of the twenty years that I had lived.'

His feelings towards her were later to influence his approach to public policy. In *My Early Life*, he writes that his awareness of how many such women, after leaving their employer, ended their lives in penury made him glad, as a minister in Asquith's Liberal government, to play a part in the introduction of old age pensions and national insurance in 1911. This measure, part of a package of far-reaching reforms initiated by the Chancellor of the Exchequer, David Lloyd George, was regarded as very radical by British public opinion, although Bismarck had pioneered it in Germany many years before. It marks the first step on the long road to the establishment of the welfare state after 1945. The credit for that great innovation lies with the Labour government of 1945–51, but its genesis was a famous report by Lord Beveridge in 1942 that was commissioned and published by the wartime coalition led by Churchill.

After a famously unsuccessful school career at Harrow, Churchill found his self-confidence and acquired the characteristics and attitudes that were to become his hallmark serving as a young officer in a British Army cavalry regiment, the 4th Hussars, in India. One was the love of reading and the omniscient knowledge of history that together enabled him to become such a successful writer and orator as well as forming his approach to politics. It was, he writes, 'when I had almost completed my twenty-second year that the desire for learning came upon me'. Thereafter, while in barracks, where his duties were very light, he read voraciously for four or five hours a day.

Beginning with Gibbon's *Decline and Fall of the Roman Empire** he moved on to Macaulay, Malthus and Darwin and touched on others, including Plato, Aristotle and Schopenhauer. This was a solitary exercise. He had no university tutor or supervisor to guide him and he formed

* He was delighted to find that Gibbon in his autobiography expressed gratitude to his old nurse.

his own conclusions as he went along; an extraordinary exercise in self-education. No such books would have been in the library of the officers' mess and he relied on his mother to dispatch them in enormous parcels from England; on one occasion eight volumes of Gibbon, on another twelve of Macaulay.

The other characteristic he acquired at that time, and which comes through strongly in *My Early Life*, was his delight in war. In those days there was almost always a small colonial war going on somewhere in the empire. Churchill invariably volunteered to go wherever the fighting was thickest, first in India and later in Africa where, in 1898, he participated in the British Army's last victorious cavalry charge at the Battle of Omdurman.* The frankness with which he records the thrill of combat and the rather casual way he writes about casualties jar with those of a less martial disposition. Books and articles about his adventures poured from his pen and turned him into a minor celebrity until he was captured during the Boer War. After a dramatic escape from the camp in which he was being held prisoner, and a hair-raising flight across hundreds of miles of enemy-controlled territory, he returned home a hero and a household name. On the back of this he was catapulted into the House of Commons in the 1900 general election and able to earn large sums of money lecturing both in Britain and the United States where his mother opened many plutocratic doors for him.

The pattern of his life was set. Politics replaced fighting. Otherwise the rhythm of action interspersed by writing and public speaking continued until the end of his life. His range was enormous, from his multi-volume account of the First World War, entitled *The World Crisis*, and his biography in four volumes of his great ancestor, the Duke of Marlborough, at one end of the spectrum to lightweight articles in the popular press at the other. All were highly paid, which helped to fund

* It is salutary to think that as a young man he took part in this cavalry charge and as an old man authorized the British hydrogen bomb programme.

his lavish lifestyle. *The World Crisis*, published in the United States as well as in Britain and serialized in *The Times*, is estimated to have earned him £25,000, or about £1,500,000 in today's money. A series of articles in the early 1930s for the *News of World* on 'Great Stories of the World Retold', from *Ben-Hur* to *Uncle Tom's Cabin*, was paid for at the rate of £330 each, or about £22,600 in today's money. Inevitably, however, his writing exposed his restless spirit, belligerent character and enormous ego. Arthur Balfour, a former Prime Minister and Cabinet colleague, mocked *The World Crisis* as 'Churchill's autobiography disguised as a history of the world'.[5]

His record in office reinforced his literary image. As Home Secretary in 1910 he earned the undying enmity of the Welsh miners by his handling of the so-called Tonypandy Riots. As First Lord of the Admiralty he initiated and was blamed for what turned out to be the disastrous Gallipoli campaign of 1915. Many were also disgusted by his frank enjoyment of the war, about which he spoke openly, as during the height of that campaign to Violet Asquith, the Prime Minister's daughter. 'I know a curse should rest upon me – because I love this war,' he told her over a dinner at the Admiralty. 'I know it's smashing and shattering the lives of thousands every moment – and yet – I can't help it – I enjoy every second of it.' During the previous month he had told her stepmother, Margot, 'I would not be out of this glorious, delicious war for anything the world could give me.' The bestselling author Arnold Bennett's lightly fictionalized portrait of him in *Lord Raingo*, a popular novel about the wartime government, brought this characteristic to the attention of the general public. His aggressive stance and divisive behaviour during the General Strike of 1925 further antagonized many people. His crossing the floor from the Conservatives to the Liberals when the latter were doing well in the early years of the century and his return to the Conservative Party in the 1920s, after the Liberal Party had collapsed, added to the aura of distrust that surrounded him.

In the 1930s India was injected into this volatile mix with calamitous consequences both for him and the country. In *My Early Life* Churchill had written in rapturous terms about his time there: the numerous servants – butler, syce, head groom and dressing boy – who 'formed the foundation of a cavalry subaltern's household', the polo matches between rival regiments and teams supported by Indian princes, the pleasures of regimental life and the thrill of skirmishing on the North-West Frontier. Shortly after the book's publication, and while it was being widely read throughout the country, the government brought forward plans to move India along the road to self-government and eventual independence.

Such plans were anathema to him. He seemed unable to grasp the extent to which India and the foundations of British power there had changed since the 1890s and opposed them root and branch. Coupled with the imperial nostalgia that suffused *My Early Life*, this created the impression of an anachronistic romantic out of touch with the temper of the times. The extreme tone of some of his rhetoric, notably when he mocked Mahatma Gandhi, the widely respected Indian advocate of non-violent resistance to British rule, as 'the half-naked fakir', damaged him badly. These errors of judgement were then reinforced by his emotional and ill-judged support for Edward VIII during the 1936 Abdication crisis. Against this background Churchill looked like a man whose time had passed; a man whose obituary would have read, had he died at that time, that he had been brilliant, but, like his father, fundamentally unstable and not to be trusted.

So, neither fellow politicians nor the public at large were disposed to listen when he insistently warned in speeches and articles about the threat posed by the rising power of Nazi Germany and the need for Britain to intensify its rearmament programme. He and his small band of followers were disregarded both in Parliament and outside. After he opposed the now infamous Munich agreement between the Prime

Minister, Neville Chamberlain, and Hitler in the autumn of 1938 hostility towards him within the Conservative Party became so great that he had to fight off a move in his constituency of Epping in Essex to de-select him as their parliamentary candidate.

The breakdown of the Munich agreement followed by the outbreak of war in September 1939 transformed the public's view of Churchill. He was proved to have been right about Germany all along and a far more acute and up-to-date observer of current European trends than his critics. His well-known love of battle was likewise transformed from being a disadvantage into exactly the characteristic the country needed. He was invited to rejoin the government as First Lord of the Admiralty, the post he had held in 1914. When, in 1940, it became obvious that Chamberlain was unable to prosecute the war effectively, Churchill, at the age of sixty-five, finally achieved his life's ambition to become Prime Minister.

There was nothing inevitable about this. Quite the contrary. Germany's military successes had badly shaken the British political establishment. When he entered No. 10 Downing Street at the head of a new National coalition government there were many more in British public life than is now generally recognized who would have preferred to look for a way out of the struggle than to fight on.

King George VI was not one of them. When France made peace with Germany he wrote to his mother, Queen Mary: 'Personally I feel happier now we have no allies to be polite to and pamper.'[6] Churchill himself was more realistic. He knew Britain had to find new allies and did all that he could to bring the United States into the war. When Soviet Russia resisted Hitler's attack in June 1941, he rushed to embrace it, although he had always opposed Communism and knew very well that its regime was as morally reprehensible as the Nazis'. Then, six months later, came the real turning point when Hitler, in a monumental act of folly, declared war on the United States a few days after the Japanese attack on Pearl Harbor. Together Britain, the Soviet Union and the United States eventually won the war against Germany and Japan, but they could never have done so if Britain had made peace or been defeated in 1940.

When it was all over Churchill, with a team of assistants, wrote a history of the conflict in six volumes entitled *The Second World War*. This time nobody could object, as Balfour had earlier done, when he put himself at the centre of the story.

Flare Path

by Terence Rattigan (1942)

Few Eggs and No Oranges: The Diaries of Vere Hodgson 1940–45,

published in 1971

Darling Monster: The Letters of Lady Diana Cooper to Her Son John Julius Norwich 1939–1952

edited by John Julius Norwich and published in 2013

The Second World War brought the British people face to face with the reality of war for the first time since the Civil War involving Charles I and Cromwell in the seventeenth century. Instead of being a safe haven from which men went out to fight on the high seas or in other countries, Britain itself became a battleground. There had been a foretaste of this during the 1914–18 war when both sides had launched aerial bombardments against each other's cities, but those had been on a small scale. The German bombing raids, the worst of which from September 1940 to May 1941 became known as the blitz, put the civilian population of major cities* as much at risk as front-line troops had ever been. The men of the Royal Air Force who fought back against the attackers and mounted counter-strikes against German cities spent their off-duty hours at airfields in the countryside in close contact with civilians. The war was part of people's daily lives, not something they read about in newspapers or letters home from the troops. These three books capture the feel of what that meant in the most personal terms.

Flare Path is a play set in 1941 in a hotel near an RAF base in Lincolnshire involving a group of airmen, their wives and the hotel staff. Terence Rattigan wrote it while himself on active service with the RAF as a flight lieutenant and it is derived from his own experience. Vere Hodgson, the author of *Few Eggs and No Oranges*, described herself as 'an ordinary commonplace Londoner'. She lived in the Notting Hill district of London, then a modest rather than a fashionable area, where she worked for a community doing religious and philanthropic work among the homeless and the poor. She wanted to keep her cousin in Northern Rhodesia (now Zambia) informed of what was happening in London, so kept a daily record of what she saw and heard, which she then dispatched by post. Lady Diana Cooper was the wife of Duff Cooper, the Minister of Information in Churchill's government during the blitz. Like many other well-to-do couples,† they had sent their son, John Julius, then aged ten, to North America to escape the bombing. She wrote her letters to provide him with a running commentary on

* Among the worst hit were London, Swansea, Cardiff, Bristol, Southampton, Plymouth, Birmingham, Coventry and Liverpool with many others also suffering severe damage.

† Although the practice was widespread, the Coopers were strongly criticized for sending their son to safety. For a government minister to do so was regarded as defeatist and, as Duff Cooper's ministry was in charge of propaganda and raising public morale, his action ran directly counter to his responsibilities.

what she and his father were doing. As an elderly man, when he had achieved fame as the author John Julius Norwich, he edited them before their publication in 2013. Vere Hodgson edited her diary herself before it was published in 1971.

Running through all three books is a theme captured by Maudie, the wife of one of the airmen in *Flare Path*. Her home in London had been bombed out and she was having to live and work in St Albans. When asked how she is managing the change, she replies: 'What I say is, there's a war on and things have got to be a bit different and we've just got to get used to it – that's all.' With everyone's life disrupted to some extent, and everyone knowing someone worse off than themselves, this response captures the mood of the time. What would have been unimaginable, not to say intolerable, in peacetime became a new normal.

This was as true of the Coopers as of others, albeit at a more privileged level than that of humbler folk. While the raids were in progress, most Londoners, men, women and children, were crammed hugger-mugger into basements, air raid shelters and Tube stations where they would often spend several nights at a stretch. The Coopers had closed their house and taken rooms at the Dorchester Hotel, then recently built and thought more likely to withstand bombs than the Ritz, Claridge's or the Savoy. The hotel's management set up dormitories below ground for its guests in the Turkish baths and the gym.

Lady Diana describes life in the latter where they are one of four couples, including the Foreign Secretary, Lord Halifax, and his wife. 'Conversations are conducted in whispers that take me straight back to childhood,' she writes. Snoring is a problem. 'If Papa makes a sound I am up in a flash and rearrange his position. Perhaps Lady Halifax is doing the same to his lordship.' Despite the difficulties they continue to give dinner parties, guests sometimes arriving 'pyjamas in hand' lest an inopportune air raid prevents them from getting home and they have to find somewhere to doss down. Later, she reports gleefully,

'The Dorchester stands up well so far. The water flows well, whereas at Claridge's no one has had a bath for a week.'

Not even the Dorchester's walls could protect its residents from the noise of the raids with the anti-aircraft guns in Hyde Park doing more to disturb Lady Diana's sleep than the bombs, unless they fell very close. Vere Hodgson makes the same complaint. At the start of the blitz both women constantly write about broken nights and how tired they are, but as it goes on they find they can sometimes sleep through the noise.

Understandably Lady Diana spares her son harrowing details of the damage and the deaths, although she does sometimes tell him when the houses of friends he knows have been destroyed and of the trouble she takes to move his father's extensive library to safety in the country. I asked John Julius in his later years whether receiving his mother's letters at his school in Toronto made him worry about whether his parents would be killed. He replied that they never did, adding, 'I must have been a very unimaginative child.'

Vere Hodgson, by contrast, is meticulous in recording the death and destruction. Her deadpan style and absence of adjectives enhances the horror. When two bombs go right through Whiteleys department store in Queensway a water main bursts and those in the shelter below who survived the blast are drowned, forty-seven in all. A direct hit on the Café de Paris at Leicester Square kills some thirty-four people dining and dancing there. Another on the Notting Hill police station kills twenty policemen. And so on, night after night. Vere Hodgson herself was never bombed out. When she writes about those who were her tone is as matter-of-fact, as if she was referring to some routine domestic drama: 'Ivy rang up and we arranged to lunch together. Said she had been bombed out again. Found it hard to believe! This is the third time.'

She lists the names of the historic churches that have been destroyed and goes for walks round different parts of London to make an inventory of the damage. A typical report reads: 'Down Whitehall, past Horse Guards, which had had a tremendous Biff and looks awful. Reached Westminster … two definite holes in the roof of the Hall. Damage to the Abbey is not apparent from the outside. Up Victoria St., Christ Church there is finished. Great crater in front of the Army and Navy Stores – fit to hold a bus. Various biffs and wonks. Station looks battered, but eventually groped our way in to a cup of tea.'

But, as is always the case, in even the most extreme situations daily life goes on. Vere Hodgson writes about how scarce oranges have become and how, when she manages to find two, she feels obliged to give one away and to share the other. Eggs, by contrast, are still available. She records how the laburnum is coming out and how a hedgehog has disappeared from her garden. On a warm day in February 1941 she buys lingerie material at Barkers in Kensington High Street and watches gulls and ducks sunning themselves by the Round Pond in Kensington Gardens. Lady Diana records buying a dress from Molyneux, one of the most fashionable couturiers, of occasional excursions to the theatre and of her delight at spending weekends in grand country houses.

The absence of oranges (and bananas), that children like me born shortly before the war had never seen, became a sort of symbol of wartime shortages. The son of Field Marshal Montgomery, who in November 1942 became a national hero after defeating the Germans at the Battle of El Alamein in North Africa, once told me that as a schoolboy he only became fully aware of just how important his father was, when, on one of his returns to this country, his father presented a crate of oranges to his school.

Vere Hodgson makes no reference in her published record to her welfare work, although, according to Jenny Hartley of the University of Surrey, Roehampton, writing in the preface, it was sufficiently important to exempt her from conscription. Lady Diana's took the form of serving in a mobile canteen on RAF bases. She writes in one letter of how 'It's lovely because RAF men rush the van and are jokey and grateful for hot teas and doughnuts, Mars bars and fruit gums.' In another she records arriving at an airfield soon after 'it has had a "dusting" from the enemy. Not one hangar has missed that duster, and when a hangar gets an explosion of course it looks far worse than a house.' In a third, she tells how, 'after my canteen [I] buzzed down to Chequers to have lunch with Clemmie Churchill', the Prime Minister's wife, a juxtaposition of activities that speaks volumes about how topsy-turvy the world had become.

Strangely, neither woman seems surprised by the remarkable way the essential services kept going. Public transport continued to run, the post was collected and delivered, the telephone still rang. They grumble about delays, such as those when Vere Hodgson goes by train to visit her family in Birmingham, but there is no mention of the astonishing work of the fire brigades nor of how quickly services were adapted and restored to work round the bomb damage. It's as if they take it for granted that, one way or another, people will cope, as indeed they did.

It seems to have been much the same in Germany. While the Luftwaffe was raining bombs on British cities the RAF was doing the same, though initially to a lesser extent, to German cities. The effects of this in Berlin were recorded in her daily diary by a young aristocratic Russian émigré called Marie Vassiltchikov.[7] Her reactions and those of people she writes about to the bombing, her inventories of the damage and her descriptions of a city adapting to the disruption caused by bombing are remarkably similar to those of her British counterparts. So is her cheerfulness. Not until 1943 and 1944, when the Allied raids reached massive proportions, creating firestorms that killed thousands of people at a time, does the tone darken. By then too her social circle, from which came those involved in the plot to kill Hitler, was in grave danger with the Gestapo arresting many of her friends.

The raids over Germany were carried out by RAF Bomber Command from airfields on the eastern side of Britain, of which the one described in *Flare Path* was typical. These raids were so dangerous that at 41 per cent Bomber Command had a higher death rate than any other branch of the British armed services. *Flare Path*, named for the lights that guided the bombers as they took off into the night, deals fundamentally with what it means for a man to have to live in a state of perpetual fear and the particular form of courage required to keep on going. To drive the point home, the man in question is a highly decorated young officer, Flight Lieutenant Teddy Graham, who, besides being widely admired for his bravery, is worshipped by his crew for his special ability to bring them home safely regardless of the damage sustained by his aircraft.

The play opens in the hotel near the airfield where some airmen, their wives and the staff are expecting a quiet weekend. To their astonishment a famous Hollywood film star called Peter Kyle arrives in search of a room. He has come, we soon learn, to reclaim Patricia, Teddy's actress wife, with whom he had formerly lived in California. His career is on the wane and he wants her back to help him adjust to his decline. She had married Teddy on the rebound and Peter has no difficulty in persuading her that she should return to him.

However, before she can confront Teddy with her decision the squadron is unexpectedly ordered to go on a raid. Their talk has to be postponed for a few hours until he gets back and he sets off to risk his life completely unaware that his wife is planning to leave him. While he is away the Squadron Leader, who has remained behind, tells her how amused he and his fellow officers are by the way Teddy speaks with so much pride about her and being married to her. She begins to realize the extent of his dependence on her and her resolve is shaken.

The following morning, she finds out for herself how much she means to him. He has had a terrifying experience. His plane was badly damaged by enemy fire and he has had the greatest difficulty bringing it home. His crew are filled with admiration at his skill and gratitude to him for their safe return. He is the hero of the moment, but obviously not well, and he won't let her call a doctor. When she tries to insist, he confesses: 'Do you know what's the matter with me? Funk. Just ordinary, common or garden, plain bloody funk.'

He knows the doctor will recognize the condition and classify him as unfit for further service. He will be reassigned as an instructor and his pupils will guess that he had buckled under the strain of combat. The shame, he tells her, would be unbearable. Yet he can hardly bear the pressure of being responsible for the lives of others while living in perpetual fear. He has reached breaking point and it is only his marriage to her that enables him to keep on going. 'It was you who got us home tonight. Not me,' he tells her. She realizes that his need for her is of a wholly different order from Peter's and that she must stay with him.

When Churchill was taken to see *Flare Path*,* he declared himself 'very moved'.[8] He also commented approvingly on the understated dialogue. This takes different forms. One is designed to downplay the dangers of the men's lives, like calling a raid a 'do' and a 'shaky do' when casualties and damage to the planes are involved. Another is the men's disdain for rhetorical posturing. When the Squadron Leader tries to tell Patricia of his admiration for her husband, he says, 'I hate all this patriotic bilge in the newspapers, but, my God, we do owe these boys something, you know.' Later Teddy is embarrassed to hear himself telling her, 'We've got to win this war somehow, you know', adding, 'God, how *Daily Mail*! I'm glad nobody heard it but you.'

The success of *Flare Path*'s London revival in 2011, when it was acclaimed by critics and audiences with no personal experience of the war, demonstrates the play's dramatic quality. It also testifies to the profundity of the question of fear and the courage required to overcome

* The play was directed by Anthony Asquith, always known as Puffin, whose father was Herbert Asquith, the first Prime Minister under whom Churchill had served before and during the First World War. His mother, Margot Asquith, accompanied her old friends Churchill and his wife to the performance.

it. To a wartime audience made up of men and women who had survived the blitz and with family members serving with the armed forces, it would have sent a direct message: that, whatever their situation, they must master their fear and carry on. As its run continued, they would have been aware of its direct links to real life. When the show opened on Broadway Rattigan had to miss the first night because he was under orders from the RAF to ferry an aircraft across the Atlantic, while the young actor who played Teddy Graham, and who was also serving in the RAF, had to be replaced during the play's run when he was posted out of London.

Flare Path ran for some six hundred and seventy performances and transformed Rattigan's career. His previous two plays had failed badly. In the view of his biographer Geoffrey Wansell, if *Flare Path* had suffered the same fate, 'he might never have risked writing for the stage again, taking refuge instead in screenplays'.[9] It relaunched his career and established him as one of the most successful commercial playwrights of the mid-twentieth century.

Cold War

Lord of the Flies by William Golding, 1954,
and *On the Beach* by Nevil Shute, 1957.

The Dead, the Dying and the Damned by D. J. Hollands, 1956.

Lord of the Flies

by William Golding (1954)

On the Beach

by Nevil Shute* (1957)

The end of the Second World War was followed almost immediately by the outbreak of the Cold War between the Soviet Union and the countries it controlled in the Communist bloc on the one hand and the Western Alliance led by the United States on the other. Initially the United States enjoyed a monopoly of nuclear weapons, but in 1949 the Soviet Union successfully tested an atom bomb. By the mid-1950s, when both Britain and the Soviet Union had acquired hydrogen bombs and China too had become a nuclear power, a full-scale war involving any two of them would have wreaked damage on an unprecedented scale. A paper considered by the British Cabinet in 1954 estimated that ten bombs dropped, one each on selected cities, in this country would cause anything up to twelve million casualties, depending on their strength.[1] Without knowing the details, which were closely

* A pseudonym. His real name was Nevil Shute Norway. He was a professional engineer and adopted a pen-name to protect himself from publicity.

guarded secrets, the general public was aware that a nuclear war would destroy not just the fabric of British society, but perhaps even eliminate life itself on the planet. The nightmares of H. G. Wells and Baldwin's warnings about the end of civilization, described in earlier chapters, had become a potential reality.

Two books published during the 1950s stand out for the extent to which they both reflect and fanned the fears of the time: *Lord of the Flies* by William Golding in 1954 and *On the Beach* by Nevil Shute in 1957. Both were bestsellers in Britain and abroad and their influence was further enhanced when they were turned into films. The former was a first novel that launched a career that culminated in a Nobel Prize for Literature and remains the book for which Golding is best known. The latter was by an established author who already had a large body of work to his credit.

They could not be more different, with each playing on a different aspect of people's fears. *Lord of the Flies* is a parable set among children about the breakdown of civilization and a reversion to barbarism. *On the Beach* is about how the last remaining survivors of a nuclear war prepare for their inevitable deaths. Both draw extensively on imagery and attitudes that would have been familiar to contemporary readers from the Second World War.

The action in *Lord of the Flies* takes place on a deserted tropical island in an unnamed ocean where an aeroplane carrying British schoolboys being evacuated from the war zone has crashed. There are no adult survivors and no girls. The boys have had no previous connection with each other. The oldest are about twelve and the youngest, as far as one can gather, about six. Other than the fact that an atom bomb has been dropped, the reader is told nothing about the war itself. The book is devoted to how the older boys respond to the situation and how they relate to each other.

When he wrote it, Golding was teaching English and Classics at a grammar school in Salisbury, which gave him an intimate understanding of how pre-adolescent boys spoke and thought at that time. He had also been deeply affected by the war, which had convinced him that, if social sanctions and prohibitions break down, most people, whatever their nationality, are capable of committing the sort of atrocities perpetrated by the Nazis. It is all a question of circumstances. Some of the views that are today freely expressed on the unregulated social media platforms and the threats made against individuals and minorities bear witness to the dark forces that lurk beneath even the most stable and sophisticated societies and lend credence to that view.

In *Lord of the Flies* Golding develops this idea by showing how, as the conventions within which they had formerly lived drop away, the boys become murderous gangsters. There are three key characters: Ralph, Jack and Piggy. When the boys, dazed and disorientated, gather together for the first time after the crash Ralph, a natural head boy, takes charge. The fat, bespectacled, asthmatic Piggy becomes his sidekick. A little later Jack turns up at the head of group of choirboys, who behave with almost military discipline, and puts himself forward as the overall leader. A vote takes place. Everyone except the choir supports Ralph and Jack grudgingly gives way. A search party is sent out, which establishes that they are on an island. Another meeting then takes place at which, under Ralph's direction, a set of rules is agreed of which the most important is that a fire must be kept alight on a hill at all times in the hope of attracting the attention of rescuers.

As time passes the choirboys become hunters who provide the meat on which the boys subsist by killing pigs that run wild on the island. As this role becomes more important and the group's memories of their previous lives fade, so Jack's resentment against Ralph and his dislike of Piggy become more outspoken. Life gets harder, Ralph's authority frays and tensions erupt over whether hunting or keeping the fire alight is the more important activity. As respect for the rules crumbles, the hunters grow more assertive. Eventually Jack is able to isolate Ralph and Piggy, who are banished from the community. The parallel with the way in which the military had ousted constitutional governments in several European countries between the First and Second World Wars would have been immediately apparent to readers.

With Jack in charge the rules are set aside and the descent into madness and cruelty begins. The boys forget the moral code they had been brought up with before leaving home. Violence for its own sake takes hold of their emotions and, like a lynch mob, they develop a fearsome rhythmic chant: 'Kill the beast! Cut his throat! Spill his blood!' While under its influence the group becomes so carried away that one of the boys is semi-accidentally killed. Under the new regime another is subjected to brutal punishment. And then Piggy is murdered.

Ralph is warned by a sympathizer that 'they're going to do you'. He tries to hide, fails and is hunted down like a pig. As he flees across the island the fire, no longer receiving proper attention, bursts out of control. At the end of his tether with the flames and his pursuers closing in on him he finally collapses on the beach expecting the blows to come raining down on him. Instead he is confronted by a British naval officer, who, complete with escort, has been sent ashore to investigate from a passing ship that has seen the fire.

As soon as the officer takes charge, the boys revert to type. Ralph pulls himself together and acts as their spokesman while Jack fades into the background; an unmistakeable reprise to contemporary readers of what had happened in 1945 when the victorious powers took control in Germany and the Nazis sought to disappear into the general population. As the island is consumed by fire the boys, sobbing with emotion, are taken off in a cutter to the warship lying offshore.

On the Beach has no such happy ending. Its story is inspired by the concluding lines of T. S. Eliot's poem *The Hollow Men*: 'This is the way the world ends/Not with a bang but a whimper'. It is set in 1963, six years into the future from when the book was published. In the previous year there had been a cataclysmic nuclear exchange between the Soviet Union and the West followed by another between the Soviet Union and China – a perfectly imaginable sequence of events at that time and eerily reminiscent of those envisaged by H. G. Wells in *The War in the Air* and *The World Set Free*.

All life in the Northern Hemisphere has been extinguished and a fatal radiation cloud is moving inexorably southwards. In Melbourne, the world's southernmost large city, people await their fate as the radio reports each day on how one by one the countries and cities in the cloud's path 'go out', like so many candles. Shute actually wrote the book while living not far from Melbourne, having emigrated from Britain in 1950, which invests his book with a sense that there is no hiding place, regardless of how far from the theatre of war a person flees or where they might happen to be.

The book's focus is on a small group of characters: a naval officer, his wife and their baby, their relations and friends, including the American commander of a nuclear submarine that escaped the holocaust and which he has placed under Australian command. When the story opens life in Melbourne and its environs is continuing very much as normal. Although the cloud is already over the northern part of Australia, shops are open, people go to work, the radio broadcasts and government functions. Scientists suggest that as the cloud moves south the radioactivity in the atmosphere might be weakening and that the southernmost parts of the globe might survive. An intermittent radio signal from a United States naval base at Edmonds on the American west coast gives rise to the hope that perhaps in some places life is hanging on.

The American submarine with the Australian naval officer and a scientist on board is sent on a Pacific cruise to investigate. It calls at various places. Some have been badly bombed. Others, when the commander peers through his periscope, look normal and untouched, except that there is nobody to be seen. At Edmonds an officer in protective clothing goes ashore to find the source of the radio signal. He is confronted by a modern Herculaneum – everything as it was at the instant the radiation struck with corpses at a desk, another sitting on the lavatory and a group gathered together at a party. At the transmitting office he finds that a loose window banging against an overturned Coca-Cola bottle on the transmitter is sending out the signals.

The scientist, meanwhile, conducts various tests, which show that the radioactivity in the atmosphere is as strong as ever. So no hope is left and the commander reports back to Melbourne accordingly. While all this is happening a sailor whose home is at Edmonds manages to escape through a torpedo hatch. The following day the commander sees him through the periscope fishing from a boat. They speak through a loud hailer and the seaman explains that as he is going to die anyway he wants to do so in his home town, among his own people and doing what he likes best.

After the submarine returns to Melbourne, the various characters, each in his or her own way, concentrate on making the best of the time left to them – tending their garden, caring for their baby, organizing and participating in a sports car race, drinking their way through their club's wine cellar and conducting a flirtation. A public debate takes place over whether the opening of the trout fishing season should be brought forward by a month, which it is, so that anglers can enjoy a final fling. The nearer the cloud gets the more they immerse themselves in their own interests. Their unemotional stoicism and their belief that that is the only way to get through the crisis recalls a somewhat idealized wartime Britain, except that there, even during the worst of the bombing, there was hope while in Australia there is none. In the background riotous parties take place, the supply of goods and services breaks down and people stop going to work.

Society, however, remains fundamentally orderly. People don't flee from one place to another in search of safety. As everywhere is doomed, it is better to prepare to die 'tidily' where one is. The American commander takes his submarine out to sea and scuttles it. For those who don't want to wait or to endure the unpleasantness of radiation sickness before dying the government makes suicide pills freely available.

There is no sex among the characters in either *Lord of the Flies* or *On the Beach*, which would have been inconceivable if they had been published at any time after the 1950s. In *On the Beach* the American submarine commander has a platonic affair with an Australian woman. She would like to sleep with him, but he is determined to go on living as if his family in the United States is still alive, buying presents for his children and remaining faithful to his wife. He asks the woman whether she thinks this is crazy. She replies that she doesn't. Everyone has to find their own way of coping with the inevitability of death. Those engaged in the riotous parties may well have sex, but we are not told about it. In *Lord of the Flies* there are no sexual relationships or activity of any kind. The nearest approach to any sexual reference occurs when the hunters giggle, after killing a sow, about how one of their spears has gone 'Right up her ass!', after which they mime her efforts to avoid it.

The quality of Golding's and Shute's writing is such that their scenarios are entirely convincing. And perhaps they are not so very far removed from how, in the situations they describe, people might have behaved.

A chilling example of the kind of violence that occurred in private schools at that time is to be found in the memoirs of my old friend Richard Luce, the former Governor of Gibraltar and Lord Chamberlain to the Queen.[2] He recalls how at Wellington College, in the early 1950s, a boy like Jack once tied his dressing gown round his neck and suspended him over the bannisters from an upper floor, a memory that has remained with him for the rest of his life. I never witnessed anything remotely comparable, but at my own prep school, King's College Choir School in Cambridge, to which I went at the age of seven in 1944, boys underwent a ritualized 'bashing up' in their second term. I remember my fear when it was my turn to be bashed and how I was just as nasty as the rest when it was the turn of others.

In her memoirs, the author Elizabeth Jenkins[3] describes events that lend credibility to some of the reactions of characters in *On the Beach*. In May 1940, as German tanks rampaged through France and the British Army retreated to Dunkirk, she and other Jane Austen enthusiasts gathered at a house near Austen's former home at Chawton in Hampshire to form the Jane Austen Society. There, while the threat of invasion loomed, they busied themselves with such matters as who should be the honorary secretary and what the subscription rate should be. In an echo of a bygone war they asked the Duke of Wellington, as a county grandee, to be their President. He replied that he was delighted to hear about the formation of the society and added, 'Thank you for making so much of me.' Today that society is among the most successful of its kind and has spawned a network of associated bodies across the world – an example of how, short of a nuclear holocaust, even the worst situations can lead to good and lasting initiatives.

The Dead, the Dying and the Damned

by D. J. Hollands (1956)

The Cold War between the Western Alliance led by the United States on the one hand and the Communist bloc led by Soviet Russia on the other, that began soon after the end of the Second World War in 1945, meant that Britain could not revert to its normal peacetime practice of relying on professional volunteers for its armed forces. It was still a major world power, one of the 'Big 3' in the jargon of the time, with the United States and the Soviet Union. It had imperial commitments in Asia, the Middle East and Africa and a key role to play in the defence of Western Europe. The regular forces by themselves could not have coped in the event of another war, which for a long time seemed quite possible, and the country needed both a large standing army and a large reserve of trained manpower.

To fill the gap a system of National Service was introduced under which, between 1945 and November 1960, over two million young men were conscripted into the armed services, initially for a period of eighteen months and from 1950 for two years. All men born between 1928 and September 1939 (coincidentally the month the Second World War began) were liable. Some were deemed medically unfit, a few were able to escape for educational or other reasons and a tiny minority were conscientious objectors, but, until the system began to run down towards the end, the vast majority served. About two-thirds went into the army, the rest into the Royal Navy or the Royal Air Force. For nearly all it was by far the most important event in their lives up to that point. For men from working-class backgrounds it was usually the first time they had ever left home.

For most, regardless of social background, it remained a defining experience for the rest of their lives, as it has for me. After it ended numerous novels were written about it, often dealing with the absurdities and futilities of service life as they appeared to men who, in their own minds, remained civilians throughout their time in uniform. It also features extensively in memoirs and autobiographies written in the 1990s and early 2000s by men looking back to a distant youth. But during the years that it lasted very few books were written about it.

One of the first, published in 1956, was D. J. Hollands' *The Dead, the Dying and the Damned*, an autobiographical novel set against the background of the Korean War in which he had served in the army as a second lieutenant in the 1st Battalion of the Duke of Wellington's Regiment* and been awarded a Military Cross for gallantry. That war, which lasted from 1950 until 1953, was by far the largest and most important conflict in which conscripts were involved; two hundred and eighty-six were killed and one thousand and fifty-six wounded. There were other engagements – the failed Anglo-French invasion

* A battalion is the basic infantry formation. Those serving in Korea generally comprised about thirty officers and six hundred and thirty non-commissioned officers and men. Officers, who hold the Sovereign's commission, range from second lieutenant up to field marshal. National Servicemen very rarely rose above second lieutenant. Non-commissioned officers (NCOs) range from lance corporal to regimental sergeant major. At the very bottom are the men with the rank of private in the infantry. The generic term for all those who are not officers is 'other ranks'.

of Suez in 1956 and operations against independence movements and other opponents of British rule in Malaya, Kenya, Aden and Cyprus – but the Korean War was in a class of its own. It began when North Korea, backed by the Soviet Union, invaded South Korea and a United States-led United Nations force, including a British and Commonwealth contingent, went to the defence of the South.* To many it seemed like a prelude to a Third World War and when China came in on the side of the North the United States contemplated a nuclear response. In the end, it petered out in a stalemate and the Korean peninsula has since remained divided between the two Korean states with the armistice line where the fighting stopped acting as the frontier between them.

Those National Servicemen who fought in Korea and the various colonial uprisings against British rule were the unlucky ones. Most never heard a shot fired in anger. Some never left the United Kingdom while others, including me, served in West Germany in the huge British Army of the Rhine ready to withstand a Soviet attack from the East. It never came, but we treated the threat and the training we undertook to prepare for it seriously.

The Dead, the Dying and the Damned has no great literary pretensions though it sold well when it came out. It reads easily, the characterization is good and the extensive battle scenes highly convincing. Through the prism of a small group – Second Lieutenant Peter Blake and some other officers and men in a single infantry battalion – it provides a microcosm of what life was like in most branches of the army at that time. The relationships between the different ranks, their attitudes to each other and their respective codes of behaviour are clearly delineated and in line with my memories of my service from 1955 to 1957.

* At this time the Soviet Union was boycotting the United Nations, which enabled the United States to carry a motion condemning the invasion and establishing a UN force under American command to repulse it.

Except in one respect: in keeping with the publishing proprieties of the time the book doesn't contain a single four-letter word. Yet among the NCOs and men no sentence was complete without one and 'fucking' was used as an all-purpose adjective at a time when the word was much less common in general conversation than it is now. Nor does the book record the imaginative verbal abuse with which drill sergeants and sergeant majors exhorted recruits marching back and forth across the parade ground, such as: 'If you don't sharpen up, Tugendhat, I'll put my fucking pace stick up your arse and turn you into walking lollipop.' Or: 'What happened when you were born, you horrible little man? I'll tell you. They threw away the fucking baby and kept the fucking afterbirth and that's you, a horrible mess of afterbirth. Now repeat after me "when I was born ...".' In my experience, the only insult that could never be directed at a man by his superior was the word 'bastard' because it might be true.

The great majority of National Servicemen joined up at eighteen. With very few exceptions all the army's recruits, regardless of class and educational background, were then knocked into shape by drill sergeants and sergeant majors during a few weeks of basic training. For nearly all of us that experience was the first time we had ever encountered contemporaries from another social class on a basis of equality.

Thereafter the road forked. In practice only those who had been to public schools and to some extent grammar schools could go on to become officers. By no means all of them passed the necessary tests and survived the additional training at officer cadet school to achieve that status.* Many did not, but nobody else could aspire to become an officer and the privileges that went with it. The contrast between the

* In the Royal Navy and the Royal Air Force, with their more demanding technical requirements, it was more difficult for National Servicemen to become officers than in the army. In some of the army's specialist corps, such as the Royal Army Pay Corps and the Army Catering Corps, class and rank distinctions were less clearly drawn. The Royal Air Force was also more relaxed.

comforts of the officers' mess with a room of one's own, eating better food and being waited upon by servants, including a personal servant, known as a 'batman', with the barrack room life of the ordinary soldier was total.

Officers in the British Army had traditionally been drawn from the more privileged and prosperous classes, those who in earlier epochs had customarily employed servants. During the two world wars the gates had had to be widened to enable men with the right qualities but the wrong backgrounds to pass through, but during the period of National Service traditional criteria were again much in evidence.

The public and grammar schoolboys were far better educated than those who had been to ordinary state schools and left to start work at fifteen. They had remained at school until they were eighteen with most entering the armed forces within a few weeks of the end of their last term, although some went to university first and deferred their military service until they had secured their degree.* Though less well educated in the formal sense than their public school contemporaries, those from state schools often knew more about life. They had earned a living and been free to enjoy sex lives that boys cooped up in single-sex public schools could only dream about.

This could create problems for young officers trying to maintain the morale of men under their command, as Peter Blake discovers. A not uncommon cause of depression among young soldiers was the arrival of a 'Dear John' letter from their girl back home announcing the end of a relationship or even of an engagement. When one of his men on the front line in Korea later receives a 'Dear John' the virginal nineteen-year-old Blake is at a loss as to how to offer comfort

---

* Medical students were able to defer until they had qualified when they would enter the forces as medical officers. Once the end of National Service had been announced most of those with university places took them up immediately and deferred their National Service in the knowledge that it would be over by the time they graduated.

or advice. Subsequently he falls in love with a Japanese woman who takes him in hand while he is on leave in Tokyo after which he receives one himself.

Military hierarchy and discipline were such that regardless of age and experience there was never any question as to who was in charge in any given situation. It was always the man with the higher rank. So, when I, as a newly minted second lieutenant, took command of my platoon in the 1st Battalion of the Essex Regiment in Germany the chain of command was clear. I was answerable to my company commander and, above him, my battalion commander, and responsible for the thirty or so men in the platoon under my command. But rank and experience were two very different things. My platoon sergeant and second in command was about twice my age and had served in the Second World War and Korea. He and I and the rest of the platoon all understood perfectly well that he knew infinitely more about soldiering than I did. I drew extensively on his wisdom and he showed great tact in proffering advice. We weren't tested in battle like Hollands and his men. The nearest we got to it was being on standby to join the Anglo-French invasion of Suez in 1956.

I have often wondered about what might have happened if we had become involved in serious fighting there. My sergeant had served in Egypt and claimed to know the people well. 'Don't ever let yourself get captured,' he warned the platoon. 'The Gyppos will hand you over to the women who'll cut off your balls.' My men believed him and, though I was sceptical, I had no basis on which to contradict him, let alone to be believed. What would have happened, if, after some hard fighting, we had taken Egyptian soldiers prisoner with my men believing what my sergeant had told them?

In his memoirs, Richard Luce, to whom I referred in relation to *Lord of the Flies*, records his experiences serving as a second lieutenant in Cyprus during the uprising there while I was in Germany.

'Certainly, prisoners were tortured to gain information,' he writes. 'But in an emergency and facing violence it is difficult not to get angry with people who shelter terrorists.'[4] A man with whom I many years later served on a corporate board told me of his experiences when fighting as a second lieutenant in the French army during the Algerian war of independence. His platoon had taken a rebel prisoner and he had agreed when his experienced sergeant said, 'Leave him to me, I'll find out what he knows.' The prisoner had died. This had weighed on my friend's conscience ever since with the weight growing heavier as he grew older. There is no mention of prisoners in Hollands' book.

Some of his most striking passages show how, despite the experience of being under fire together, the social gap between a man who had served as an officer and one who had been under his command remained unbridgeable for as long as both were under the influence of the army. At the end of the book Blake and another National Serviceman who had risen to the rank of sergeant are passing through London on their way home to the north. They like and respect each other. In the army, the sergeant would have addressed Blake as Sir. Now, civilians once again, he says Mr Blake while Blake calls him by his nickname.

Whatever their other differences of rank and character, almost all National Servicemen had one big thing in common. They couldn't wait to leave the army and get on with their own lives. 'Roll on demob' was the phrase we used. This didn't mean that the National Servicemen performed any less well than their regular comrades in battle. In Hollands' book the only young officer to be overcome by fear while under fire is a regular and Blake is warned against a particular regular sergeant who might let him down when out on patrol. All the evidence suggests[5] that the National Servicemen of all ranks were as good as the regulars and sometimes more resourceful. A number, like Hollands, were awarded medals for gallantry.* But it did mean that they sometimes had a different approach from the regulars to disciplinary issues.

Hollands provides two telling examples. One involves a soldier under Blake's command, who has, without realizing the implications of what he was doing, signed a document indicating that, if asked, he might be willing to extend his service. When he is ordered by senior officers to sign on again, Blake, to their uncomprehending fury, advises him that he is not legally obliged to do so and he refuses. Another occurs when Blake himself refuses to accept his senior officer's explanation of why he and his men had been subjected to a prolonged bout of 'friendly fire' during an engagement and asks to be removed from that officer's command, a breach of military etiquette. The senior officer exacts an unscrupulous revenge that could easily have resulted in him being killed in action.

For their part, the regular officers and NCOs couldn't wait to see the back of National Service. They looked forward to returning to the traditional British practice of a professional volunteer army. If ever there was a case of 'beware of what you wish for' this was it. National Service enormously increased the size of the army thereby increasing the regulars' promotion opportunities. It also created jobs running training programmes and dealing with the administrative burdens of new intakes coming in and old ones going out at fortnightly intervals. The removal of these tasks meant that many of the regular officers and NCOs who had carried them out found themselves being 'bowler hatted', to use the euphemism of that time for early retirement, when National Service came to an end.

* The highest, a Distinguished Service Order (DSO) for gallantry, second only to the Victoria Cross (VC), was awarded to Second Lieutenant William Purves of the King's Own Scottish Borderers, whom I knew well in later life when he was Chairman of the HSBC bank and I was Chairman of Abbey National.

The demobilization of the last National Servicemen, including those who had signed on for an extra year to get the additional pay that went with it, represented a landmark for the country as well as the armed services. When they returned to civilian life in 1962 and 1963 the roll call of veterans extended back through the two world wars to a small number of octogenarian survivors of the Boer War at the turn of the twentieth century. Never since has such a large proportion of the male population shared a common experience, except for the ephemeral thrills of great British sporting successes.

Imperialist Complexities

Heart of Darkness by Joseph Conrad, 1902.

Our Island Story by H. E. Marshall, 1905,
and *Scouting for Boys* by Robert Baden-Powell, 1908.

A Passage to India by E. M. Forster, 1924,
and *Altogether* by W. Somerset Maugham, 1931.

The Last September by Elizabeth Bowen, 1929.

Remote People by Evelyn Waugh, 1931, and *So Rough a Wind: The Kenya Memoirs of Sir Michael Blundell*, 1964.

Heart of Darkness

by Joseph Conrad (1902)

Joseph Conrad's *Heart of Darkness*, published in 1902,* runs to only thirty-eight thousand words. It is a short story or novella rather than a novel. Yet it is one of the most influential texts of the twentieth century. It deals with the moral issues that arise when, thanks to technology and superior strength, people of one nation acquire unrestrained power over another, issues that lay at the heart of imperialism when it first appeared and still cast a long shadow over our historical perspective of that period. In the words of his most recent biographer, the American historian Maya Jasanoff: 'Conrad's book has become a touchstone for thinking about Africa and Europe, civilization and savagery, imperialism, genocide, insanity – about human nature itself.'[1]

It is about the exploitation of Africans by Europeans and to some Conrad's use of the words 'niggers' and 'savages' in describing Africans is so objectionable as to outweigh the book's qualities. The Nigerian novelist Chinua Achebe dismisses him as a racist. Yet, offensive as they are, those words did not carry the same meaning for Conrad as they do today. They were the ones in general use at the time, which is a reflection

---

* It first appeared as an article in *Blackwood's Magazine* in 1899. A final revised version first appeared in book form in 1902 as one of a number of stories by Conrad in a volume entitled *Youth*.

on the age rather than the man. As a student the future President of the United States, Barack Obama, was able to see through them to Conrad himself. When rebuked by a fellow student for reading a racist tract, he replied: 'See, the book's not really about Africa. Or black people. It's about the man who wrote it. The European. The American. A particular way of looking at the world.'[2] He saw that the point of *Heart of Darkness* is that people of all races share a common humanity and that evil is no less evil when the sufferers are black than when they are white.*

In this respect Conrad was way ahead of his time. In the United States the lynching, often carried out with great savagery, of black men by white mobs was a common occurrence in the Southern states of the United States – more than a hundred in 1901 alone – while the European empires in Africa and Asia were based on the assumption of white racial superiority.

It is not only in terms of our understanding of the past and of human nature that Conrad's story is memorable. It has also exercised considerable literary influence. Among the authors to have derived inspiration from it are T. S. Eliot and Graham Greene, while Francis Ford Coppola's film *Apocalypse Now*, set during the Vietnam War, draws heavily on it. In 1932, Graham Greene wrote in his diary of *Heart of Darkness*: 'It makes me despair of the book I am finishing, of any book I am now likely to write, but at the same time filled me with longing to write finely.' Another admirer was the French author and Nobel Prize-winner André Gide. He dedicated his own *Travels in the Congo* (1927) 'To the Memory of Joseph Conrad' and wrote, 'I am re-reading *Heart of Darkness* for the fourth time. It is only after having seen the country that I realize how good it is.'

---

* It is interesting to compare the attitudes of Achebe and Obama with those of the Nigerian novelist Chimamanda Ngozi Adichie who has described Graham Greene's novel *The Heart of the Matter*, which is set in colonial-era Sierra Leone and makes frequent use of the n-word, as 'close to my idea of the perfect novel. It is beautifully written and has a wonderful grave quality.' See Parul Sehgal, 'A Conversation with Chimamanda Ngozi Adichie', *Tin House*, summer issue, 2013.

The story opens with the narrator, Philip Marlow, like Conrad a retired master mariner on the last generation of sailing ships, sitting with a group of friends on the deck of a boat moored in the Thames estuary. As the sun goes down on a scene of utter tranquillity Marlow embarks on a tale of violence and horror about a voyage he had once undertaken on the River Congo, which at that time flowed through a territory owned and run by a company controlled in a personal capacity by King Leopold II of the Belgians. The company, like other imperial enterprises, claimed to have a civilizing mission, but its operations had acquired a reputation for avarice and cruelty on a monumental scale. Marlow's voyage, which was based on one that Conrad himself had undertaken a few years earlier, had brought him face to face with the worst of the atrocities. The contrast between the surroundings in which the story is told and those to which it relates creates an hallucinatory effect in the mind of the reader. One feels one is experiencing a nightmare, but without wishing to awake as the prose is so mesmerizing.

The purpose of Marlow's voyage as captain of a riverboat was to find and bring back Kurtz, the company's star agent, who it is feared is sick or perhaps even dead. As he proceeds upriver so the yawning gulf between the company's ostensible civilizing mission and its actual practices becomes apparent. When he stops at the first of its trading stations he is shocked to see Africans lying about in various grotesque positions – 'black shadows of disease and starvation' – as, no longer fit for work or of use to the company, they await death. The scene he goes on to describe is eerily similar to the eyewitness account of the Nazi death camp for Jews at Belzec in the memoirs of the Polish resistance fighter Jan Karski.[3] In both what chills the reader's blood is the contrast between the dying lying hugger-mugger on the ground, shorn of any semblance of human dignity while the SS men and company officials go casually about their business untouched by the suffering around them.

From the moment he arrives in Congo Marlow is told by those he meets of Kurtz's remarkable qualities – how he 'sends in more ivory than all the others put together', how he 'is an emissary of pity and science and progress' and how he is destined to rise to the top of the company. Marlow also learns that, 'All Europe contributed to the making of Kurtz.' His mother was half-English, his father half-French and he was partly educated in England; he is the personification of the great imperial powers. So great is his reputation that he has been entrusted by the International Society for the Suppression of Savage Customs with the preparation of a report for its future guidance.

Which makes the reality of his activities and his abuse of power all the more dreadful. Far from suppressing the customs the society regards as savage, Kurtz has been perpetrating the most savage practices of his own. A white man, a Russian, whom Marlow encounters as he sails upriver, explains how Kurtz came to the Africans with 'thunder and lightning', how 'they had never seen anything like him' and how 'very terrible he could be'. 'There was nothing on earth to prevent him killing whom he jolly well pleased.' The Russian himself was forced to hand over his ivory on pain of being shot. Yet so charismatic is Kurtz that he still fell under the man's spell when he spoke to him of his dreams and of love.

When Marlow finally arrives at Kurtz's station he is confronted with the reality of the man's power. What had appeared from a distance to be ornamental knobs on pillars around his house turn out to be the severed heads of those he has had executed. By virtue of the strength of his personality and the power and machinery at his disposal he has acquired both a physical and a psychological domination over the local population. The chiefs crawl when they approach his presence and he has the status of a demon god. Sick and bedridden though he has become, they are fearful of what may befall them without him to rule over them. When Marlow takes him away they lament his departure with exotic expressions of grief.

On the return voyage Kurtz becomes delirious. His dreams of the good he might have done and his belief in the importance of always having the right motives mingle with his terror as he faces up to what he actually did. He asks for the shutter to be closed so that he can't see the passing jungle. 'I can't bear to look at this,' he cries. Marlow is gripped by the expression on his face of 'sombre pride, of ruthless power, of craven terror – of an intense and hopeless despair'. His last words, now famous for defining his legacy and the message of the novella are: 'The horror! The horror!' Marlow is deeply moved by the fate of a man, who, because he understands the difference between good and evil and chose the latter, is overwhelmed by the horror of what he has done.

On his return to Europe Marlow goes to the company's headquarters in Brussels, 'a city that always makes me think of a whited sepulchre', a term which in biblical language implies hypocrisy. Its representatives press him to hand over commercial information they believe he has received from Kurtz. They are not interested in the circumstances of his death or the events surrounding it. He also visits the woman Kurtz had intended to marry in order to give her a packet of personal papers. When he hears her talk of Kurtz, 'of all his promise, and of all his greatness, of his generous mind, of his noble heart' and of how 'his goodness shone in every act' he feels he must spare her the truth and confirm her illusions. Those illusions are genuine and represent the dream of what in the right hands colonialism might achieve. The exclusive concern of the company's representatives with commercial information represents the reality.

The lesson of Kurtz, Marlow reflects, is of how, in the absence of restraints, a man with unlimited power can give way to 'the gratification of his various lusts'. What the absence of restraints can lead to is a recurring theme in the book. At the outset of his story Marlow recalls that the Thames must once have seemed as savage to the Romans as the Congo does to him and his contemporaries. He reflects on how, when they came to Britain, 'they grabbed what they could get for the sake of what was to be got'. He tells too of meeting a group on his voyage upriver called the Eldorado Exploring Expedition. 'To tear the treasure out of the bowels of the land was their desire, with no more moral purpose at the back of it than there is in burglars breaking into a safe.' In both cases, the Romans and the Eldorado, 'They were conquerors and for that you want only brute force – nothing to boast of, when you have it, since your strength is just an accident arising from the weakness of others.' In the age of empire, when the white races held sway over all others and many among them believed it to be ordained by God that they should do so, these were deeply unconventional sentiments.

But then Conrad was a deeply unconventional man. Marlow is portrayed as an easily recognizable type of seafaring Englishman. But his creator hailed from a totally un-English cultural and intellectual tradition. Joseph Conrad, whose original name was Józef Teodor Konrad Korzeniowski, was born in 1857 to Polish parents living in a part of their traditional homeland that was then occupied by Russia. They conspired against Russian rule for which they were exiled to a remote province, taking him with them, when he was four years old. Both parents died while he was still a child, leaving him in the care of an uncle. He nursed the extraordinary ambition for one born in such a landlocked territory of going to sea and in 1874 left home for Marseilles, as French was his second language, to join the French merchant marine as a steward. In 1878 he switched to the British service, perhaps because, as a Russian citizen, he needed the permission of the Russian consul to serve under the French flag. Serving on British ships he in due course gained his master's certificate, acquired British nationality and changed his name. When, while still at sea, he began writing novels in English it was his third language. He is said to have wished he could have been a French novelist and to have regretted being unable to make the change.

Many books written by British writers during the first sixty years of the last century were set abroad in the empire and elsewhere; Somerset Maugham, E. M. Forster, Graham Greene and Lawrence Durrell come to mind. But, however cosmopolitan their characters and settings, and whatever their own attitude to imperialism, these men saw the world through British eyes and their judgements inevitably owed much to the culture in which they had been brought up. They took it for granted that the terms on which white people interacted with others would be set by the whites. Conrad would have understood this to be the reality as well as anyone, but he would also have had a different perspective. As a Pole he knew from personal experience what it meant to be a member of a subject people – a people very unlike the victims in *Heart of Darkness*, but, like them, at the mercy of an arbitrary and unrestrained overlord.

Our Island Story

by H. E. Marshall (1905)

Scouting for Boys

by Robert Baden-Powell (1908)

The purpose of these two books, published in the first decade of the twentieth century, was to foster a sense of common identity and shared interest among young people throughout the British empire. Their message was that, wherever they might be living, if they had roots in the United Kingdom, which at that time included the whole of Ireland, they were part of one large family. In *Our Island Story*, published in 1905, H. E. Marshall, always known by her initials rather than as Henrietta, puts the emphasis on this worldwide kinship while treating other races as colourful background, like extras in a film. In *Scouting for Boys*, published in 1908, Robert Baden-Powell adopts a different approach. He wants to encourage boys in this country to draw inspiration from the way men live in the wilder parts of the empire so that they are equipped to defend Britain against an invader. He also wants to inspire them, whether they live here or in the colonies, to uphold British rule over other races.

Both books enjoyed phenomenal sales and have been reprinted many times over. As the basic text of the scout movement that originated in this country, each new edition of *Scouting for Boys* was adapted to take account of changing circumstances and social mores and of the spread of scouting across the world. The overtly racist and militaristic characteristics that are so prominent in the original edition were toned down and then edited out. By contrast the original text of *Our Island Story* remained unchanged from one edition to the next with new chapters being added to bring the story up to date. The most recent re-publication was in 2005 with a foreword by the popular historian Antonia Fraser, after which it enjoyed something of a revival with a further boost in 2014 when the then Prime Minister, David Cameron, said when he was a boy, 'it really captured my imagination'.*

Our Island Story begins in Australia, though this is not explicitly stated, with a father telling his two children that he is opening a letter 'from home'. As they are in their own house, they don't understand what he means by home. He explains: "I mean 'the little island in the west' to which we belong, and where I used to live". The children respond that they live in a big island, so how can they belong to a little one? The father replies that 'the big island and the little island belong to each other'. The children want to know more and the book is the story they are told.

At the outset Marshall makes clear that her book is 'not a history lesson, but a story book' and that some of the stories 'are only fairy-tales and not history'. The text, however, rarely distinguishes between the two. Both, she argues, are part of *Our Island Story*. The result is a charming, discursive and clearly written chronological account of British history from mythical origins in the mists of time until the beginning of the twentieth century. Fact and legend are interwoven to create an idealized narrative of how the English, Welsh, Scots and Irish came together. The battles by means of which the English largely brought this about are mentioned, but unpleasantness is glossed over

* In a speech campaigning against Scottish independence as reported in the *Guardian*, 7 February 2014.

and the end result is all for the best. Thereafter the country, combining the four nations in a common allegiance to the Crown, goes on to build a worldwide empire.

Reading *Our Island Story* is like coming across familiar paintings in an art gallery or wandering round the Houses of Parliament and looking at the pictures there that illustrate significant moments in our national history, like the plucking of the red and white roses to mark the start of the Wars of the Roses or the departure of the pilgrims for North America. It includes all the old familiar tales, such as King Alfred burning the cakes, the Scottish king, Robert the Bruce, defeating the English at the Battle of Bannockburn and Francis Drake finishing his game of bowls before boarding his ship to take on the Spanish armada. Besides aiming to inform and hold her readers' interest, Marshall has one overriding objective. She wants them to feel that wherever they live in Britain or the empire they have an equal stake in the great continuing national saga.

This involves omissions and interpretations, some of which now look distinctly weird. One would, for instance, never suppose from reading *Our Island Story* that within a couple of decades of it being written the Irish would revolt against the United Kingdom and establish their own separate state.* Her handling of events in South Africa at the time of the Boer War between Britain and the Afrikaans-speaking settlers of Dutch origin, known as Boers, and the peace treaty in 1902 that ended it is concerned only with the two white groups. She doesn't refer to the black South Africans, who outnumbered both, whose interests were ignored and whose battle against oppression would, in due course, become the dominant feature of South African politics as the century progressed.

In this Marshall was typical of her time. Whether in Africa or elsewhere, she mentions indigenous peoples only insofar as they temporarily impede the spread of Britain's beneficent influence through

---

* The Irish Free State was established in 1922 and in 1949 the present Republic of Ireland was declared.

the acquisition of their territories. She accords them no rights or interest in how they are governed. She ignores their injustices. Nor does she take much account of the influence of economic and social factors in how Britain and the empire evolved. History for her is made by great men, and occasionally women, and epochs defined by ruling dynasties. That is how history was still taught when I started school in the 1940s. As that approach changed, and as the empire was wound up in the late 1950s and early 1960s, so the book went out of fashion. It owed its revival not to a return to early twentieth-century attitudes, but to a resurgence of interest in a chronological, as distinct from a thematic, approach to history and to the clarity and charm of its narrative.

Scouting for Boys is a completely different sort of book. Its subtitle is *A Handbook for Instruction in Good Citizenship*. As such it provides us with an insight into what constituted that concept in the reign of Edward VII. Its aim, conveyed through a sequence of 'Camp Fire Yarns', was to teach boys how to become responsible citizens primarily by learning how to look after themselves in the wild, or at least the British countryside, as members of organized scout troops led by an adult. This involved mastering such practical arts as tracking, woodcraft, signalling, marksmanship, lighting fires and first aid. It also meant subscribing to a Code of Honour and refraining from such bad practices as smoking, eating and drinking too much and cruelty to animals. The sense of being part of a disciplined elite group engaged in adventurous activities that appeals to so many boys is powerfully conveyed. Even so, it is hard to imagine how this worthy but prosaic agenda could have had such an impact that within a year of the book's publication the Scout Movement had attracted over a hundred thousand members.

The answer lies in the immense prestige of its author, the Boer War hero Lieutenant General Robert Baden-Powell. Like his younger contemporary Winston Churchill, Baden-Powell had embellished his military career with self-promoting journalism so that when the Boer

War broke out he was already well known. The war then turned him, like Churchill, into a celebrity.* He was in command of the town of Mafeking when the Boers laid siege to it in 1899. His defence and ultimate victory after two hundred and nineteen days was the first British triumph in a hitherto unsuccessful war and led to immense national rejoicing. The book draws on what happened during the siege and on the ingenuity of the defenders, including a cadet corps of boys that 'did very useful work'.

Baden-Powell asserts his book's patriotic purpose at the outset with the statement, 'I suppose every British boy wants to help his country in some way or other. There is a way in which he can easily do that and that is by becoming a scout.' He then presents scouting as being in a direct line of descent from such heroic figures of the past as the fictional King Arthur and his knights, Richard Cœur de Lion and the Crusaders, Francis Drake and, a particular favourite of his, Captain John Smith,† who played a leading role in the foundation of Virginia, England's first North American colony, in the early seventeenth century. The exploits in India of Rudyard Kipling's character Kim in the novel of that name are invoked as an example of what an individual boy can singlehandedly achieve to further the imperial cause.

Inspiration is also drawn from the empire. The way of life of big-game hunters, trappers and explorers in its wilder reaches is held up as an example to be emulated. So too are colonials in general for being more 'open and cheery' than stay-at-home Britons and because 'in the Colonies boys think more about shooting than their games, because the shooting is for their *country* the games for themselves'. The character of John Buchan's hero Richard Hannay‡ is prefigured in Baden-Powell's eulogy of the qualities engendered by colonial life.

---

* See essay on *My Early Life* by Winston S. Churchill.

† Claimed by Baden-Powell's mother to be an ancestor.

‡ See essay on *The Riddle of the Sands* by Erskine Childers and *The Thirty-Nine Steps* by John Buchan.

Colonial means white. Scouts are enjoined to learn from Zulus, Native Americans and others about tracking, hunting and how to live in the wild. But white racial superiority and the importance of maintaining it are recurring themes throughout the book. Scouts are urged to practise the technique of imposing their will on subject people by means of staging plays. In one example John Smith, through sheer force of character, persuades a Native American chief in Virginia to accept British rule. In another a middle-ranking British official humiliates an Indian prince who had failed to show proper respect by keeping his shoes on when he came into the official's presence.

The assertion of white racial superiority is combined with a deep underlying unease about the future. Thanks to the improved statistics that were becoming available at that time the political class was being made aware, as they had not been before, of the poor health of the great mass of the population. They tended to assume that it was a recent phenomenon whereas in fact it had existed since time immemorial. To Baden-Powell the conclusion was clear. 'Recent reports of the deterioration of our race ought to act as a warning,' he wrote in *Scouting for Boys*. The healthy outdoor life of scouts, he suggested, was part of the solution.

Another cause of concern in the early years of the twentieth century was the extent to which Britain had found herself isolated during the Boer War with public opinion on the Continent and in the United States favouring the Boers. This was mainly because the Boers were perceived to be a gallant David up against an overbearing Goliath rather than a manifestation of active hostile intent towards the United Kingdom. Nonetheless, Baden-Powell was reflecting a widespread public unease when he wrote: 'We have many powerful enemies round about us in Europe who want very much to get hold of the trade in our great manufacturing towns, and of the vast farmlands in our colonies.' He thought it 'quite likely that England will some day be attacked just as Mafeking was, unexpectedly and by a large number of enemies'.

Scouting, he contended, could help to counter this threat. In a Camp Fire Yarn about signalling, scouts are told, 'if it should ever happen that an enemy got into England, the Boy Scouts would be of the greatest value if they have practised this art'. Under the heading 'How the Empire Must Be Held', they are told, 'Don't be disgraced like the young Romans, who lost the empire of their forefathers by being wishy-washy slackers without any patriotism in them.' In an extraordinary passage he writes, 'we ought really not to think too much of any boy, even though a cricketer and footballer, unless he can also shoot, and can drill and scout. That is the fellow who is going to be useful if England is attacked.' 'So,' he urges, 'make yourself good scouts and good rifle shots in order to protect the women and children of your country if it should ever become necessary.'

The call to arms and overt racism of the original edition of *Scouting for Boys* are a far cry from what the scouts came to stand for in Britain and abroad as the twentieth century progressed. As times changed and the Scout Movement gained in popularity across the globe, including in countries that were not exclusively white, so each new edition was modified. The imperialistic and paramilitary aspects, which had featured so prominently at the beginning, were played down and eventually disappeared. The camp-fire camaraderie and moral code aspects were brought to the fore. Over time, scouting came to be regarded simply as an enjoyable way for boys, particularly from urban backgrounds, to learn social skills and self-reliance and to be kept out of trouble while camping in the countryside. Meanwhile, girls were catered for separately in the Girl Guides, founded as early as 1910, with first Baden-Powell's sister and then his wife at their head.

In their original form, *Our Island Story* and *Scouting for Boys* reflect two sides of the same coin. The former represents the glory, grandeur and self-confidence of the British at the high noon of empire, which is generally how we look back on the Edwardian era; the latter displays the anxieties gnawing away beneath the surface and the belief that it was from the colonies that strength and inspiration could be drawn to save it. Neither Baden-Powell nor Marshall lived to see the end of empire. Both died in 1941; he with a knighthood, a peerage and other honours, she unsung and largely forgotten.

A Passage to India

by E. M. Forster (1924)

Altogether

by W. Somerset Maugham (1934)

The British Empire was a huge enterprise. At its greatest extent after 1919* it covered a quarter of the earth's surface and a fifth of its population. There were two distinct forms of membership. On the one hand there were what were then known as the 'self-governing dominions' – Canada, Australia, New Zealand and South Africa – which between the two world wars became fully independent states linked to Britain by a shared allegiance to the Crown. On the other there were numerous colonies and dependent territories of various kinds, of which by far the most important was India. There the British sovereign ruled as Emperor with a Viceroy in Delhi, once the seat of the Mughal emperors. In schools throughout Britain there were maps and globes, large portions of which were coloured pink to show that they 'belonged to us'. They formed the basis of my earliest geography lessons.

---

* When, as part of the peace settlement, several former German colonies and other former enemy territories were awarded to Britain under the guise of mandates from the League of Nations.

The Dominions were populated largely, but not exclusively, by people who had emigrated from this country, except for South Africa, where a majority of the whites were Afrikaners of Dutch and Huguenot origin and Africans formed the overall majority. In most of the rest where the British went to work rather than to settle, people from this country were few and far between. According to the 1931 census, there were some three hundred and fifty million Indians.* Yet the Indian Civil Service, which administered the country on behalf of the imperial power, never numbered more than about twelve hundred men. The total number of British officials of all kinds and of British troops in the subcontinent was generally of the order of twenty thousand. Again according to the 1931 census, all the British in India – that is to say businessmen, professionals, tea planters, missionaries and those providing services of various kinds plus their families as well as the officials and their families – totalled less than a hundred and fifty thousand with men outnumbering women by two to one.

It was a source of wonderment and envy to both Hitler and Stalin that such a small number of British officials and military should be able to dominate such a large territory as India with its huge population.[4] That they were able to do so is tribute to the efficiency and beneficence of their administration, notwithstanding their racial prejudice. It also reflected the extent of the numerous divisions that existed within Indian society, of which that between Hindus and Muslims was only the most conspicuous.

In Britain's other Far Eastern territories, such as Burma (now Myanmar), which was run as an adjunct to India, Malaya (not then part of Malaysia) and Ceylon (now Sri Lanka) the British were similarly

* The India over which Britain ruled comprised India as it is today plus what is now Pakistan and Bangladesh, which broke away from Pakistan in 1971. The British administration of Myanmar, formerly Burma, was also subordinate to the Viceroy's government in Delhi.

thin on the ground and scattered over a wide area. When the twenty-eight-year-old Leonard Woolf (Virginia's future husband) became an Assistant Government Agent in Ceylon in 1908 he was in charge of a district of a thousand square miles with a population of a hundred thousand people. His nearest fellow countryman was twenty miles away through the jungle.[5]

In different ways E. M. Forster's novel *A Passage to India* and Somerset Maugham's Malayan short stories in *Altogether*, both set in the 1920s, are about the effect it had on individuals to conduct their working lives in circumstances in which they were at the same time members of a ruling caste, overwhelmingly outnumbered and temporary rather than permanent residents. With rare exceptions, all the British in the East during this period went out when they were young, around the age of twenty, and returned home to retire, which in the case of the Indian Civil Service was between the ages of forty-seven and fifty-eight.

The men spent their initial years as bachelors and would meet their wives either when they returned to Britain for a 'home leave'* or from among the young women who went out in search of husbands in what were known as 'the fishing fleets'. All those who could afford to, which includes the characters in these two books, sent their children back to Britain to be educated. Before the era of air travel it was impossible for the children to return for the holidays so parents and children would, in most cases, not see each other for years at a stretch. Each generation started out afresh and family life in the sense of parents and children living together was confined to the earliest years of childhood up to about seven. It is no wonder if subsequent generations should find people living in this way eccentric and strange.

Forster made two prolonged visits to India, the first in 1912–13, with introductions from a young Muslim aristocrat, Syed Ross Masood,

* In the 1960s I dated a girl whose mother had many years earlier established a marriage bureau, as dating agencies were then called, aimed at this market.

to whom he dedicated the book. During the second in 1921 he served for six months as the private secretary to the Maharajah of one of the princely states that enjoyed limited autonomy within the framework of British rule. So, on both occasions he was in India largely under Indian auspices and thus able to move on both sides of the social wall that divided the British, or Anglo-Indians as they were often known, from the 'natives'. This was unusual. Most Britons would have been firmly on the British side and able to meet Indians socially only under contrived and artificial circumstances.

It is an attempt by two visiting British women to break free from this convention that sparks the sequence of events that form the story of *A Passage to India*. One is Adela Quested, who, having met the City Magistrate of Chandrapore, Ronny Heaslop, in Britain has come out expecting to marry him. The other is her chaperone, Heaslop's mother. They want to see the 'real India' and to socialize with Indians as they would with people at home. They are told that is not the way things are done. All that can be arranged is a 'Bridge Party'. Indians are forbidden to enter the British club and so are invited to tea on its lawn where they can be suitably patronized and later mocked after their departure. This is not enough for the ladies who, to the massive disapproval of their hosts, accept an invitation from a young Muslim, Doctor Aziz, to go on a picnic to the nearby Marabar Caves.* This ends in disaster when Adela Quested alleges she has been the victim of an attempted assault without being able to say who by.

The deepest prejudices of the British community are aroused. Without any evidence or even a warrant, Aziz is arrested. The case provokes a crisis in communal relations that threatens to become a political cause célèbre with consequences far beyond the city. Everything hinges on the outcome of the trial: the British are determined to make

* Based on the real-life Barabar Caves in the Jehanabad district of Bihar.

an example of Aziz while the Indians want to win a great victory over the imperial power. But while the crisis builds Adela Quested has increasing doubts about what actually happened, whether she can go ahead with her marriage and whether she can bear to become the wife of a British official. She breaks down on the witness stand, admits her doubts about the accusation and the case collapses. The British are horrified and the Indians exultant. The marriage is called off and she leaves the country.

It is not, however, these events nor their dramatic denouement that lie at the heart of this enthralling and beautiful novel. They are the backdrop against which Forster develops his central message, which is that for as long as the British control India it will be impossible for Britons and Indians to understand each other as human beings or to form real friendships. He illustrates this through the relationship between Aziz and the schoolmaster Fielding, the most sympathetic of the British characters, who want to like and trust each other but whose efforts to do so are constantly thwarted by circumstances.

There is also a poignant recollection by an elderly Indian of how, in his youth, he had felt part of an English family who had befriended him when he was studying in England, but now that their grown-up son has come out to India he dare not approach him for fear of being snubbed and suspected of taking advantage of the earlier relationship. Heaslop's mother asks her son why she can't seek to be pleasant and make friends with Indians in Chandrapore as she would if she had arrived at somewhere new in England. He explains: 'We're not out here for the purpose of behaving pleasantly … We're out here to do justice and keep the peace … We're not pleasant in India and we don't intend to be. We've something more important to do.'

Forster is just. He shows that Heaslop works hard and does his best to administer justice in a society in which Hindus and Muslims, different castes of Hindu, other sects and landowners and peasants are all constantly striving to take advantage of each other. He portrays

Indian society as deeply divided and his judgements foreshadow the division of British India some twenty-five years later into India with a Hindu majority and Muslim Pakistan. He reveals flaws in his Indian characters and deplores the ruthlessness with which they take advantage of Aziz's acquittal to humiliate Adela Quested. But above all as a Briton, he is horrified by the distorting effects that being the ruling caste has on the minds and attitudes of his compatriots – the sense of racial superiority over the Indians and disdain for their culture that it engenders; the suspicion of their motives and contempt for their characters that it breeds. In short, what today is called racism.

Much of the action among the British characters takes place in their club, what George Orwell, who served in the Burma Police, described 'as the spiritual citadel, the real seat of British power, the Nirvana for which native officials and millionaires pine in vain'.[6] It was where men and women could rant about their surroundings, where prejudices were reinforced, characters assessed and standards set. When a crisis erupted in a district, it was where the local Anglo-Indian community gathered to form a united front.

The constant references by the British characters in *A Passage to India* to the Indians 'hating them', in fact far too strong a word, to how useless the Indians are and to their own indispensability come across not as self-confidence, but as the refrain of people aware of their own vulnerability and needing to justify their own existence. The women are particularly intolerant and damning of the Indians, which is why Fielding rarely goes to the club. 'He had discovered that it is possible to keep in with Indians and Englishmen, but that he who would also keep in with Englishwomen must drop Indians. The two wouldn't combine … He found it convenient and pleasant to associate with Indians and he must pay the price.'

In his novel *Burmese Days*, based on his experiences serving in Burma, Orwell also describes the reactions of the members of a British club to a local crisis that pits the British against the locals. There are similarities between the two accounts and Orwell too has a character who runs into trouble with his compatriots because of his friendship with an Indian, but Orwell's British characters are more hostile to the 'natives' and their racism is expressed in stronger language than those in Forster's novel, perhaps reflecting the fact that *Burmese Days* is set in a more isolated and out-of-the-way location.

Unlike Forster, who set his novel in a town, Maugham focuses on people living on isolated rubber plantations and in remote administrative outstations surrounded by servants and employees, often without seeing another white face for weeks or more at a time. He made two visits to Malaya, each of several months, with his lover Gerald Haxton and made no secret of the fact that he was looking for material, which he acquired partly by extensive travel and partly from the hours he and Haxton spent in bars and clubs. As both were good listeners and those they met were flattered to be in the presence of a famous writer, they were told a good deal. Although he fictionalized what he heard, his characters were based on real people. When his stories were published his local readers recognized what they read and denounced him not for inventiveness but for disloyalty and betraying his hosts. Maugham didn't care. In her biography of him, Selina Hastings quotes him as saying: 'If they didn't like the way I honestly thought them to be, then to hell with them.'[7]

Loneliness and boredom and how to maintain some connection with 'home' are recurring themes in the stories. In this connection newspapers and periodicals, though delivered six weeks or more late, played an important role. So did food. The impression conveyed by these stories is that most of the British insisted on their cooks producing English meals, however inappropriate to the climate and however much it involved relying on tinned rather than fresh ingredients. Some took the ritual of meals a step further. The principal character in 'The

Outstation' is an official who always wears evening dress for dinner, although he is often alone for months on end.

Class and background were very important. Officials were acutely aware of where in the social hierarchy in Britain their colleagues hailed from. Those who had been to the smartest public schools, like Winchester and Harrow, were always at pains to advertise the fact. In the aftermath of the First World War the regiment in which a man had served became important. But the trump card was to be able to demonstrate a connection, by family or friendship, with the aristocracy.

By far the biggest problem arising out of loneliness was sex. As most young men spent their first years in Malaya as bachelors it was common for them to take a 'native' mistress, which frequently led to the fathering of mixed-race children. Though officially frowned upon, this practice was widely condoned. A man was expected to send his mistress and children back to their kampong, or 'native' quarters, when another white person came to visit, but it was understood that few young men would wish, or be able, to remain celibate and alone in the circumstances in which they lived. This frequently led to horrible misunderstandings when young wives found out what their husbands had been up to as bachelors.

One of the saddest stories is 'Force of Circumstance', which tells of a wife newly arrived from England, who rejects the husband she loves when she learns that he had had a mistress and actually sees the woman with her children living not far from her own home. She cannot bear the prospect that they should continue in such close proximity. Although she recognizes that her husband was lonely and without any emotional or intellectual support, she cannot forgive him and, to the great distress of them both, they part. Selina Hastings writes that the problem of wives only discovering about their husbands' bachelor days after their arrival in the country was of sufficient concern among the white community as to be openly discussed in their newspaper, the *Malay Mail*.[8]

Neither a mistress nor the children were accorded any rights or status. While some men made financial provision for them others did not and, whatever their financial circumstances, the children generally had to grow up as outsiders on the margins of society. Occasionally, in an earlier period before the colour bar became as established as it did in the 1920s, a man might send his mistress or children back to Britain to be looked after by his family there.

One of the stories, entitled, with malicious irony, 'The Yellow Streak', is about just such a child, who, after being educated at Harrow and serving in a smart regiment during the war, returns to Malaya to take up a career as an official. He is popular and successful and, thanks to his school and regiment coupled with his own charm, enjoys an impregnable social position. But he is obsessed by the fear that one day his antecedents will be exposed and his life ruined. Eventually, as a result of a moment of panic and cowardice during an accident on a river and his attempt to cover up what really happened, a South African with whom he is travelling guesses the truth. The story ends with the reader left not knowing whether the secret will be revealed to others or not.

The scarcity of white women and the monotony of plantation and administrative life inevitably led to affairs, a source of endless fascination to Maugham. Two of his stories are about murders that resulted from them. Both, he writes in the preface to *Altogether*, 'were told to me and I had nothing to do, but to make them probable, coherent and dramatic'. One, entitled 'The Letter', involving a woman who shoots her white lover because he had thrown her over for a Chinese woman and then concocts a story that he had tried to rape her, is based on a trial that actually took place in 1911. She was found guilty, for which, given the law at the time, she should have hanged, but she was granted a reprieve. In his story Maugham draws on the details but alters the outcome by having the husband buy a letter from the Chinese woman's family that would have destroyed her defence, thereby enabling her to escape justice.

In 'Footprints in the Jungle' Bronson invites his old friend Cartwright, who has lost his job, to stay with him and his wife at their plantation until he finds another. The Bronsons are childless and when Mrs Bronson becomes pregnant by Cartwright they arrange the husband's murder in such a way as to make it appear that he has been killed by his own workers. The police investigation runs into the sand and in due course the case is closed. After a lapse of time new evidence comes to light that convinces the local Police Chief of Cartwright's guilt, but it is too degraded to be credible in a court of law. Some years later the Police Chief is transferred to a small town where, as a matter of course, he joins the local club. Mr and Mrs Cartwright, as they have become, are already members and they become his regular bridge partners.

Maugham's stock-in-trade as a writer was the vagaries of human nature while Forster's was the clash of irreconcilable values and interests. Both found much to engage them in the peculiar circumstances in which British people pursued their careers in the British empire in Asia. When, at the end of those careers, they returned 'home' they often found it hard to settle down. They were shorn of their status and role, conditions were so different from what they were used to and nobody who had not been involved in the empire was interested in what they had done. Many of those who had looked forward for many years to returning 'home' found themselves disappointed by what they found.

The Last September

by Elizabeth Bowen (1929)

When great empires begin to crumble they generally do so first at the edges, as happened to the Roman, Ottoman and, most recently, Soviet empires, to name but three. The British empire was an exception. The first province successfully to challenge the imperial power was Ireland, the one closest to the centre, which achieved independence as the Irish Free State in 1922, two years before the publication of *A Passage to India*, twenty-five years before India and some forty years before the empire finally came to an end in the early 1960s.

In some respects, the breach with Ireland was the most painful. There were so many with a foot in both camps. Erskine Childers, whose experiences are described in an earlier chapter, was one.* The writer Elizabeth Bowen was another. In *The Last September*, published in 1929 and set in 1920 at the height of the Irish rebellion, she draws on her own experience to show what that rebellion meant for the British landowners in Ireland, who had been settled there for centuries and become known as Anglo-Irish.

Her family was typical of that group. They were descended from a Welsh colonel who had served under Oliver Cromwell during his

---

* See earlier essay on *The Riddle of the Sands*.

pacification of Ireland in the 1650s. As a reward for his services the colonel was granted land in Co. Cork confiscated from its original owners. In 1776 his descendants built a house there called Bowen's Court, which had passed down from father to son until Elizabeth herself inherited it after the events described in this novel.* Many other such 'Big Houses', as they were known, were to be found all over Ireland belonging to families whose Protestant ancestors – English, Welsh and Scottish – had taken part in the various incursions by English rulers into Ireland. Their descendants remained Protestant and the houses dominated the rural Catholic communities around them.

These families had put down roots of their own in Irish soil and identified both with their British heritage and with their Irish surroundings and backgrounds. They stood to lose more than anyone from the rebellion against British rule. But at the heart of Bowen's novel is their ambivalence in confronting it. Irish nationalists disdained this duality. They regarded the 'Big Houses' as the physical manifestation of alien rule. During the War of Independence, a largely guerrilla or terrorist affair, the Irish Republican Army, commonly known as the IRA, burned a large number to the ground, though not Bowen's Court.

The Last September is not about that war as such. It is a study of the war's impact on the Anglo-Irish and how they reacted to it. The setting is a 'Big House' in Co. Cork called Danielstown that is derived from Bowen's Court. The principal characters are the owners, Sir Robert and Lady Naylor, their nineteen-year-old niece, Lois, their guests and British officers in the neighbouring garrison. Lois is a couple of years younger than Bowen was at the time the book is set and, like her creator, falls in love with a British officer. In both cases aunts step in to

* A description of Bowen's Court and an account of its history and that of the Bowen family may be found in *Bowen's Court* by Elizabeth Bowen, first published by Longmans, Green & Co. in 1942. A second edition with an afterword was published in 1964 and republished by Vintage in 1999 along with a memoir of her childhood in Dublin entitled *Seven Winters* and an introduction by Hermione Lee.

halt the romance, but whereas Bowen was sent to Italy to get over her attachment, Lois' boyfriend is killed before she can be sent away.

The Last September is an outstanding novel imbued on the one hand with a sensitivity derived from Bowen's own feelings and memories and on the other with the objectivity of the London literary figure that, by 1929, she had become. The literary critic and Oxford academic Maurice Bowra praised her for combining 'a historian's impartiality with a novelist's commitment'.* Her description of the emotions, absurdities and dilemmas of the Naylors, a family emblematic of their caste, shows how painful and difficult it was for the Anglo-Irish landowners to grasp that their world and their hegemony were collapsing until finally forced to face up to reality when their house is consumed by flames.

Until then they try to minimize the horrors going on around them. At one moment Sir Robert says, 'There should be less of this ambushing and skirmishing and hey-fidadding now that the days are drawing in', as if they were merely some kind of summer madness. At another Lady Naylor complains that the parents of the girls Lois had been at school with in England won't send them over to stay because 'something said in the English press has given rise to an idea that this country is unsafe'.

When neighbours and some officers and their wives come over to Danielstown to play tennis the conversation over tea turns to a recent attack on a nearby police barracks that had left several policemen dead. One of the officers' wives seeks to reassure the Anglo-Irish round the table that 'we're here to take care of you' and is disconcerted at the lack of a grateful response. To the Anglo-Irish the atrocity is more in the nature of an embarrassment to be passed over as quickly as possible. When an incident touches themselves, they seek reassurance by seizing on any explanation except the most likely. So, when a house guest at Danielstown reports that a raid has taken place at the neighbouring Castle Trent, the

* Quoted by Victoria Glendinning in her introduction (p. 6) to the Vintage edition of *The Last September*, published in 1998.

Trents' explanation that it was done by a gardener's cousin who hates the family rather than by the IRA is accepted. 'He left a quite unnecessary message behind with a skull and crossbones,' says the woman who conveys the news, adding, 'he sounds to me a rather silly man'.

In theory, the position of the Naylors, their family and friends should be clear. The rebels are trying not just to establish an independent state, but to subvert the existing social order as well. The army, the police and the notorious auxiliaries sent over to Ireland by the British government, called Black and Tans, are defending the status quo of which their houses and way of life are a prominent part. The Naylors and their neighbours also entertain the army officers and their wives in their homes and are entertained by them at the military base. Yet, in practice the Anglo-Irish see the situation in more complicated terms. They want life to return to normal, but they also worry about how the forces of the Crown are harassing and causing suffering to their tenants for whom they feel responsible and have known all their lives. Nor do they see the behaviour of the two sides in clear-cut terms. The disorderly and unpredictable behaviour of the Black and Tans is such that they fear being stopped by a Black and Tan patrol when they leave their estates as much as by the rebels.

This conflict of loyalties is poignantly illustrated by the relationship between the Naylors and their tenants, the Connors. When Lois asks after Michael Connor's wife and whether they have yet heard from their son, Peter, who is away from home, both she and Connor know Peter is a rebel on the run, but neither refers to that fact. A short time later, while at lunch with the Naylors, Lois' boyfriend, Lieutenant Lesworth, announces proudly that while on patrol the previous night he raided the Connors' house and arrested Peter. He expects to be congratulated for capturing a terrorist. Instead Sir Robert says how sorry he is; he knows Lesworth must do his duty, but Peter's mother is dying and this will be a terrible blow to her. In a futile and almost feudal gesture, he adds that he must send the family some grapes. Lesworth is left gasping: 'I had no idea these people were friends of yours.'

Even in the case of strangers the Anglo-Irish behaviour, as depicted by Bowen, is ambivalent. While out for a walk Lois and a woman house guest come across a man sleeping in the woods. He wakes, points a pistol at them and asks who they are and what they've seen. When they tell him where they're from he warns them to 'keep to the house while y'have it' and to stop their walks. He then lets them go. They promise not to tell anyone about seeing him and stick to their undertaking when they get home rather than reporting the incident to the authorities.

When, a short time later, Lesworth is killed in an ambush one wonders whether this man might have been responsible. Lois makes no such connection, but Sir Robert immediately thinks of 'Peter Connor's friends – they knew everything, they were persistent: it did not do to imagine ...' He feels powerless in the face of events that have run beyond his capacity to comprehend.

A big part of the Naylors' problem and of others like them was their social isolation. They were part of a caste of closely related and intermarried families who knew each other intimately, but other people scarcely at all. They had friends and relations who had gone out into the wider world and achieved success in the professions and other fields in Ireland, England and the empire, but those who had stayed within their own demesnes, as their estates were called, had become cut off from the changes that were transforming society on both sides of the Irish Sea. Their contacts with their tenants, those who worked for them and the local trades people were conducted on the basis of an impenetrable deference and politeness that masked the fundamental changes taking place beneath the surface.

As hereditary landowners, they looked down on the officers and their wives from suburban and Home Counties backgrounds with a snobbish disdain and, behind their backs, mocked their social solecisms. Discussing with a friend the fact that Lesworth comes from Surrey, Lady Naylor says,

'One cannot trace him ... Practically nobody who lives in Surrey ever seems to have been heard of, and if one does hear of them they have never heard of anybody else who lives in Surrey.' She wonders whether his 'people are in trade', but 'I should never say a thing like that without foundation'.

After the establishment in 1922 of the Irish Free State, the forerunner of today's republic,* those 'Big Houses' that survived became increasingly hard to maintain. Over time, with a few exceptions, they and the way of life based on them faded away. Many were sold. Some of the previous owners stayed in Ireland. Others departed for Britain or to the six counties of Ulster that remained part of the United Kingdom. Elizabeth Bowen was based in London when she inherited Bowen's Court in 1930. She visited it regularly and entertained her London literary friends there. In 1934 these included Virginia Woolf, who found it very run-down and recorded in her diary that it was 'pompous & pretentious & imitative & ruined'.[9] Bowen tried hard to keep it up, but eventually the struggle proved too much. In 1959, she sold it to a local farmer, who demolished it in the following year. She felt that to be 'a clean end. Bowen's Court never lived to be a ruin.'[10] In later years, after Ireland had become prosperous, some of the other former 'Big Houses' were converted into country house hotels, a fate she would have hated to befall Bowen's Court.

Bowen herself embodied the duality of the Anglo-Irish as she demonstrated during the Second World War when she travelled regularly from London to Ireland reporting back to the Ministry of Information on the situation there. This has since been condemned by Irish nationalists as spying. Yet in London, where Irish neutrality was widely resented, she championed Ireland's right to be neutral as a means of achieving national self-respect after centuries of British domination.

* The Irish Free State was established as a Dominion owing allegiance to the King, like Canada or Australia. In 1937, it adopted a new constitution with an elected non-executive President as head of state. In 1949, it was officially declared a republic when it also formally left the Commonwealth and severed all formal ties with the British Crown.

Remote People

by Evelyn Waugh (1931)

So Rough a Wind

by Sir Michael Blundell (1964)

When I read history at Cambridge in the late 1950s I took an optional course entitled The Expansion of Europe. It dealt with the mass migration of people from Europe over the previous four hundred years and their creation of new states in North and South America, Australasia and Africa. It dwelt much more on the achievements of the Europeans in their new habitats than on the fate of the indigenous peoples, who were either subjugated, sidelined or largely eliminated. It was a popular course because of its topicality: we could see that this long historical process was suddenly and painfully coming to an end.

In Algeria, where a large French population had been living for generations, the French army was fighting a bitter war that was shortly to end in defeat and the withdrawal of the settlers. In Kenya the British were simultaneously putting down a revolt by a section of the African population while defying the wishes of the colony's white settlers by promoting political reforms designed to lead to African majority rule. In the Central African Federation, made up of Southern Rhodesia (now Zimbabwe), Northern Rhodesia (now Zambia) and Nyasaland (now Malawi), British ministers were trying to bring about a settlement between whites and blacks that recognized the rights of the black majority. This was to lead to a revolt by the whites in Southern Rhodesia, who in 1965 established an illegal state that lasted until black majority rule was finally achieved in 1980. In South Africa the white minority government was clamping down on the growing assertiveness of the black majority by means of the oppressive and discriminatory apartheid regime.

These conflicts put Africa and the issue of decolonization at the forefront of British politics. The left and younger people on the right were generally in favour of African advancement while older people and the Conservative right wanted the British government to support those in the colonies and South Africa who were trying to resist it. The debate was sharp and bitter because the white people in Kenya and Rhodesia and many of those in South Africa were, in the phrase of the time, 'our kith and kin'. They were British by race and retained strong family and other links with this country. In January 1961 the Prime Minister, Harold Macmillan, wrote in his diary of his fear that, 'From the party point of view Kenya is going to create a big problem. We might even split on it. Lord Salisbury and Lord Lambton could easily rally a settler lobby here of considerable power.'[11]

According to one view, the settlers in Kenya and Rhodesia deserved support because they were British. According to the other they had to be opposed because they were acting in defiance of the principles of democracy and equality before the law on which our society is based. Besides which, in realpolitik terms – and this was crucial – they were holding up the conversion of the colonial empire that Britain could no longer afford into a commonwealth of independent nations, a policy that became a major British priority in the 1950s.

So Rough a Wind, published in 1964, is the autobiography of Michael Blundell, a leading white politician in colonial Kenya who had arrived there as a young man from Britain in 1925. It traces the evolution of his thinking from an assumption of white mastery through the idea of partnership between Africans and Europeans, as the British settlers* described themselves, to an acceptance of black leadership as the only way in which white people would be able to remain. In his travel book *Remote People*, published many years earlier in 1931, the novelist Evelyn Waugh records his impressions of a visit to Kenya when the settlers were in their heyday. He applauds their way of life and their desire for the colony to be run in their own interests. He also expresses his support for the idea of white, in particular Anglo-Saxon, racial superiority. Yet in the same breath he forecasts, in defiance of all expert opinion at the time, that the colonial venture would not last beyond the 1950s.

Michael Blundell's journey across the political spectrum earned him a knighthood from the British government, but the enmity of his fellow settlers. Many in the white community ostracized him and accused him of being a traitor. On one occasion when he returned from a conference in London he was greeted by a European crowd at Nairobi airport with shouts of 'Judas' and thirty silver coins were thrown at him. In later years, after Kenya had become independent, the wheel turned full circle as those Europeans who had remained often looked to him to intercede on their behalf with the African government.

As he looks back over his career Blundell shows understanding of the aspirations and dilemmas of both races as well as of the traders and businessmen from the Indian subcontinent who had settled in the colony and become objects of suspicion to black and white alike, despite

* A few were Scandinavian, including Karen Blixen, the author of the famous book *Out of Africa*, who was Danish. My wife, whose father was a colonial administrator in the neighbouring territory of Tanganyika, went to boarding school in Nairobi, the capital of Kenya, where her best friend was the daughter of Swedish settlers in that country.

their indispensable role in running the economy. Yet, as one reads his account, with the benefit of both his and history's hindsight, it is hard to escape the conclusion that there were three rocks on which the project of a permanent place for the white settlers was always bound, sooner or later, to founder. One was the question of to whom did the land rightfully belong. The second was that the blacks outnumbered the whites by a hundred to one or more. The third was the enduring racism of the white community.

In the nineteenth century the land question would have been settled by force of arms as it was in the United States, Australia, South Africa and other areas of white settlement. In those places where the indigenous people were weak, as in the first two, they were left on the margins of society with scraps of land the white people didn't want. Even where they were strong enough to put up a significant fight, as in South Africa, they lost out badly. In all cases they were denied political rights. As late as 1910 Britain granted self-government to South Africa with power being handed over exclusively to the white minority without much regard to the interests of the black majority.

It was against this background that white settlers began to move informally into Kenya in the 1890s. In 1902 the British government initiated a consistent settlement policy awarding incoming whites land that had been appropriated from the Africans. After the First World War army veterans were granted land under the British government's Soldier Settlement Scheme. This was followed after the Second World War by another scheme for ex-servicemen to settle on land reserved exclusively for Europeans. All these settlers, and others who arrived independently, believed they were putting down roots in a territory that would remain under British control for as far ahead as they could see. Indeed, the post-1945 scheme was explicitly designed to run for forty-four years. They assumed too that those parts of the country, notably the highlands, that were reserved for Europeans would remain so. In the nineteenth century their interests would have prevailed against all others. Their mistake was to believe that this would still be case in the twentieth.

The early settlers had to create everything from scratch. When Blundell began he worked for another settler, lived in a mud and wattle hut and helped to build his boss' house before going on to acquire a farm of his own. They were as much pioneers as those who opened up the American West. Later arrivals sometimes, but not always, acquired farms that were already going concerns. They too had then worked hard to develop them in conditions where the vagaries of the climate and the fluctuations in the price of their products on world markets made for a very uncertain life. They believed they had a right to what they owned both because it had been legally granted to them and because of the work they had put into it. They also believed that they had a right to look to the British government for protection.

For their part the Africans believed that the land rightfully belonged to them and that it had been taken from them against their will by force backed up by legal means that at the time they did not fully understand. They further believed, and not without reason, that over the years government policy and subsidies had favoured European over African farming and that it was, in any case, outrageous that parts of the country should be reserved exclusively for Europeans. They also resented the presence of the large Indian community in the colony. They too believed that they had a right to look to the British government for redress and that, as they constituted the overwhelming majority of the population, their will should prevail.

Blundell was among the first Europeans to grasp that the war marked a watershed in the relationship between the races. Before 1939 African nationalism was weak and the bulk of the African population had neither the skills nor the confidence to challenge the white supremacy. After 1945 this had ceased to be the case. The Africans were no longer willing to be treated as a 'junior partner' in their own country.

He commanded African troops serving initially in Ethiopia against the Italians and later in India. He saw how their experiences outside their own country led the men serving under him to question their old assumptions. 'They asked why only Europeans were officers in the East African Army and why the food scales were different as between white and black soldiers. They learnt that courage, fear, hunger and physical exhaustion were common to men of all races.' And they began to apply the Allied wartime propaganda about fighting for freedom and democracy to their own situation. In 1945 he read a letter from an African soldier that made a big impression on him. After describing the many disadvantages under which Africans laboured in their own country it ended 'with a passionate and bitter cry "Long hair, long hair (i.e. European hair) has stolen my country away." I was face to face with the smouldering thoughts of a new Africa.'

Even so it took Blundell some time to adjust his ideas to the new reality. In 1948, when he first stood for election to the colonial legislature, he still argued in favour of 'European leadership, reservation of the European highlands and a communal or racial role for election purposes', a device to ensure that the European minority would always have as many seats in the legislature as the other races combined.

Sir Philip Mitchell, the colony's Governor from 1944 to 1952, helped to change Blundell's mind by posing the question: 'What then is the wise course for a European population of some 45,000 set among 100,000 Asians and 5,000,000 Africans? … If it insists on separation and special rights and refuses genuine co-operation with other races, it will isolate itself, stimulate African nationalism and almost certainly drive Asians into that camp.' To persist in that course, the far-sighted Governor warned, would lead the whites to rebel against Britain, as would later happen in Southern Rhodesia where the whites could rely on the support of neighbouring South Africa, an advantage the Kenya whites did not have.

It was because he faced up to this reality ahead of most other Europeans that Blundell came 'to realize that the role of the white man must change from undisputed leader to associate and friend of the new forces which were emerging in our country'. In 1960, by which time there were sixty thousand Europeans to six million Africans, he had reached the point, under pressure from the British government, of accepting that 'Kenya was destined to be an African country'.

Which raises the question of why other Europeans had such difficulty in coming to the same conclusion. As Blundell puts it, 'They believed firmly in the benefit of British rule to the African and were proudly conscious of what they had achieved in turning chunks of raw Africa into smiling farms and prosperous valleys.' In a speech in London in 1960, he himself claimed that it was a 'country we had created', without mentioning the contribution of Africans and Asians. But at bottom, as he admits, lay their enduring racial prejudice – 'the dark chasms in the minds of the (white) electorate over race'. The issue lurks beneath the surface of the book without ever being tackled head-on. For that one must turn to Evelyn Waugh.

In *Remote People*, published in 1931, Waugh is enchanted by the Kenya settlers; in his view, 'perfectly normal, respectable Englishmen' trying to re-create 'the traditional life of the English squirarchy', that was going out of fashion in their own country. He praises the endeavour and regards it as perfectly natural that they should want to reserve the colony for people like themselves and not be required to share power or amenities with either Africans or Asians.

That those other races, regardless of an individual's sophistication, education or wealth, should be denied political rights and not allowed to use the same hotels and restaurants or travel in the same part of a bus or train as white people seemed to him, as to the settlers, to be part of the natural order of things. It was, after all, the practice not only in neighbouring South Africa, but also in the Southern states of the United States, as well as Washington DC.

In a passage that makes for painful reading today, but accurately reflects the attitudes of the period, Waugh points out with characteristic bluntness that wherever Anglo-Saxons lived in close proximity with other races – he cites India and Virginia as examples – 'the reality of racial antagonism' exists. 'It is not a matter one can be censorious about. Gentle Reader, you would behave in just the same way yourself after a year in the tropics.' He then suggests that because it is so widely felt, 'It is just worth considering that there may be something valuable behind the indefensible and inexplicable assumption of superiority by the Anglo-Saxon race.'

To hold such views in the 1930s was commonplace. They were among the assumptions on which the empire was based. By the 1950s they had become lethal to the settlers' own long-term interest, but the pace of change had been too fast for many of them to realize this. They wanted to continue to live as nearly as possible as they always had. They could not understand the insistence of British ministers that the only way to avoid bloodshed was to bring the colony to independence on the basis of black majority rule. Nor did they grasp that, although a vocal minority in Britain spoke up for them, the majority did not care what happened to them.

This was the outcome foreseen by Waugh. He concludes his discussion of racial attitudes in *Remote People* by suggesting that 'it is uncertain whether the kind of life the Kenya settlers are attempting to re-establish is capable of survival; whether indeed the European colonization of Africa will survive in any form; whether there may not be in the next twenty-five years a general Withdrawal of the Legions to defend Western civilization at its sources'. Whether that would be because of those attitudes or despite them he does not say. Either way it was a remarkable prognostication.

Provincial Life

Anna of the Five Towns by Arnold Bennett, 1902, *The Condition of England* by C. F. G. Masterman, 1909, and *The Ragged-Trousered Philanthropists* by Robert Tressall, 1914.

Love on the Dole by Walter Greenwood, 1933, and *Saturday Night and Sunday Morning* by Alan Sillitoe, 1958.

Room at the Top by John Braine, 1957, and *This Sporting Life* by David Storey, 1960.

Anna of the Five Towns

by Arnold Bennett (1902)

The Condition of England

by C. F. G. Masterman (1909)

The Ragged-Trousered Philanthropists

by Robert Tressall (1914)

Despite the fear of war and the general sense of insecurity described in the chapters on the build-up to the First World War, the period between the death of Queen Victoria in January 1901 and the outbreak of the First World War in August 1914 is suffused in British folk memory with a golden glow. It is regarded not just as the calm before the storm but as a period of serenity and contentment epitomized by the plump and pleasure-loving figure of King Edward VII, who ruled for most of it. The struggles turning to violence of the suffragettes, the industrial disputes and strikes, and the extent to which politics was embittered by the dispute over Home Rule for Ireland are overshadowed by the horrors of what followed. In later years the memoirs of those who survived the war tended to describe their lives before it broke out in idyllic terms. Popular television dramas such as *Upstairs, Downstairs* and *Downton Abbey* have embellished these recollections and embedded them in the public mind.

But those whose memoirs were published were nearly always members of the prosperous and privileged classes. The television dramas also focus on those classes and their retainers. For the aristocracy, the rich and the well-to-do the Edwardian age was indeed a wonderful time to be alive. Their love of luxury and self-indulgence has become the stuff of legend and contributed disproportionately to our image of the age. These three books – an outstanding novel by Arnold Bennett, a political tract in the guise of a novel by Robert Tressall* and a comprehensive survey of the state of the nation by the Liberal MP and journalist Charles Masterman – deal with men and women who do not appear in the memoirs of the period. They are set in different parts of the country and among different types of people. Together they show how harsh life was for most people and how severe the penalties for failure and misfortune.

Masterman researched and wrote his book soon after the election of a reforming Liberal government in 1906. By the time it was published in 1909 he had become a junior minister. His title invoked a famous phrase coined in 1839 by the historian and philosopher Thomas Carlyle to describe the working class during the Industrial Revolution, which has since become a generic cliché to describe books that set out to analyse contemporary politics, economics and society. His aim was to influence public opinion in favour of the government's reforms.

His report on the countryside is particularly striking. Far from being the unspoilt arcadia of popular imagination, it was, to paraphrase the hymn 'Jerusalem', no 'green and pleasant land'. Conditions there were

---

* His real name was Robert Noonan. He signed the original manuscript as Robert Tressell, which is how it appeared on later editions. But it was printed as Tressall on the first edition, published in 1914, which is why I have adopted it here.

in fact worse than in 'the dark satanic mills'* of the great industrial cities. 'Rural England,' he writes, 'beyond the radius of certain favoured neighbourhoods, and apart from the specialized population which serves the necessities of the country house is everywhere hastening to decay.' The main underlying reason for this was the opening up of North and South America and Australia in the latter half of the nineteenth century and the development of fast steamships and refrigeration that enabled their produce to be delivered to Britain at prices with which local production could not compete. This had created a crisis for the rural economy.

Masterman has little to say about these causes, which is understandable as the Liberals were in favour of continued free trade while the Conservatives wanted to introduce tariffs that would have helped the rural economy to recover but at the cost of higher food prices. This was one of the big political issues of the day. Rather he blames everything on the large landowners and farmers. He points out that much of the landowners' wealth, whether aristocrats or the newly rich, derived from investments in trade, industry and finance. He berates them for deserting agriculture in favour of parks and avenues with woods devoted to the breeding of game birds for shooting and stretches of land left open for hunting. He sees these as both the cause and the symbol of what had gone wrong. He is equally scornful of 'the great farmers' who had bought up their less successful neighbours, enclosed and taken over common land and created large fields surrounded by hedges to achieve economies of scale.

These developments were draining the life out of the countryside, 'with village after village in which no new cottages have been built for a hundred years; crumbling walls falling into decay; crowded families with all the starved life and degradation inevitably associated with such overcrowding; the whole presenting an aspect of fatigue and decline'.

---

* 'Jerusalem' by William Blake.

The more energetic either went off in search of work in the cities or emigrated to Australia, Canada or the United States. Those who remained were at the mercy of the landowners, who not only employed them but, for the most part, also owned the cottages in which they lived. To lose a job, therefore, usually meant losing the home that went with it. Being rendered homeless was an ever-present fear, especially for elderly men and women faced with the prospect of ending their days in the workhouse where husbands and wives were generally separated. Masterman describes the rural population as being so cowed as to resent the intrusion of politicians and trade unionists campaigning for better conditions for fear of retribution from their landlords.

To illustrate his point, he recounts a recent incident in Oxfordshire where a Liberal MP had persuaded villagers in his constituency to go to court to resist the enclosure by the landlord of a right of way. 'The resistance was sustained, and the village preserved its ancient privilege. But all six witnesses were dismissed from their occupations and driven from the district. And indignation fell, not on the landlord who thus revealed his power, but on the member of Parliament who revealed his impotence.' For all its good intentions and, despite pioneering old age pensions and unemployment benefit, the Liberal Party had no answer to problems of this kind, whether in agriculture or industry, thereby leaving the way open for the emergence of the Labour Party sponsored by the trade unions.

Robert Tressall's *The Ragged-Trousered Philanthropists* was one of the Labour Party's earliest inspirations. Writing in 2011, the former Labour Cabinet minister and icon of the left Tony Benn described it as 'a major Socialist novel that has influenced thousands of readers since it was published in 1914'.[1] From the other end of the political spectrum the World Economic Forum in Davos in 2016 listed it among nine novels 'that have changed society' because of the influence they had on 'the drive for social reform at the start of the last century'.[2] It fully achieves its author's aim, set out in his preface, to produce 'a readable story full of human interest and based on the happenings of everyday life' to convey his message that socialism was the answer to injustice and exploitation. Its policy prescriptions have long since lost their relevance, but its account of working-class life in the early years of the twentieth century retains all the clarity of a photograph.

The author was the illegitimate son of a prosperous Dubliner, who received a good education before it was cut short when his father died, after which, resenting his mother's marriage to another man, he emigrated to South Africa. On returning to Britain he became a signwriter and house painter in Hastings, where the novel is set. The original version was eighteen hundred pages long and it was not until three years after his death from tuberculosis that his daughter secured the publication of a shortened version of three hundred and ninety-one pages. Later editions include more of the original text, but it was the shorter version that established the book's fame and it remains the most readable. The title was meant to be a sardonic reference to the way in which poor men gave away their labour to richer men for much less than it was worth, thereby colluding in their own exploitation. His renaming of Hastings as Mugsborough drives the point home.

The action is set among a group of employees of a building firm called Rushtons who are working on the renovation of a large house known as The Cave. The central character, Frank Owen, is, like the author, a signwriter and house painter, a socialist, an atheist and suffering from the early onset of tuberculosis.*

The men's lives are dominated by debt. It overshadows every aspect of their existence. All owe money for food, clothing or furniture and

---

* In her autobiography *Walking in the Shade* (p. 88) Doris Lessing writes of staying in a hotel in Hastings in the 1950s that was reputed to have been the house on which Tressall based The Cave. There she was shown 'a beautiful ceiling' that was said to be 'a possible work' by him.

often for all three. To be in arrears on their rent is normal and their possessions move in and out of the pawnbrokers as need dictates. When they are in work they pay down their debts. When they are out of work their debts increase. Their heads are never above water as whenever they approach the surface another setback pushes them under. Their ever-present fear at a time when there was no unemployment benefit* is of being out of work, which they frequently are. By its very nature the building trade is seasonal so that work was harder to find in winter than in summer and, as soon as a big job like The Cave finished, they were likely to be laid off until their current employer, or one of the others in the town, won another big contract.

Their wives are responsible for managing the family's finances, which means facing up to the rent collector and shopkeepers to whom they owe money, juggling the debts and eking out what is left. What that meant in practice is shown when one of the characters called Easton and his wife review their situation after he has been taken on at The Cave at twenty-five shillings a week (about £133 in contemporary money)† compared with the eighteen shillings, taking good times with bad, that he had averaged over the previous year. They find they are four weeks in arrears with their rent, which amounts to twenty-four shillings, face a demand for rates‡ of nearly twenty-five shillings, owe twelve shillings for furniture bought on hire purchase, and about thirty shillings to the grocer, butcher, baker, milkman and greengrocer. Easton rebukes her for mismanagement, only to get into the habit of going off to the pub with his mates after receiving his weekly wages instead of taking them home to her, a not uncommon phenomenon. The Eastons were not long

* It was introduced in 1911, the year the author died.

† Until the decimalization of the currency in 1971 the pound was divided into twenty shillings, which were in turn divided into twelve pence. For the sake of simplicity I have only used shillings in respect of the men's finances. A guinea was worth one pound one shilling.

‡ A property tax, the nearest equivalent to which is today's council tax.

married with only one child. Other couples with the large families that were normal at that time would have faced greater challenges.

These mountains of debt put men at the mercy of those with the power to hire and fire, towards whom they behave with fawning obsequiousness and loathing in their hearts. Yet those managers and foremen were themselves at the mercy of the men who owned the building firms and were under constant pressure to cut costs in order to win contracts. If they failed, they too would lose their jobs. One of the most poignant episodes in the book is the suicide of the manager who tyrannizes the workers at The Cave when, in a fit of despair, he can no longer make his figures add up. Because of the constant pressure on costs the work is always being 'scamped' instead of properly done, with too few coats of paint being applied and inferior materials substituted for those in the contract. When one of the men takes too much trouble over a task and so too long to finish it, he is sacked. Safety is ignored with the result that a man dies falling from an upper storey because a frayed rope hasn't been replaced. At the inquest his workmates perjure themselves rather than reveal the cause of the accident for fear of reprisals from their employer if they tell the truth.

Better educated and more articulate than the others, Frank Owen veers between fury with them for their passivity in the face of such conditions and sympathy for their inability to understand what's wrong and to rebel against it. During their lunch breaks he explains how the system works whereby the benefits flow disproportionately to the owners of the businesses while those who do all the hard work earn so little and are discarded when no longer needed. In a memorable chapter entitled 'The Money Trick', he at last manages to rouse their indignation, but the moment is lost when the bell rings to summon them back to work. Otherwise they listen to him with amusement or scepticism and in some cases, notably the foreman, impatience for being too clever by half for an ordinary working man.

The idea of thinking about how industry or society might be changed doesn't interest them or, at least, not for more than a few moments at a time. In the mines, the docks and the railways trade unions had already become powerful and strikes were endemic in the years leading up to the outbreak of war, but in less organized industries, such as the building trades and agriculture, men like Owen found it hard to convince their colleagues to organize so that their combined strength could be used to secure better terms and conditions. Because his workmates like him, they let him speak, but when a group of socialists arrives in the town to canvass support they regard them as troublemakers and drive them out.

It is not only at work that the men and their families are exploited. Tressall shows how as ratepayers they lose out too through their employers' control of the local council. The owner of The Cave arranges for the council to pay for linking its drainage to the municipal system and the members of the council line their own pockets through arranging the merger of the local gas and electricity companies while paying off the officials who facilitate the process on their behalf. The fifty guineas, or 1,050 shillings, that one receives for his help in this matter stands in stark contrast to the weekly wages of the workers.

Tressall's strongest anger is reserved for the Nonconformist Shining Light Chapel where the great men of the town preside and parade their Christian principles by taking the Sunday school and in other ways. The pastor is hand in glove with them. Owen is nauseated to hear him telling the underfed and ill-clothed children of the workers to thank God for having been 'made happy English children' while their parents are expected to contribute to the chapel's upkeep. They are also asked to subscribe to a fund to enable the pastor to have a holiday in the South of France, which raises a sum of money that could have made a huge difference to the poorest of the parish. The preacher who stands in for him is paid at the rate of eighty-four shillings a service whereas the chapel's widowed caretaker receives a derisory six shillings a week with which she has to feed her son, who as an apprentice works for almost nothing, as well as herself.

At the end of the book, when the tuberculosis is taking hold of Owen and he fears he may soon die, he agonizes at the prospect of his wife and son being left 'alone and defenceless in the midst of the "Christian" wolves who were waiting to rend them as soon as he was gone'.

Arnold Bennett took a similarly jaundiced view of the Methodist brand of Nonconformism practised in the Staffordshire pottery towns where he was brought up and where *Anna of the Five Towns* is set.* The novel has two interweaving themes. One is the ruthlessness displayed towards each other by the town's leading businessmen and how far it diverges from the doctrines they espouse and preach at the chapel of which they are all members. The other is the mastery of men over women. The two are brought together in the relationship between the eponymous Anna and her father, the miser Ephraim Tellwright. Bennett is particularly good at portraying women and conveying the dilemmas they faced as a result of their subordinate status. He understood how the conventions of the time made it so difficult for them to turn independent thought into action against the will of a dominant man, regardless of their legal rights.

Anna and her younger sister, Agnes, live with the widowed Tellwright, whose 'surly and terrorizing ferocity' dominates their lives. He was a man who 'could recall the fearful timidity of his mother's eyes without a trace of compassion' and, in a telling phrase, 'belonged to the great and powerful class of house-tyrants, the backbone of the British nation'. When, on her twenty-first birthday, Anna inherits a portfolio of shares and properties worth £50,000 (about £6,000,000 in contemporary money) from her maternal grandfather she cannot

* There were in fact six towns, which in 1910 were incorporated into a new county borough called Stoke-on-Trent, which became a city in 1925.

help but allow him to continue to administer it. She then has to watch helplessly as, in her own financial interest but against her wishes and her conscience, he drives a tenant who owes her money to financial ruin and suicide. As the screw tightens we do not condemn her for being weak; we sympathize with her for her inability to be strong.

It is not just her conscience that suffers; her emotions are engaged as well. She had fallen in love with the tenant's son, Willie Price, after witnessing his courage in standing up for his father against her own. But because of the circumstances that have brought them together, and because a woman could not possibly take the initiative in declaring such an emotion, she fails to act. Instead she allows herself to be manoeuvred by kindly neighbours into committing herself to their highly suitable, but, as yet, impecunious young cousin, Henry Mynors, whose business success will be assured with her money behind him. 'She had sucked in with her mother's milk the profound truth that a woman's life is always a renunciation, greater or less. Hers by chance was greater.' Her thoughts, after marriage, 'often dwelt lovingly on Willie Price', who, following his father's death, had told her he was off to Australia. She had given him £100 in a sealed envelope not to be opened until he reached his destination. What she will never know is that instead of emigrating, his shame at his family's disgrace had led him to commit suicide by throwing himself down an abandoned mine shaft.

The novel is about the life of a community Bennett knew intimately and, besides the dramas of its plots, it contains some memorable scenes of life within it. When Mynors shows Anna round his works, which he had designed himself, it is to him a thing of beauty and to her a source of wonder. The reader sees it through the eyes of both and there can rarely have been a more lyrical description of an industrial process. Another is the revivalist meeting and the fervour with which the preacher calls on God to save the congregation's souls and on the congregation to give generously to the collection. In the chapel 'the atmosphere was electric, perilous, over-charged with spiritual emotion' as, one after another, seventeen people left the pews to go forward to be saved.

A third is the special tea at which the family who brought Anna and Mynors together celebrate their engagement. 'Such a meal as could only have been compassed in Staffordshire or Yorkshire', the array of delicacies is described in loving detail, from 'the fowl which had been boiled for four hours' at one end of the table to 'a hot pork pie, islanded in liquor' at the other. This was the world she was moving into and the contrast between its lavishness and the fate of those whose businesses failed is stark.

Anna of the Five Towns was Bennett's third novel and established his reputation as one of the leading and most prolific novelists of his generation. After his death in 1930 it went into a decline from which – unfairly in my view – it has never recovered. He was a great bon viveur who loved grand hotels and is now remembered, if at all, mainly for the Omelette Arnold Bennett,* a delicious concoction that the chef at London's Savoy Hotel named in his honour. It may still sometimes be found on the menu at traditional establishments and, whenever I come across it, I order it.

---

* Its ingredients are egg, smoked haddock, a hard cheese such as parmesan or gruyère, milk, butter and flour.

Love on the Dole

by Walter Greenwood (1933)

Saturday Night and Sunday Morning

by Alan Sillitoe (1958)

Love on the Dole, published in 1933, and *Saturday Night and Sunday Morning*, published in 1958, stand in relation to each other like the before and after images in an advertisement for washing powder. Both are about working-class life in a community that revolves around a great manufacturing company. In the former it is the Hanky Park district of Salford, now part of Greater Manchester, beginning in 1926 but mainly in the Depression-hit early 1930s. In the latter it is Nottingham in the mid-1950s shortly before the then Prime Minister, Harold Macmillan, famously claimed that 'most of our people have never had it so good'.*

How right he was! The contrast between the lives of the characters in these two books is immense and shows the extent to which the way of life of the British industrial working class was transformed during the twenty-five years between their publication. Those in *Love on the Dole* live in extreme penury with every aspect of their existence dominated by

---

* Speech 20 July 1957 at Bedford.

the impact of long-term unemployment. In their wildest dreams they would not have been able to imagine the lavish spending and freedom from insecurity enjoyed by Arthur Seaton, around whose life *Saturday Night and Sunday Morning* revolves. Their lives are much closer to the pre-First World War conditions described in *The Ragged-Trousered Philanthropists*,* although unemployment benefit – the dole – and means-tested relief had somewhat mitigated the hardship of unemployment.

This great transformation had taken place despite the Second World War and was the result of both international and domestic factors. Just as the problems of the 1930s had above all been caused by the collapse of the world economy, so the prosperity of the 1950s was primarily the result of the rapid expansion in the world economy that began after the war. All industrialized countries benefited. Britain in fact grew richer at a somewhat slower pace than some others while doing sufficiently well to ensure full employment. On top of this there was the welfare state, introduced by the 1945–51 Labour government, which benefited all classes, but above all those who had previously been the least well off.

Both authors were writing about their own people. Greenwood, born in 1903, lost his father when he was nine, his mother worked as a waitress and he left school at thirteen. By the time he was thirty, when *Love on the Dole* was published, he had worked at a variety of low-paid jobs without ever earning as much as £2 a week (about £130 in today's money), alternating with long periods of unemployment. His book was drawn directly from life, which makes his descriptions of urban poverty and the dialogue of his characters so realistic.

Sillitoe, born in 1928, also experienced extreme poverty. After his father lost his job the family was reduced to transferring their belongings from one refuge to another in a handcart. After leaving school at fourteen he was for some time a piece worker in the bicycle

---

* See previous essay.

factory in which the central character in his novel, Arthur Seaton, later works. His life was transformed by a prolonged period of convalescence from tuberculosis while doing his National Service. Unpleasant though this must have been, it provided him with the opportunity to read widely and to return to civilian life with a small pension that enabled him to devote his time to writing.

The two authors differ from other writers with whom they are often classified. In Greenwood's case that is George Orwell, an infinitely more accomplished writer whose classic *The Road to Wigan Pier** has come to be regarded as the definitive account of working-class life during the Depression while *Love on the Dole* is largely forgotten. But as a middle-class radical intellectual, Orwell was writing from the point of view of a visitor from another social planet not as a 'native'. He was, moreover, following in Greenwood's footsteps.

The distinction between Sillitoe and the other writers with whom he is often grouped as part of the 1950s working-class movement, such as John Braine, David Storey† and Stan Barstow, is more subtle. As none of them had been to a public school they regarded themselves, and were regarded by others, as outsiders in the literary world. But, unlike Sillitoe, they had been educated at perfectly good grammar schools. These lacked the social cachet of public schools, but in educational terms were often just as good and in some cases better. Sillitoe, by contrast, was largely self-educated.

Love on the Dole is about the hopelessness of the Hardcastle family, typical members of the community in which they live in the sense of always being victims of circumstances beyond their control. This derives from the impossibility of ever finding sufficient regular work to bring in enough money to secure more than a subsistence existence and the

* Published by Victor Gollancz in 1937.

† See following essay on John Braine's *Room at the Top* and David Storey's *This Sporting Life.*

constant fear of losing even that. The father, an ex-miner whose pit has closed, is consumed with shame at being unable to provide for his children. The mother defies his injunction never to get into debt in order to buy their son, Harry, the suit he yearns for. Harry later loses his job at the local engineering works as the firm always sacks young men as soon as they finish their apprenticeship and qualify for an adult wage, in order to replace them with other apprentices able to work for a lower rate. Shortly afterwards his girlfriend, Helen, becomes pregnant and they have to marry with minimal means of support.

The answer to these problems is provided by his beautiful sister, Sally. She had been hoping to marry the local Labour Party organizer with whom she was in love, but when he dies as a result of a combination of pneumonia and being roughed up by the police while leading an unemployment march (based on one that actually took place in October 1931), she agrees to become the mistress of the local bookmaker in order to save the family. As the richest and most influential man in the neighbourhood, he secures jobs for her father and brother with the local bus company and provides her with a financial settlement. Such a plot could easily descend into maudlin melodrama, but the rawness of their language and dialect and the brutal realism with which the characters confront their lot save it from doing so.*

Hanky Park was representative of conditions throughout the industrial North of England and the significance of *Love on the Dole* derives from the light it casts on the daily life of the urban poor. The abuse of the apprenticeship system by employers is one such example. Another is the central role played by the pawnshop in the life of the community, just as it had a generation earlier as described in *The Ragged-Trousered Philanthropists*. It provided a service whereby women – and

* Links are sometimes drawn between Greenwood's descriptions of life in Hanky Park and L. S. Lowry's paintings of the same period of life in Salford on which the novel was based.

it is always the women – can hand over clothes, or other household goods for which they have no immediate need in return for cash and then redeem them for a slightly larger sum when they are in funds. A normal practice was for a wife to take in her husband's suit on Monday to get money to tide them over to payday on Friday when it could be redeemed for the weekend. Money, such as it was, was always the wife's responsibility. On payday the convention, not always observed, of course, was for those members of the household in receipt of wages or benefits to hand them over to her to deduct what she needed for housekeeping before returning the small change remaining for spending money.

Some households were extremely large. Helen has eleven siblings all sharing a four-room dwelling with their parents. In such conditions privacy was impossible and there could be no secrets. When the young men in the community talk about sex they joke about what they've seen and heard their parents do. It is above all in order to escape from hearing her parents having sex in the next room that Helen wants to leave home.

This aspect of communal living has rarely been dealt with in literature.* In drawing attention to it Greenwood brought home to his middle-class readers the horrors of poverty in a particularly forceful manner. He did not, however, mention the incest between fathers and daughters to which the overcrowding sometimes gave rise. That would have been going too far. Yet, as I recount in a later chapter, the campaigner for women's rights and future Cabinet minister Margaret Bondfield had explicitly drawn attention to the problem in 1910 in her report to the Women's Labour League on conditions in the Yorkshire woollen industry.

Arthur Seaton, the twenty-two-year-old anti-hero of *Saturday Night and Sunday Morning*, would have been born at about the same time as Harry's and Helen's child, but by the time he has grown up the Hardcastles'

---

* Another example is Graham Greene's novel *Brighton Rock*, published by Heinemann in 1938. Its central character, Pinky, a brutal teenage murderer, is haunted by memories of what he witnessed his parents do in bed.

miseries are a distant memory. He is aware that his parents' generation have had difficult lives from which they still bear scars and is somewhat awed by the experiences of one of his aunts, but, like anyone else of his age, he lives in the present. At a time of full employment, he takes his job for granted and thinks about it only in terms of how to manipulate the piecework system by which he is paid in order to maximize his earnings. He is on terms of guarded equality with the foreman, who supervises his work; a big change from the pre-war years and those of *The Ragged-Trousered Philanthropists* when, as a man with the power to hire and fire, a foreman inspired fear among those who worked under him.

While at work Seaton's thoughts are on the two older married sisters, Brenda and Winnie, with whom he is having affairs, where to get drunk at the weekend and what clothes to buy and wear. His life is devoted to self-indulgence interspersed with random acts of violence against those who annoy him. When a small car nearly runs into him, he and his brother turn it over. When an old woman in the street where he lives gossips about him, he wounds her by shooting her with an airgun. He rejects all authority and accepts no obligations or responsibilities, except to his extended family and to giving pleasure to women he is sleeping with. 'Make a woman enjoy being in bed with you – that's a big part of the battle – then you were well on the way to keeping her with you for good. Christ, that's the best thing I've ever done,' he soliloquizes. Eventually, however, retribution catches up with him when Winnie's soldier husband comes home on leave and with a mate beats him up in a dark alley. By then he has met Doreen, a girl younger than himself who takes him in hand and to whom, in a chastened mood, he becomes engaged.

The book received a sensational reception for two reasons that cast light on the social attitudes of the time. One was the portrayal of Arthur, who came to be regarded as an iconic figure of what was called 'working-class literature'. The other was the graphic account of

Brenda's successful attempt to terminate her pregnancy by the time-honoured method of lying in a bath of very hot water while drinking her way through a bottle of gin. This passage is thought to have played some part in influencing public opinion in favour of the legalization of abortion that came a few years later. Subsequent generations must also be struck by the furtiveness and embarrassment involved in those days in the purchase of contraceptives, which, of course, led to many unwanted pregnancies, backstreet abortions, illegitimate babies and forced marriages.

There are several other insights into what it was like to live in the 1950s. The acquisition of a television set is still something to be very excited about and it is still rare for anyone in Arthur's circle to own a car. Nobody yet goes abroad on holiday. The army casts a long shadow. Winnie is lonely and open to Arthur's charms because her husband is away serving in Germany in the British Army of the Rhine. Arthur's earlier two years of National Service in the army and the two weeks each year for some years after that which he is required to spend at Territorial Army camps are the only times in his life that he ever leaves home.

That there might be another war is a recurring subject of speculation and leads to passages in the book that are completely at variance with the heroic terms in which the war is conventionally portrayed. Being tall, Arthur was drafted into the Royal Military Police, or Redcaps, but this in no way diminished his anarchic tendencies. He looks back with admiration on the exploits of his older cousins, who had deserted during the war rather than fight: 'Tall grinning army deserters caught time and again by Redcaps or police, but always escaping, on the run, in hiding, living with whores, thieving for food and money because they had neither ration-books nor employment cards. A shaky game … But they had been right, he knew that, because they were still here, alive, at work, earning a good living in spite of the army.' They had said why should they fight after the years of unemployment and hardship they had endured before the war. He is resentful because he is paid much less when on military service than in his factory. 'But let them start a war, he thought, and see what a bad soldier I can be.'

I have no idea how widespread such sentiments were. During the weeks of my National Service basic training in the Royal Armoured Corps I shared a hut and all my waking hours with some thirty men from different parts of the country with backgrounds like Arthur's and met many more. Yet I never heard anything remotely along these lines. Some rancour and resentment and plenty of homesickness, but nothing incendiary. During the Korean War and in the various colonial engagements with which the army was involved National Servicemen fought well.*

During the Second World War the desertion rate never reached even one 1 per cent a year, although, given the enormous size of the armed forces at that time, that still amounted to a significant number of men. By 1945 the total number of men on the run as deserters is estimated to have reached nearly a hundred thousand.† Some suffering from traumas of one kind or another wanted only to hide. Others became involved in crime, often violent, and the twenty thousand deserters estimated to be at large in London were a major source of trouble to the police.

In another respect too, *Saturday Night and Sunday Morning* differs from other records of the 1950s. It was published in the same year as the Notting Hill race riots in London and when, as described in a later chapter, racial discrimination was rife in the capital.‡ Yet a sergeant from the Gold Coast (now Ghana), whom one of Seaton's cousins had met in the army, is invited to spend Christmas with his family and

---

* See essay on *The Dead, the Dying and the Damned.*

† Figures taken from sources at the National Archives and reproduced in David French, 'Discipline and the Death Penalty in the British Army in the War Against Germany During the Second World War, *Journal of Contemporary History*, October 1998, Vol. 33, No. 4, p. 541.

‡ See essay on *The Lonely Londoners* by Sam Selvon and two novels by Colin MacInnes.

receives a warm welcome. This could perhaps be attributed to military solidarity, but the presence of an Indian man as a permanent lodger in Doreen's mother's house without anyone seeming to mind suggests that, so far as individuals at least were concerned, racial discrimination was still quiescent in the circles Sillitoe was writing about.

Both *Love on the Dole* and *Saturday Night and Sunday Morning* were first novels which, after being rejected by a number of publishers, achieved instant success and were later turned into films. Their authors went on to write a good many other books and, in Greenwood's case, plays and television scripts, without achieving anything like the same success. Sillitoe was acclaimed in the Soviet Union, which would have liked to use him for propaganda purposes as a voice of the British working class. Far from responding, he became a critic of Soviet human rights abuses and campaigned on behalf of political prisoners in the Communist bloc countries and individual Jews who were prevented from leaving for the West.

Room at the Top

by John Braine (1957)

This Sporting Life

by David Storey (1960)

John Braine's *Room at the Top*, published in 1957, and David Storey's *This Sporting Life*, published in 1960, have much in common with Alan Sillitoe's *Saturday Night and Sunday Morning* in the preceding essay. All are first novels by young men with no literary training or experience that enjoyed instant critical acclaim and commercial success that was further compounded by hugely popular films. Their heroes are working class and they are set in surroundings their authors knew well from personal experience. Taken together, and along with others of the same genre, they opened the eyes of many middle- and upper-class readers to an unfamiliar world with different values from those they were accustomed to read about. They are as readable today as when they first appeared, while the films they inspired remain landmarks of British film-making. They also throw light on the power structure in northern cities in the 1950s and, in the cases of *Saturday Night and Sunday Morning* and *Room at the Top*, on a surprising attitude towards the war.

They cover a wider canvas than *Saturday Night and Sunday Morning* because their heroes, Joe Lampton in *Room at the Top*, and Arthur Machin in *This Sporting Life*, break away from their social backgrounds, albeit only temporarily in the latter case, while Arthur Seaton in *Saturday Night and Sunday Morning* is content to remain in his. As a result, through their eyes and experience, we gain vivid and unvarnished glimpses into the power structure as well as the social life in northern industrial towns in the now forgotten era when their woollen mills and manufacturing industries were still large employers. This was before much of their economy had fallen under the control of multinational companies and large London-based combines; an era when the companies that ran those industries were largely locally based while the men who owned and controlled them lived in the big houses on the hills above the towns – the Top, or 'T'Top', as they say in Yorkshire – and dominated much of the life in the communities around them. The workers were at the bottom near the works and social prestige could be measured by where on the gradient one lived.

Before writing *Room at the Top* John Braine was a librarian at the Public Library in the Yorkshire textile and market town of Bingley. The novel begins in 1947 with Joe Lampton arriving in a town called Warley to take up a post at the Municipal Treasury and to lodge not far below 'T'Top' with a master at the local grammar school and his wife. The couple had lost their only son during the war and are pleased to have Joe, who, like their son, had been in the Royal Air Force, to fill the gap left in their lives. Joe is thrilled. Having come from a poor working-class background in a neighbouring city, Joe has never been in such a well-appointed house before and is determined to use his new professional and social position as a launch pad to rise still further. He describes his ambition to himself as being 'as clear and compelling as the sense of vocation which doctors and missionaries are supposed to experience, though in my instance, of course, the call ordered me to do good to myself not others'.

Joe's initial jump from the backstreets into the professional class had been brought about in circumstances that are hard to imagine today. It was the result of having been shot down while on a bombing raid over Germany and spending three years there as a prisoner of war. During that time, under the auspices of the International Red Cross, he was able to qualify as an accountant and to accumulate £800 in back pay, a modest capital that he would never otherwise have been able to acquire. Food was short in the camp and he remembers how hungry he had been, but he has no doubt that captivity had been his lucky break.

When he is upbraided for not having tried to escape, like Jack Wales, the son of one of the local grandees who had earned a gallantry medal, he responds in a powerful passage that is totally at variance with how the war and being a PoW are conventionally portrayed: 'It was all right for him to escape. He had a rich daddy to look after him and to buy him an education. He could afford to waste his time. I couldn't. Those three years were the only chance I'd get to be qualified. Let those rich bastards who have all the fun be heroes. Let them pay for their privileges. If you want it straight from the shoulder I'll tell you: I was bloody well pleased when I was captured. I wasn't going to be killed trying to escape and I wasn't going to be killed flying again.' Even by the standards of Arthur Seaton's admiration in *Saturday Night and Sunday Morning* for those of his relations who had deserted from the armed forces to engage in the black market, this is very far removed from how it is now thought people in the 1940s thought and spoke about the war.

Taking and passing exams while in captivity was not unusual. Anthony Barber, who served as Chancellor of the Exchequer in Ted Heath's government from 1970 to 1974, was among those who did so. Before the war he was an articled clerk in a provincial solicitor's office. While in captivity from 1942 to 1945 he achieved a first-class law degree from London University through the good offices of the International Red Cross. As a result, when finally liberated he was awarded a grant to go to Oxford from which he went on to become a barrister in the Inner Temple; a less transformational rise than Joe Lampton's, but still something he would have been unlikely to have achieved in peacetime. Unlike Joe, however, Barber combined his studies with attempts to escape* and helping others to do so, for which he was mentioned in dispatches, the next best thing to a gallantry medal.

The vehicle by means of which Joe pursues his ambition is again very much of its time. He joins the town's amateur dramatic society, an institution which in those pre-television days flourished in provincial towns and cities. In this respectable milieu, bound by its very nature to forge bonds between the participants, he is brought into contact with a wide range of people: fellow professionals in different walks of life and their wives, women in search of an interest outside the home and Susan Brown, the rather childish and innocent nineteen-year-old daughter of one the town's important industrialists and influential members of the town council, Councillor Brown.

She becomes his target. Marriage to her and with it a position in her father's firm will, in one bound, take him straight to the Top. He faces two great obstacles, one emotional the other practical. The emotional is that having embarked on a 'no commitments on either side' affair with Alice, one of the married women in the group, he falls in love with her and she with him. The practical is that Susan's parents want her to marry Wales and don't regard him as at all a suitable match. The terms in which they and Wales snub, patronize and belittle him on social occasions are illustrative of the social mores of the time. Joe's boss warns him that if he crosses Councillor Brown it could damage his career while, if he gets on the right side of the Councillor, it will be to his benefit; a warning that would deter most young council employees from

* One of the attempts in which he was involved inspired the film *The Wooden Horse*, according to the *Oxford Dictionary of National Biography* account of his life by Denis Kavanagh.

pursuing the Councillor's daughter. But Joe perseveres while continuing his affair with Alice until a denouement is reached when he all but rapes Susan, who then triumphantly tells him he won't need Alice any more.

Soon after, he is summoned by Councillor Brown to the local Conservative Club, portrayed as the luxurious inner sanctum of the rich and powerful, a far cry from the seedy decay of so many of the provincial Conservative clubs of today. Brown offers to set him up in business and to provide him with customers if he will leave Susan alone. When Joe refuses, Brown immediately changes tack, says he 'wanted to see what you were made of' and tells Joe that he and Susan should marry right away. It then emerges that Susan is pregnant and that she hadn't told Joe because she hadn't wanted him to marry her 'out of a sense of duty'.

As Brown makes clear, it is not the way in which he had hoped his daughter would marry, but he is easily reconciled to the fact. He recognizes that Joe is an able and ambitious young man who is worth backing anyway. He also recognizes something of himself in Joe as he too had come from nothing and furthered his own career by marrying into his wife's established county family. The one condition he imposes, not unreasonably, is that Joe should sever all connection with Alice.

At this point tragedy intervenes. While Joe is still revelling in his success, he hears that soon after he and Alice had had their acrimonious final meeting she had gone on a drunken binge, crashed her car into a wall and died a lingering death. Her best friend, whose flat he and Alice had borrowed for their love-making, accuses him of being responsible and tells him how much she had loved him. He knows that to be true, and himself goes on a drunken binge during the course of which he narrowly escapes being beaten up. When friends find him, he blames himself for murdering Alice and when they say she would have ruined his life and 'nobody blames you' their sympathy intensifies his remorse.

Big-hearted, impetuous, unable to understand the feelings of others, let alone manipulate them, and given to violence, Arthur Machin, the hero of *This Sporting Life* is the polar opposite of Joe Lampton. He is a professional rugby league player. Among the toughest of team sports, rugby league football, not to be confused with rugby union, is in this country a North of England sport. In the 1950s it was an integral part of working-class culture there and it remains a distinctive regional feature dividing north and south. David Storey had himself been a professional rugby league player, though a most unusual one, as he had combined playing for Leeds Rugby League Football Club with studying at the Slade School of Fine Art in London. It is hard to imagine a man straddling a wider cultural divide. His book is the only literary novel written by a professional player of any form of football and, as such, something of a literary curiosity.

The opening lines put the reader at the heart of the action: 'I had my head to Mellor's backside, waiting for the ball to come between his legs. He was too slow. I was moving away when the leather shot back into my hands and before I could pass, a shoulder came up to my jaw. It rammed my teeth together with a force that stunned me into blackness.' The trainer takes him off and tells him his front teeth are broken, despite which he returns to the pitch to finish the game.

Arthur is a valued player. As soon as the game is over Weaver, a local magnate, and one of the two men who control the club, whisks him off in his Bentley to the dentist and then, to add lustre, to his Christmas party at his house at the Top. Arthur still works as a lathe operator in Weaver's works, but as a football star he transcends class – for as long as he is on form and in favour. As he soon discovers, however, for Weaver and his partner-cum-rival, another big local industrialist called Slomer, the club is 'their mutual toy. They bought and sold players, built them up and dropped them, like a couple of kids with lead soldiers.'

Arthur's fate, like that of most other professional sportsmen at that time, was always to remain one of the lead soldiers. Without the education or ability to use his temporary fame and earning power to create a long-term career for when his playing days come to an end, his only assets are his youth, skill and strength. In the pre-television age rugby league was too local a sport and the wages and celebrity status of its stars too circumscribed for a player to earn the sort of money that could transform his life.

Even football stars with a national and international reputation were infinitely less well off than they are today as their wage rates were capped in the interests of the clubs that employed them. One of the greatest players of the 1950s was Tom Finney, still regarded by some as the most complete footballer ever to have played for England, who was knighted in 1998, thirty-eight years after his retirement. In 1952 he was earning £12 a week and in 1960 £20 – the equivalent to about £340 and £450 in today's money. He had been apprenticed as a plumber before becoming a professional footballer and after his retirement ran his own plumbing and heating firm in his home town of Preston.

This was exceptional. The lucky ones might take over a pub, a possibility Arthur discusses with one of his team-mates. Others, for the most part, reverted to being wage earners of one sort or another. The question at the heart of *This Sporting Life* is whether, in the circumstances of its time and place, the temporarily glamorous life it describes was worth the pain and the price involved.

The parabola of Arthur's career is traced through episodes on and off the field. At the outset there is an excruciating act of violence when an older player on his own side, jealous of his talent, sets out to starve him of the ball. Arthur awaits his chance. Then, while they are both heads down in the scrum and the referee can't see, 'I swung my right fist into the middle of his face. He cried out loud. I hit him again and saw the red pulp of his nose and lips as my hand came away.' The referee blames a player in the opposing team and the man leaves the field with a broken nose. Thereafter Arthur plays a blinder and, though they have a fair idea of what happened, the club officials sign him up as a professional.

When he is established in the first team and so fit that he can come off the field 'fresher than when I went on', he recalls an incident when he scores a try. 'I went straight for the full-back, and when he came in I gave him the base of my wrist on his nose. The crack, the groan, the release of his arms, all coincided with a soaring of my guts. I moved in between the posts keeping my eye on the delight of the crowd as I put the ball down.' Towards the end of his career the roles are reversed. He is trying to prevent an opponent scoring, misses his man, falls and, as the crowd roars 'its pain like a maimed animal', is left to 'stare unbelievingly at my legs, which had betrayed me'. In the dressing room afterwards, Arthur watches the new young star being ceremoniously doused under the cold water tap to celebrate his success while his own ankles are being strapped and he is putting his false teeth in. He knows his glory days are over and that he has nothing to fall back on.

In the town, which is too small to be Leeds and may be based on Storey's home town of Wakefield, Arthur in his prime is a celebrity. He is recognized wherever he goes, welcome in the clubs and restaurants frequented by the local elite and, with Weaver's help, able to buy his car and a television at a discount. It gives him self-confidence and a swagger but cuts him off from his parents and creates a barrier between him and the woman he falls in love with, a young widow in whose house he lodges. He gives her a fur coat and a television and takes her and her children for trips in his Jaguar to expensive restaurants. She sleeps with him but worries about becoming overwhelmed and a mere appendage. When she tries to explain her doubts about committing to him, 'I couldn't think why she should say all this, and the shortest way of stopping it was to hit her. I cracked her hard across the face, and I wanted to apologize when I saw the mark.' What works on the football field doesn't with her. She throws him out of her house. Later, when she contracts a fatal illness, he pays for her to have private treatment but her death leaves him again with nothing.

A tantalizing aspect of the rivalry between Weaver and Slomer, and of the attitude of others towards them that Storey touches on but fails to elaborate upon, is the position of Catholics in the town. At an early stage in their relationship Arthur mentions to the widow that Slomer has a lot of money. 'And you're satisfied with that sort of money? He's a Catholic,' she replies, as if the mere fact of his religion makes his money disreputable. Arthur wonders, 'how far that should affect me … a Catholic more or less represented a foreign agent. They might be on your side. On the other hand they might not. It was better to treat them all as enemies, then you could be sure.' Later Slomer asks Arthur if he has ever thought of becoming a Catholic: 'It's got a lot of advantages for a young man like you. It has organization for one thing,' he explains. Arthur doesn't pursue the matter and there is no further reference to it. In Scotland the sectarian divide was deeply embedded and expressed through football* until well into this century; to a lesser extent, that was true of Liverpool as well. But that Storey, drawing on his own experience, should represent it as influencing power struggles within a Yorkshire rugby league club and social attitudes within the local community during the 1950s is surprising.

After achieving great success with their first novels the careers of John Braine and David Storey went in opposite directions. Braine, who died in 1986, never repeated his initial triumph. By contrast, Storey, who died aged eighty-three in 2017, went on to write many successful novels and to become a distinguished playwright and screenwriter as well. In his later years he returned to painting and drawing and an exhibition of more than four hundred of his works was held in Wakefield a year before his death.

---

* Catholic Celtic vs Protestant Rangers in Glasgow and, less well known, Protestant Heart of Midlothian vs Catholic Hibernian in Edinburgh.

Early Feminism

Suffragette Sally by Gertrude Colmore, 1911,
Testament of Youth by Vera Brittain, 1933,
and *A Life's Work* by Margaret Bondfield, 1948.

A Room of One's Own by Virginia Woolf, 1929,
and *Three Guineas* by Virginia Woolf, 1938.

The Golden Notebook by Doris Lessing, 1962.

Suffragette Sally

by Gertrude Colmore* (1911)

Testament of Youth

by Vera Brittain (1933)

A Life's Work

by Margaret Bondfield (1948)

History is written by the victors, or so the saying goes.† Of no subject is this more true than the battles fought on many fronts, political, in the workplace and in the home, for women's rights and aspirations in the early years of the twentieth century. It is the suffragettes' campaign for the right to vote in parliamentary elections that dominates the national memory. It is their exploits – the violence they perpetrated and the suffering they endured – in the years immediately before the First World War that have been recorded and dramatized in countless

* A nom de plume. Her real name was Gertrude Baillie-Weaver.

† It is attributed to different authors, including Winston Churchill, but I have not been able to discover who used it first or when.

books, documentaries and films. It is the statue of their leader, Emmeline Pankhurst, that has stood in Victoria Tower Gardens beside the Houses of Parliament since 1930. In his great classic on pre-1914 politics, *The Strange Death of Liberal England*, George Dangerfield writes that Mrs Pankhurst and her followers must be 'enrolled among the makers of history'.*

Millicent Fawcett, the doyenne of campaigners for women's suffrage, who abhorred the violence of the suffragettes, which she regarded as damaging rather than helpful to bringing about reform, was, until the installation of her statue in London's Parliament Square in 2018, a largely forgotten figure. Yet her life had been devoted to campaigning for women's suffrage since 1865, when, as a young woman, she had helped to gather signatures for the petition that in 1866 first put the issue onto the political agenda. In 1913 the National Union of Women's Suffrage Societies (NUWSS), which she led and which sought to bring about change by constitutional methods, enormously outnumbered the Women's Social and Political Union (WSPU), the official name for the suffragettes. Figures vary, but some estimates give the former up to one hundred thousand members compared with two thousand for the latter.

Still forgotten, and in many ways still more remarkable, is Margaret Bondfield, who in 1929 became the first woman Cabinet minister. While Emmeline Pankhurst and Millicent Fawcett were securely anchored in the prosperous middle class, she was a working-class woman with little education and nothing but her wits and her energy to support her. When she began work as a shop assistant in 1887 shop assistants were among the most exploited of working women. Her campaigns, initially on their behalf, and, later, on behalf of women in other industries,

* George Dangerfield, *The Strange Death of Liberal England*, Harrison Smith and Robert Haas, 1935, p. 147. This was in New York where it quickly went out of print. It only achieved fame when republished in the United Kingdom in the following year, since when many other editions have been issued.

helped to pioneer effective trade union action on behalf of women; action which brought about tangible improvements in their lives and working conditions long before the vote, and the political clout that went with it, was achieved.

The significance of these battles in the political and industrial arenas during the late nineteenth and early twentieth centuries can now be appreciated. At the time they were far removed from the concerns of women trying to break free from their traditional role within their own families. Among the most outstanding twentieth-century autobiographies, and one of the finest chronicles of the First World War, is Vera Brittain's *Testament of Youth*. Published in 1933, it became an instant bestseller and is still widely read today. Between the wars she was an inveterate campaigner for the League of Nations and other anti-war causes. Yet in her account of her early years before 1914 she barely mentions the political debate about whether women should have the vote and the activities of women trade unionists completely passed her by. Her ambitions were solely directed at persuading her parents to allow her to go to Oxford, an extremely unusual aspiration for a young woman from a prosperous provincial background at that time, and to passing the exams required to get there.

Vera Brittain was born in 1893. By the turn of the century it was no longer unusual for girls from well-to-do families to attend school though many were still being educated at home. During the previous thirty years or so a tiny minority had gone on to university. A few had even become academics and doctors; Britain's first woman doctor was Fawcett's sister, Elizabeth Garrett Anderson. Most professions, however, other than school teaching and nursing, which did not require university degrees or similar qualifications, were still closed to women. In the prosperous classes parents neither wanted nor expected their daughters to earn their own living and saw no need for them to acquire qualifications; rather the reverse. It was widely believed that if a woman was too well educated it would harm her marriage prospects and distract her from the domestic duties that were held to be her true vocation.*

Vera Brittain's family were typical in not taking her education seriously and in wanting her to grow up 'as an ornamental young lady'. While her father regarded it as axiomatic that her younger and less intellectual brother should go to university, he was adamantly opposed to his daughter doing so. He was happy to buy her a grand piano and to spend money on music lessons but begrudged every penny that went on her tuition. Her school friends regarded her ambition with incomprehension while the women in her parents' social set in the Derbyshire town of Buxton considered it to be 'ridiculous' and described her in the contemptuous term of the time as a 'bluestocking'. To overcome such a battery of conventions and prejudices required courage and determination. Her measured account of how she gained her parents' acquiescence, found out what exams she had to take and worked to pass them explains why so few tried and the nature of the constraints on a young woman in even a loving and prosperous home.

Tragically, no sooner had she reached her promised land than war broke out. The authorities at Somerville College, Oxford, exhorted their undergraduates to continue with their studies and not allow the war to distract them. Most did so. Brittain again defied convention by volunteering to become a nurse and only returning to Oxford when peace was restored. By then her fiancé, her brother and her two other closest men friends had all been killed.

As I write, more than half the young people going to university in this country are women. The days when they had to overcome a wall of parental prejudice and other obstacles to get there seem like a distant memory. In fact, they continued until well into the 1960s. Some of the most intelligent and intellectually active women that I know in my own

---

* See later essay on *A Room of One's Own* by Virginia Woolf for more on this subject.

generation were not allowed to go to university by their parents in the belief that it wasn't the right thing for a girl to do. Finishing schools and secretarial colleges were deemed to be more appropriate. Fathers, like Margaret Thatcher's, who, in the 1940s, determined that she should go to Oxford, remained very much the exception until well into the 1970s, shortly before Mrs Thatcher herself became Prime Minister.

Suffragette Sally, published in 1911, is a very different sort of book. Its aim was to propagandize on behalf of the suffragette movement and to encourage recruits to join its ranks. Though a novel, it is hard to separate fact from fiction. The demonstrations and confrontations between the suffragettes and the police that it describes are taken from life, as are the horrific experiences of those women who were sent to prison and suffered in other ways. The women described as the movement's leaders in the book, are clearly Mrs Emmeline Pankhurst and her allies lightly disguised. Of the three main characters, the aristocratic Lady Henry Hill is derived from Lady Constance Bulwer-Lytton while the working-class Sally Simmonds and the upper-middle-class Edith Carstairs are composite figures drawn from the author's experience.

As a piece of propaganda *Suffragette Sally* scores highly, portraying the suffragettes as a dedicated group drawn from every social class battling on behalf of all women and open to women of all classes. Class distinctions are dealt with very subtly. Far from being eliminated they provide inspiration and reassurance. Sally herself, a former maid of all work, is inspired to find herself working for the same cause as, and coming into personal contact with, Lady Henry while Lady Henry's charm and position give Edith Carstairs the courage to oppose her family's wishes and even to stifle the mockery of her brother.

One of the book's most trenchant messages was that, whatever her class, a suffragette would often find that the most intense opposition she had to face would be from her own relations and social circle. When Edith Carstairs, after finally overcoming her doubts, participates in a demonstration, she is arrested. Her mother is horrified and deeply hurt. Her clergyman uncle and aunt forbid her to enter their house because she has brought disgrace on the family. This reaction reflected the way many respectable people reacted to the suffragettes' methods. The great majority of women, whether in favour of the vote or not, disapproved of and were indeed often shocked by their methods, which was why the other women's groups campaigning for the vote, known as suffragists, thought the suffragettes' tactics were counter-productive. The ridicule, insults and social ostracism to which Edith Carstairs and Sally were subjected varied in tone but not in intensity from one class to another.

The book conveys in graphic detail both the nature of the suffragettes' protests and the punishments they received. The former ranged from demonstrations and marches in the streets, disrupting political meetings and harassing individual politicians to stone-throwing, breaking windows, vandalizing golf courses and setting fire to empty buildings. The usual punishment was a short prison sentence. To protest against being imprisoned for, as they saw it, demanding the right to vote rather than for a crime, a number of those who were arrested went on hunger strike. This led to a form of forced feeding that amounted to torture.

The authorities were, however, determined that no embarrassing accident should befall women from the upper classes. As a result, while 'common' or 'working women' were subjected to this harrowing experience as a matter of course, 'ladies' were often given a medical examination on the basis of which they would be discharged. In an incident based on the real-life experience of Lady Constance, Lady Henry exposes this injustice by getting herself arrested under a pseudonym and then publicizing her experiences after her release from prison, which helps to bring about a change of policy. Lady Henry recovers from her ordeal, but Lady Constance's health was broken, as happened to many others. Sally herself dies after a prolonged illness caused by being kicked in the stomach by a policeman during a demonstration.

A point that does not emerge from *Suffragette Sally* is the precise nature of the franchise for which the WSPU was campaigning. In fact, it was not arguing for the vote for all women and Sally herself would have been excluded from the franchise its members were campaigning for. At that time, the vote was not only restricted to men; there was a property qualification as well that excluded a significant proportion of working-class men. What the WSPU wanted was votes for women on the same basis as men. They were not arguing for a universal adult suffrage.

This brought them up against the redoubtable Margaret Bondfield, who chaired the Adult Suffrage Society. Her view, as explained in her autobiography, *A Life's Work*, was that if only well-to-do women won the right to vote, it would tip the political scales still further against the workers by strengthening the power of the rich and powerful. 'I have never been able to approach the question [of women's suffrage] from the standpoint of women's rights,' she wrote. What she wanted was for all men and women above the age of twenty-one to be given the vote.

She was one of the most remarkable women of her age and it is surprising to me that she is not more honoured in the feminist pantheon. Born in 1873, one of eleven children of a Somerset lace-maker and his wife, she left school and started work as a shop assistant at fourteen. In 1929, after a lifetime campaigning on behalf of the poorest and most disadvantaged women, she became the first ever woman Cabinet minister. Her autobiography, published in 1948, is badly constructed and difficult to read, but is nonetheless an important historical record of how much effective campaigning and political activity some women were engaged in, long before getting the vote.

Her first campaign was on behalf of shop assistants like herself, who were subjected to the rigours of the 'the living in' system whereby unmarried staff were obliged to live in single-sex dormitories owned and run by the employers. Their wages were reduced accordingly to cover the cost. The food and hygiene were notoriously bad and, as she describes in her book, the overcrowding was dreadful. The practice enabled the employers to control every aspect of their employees' lives. When she was living in, she worked 'for about sixty-four hours a week for which she was paid between £15 and £25 per annum' (£2,000 and £3,200 in today's money), which could at any time be arbitrarily reduced if she broke any one of the numerous rules for which her employer could impose a fine. She gives examples of these gleaned from a number of different firms in London and elsewhere – being late for work or for meals, not serving a customer quickly enough, addressing a customer as Miss when it should have been Madam, not using paper or string with economy, sleeping out without permission and using candles when the bedroom gas is turned off.

Instead of knuckling down under what she regarded as 'humiliating and degrading' conditions, she joined a trade union,* which brought her into contact with women who told her about working practices in other firms. Under the pseudonym Grace Dare she began writing short stories for the union journal, *Shop Assistant*, about the conditions under which its members worked. She did this at night by candlelight behind a towel while her room-mates were asleep and relied on them not to give her away. Had she been discovered she would have been summarily dismissed.

As it was, she went on to be recruited by the privately funded Women's Industrial Council, which carried out covert investigations into women's working conditions, the results of which were published in a national newspaper as part of a campaign to change the law. In 1901 this led to her giving evidence before a select committee of the House of Lords, an early step on the road to becoming a public figure.

* The National Union of Shop Assistants, Warehousemen and Clerks (NUSAWC).

Thereafter, the campaign with which she had been associated began to bear fruit. In 1904 the Shop Hours Act limited shop-opening hours while in 1907 the first steps were taken to end the practice of 'living in'.

Her career thereafter shows how politically active and effective it was possible for an exceptional and determined woman to be, even without the right to vote. She became a professional campaigner as organizing secretary of the Women's Labour League and a member of the Women's Co-operative Guild, which exposed her to what was happening across the industrial landscape. In 1910 when she enquired into conditions in the woollen textile industry in Yorkshire she was shocked by the incidence of incest in the overcrowded slums where the workers and their families lived. Among the examples she quotes: 'One family [that] consisted of a mother with two girls, a boy of nineteen and a boy of twelve, all lying in the same bed. Both girls had children to brothers.' She had long campaigned for a minimum wage and for equal pay for women. This experience led her to widen her agenda to include demands for maternity and child benefit and measures to reduce child mortality.

She also became involved with the international aspects of the Labour movement. In 1910, she visited the United States to tell women's organizations there about the work of the Women's Labour League. In 1915, she went as a member of the Women's Peace Council to a conference in Switzerland organized by the Women's International of Socialist and Labour Organizations to call for a negotiated peace to end the war.

In 1923, she became the first woman to chair the Trades Union Congress (TUC) and one of the first three Labour women to be elected to Parliament. In 1924, she joined the short-lived first Labour government as a junior minister and five years later, after the 1929 election, became a Cabinet minister in the second Labour government. Her political career came to an end when that government fell in 1931, after which she continued to be active in the trade union movement until 1938. Despite all her achievements, when she sets out a list of her siblings and their careers in her book she describes herself simply as 'Spinster. The writer of this book.'

The principle of votes for women was decided by the First World War. Their contribution to the war effort made it impossible to deny their claim any longer, but it was granted only partially and grudgingly. The Representation of the People Act of 1918 extended the right to vote in parliamentary elections to all men aged twenty-one and over, whether or not they owned property, while women had to be aged thirty and to meet a residual property qualification. Only in local elections were both sexes allowed to vote on equal terms at age twenty-one without a property qualification. In 1928 this arrangement was extended to parliamentary elections and women finally achieved the same rights to vote as men.* Margaret Bondfield rejoiced in these victories, but other battles, including equal pay, were still far from won when she died in 1953.†

* The qualifying age has since been lowered to eighteen.

† I possess a souvenir of her life in the form of a copy of John Maynard Keynes' book, *The Economic Consequences of the Peace* (see later essay), with her ownership inscription on the flyleaf.

A Room of One's Own

by Virginia Woolf (1929)

Three Guineas

by Virginia Woolf (1938)

Who's Afraid of Virginia Woolf is the title of a well-known play by the American Edward Albee first performed in 1962. It's about the complexities of a marriage and has nothing to do with Virginia Woolf herself, but the words of the title convey her daunting reputation and the way people tend to think of her. Her name has come to personify the most rarefied intellectualism and sensitive aestheticism. Her ethereal face with its large, expressive eyes provides their physical manifestation.

Her fame derives both from her books and from the circle in which she moved. Her most famous stream-of-consciousness novels, *Mrs Dalloway*, *To the Lighthouse* and *The Waves*, which deal more with what's happening in their characters' minds than with what they are doing or what is happening around them, are among the key books of the modernist movement. Like the works of James Joyce and Marcel Proust, all serious readers feel they ought to have tackled them and tend to be apologetic about admitting it when they haven't or gave up the attempt.

A Room of One's Own and *Three Guineas* pose no such problems. They are extended essays and easy to read. Together they provide the foundation on which her reputation as one of the century's pioneering feminist (a word she hated) thinkers and writers is built. Hermione Lee, the Goldsmiths' Professor of English Literature at Oxford and biographer of Woolf, describes *A Room of One's Own* as 'probably the most influential feminist essay of the twentieth century'.[1] *Three Guineas* is less famous, but marks a point at which women, having achieved the vote and enhanced educational opportunities, began to turn their attention to breaking down the barriers against them in the professions.

As described in the essay on Lytton Strachey and *Eminent Victorians*, Virginia Woolf with her sister, the artist Vanessa Bell, formed the hub around which the famous Bloomsbury Group of writers, artists and intellectuals gathered before, during and after the First World War. Besides Strachey and such well-known individuals as the great economist John Maynard Keynes and the artists Duncan Grant and Roger Fry, it included her husband, Leonard Woolf.

He was crucial to her success as a writer. Throughout her adult life she was prone to mental instability and breakdowns, which some believe may have been exacerbated by abuse she suffered as a child at the hands of her half-brothers, George and Gerald Duckworth. When she was afflicted Leonard sustained her; when depression threatened he helped her to deal with it. He also founded the Hogarth Press, a private venture which published many of her books as well as those of other leading writers of the period. Given her delicate mental balance and the stress bringing a book to publication always caused her, it must be doubted whether she would have been able to produce the body of work that she did if her husband and his press had not been there to ease the strain. Despite his care and help, life eventually became too much for her to bear. In 1941, at the age of fifty-nine, with worries about the war adding to her mental distress, she gave up the struggle and drowned herself in a river that ran by their country cottage at Rodmell in Sussex.

The Woolfs and their friends were people of independent means, not rich and certainly not lavish spenders, but ultimately not dependent on what they earned for how they lived. Virginia Woolf's advocacy of women's rights kept within the comfort zone of her social class. She did not write on behalf of the great mass of women at that time working in factories, shops and domestic service or struggling to feed numerous children on a working man's wages, or less if their husbands were unemployed; the women for whom Margaret Bondfield campaigned. Her focus wasn't on the gap between rich and poor or the problems of the poor. It was on the injustices perpetrated throughout history on the women she describes in *Three Guineas* as 'the daughters of educated men'; in other words, women whose families employed servants.

Within that class, she argued, the single most important reason why women had always been disadvantaged and demeaned by men was their lack of financial independence and the means to acquire it. Not until the Married Women's Property Act was passed in 1882, the year Woolf was born, did married women become entitled to own and control property in their own right. Until then their fathers, before they married, and then their husbands had always controlled the purse strings so that, ultimately, they had to do as they were told. Fathers could prevent their daughters from marrying or, if they insisted, determine who they should marry. Husbands could dictate the way and the values by which they should live. Access to books and the right to write and to express independent views were at the discretion of fathers and husbands. The 1882 Act changed the legal status of married women, but old attitudes persisted well into Woolf's adulthood and beyond while in many families daughters remained as much under parental control as ever they had.

Her indignation and rage against the constricting effect that lack of independence had on women's lives suffuses both books. In a famous passage in *A Room of One's Own* she illustrates the point by imagining the disapproval, frustrations and blighted hopes culminating in suicide that might have faced a fictional sister of Shakespeare, if she had had the same talents and aspirations as him. Prefiguring and demonstrating the need for what are now known as Women's Studies, she writes about what little was known of the lives of a few seventeenth- and early eighteenth-century women writers and of the social significance of the emergence, towards the end of the eighteenth century, of middle-class women writing for money; a development, she argues, that deserves more attention in the history books than the Crusades or the Wars of the Roses.

Two of the best and most famous of the nineteenth-century writers were Jane Austen and Charlotte Brontë. But their success did not enable them to break free from the conventions of their time. Far from it. As an unmarried woman living with her family, Jane Austen had to write her books in the general sitting room. Whenever she heard someone approach she would hide her manuscript under a piece of blotting paper as she would have been embarrassed if servants or visitors or anyone beyond her immediate family should have known what she was doing. Charlotte Brontë's problem was of a different kind. Her father simply forbad her for some years to marry the man she loved and she had to acquiesce.

A Room of One's Own is based on two papers delivered in 1928 to societies at Newnham and Girton, at that time the only two women's colleges at Cambridge and thus the only ones where women could study at that university. It is concerned with creating the conditions that would enable women to attempt to write fiction, whether prose or poetry. To do so, Woolf argues, 'a woman must have money and a room of her own'. By money she means £500 a year, which equates to about

£31,000 a year in today's money. Her own earnings only attained that level in 1926, the year after the publication of *Mrs Dalloway* and eleven years after the publication of her first novel in 1915. Thereafter they increased substantially.

Besides money and a room, she believed that, in order to write, a woman also had to have had an education. Hence her anger, expressed forcibly in both these books, at the way middle- and upper-class families had always spent large sums educating their sons and virtually nothing on their daughters. Girls' schools were still quite a new phenomenon when she was a child and, like many of her contemporaries, she was kept at home where her father, Sir Leslie Stephen, the founding editor of the *Dictionary of National Biography*, took charge of her education and gave her the run of his library until, at the age of fifteen, she attended a few Greek classes under the auspices of King's College London. Hermione Lee argues that 'she would not have been the writer she was, with the subjects she chose, if she had had a formal education'.[2] That must be true, but, as Woolf knew, most girls, whether at school or at home, received much less of an education than their brothers and were correspondingly intellectually handicapped in adulthood.

Woolf illustrates the continuing inequality between men and educated women in her own time by recording a visit to 'Oxbridge' where she has lunch in one of the old colleges that only men could attend. She describes the beauty of the buildings, the perfection of the grounds, the lavishness of her meal and how she is turned away from the library as women could only enter 'if accompanied by a Fellow of the College or furnished with a letter of introduction'. This leads her to speculate about 'the unending stream of gold and silver' in the form of endowments, bequests, gifts and tithes that these colleges had received from rich and powerful men over the centuries on the basis of which 'Oxbridge' has been able to establish chairs, lectureships and fellowships and to stock its libraries and equip its laboratories and observatories.

She ends her day at a women's college where the gardens are bedraggled, the building undistinguished, the dinner plain and resources limited. The first women's colleges were established at Oxford and Cambridge between 1869 and 1875, but women remained second-class citizens for long after that. At Oxford they were only allowed to participate in degree ceremonies in 1920 and at Cambridge not until 1947. Because women in previous generations had not been able to amass fortunes there were no potential female benefactors to call on and Woolf didn't expect men to fill the breach.

The purpose of the essay is, however, more far-reaching than to inveigh against past and continuing inequalities. It is to argue that because all but a tiny fraction of the books that formed the intellectual and cultural basis of the society in which she and her readers lived had been written by men, that society reflected male values, attitudes and assumptions. It not only gave men power over women, it also accorded particular prestige to military prowess, the pursuit of power and the accumulation of large fortunes. If women had been equal rather than subservient, they would have countered these values and cut men down to size. Instead, their subservience led them to nurture and encourage male vanities and ambitions like 'looking glasses possessing the magic and delicious power of reflecting the figure of the man at twice its natural size'. It was because so many women had been brought up to believe that their role in life was essentially to support their menfolk that they often opposed, or at least did not support, reforms aimed at achieving equality between the sexes.

Three Guineas is couched in the form of a response to an 'educated man' who has written a letter to Woolf asking her to support his efforts to prevent a war. She does so by considering, in the light of his letter, which of three organizations that have asked her for money should receive her guinea – an anti-war society, a women's college building fund or a society promoting the employment of professional women.

The essay is diffuse and repetitious and its tone is harsher than *A Room of One's Own*, perhaps because she was mourning the death of her nephew, Julian Bell, in the Spanish Civil War while she was writing it. The absolutism of her pacifism makes no allowance for the seriousness of the Nazi threat facing Britain, which offended a number of her friends, including Keynes, while Leonard thought it her worst book. However, in the opinion of the literary biographer Lyndall Gordon, 'her attack on war as a pastime of men in power'* has in the long run been helpful to her reputation rather than the reverse.

In the essay she makes fun of the way men in power dress up in colourful uniforms and ceremonial robes of office, a particular foible of the British though not confined to them. She suggests that this feeds their sense of self-importance and exclusivity and thus their reluctance to allow women an equal share of life's prizes. Most professions had been obliged to admit women under the Sex Disqualification (Removal) Act of 1919, but as she shows the pace of their advance up the professional ladder had been painfully slow. A few professions even managed to remain closed to women until after her death. The Foreign Office did not accept women until 1946 and, until 1973, obliged them to resign on getting married, while the Jockey Club refused to grant licences to women to train racehorses until a court case in 1966.

Woolf holds up the Church of England as an example of how men could decide among themselves on the basis, in her view, of prejudice and tradition to keep women out. In 1935 it set up a commission to look into the question of women priests. It concluded, she writes, that while there was no inherent reason why women should not be ordained, 'we believe that the general mind of the Church is still in accord with the continuous tradition of a male priesthood'. Not until 1994 were the first women priests ordained.

---

* *Oxford Dictionary of National Biography* entry.

In other fields the whim of an employer could decide whether or not women should even be hired. As late as the 1950s the editor of the *Financial Times*, in other respects a most enlightened man, was reluctant to give women editorial jobs. I joined the paper in 1960 and well remember the stir it caused when this policy began to be relaxed and women to take their place among us.

That these barriers took so long to come down is evidence of how far ahead of her time Woolf was in assaulting them. She was equally, if not more, advanced in challenging the widespread practice of paying women less than men in the same position or doing the same work, a practice often justified on the grounds that a man had a family to support. In response she argued that as tax was levied at the same rate for women as for men they should be paid at the same rate and that in any case unmarried men always received the same salary as those who were married. As in *A Room of One's Own*, she bases her case both on fairness and on the need for women to have the means to escape from the control of their fathers and husbands so as to be able to lead lives of their own.

Looking back from the twenty-first century it is surprising for how long after Woolf's death educated women continued to put up with inequalities at work. The late Diana Athill, a famously successful editor from the 1940s to the 1980s at the André Deutsch publishing house, provides a partial explanation in her memoirs: 'Obviously it is true that indifference to status and pay is not found in all women, but I have seen it in a good many, who, like me, enjoyed their work. All my colleagues in the sixties and seventies admired and sympathized with women who were actively campaigning for women's rights, but none of them joined in as campaigners: we could see the injustice, but we didn't feel the pinch because we happened to be doing what we wanted to do.'[3] It was only when the majority of women ceased at a subconscious level to regard being able to work at what they liked doing as a privilege and started to think of themselves as having the same basic rights to fulfilling careers as men that equality began to come within reach.

Virginia Woolf believed that women had a mission to change and improve society through their writing and by becoming more active in the professions. To do that she wanted them to think of themselves as outsiders and not to adopt existing practices, values and assumptions. In accordance with this principle she refused all honours: to give the prestigious Clark Lectures at Cambridge that her father had once given, appointment as a Companion of Honour and honorary degrees from the universities of Manchester and Liverpool. 'It is an utterly corrupt society,' she wrote in her diary on 25 March 1933, '& I will take nothing that it can give me.'[4] In these two essays, as well as in other writings, she sought to bring about far-reaching change. With women's suffrage and access to the professions achieved, she played an important role in opening up the new front of equal opportunity, albeit that she was concerned only with the interests of 'the daughters of educated men' and not with women from other social classes.

The Golden Notebook

by Doris Lessing (1962)

Doris Lessing's novel *The Golden Notebook*, published in 1962, is one of the most celebrated books of the mid-twentieth century and widely regarded as a feminist bible. In his 1979 anthology, *Ninety-Nine Novels: The Best in English Since 1939*, the author and critic Anthony Burgess described it as 'the most massive statement made up to that time on the position of women in the modern world'.[5] In 2007, when the Swedish Academy awarded Lessing the Nobel Prize for Literature, its citation declared that *The Golden Notebook* 'belongs to the handful of books that informed the 20th century view of the male-female relationship'.[6] In January 2017, shortly before leaving the White House, Barack Obama, in an interview with the *New York Times*, said that it was one of the books he had put on the Kindle he had recently given his daughter Malia.[7]

There can be few books less suitable for reading on a Kindle than *The Golden Notebook*. Not only is it extremely long – five hundred and sixty-seven pages in the original edition – it has a complex and unusual structure that requires frequent cross-checking. As Lessing explains in the preface to the 1972 edition: 'There is a skeleton, or frame, called *Free Women*, which is a conventional short novel, about 60,000 words long, and which could stand by itself. But it is divided into five sections and separated by stages of the four Notebooks, black, red, yellow and blue', that are kept by Anna Wulf, the central character in *Free Women*.[8] After having written one successful novel, Anna is suffering from writer's block. The notebooks with their different coloured covers are a device by means of which she hopes to overcome it. In the black she writes about her life as a writer and in the red about politics. In the yellow she makes up stories derived from her own experiences while the blue is a sort of diary. From out of their fragments comes the new and original golden notebook, which constitutes the catharsis that enables her to come to terms with her life, to give up writing and to become an untrained marriage guidance counsellor.

The result is an enormous canvas, a profusion of characters and several different yet overlapping texts and stories. If Lessing did not write so clearly and so well, the novel would be unreadable. Unless Malia Obama is extremely adept at jumping back and forth on her Kindle, she must at times have found it difficult to keep a handle on the different characters and where they fit into the overall framework. Directly and indirectly *The Golden Notebook* deals not just with the role and aspirations of women, for which it is famous, but also with the end of the Communist dream, life in colonial Africa during the war years and the ideas and attitudes of left-wing intellectuals in London in the 1950s. On all these matters it holds up a mirror to the age in which it was written that is of enduring interest.

Lessing set out to write a classic, but not the one *The Golden Notebook* has become. In her preface to the 1972 edition,[9] she writes that she wanted to describe the intellectual and moral climate of her time as, in the nineteenth century, Tolstoy had done for Russia with *Anna Karenina* and Stendhal for France with *The Red and the Black*. When she embarked on her project in the late 1950s the position and aspirations of women were not in the forefront of her mind. Her main concern was with the disillusionment and emotional crisis through which she and many of her friends and associates were passing owing to the collapse of the moral authority of Communism and, with it, of Soviet Russia, following the exposure of Stalin's crimes by his successor, Nikita Khrushchev. Great tracts of the novel are devoted to their agonizing.

She describes her feelings at the time that she was writing it in her autobiography: 'All around me, people's hearts were breaking, they were having breakdowns, they were suffering religious conversions or – very common, this – formerly hard-line communists were discovering a talent for business and making money, because an obsession with the processes of capitalism was the best of preparations for a career in commerce. The point was, I was seeing people who had put all their eggs in one basket come to grief. What had been shut out of their thinking was rushing in, sometimes in the form of madness.'[10]

The crisis in Lessing's political life coincided with one in her emotional life. In her autobiography she writes that she had 'been dragged to her emotional limits'[11] by two men and was also affected by the growing up of her third and last child. In her own mind at that time breakdown and the self-healing to which it can lead, as exemplified by the golden notebook, was a central theme of the book.

The Golden Notebook was badly received. In the 1972 preface, ten years later, she gives vent to her resentment that 'nobody so much as noticed this central theme'. She also complains that the book was 'belittled' for being about the sex war and that she was accused of being 'unfeminine' and a 'man-hater'.[12] In her autobiography she recalls that 'Women at first certainly did not rush in to approve the book. On the contrary some distanced themselves from it, including personal friends.'[13]

A contributory factor was the frankness with which she wrote about sex – philosophizing on the nature of vaginal and clitoral orgasms, describing the wetness between Anna's thighs when attracted to a man, her analyses of the performance – usually the incompetence – of the various men with whom Anna and other characters go to bed, the casual way in which they decide to do so and the distinction between giving and receiving pleasure. These matters are now commonplace in women's magazines and advice columns as well as in novels. In 1962, only two years after the court case that resulted in *Lady Chatterley's Lover* being cleared for publication in this country, they were still dynamite. Inevitably they distracted attention from other aspects of the book, as I remember well from the way it was discussed at the time.

Another of the book's problems was the absence of general interest in what Lessing regarded as the great historic event of the end of the Communist dream. The trauma afflicting her and her Communist and ex-Communist friends who, as she puts it in her autobiography,[14] had been dreaming of a golden age, which they had thought had been almost within reach, left most readers and critics cold. Her contemporary, the editor and memoirist Diana Athill, spoke for many when, asked by the *Guardian* in 2012, on the 50th anniversary of its publication, what *The Golden Notebook* had meant to her when she first read it. 'I soon became impatient,' she replied, 'with a book full of minute analysis of the dismay and distress of party members when they had to face the ugly truth which had been accepted by everyone else for years. Their situation was interesting, but not so tremendously interesting as all that. Lessing's involvement with it made me think of the Holy Roman Emperor's supposed comment on an opera by Mozart: "Too many notes". On this subject Lessing had written too many words.'[15]

Lessing herself recalls in her autobiography that what transformed the book into a success was its discovery by the feminists in Britain, the United States and Scandinavia, as a result of which it became 'the Bible of the Women's Movement'. This left her feeling in a false position. On the one hand she supported the movement and was pleased to become an instrument for its advancement; on the other she was embarrassed because her book had not been intended as 'a trumpet for Women's Liberation'.

Looking back over the nearly sixty years that have elapsed since its publication it is hard to understand why it should have acquired that role. Apart from the involvement of its female characters in political arguments and activities, *The Golden Notebook* defines women's freedom almost entirely in sexual terms. It asserts their right to the same sexual licence as men had traditionally enjoyed and to be untrammelled by their consciences when they sleep with whoever they want, whether in response to purely physical or emotional needs. In this respect it captured and put into words what many women felt should be the case and were beginning to say. Its timing coincided with the change in sexual mores that marked the beginning of the 1960s and the birth of what came to be called the 'permissive society'.

But there is not a word in *The Golden Notebook* about how essential it is for women to acquire the economic independence without which other forms of independence cannot be sustained. Without work and the income it yields, or at the very least the skills that enable her to work and to earn a living, a woman without money of her own must inevitably be dependent on a man, a theme that runs through Victorian literature. Nor is there anything about a woman's right, not just to work, but to equal recognition, opportunities and rewards. It is as if Virginia Woolf's *A Room of One's Own* and *Three Guineas* had never been written and as if women were not already debating these issues among themselves.

The idea that a woman might wish to be as serious about a career as a man, and to gain from it the kind of self-fulfilment that enables a person to define themselves in relation to their work, as many men have done since time immemorial, is outside *The Golden Notebook*'s frame of reference. This is ironic since Lessing herself was a totally committed professional writer, who defined herself as such and lived entirely from her own earnings. By contrast, the book's two principle characters, Anna and her friend Molly, have no deep attachment to their work and do not regard it as being a significant element in their personalities.

On the evidence available to us, both are financially dependent. Molly lives with her son in the Earl's Court area of London, not as expensive then as it is now, but definitely middle class. She is a small-time actress and her son's school fees are paid for by her ex-husband. At the end of the book, when her son has moved away, she decides, without any pretence of love, to marry a rich businessman who can support her. Anna lives nearby. Her income, we are told, is derived from the declining earnings of her book and rent from a room she lets out in her flat. Yet she is able airily to dismiss the offers she receives for film and television rights regardless of how much difference the money might make to her life.

When her daughter wants to go away to boarding school, Anna agrees and buys the uniform her daughter asks for, even though it is optional, without expressing any anxiety about how the fees are to be paid or whether she can afford them. Either the girl's father is paying, or she must have a private income of some sort, or Lessing doesn't believe such mundane matters merit explanation. Nor does Anna worry about how to reconcile her left-wing principles with sending her daughter to a private instead of to a state school. Many other left-wing people, both then and since, have made the same choice, but usually with a certain amount of soul-searching.

In another respect *The Golden Notebook* reflects one of the characteristics of its time that in retrospect look very odd. Both in *Free Women* and in Anna's notebooks there is a good deal about racial discrimination and the exploitation of Africans in colonial Africa, which draws on Lessing's own experience as a young woman in Southern Rhodesia (now Zimbabwe) and her lifelong sympathy for Africans and the cause of African freedom. Yet there is no reference in any part of the novel to racial issues in Britain, although the Notting Hill race riots of 1958 took place while it was being written and Lessing herself had lived in that part of London. One of the ironies of the period, as illustrated by *The Golden Notebook*, is that, while those on the left and liberal-minded people in general were extremely concerned about

British policy in Africa and the actions of the colonial governments in Kenya, Nyasaland (now Malawi) and Rhodesia, it took a long time for them to take an interest in the plight of black and minority ethnic people in Britain. In ignoring them Anna and her creator were typical of their time.

On another matter, however, Anna was very untypical. As an immigrant to Britain with first-hand experience of a repressive colonial regime, Lessing didn't take British freedoms for granted. In several passages Anna reflects thankfully on the cost-free nature of being, or having been, a Communist in this country in a way it is hard to imagine that someone born and brought up here would have done. In some she compares the position of herself and her friends with what she has heard has happened in the Communist countries of Eastern Europe where disagreements had led to purges, with people in authority finding themselves having to execute former friends. In others the comparison is with the United States where, shortly before the book was written, the notorious Senator Joe McCarthy had carried out his anti-red witch-hunt as a result of which many in the creative industries who had once been Communists or Communist sympathizers lost their jobs and became unemployable. They and other Americans with left-wing leanings often ended up in London. Lessing draws on them for several of the characters who become Anna's lodgers and lovers.

Sex and Relationships

Married Love by Marie Stopes, 1918,
and *Lady Chatterley's Lover* by D. H. Lawrence, 1928.

Maurice by E. M. Forster, 1914,
The Well of Loneliness by Radclyffe Hall, 1928,
and *The Charioteer* by Mary Renault, 1953.

Married Love

by Marie Stopes (1918)

Lady Chatterley's Lover

by D. H. Lawrence (1928 privately in Italy and 1960 in Britain)

Between them these two books have probably provoked more indignation and controversy than any others published in English during the twentieth century. Both are famous for their treatment of sex, primarily from the woman's point of view. Each in its own way was a pioneering work that altered attitudes and, in the case of *Married Love*, the way people lived their lives. The furore they created when they were published speaks volumes about how people thought in those days.

Married Love was published in April 1918 at a critical stage in the war. In the previous month, the Germans had launched a massive attack on the Western Front, which, for a while, looked as if it might carry them to victory. They overreached and the Allies were able to strike back. But in April the outcome of the battle was still uncertain. Despite this national drama, *Married Love* provoked a storm of controversy and became an immediate bestseller. Over two thousand copies were sold within a fortnight. Five further editions had to be printed within the next ten months. By 1931 the book had gone through nineteen editions and sold seven hundred and fifty thousand copies in the United Kingdom. In the same year, it was published in the United States where, until then, it had been banned on grounds of obscenity. Marie Stopes herself became a national celebrity and the nation's first agony aunt, with men as well as women writing to her for advice about their sexual problems.

Nothing like it had been seen before. It was the first book ever published in English by a respectable publisher about sex technique. Although its language now seems coy and archaic, its meaning throughout is absolutely clear. Its purpose was to strip away the prejudice and superstition that surrounded the subject and to inform both men and women about the actions, emotions and sensibilities that would enable them to experience the joy of sex. Its impact on readers may be judged by the reaction of the young Naomi Mitchison, who later became a successful popular novelist. She was married in 1916 and read the book when it came out. As soon as she had done so, she sent a second copy to her husband serving with the army in France with a covering note urging him to 'read this before we meet again'.[1]

At a time when prostitution of every sort was rife and sexually transmitted diseases common, it was widely maintained among the middle and upper classes that respectable women should regard sex in marriage as a duty rather than a pleasure. 'The idea that woman is lowered by sex intercourse is very deeply rooted in our society,' Marie Stopes wrote. She also blamed women's education for 'encouraging the idea that sex-life is a low, physical, and degrading necessity which a pure woman is above enjoying' – attitudes that make it no wonder that their husbands so often resorted to professionals.

Among these classes there was an iron rule that young women should remain virgins until marriage. In many families it was further believed that they should be protected from all knowledge of sexual matters. All too often, therefore, they married in a state of complete sexual ignorance. As a result, Stopes argued, their initiation either became almost tantamount to rape or they were treated with such forbearance as to be left sexually unsatisfied. Either way, she claimed, '70 or 80 per cent of our married women [by which she meant the middle and upper classes] are deprived of full orgasm'. She had no possible means of knowing what the figure was, but, as her subsequent postbag bore out, large numbers were being so deprived owing to their own and their husbands' ignorance.

Rules are one thing, behaviour quite another, especially where sex is concerned. The rules were certainly not universally respected. While still a Cambridge undergraduate a young woman called Amber Reeves embarked on a celebrated affair with the author H. G. Wells, a man many years her senior who fictionalized the experience in his novel *Ann Veronica*. A woman who took matters into her own hands was the mother of the future Cabinet minister Denis Healey. She was a respectable teacher in Gloucester, but when Denis Healey's father, Will, proposed to her in 1914, she insisted that before they finally committed themselves they should first have a trial run on a holiday on the Isle of Man. Her mother was so shocked she wouldn't speak to her for months.[2] At the other extreme was Vera Brittain, whose autobiography, *Testament of Youth*, is discussed in an earlier chapter. She and her fiancé, she recorded, had never even kissed before he left her to fight and die in France.

In any case these niceties were only for those who lived in houses with enough room to allow for some privacy. They had no place in the slums of the industrial cities where large families were packed into tiny houses, as two other books in this anthology make clear: *Love on the Dole*, in which a young woman hates having to hear her parents having sex together, and Margaret Bondfield's account in her autobiography of incest in the Yorkshire woollen towns.

In the preface to *Married Love* Marie Stopes claims, 'in my first marriage I paid such a terrible price for sex ignorance that I feel that knowledge gained at such a cost should be placed at the service of humanity'. That cost, she claimed, included non-consummation, the grounds on which she secured an annulment in 1916 after five years of marriage. This claim was good publicity for the book, as was another, that she had only learned the literal truth about sex in 1913, two years after her marriage, by poring over medical tomes in English, French and German in the restricted access section of the British Museum Reading Room. They are, however, hard to credit. After his death a statement by her first husband was deposited in the British Library which, according to the *Oxford Dictionary of National Biography*, 'tells a rather different, though not necessarily more plausible story'.* Another piece of evidence is a letter written to her only a few months after her first marriage by a clergyman in which he refers to the birth control advice she had offered him while they were travelling together to a scientific congress in Stockholm.

From promoting the joy of sex, Marie Stopes moved quickly on to advocating birth control with the publication of Wise Parenthood in 1919. Thereafter, with the support of her second husband, Humphrey Roe, she devoted much time and energy to the cause. They opened their first clinic in 1921 and others followed.

Her motives in advocating birth control were mixed. Enabling the readers of *Married Love* to enjoy a more liberated sex life was one. Another was to help working-class women escape from the terrible burden of frequent pregnancies and numerous children. A third arose from her involvement with the eugenics movement, which believed in trying to improve the quality of the British race by restraining those with the physical, mental and character defects usually associated with poverty and malnutrition from breeding. This connection led Stopes into the treacherous waters of racial theories, which has cast a shadow

* *Oxford Dictionary of National Biography*, entry by Lesley A. Hall.

over her reputation. Her clinics also ran into financial trouble after her death in 1958, but her name lives on as that of the NGO Marie Stopes International, which carries on her work both in this country and abroad.

Married Love and her advocacy of birth control made Marie Stopes famous, but long before embarking on sex education in her late thirties she had built up a substantial academic reputation in a quite different sphere of activity. At the age of twenty-two she gained a first in botany and geology from University College London, after which she became the first woman to be awarded a Ph.D. in botany at Munich University, where she defended her thesis in German. In 1904 she was the first woman to be appointed to the faculty at the University of Manchester and in 1905 she became the youngest Doctor of Science in Britain.

She went on to make a successful career in palaeobotany, the study of fossil plants, undertaking work in Japan and Canada. During the First World War, she carried out research for the government into the composition of coal, arising out of which she co-authored a monograph on its chemical and palaeontological properties for the Department of Scientific and Industrial Research. It too was published in 1918 and led on to a further paper on the ingredients of coal that was published by the Royal Society in 1919. By virtue of the range of her activities as well as their pioneering quality, in science as much as sex education, she was one of the most remarkable women of her time.

Despite the path blazed by *Married Love*, there could be no question of D. H. Lawrence's novel *Lady Chatterley's Lover* being published in Britain, or the United States, when he completed it in 1927 while living in Italy. Instead an Italian bookseller friend of his in Florence, Pino Orioli, produced a handsome edition for private circulation to subscribers. It turned out to be extremely profitable, but inevitably, and to Lawrence's great annoyance, was immediately reissued in a variety of pirate editions. In an attempt to counter them he published a cheap popular edition in Paris in 1930.

The book broke new ground and shocked contemporary opinion at several levels. To begin with it attempted to describe the female orgasm in a way that had never been attempted before in serious English literature and, in so doing, established an imagery on which novelists still draw. It featured a heroine who is liberated by her adultery instead of being punished for it like Anna Karenina and Emma Bovary. It used four-letter words – fuck, cunt, shit – that were regarded as beyond the pale on the printed page. It was also a glorification of sex. As Lawrence wrote in his introduction to the Paris edition: 'And this is the real point of this book. I want men and women to be able to think sex, fully, completely, honestly and cleanly.'

In 1960 Penguin Books published the book in Britain and were immediately prosecuted under the Obscene Publications Act. The trial at the Old Bailey turned out to be a critical battle between the standards of a more straitlaced and inhibited past and the emerging mores of a more permissive future. The jury's verdict of not guilty stands as one of the landmarks of when the so-called 'permissive society' began to emerge. The trial lasted six days and was a great public spectacle as those for and against publication appeared to vie with each other in the absurdity of their opinions. The chief prosecuting counsel, Mervyn Griffiths Jones QC, became a national laughing stock when he asked the jury 'if it was the kind of book you would wish your wife or servants to read'. The celebrated sociologist and lecturer in English at the University of Leicester, Richard Hoggart, provoked astonishment when he called the book 'highly virtuous, if not puritanical'. The trendy Bishop of Woolwich, John Robinson, found himself trapped into saying it was a book all Christians should read.

Reading *Lady Chatterley's Lover* after the trial is something almost everyone of my generation can remember doing; a shared generational memory, like where one was when President Kennedy was assassinated three years later. We did so, of course, for the sex scenes that were unlike anything we had seen, or read, before. It is for these that those who haven't reread the book since will always remember it, which is a pity. The affair between Connie, as Lady Chatterley is always called, and her husband's gamekeeper, Mellors – never Oliver – is the relationship around which the novel revolves and the glorification of sex is its central message. But there is far more to the book than that, in addition to which it casts a penetrating light on the social mores of the 1920s.

Connie's misfortune is that her husband, Sir Clifford, had returned from the war paralysed from the waist down and impotent. Lawrence, who didn't serve in the war, presents him as mean-minded, artificial, possessive and intellectually and socially arrogant; so unpleasant in fact as almost to deserve his wife's infidelity. One wonders what, if they were not too carried away by the sex scenes, contemporaries made of this unsympathetic portrait. All over Britain at that time hundreds of thousands of families – wives, parents and children – were trying to cope with mutilated and disabled men and the effects of their injuries on their characters and on those around them. This aspect of the book has since attracted little attention, but in the 1920s it must have had a good deal of resonance with many women of all classes facing dilemmas similar to Connie's.

The progress of her affair with Mellors is matched by Sir Clifford's own regeneration thanks to the ministrations of his nurse, Mrs Bolton, a relationship that provides some of the book's most interesting passages. Mrs Bolton is a widow, her husband having been killed some years earlier in an accident in one of Sir Clifford's coal mines. Despite this tragedy, restoring Sir Clifford's self-confidence, and thereby enabling him to resume his responsibilities as a coal and land owner, become her mission in life. Yet, all the while that she is helping him she harbours a deep visceral resentment against the ruling class, exults at having the man who owns the neighbourhood dependent upon her and rejoices when she learns that it is a local man from her own village who is cuckolding him.

Not that Mellors is an ordinary local man or an ordinary gamekeeper. During the war he had risen from the ranks and been commissioned as an officer. If he had wished he could have cut himself loose from his background and joined the middle class instead of returning to his origins. Before she embarks on her affair with him, Connie notices and tells her husband that, 'The game-keeper, Mellors, is a curious kind of person ... he might almost be a gentleman.' This observation is key to everything that follows.

The nature of their affair and the conversations she has with him are such that it is impossible to believe Connie would have given herself to him, let alone that their physical affair would have mutated into a love so deep that she wants to marry him, if he had been an ordinary working man. Her father and sister are at first appalled that she should have taken up with a servant. The sister feels humiliated by it and the prospect of the scandal involved. But Mellors' social self-confidence and ease of manner when he meets them on their own ground see him through. When he and Connie's father dine together at the latter's club, they are soon on a comfortable footing and her sister too is mollified. Mellors, like Connie, has to secure a divorce, though he has long been separated from his wife, and the book ends with the two of them waiting out the time they have to spend apart that the law in those days required before a divorce could be granted.

Lawrence's reputation since his death in 1930 has had its ups and downs. Initially it went into decline until in the 1950s the Cambridge academic and critic F. R. Leavis, one of the most influential teachers of the day, hailed him as one of the great writers of the twentieth century. Now it is more mixed. *Lady Chatterley* has never been regarded as one of his major novels, like *Sons and Lovers* or *The Rainbow*, but it will ensure that he is never forgotten.

Maurice

by E. M. Forster (completed 1914 and published 1971)

The Well of Loneliness

by Radclyffe Hall (1928)

The Charioteer

by Mary Renault (1953)

'What is the love that dare not speak its name?' prosecuting counsel asked Oscar Wilde when in 1895 he was on trial for gross indecency, by which was meant sex with other men. His impromptu response was: '"The love that dare not speak its name" in this century is such a great affection of an elder for a younger man as there was between David and Jonathan, such as Plato made the very basis of his philosophy, and such as you find in the sonnets of Michelangelo and Shakespeare.'[3] The spectators in the gallery applauded and the jury could not agree on a verdict, but Wilde did not walk free. He was remanded in custody before being released on bail until at a second trial he was found guilty. The phrase, originally the title of a poem by Wilde's lover, Lord Alfred

Douglas,[4] entered the language as a way of referring to sexual relations between men.

Maurice by E. M. Forster, written in 1914 and published in 1971, and Mary Renault's *The Charioteer*, published in 1953, are novels about what it was like to be gay when for men to have sex together was a criminal offence, as it remained until 1967. Lesbianism was not illegal but attracted a similar degree of prejudice and opprobrium. When Radclyffe Hall's lesbian novel, *The Well of Loneliness*, was published in 1928, a government official told the publishers, Jonathan Cape, it was 'inherently obscene ... it supports a depraved practice [and] is gravely detrimental to the public interest'.[5] Sir William Willcox, a distinguished toxicologist at St Mary's Hospital London, told the court that 'lesbianism was a vice which, if widespread, becomes a danger to the well-being of a nation'. Radclyffe Hall, as she was always known, though her first name was Marguerite and in private she liked to be called John, was herself a lesbian, as was Mary Renault, while E. M. Forster was gay.

Despite the law and prejudice there were, of course, many practising gays and lesbians as the biographies of John Maynard Keynes, Somerset Maugham, Benjamin Britten and Vita Sackville West, to name but four, show. Nor were they by any means confined to what might be termed bohemian, artistic and literary circles. Two senior executives in the oil company run by my father lived openly together in the 1940s and 1950s in a large house at Westerham in Kent. In Ongar, the Essex village near where we lived when I was growing up, two women who had served together during the war in the women's branch of the Royal Navy set up house together and ran a small craft shop. There were myriad other such couples sharing their homes and lives up and down the country without running into trouble, although, as in these two cases, plenty of snide comments were exchanged behind their backs.

Men who went in search of new partners and, above all, those looking for adventure and/or paid sex ran great risks. Between 1945 and 1955 the number of annual prosecutions for homosexual offences of various kinds rose from eight hundred to two thousand five hundred, according to the Wolfenden Report published in 1957.[6] In 1952 Alan Turing, the computer scientist whose work during the war had contributed greatly to Bletchley Park's success at breaking the German codes, and in 1953 the celebrated actor John Gielgud were among those prosecuted, found guilty and fined. When Lord Montagu of Beaulieu, later famous for founding the National Motor Museum, and two of his friends were convicted in 1954 they were sent to prison.

The fact that sex between men was a criminal offence meant that those who practised it beyond the restricted circle of those they knew well were at constant risk of blackmail. Besides which both gays and lesbians were aware that they might at any time run up against prejudice and social ostracism. These three authors were all therefore writing from within and about a besieged and, by many, despised community.

Maurice and *The Well of Loneliness* share a common theme. They chart journeys of self-discovery as their principal characters progress from realizing that they are different from the generality of people to understanding the nature of their sexuality. Their reactions differ, but in both cases the nature of their agonizing and the intensity of their emotions, as they grapple with what this means, are bound to seem strange, if not incomprehensible, to those accustomed to living in a society in which sexual relations between people of the same sex has long since ceased to be a taboo.

Clive Durham, with whom the eponymous Maurice has a platonic affair while they are both undergraduates at Cambridge, exemplifies the difference between then and now. He is deeply religious and when he finds that his 'impulse' is homosexual he determines 'that it should not ever become carnal'. He also feels obliged 'to throw over Christianity'. 'He wished Christianity would compromise with him a little and searched the Scriptures for support. There was David and Jonathan; there was even the "disciple that Jesus loved". But the Church's interpretation was against him.' To overcome 'the horrors of the Bible' he turns to Plato's *Phaedrus* in which Socrates and Phaedrus discuss love between men and the distinction between true love and the simple pursuit of pleasure. How different from today when, instead of feeling obliged to throw over Christianity, gay Christians expect the Church to embrace them.

The first part of Forster's novel is dominated by the unconsummated affair between Clive Durham and Maurice Hall. They kiss, cuddle, lie in bed together and exchange love letters, but never actually 'unite'. Initially it is Clive who awakens Maurice's sexuality and later it is he who terminates their affair with a letter announcing, 'Against my will I have become normal. I cannot help it.' His next step is marriage. Maurice is left feeling abandoned and resentful and also, to his horror, recognizing that when a man attracts him it is 'lust' that he feels.

He must, he believes, find a cure for his condition and turns first to an old man who had formerly been his family's doctor. 'I'm an unspeakable of the Oscar Wilde sort,' he explains. 'I want to be cured. I can't put up with the loneliness any more.' The doctor cuts the conversation short. 'Never let that evil hallucination, that temptation from the devil occur to you again,' he responds and calls for his servant to give them both a whisky. Maurice then finds an American doctor, who, through hypnosis, specializes in curing men suffering from what he describes as 'congenital homosexuality' with, he claims, a 50 per cent success rate. Men continued to seek medical advice in such circumstances for long after *Maurice* was written. The distinguished historian Sir Michael Howard recalls in his memoirs[7] how, in 1945, on returning to civilian life after wartime service in the army, he went to see a Harley Street specialist. After describing some possible treatments the specialist told him, 'Frankly I shouldn't worry. There are a lot of people around like you', adding that he should get on with his life. 'Seldom has money been better spent,' writes Howard, as the consultation enabled him to come to terms with himself.

Maurice gets on with his life in more dramatic fashion. While on a visit to the Durhams at their country estate he falls for the gamekeeper, Alec Scudder, and they have marvellous sex together. On his return to London he fears that he has laid himself open to blackmail and Alec indeed sends him a threatening letter. They meet to resolve the matter. One thing leads to another and, after a rapturous night together in a hotel, they declare their love for one another. Alec, who had been planning to emigrate, decides not to, while Maurice announces that he will give up his profession as a stockbroker and leave his family. They determine to live privately together in the countryside defying convention in terms both of their sexuality and class distinctions.

This highly romanticized ending is not how most men in that situation would have behaved. They would have been far more likely to have found a way of continuing with their lives so as to observe the conventions while continuing their connection. Forster's own life is a case in point. He too fell in love with a man from a different class, a policeman called Bob Buckingham, in 1930. Their relationship continued after Bob's marriage and when Forster died in 1970 his ashes were scattered in the Buckinghams' garden. But the relationship between the two men was always kept secret from the general public. When a friend criticized him for this, pointing to the example of André Gide, he replied, 'But Gide hasn't got a mother',[8] a reply that would have resonated with many of Forster's generation and others before and afterwards. Even after his mother's death in 1945 he preferred to remain discreet and did not wish to face the controversy that publishing *Maurice* would have provoked, with the result that the book did not see the light of day until after he too had died.

In the mid-1920s Forster and Radclyffe Hall were the only two writers to have won two of the most prestigious literary prizes of the time, the Femina – Vie Heureuse, a prize awarded to British writers between 1920 and 1940 by the French Hachette publishing group, and the James Tait Black Memorial Prize – he for *A Passage to India** and she for *Adam's Breed*, which had immediately preceded *The Well of Loneliness*. Otherwise they were chalk and cheese. Hall lived openly as an invert, as lesbians were generally called and called themselves (the word was also used for gay men), and she wanted to use her fame 'to encourage inverts to face up to a hostile world in their true colours, and this with dignity and courage'.[9] 'Having attained literary success, I have put my pen at the service of some of the most persecuted and misunderstood people in the world,'[10] she wrote to one of the publishers who turned the book down.

Hall believed herself to be a man trapped in the body of a woman and the hero of her novel, Stephen Gordon, is a reflection of this. She is given a boy's name at birth because her father, a wealthy country landowner, had expected to have a son. As she grows up in Worcestershire she comes to realize that she is not like other girls and wishes she was a boy. She becomes a skilful fencer, excels on the hunting field, starts to wear masculine dress and has an affair with a woman that ends disastrously. She moves to London and, after writing a successful first novel, to Paris, where she joins a lesbian salon. When the First World War breaks out, she serves courageously with an ambulance unit in France and is wounded in the face. She also falls in love with a much younger colleague, Mary Llewellyn.

Hall hoped that her book would encourage understanding and sympathy for those she was writing about. Instead it attracted controversy, obloquy and mockery led by a hate campaign in the *Sunday Express*. Arguing for its suppression, the paper's editor wrote: 'I would rather give a healthy boy or a healthy girl a phial of prussic acid than

---

* See essay on *A Passage to India* and *Altogether*.

this novel. Poison kills the body, but moral poison kills the soul.'[11] People rushed to buy the book before it could be banned as it promptly was by a magistrate's court with the verdict being upheld on appeal. Meanwhile, a spate of lampoons, satires and cartoons made Hall and the cause she was promoting look ridiculous. Despite the seriousness of her purpose, *The Well of Loneliness*' reputation has been indelibly marked by the mockery. I think unfairly, although its style and the author's deeply conservative social values in matters other than sex do not wear well today.

It was not the book's descriptions of what people do in bed that gave offence. There are none. The nearest approach comes in a scene where 'Stephen bent down and kissed Mary's hands very humbly, for now she could find no words any more … and that night they were not divided.' Proust's great multi-volume novel *A la recherche du temps perdu*, English translations of which were being published during the 1920s, deals extensively with lesbianism and homosexuality and is far more explicit. Yet it was never prosecuted. What gave offence in Hall's case was her defiance. She presents lesbians as brave and practical women who did more than their fair share during the war and are treated unfairly and hypocritically by society, while Stephen is portrayed as a heroic figure by turns courageous, tender and self-sacrificing.

So self-sacrificing in fact that, when it becomes apparent to her after the war that for as long as their affair lasts Mary will be identified as a lesbian and thereby denied a normal social life, Stephen makes the ultimate sacrifice of giving her up. She colludes with a man who has fallen in love with Mary to be on hand when Stephen deliberately drives her into his arms by pretending to be unfaithful in a particularly hurtful manner. The book ends with Stephen, lonely and bereft, uttering a private prayer: 'Acknowledge us, oh God, before the world. Give us also the right to our existence.'

Mary Renault, whose real surname was Challens, falls between Forster and Hall. She lived openly with her partner, Julie Mullard, whom she had met when they were both training to become nurses, but did not adopt a public position as a lesbian. She is best remembered for her historical novels set in ancient world, but before turning her hand to those she wrote contemporary novels, for one of which, *Return to Night*, MGM bought the film rights for $125,000 thereby enabling her and Julie to emigrate to South Africa. They were already settled there when, in 1953, *The Charioteer* came out. The publishers, Longmans, Green, were brave to hazard their reputation on a book about homosexuality in the armed forces during the war at a time when prosecutions for homosexual offences were rising sharply. It served as a timely reminder that 'queers', as they were called and referred to themselves, had played their part as much as anyone, and thus made a modest contribution to the campaign for homosexual law reform that was beginning to gather momentum.

Much of the novel is set in a military hospital like that in which Renault herself worked during those fraught months after the British Army's evacuation from Dunkirk in June 1940. Its central character, Laurie Odell, is there undergoing treatment on one of his legs that was badly damaged during the fighting. The naval commander of the small boat that had brought him back to England was the former head boy of his public school, the charismatic Ralph Lanyon, who had been expelled for a homosexual offence. Laurie had hero-worshipped him and carried into action a copy of *Phaedrus* that Ralph had given him before leaving school inscribed with the words, 'It doesn't exist anywhere in real life, so don't let it give you illusions. It's just a nice idea.'

Each holds a mythic place in the mind of the other and when they meet again at a gay party in the town near the hospital the effect on both is traumatic. But by then Laurie, who is aware of his homosexuality, has fallen in love with Andrew Raynes, an innocent young man, who is one of a team of Quaker conscientious objectors working as orderlies in the hospital. The novel is primarily about how that situation is resolved.

Ralph has no hang-ups about his sexuality. His view is 'It's not what one is, it's what one does with it' that matters. What he wants is to give up the promiscuity epitomized by the party for a monogamous relationship with Laurie. Laurie has difficulty in responding. He is emotionally and physically attracted to Ralph and they make love together. But the pure and protective nature of his relationship with Andrew and horror of hurting him pulls the other way. So too does his reluctance to put himself in a position that he feels will mean that the world will define him primarily by his sexuality. Ralph displays considerable forbearance and understanding as Laurie agonizes, and eventually wins out in a dramatic denouement.

As the story unfolds aspects of the gay predicament that continued untouched by the war are illuminated. At an emotional level, Laurie, while coming to terms with the fact that his wound will leave him permanently lame, wants to tell his widowed mother that this is more than made up for by falling in love with Andrew and is deeply hurt by the realization of how shocked she would be if he did. On a practical level, he hears two of Ralph's friends discuss the blackmail of someone they know. One argues that for the sake of their self-respect victims should never give in to it. The other responds, echoing Forster, 'What about his job, what about dependants, what if his mother's got a weak heart and the news will kill her?'

Whether in uniform or not, gays were as much at risk of arrest, and so of blackmail, as before the war. In fact, the annual rate of prosecutions was higher during the war than in the 1930s though lower than in the 1950s. They were also at constant risk of exposure and insult as Laurie realizes when Ralph, in naval officer's uniform, accompanies him to his mother's remarriage and the circumstances of his expulsion from school are about to be revealed before a distraction intervenes.

The Charioteers is about gays and what it meant to be gay. But that aside, it conveys very well the atmosphere during those tense months in the autumn of 1940 when life went on as normal in so many ways while the Battle of Britain raged overhead and invasion seemed imminent. It is particularly good on the conscientious objectors, men who would not bear arms for reasons of conscience and were conscripted to fulfil various functions, such as hospital orderlies, stretcher-bearers and ambulance drivers. They were widely viewed with contempt. When the men in Laurie's ward hear that 'conchies' are to replace the maids, who had previously assisted the nurses, they are appalled. The man in the next bed to Laurie's voices their feelings when he declares that he would prefer German prisoners, who had 'done their duty as they see it, same as us. Not like those creeping-Jesus, knock-kneed conchies.'

When Laurie and Andrew become friends, it is not the possibility of sexual attraction that worries the other men in his ward. It is the fear that Andrew will try to undermine Laurie's military loyalty. Renault, who, as a nurse, would have worked closely with many conscientious objectors, portrays them as brave, trustworthy men standing by their beliefs and working on behalf of others. Some of the passages in which Andrew and Dave, who is in charge of the Quaker team, express their own inner doubts and what drives them are among the most sensitive in the book.

Race and Immigration

The Foundations of the Nineteenth-Century
by Houston Stewart Chamberlain, 1911,
and *The Alien Corn* by W. Somerset Maugham, 1931.

The Story of Art by Ernst Gombrich, 1950,
and *The Buildings of England by Nikolaus Pevsner*, 1951–74.

The Lonely Londoners by Sam Selvon, 1956,
City of Spades by Colin MacInnes, 1957,
and *Absolute Beginners* by Colin MacInnes, 1959.

The Foundations of the Nineteenth Century

by Houston Stewart Chamberlain
(1899 in German and 1911 in English)

*The Alien Corn**

by W. Somerset Maugham (1931)

Britain has always taken pride in the fact that, unlike some other European countries during the inter-war period, extremist political parties and vicious anti-Semitism never took root here. Oswald Mosley and his Blackshirts, who looked to Nazi Germany and Fascist Italy for inspiration, never progressed beyond the outer reaches of the political fringe. It therefore comes as something of a shock to find that one of the inspirations behind the Nazis, and thus a man whose influence was later to be felt across Europe was British. His name was Houston Stewart Chamberlain† and his book *The Foundations of the Nineteenth Century*.

---

* First published in 1931 by Heinemann with five other short stories under the title *First Person Singular*.

† No relation to Neville Chamberlain, Prime Minister from 1937 to 1940, whose father, Joseph, and half-brother, Austen, who were also Cabinet ministers.

On his 70th birthday in 1925 the Nazi newspaper *Völkischer Beobachter* described it as 'the gospel of the National Socialist movement'. In 1927 Hitler and Goebbels visited Chamberlain on his deathbed at the Wagner family property at Bayreuth where he lived with his second wife, the composer's stepdaughter Eva. Three years later Arthur Rosenberg, often described as the principal philosopher of Nazism, published *The Myth of the Twentieth Century* as a homage to Chamberlain, whom he hailed as 'the pioneer and founder of a German future'.*

Described by his biographer Geoffrey Field as 'The Evangelist of Race',[1] Chamberlain initially came to prominence during the reign of Kaiser Wilhelm II before the First World War. On receiving a copy of his book the Kaiser wrote, 'God sent your book to the German people, just as he sent you personally to me, that is my unshakeable conviction.' He went on to praise Chamberlain as his 'comrade-in-arms and ally in the struggle for Teutons against Rome, Jerusalem etc'[2] and provided practical help by organizing subsidies for a popularly priced edition. There wasn't anything particularly new in Chamberlain's book. Others in Germany, Austria and France, where the Dreyfus case that began in 1894 had unleashed a wave of anti-Semitism, were preaching along the same and similar lines. It was the power of his exposition that, in Field's words, 'turned Chamberlain almost overnight into the prophet of race for educated laymen in Central Europe'.

An English translation of *Foundations* was published in Britain in 1911. Lord Redesdale (the paternal grandfather of the Mitford sisters),† a former diplomat, acknowledged authority on international affairs and prominent in artistic and literary circles, provided a eulogistic introduction and it was widely reviewed. The playwright George Bernard

* The references in this paragraph are drawn from the *Oxford Dictionary of National Biography* entry on HSC by Michael Biddiss.

† This connection must have been of some help to Unity Mitford in gaining access to Hitler's circle when she settled in Munich in 1924 with that intention.

Shaw, then at the height of his fame, described it in the left-wing *Fabian News* as 'a masterpiece of really scientific history'.[3] The *Spectator* called it 'a monument of erudition, and the skilful handling of erudition'.[4]

Chamberlain's central thesis was clear. It was that when the Roman empire collapsed it left behind a 'a chaos of peoples', all of whom had become hopelessly mongrelized apart from the Jews, who alone had retained their racial purity. Their counterparts, also pure and undefiled, were the Teutons, who broke into the empire's territories at that time. He rejected the general concept of human progress. Rather, he attributed all that had been achieved since the fall of Rome to the Teutons through 'constant struggle between Teuton and non-Teuton'. As a result, 'Our present civilization and culture are specifically Teutonic, they are exclusively the work of Teutonism … this is the great primal truth, the "concrete" fact, which the history of the last thousand years teaches us on every page.' Events in other parts of the world did not interest him. His focus was on Europe, an attitude that now seems absurd, but which was not uncommon at the time.

According to his theory all European peoples could be grouped into the Aryan race at the head of which came the Nordic or Teutonic peoples led by 'the most highly gifted group', the Germans. The Latin peoples and the Slavs he regarded as markedly inferior. To explain the genius of historic figures from outside the Teutonic elite he found grounds to endow them with a Teutonic heritage. Thus, Dante and Michelangelo, to take two examples, owed their genius to being descended from the Goths. Christ, who lived before the Teutons appeared on the scene, was, he claimed, despite being Jewish by education and religion, not Jewish by race as 'the national character of the Galileans was essentially different from that of the Jews'.

Perpetually opposed to the Teutons stood two massive and implacable enemies, the Catholic Church and the Jews. The Church he accused of constantly seeking 'to subjugate all our power, freedom, property, bodies and souls and through us (had God not prevented it) the whole world'. However, by the nineteenth century, thanks to two great Germans, Luther and Kant, the Church had been humbled, its pretensions exposed and its power greatly weakened. The Teutons had been 'emancipated' from Rome. But the Jews remained. In Chamberlain's eyes they faced the Teutons as the perpetual other, locked in continuous struggle. Whereas the fight with the Catholic Church was about power, namely the Pope's claims to authority, the fight with the Jews was about race. There was no identifiable *casus belli* and no grounds on which a peace treaty could be negotiated. Rather, two pure races, the oldest and the youngest, were fated to be forever in conflict with each other. The parallel with that between Good and Evil is inescapable.

It followed from this view of the world that Jews could not be trusted as fellow citizens, that they worked only for themselves regardless of the interests of others and that marriages between Gentiles and Jews should not be permitted. Unlike some other anti-Semites at that time, including by 1903 some members of the Russian government,[5] Chamberlain showed no interest in Zionism as a means of resolving the conflict by persuading Jews to migrate from Europe to Palestine. So we shall never know whether he would have approved of Hitler's Final Solution or been appalled by it. His praise for 'the annihilation of the Indians in North America' that paved the way for 'the later development of a thoroughly Teutonic nation upon that soil' suggests he might have approved while giving Americans some food for thought about their own history.

With what we now know about the Holocaust it is hard to believe that the theories propounded by Chamberlain could have been taken at all seriously by people in this country. But in 1911 such an outcome was unimaginable and circumstances were propitious for his book. On the one hand, with the empire at the plenitude of its power, the idea that the white races in general and the British in particular were inherently superior to all others, was taken for granted by most of the population. On the other there was unease about the extent to which newly rich Jewish individuals of foreign origin were becoming prominent in British life.

Edward VII's welcome of such men as Sir Ernest Cassel, Sir Julius Wernher, Lord Rothschild and the Austrian Baron Hirsch into his inner circle had been widely disapproved of. In some parts of the press it was suggested that British soldiers had died during the Boer War to defend the investments of Jewish financiers in South Africa. In 1912 came the Marconi scandal in which two Jewish ministers, as well as others, were accused of profiting from inside information on a government contract. Politics was convulsed and an anti-Semitic outburst triggered in some sections of the press. The temper of the times may be judged from a proposal put forward in 1911 by the popular novelist Hilaire Belloc, who argued that Jews were infiltrating British society while disguising their growing influence by adopting English names. He proposed to counter this by obliging them to enter their names on a national register with false ones being punished by law and to bar them from military service.

The kind of vicious anti-Semitism that could so easily mutate into persecution and ultimately the Holocaust did not take root in Britain. The British variant was of the type that demeaned, mocked and joked about Jews. It also implied, or even asserted, that, however much they might wish to, Jews could never become real Britons or fully integrate into British society. They might join the government, acquire titles or become great landowners, but would always be outsiders vulnerable whenever trouble arose.

In his *Trials of the Diaspora*, probably the most comprehensive study of anti-Semitism in Britain ever published, Anthony Julius[6] cites the example of the then Secretary of State for India, Edwin Montagu, after he had sacked a general responsible for ordering his troops to fire on an unarmed crowd and killing many men, women and children, the infamous Amritsar massacre of 1919. He quotes Montagu's Cabinet colleague Austen Chamberlain, writing in his diary, that to Conservative MPs Montagu's Jewishness meant that the issue had become not a question of justice or discipline, but of 'a Jew, a foreigner rounding on an Englishman and throwing him to the wolves'. More than sixty years later, in 1985–6, when my friend Leon Brittan, as Secretary of State for Trade and Industry, was at the heart of the Westland controversy that briefly threatened to bring down Margaret Thatcher, there was more than a whiff of anti-Semitism behind some of the attacks on him from the backbenches. When Brittan had to leave the government the backbench Conservative MP John Stokes demanded that his replacement should be 'a red-blooded, red-faced Englishman, preferably from the landed interests'.*

Somerset Maugham's short story *The Alien Corn*, set in the 1920s, is about whether integration is possible. Both the title and the text say much about attitudes at that time. It concerns two branches of an immigrant Jewish family. One, headed by Sir Adolphus Bland, always known as Freddy, lives in a lovely Elizabethan house with a large estate in a part of Sussex where he is the local MP. Their way of life and values are those of the landed aristocracy. Lady Bland, Muriel to her friends, refers often to her convent education and their sons go to Eton and Oxford. They want the eldest, George, to make a suitably aristocratic marriage. Everything appears to be as settled and as English as can be. Yet to their friend, the narrator, nothing in the house is quite as it should be – it is all too contrived and has none of the patina of age and inheritance. And there's the rub. The family's name was originally Bleikogel, Freddy was originally Adolph, Muriel was Miriam and the family's ownership of the estate is of recent origin.

---

* As quoted in the *Daily Telegraph* obituary of Sir John Stokes, 30 January 2003. A former Conservative MP has told me of the shock he felt when he heard Stokes utter these words at a meeting of the 1922 Committee of backbench Conservative MPs.

The narrator juxtaposes the Blands with Freddy's uncle, Ferdy Rabenstein, whom he also knows, and his mother, old Lady Bland. Ferdy is a debonair bachelor with a 'fine Semitic profile', who moves easily in the highest reaches of society where he enjoys great success with women while making a point of drawing attention to his Jewishness by telling Jewish jokes and wearing flashy jewellery – 'After all I am an Oriental,' he was in the habit of saying. And 'I can carry a certain barbaric magnificence.' Whereas the Blands want desperately to be indistinguishable from those around them, Ferdy glories in his difference and is welcomed as an exotic outsider. The Blands strongly disapprove of him for retaining his overt Jewishness and for not having changed 'his horrible German name' during the war. They don't want their children to meet him, although George disobeys them and does so. The matriarchal old Lady Bland, Ferdy's sister, speaks with a guttural German accent, calls her daughter-in-law Miriam and wants her grandson to marry the daughter of another self-made Jewish millionaire who has retained his German name.

The principal drama of the story centres on George, who, with the world at his feet, rejects his English upbringing and prospects. He wants to revert to a German Jewish identity and to devote his life to becoming a great pianist. This brings the two branches of the family together, both equally horrified that so much that has been achieved should be thrown away and neither believing that he has the talent to fulfil his ambition. After much toing and froing the old lady brokers a deal whereby the parents agree to his studying in Munich for two years at the end of which he will submit himself to the judgement of a professional pianist. If the professional believes that he will in due course make the grade, he will be allowed to continue. If not, he will revert to the life of an English gentleman. He fails the test. The professional says he will never be first rate and he knows in his heart that this is true. His parents are devastated on his behalf and even willing to let him continue with his music, but he cannot live without the hope of his ambition being fulfilled and shoots himself.

The secondary drama concerns the unravelling of the Blands' integrationist dream and the extent to which, when gathered together, the two branches are so alike, with the old lady the ultimate authority whom none will defy. On the day of the test they all lunch with the famous Jewish woman pianist who is to conduct it. The narrator is the only Gentile present. 'All but old Lady Bland spoke perfect English,' he recounts, 'yet I could not help feeling that they did not speak like English people; I think they rounded their vowels more than we do, certainly spoke louder, and the words seemed not to fall, but to gush from their lips. I think if I had been in another room where I could hear the tone but not the words of their speech I should have thought it was in a foreign language they were conversing.'

This passage is part of a picture the first brush stroke of which had been Ferdy's profile. It is followed by Freddy bursting into tears when thwarted by his son, a spectacle that prompts the narrator to observe, 'he didn't behave very much like Sir Adolphus Bland, Bart., and the good old English gentleman he so much wanted to be, but like an emotional Adolph Bleikogel'. Finally, the narrator observes how 'her fleshy nose, the shape of her face and the back of her neck' revealed that the fair-haired, blue-eyed Muriel 'could not possibly be an Englishwoman'. In these and other references, as the story unfolds, attention is drawn to what the narrator regards as inherently Jewish features and characteristics and the enduring differences between alien and home-grown corn.

This was in accordance with the literary conventions of the time. References to stereotypical Jewish physical features and character traits are to be found in the works of almost all authors writing during the inter-war years. They reflected the way people thought and spoke. In some cases, the writer was anti-Semitic, but not necessarily, and the presumption should not be made on the basis of words attributed to fictional characters. Not until the end of the Second World War did the convention change.

In his book *Our Age*, an outstanding study of the generation born in the first two decades of the twentieth century, Noel Annan writes: 'The end of the war marked a change of manners concerning one topic. The revelation of the Holocaust in the concentration camps altered the way the educated classes spoke and felt about Jews. Anti-semitism never dies; like other forms of xenophobia it festers and erupts on strange issues. But at any rate after 1945 it became bad form and was regarded as disgusting to talk in a derogatory way about Jews, still less discriminate in public against them.'[7]

In the period after 1945 there was also a notable increase in the Jewish contribution to many aspects of British life through the work of those Jews who had fled to this country from the continent to escape the Holocaust. This is the subject of the following essay. But as I complete the writing of this book during the winter of 2018–19 against the background of the row over anti-Semitism in the Labour Party I have Annan's point about festering and erupting on strange issues ringing in my ears.

The Story of Art

by Ernst Gombrich (1950)

The Buildings of England

by Nikolaus Pevsner (1951–74)

Ernst Gombrich was born in Vienna in 1909, and Nikolaus Pevsner in Leipzig in 1902. They died in London in 2001 and 1982 respectively, loaded with honours awarded for their great contributions to British cultural life. Few individuals have exercised a more enduring influence on how people view and react to art and architecture than they. 'More people … have been introduced to the world of fine art in the last 45 years through Ernst Gombrich's *The Story of Art* than through any other single book,' wrote the Professor of Cultural History (and later Rector) at the Royal College of Art, Christopher Frayling, in 1995.* Reviewing a biography of Pevsner, the author and critic A. N. Wilson described him as 'one of our greatest cultural historians'.[8] They came to Britain in the 1930s and worked and wrote in English because they were Jews who had to flee from the Nazi persecution of the

* As quoted in the endorsements to the 16th edition of *The Story of Art*, Phaidon Press, 1995.

Jews that had begun in Germany and Austria and would culminate in the Holocaust.

They were part of an incredible transfer of talent to Britain from the countries that fell under Hitler's control. The actual numbers were small. Some estimates suggest around sixty thousand, but they were hard to count. Some, like Gombrich and Pevsner, arrived as adults with family members as a direct result of the Nazis' actions. Others, like the famous philosopher Ludwig Wittgenstein and my own father, both from Vienna, were working and established here before the Nazis came to power and decided to stay. Then there were those for whom Britain was a staging post en route to the United States, like the author Stefan Zweig. And there were unaccompanied children sent by parents who themselves could not escape, like my colleague in the House of Lords and former Labour opponent in two parliamentary elections, Alf Dubs. They were the lucky ones. As the Nazis tightened their grip it became increasingly hard for those without qualifications, connections or wealth to find a country that would take them in. By the end of 1940, when the Germans had overrun most of continental Europe, escape was almost impossible.

Their impact was out of all proportion to their numbers and benefited all branches of the arts, sciences, academia and business. In his standard work on the subject, *The Hitler Emigrés*, Daniel Snowman writes that by 1992 they or their children had won sixteen Nobel Prizes while seventy-four had become Fellows of the Royal Society.[9] There were many others who achieved great success in diverse fields. Three of the most notable were the artist Lucian Freud, who came with his family at the age of seven, Siegmund Warburg, the most innovative banker in the City of London for forty years after the Second World War, and George Weidenfeld, an equally innovative publisher for much longer. The economist Friedrich Hayek and the philosopher Karl Popper, who together provided Margaret Thatcher with much of her inspiration, were also refugees. The list is almost endless and so is the range of activities. It includes my father, Georg Tugendhat, who, together with a fellow émigré, Franz Kind, established a company that pioneered oil refining in the United Kingdom.

Many received British honours in recognition of their work as well as medals and prizes from other countries, including, after the war, those from which they had fled. Few garnered more than Ernst Gombrich, whose haul, as well as a knighthood and various academic distinctions, included the Order of Merit, one of the most exclusive British awards because there can be no more than twenty-four members at any one time. His output of books, articles and lectures was considerable, but the foundation on which the edifice of his fame and reputation was built is *The Story of Art*. Since it first appeared in 1950 it has never been out of print, has run into sixteen editions and been translated into more than thirty languages.

In 1995 Neil MacGregor, then Director of the National Gallery and later of the British Museum, wrote: 'Like every art historian, my way of thinking about pictures has been in large measure shaped by Ernst Gombrich. I was 15 when I read *The Story of Art* and like millions since, I felt I had been given a map of a great country, and with it the confidence to explore further without fear of being overwhelmed.'* This captures the essence of what Gombrich is about. He doesn't tell his readers what to think or like; he provides the means by which they can form their own judgements.

As it happens, when MacGregor read *The Story of Art* he was at the age that Gombrich was aiming at when he wrote it. As he explains in the book's preface: 'The readers I had first and foremost in mind were boys and girls in their teens who had just discovered the world of art for themselves.' To this end he was determined to 'avoid any

* As quoted in the endorsements to the 16th edition of *The Story of Art*, Phaidon Press, 1995.

trace of pretentious jargon or bogus sentiment', characteristics that all too often disfigure books on art, wine and other subjects in which connoisseurship is highly prized.

Reading *The Story of Art* is like being taken round a gallery by a curator who picks out the most important pictures, explains what makes them so, what to look for in them and how they relate to the other works around them. Great emphasis is placed on the importance of understanding what it was the artist was trying to achieve and the social, political and economic context within which he was working. A picture, Gombrich argued, should not be regarded as an object in isolation; it should be appreciated within the context in which it was created. It should be seen as an attempt by an artist, working in a particular time and place and governed by a set of beliefs to which he in some measure subscribes or rebels against, to convey an idea, story, concept or way of viewing the world around him.

The book is a phenomenal feat of memory. Because of the disruption caused by the war and post-war travel restrictions Gombrich would not have seen any of the pictures, sculptures and buildings outside this country about which he was writing for many years. He would have been able to look at photographs, but, like those in the original edition, they would almost all have been in black and white from which it is difficult to pick out details and finer features unless one knew them already and could remember where they were. In the 1950s his readers would have appreciated that. They wouldn't have been able to travel outside Britain either, except on active service during the war. The treasures he laid before them would have seemed out of reach in a way that is difficult to imagine today when foreign travel has become so easy.

Anyone now reading *The Story of Art* for the first time might be struck by the absence of any reference either to the destruction wrought by the war on Europe's architectural heritage or to the looting of works of art on a grand scale first by the Nazis and then by the Russians.

Many masterpieces had been lost and some have even now not been recovered. But this lacuna was symptomatic of the time when it was written. In the aftermath of the war people did not need to be reminded of its horrors. The memories were fresh and the scars in the form of bombsites were all around them in London and other British cities as well as on the Continent. In all countries people wished to blot out the worst of what had happened and to get on with rebuilding their lives and societies. Even in Israel in the 1950s, as Ari Shavit has written, 'The Holocaust was not to be mentioned and war was a heroic memory.'[10]

The structure of the book is chronological. Its twenty-seven chapters begin with pre-history and march steadily through the Egyptians, Greeks, Romans and each succeeding school and period of Western European art until tailing off in the twentieth century. Once the early periods are out of the way the emphasis is very much on pictures rather than sculpture or architecture. Gombrich was already in his lifetime criticized for not writing enough about women and for being too Eurocentric. On both he was representative of an era that still had many years to run. When, in 1969, Kenneth Clark presented his famous and ground-breaking thirteen-part BBC television series entitled *Civilisation*,* which is still the single most famous television production ever devoted to the arts, it dealt only with Western Europe and women barely featured.

Nikolaus Pevsner wanted to become an art historian from an early age. At sixteen he wrote in his diary of 'the dream I had been cherishing for some time: to see myself as a professor of art history, in a small house of my own, with the lady wife and a child, teaching, going about my business, maybe now and again writing – a German idyll'.[11] The German aspect of this ambition was denied him when, after being

* Shortly afterwards he received a peerage and took the title of Lord Clark of Saltwood. Both then and since, however, he has always been known as Lord Clark of Civilisation.

elected to power in 1933, the Nazis introduced race laws that prevented Jews from holding academic appointments as well as barring them from many other activities. But in Britain he was able to bring the art historical aspect to fruition.

While being interned for a short while as an 'enemy alien', like many other German and Austrian refugees (including an uncle of mine), he embarked on a book entitled *An Outline of European Architecture*, which was published after his release in 1942. Only a hundred and sixty pages long, it has since gone into seven editions and been translated into sixteen languages. It came out under the Penguin Books Pelican imprint and marked a turning point in his long and happy relationship with the firm's founder, Allen Lane.

As the war drew to an end Lane asked him for ideas. He came up with two. One was for a Pelican History of Art series and the other, which must at the time have sounded the more modest, was for a series of county-by-county guides to British architecture. The History of Art series, which aimed to encompass the whole world, was launched under Pevsner's editorial guidance in 1953. It achieved considerable success, but it is to the latter, entitled *The Buildings of England*, that Pevsner owes his enduring reputation. The guides have become so much of an institution that they – the originals, the revisions and the later ones written by his successors – are known and referred to as 'Pevsners'. For many they are the template against which other guides are judged.

The idea was not original. It was inspired by a handbook of German artists that dated back to 1900. There had also been county guidebooks before, notably those published by the Shell oil company to boost petrol sales. But these had been mostly written by amateur enthusiasts whereas Pevsner was a recognized scholar with his architectural book to his credit. The first volume on Cornwall appeared in 1951 to be quickly followed by two more. Timing was a key factor in the venture's early success. In 1950 petrol rationing had finally come to an end so that, for the first time since 1939, people could think about driving for pleasure instead of keeping their ration for work purposes and emergencies. It was in its way a liberation and Pevsner gave them a reason to take advantage of it by exploring their own country. As foreign travel was still very restricted because of the limits imposed on the amount of money individuals could take out of the country, there were many who wished to do so.

Pevsner's modus operandi became legendary and inspired many legends. Two German refugee ladies, later succeeded by graduate assistants, would gather all the material they could find on the target county. Pevsner, usually driven by his wife Lola until her death in 1963, would then visit all the places of interest that they had identified. The pace was frantic. One of those who drove him round Warwickshire recalled, 'Our record was nineteen parishes in a day, that is nineteen churches, say some forty other buildings and an assortment of other features of interest.' In the evening, 'the Professor went to his room and wrote up everything he had seen that day … so when we got back to London the book was finished and needed only an introduction'.* Pevsner and whoever was accompanying him always stayed in modest accommodation and, rather than interrupt his work schedule, he never accepted social invitations. In this way, between 1951 and 1974, he completed forty-six volumes of which he wrote thirty-two alone and the remainder with the help of an assistant. A truly Stakhanovite achievement.

Since Pevsner's retirement and death a succession of other authors has produced them. The originals have been revised and enlarged to take account of new material, new areas have been introduced and the series has been extended to include Scotland, Wales and Ireland. Whether readers agree with the views and judgements expressed in the Pevsner guides is immaterial. Their value lies in providing a yardstick against

---

* *Oxford Dictionary of National Biography*, entry by Brian Harrison.

which readers can form their own views and a means of ensuring that when they embark on an exploration of a town or region they see all there is to be seen.

Gombrich's and Pevsner's great contribution to this country – the country of their adoption – can be summed up in seven words: they opened the eyes of the British. Art and guidebooks galore had existed before they arrived here. But, though English was not their mother tongue, they found ways of conveying information and guidance in a clear and accessible way that enabled more people than ever before to appreciate and understand what they were looking at. This was perhaps because they had been brought up in German, which, until the Second World War, had always been the principal language of art history. When Clark began his career in the 1920s Bernard Berenson, the American who was at that time the most famous connoisseur in the world, advised him that if he wanted to write about art he would have to read the great art historians in their own language.[12]

I have written about Gombrich's and Pevsner's success. But, like all who came to Britain to rebuild their lives in exile, they experienced difficult adjustment periods. At one point after his internment Pevsner had to work as a labourer clearing rubble from bombed London streets. All had to adapt to a new language and environment and usually to having much less money than they had been used to. They had to put their former habits and ambitions behind them and set themselves new goals. Some could not do so. Gombrich and Pevsner, and the others whose names are mentioned in this essay, succeeded magnificently and Britain has gained accordingly. But they are the ones who stand out. There were many for whom migration resulted in blighted hopes and disappointing lives. And, whether successful or not, all had to contend with the knowledge of how the relatives and friends they left behind had suffered and died. 'I think of it every day,' I heard Claus Moser say at his 90th birthday celebration in 2012. He had arrived in this country in 1936 at the age of fourteen. After a long and successful career as a statistician, academic, adviser to governments, head of an Oxford college, chairman of the Royal Opera House, member of the House of Lords and much else, the memory continued to weigh heavily upon him, as it did on many others until the day they died.

The Lonely Londoners

by Sam Selvon (1956)

City Of Spades

by Colin MacInnes (1957)

Absolute Beginners

by Colin MacInnes (1959)

Of all the changes that have taken place in this country during my lifetime the most visible is in the composition of the population. Until the arrival of black American troops during the Second World War few Britons would ever have set eyes on a person of a different colour. The American army at that time was segregated into all-black and all-white formations and I can still remember, with some embarrassment, how my nanny and I stared at a large contingent of black troops camped in a park in rural Essex through which we were being driven to a children's party. When the war ended and life began to return to normal, some American military remained and a trickle of students from the colonies started to arrive, but the figures were very small. It is thought that the total number of people of non-European ethnic origin resident in this country was only about twenty thousand, although there are no reliable statistics to draw on.*

A sense of how rarely most people encountered members of this minority and how they were regarded is conveyed by a diary entry in the Mass Observation Project *Our Hidden Lives: The Everyday Diaries of Forgotten Britain, 1945–1948*, an invaluable record of how ordinary people felt and thought on issues of every kind in those years. On 12 December 1946 Maggie Joy Blount, a freelance writer and public relations agent, records an evening at the theatre in Windsor: 'The part of coloured servant played by a real Negro. When company took their call at the end they stood in line as usual, hand in hand, all except the Negro who stood separately a little behind them.'[13]

The turning point came in 1948. The British Nationality Act of that year conferred British citizenship and the right to enter and settle in the United Kingdom on all people living in the Commonwealth. On 22 June, while it was still being debated in Parliament, a ship called the *Empire Windrush* docked at Tilbury and some five hundred Jamaican immigrants, many of whom had served in the British forces during the war, disembarked. This is generally taken to be the moment when large-scale immigration from the Commonwealth began though few realized it at the time. The Colonial Secretary, Arthur Creech Jones, said he didn't expect the *Windrush* passengers to last more than one winter and many of them were in any case not intending to make their lives here.[14]

At first the flow of immigrants arriving each year increased slowly, but, as the 1950s progressed, the combination of full employment and an expanding economy stimulated a demand for cheap immigrant labour, especially in such state-run services as the NHS and London Transport. By comparison with conditions in the West Indies, parts of the Indian

---

* The 1991 UK census was the first to include a question about ethnicity.

subcontinent and Africa, prospects in Britain looked enticing and the number of new arrivals rose sharply – in the case of West Indians alone from two thousand in 1953 to twenty-seven thousand five hundred in 1955.[15] These three documentary novels, published in 1956, 1957 and 1959, are set in London during the period when the first arrivals were finding their feet and Londoners were coming to terms with what it meant to have strangers of another colour in their midst.

The barbed and uneasy relationship between the old and the new communities is encapsulated in two conversations. In Sam Selvon's *The Lonely Londoners* the Trinidadian Moses Aloetta, who has been in London some time, explains the realities of life to the recently arrived Galahad: 'It had a time when I was first here, when it only had a few West Indians in London, and things used to go good enough. These days spades all over the place, and every shipload is big news, and the English people don't like the boys coming to England to work and live.' Galahad asks if, 'Things as bad here as in America?' Moses replies that discrimination is less overt, but nonetheless real: 'In America you see a sign telling you to keep off, but over here you don't see any, but when you go in the hotel or the restaurant they will politely tell you to haul – or else give you the cold treatment.' In fact, as the immigrant population increased so did notices, especially at lodging houses, proclaiming 'No Blacks', 'No Coloureds' or, most notorious of all, 'No Blacks, No Irish, No Dogs'.

In *City of Spades* by Colin MacInnes, the white intellectual Theodora Pace declares her love for the Nigerian student dropout Johnny Fortune, after which they somewhat bizarrely embark on a discussion about the implications of immigration. 'We'd better change our immigration laws,' she says. 'Otherwise we'll soon have a half-caste population.' His response goes to the heart of the British dilemma: 'Always you preach in England against colour bars in other countries! Now you can practise what you preach at home.'

Sam Selvon and Colin MacInnes approached the subject from different and complementary standpoints. Selvon was among the first wave of West Indians to reach this country, arriving in 1950. MacInnes was an upper-class Englishman. Neither, however, was typical of his tribe. Selvon, who was of largely Indian ancestry with a dash of white, had been a successful journalist in Trinidad and his first novel, *A Brighter Sun*, which was set there, was published in London in 1952. MacInnes, who had been educated in Australia, was openly gay when homosexuality was still against the law. He was also one of the white 'slummers' of both sexes, who went in search of sex and excitement among the West Indian community. Darcus Howe, one of this country's foremost campaigners for black rights for many years before his death in 2017, was, as a young man, among those MacInnes propositioned, in this case unsuccessfully.[16] But, unlike most such 'slummers', MacInnes recognized a responsibility towards the black community as he showed when becoming one of the founders of the legal charity Defence, set up to help black people who had been arrested or harassed by the police.

Selvon sets out to chronicle what it was like to be a West Indian immigrant by fictionalizing the experiences of a group of young men among whom he lived when he first came to London. Initially he tried to write in standard English. When he found that wouldn't work he created a sort of fusion between the idiom of the people he was writing about and the way English is written, an effective device that has since been followed in varying degrees by other writers. Nearly all the action takes place in the area where the West Indians first congregated, bounded in the west by 'the Gate' (Notting Hill), in the east by the 'Arch' (Marble) and in the north by 'the Water' (Bayswater).

That practically all the characters are young men reflects the fact that, whenever large numbers of people start to move from one part of the world to another, it is young men who lead the way. Women and families follow and not many had done so at the time about which

Selvon is writing. Only one family features in *The Lonely Londoners* though Moses feels a sense of failure when he sees other men, who have been in London for less time than he, saving up enough money to bring their families over.

He is sometimes asked by people in Trinidad to meet new arrivals. They get off the boat train at Waterloo station in summer suits, clutching cardboard suitcases and thinking they know what to expect because Britain, the mother country of the empire, has loomed so large in their education and in the lives of the colonies from which they come. In fact, they are completely unprepared for the cold, the fogs, which are brilliantly evoked, the food and the mix of metropolitan glamour on the one hand and squalor on the other that characterized London at that time. They have to learn that a sum of money that would represent wealth at home buys little in London, so that the high wages they thought they were coming to earn are actually quite modest, and that in any case jobs are harder to find and pay less for black men than for white.

At the employment office, Moses explains to Galahad: 'Suppose a vacancy come and they want to send a fellar, first they find out if they want coloured fellars before they send you. That save a lot of time and bother, you see. In the beginning it cause a lot of trouble when fellars went and said they came from the labour office and the people send them away saying it ain't have no vacancy. They don't tell you outright that they don't want coloured fellars, they just say sorry the vacancy get filled.' When another veteran finds a job for a recently arrived relative, he explains, 'the work is a hard work and mostly is spades they have working in the factory, paying lower wages than they would have to pay white fellars'.

Selvon describes how the immigrants cope with this strange and hostile environment – crowding together for company to talk about home, to eke out scarce resources and to eat rice and peas; how they learn to navigate the city, to find jobs, to adjust to prejudice and where to buy 'weed'. There is nothing self-pitying or sentimental about his account. Some prosper as hustlers or in more or less legitimate businesses, others rub along on whatever wages they can pick up. One resourceful character, living in a top-floor room in what is today the exclusive Dawson Place, in Notting Hill, finds a way to save money on food by trapping and cooking seagulls. Like many working-class people in those days before the lottery, the immigrants do the weekly football pools and dream of winning the top prize of £75,000 (almost £2 million in today's money).*

They dream of, and often succeed in, dating English girls – a 'skin' or 'a sharp piece of skin', a 'frauline' (sic), a 'cat', a 'number', a 'chick' or 'white pussy'. On his way to his first date with a white girl, 'a nice piece of skin waiting under the big clock at Piccadilly Tube Station', Galahad rhapsodizes: 'This is London, this is life oh lord, to walk like a king with money in your pocket, not a worry in the world.' But mostly the contacts are less romantically tinged as white women seek out black men for experience and excitement and black men take advantage of the opportunities at illicit drinking clubs known as shebeens or private parties. As Darcus Howe later remembered it: 'The girls were Australian, Swedish, whatever – it was black men and white girls – mine was Italian. That's how it was.'[17] In his books Colin MacInnes describes other parties of a more louche variety that take place in white people's homes.

Then there was the Bayswater Road, in those days famous for the large number of prostitutes who solicited openly from the 'Arch' to the 'Gate'.[18] The women often took their clients into the park, in the quieter parts of which others too engaged in sexual activities and assignations of various sorts.

The most striking passage in *The Lonely Londoners*, extending over ten pages without a full stop, is Moses Aloetta's stream-of-consciousness

* A complex form of betting through a pool on the results of the following Saturday's football matches.

reminiscence of his own and others' experiences in the park during the warm summer months. From buying sex from prostitutes for a pound, to white women looking for black men to have sex with there or to take home, to voyeurs offering to pay him to have sex with their wives while they watch, to 'white fellars who feel is a big thrill to hit a black number and the girls does make them pay big money' – 'people wouldn't believe you when you tell the things that happen'. Significantly, this is not a happy memory. As the reminiscence ends, 'Moses sigh a long sigh like a man who live life and see nothing at all in it and who frighten as the years go by wondering what it is all about.' In this and numerous other passages, Selvon conveys the pain and perplexity felt by so many immigrants who had come to London to seek their fortune only to end up trapped in lonely and aimless lives.

There is no violence in *The Lonely Londoners*. That came later when, in the late summer of 1958, the resentment Moses had referred to in his conversation with Galahad reached boiling point in the form of the so-called Notting Hill race riots. In *Absolute Beginners*, which is mainly about what, in the 1960s, came to be called 'swinging London' rather than the black community, MacInnes captures the atmosphere of sinister foreboding that preceded the riots and how they escalated from individual acts of violence by white on black to ambushes and pitched battles.

The book's white narrator is attacked for being a 'Darkie-luvver' when he is found talking to a group of black men. Among other violent incidents that are described, a particularly arresting image is that of a black youth fleeing from a white mob down Bramley Road and seeking refuge in a greengrocer's shop whose elderly white female proprietor then confronts his pursuers as they shout, 'Bring him out' and 'Lynch him'. In *Having It So Good*, about the 1950s, the contemporary historian Peter Hennessy records being told by a West Indian, who had served in the RAF during the war and returned to live in Notting Hill, of white gangs rampaging down Portobello Road and Colville Road chanting,

'Kill the niggers!'[19] The diarist and future Labour Cabinet minister Tony Benn, who lived nearby, was appalled by the gangs' use of petrol bombs, iron bars and razors during the riots.[20]

The impact of the riots on public opinion was profound and among the factors that, in the 1960s, led to political action on two fronts: the imposition of restrictions on immigration and the introduction of laws against racial discrimination. Both were progressively tightened over the following decades. Also during those decades, as Britain became more prosperous, parts of the area in which the immigrants had settled were 'gentrified' and gradually transformed into the fashionable area that the name Notting Hill conjures up today. The immigrants moved to other parts of London. Today only the annual August Bank Holiday Carnival remains as a reminder of its West Indian past.

City of Spades is a play on words, the description given by one of the book's white characters to 'a world where you've never set foot before' – the 'spade city' being created by West Indians, Africans and American GIs in the heart of London. MacInnes describes it with all the relish of a man who enjoys the milieu and wants both to convey that enjoyment and to shock his readers. It is a world of loosely disguised and, for those familiar with the scene, instantly recognizable clubs, pubs, restaurants and dance halls where black people gathered and black and white mixed. But the black characters are by no means representative. There are no ordinary individuals in boring jobs and struggling to look after the families, which, by the late 1950s, were beginning to arrive. They are colourful rogues engaged in petty thievery, drug trafficking and prostitution with always a hint of violence just below the surface. MacInnes clearly got a kick out of consorting with them and deals amusingly with the fumbling ineptitude of his white characters as they try to find their way around.

The result is a book damaging to race relations in two respects. The nature of its characters and the activities they are engaged in confirmed the prejudices held by whites about the alleged fecklessness, lawlessness and unreliability of black people. And, for that reason, it diminished the impact of his accounts of how the police abused their powers when dealing with black people, a problem that was to blight race relations for many years afterwards.

City of Spades represents a landmark as the first novel by an established white writer set mainly among black people. Moreover, it is the black rather than the white characters who, for the most part, set the terms of engagement between them. Individual black and ethnic minority characters were beginning to appear in plays and novels in the late 1950s. Shelagh Delaney's play *A Taste of Honey*, first shown in 1958, and Alan Sillitoe's *Saturday Night and Sunday Morning*, published in the same year,* are two examples, but *City of Spades* is of an altogether different order. That it should have been a voyeur's guide to the seamier side of life in itself speaks volumes about how white people regarded black and the disadvantages the newcomers were up against.

* See essay on *Love on the Dole* and *Saturday Night and Sunday Morning*.

Diverse Perspectives

The Doctor's Dilemma, 1906, to which is linked the *Preface on Doctors*, 1911, by George Bernard Shaw, and *The Citadel* by A. J. Cronin, 1937.

The Green Hat by Michael Arlen, 1924, and *The Vortex* by Noël Coward, 1924.

The Old School edited by Graham Greene, 1934.

Scoop by Evelyn Waugh, 1938, and *Brideshead Revisited* by Evelyn Waugh, 1945.

Strangers and Brothers by C. P. Snow, 1940–70, and *The Two Cultures and the Scientific Revolution* by C. P. Snow, 1959.

A Book of Mediterranean Food by Elizabeth David, 1950.

The Doctor's Dilemma (1906) and the *Preface on Doctors* (1911)

by George Bernard Shaw

The Citadel

by A. J. Cronin (1937)

Few books have so comprehensively captured the mood of the moment when they were published as A. J. Cronin's *The Citadel* in 1937. Within four months this novel excoriating the medical ethics and practices of its day had sold over one hundred and fifty thousand hardback copies. In the following year, a Gallup poll reported that it 'impressed' more people than any other book except the Bible.[1] It traces the career of Andrew Manson, a young Scottish doctor, from being an assistant general practitioner, or GP, in South Wales to a rich London practice and draws heavily on the experiences of its author, a Scottish doctor who had himself started in South Wales in the early 1920s and later practised in London before retiring to write novels. *The Citadel* was his fifth and most successful.

George Bernard Shaw was already established as a leading playwright when *The Doctor's Dilemma* was first performed in 1906, since when it has been frequently revived. It is a satire on both the ethics of the medical profession and on the artistic temperament as personified by the brilliant and corrupt Louis Dubedat, an artist dying of tuberculosis. It also deals with the issue of trying to weigh the value of one individual's life against another's, the dilemma that gives the play its title, and with the blindness of romantic love. Depending on the production, the medical ethics issues can become somewhat overshadowed by other aspects of the play. Shaw, however, attached such importance to them that in 1911, when the play was published in book form, he added a *Preface on Doctors* of nearly a hundred pages. In this he sets out his criticisms of the medical profession's methods and ethics as well as expounding some theories of his own.

He approached these matters as a sceptic about how much doctors could achieve or indeed really understood about what they were doing, an attitude attributed by some to his having caught smallpox as a young man after having been vaccinated against it.[2] His circle of friends, however, included the celebrated bacteriologist Sir Almroth Wright and the play was inspired, at least in part, by a visit he paid to Sir Almroth's laboratories at St Mary's Hospital in London and the discussions he had with those working there. The character of Sir Colenso Ridgeon in the play draws on that of Sir Almroth, who, it is believed, helped Shaw a good deal with its technical medical details.

Shaw's central concern in the *Preface* is with the conflicts of interest inherent in the provision of medical services in return for money. He deals first with the relationship between rich patients and their doctors where, he argues, it will always be in the doctor's interest to prescribe the most expensive form of treatment. He rejects as hypocritical the profession's claim to be impartial in making this choice. By that he doesn't mean doctors deliberately putting their own financial interest ahead of the welfare of their patients or recommending harmful courses of treatment in order to earn more money, although, of course, there must always be the risk of that. He has in mind something more nuanced.

He believed that, 'As to the honor [sic] and conscience of doctors, they have as much as any other class of men, no more and no less.' They are therefore, he argues, as likely as other men (they are all men in both the *Preface* and the play) to believe that a particular course of action is objectively the best if it also happens to coincide with their own pecuniary interest. The extent to which their judgement may be swayed by this consideration will vary from one individual to another, but it must always, he believed, play some part, consciously or subconsciously, in a doctor's diagnosis and prescription. As there is so often more than one valid course of action in treating a condition, it will always be possible to make the case, and genuinely to believe, that the most expensive treatment is the most appropriate.

The temptation to err on the side of profit is enhanced by the propensity of consumers of all forms of goods and services to equate price and fame with quality. This is especially true of medicine about which most people know very little. The more fearful a person is, Shaw argues, either on their own behalf, or that of a loved one, the more likely they are to demand 'the best' regardless of cost in the hope of avoiding suffering and death. When they are advised that the newest treatment, or the most expensive, or the most fashionable, which are often one and the same, is the most suitable for their condition, it is often what they want to hear. If, nonetheless, the loved one dies, a large bill can reassure the survivor that no effort or expense was spared.

An incident in *The Citadel* illustrates this point. Andrew Manson refers a patient to a fashionable and expensive but incompetent surgeon with whom he has a financial relationship. The patient dies during the operation and Manson is overcome by remorse. But when he tries to apologize to the patient's widow for referring her husband to such an incompetent, she will have none of it. She is proud that her husband had been in the hands of a famous surgeon, she has boasted about it to her friends and she is happy in the belief that everything money could buy was done on his behalf.

Shaw argues that there will always be those among the rich and privileged who, when sick or caring for someone who is, will seek out the most famous doctor in the relevant field and invest a blind faith in his powers, as Mrs Dubedat does in the play when she pleads with Sir Colenso to save the life of her husband. That she is not, in fact, rich is incidental. She comes from the social class of people who are and is confident that Sir Colenso will attach as much worth to her husband's talent and future fame as he would to money.

This credulity, Shaw suggests, is often misplaced. Among the characters in the play, Sir Colenso has earned respect for his new treatment for tuberculosis. But Sir Ralph Bloomfield Bonnington, who takes on Dubedat's case when Sir Colenso says his hands are full, is casual to the point of negligence in his methods while the dandified surgeon Mr Cutler Walpole is a fraud. Shaw created these characters for dramatic effect, but their banter about misdiagnoses and operations that have gone wrong or served no useful purpose give substance to a serious accusation he makes against the medical profession in the *Preface*; namely that its members will always support each other when a mistake occurs: 'The only evidence that can decide a case of malpractice is expert evidence: that is, the evidence of other doctors; and every doctor will allow a colleague to decimate a whole countryside sooner than violate the bond of professional etiquette by giving him away.'

This was a fair point. Not only in medicine but in other professions too professional solidarity took priority over the public interest in Shaw's day. Today codes of behaviour, reporting procedures and regulatory structures are much stronger, but professional solidarity still exercises a powerful influence and abuses can still occur. Constant vigilance is required and whistle-blowers have a vital role to play.

If the practice of medicine was distorted by too much money among the rich, the opposite, Shaw argues in the *Preface*, was the case among the poor. When a poor man can't afford to pay more than a pittance, 'it is kinder to give him a bottle of something almost as cheap as water and tell him to come again with another eighteenpence if it does not cure him' than to suggest remedies that are beyond his means. In the play Dr Schutzmacher, who had begun his career working among the poor, boasts of how he had always prescribed the same medicine regardless of a patient's condition: 'Parrish's Chemical Food: phosphates, you know. One tablespoonful to a twelve-ounce bottle of water: nothing better, no matter what the case is.'

Whereas the rich were desperate to use their wealth to try new remedies, the poor, Shaw believed, were in thrall to ideas handed down from the past and suspicious of new ideas. 'The doctor,' he warns, 'learns that if he gets ahead of the superstitions of his patients he is a ruined man; and the result is that he instinctively takes care not to get ahead of them.' So, among both rich and poor there was a conspiracy between doctors and patients – among the rich to prescribe what is newest and most expensive, among the poor to stick with familiar remedies and the time-honoured bottle of coloured fluid.

Manson learns these lessons when he arrives in South Wales straight from medical school as an assistant GP full of enthusiasm and new ideas. He is shocked to find the surgeries, including that of the doctor for whom he works, dispensing medicines that are little more than coloured water. He is disappointed by his patients' reluctance to try unfamiliar remedies, sometimes with tragic results. When he advises a miner whose arm had been badly scalded by boiling water on how to treat it his prescription runs counter to the traditional remedy proposed by the District Nurse, a respected figure in the community. When he perseveres, he is told he is no longer wanted, with the result that the man is left with a permanently disabled arm and Manson loses a patient.

Another problem is the unwillingness of the local District Medical Officer of Health to stand up to the local council if that involves incurring expenditure, which leads to one of the most celebrated incidents in *The Citadel*. When Manson and another doctor identify contaminated water from a particular sewer as the cause of an outbreak of typhoid the Medical Officer fails to press the council to replace it. The two doctors thereupon take matters into their own hands by blowing up the sewer and successfully blaming the explosion on its own inert gases, thereby forcing the construction of a new one.

Over time, through sheer hard work and following a few spectacular successes, Manson wins the confidence of the local people, initially in one small town and then in another nearby. On one occasion he revives a baby the midwife had given up as stillborn. On another he saves a man from being certified as insane when he identifies and treats the illness that has given rise to the mental disorder. On a third he goes underground to amputate a miner's arm that that has been trapped under fallen rubble thereby freeing the man himself to be brought to the surface.

Yet his career cannot progress. In his first post the doctor for whom he works as an assistant has been incapacitated by a stroke and will never be able to resume his duties. Because there is no mechanism to remove him Manson does all the work while the doctor's wife* pockets the proceeds out of which she pays him a small salary. He moves to a neighbouring town to work for one of the medical aid societies set up by the miners' trade union. There he runs into more problems. His refusal to sign sick notes for malingerers and the methods by which he pursues his private research into the causes of lung disease among miners make him powerful enemies and he feels obliged to leave. His research enables him to secure a post in London with an official body

* This character in *The Citadel* so closely resembled the wife of the doctor for whom Cronin had worked as an assistant in South Wales that she successfully sued for libel. Cronin settled out of court and in subsequent editions wife was changed to sister.

concerned with the health of miners. He believes this will be his great opportunity, but soon discovers that it is controlled by the mine owners and he is sidelined as a troublemaker.

Manson at last achieves professional recognition when he buys a small general practice in a modest part of London with the intention of serving the local community. Here he comes into his own in a community that respects his talents. His reputation spreads and increasing numbers of prosperous people from other parts of London flock to consult him. At this point his moral compass deserts him.

He becomes infatuated by money and involved with a clique of self-serving physicians and surgeons who pass patients from one to the other, pander to hypochondriacs, promote pseudo-scientific remedies on behalf of their manufacturers and prescribe the most expensive treatments and operations. Only when one of his seriously ill patients dies while being operated on by an incompetent member of the clique in the incident referred to above are Manson's eyes opened. Appalled and remorseful, he decides to leave London and, with two old friends, to set up a new practice in the Midlands based on the most modern ideas.

Before he can do so disaster strikes and the novel reaches its crescendo. Manson had had under his care a young woman, the daughter of a dear friend, suffering from tuberculosis. Believing that the treatment she was receiving at a leading London hospital was doing her no good he had removed her to one run by an American pioneer of a new form of treatment. Together they had performed a procedure on her that had been entirely successful. But the American was not a formally qualified and registered doctor. His former associates, out to get him, report him to the General Medical Council for a breach of medical ethics and he is put on trial for his professional life. Friends and foes alike expect him to be struck off, but in a dramatic denouement he convinces his judges that he was acting in the best interests of his patient and is allowed to continue with his career. Thus, the book ends on a hopeful note with the medical establishment showing itself, on this occasion at least, willing to defy professional solidarity in favour of the outsider.

Cronin and Shaw can both reasonably be accused of unfairness and lack of balance in their portrayal of contemporary British healthcare. But they were not aiming at objectivity. They were polemicists inveighing against long-standing and deep-seated abuses and drawing attention to issues that needed to be tackled. They largely agreed on their diagnoses but differed on the remedy.

In the *Preface* Shaw argues that 'Until the medical profession becomes a body of men trained and paid by the country to keep the country in health it will remain what it is at present: a conspiracy to exploit popular credulity and human suffering.' He therefore welcomed the introduction of the National Health Service in 1948, two years before his death at the age of ninety-four. In *The Citadel*, when Manson reflects on the inadequacies of the hospital system he asks himself whether a state system might be the answer but rejects it: 'No damn it, that's hopeless – bureaucracy chokes individual effort – it would suffocate me.' The nearest he comes to setting out a reform programme is in his impassioned speech at the GMC in which he argues, 'We ought to be arranged in scientific units. There ought to be a great attempt to bring science into the front line, to do away with the old bottle-of-medicine idea, give every practitioner a chance to study, to co-operate in research.' He insists that commercialism must be taken out of medicine but does not suggest how that should be done.

Despite this, *The Citadel* helped to create the climate of opinion that, after the Second World War, led to the creation of the NHS. It also achieved fame and influence of a less welcome sort. In Germany during the war it was used with Cronin's other novels to discredit Britain. In April 1944 the Jewish diarist Victor Klemperer, who, despite dreadful privations and persecution, was still living in Dresden, wrote in his diary: 'Propaganda: English novels are banned of course;

but there are books by A. J. Cronin in every shop window: he's Scottish and exposes shortcomings of social and public services in England.'[3] Ironically Cronin himself was at that time propagandizing on behalf of the British war effort while working for the Ministry of Information in Washington.

The Green Hat

by Michael Arlen (1924)

The Vortex

by Noël Coward (1924)

In the mid-1920s Michael Arlen and Noël Coward, the one destined for obscurity, the other for immortality, were on a roll together. Arlen's novel *The Green Hat* was the literary sensation of 1924 while Coward's play *The Vortex* was its counterpart on the London stage. There was no doubt as to who was the bigger star. Coward had been unable to find a leading London theatre management to back his play and was only able to put it on at a small Hampstead theatre thanks to a loan from Arlen of £250 (£15,000 in today's money).[4] It was an immediate success, soon transferred to the West End and became his breakthrough into the big time. But when, in the following year, it opened in New York in the same week as a dramatized version of *The Green Hat* the *New Yorker* magazine reported, 'The Green Hat was consuming most of the attention with the opening attracting "every bigwig of Broadway", including Irving Berlin.'[5] In 1928 a film adaptation entitled *A Woman of Affairs* was produced, starring Greta Garbo.

It was not only in terms of sales and celebrity status that Arlen was highly regarded. In his memoir, *A Moveable Feast*, about his time in Europe in the 1920s, Ernest Hemingway records driving from Lyons to Paris with Scott Fitzgerald. 'Scott was very cheerful and happy and healthy and told me the plots of each and every one of Michael Arlen's books. Michael Arlen, he said was the man you had to watch and he and I could learn much from him.'[6] Sometime after this trip Hemingway sent Fitzgerald the draft of his first novel, *The Sun Also Rises*. Fitzgerald replied, 'You've done a lot of writing that honestly reminded me of Michael Arlen', which led Hemingway to cut out its first fifteen pages.[7] Even so his character Brett Ashley was considered by many American critics at the time to be derived from Iris Storm, the principal character in *The Green Hat*, although in fact she probably owed more to Lady Duff Twysden with whom Hemingway had been travelling in Spain.

Anthony Powell was another who fell under Arlen's spell. He recalls in his memoirs that when he arrived in London from Oxford in 1926 he decided not to live in the areas chosen by most of his friends and contemporaries. 'I had my own ideas, though I might not have admitted to everyone that the Shepherd Market seduction scene which opens Michael Arlen's novel, *The Green Hat* (1924) chiefly caused me to set my sights on that small enclave (also described in Disraeli's *Tancred*) so unexpectedly concealed among the grand residences of Mayfair.'[8] In *A Question of Upbringing*, the first novel in his own famous A Dance to the Music of Time sequence, which is set in the 1920s, Powell has two Oxford undergraduates discuss *The Green Hat* with one borrowing it from the other in the belief that it will unlock the secrets of what goes on in fashionable London society.[9]

The Green Hat is the story of Iris Storm, twice widowed and famously promiscuous. It was the first novel about the Bright Young Things of the 1920s – their parties, extravagances, fast cars, nightclubs and frivolity – to become a bestseller. Evelyn Waugh's *Vile Bodies*, published in 1930, has long since become the most famous example of the genre and a symbol of the decade. But in the decade itself it was *The Green Hat* which held that position. In the words of Waugh's novelist brother Alec, Michael Arlen was both 'the spokesman of a new type of woman who was demanding a man's right to live her life in the way she chose' and 'the spokesman of a disenchanted generation'.[10]

In the opening scene Iris Storm, wearing her signature green hat, arrives in Shepherd Market in her yellow Hispano-Suiza, one of the most glamorous cars of the period, to visit her alcoholic brother. The narrator, who lives in the flat below, shows her the way and, when they find him in a drunken stupor, is rewarded by spending the night with her. As the novel unfolds her history emerges. On her wedding night, when she was only nineteen, her husband fell to his death from their bedroom window. Her explanation, that he did so 'for purity', is widely taken to mean that he had committed suicide after finding that she wasn't a virgin. She bears out this interpretation by embarking on a string of affairs. Her second marriage, to an army officer with a Victoria Cross, is quickly cut short when he deliberately courts death in a shootout against Sinn Fein rebels in Ireland, thereby giving rise to more rumours and insinuations. Finally, after various other adventures, she has a miscarriage after sleeping with Napier Harpenden, an up-and-coming young diplomat she has known since childhood. They decide to elope, which, given the conventions of the time, means the destruction of his career and the hopes his father had for him as well as the end of his marriage.

The moral of the book lies in the last chapter, in which she and Napier's father confront each other. She reproaches him for having forced Napier to give her up when they were in love as eighteen-year-olds because he believed that with her as his wife Napier would be unable to fulfil the paternal ambitions he had for him. This had changed the course of her life. Though she had slept with many men since, 'I have only told one that I loved him', and that was Napier. She had married her first husband simply because she needed sex. The reason for his suicide was that he had syphilis and hadn't wanted to infect her. Her second went to his death because he had heard her declare her love for Napier in her sleep.

She denounces the father's values and the ambitions he held for his son. 'I despise your England,' she tells him and denies the right of old men like him to impose their ideas on the young since it was those ideas that 'have sent all Europe to the devil'. She rejoices in breaking Napier's diplomatic career because it was inherent in the nature of the diplomacy of the time that the world had been plunged into war. When they were young the father had been able to impose his will. But, instead of submitting as tradition demanded, Iris had rebelled. She had defied convention by her way of life and now at the age of thirty she is reclaiming the man she had always loved.

However, in a metaphor for the period, it is the old conventions that triumph in the same pyrrhic fashion as the Allied victory in the recent war. The unexpected arrival of Napier and his wife, who has acquiesced in the elopement, destroys her resolve. Iris flees back to her car, drives away at high speed and crashes into a tree beneath which she and Napier used to play as children. The narrator finds her green hat lying near the wreckage. Everybody has lost.

Today the way Arlen links the tragedy of Iris and Napier with the causes of the recent war and the great moral issues of the period seem absurdly over-dramatized and over-written. In 1924, coupled with Iris' scandalous behaviour, that link helped to propel the book up the bestseller lists while Arlen himself inspired the admiration of one of the greatest American writers of his generation.

The Vortex too is about intergenerational conflict, with cocaine as well as sex deployed to shock the audience. The chief protagonists are an ageing socialite mother with a much younger lover, the latest in a long line, and her drug-addict son, Nicky, the part Coward wrote for himself.

It begins as a light-hearted comedy of manners titillating the audience as a take-off of high society decadence and develops into a deeply serious confrontation between the mother and son as the son forces her to face up to the consequences of her selfish and immoral behaviour on those around her and above all on him. She is forced to accept her share of responsibility for him having become a drug addict and the play ends with both promising to try to overcome their addictions.

Both *The Green Hat* and *The Vortex* were entertainments, not political or social tracts, yet their popularity was a manifestation of the widespread post-war ambivalence about traditional values coupled with unease about their decline. The connection drawn between Napier's father's ambitions for his family and the attitudes that led to the horrors of the First World War struck a chord with Arlen's readers. When Coward presented high society as shallow and corrupt, his audiences both laughed and fretted that the country was losing its bearings.

The play transformed Coward into an icon of the age. Men everywhere wanted to ape the manners and appearance of Nicky, an image as far removed from the correct and upright ideal of the pre-war years as it is possible to imagine. As the famous photographer and arbiter of fashion Cecil Beaton puts it in his book *The Glass of Fashion*: 'All sorts of men suddenly wanted to look like Noël Coward – sleek and satiny, clipped and well groomed, with a cigarette, a telephone, or a cocktail at hand ... Coward's influence spread even to the outposts of Rickmansworth and Poona';[11] in other words to the outer London suburbs and to the best-known hill station of the British Raj in India. So ubiquitous was the image that it became one of the hallmarks of the decade.

The Vortex, in the words of his biographer Sheridan Morley, 'gave Coward as actor and as playwright his name, his reputation and his future'.[12] Arlen recognized the play's quality. 'If I had written that,' he said when he went backstage after the first night, 'I should have been so very proud.'[13] When their two plays were running together in New

York, rumours began to circulate that jealousy had come between them. To show that this was not so, they decided to dine together once a week at a nightclub.

Thereafter their careers diverged. With each succeeding decade Coward was able, with only a few mishaps, to capture the public mood on both sides of the Atlantic as one success followed another. His total output was enormous. At his death in 1973 it was estimated to include some forty plays and musicals, ten films and television scripts, fifteen musical reviews and cabarets plus books, short stories and memoirs. His 1942 film *In Which We Serve*, about a Royal Navy destroyer and its commander, based on the Duke of Edinburgh's uncle Lord Louis Mountbatten, and his ship, HMS *Kelly*, is one of the great classics of British wartime cinema. In 1964, forty years after his initial triumph, he was invited to direct his 1925 play *Hay Fever* at the National Theatre, the first living dramatist to be produced there.

Arlen was never able to repeat the success of *The Green Hat*, but he continued to write books and short stories that were highly popular both in Britain and the United States. Some were turned into films and he made a great deal of money. He also achieved indirect success when the lyricist and song writer Eric Maschwitz 'stole' and slightly adapted the title of one of his short stories to 'When the Nightingale Sang in Berkeley Square', which became one of the romantic classics of the 1940s on both sides of the Atlantic. Arlen, Maschwitz records, 'was genuinely delighted and insisted that the printed version of it should be dedicated to him'.[14] During the 1930s, Arlen enjoyed the fruits of his success, living with his family in some style near Cannes where Somerset Maugham, H. G. Wells, P. G. Wodehouse, Aldous Huxley and other famous writers had houses.

When war broke out in 1939, he and his family immediately returned to Britain. His wife joined the Red Cross and he was appointed Civil Defence Public Relations Officer for the East Midlands. However, when Bulgaria entered the war on the German side, questions were raised in the House of Commons about his loyalty, for Arlen had been born in that country of Armenian parents and his original name was Dikran Kouyoumdjian. In 1901, six years after his birth, his parents had moved to England and given him a public school education at Malvern College, after which he had acquired British nationality and changed his name. There had never been any secret about this. He himself had often[15] drawn attention to his foreign origins, in words calculated to raise a smile and disarm criticism, by describing himself 'as every other inch a gentleman'.* But faced with such questions he and his wife decided to leave the country. They settled in New York where, in the 1950s, Alec Waugh found him holding court every day at lunchtime in the King Cole Room of the St Regis Hotel. He died in 1956, while Noël Coward went on from one success to another.

---

* *Oxford Dictionary of National Biography*, entry by M. R. Bellasis, revised by Rebecca Mills.

The Old School

edited by Graham Greene (1934)

'Just as the heart of England is the middle class, so the heart of the middle class is the public school system,' wrote E. M. Forster in *Notes on the English Character* in 1920.[16] That is still true as I write nearly a hundred years later, which would have surprised many in the 1930s and 1940s. I remember the author and scientist C. P. Snow telling the Cambridge Union during a debate in the late 1950s that when the war ended he had been sure that, whatever else might happen in the coming years, the public schools would disappear and how surprised he was that they hadn't. In the early 1930s, Graham Greene, then at the outset of his literary career and himself the son of a headmaster,* was sure that they would. In his preface to *The Old School*, published in 1934, he writes, 'there can be no small doubt that the system which this book represents is doomed. Too few people can afford the fees of a public school.' He also believed that the class distinctions in society on which the public schools were based 'will not remain unaltered'.

Greene intended this collection of essays by various writers recalling their own school days to be the system's memorial, 'like a family photograph album'. For the purposes of comparison, it includes

* Of Berkhamsted School.

a few recollections by men who went to other sorts of school and by women who went to girls' schools, but the classical boys' public schools to which Forster referred form its core. The essays describe what it was like to be a public school boy – there were no girls – and what the schools were trying to achieve during the first quarter of the twentieth century.

The poet W. H. Auden, who was very happy at Gresham's School, Holt, in the early 1920s, describes their purpose as being 'the mass-production of gentlemen'. Another contributor, J. N. Richards, who went to Winchester, quotes with approval a suggestion that 'the public school system might be likened to a sausage machine – all kinds of meats were put into it, but only a monotony of sausages came out at the other end'. The diplomatic historian and diarist Harold Nicolson, who went to Wellington College in 1900, describes their aim in more hyperbolic terms as being 'to provide a large number of standardized young men fitted for the conquest, administration and retention of a vast Oriental Empire'.

Parents sent their sons to public schools so that, whatever their own background, their boys should emerge as gentlemen. That is to say as men instantly recognizable by their accent and manner as entitled to give orders, to employ others and to be treated with deference and respect by those who did not possess the same attributes. For some that was a sufficient basis on which to make a life. Richards, about whom I have been able to discover nothing, concludes his essay with an expression of gratitude to Winchester for an education that 'has admirably suited me to the life of leisure which I find most congenial to my temper'. For others it provided the foundation for building a successful career, whether, as Nicholson suggests, in running the empire, or in the arts, sciences, the professions, business or government.

There were men who had not been to public school at the apex of all these activities, more indeed than is often supposed. But they were always the exceptions who had had to overcome considerable difficulties to reach the top whereas public school old boys had been on an inside track. Whether or not a man's parents were well-established members of the middle and upper classes or new money, if he had been to a public school that fact in itself established him as a gentleman with all its consequential advantages. Some schools were, of course, more prestigious than others. To have been to Eton or Winchester provided access to better networks and more opportunities than Gresham's or Berkhamsted. Those who had been to the former would have looked down on those who had been at the latter. Nonetheless, for a man the crucial distinction between being a member of the upper or the lower orders – the leaders and the led – was whether or not he had been to a public school.

This privilege came at a price and not just in parental money. By the standards of today life at the public schools, though better than in Victorian times, was in some respects very harsh. Two features stand out: fagging and beating. Fagging was a system whereby junior boys acted as servants to their seniors. It took different forms at different schools, but often included such chores as cleaning the senior boy's study, lighting its coal fire and toasting crumpets for his tea. Sometimes they were more esoteric as the children's writer Roald Dahl recalls in his autobiography. At Repton in 1929 the lavatories were in an unheated outhouse where he was obliged each morning to sit on a seat to warm it before a senior boy used it.[17]

In some schools the juniors were at the permanent beck and call of their seniors so that if, for instance, a senior boy wanted a letter posted or a message delivered to some distant part of the school, he could stand in a corridor and shout 'Fag' at the top of his voice. The small boys would then have to interrupt whatever they were doing, including studying, and come running, with the last to arrive being assigned the task. When Anthony Powell, famous now for his great sequence of novels A Dance to the Music of Time, was at Eton, he found responding to summonses of this sort while trying to study 'very irksome', but this was more than made up for by the enjoyment of exercising power when he became a senior. 'Who again,' he writes in his essay, 'will be in a position to summon by a shout fifteen servants who know that physical agony will be the price of disobedience?'

By physical agony he meant a beating. Corporal punishment was commonplace in all public schools. It could be administered both by masters and by those senior boys who, as prefects or monitors, assisted the masters in maintaining discipline. The regime varied from one school to another, but in most it was often meted out for the most trivial offences, such as failing to respond to a senior boy's call, breaching a dress code or being late for an engagement. L. P. Hartley, now best remembered for his novel *The Go-Between*, records that, while at Harrow from 1910 to 1915, he was 'whopped for being late for House singing'. Later he became Head of House in which capacity he 'did not mind whopping delinquents' and would take 'practice shots against the curtain of my bed to get my hand in'.

Modern readers, who did not experience corporal punishment at school, will be surprised by the matter-of-fact tone in which the contributors to *The Old School* refer to beatings and the reasons why they were administered. They were regarded as part of daily life and none of them claims to have suffered any lasting ill effects because of them. This accords with my own experience between 1950 and 1955 at Ampleforth where, like many others, I was subjected both to beatings on my behind with a cane and on my hands with a leather strap, depending on the nature of the offence. Much as we disliked it, we did not, as I recall, consider it to be any big deal. In accordance with the psychological theories then becoming fashionable, the literary editor of the *Spectator* in the 1930s, Derek Verschoyle, who was at Malvern in the mid-1920s, provides an explanation for the prevalence of corporal punishment. He suggests, 'The tradition of corporal punishment grew up side by side with the tradition of unmarried masters', and that it provided a form 'of acute sexual release'. He also notes that 'with the increasing number of married masters, there has been a decline in the amount of corporal punishment inflicted'.

Another theme that runs through most of the contributions is sport. Auden gives thanks for the fact that at his school 'athletics were treated as they ought to be treated, as something to be enjoyed not made a fetish of'. This was by no means common. At many other schools, sport played a central, not to say dominant, role in the lives of the boys. It was the principle yardstick by which success was judged and prestige earned. Around it was constructed a culture of *esprit de corps* and loyalty to the school and the houses into which it was divided that was supposed to be a template for the emotions they would later be expected to feel towards their country and whatever institutions they became part of.

At Rugby during the First World War, the novelist, poet and critic William Plomer gained the impression 'that the ritual of the cricket field was more elaborate and just a trifle more sincerely performed than that of the chapel'. This is obviously somewhat tongue in cheek, but there is real resentment in Harold Nicolson's recollection that at Wellington his scholastic promise counted for nothing beside his inability to succeed at any sort of sport. He felt that it 'retarded the growth of any self-confidence or "will" or even "character for seven shrouded years"'. Others must similarly have suffered.

Other themes recur with varying degrees of frankness. Vice, by which was meant homosexual acts between boys, and the measures taken to combat it, such as the absence of doors on the lavatories at Malvern or the removal of their locks at Berkhamsted, receive only passing references. It was such a well-known feature of public school life during this period that it could not have been completely ignored, although most of the references are somewhat oblique. An exception is Verschoyle when he states: 'The fact of homosexuality is a natural and transitory condition of adolescence, and that the very conditions of school life designed to suppress it are the ones most likely to produce homosexual fixation, is naturally not recognized nor taken into consideration' by the school authorities. To express such an opinion showed how much times had changed since 1917 when Alec Waugh had brought a storm of obloquy down on his head as a result of the very circumspect references in *The Loom of Youth*[18] to homosexual relationships between boys at Sherborne, where he had been at school.

Most public schools had imposing chapels. Religious education and the formal practice of the Anglican religion were conspicuous features of their culture. It was not uncommon for headmasters to be clergymen and to go on to become bishops. The Headmaster of Rugby in Plomer's day, Albert David, later became Bishop of Liverpool. As late as after the Second World War Michael Ramsey followed Geoffrey Fisher as Archbishop of Canterbury, having earlier succeeded him as Headmaster of Repton. Even so, Auden captures a general sense that comes through in other contributions when he writes that 'a Christian world view has broken down among schoolmasters'. Religion had become a formality.

Catholics were forbidden by their own bishops from going to Protestant schools unless they received a special dispensation. Instead they went to exclusively Catholic establishments run on the same lines by the religious orders of which the Benedictine Ampleforth and Downside and the Jesuit Stonyhurst and Beaumont were the best-known. Some, though not all, other schools accepted Jews. The nature of the tensions this could cause can be detected from a revealing passage in Powell's essay. When he arrived at Eton in 1919, he found that his house had a poor reputation. This was in part due to lack of sporting success. But, 'Worse still there had been a period in the immediate past, happily drawing to a close at the time of my arrival, when the non-Aryan proportion in its membership seemed to many unnecessarily high.'

As most of the contributors were at school during or soon after the First World War, it is not surprising that the Officers' Training Corps, generally known as Corps, features in several of the memoirs. Designed to provide boys with a rudimentary understanding of military matters and weaponry, it involved parading in khaki at set times each week for drill and martial exercises of various kinds plus field days when mock battles were fought, and a summer camp with an army unit. It loomed equally large in the lives of those of us who were at school during the Second World War and the Cold War.

I believe that at some schools it was possible to get out of Corps on grounds of conscience. At Catholic schools that was not the case as the monks who ran them regarded themselves as experts on such matters. At Ampleforth, when we paraded on Monday and Friday afternoons and at other Corps occasions, Father Peter, the Housemaster of the Junior House, metamorphosed into Lieutenant Colonel Utley with other monks as his subordinate officers in military uniforms with badges of rank. As, unlike most men of their age, they had not fought in the war because of being in Holy Orders, this was somewhat ironic. The real work was done by a former regular army sergeant major.

Several contributors pay tribute to a particular master who inspired them. Auden, Powell and the writer and critic Arthur Calder-Marshall, who was at St Paul's in the early 1920s, all commend in varying degrees the quality of the teaching they received. Nicolson, on the other hand, has 'no affection for, nor gratitude towards, my own old school' though when he revisits it in the 1930s he finds it somewhat improved. Exams, which now mean so much to the schools, parents and pupils – as they did to us in the 1950s – are never mentioned. Nor is there any reference as to whether they weighed on the minds of the contributors during their school days or what passing or failing ever meant to them. It was the fact of having been at a public school that above all determined the opportunities a man would have in life, not the exams he took while there.

However, nearly all the contributors express views on the curricula their schools followed, believing them to be out of date and with too much emphasis on the Classics. They also express regret at the class-consciousness with which they had been so thoroughly imbued. In this context the contribution by the poet Stephen Spender, about University College School in London, where he was a day boy, stands out. Most unusually 25 per cent of the boys there had won scholarships from state schools and some came from very poor backgrounds. As a result, he felt he had a better idea than those who went to conventional public schools of how privileged his family was and of how most of the country lived. For his part Graham Greene looks forward to a more radical reform of the system than extending the UCS model. In his conclusion, he holds up Norway with its almost universal system of state education in the hands of non-political civil servants as the example Britain should follow.

Scoop

by Evelyn Waugh (1938)

Brideshead Revisited

by Evelyn Waugh (1945)

Evelyn Waugh was one of the best writers in the English language anywhere in the world during the twentieth century. His novels are a joy to read, his characters memorable, his satire coruscating and his scorn venomous. But it is for the beauty and clarity of his prose that he earns his place in the pantheon of greats. In the words of the Australian essayist and critic Simon Leys, 'the way in which Waugh manipulates language is akin to the poetic mode of literary creation: his is first of all an art of words'.[19]

His output was considerable. Besides the novels for which he is most famous, it includes travel books and biographies, some of which cast a penetrating light on the times in which he lived. As I have already described in an earlier chapter, he displayed the most remarkable foresight, when in his 1931 travel book, *Remote People*, he raised the question of whether the European colonization of Africa would survive for more than another twenty-five years. In these two books, *Scoop*, published in 1938, and *Brideshead Revisited*, published in 1945, he tackles two quite different subjects.

Scoop, as its title indicates, is about newspapers. It exposed their methods and satirized their morals and mores, the people who worked for them and the tycoons who owned them. As such it is unique. No other British author has mounted so powerful an attack on the press on such a wide front. Some have attacked the proprietors, others have mocked journalists. Waugh went for both simultaneously and he did so at a time when the press was at the height of its power. With radio still quite a new phenomenon in the 1930s, newspapers were the nation's principal source of news, the prism through which people saw and learned about the world and the catalyst for their political opinions and judgements.

Their proprietors were larger-than-life characters, who used their newspapers to wield political influence and who themselves sometimes became directly involved in politics. During the First World War Lord Rothermere of the *Daily Mail* and Lord Beaverbrook of the *Daily* and *Sunday Express* had both served in Lloyd George's government while Beaverbrook would do so again in Churchill's during the Second World War. The press and its proprietors could turn their fire on whoever they chose but were themselves to a great extent immune. As authors depended on newspapers for reviews, coverage and commissions, it took unusual courage or recklessness for a writer to make them and their owners objects of ridicule.

That is what Waugh did. His portrait of Lord Copper, the proprietor of the *Daily Beast*, is both mocking and patronizing. Within his own empire Copper is an omnipotent dictator whose employees quail before him. 'Up to a point, Lord Copper', the words his foreign editor uses to indicate dissent when his proprietor says something blatantly wrong, has entered the language as the epitome of obsequiousness. Yet Lord Copper is largely unaware of anything beyond his own interests, in awe of society hostesses and putty in their hands. He cares nothing for either the moral issues at stake in the news his papers carry or for the veracity of their reports. When a war breaks out abroad he is concerned only with whether it will be a 'promising' source of copy. What he wants is for his journalists to scoop the opposition in order to generate the excitement that will boost circulation and profits.

Contemporaries would have immediately recognized the *Daily Beast*'s office as being based on the Express Group's black-glass palace in Fleet Street. Lord Copper is a more composite figure embodying aspects of, among others, both Beaverbrook, who threatened to sue when he saw the original dust jacket of *Scoop**, and Rothermere. The *Daily Beast* and its great rival the *Daily Brute* are obviously modelled on the *Daily Express* and the *Daily Mail*.

The novel is built on a misunderstanding. To please the society hostess Mrs Stitch, Lord Copper agrees to send her protégé, the fashionable young novelist John Boot, to cover an African civil war. When the foreign editor receives the instruction, he thinks his proprietor must be referring to William Boot, the young man who writes the paper's weekly nature notes. William is accordingly dispatched to the war zone with an unlimited expense account and a mountain of expensive equipment that provides Waugh with a running joke. A comic farce then unfolds. The hapless William Boot, with no idea of what he is supposed to be doing and outmanoeuvred at every turn by the ruthless professionals of rival papers, stumbles from one absurd misadventure to the next. Finally, however, through a mix of good luck and good nature, he secures the story about a British financier outwitting foreign competitors to obtain a vital minerals concession that is the scoop that gives the book its title. As a result, he returns home a celebrity.

Like all true satire, *Scoop* is not pure invention. The central features of the story are loosely based on facts, which Waugh embroiders and exaggerates to render ridiculous. The African civil war is drawn from his experience covering the 1935 Italian invasion of Abyssinia (as Ethiopia

* The book's original dust jacket, a clear pastiche of the *Daily Express* masthead, was quickly withdrawn and replaced by another. Very few of the originals survive.

was then known). He had done this for the *Daily Mail*, an assignment he had secured thanks to Lady Diana Cooper, the society beauty on whom Mrs Stitch is based, intervening on his behalf with Lord Rothermere. William Boot is, to a great extent, based on the young and totally inexperienced Bill Deedes, who went out to Abyssinia for the *Morning Post* without achieving Boot's success. Waugh's descriptions of how the journalists competed with each other by spoiling each other's stories, stealing each other's cables and filing eyewitness accounts of events before they had taken place were derived partly from his experiences covering the Italian invasion and partly from his earlier assignment in Abyssinia reporting on its Emperor's coronation.*

Almost seventy years after the publication of *Scoop*, Deedes, who by then had achieved the unique distinction of having been both the editor of a national newspaper and a Cabinet minister, wrote a memoir[20] describing the incidents and characters that provided Waugh with his raw material. This includes how, like Boot, he had been taken to a London store to acquire a mountain of equipment, in his case weighing six hundred pounds, that required two taxis to take away. He also provides details of the incident that inspired Boot's scoop. In real life it was obtained by one of the professional journalists Waugh mocks in the novel, with Waugh himself completely out of touch with what was happening.

Deedes doesn't dwell on how the journalists in the novel were able to make so much money from their expenses but I can provide supporting evidence for that. The culture of treating expenses as a tax-free supplement to salary was still going strong on some papers in the early 1960s when I was offered a job on the *Daily Express*' 'William Hickey' gossip column. 'You can double your money on expenses,' its editor told me, adding, 'and girls will do anything for you'. Despite these inducements, I declined and remained on the *Financial Times*.

---

* This led to his novel *Black Mischief*, published by Chapman & Hall in 1932.

Scoop is about a world Waugh despised. By contrast *Brideshead Revisited* is a lament for a lost world of great country houses, privilege, luxury and ease that he adored. The great French statesman Talleyrand is reputed to have said in old age, 'He who did not live in the years before the Revolution cannot understand what the sweetness of living is.' In 1945 many members of the middle class and aristocracy – the book-buying classes – felt the same when they looked back to their pre-war world. They rejoiced in Britain's victory, but mourned the loss of their comforts and privileges that the war had brought about. Their servants had disappeared, their taxes had risen steeply and they suffered the same privations as everyone else from food, clothes, petrol and coal rationing. As Waugh himself later put it, 'the book is infused with a kind of gluttony, for food and wine, for the splendours of the recent past'.* When they read of the way of life he describes and, above all, of the meals the book's characters consume, his British readers were transported back to happier days. It cast their pre-war world in a golden haze of romanticism and they flocked to buy it.

Not only those readers; its appeal went and continues to go much wider. It was published in the United States a few months after the United Kingdom and was an immediate success there too, selling over half a million copies as a Book of the Month choice and thereby transforming Waugh's finances. It has remained one of his most widely read novels ever since, above all because it is a brilliant exercise in nostalgia that conveys the excitement he himself felt when breaking into fashionable society during the inter-war period. The evocative 1981 Granada Television series and the less good 2008 feature film based on it have generated further sales, but these were inspired by the book's enduring popularity, they did not create it.

---

* Preface written in 1959 for the new Penguin edition of *Brideshead Revisited*.

When he wrote *Brideshead* in 1944 Waugh was a captain in the army on six months' unpaid (at his request) leave. It opens with the narrator, Captain Charles Ryder, arriving at an unknown destination where his battalion is to be billeted. With a shock of recognition he realizes it is Brideshead Castle, which before the war he had known well when it was the home of the aristocratic Flyte family. Memories come flooding back, beginning with a blissful holiday he spent there in 1923 with his lover, the beautiful and eccentric Lord Sebastian Flyte, and their time together as Oxford undergraduates. This is the most important relationship in the book; everything else flows from it.

Throughout, the parallels with Waugh's own life are close. At Oxford he had an affair with a young man called Alastair Graham, who shared both Sebastian's beauty and his addiction to drink. After Oxford Ryder's connection with the Flyte family plus his burgeoning reputation as an artist enable him to climb from his Bayswater background into aristocratic circles. Waugh made a similar progression from the environs of Golders Green, where he was brought up, thanks to his burgeoning reputation as a novelist and his friendship with the aristocratic Lygon family among others. Apart from its chapel, the Lygons' stately home at Madresfield bears no resemblance to Waugh's description of Brideshead, but the head of their family, the Earl of Beauchamp, lived abroad because of an earlier scandal, as does Lord Marchmain, the head of the Flyte family. Both return home in order to die with Marchmain's death playing a crucial role in the novel's denouement.

The book is a mine of period detail and social nuance of the most varied kinds. For instance: if, after a drunken evening, of which Sebastian and Ryder have many, an undergraduate leaves vomit on the floor of his room for his College servant to clear up, he should tip the servant five shillings (about £15 in today's money). And: although Sebastian's sister, Julia, is the daughter of a Marquess and one of the most beautiful debutantes of her year, there were grand families who would not regard her as a suitable match for an eldest son because the Flytes are Catholic.* Partly for this reason she marries a worldly and ambitious Canadian, who, having amassed a fortune, is making his way in politics.

It is on their commitment to the austere and authoritarian form of Catholicism that held sway among English Catholics at that time, and to which Waugh himself was devoted, that the book turns. In the end, whatever they might have done to resist it, their religion determines the fate of each of the major characters in a way that Waugh later described as 'the operation of divine grace'.† When, after years as an alcoholic bumming around the Mediterranean and having lost his male lover, Sebastian can no longer cope with life, he persuades a monastery in Tunisia to take him in. When Lord Marchmain, having deserted his wife and his faith many years before, returns, accompanied by his mistress, to die at Brideshead, he accepts a priest's absolution and the last rites of the Church on his deathbed.

The drama and symbolism of this event have a profound effect on Julia. By then divorced and having left the Church, she is having an affair with Ryder and planning to marry him. The circumstances of her father's death force her back to her original beliefs and to throw Ryder over. 'I need God. I can't shut myself off from his mercy,' she explains. To go ahead with the marriage would, she feels, be 'to set up a rival good to God's' and she cannot do that. The non-Catholic and sceptical Ryder is left speechless and denied the shared inheritance of Brideshead that would have been his if the marriage had gone ahead. Yet in the final pages, when he is back at the Castle in uniform we learn that he too has become a Catholic.

---

* Though not precisely analogous, the disapproval of the Duke and Duchess of Devonshire when, during the war, their eldest son, the Marquess of Hartington, wanted to marry Kathleen Kennedy, the Catholic daughter of the immensely rich former United States Ambassador to Britain, Joe Kennedy, illustrates this point. The Kennedys disapproved even more strongly, but the wedding went ahead. Hartington was killed in action shortly afterwards and she died in an air crash in 1948. Her brother, Jack, became President of the United States in 1960.

† Preface for the 1959 Penguin edition.

When the book came out Waugh was abroad with the army. His friend, the writer Nancy Mitford, reported to him on what their mutual friends thought of it. Many, like her, admired it, but a common reaction was 'too much Catholic stuff'.[21] Waugh did not allow that to put him off. His subsequent and much-admired Sword of Honour trilogy about the Second World War also has a strong Catholic theme.* Catholicism, to which he had converted in 1930, was integral to his life and gave it a purpose and meaning that is reflected in the character of Guy Crouchback, the central figure in the trilogy. Readers in a post-religious age find this aspect of his novels hard to understand and tend either to ignore it, as the television and film directors did, or to feel uncomfortable with it. It has, I think, contributed to him being taken less seriously as a novelist than he deserves.

More damaging blows to Waugh's reputation have, however, been delivered by his views on other matters and by his own behaviour. His love of the aristocracy, with which he so much wanted to be identified and which permeated his life as well as his work, attracted mockery even when *Brideshead* was published. The patronizing contempt with which he writes about Africans in *Scoop* and *Black Mischief* was in tune with public attitudes when the books were published; now it is completely unacceptable. Throughout his life he consumed vast quantities of alcohol. These took their toll. In his later years he was deeply depressed and seemed determined to present himself to the general public in the most reactionary and misanthropic colours.[22] When his diaries[23] were published in 1976, eleven years after his death, they confirmed this impression of him. That, despite such handicaps, his novels continue to be so widely read and enjoyed throughout the English-speaking world is a tribute to his skill as a novelist and to the beauty and clarity of his prose.

---

* *Men at Arms* (1952), *Officers and Gentlemen* (1955) and *Unconditional Surrender* (1961). All published by Chapman & Hall.

Strangers and Brothers

by C. P. Snow (1940–70)

The Two Cultures and the Scientific Revolution

by C. P. Snow (1959)

C. P. Snow, as he was always known, introduced two phrases into the English language, 'the Corridors of Power' and 'the Two Cultures', that continue to be used long after their origins have been forgotten. The first is the title of one of the novels in his *Strangers and Brothers* sequence, the other an abbreviation of the title of a celebrated lecture, 'The Two Cultures and the Scientific Revolution', that he gave at Cambridge in 1959. In his heyday, in the twenty years after the Second World War, his novels were bestsellers in Britain, widely read abroad, particularly in the United States and the Soviet Union, and adapted for stage and television. His lecture on the gap that existed between scientists and, in his words, 'literary intellectuals' – the two cultures – and their mutual incomprehension and disdain for each other influenced opinion and aroused controversy across the world. In the United States the soon to be President Jack Kennedy described it as 'one of the most provocative discussions I have ever read of this intellectual dilemma, which at the same time is of profound consequence to public policy'.[24]

Snow himself was a polymath with a foot in both cultures. As a young academic scientist in the 1930s he worked at the Cavendish Laboratory in Cambridge during its golden age of research into nuclear fission. When war broke out in September 1939 he wrote a far-sighted article forecasting that, if an atomic bomb could be developed, it would most likely be in the United States while warning of the danger that Germany might get there first.[25] The government brought him into Whitehall to mobilize scientists to work on the British nuclear programme as well as radar and other high-priority technology projects. After the war, besides devoting himself to his writing, he took up a position with English Electric, then one of the country's largest industrial companies. When Labour won the general election in 1964 he became a government minister with a seat in the House of Lords. Few novelists have enjoyed such a varied career.

Strangers and Brothers is a sequence of eleven overlapping novels chronicling the life and times of their narrator, Lewis Eliot. They span the years from 1914 to 1968 with the emphasis on the 1930s, 1940s and 1950s and were published between 1940 and 1970. Like Snow, Eliot was born and brought up in a lower-middle-class family in a provincial city (in Snow's case Leicester). He breaks free as the result of receiving a small legacy and by qualifying as a barrister. Marital problems make it difficult for him to pursue this profession and he puts together an alternative, which involves dividing his time between a fellowship at a Cambridge college (based on Christ's where Snow was a fellow) and part-time work for a large company in London.

When war comes Eliot, like Snow and many others, is swept up into Whitehall where he achieves success as a civil servant involved with the bureaucratic aspects of the British nuclear programme. In the post-war years he attains an important but shadowy role at the interface between defence and science policy, but declines an offer of a ministerial post under the Labour government elected in 1964. By the time Snow came to describe that incident in *Last Things*, published in 1970, he had himself left office. Inevitably, this gives the impression that Eliot's decision reflected a feeling on his part that he had made a mistake in becoming a minister. His element, and Eliot's, was the bureaucracy, not politics.

Both Snow and Eliot enjoyed unusually successful and diverse careers, but there were many others of that generation whose lives were transformed for the better by the war. It gave British society a huge shake-up that broke down barriers between classes and occupations. For those lucky enough to have the right attributes, military or civilian, and to be in the right place at the right time, it opened up previously undreamed-of opportunities. Snow was very conscious of this and of his good fortune. What it meant to rise from obscurity to the heart of the British Establishment is a constantly recurring theme in the novels.

He and his alter ego remained firmly on the left in politics. They welcomed the social changes brought about by the war and the 1945 Labour government. But, far from rejoicing in the pain of those whose privileges were being stripped from them, as many on the left did, Snow admired their grace in making sacrifices in the national interest. In *The New Men*, set during the war, he has Eliot record his admiration for the way in which the aristocracy and well-to-do put the national interest before their own class interest. This is often now taken for granted, but it was a point that at the time impressed overseas observers of the British scene. One such was the Canadian diplomat Charles Ritchie, who, in April 1941, wrote in his diary: 'They are Englishmen before they are capitalists or landlords (unlike the same class in France) … England's ruling class are committing suicide to save England from defeat.'[26]

The most famous of Snow's novels is *The Masters*, published in 1951. Although set in Eliot's Cambridge college, it has nothing to do with undergraduates. Nonetheless when I first read it in 1955, between leaving school and joining the army for my National Service, it made me frantic with worry that I might be prevented by another war from ever taking up my place there, or be inordinately delayed, as happened to so many in 1939. It revolves round the election of a new Master of the college in the late 1930s and deals in enthralling detail with the machinations, clash of personalities and points of contention involved. These have nothing to do with the great ideological issues of the period. It is a study of pure politics in the sense of how men (women were confined to separate colleges at that time) succeed and fail to get their way within a closed community. As such it is a classic of its kind. The same is true, except that it is less good, of *The Affair*, about how the college deals with a miscarriage of justice involving a piece of abstruse scientific research in the early 1950s.

The same theme is pursued in a completely different context in *The New Men*, published in 1954, which deals with the development of nuclear fission and the atomic bomb during and immediately after the war. The action is all behind the political scenes at the research establishment where the work is taking place and in Whitehall, Snow's home ground. Besides the rivalries and personality clashes of the college novels, the plot involves the conscience-stricken agonizing of the scientists as they confront the possible implications for the human race of what they are doing while being driven forward by their own determination to resolve technical problems and the overwhelming need to win the war. Everything comes to a head when two atomic bombs developed by their American colleagues are dropped on Japan, a Soviet spy is uncovered in their midst and the government decides to develop an independent British nuclear capability. *The Corridors of Power*, set in 1958 and 1959 and published in 1964, is on a related matter: the downfall of an ambitious young Conservative minister who wants Britain to relinquish the bomb.

The other books in the sequence relate to Lewis Eliot's previous life as he progresses from the provincial backstreets to Cambridge and London. The first, originally called *Strangers and Brothers* but renamed *George Passant* when that title was given to the whole oeuvre, is about the efforts of a charismatic but flawed solicitor's clerk in a provincial city to encourage the young people around him to make the most of their lives. *Time of Hope* and *Homecomings* are about Eliot's early career and his unhappy first marriage culminating in his wife's suicide, which is followed by an affair with a married woman that leads to a second marriage and middle-aged fatherhood.

The Light and the Dark explores the character and dilemmas of a brilliant but manic-depressive Cambridge scholar of oriental languages, who, when told that RAF Bomber Command is where a man is most likely to meet an early death, volunteers for it and is duly killed while on a mission over Germany. *The Conscience of the Rich* is a study of a rich Jewish family in the 1930s and the oppressive effect of their wealth on their eldest son, a barrister friend of Eliot's, who decides to give up his life of privilege to become a doctor in the East End of London.

When Snow was approaching the halfway mark in the *Strangers and Brothers* sequence the political columnist Henry Fairlie, writing in the *Spectator*,[27] coined the term 'The Establishment' to describe the informal network of influential individuals who, working through informal as well as formal channels, made the country tick. That was Snow's world.

His Cambridge and Whitehall novels provide a direct insight into how those individuals thought, acted, spoke, behaved towards each other, deployed arguments and took decisions during the period between the late 1930s and the early 1960s. Reading his dialogue is like listening into their conversations. He also provides a wealth of period detail, such as how, during the wartime winters, when there wasn't enough coal to heat Whitehall offices, officials wore their overcoats at work, how it was customary for even the closest of colleagues to address each other by their surnames and how, in some of the circles in which Eliot moved, men were expected to shake hands on meeting and in others not.

In his lifetime Snow's novels were often compared with those of Trollope, through the prism of which we enter the lives of mid-Victorian churchmen and politicians. The difference between them is that Trollope was not a player in the worlds about which he wrote whereas Snow was. Trollope, however, had a better understanding than Snow of the link between the public and the private sphere in men's lives. In the worlds in which both men operated women played no official part, but Trollope understood that they could wield considerable influence behind the scenes, as does Mrs Proudie in the Barchester novels and Lady Glencora (later Duchess of Omnium) in the political ones. Snow's novels demonstrate no such understanding. Nor, unlike Trollope, did he create memorable characters that live on in the minds of his readers like those two women and several others.

Trollope's reputation declined after his death and did not fully recover until he came into vogue during the Second World War, since when it has remained high. The beginning of the decline in Snow's literary reputation was a vitriolic attack launched on him in 1962 by F. R. Leavis,[28] the leading Cambridge academic and literary critic, who took exception to his lecture on the 'Two Cultures'. Leavis had many followers among the younger generation of academics and critics among whom it became fashionable to denigrate Snow's work. By the time of his death in 1980 to say that one liked his novels was to define oneself as a philistine.

A different and, I think, fairer view than that of Leavis and his acolytes was expressed by the novelist and author of *A Clockwork Orange*, Anthony Burgess, who in 1984 included *Strangers and Brothers* in his anthology *Ninety-Nine Novels: The Best in English Since 1939*. 'This sequence,' he wrote, 'is a very considerable achievement, despite the flatness of the writing … it deserves to be reconsidered as a highly serious attempt to depict the British class system and the distribution of power. The work has authority: it is not the dream of a slippered recluse but of a man actively involved in the practical mechanics of high policy-making.'[29] A more recent accolade has come from another novelist, Zadie Smith. In 2017, in an obituary tribute to Bob Silvers, the legendary editor of the *New York Review of Books*, she wrote: 'Many of Bob's writers were Nobel Prize winners, true geniuses, all rounders of the C. P. Snow variety.'[30]

The Two Cultures and the Scientific Revolution itself lives on and continues to be cited in the United States[31] as well as Britain more than half a century after it was delivered. The mutual incomprehension of scientists and non-scientists, and the inability of political and business leaders educated in the arts and humanities to take scientific factors sufficiently into account in their decision-making, are as much a cause of concern in both countries today as they were then.

The terms in which the lecture is couched are redolent of the intellectual climate and assumptions of the 1950s. To read it now is to be transported back to the arguments it provoked in those days in newspaper leading articles, politics, university common rooms and among the chattering classes. It assumes that, if the West can't resolve the problems of poverty in Africa and Asia, 'the Communist countries will'. The permanence and continuing success of Soviet Communism is taken for granted. British performance is measured only against developments in the United States and the Soviet Union. There is barely mention of the economic transformation being wrought at that time in Western Europe and of the challenges and opportunities posed for Britain by the newly formed European Economic Community, as it was then called. In this Snow was typical of the British Establishment, which completely failed to appreciate the importance of what was happening on the Continent or to foresee that in the following decade the question of whether or not to join that Community would become a central issue in British politics.

In the early 1970s my wife and I lived a short distance away from Snow and his wife, the novelist Pamela Hansford Johnson, and we became friends. We kept in touch after I became a European Commissioner and our move to Brussels. When I acquired a first edition of the original *Strangers and Brothers* novel I telephoned to ask Snow to inscribe it for me on my next visit to London. When I arrived at his house to take him out to lunch I was told by Pamela that he had died a few hours earlier.

A Book of Mediterranean Food

by Elizabeth David (1950)

Traditionally in Britain the preparation, presentation and eating of food has not been regarded as a means of expressing creativity. In France and Italy, they have for long been an integral part of popular culture and even attained the status of an art form. What the British traditionally wanted was plain fare and plenty of it, with quantity rather than creativity denoting wealth and status. Our popular culture has for long been the tending and creation of gardens, which, in the right hands, can also be an art form.

In recent decades tradition has been turned on its head. While gardening and gardens remain a national obsession, there are now millions of people interested in how to cook, present and enjoy food. Programmes on every aspect of these subjects have become a staple of television and the shelves in bookshops groan under the weight of cookery books. The stars of the former and authors of the latter become celebrities and chefs can achieve the status, or nearly so, of leading sportsmen and women. Eating out is a popular pastime and the quality of food served in restaurants at all price levels is infinitely better than it used to be. Such a massive change in popular culture can only be the result of several factors. Rising living standards, the arrival here of people from other countries and foreign travel have all played a part. But if there is one person above all others who can be credited with kickstarting the process it is Elizabeth David with *A Book of Mediterranean Food*, published in 1950.

Her biographer, Artemis Cooper, claims that she 'was the best writer on food and drink this country ever produced'.* That is impossible to prove, but she is certainly among the most celebrated. In 2012 to mark the Queen's Diamond Jubilee she was chosen by BBC Radio 4 as one of the sixty Britons who had been most influential during the sixty years of the Queen's reign. In 2013 her portrait was on one of the first-class stamps honouring ten 'Great Britons'. A film has been made about her life† and she has been the subject of a novel.[32] Her fame spread to the United States where her papers are now housed in the Schlesinger Library at the Radcliffe Institute for Advanced Study at Harvard University.

Yet in the year of its publication, *A Book of Mediterranean Food* was not so much a cookery book as a book of dreams – hers and her readers'. It would in practice have been impossible to produce most of her recipes. With the system of food rationing introduced in 1940 still in full swing, such basic foods as meat, bacon, butter, cheese, sugar and tea could only be purchased in the small quantities that each person was permitted to buy. Olives, olive oil, garlic, cloves, aubergines, lemons and other staple ingredients of Mediterranean cooking, though not rationed, were virtually unobtainable except in very limited amounts from obscure shops in Soho. I still remember the conspiratorial way in which the head waiter at Manchester's Midland Hotel whispered to my father, a frequent and highly valued guest, as we took our seats in the dining room in September 1950, that some black olives had been specially saved for him.

---

* *Oxford Dictionary of National Biography*.

† *Elizabeth David: A Life in Recipes*, written by Amanda Coe, directed by Catherine McCormack and first screened by BBC2 on 3 January 2006.

As David herself wrote in a preface to the book's second and revised edition published in 1958, 'even if people could not very often make the dishes here described, it was stimulating to think about them; to escape from the deadly boredom of queueing and the frustration of buying the weekly rations; to read about real food cooked with wine and olive oil, eggs and butter and cream, and dishes richly flavoured with onions, garlic, herbs, and brightly coloured Southern vegetables'. Her readers could not produce the dishes she described, but they were transported into another world in the same way as when they read a novel set in an exotic location.

A Book of Mediterranean Cooking was a long time in the making and grew directly out of Elizabeth David's adventures during the war years. These began in the early months of 1939 when, despite the looming threat of war, she had set off in a small yacht with her lover, Charles Gibson Cowan, to sail to Greece, an extremely unconventional thing for a young (she was twenty-five), unmarried, upper-class woman to do at that time. When they reached Marseilles she fell under the spell of the then famous author and traveller Norman Douglas to whom the enjoyment of food was as integral a part of a civilized life as appreciation of the arts. He became her mentor. As Artemis Cooper puts it, 'Norman taught her that with a little care and attention, one could eat good food every day. He also taught her how to search out the best, insist on it, and reject all that was bogus and second rate.'[33]

In 1940, as the German army advanced into France, she and Gibson Cowan resumed their journey only to be stopped and briefly interned as enemy aliens by the Italians, who had just entered the war on Germany's side. Eventually, after their boat was impounded, they were put on a train to still neutral Greece where he found a job as an English teacher on the island of Syros. There, with very little money, she learned to cook using only the ingredients available on the island and drawn from the sea around it, the most practical possible course in

Mediterranean cooking and a complete contrast to the sophistication of the South of France.

It did not last long. After a few months, the Germans invaded Greece and they again had to flee, this time to Crete. From there they were evacuated by the British Army to Egypt, where she and her lover decided to separate.

As a former debutante with aristocratic connections in England and speaking good French and German, Elizabeth David was quickly able to find a job working for the vast British military establishment in Cairo. She also joined the glittering and cosmopolitan society that surrounded it, a world immortalized by Lawrence Durrell in those of his novels known as the Alexandria Quartet and by Olivia Manning in her Levant Trilogy. Both became friends. Now she had servants to cook for her. The supply of food was plentiful and varied and from them she learned a great deal. She also cooked herself and, unlike most British women in her position, scoured the bazaars for the ingredients she needed rather than relying on the servants to do her shopping for her. It was during this time that she married an army officer called Tony David and acquired the name by which she was to become famous. However, by the time she returned to Britain when the war ended they were, to all intents and purposes, already separated.

After the warmth of the Mediterranean and the glamour and plentiful food of her life in Cairo, she found the cold, the shortages and the sheer grimness of post-war London hard to bear. Writing her book was a form of therapy. For many years she had collected recipes and when she and a lover from her Egyptian days were trying to find some escape from the horrors of London in a hotel in Ross-on-Wye in November 1946, he suggested that she put them down on paper. The hotel was warm, but its food dreadful. Recalling the recipes she had once enjoyed helped her, David later wrote, 'to work out an agonized craving for the sun and a furious revolt against that terrible, cheerless heartless food by writing down descriptions of Mediterranean and Middle Eastern cooking. Even to write words like apricot, olives and butter, rice and lemons, oil and almonds produced assuagement';[34] the same feelings Evelyn Waugh records having experienced when he was writing *Brideshead Revisited* two years earlier.*

Several publishers turned the book down, with one suggesting that it needed a linking text. It was this that provided David with an inspiration. She decided that instead of writing the links herself, she would interweave what she had already written with apposite extracts drawn from the works of a wide range of authors. These included her friends Norman Douglas and Lawrence Durrell, some who were famous, like Henry James, Arnold Bennett and D. H. Lawrence, and others who were not. They injected a further element of romance into her lists of ingredients and instructions on how to use them while giving the book something of the character of a literary anthology. They also conjured up visions of travelling in the countries from which the recipes came and consorting with their inhabitants; in that respect giving it something of the same appeal to the imagination as Durrell's Alexandria novels which came out a few years later.

The publisher John Lehmann accepted David's amended manuscript and commissioned the artist John Minton to do the illustrations. This proved to be another inspiration and one that played a significant role in the book's success. His cover, depicting a table loaded with bottles of wine, a lobster, melon and other delicacies set against the background of a harbour on a bay encircled by mountains, evoked memories among those who had been to the Mediterranean before the war and dreams among those who yearned to see it.

The book's timing turned out to be ideal. Rationing had been popular during the war when it enabled the whole population and not

---

* See essay on *Scoop* and *Brideshead Revisited*.

just the well-to-do to enjoy a balanced and sufficient diet. By 1950, five years after the war had ended, people had become thoroughly fed up with it and with the austerity foods, such as dried eggs, dried milk and whale meat that went with it. They couldn't wait for it to end.

Within a year of the book's publication a new Conservative government committed to abolishing rationing and loosening the rules that severely restricted the amount of money that individuals could take out of the country was elected. More people began to go abroad and to envisage producing meals derived from ingredients they had tasted there. There was not a mass market for either. Far from it. Nobody, except the well-to-do, would have contemplated travelling abroad for a holiday or experimenting with unfamiliar recipes. But those who could needed help and there were sufficient of them to generate a large demand for David's book. Before the war, the people who bought it would have had cooks and other servants. In the post-war world they had to do their own cooking, housekeeping and shopping.

As the 1950s progressed and scarcity gradually gave way to plenty, there was a growing demand for advice among the more prosperous classes, especially the younger generation, on how to improve their cooking skills. Elizabeth David produced articles for magazines and periodicals and wrote further books, *French Country Cooking* and *Italian Food*, during the preparation of which she travelled extensively in both countries. She then turned her attention to books on various aspects of English cooking. Where she led, others followed and became well known in their own right. In the years after we married in 1967, my wife's favourites were Robert Carrier for his books and Fanny Cradock on television.

Over time cookery books were transformed from a niche into a mass market, television cookery programmes built up vast audiences and chefs and writers on food and drink became celebrities. But none matched the influence of Elizabeth David either on the way the genre developed or in their influence over other writers. And not just in this country. Alice Waters, sometimes described as the 'mother of modern American cooking', has described David as 'her greatest inspiration': 'When I go back and read her books now I feel I plagiarized them,' she was quoted as saying on David's death in May 1992.[35] Nor did other writers achieve a similar cult status of the sort illustrated by a 1999 Channel 4 television documentary. Entitled *In the Footsteps of Elizabeth David*,* it featured the former Cabinet minister and the last Governor of Hong Kong Chris Patten visiting the various places mentioned in her books as he recalled how, in the early days of their marriage, he and his wife had worked their way through her canon. There were many other less famous couples who did the same.

---

* Shown on Channel 4, 26 and 27 December 1999.

Conclusion

The Economic Consequences of the Peace by J. M. Keynes, 1919, and *The General Theory of Employment, Interest and Money* by J. M. Keynes, 1936.

Homage to Catalonia by George Orwell, 1938,
Animal Farm by George Orwell, 1945,
and *Nineteen Eighty-Four* by George Orwell, 1949.

The Economic Conequences of the Peace

by J. M. Keynes (1919)

The General Theory of Employment, Interest and Money

by J. M. Keynes (1936)

John Maynard Keynes – always Maynard to his friends – was the twentieth century's most famous economist as well as one of its most innovative and influential. His great work, *The General Theory of Employment, Interest and Money*, published in 1936, changed the terms in which economic theory and issues were discussed and policy implemented and continues to influence policy-makers all over the world. He is one of that select body of individuals whose ideas have had such a far-reaching impact that a belief system has been named after them – Keynesianism, like Marxism. Marx explained how capitalism must inevitably collapse under the weight of its contradictions and lead via revolution to socialism. During the Great Depression in the 1930s this outcome, with Soviet Russia as its model, began to appear increasingly likely and, to many, desirable, if not in itself at least as an alternative to the Fascism of Nazi Germany. Keynes provided a countervailing theory that has helped capitalism to adapt and to avoid a recurrence of that form of economic collapse.

The Economic Consequences of the Peace, published in 1919, was directed at the crucial issue of how to enable Europe to rebuild a viable and prosperous economy after the devastation wrought by the First World War. Had its warnings and analysis been heeded the conditions that led to the rise of Nazism in Germany and thus to the Second World War might have been avoided.

Robert Skidelsky subtitles the second volume of his magisterial three-volume biography of Keynes *The Economist as Saviour*.[1] That is what Keynes aspired to be. He regarded the management of the economy as providing the underpinning of a civilized society, just as plumbing does for life in the home. When it breaks down or ceases to function in the public interest the way is opened for violence and revolution. His huge output of books, treatises and articles culminating in *The General Theory* was aimed at resolving the economic problems that threatened peace and stability internationally as well as nationally. They were leavened by his experience working in the Treasury during the First World War (he returned during the Second) and at the Paris Peace Conference that followed it. They were reinforced by his ability to combine an active participation in public life with his teaching and other responsibilities at Cambridge.

The Economic Consequences of the Peace arose out of Keynes' experiences at the Paris Peace Conference, which led to the Treaty of Versailles that formally ended the First World War. He served there as the Chancellor of the Exchequer's deputy on the committee dealing with economic issues and was therefore both a participant and a ringside spectator. Nobody in such a position had ever before exposed the inner workings of international diplomacy to the public gaze. The book created a sensation. It immediately became an international bestseller and continues to provide the principal prism through which the treaty is studied and judged. It also created a precedent for politicians and officials to write about events in which they have participated and to argue their case in public as well as behind closed doors.

The book was very much a personal statement. Its style, in Skidelsky's words, is 'angry, scornful and, rarely for Keynes, passionate'.[2] This reflected his belief that the treaty was ill-conceived and would have disastrous consequences. Personal considerations were involved as well. He was a member of the Bloomsbury Group of intellectuals surrounding Virginia Woolf described in earlier chapters. Many of its members had been conscientious objectors during the war. His own views on the war had been complex and he had felt guilty about serving a government so determined on victory at any price that it would not countenance a negotiated compromise peace. His conscience and his yearning for the approbation of his friends both demanded that he should do all that he could to create the conditions in which such a war could never happen again and be seen to condemn those responsible if the attempt failed.

He evokes the atmosphere of the meetings and negotiations and portrays the principal characters – Lloyd George for Britain, Clemenceau for France and Woodrow Wilson for the United States – in vivid and unforgettable terms. His description of how the pre-war European economy, including Britain's, revolved round the pivot of Germany is a model of clarity and his recollection of the material benefits it yielded is a delicate combination of analysis and nostalgia. The subsequent chapters with their tables, statistics and technical arguments about the financial and economic arrangements on which the treaty is based are harder to read. But the way in which he marshals his material to make his case provides a masterclass in the art of advocacy.

The first plank of that case was that the treaty imposed such harsh conditions on Germany that it would not be able to resume its role as the pivot of the European economy. In setting out to punish Germany for starting the war, Britain and France were not only condemning the

Germans to deprivation and instability, they were denying their own citizens, and the rest of Europe, the means to rebuild the integrated European economy that was essential if their own national economies were to prosper. The United States was equally culpable, but protected from the full consequences of its actions by the scale and self-contained nature of its economy on the other side of the Atlantic.

The second plank was a powerful warning of how the Germans might react against these conditions: 'If we aim deliberately at the impoverishment of Central Europe, vengeance, I dare predict, will not limp. Nothing can then delay for very long that final civil war between the forces of Reaction and the despairing convulsions of Revolution, before which the horrors of the late German war will fade into nothing, and which will destroy, whoever is the victor, the civilization and the progress of our generation.'

Nothing is inevitable. If some of the initiatives taken and proposed by various statesmen during the 1920s had succeeded and, above all, had the Great Depression that began in the United States in 1929 been avoided, all might have been well. The European economy might have recovered its equilibrium and again provided the basis for Europeans to live in peace with each other. As it was, Germany's descent into inflationary chaos in the first part of the decade opened the way for extremists, which in due course led to the Nazis coming to power, Hitler's revanchism and the Second World War. To that extent Keynes' judgement was vindicated. The consequences were not, as it turned out, as catastrophic as he and many others had feared,* but they easily might have been.

A fundamental problem at the conference was that the political leaders attending it had not grasped the extent to which political and economic stability in each of their own countries was influenced by what happened in other countries. They did not understand the implications

* See essay on *Challenge to Death* edited by Storm Jameson and *Guilty Men* by 'Cato'.

of economic interdependence adumbrated by Norman Angell before the war in his book *The Great Illusion*, which I discussed in an earlier chapter. They were still for the most part living in an earlier era when national economies in Europe were much less interdependent than they had become in the early twentieth century. In their minds what mattered after a war was the distribution of territory and populations. In Keynes' words: 'The future life of Europe was not their concern; its means of livelihood was not their anxiety. Their preoccupations, good and bad alike, related to frontiers and nationalities, to the balance of power, to imperial aggrandisements, to the future enfeeblement of a strong and dangerous enemy, to revenge, and to the shifting by the victors of their unbearable financial burdens on to the shoulders of the defeated.' They thought in old-fashioned balance-of-power terms rather than those of economic interdependence.

They were also being driven by the demands of their electorates for revenge, in France more strongly than in Britain, a factor to which Keynes does not give sufficient weight. Both countries had suffered a terrible loss of life, but the war had not touched either the British or the German national territory. It had been fought on French soil causing severe damage to the manufacturing industry, coal mines and agriculture of eastern France. The French wanted compensation and to secure a competitive advantage against Germany when peacetime conditions were restored. For these reasons as well as their own inclinations the leaders could not see what was required through the same objective eyes as Keynes. When the Second World War ended there was a much better understanding of what was required. In the words of Alec Cairncross, Head of the Government Economic Service in the 1960s: 'Keynes's thinking in 1919 was remarkably similar to the thinking behind the Marshall Plan in 1947.'*

* *Oxford Dictionary of National Biography.*

The General Theory was conceived and born in very different circumstances from *The Economic Consequences of the Peace*. It was not an attack on a fait accompli. It was an attempt to solve the overriding economic problem of the day. And, like its predecessor, it was influenced by personal considerations. In the final chapter Keynes expresses the fear that unless the crisis of capitalism can be resolved people will turn away from democracy to 'authoritarian state systems', which would mean 'Dictators and others such, to whom war offers, in expectation at least, a pleasurable excitement'. That some of the brightest young men he knew at Cambridge* were already subscribing to Communist ideas and even becoming Communists appalled him and intensified his fears.

He was in no doubt about the importance of what he was doing. In 1935, he wrote to the playwright George Bernard Shaw: 'I believe myself to be writing a book on economic theory which will largely revolutionize – not, I suppose, at once but in the course of the next ten years – the way the world thinks about economic problems.'[3] To do that, he believed, he had first to convince his fellow economists. He states in the preface that he is addressing them rather than the general public and the book is correspondingly hard to read.

Yet its central – and at the time revolutionary idea – emerges very clearly. It is that governments both can and should act to prevent economic depressions, a concept now so much part of the conventional wisdom that it is hard to believe it was ever revolutionary. Until *The General Theory*, the prevailing economic orthodoxy was that governments were largely at the mercy of economic forces, as sailing ships had been at the mercy of the winds. Just as their captains could influence neither the force nor the direction of the winds but had to adjust their sails accordingly, so governments had to trim their policies to economic

* They included two men who later achieved notoriety as Soviet spies – Guy Burgess, who escaped to Moscow in 1951, and Anthony Blunt, who was 'outed' by Margaret Thatcher in 1979.

forces. Keynes introduced the idea of counter-cyclical policy. When the economy was sinking, he argued, governments did not have to wait until unemployment had risen and wages fallen to the point where the supply and demand for labour were again balanced. They could pump money into the economy by undertaking investment on their own account and, by cutting taxes, printing money and keeping interest rates low, encourage the private sector to do the same.

The idea challenged two core concepts of prevailing economic orthodoxy. These were that governments should always try to balance their budgets by maintaining an equilibrium between income and expenditure and that the supply of money should not outstrip the reserves of gold available to back it. These rules had been broken by governments in time of war when the integrity and what were thought to be the vital interests of their state were threatened, leading to an increase in their national debt and a reduction in the value of their currency. But that was regarded as a matter of necessity the consequences of which should be corrected as soon as possible.

Keynes' suggestion, that as a deliberate act of policy in peacetime a government should increase its debt and, if necessary, reduce the value of its currency in order to create demand and so reduce the level of unemployment, was as shocking to the economic establishment as Luther's assault on the doctrines and practices of the Catholic Church had been to Catholics in the sixteenth century. Such a policy, it was argued, would not achieve its objective, would saddle the country that adopted it with debt and would lead to inflation. Besides which, it would result in an increase in the power of the state at the expense of the individual as in a dictatorship. Keynes countered this last criticism by claiming that only by some 'enlargement of the functions of government' could 'existing economic forms in their entirety and as the condition of the successful functioning of individual initiative' be maintained. The same thought is expressed more concisely by a character in Giuseppe

Tomasi di Lampedusa's novel *The Leopard*, in the famous line, 'If we want things to stay as they are, things will have to change.'[4]

The younger generation of economists was for the most part as excited by Keynes' proposition as the Establishment was shocked precisely because they thought he had found the means by which prosperity could be achieved without recourse to revolution and dictatorship. In the words of the American economics Nobel Prize-winner Paul Samuelson, it 'caught most economists under the age of thirty-five with the unexpected virulence of a disease ... Economists beyond fifty turned out to be quite immune to the ailment.'[5] One of Keynes' own postgraduate students spoke for many of the younger generation when he wrote, 'what Keynes supplied was hope: hope that prosperity could be restored and maintained without the support of prison camps, executions and bestial interrogations'.[6] At a time when it was widely feared that the future might lie between Nazi Germany and Soviet Russia – between Hitler and Stalin – hope was something the younger generation badly needed.

It was the outbreak of the Second World War rather than the policy prescriptions in *The General Theory* that brought the Great Depression to an end. But because measures of a Keynesian nature, introduced on an ad hoc basis rather than as part of a coherent theory, mitigated its worst effects they helped to validate his theory. President Roosevelt's New Deal, launched in the United States in 1933, was the most important. Rearmament in the United Kingdom during the build-up to war was another. When people saw how effective these were at reducing unemployment, it made them more receptive to the idea that similar government expenditure on other public works could achieve the same result.

The golden age of Keynesianism came after 1945. Those who had been young in the 1930s had by then risen to positions of authority, while during the war the British and American governments had shown how effective they could be at mobilizing the total resources of the state in pursuit of victory. Throughout the Western world Keynesianism exercised a great influence on governments and nowhere more so than in Britain where it provided the framework for policy-making and was credited with the sustained economic growth that characterized the post-war years.

This lasted until the late 1960s when, under the pressure of events, the criticisms originally levied against Keynesianism began to gather renewed strength. Inflation was becoming more of a worry than unemployment as trade unions used the power that full employment gave them to drive up wages with a knock-on effect on prices to a degree Keynes had not foreseen. Limits were also reached on the extent to which governments could run annual deficits. Over time the control of inflation and the reduction of deficits once again became the dominant considerations and the policy prescriptions associated with Keynes no longer attracted the support they once had. But his central idea that, when faced with the threat of a depression, the government must do all in its power to prevent it remains embedded in the national consciousness, as shown by the way in which the government responded to the financial crash of 2008 by comparison with its predecessor's reaction to the Great Depression in 1929 and will be again in the face of future crises.

Keynes died in 1946 at the age of sixty-two, worn out by his efforts in two important sets of negotiations. One, held in 1944 at Bretton Woods in the United States, successfully laid the foundations for post-war international economic relations, in sharp contrast to what had happened after the First World War. The other secured loans from the United States that kept Britain afloat immediately after the war. He was honoured with a memorial service in the National Cathedral in Washington as well as one in Westminster Abbey where his parents led the mourners, a sad and unusual distinction. Had he, like them, lived on into his nineties, he would have come up with new and, most likely, unexpected ideas about how to tackle the economic and social problems that bedevilled the country in the decades after the war. As it is, he remains a prophet in his own country as well as being revered across the world.

Homage to Catalonia

by George Orwell (1938)

Animal Farm

by George Orwell (1945)

Nineteen Eighty-Four

by George Orwell (1949)

George Orwell, whose real name was Eric Blair,* is one of the giants of the twentieth century, famous throughout the world for *Animal Farm*, published in 1945, and *Nineteen Eighty-Four*, which appeared four years later. Both were instant bestsellers in Britain and the United States and have since been translated into more than sixty languages and sold many millions of copies. They are universally recognized as being among the most powerful works of literature in defence of freedom and against totalitarianism, which is why they were banned in the Soviet bloc countries of Eastern Europe until after the fall of Communism

* His biographer Bernard Crick writes in the *Oxford Dictionary of National Biography* that he adopted the pseudonym when he started writing to avoid embarrassing his parents and as a hedge against failure. He also disliked the name Eric.

in 1989. The word 'Orwellian' has become a synonym for attempts by governments to subvert democratic institutions and to distort facts and news. The extent of its continuing grip on people's imagination was shown in the United States when President Trump was inaugurated in 2017. A new edition of *Nineteen Eighty-Four* was rushed out in response to the fears of liberal-minded Americans. They bought it in such numbers that it went straight to the top of the Amazon bestseller list.

Homage to Catalonia, published in 1938, is in a different category. It is about his time fighting in the Spanish Civil War in 1936 and 1937, which Orwell later described as the defining experience of his life. 'Thereafter I knew where I stood,' he wrote in 1946 in his essay 'Why I Write'. 'Every line of serious work I have written since 1936 has been written, directly or indirectly, against totalitarianism and for democratic socialism.'* The book is one of the best eyewitness accounts of a war that sparked immense controversy and division in Britain. The reasons why left-wing circles in London rejected it and ostracized him for expressing the views it contains tell us much about British political attitudes in the late 1930s.

I cannot think of another author whose sales and reputation are so much higher in death than in life. For most of his career Orwell's books sold in small numbers, including *Homage to Catalonia* and *The Road to Wigan Pier*, about poverty in the North of England, which has since become a classic of its kind. He lived a hand-to-mouth existence from journalism and writing, was helped by friends and worked at various times as a school teacher and in a second-hand bookshop. In the late 1930s his essays put him on the literary map in a minor way. When war broke out in 1939 he was, despite his best efforts to join up, rejected by the army on health grounds. Thereafter he became known to a wider

* First published in the summer 1946 issue of the magazine *Gangrel* and subsequently widely republished. In the collection of his essays entitled *England Your England*, published by Secker & Warburg in 1953, the original date is given as 1947.

public through his articles in the left-wing weekly *Tribune*, the literary journal *Horizon*, the *Observer* and the *Partisan Review* in New York. He also broadcast on the BBC. But he was still, in the words of his biographer D. J. Taylor, 'a faintly marginal figure'[7] when in 1945 *Animal Farm* catapulted him into the limelight.

He had little chance to enjoy it. His wife had died* shortly before its publication, leaving him with the task of caring for a newly adopted son while the tubercular problems from which had been suffering for some years were getting worse. He felt he had to get away from London to concentrate on his writing and retreated with his son and his sister, to look after the child, to a primitive cottage on the island of Jura off the west coast of Scotland. The production of *Nineteen Eighty-Four* was literally a life-and-death struggle, which he won in the sense that his death at the age of forty-six in January 1950 occurred just a year after finishing the manuscript and seven months after its publication.

It was not only in literary terms that Orwell was a marginal figure before *Animal Farm*. It was true politically as well because of his unremitting hostility to Stalin's Soviet Union, whose iniquities and cruelties he grasped long before most others on the left and never ceased to denounce. To many on the left in the 1930s this was tantamount to blasphemy. The tone was set by people like Sidney and Beatrice Webb, who had helped to set up the London School of Economics, the Fabian Society and the *New Statesman* periodical. After visiting the Soviet Union, they published a book in 1935 hailing it as a new civilization, a view that was widely welcomed in left-wing circles. The left also looked to the Soviet Union as a bastion against Hitler and the evils of Fascism. Even as hard-headed a man as Denis Healey, who in the 1960s and 1970s became a notably tough-minded Labour Minister of Defence and Chancellor of the Exchequer, was sufficiently carried

---

* While in University College Hospital, London, he married Sonia Brownell in October 1949, three months before his death.

away by these attitudes to become a member of the Communist Party. *Homage to Catalonia* brought Orwell into direct conflict with them.

As with most civil wars the politics that lay behind the war in Spain were extremely complicated, with numerous groups reflecting different interests and opinions struggling against each other in what was then a very backward society. But in Britain and other democracies it was seen among the intelligentsia and in left-wing circles as a definitive struggle between good and evil – a war, in the words of the historian of ideas Noel Annan, in which 'justice was solely on one side, perhaps the only such war known in history'.[8] The elected left-wing republican government represented good, the right-wing rebels seeking to overthrow it, led by General Franco and backed by Hitler and Mussolini, represented evil. To Orwell, when he and his wife arrived in Barcelona in December 1936, 'here at last, apparently, was democracy standing up to Fascism' after Hitler's accession to power in Germany, Japan's invasion of Manchuria and Italy's invasion of Abyssinia. He was one of thousands of volunteers from this country and across Europe and the United States who flocked to fight for the republic.

He was entranced by what he found. 'Everyone called everyone else Comrade' and 'waiters and shop-walkers looked you in the face and treated you as an equal'. Practically everyone wore rough working-class clothes and it looked as if the wealthy classes had either fled or turned themselves into proletarians. A revolution appeared to be in full swing and 'I did not realize that there were serious differences' between the plethora of political parties and trade unions 'with their tiresome names'. His credentials had been issued in London by the far-left Independent Labour Party so, as a matter of course, he joined the militia of the Spanish party to which it was affiliated, known by its initials as POUM.*

* Partido Obrero de Unificación Marxista.

His socialist idyll continued when he was sent to the front. 'Everyone from general to private drew the same pay, ate the same food, wore the same clothes and mingled on terms of complete equality.' The cold, the dirt, the lice and the shortage of cigarettes were hard to bear. But he enjoyed the comradeship and political discussions with men of different nationalities and backgrounds and felt he was experiencing what the first stages of a socialist society would be like. Fortunately, there was very little actual fighting and this unconventional form of military organization was not put to the test.

His problems began when he returned to Barcelona, where his wife had been waiting for him, to find that class distinctions had reappeared. From the start of the war the government of the republic had relied on the Soviet Union for arms. While Orwell was away at the front the Spanish Communist Party, manipulated by Soviet agents, had taken control. Its priority was winning the war rather than promoting revolution. In order to gain the support of the wealthier classes and those elements of the regular army that had not opted for Franco, it was clamping down on the more extreme parties and their militias. Foreign volunteers and men Orwell had served with at the front had been thrown into jail and he too was in danger of being arrested.

Although deeply disillusioned, he still felt nothing could be worse than a Fascist victory and that he must fight on. Accordingly, he returned to the front line where he was wounded and briefly hospitalized. On his release, with the Communist purge intensifying, he and his wife went on the run until, after various adventures, they reached France. His first action was 'to rush to the tobacco-kiosk and buy as many cigars and cigarettes as I could stuff into my pockets. Then we all went to the buffet and had a cup of tea', a suitably British ending to a foreign adventure. A short time later both Orwell and his wife were indicted in absentia under their real names of Eric and Eileen Blair at a court in Valencia for being Trotskyite rebels.

His reports were not well received when he returned to England. Most of the press favoured Franco. Those on the left were solidly behind the republican government and its Soviet backers. Far from being seen as the villains of the piece, the Communists were regarded by the left as essential to the government's success in the war while POUM and other dissident parties and their militias were seen as troublemakers.

Orwell's articles were rejected by the *New Statesman*, the flagship periodical of the left, and he had to settle for the lesser *New English Weekly*. His regular publisher, Victor Gollancz, turned down the manuscript of *Homage to Catalonia* sight unseen because he had been a member of POUM. Fredric Warburg, who had recently established Secker & Warburg, took it on, but their high hopes for it were disappointed when it sold only seven hundred copies. By contrast a Penguin Special taking a straightforward pro-government line by the colourful Duchess of Atholl sold one hundred thousand copies in a week.

The publication of *Animal Farm* turned out to be even more fraught. Orwell wrote it between November 1943 and February 1944, before the Allied invasion of France and at a time when the Soviet army was at last pushing back the German invader. The mood of the nation was epitomized when, as Orwell was starting to write, Churchill presented Stalin with a bejewelled sword inscribed by King George VI, as a token of homage from the British people to the heroic Soviet defenders of Stalingrad during the siege of that city a few months earlier. There could not have been a worse moment to embark on a bitter satire of the Russian revolution in general and of Stalin in particular.

Gollancz again rejected the manuscript, as did Faber and Collins. Jonathan Cape decided to take it, but were persuaded to change their minds by an official from the Ministry of Information, the body charged with wartime propaganda, who later turned out to be a Soviet spy. For a while Orwell toyed with the idea of publishing it himself as a pamphlet with money borrowed from the proprietor of the *Observer*,

David Astor. Finally, Warburg again came to the rescue and the book was published in August 1945. The war in Europe had ended in May and attitudes towards the Soviet Union were no longer the same as eighteen months before. Not just commercially, but critically too, the book was an immediate success, with established authors as diverse as E. M. Forster and Evelyn Waugh writing congratulatory letters.[9]

Animal Farm is only ninety-three pages long and subtitled *A Fairy Story* in British editions, although not in the American and most others. It tells the story of how a farm is taken over by the animals, who expel the farmer and his workers and run it themselves, led by the pigs. They are inspired by a dream recounted by an old boar shortly before his death of how the farm could be run for the benefit of the animals rather than the humans. The terms in which he does so could perhaps have been inspired by the chapter entitled 'The Great Money Trick' in Robert Tressall's *The Ragged-Trousered Philanthropists*, which I cover in an earlier essay.

At first all goes well in an atmosphere that recalls Orwell's early days in Spain. But over time the pigs tighten their grip and the farm becomes a dictatorship led by a brutal tyrant in the shape of a boar called Napoleon. The other animals end up worse off than they were before the revolution though persuaded by his regime's lies and false statistics that their lives are much better. The pigs, meanwhile, have taken over all the privileges previously enjoyed by the farmer and, after teaching themselves to walk on two legs, become indistinguishable from humans. At the end of the book they invite the neighbouring farmers to a party in the farmhouse where they carouse together while the other animals peer through the windows unable to distinguish pigs from humans.*

The story of *Animal Farm* tracks that of the Russian revolution up to 1945. Another boar represents Trotsky, the rival Stalin had driven

* Ironically, in the Soviet Union in the 1930s Stalin had prosperous farmers portrayed as pigs on propaganda posters when preparing the way for them to be expropriated and persecuted.

into exile. There are purges and show trials as Napoleon establishes his power like those Stalin held in the 1930s. Many who were previously heroes are discarded, history is rewritten and the ideals of the revolution are trampled on. The 1939 alliance between Stalin and Hitler, known as the Ribbentrop–Molotov pact, is reproduced in a deal between Napoleon and a neighbouring farmer. It is followed by that farmer's double-cross and an attack on Animal Farm that recalls Hitler's subsequent invasion of Russia.

All would have been instantly recognizable to contemporary readers as would Napoleon's resemblance to Stalin. Orwell intended the book to be read as an attack on Stalin both personally and for the way in which he had betrayed the principles of the revolution that had brought the Communists to power in 1917. It was the revenge of a democratic socialist against the abuse of power in the name of socialist principles. He also intended it to be seen as a satire on all revolutions based on principle that end up as simply a change from one set of power-hungry masters to another. The satire is bitter, but the language throughout is couched in a gentle and ironic tone appropriate to a fairy story about animals.

Nineteen Eighty-Four is altogether different. In a report to his staff, Frederic Warburg described it as 'amongst the most terrifying books I have ever read'. He thought it was a 'great book, but I pray I may be spared from reading another like it for years to come'.[10] Later he told friends that some of the booksellers who had received advance copies had been so frightened that they were unable to sleep.[11] It remains a terrifying book to this day, but its impact would have been much greater in 1949 than in more recent decades. It is in many ways a compendium of the nightmares of that period to the point where some might almost have wondered whether they were reading faction rather than fiction.

Set in 1984, the story is about Winston Smith, who works at the Ministry of Truth in London, the capital of a province of Oceania, a state basically comprising the English-speaking countries and one of the three great powers into which the world is divided. They are in a permanent state of low-level war as a result of which rocket bombs periodically fall on residential areas, the necessities of life are rationed and constant propaganda exhorts the citizens to hate the enemy – siege conditions that the ruling party wishes to prolong as they help it to maintain its iron grip on society. Presided over by Big Brother, the Party's sole purpose is power for its own sake, which requires the total subordination of the human spirit and the obliteration of independent thought or action among its members.

Among its most useful instruments are two-way television screens installed in every room of every building that can both broadcast propaganda and enable the Thought Police to keep whoever they wish under surveillance at any time. Party members, like Smith, know that they can never know when they are being watched. Another is the constant rewriting of the past, both short and long term, to ensure that it complies with current orthodoxy. Smith's job at the Ministry is devoted to falsifying back numbers of *The Times* and air-brushing from history those who have fallen out of favour with the party.

Because of his work he knows that, contrary to what the Party claims, it has not always been in charge and that reality, history and facts are all subject to change and revision whenever the Party deems that to be necessary. Unfortunately for him, he is also still able to think for himself and to act independently. He begins to ask old people about the past, to recall his own childhood in the days before the Party was in full control and to look out for old objects no longer in use. He then commits the heinous crime of falling in love and having enjoyable sex with a woman, two activities forbidden because they create a world of their own outside the Party's control, sex being permitted only for the purposes of joyless reproduction. They are arrested and subjected to interrogation and torture. Smith betrays the woman and has the will to think for himself beaten out of him. The Party demands that regardless of any evidence to the contrary its members must believe – not passively accept but believe – whatever they are told to believe.

In 1949 much of this would have reflected the lives and fears of contemporary readers. Post-war London was still shabby and unkempt with rows of bombed-out houses, as described in Orwell's text. Food, clothing and fuel were still tightly rationed. Mysterious shortages of everyday items, such as the razor blades that Smith hoards, were a common occurrence. The disgusting meals in the Ministry canteen are only a few degrees more unpleasant than the institutional food of the late 1940s. Rocket bombs raining death and destruction from the skies were a recent memory and the unremitting wartime propaganda described in the book is a greatly exaggerated version of what they would have become used to during the war.

To the generation who had lived through the two world wars and was becoming accustomed to a Cold War that might at any time become hot, the idea of a perpetual war would not have seemed incredible. Nor would the concept of a world divided between three superpowers. If Britain had been defeated in 1940 and Germany had gone on to defeat the Soviet Union, Eurasia and Africa would in practice have been divided between German and Japanese spheres of influence with the United States left in control of the two American continents. That, of course, didn't happen, but when Churchill, Roosevelt and Stalin met in Tehran in 1943 Orwell felt that they were parcelling up the world into spheres of influence that would lead to all kinds of future trouble.

The Party's subordination of the human spirit and insistence on pain of death on absolute conformity to its wishes was not so very far removed from what had been the case in Nazi Germany and continued to be so in Communist Russia. If Germany had occupied Britain people believed that a regime backed up by executions and torture would have been imposed and they feared that the same would apply if the Cold

War should turn hot and the West be defeated. It was not as surprising as it might now seem that nervous booksellers should have been kept awake at night after reading *Nineteen Eighty-Four*.

Because of that title it is often supposed that Orwell was endeavouring to forecast the future. This was not his intention. The book is a satire on totalitarian and authoritarian forms of government and a warning of the horrors they could lead to. As with *Animal Farm* its model is Stalin's Soviet Union and the description of Big Brother's moustache in his ubiquitous portraits drives home the point. In the United States right-wing circles, ignoring his statement of belief in 'Why I Write', mistakenly believed Orwell to be anti-socialist as well as anti-Communist, which led some socialists to brand him a traitor. Later, in the 1950s, after Stalin's crimes had been fully exposed, he was posthumously attacked by some ex-Communists for being 'prematurely correct',* an accusation that might well have given him sardonic pleasure.

The irony is that while Orwell was writing *Nineteen Eighty-Four* democratic socialism was enjoying an apotheosis in Britain. At home, while post-war conditions remained hard and the cities scarred by bomb damage, the Labour government, elected to power in 1945, was introducing the National Health Service and the welfare state that over time would transform the lives of the great mass of the people. Abroad, in conjunction with the United States, it led the opposition to the Soviet Union and the spread of Communism while beginning the dismantlement of the empire that Orwell had always wanted.

---

* Crick, *Oxford Dictionary of National Biography*.

Acknowledgements

I have been helped and encouraged in many ways by good friends during the years it has taken me to write this book. In particular I thank Chas Foulds for putting the idea into my head in the first place and Kenneth Baker, John Eidinow, Peter Hennessy, Giles Radice and Robert Skidelsky for help in enabling me to overcome self-doubt as I pursued my project and in other ways as well. I am also grateful to John Bond, George Edgeller, Richard Collins and all at whitefox for bringing it to fruition and to Ruth Killick for her work in publicising it.

My two sons, James and Gus, have provided invaluable technical assistance as well as encouragement. Above all I thank my wife, Julia. We met and married while I was writing my first book in the 1960s. Since then she has been my constant support in everything I have ever done and my love and gratitude know no bounds.

Notes

Introduction

1 L. P. Hartley, *The Go-Between*, Hamish Hamilton, 1953, p. 9.

Debunking Victorianism

1 Introduction to the Penguin Classics edition of *The Way of All Flesh*, reprinted 1986, p. 7.

2 Leonard Woolf, *Sowing: An Autobiography of the Years 1880 to 1904*, Hogarth Press, 1960, p. 166.

3 Samuel Butler, *Samuel Butler: Victorian Against the Grain: A Critical Overview*, ed. James G. Paradis, University of Toronto Press, 2007, p. 363.

4 Samuel Butler, *The Way of All Flesh*. Essay by Brooke Allen, *Barnes & Noble Review*, 7 January 2008.

5 James Southall Wilson, 'Time and Virginia Woolf', *VQR*, Spring 1942, quoting an article from *The Nation and the Athenaeum*, December 1928.

6 BBC Home Service Talks for Schools, 15 June 1945. Reprinted in *The Complete Works of George Orwell*, Vol. 17, *I Belong to the Left: 1945*, ed. Peter Davison, Secker & Warburg, 1998, p. 186.

7 *The New Republic*, 21 September 1932.

8 Cyril Connolly, *Enemies of Promise*, George Routledge & Sons, 1938.

9 Michael Holroyd, *Lytton Strachey: A Critical Biography*, Vol. 2, *The Years of Achievement*, Heinemann, 1968, p. 264.

10 Ibid., p. 250.

11 The Romanes Lecture, June 1918, entitled 'Some Aspects of the Victorian Age'.

12 For an account of the event as well as a more objective portrait of Manning see Robert Gray, *Cardinal Manning: A Biography*, Weidenfeld & Nicolson, 1985.

War 1 – Warnings and Reality

1 Published for Queen Victoria's Diamond Jubilee, it first appeared in *The Times*, 17 July 1897.

2 Official Report, House of Commons, 18 February 1901: col 407.

3 Jim Ring, *Erskine Childers*, John Murray, 1996, p. 153.

4 Ibid., p. 289.

5 Lady Diana Cooper, *Darling Monster: The Letters of Lady Diana Cooper to Her Son John Julius Norwich, 1939–1952*, Chatto & Windus, 2013, p. 2.

6 Alan Judd and David Crane, *First World War Poets*, National Portrait Gallery Publications, 1997.

7 Ronald Blythe, *Akenfield: Portrait of an English Village*, Allen Lane The Penguin Press, 1969, p. 38.
8 John Bew, *Citizen Clem: A Biography of Attlee*, riverrun, 2017, p. 78.

War 2 – Warnings and Reality

1 Richard Overy, *The Morbid Age: Britain Between the Wars*, Allen Lane, 2009, p. 221.
2 Official Report, House of Commons, 10 November 1932.
3 Rodric Braithwaite, *Armageddon and Paranoia*, Profile Books, 2017, p. 43.
4 Roy Jenkins, *Churchill: A Biography*, Macmillan, 2001, p. 429.
5 William Manchester, *The Last Lion, Winston Spencer Churchill*, Vol. 1, Little, Brown & Co., 1983, p. 768.
6 John W. Wheeler Bennett, *King George VI: His Life and Reign*, Macmillan, 1958, p. 460.
7 Marie Vassiltchikov, *Berlin Diaries, 1940–1945*, Alfred A. Knopf, 1987.
8 Geoffrey Wansell, *Terence Rattigan: A Biography*, Fourth Estate, 1995, p. 126.
9 Ibid., p. 126.

Cold War

1 Peter Hennessy, *Having It So Good*, Allen Lane, 2006, p. 320.
2 Richard Luce, *Ringing the Changes*, Michael Russell, 2007, p. 26. In a remarkably varied and successful career he has also been a government minister and Vice-Chancellor of the University of Buckingham. We met at the Eaton Hall Officer Cadet School in 1956 while doing our National Service and have been friends ever since.
3 Elizabeth Jenkins, *The View from Downshire Hill*, Michael Russell, 2004, p. 96.
4 Luce, *Ringing the Changes*, p. 33.
5 For further information on this and other matters relating to conscription, see Richard Vinen, *National Service, Conscription in Britain, 1945–63*, Allen Lane, 2014.

Imperialist Complexities

1 Maya Jasanoff, *The Dawn Watch: Joseph Conrad in a Global World*, William Collins, 2017, p. 4.
2 Barack Obama, *Dreams from My Father*, Canongate, 2008, p. 103. In 2014, President Obama visited a Washington bookstore with his family to publicize his support for independent retailers. Among the books he purchased was *Heart of Darkness*, MailOnline, 30 November 2014.
3 Jan Karski, *Story of a Secret State*, Hodder & Stoughton, 1945, pp. 277–94.
4 David Gilmour, *The Ruling Caste: Imperial Lives in the Victorian Raj*, John Murray, 2005, p. xiii; Ian Kershaw, *Hitler 1936–45: Nemesis*, Allen Lane The Penguin Press, 2000, p. 401.

5 Leonard Woolf, *Growing: An Autobiography of the Years 1904–1911*, Hogarth Press, 1961, p. 174.
6 George Orwell, *Burmese Days*, Victor Gollancz, 1935, p. 19.
7 Selina Hastings, *The Secret Lives of Somerset Maugham*, John Murray, 2009, p. 280.
8 Ibid., p. 276.
9 *The Diary of Virginia Woolf*, Vol. IV, *1931–1935*, Hogarth Press, 1982, p. 210.
10 Elizabeth Bowen, *Bowen's Court & Seven Winters*, with an introduction by Hermione Lee, Vintage, 1999, p. 459.
11 *The Macmillan Diaries: Prime Minister and After, 1957–66*, ed. and with an introduction by Peter Catterall, Macmillan, 2011, p. 356.

Provincial Life

1 *Guardian*, 3 February 2011.
2 '9 novels that changed the world' by Rosamond Hutt, World Economic Forum, 3 March 2016. The others are: *Uncle Tom's Cabin* by Harriet Beecher Stowe, *The Jungle* by Upton Sinclair, *All Quiet on the Western Front* by Erich Maria Remarque, *Things Fall Apart* by Chinua Achebe, *The Grapes of Wrath* by John Steinbeck, *Nineteen Eighty-Four* by George Orwell, *To Kill a Mockingbird* by Harper Lee and *Beloved* by Toni Morrison.

Early Feminism

1 Introduction to the single-volume edition of *A Room of One's Own* and *Three Guineas*, Vintage, 2001, p. VII.
2 Hermione Lee, *Virginia Woolf*, Chatto & Windus, 1996, p. 148.
3 Diana Athill, *Stet: An Editor's Life*, Granta Books, 2000, p. 57.
4 *The Diary of Virginia Woolf*, Vol. IV, *1931–1935*, ed. Anne Olivier Bell, Hogarth Press, 1982, p. 147.
5 Anthony Burgess, *Ninety-Nine Novels: The Best in English Since 1939 – A Personal Choice*, Allison & Busby, 1984, p. 86.
6 Motoko Rich and Sarah Lyall, 'Nobel to Lessing, Incisive Voice of Women's Fate', *New York Times*, 12 October 2007.
7 Michiko Kakutani, 'President Obama on What Books Mean to Him', *New York Times*, 16 January 2017.
8 Preface to the 1972 edition of *The Golden Notebook*, published by Fourth Estate, p. 7.
9 Ibid., p. 10.
10 Doris Lessing, *Walking in the Shade: Volume Two of My Autobiography, 1949–1962*, HarperCollins, 1997, p. 305.
11 Ibid., p. 308.
12 1972 preface to *The Golden Notebook*, p. 8.
13 Ibid., p. 9.

14 Lessing, *Walking in the Shade*, p. 309.
15 'Doris Lessing's Golden Notebook, 50 years on', *Guardian*, 6 April 2012.

Sex and Relationships

1 June Rose, *Marie Stopes and the Sexual Revolution*, Faber & Faber, 1992, p. 116.
2 Denis Healey, *The Time of My Life*, Michael Joseph, 1989, p. 6.
3 Richard Ellman, *Oscar Wilde*, Hamish Hamilton, 1987, p. 435.
4 Ibid.
5 Jago Morrison and Susan Watkin, *Scandalous Fictions: The Twentieth-Century Novel in the Public Sphere*, Palgrave Macmillan, 2007, p. 63.
6 Report of the Committee on Homosexual Offences and Prostitution chaired by Sir John Wolfenden, Cmnd 247, Her Majesty's Stationery Office, 1957. The offences are listed under three headings: Buggery, Indecent Assault and Gross Indecency, of which the last two covered a range of activities.
7 Michael Howard, *Captain Professor*, Continuum, 2006, p. 128.
8 Introduction by David Leavitt to the Penguin Classics 2005 edition of *Maurice*.
9 Diana Souhami, *The Trials of Radclyffe Hall*, Weidenfeld & Nicolson, 1998, p. 151.
10 Ibid., p. 167.
11 *Sunday Express*, 19 August 1928.

Race and Immigration

1 Geoffrey Field, *The Evangelist of Race: The Germanic Vision of Houston Stewart Chamberlain*, Columbia University Press, 1981.
2 John C. G. Rohl, *The Kaiser and his Court*, Cambridge University Press, 1994, p. 205.
3 *Fabian News*, June 1911.
4 *Spectator*, 25 February 1911.
5 Shlomo Avineri, *Herzl*, Weidenfeld & Nicolson, 2013.
6 Anthony Julius, *Trials of the Diaspora*, Oxford University Press, 2010, p. 237.
7 Noel Annan, *Our Age: Portrait of a Generation*, Weidenfeld & Nicolson, 1990, pp. 207, 208.
8 Review of Susie Harris, *Nikolaus Pevsner: The Life*, *Financial Times*, 10 August 2011.
9 Daniel Snowman, *The Hitler Emigres*, Pimlico, 2003, p. 104.
10 Ari Shavit, *My Promised Land*, Scribe, 2014, p. 347.
11 Susie Harris, *Nikolaus Pevsner: The Life*, Chatto & Windus, 2011, p. 40.
12 James Stourton, *Kenneth Clark: Life, Art and Civilisation*, William Collins, 2016, p. 47.
13 *Our Hidden Lives: The Everyday Diaries of a Forgotten Britain*, ed. Simon Garfield, Ebury Press, 2004, p. 323.
14 Richard Cavendish, 'Arrival of SS *Empire Windrush*', *History Today*, Vol. 48, 6 June 1998.

15 Peter Hennessy, *Having It So Good*, Penguin Books, 2007, p. 223.
16 Robin Bruce and Paul Field, *Darcus Howe: A Political Biography*, Bloomsbury, 2014, p. 95.
17 Ibid., p. 96.
18 Soliciting in the street became illegal as a result of the Street Offences Act, 1959. Details of the kind of thing that went on in Hyde Park may be found in Julia Laite, *Common Prostitutes and Ordinary Citizens*, Palgrave Macmillan, 2012, chapter 10, p. 171.
19 Hennessy, *Having It So Good*, p. 498.
20 Tony Benn, *Years of Hope: Diaries, Letters and Papers 1940–62*, ed. Ruth Winstone, Hutchinson, 1996, p. 286.

Diverse Perspectives

1 Ross McKibbin, 'Politics and the Medical hero: A. J. Cronin's *The Citadel*', *English Historical Review*, Vol. 123, No. 502, June 2008.
2 Sally Peters, 'Bernard Shaw's dilemma: marked by mortality', *International Journal of Epidemiology*, Vol. 32, Issue 6, 1 December 2003.
3 *To the Bitter End: The Diaries of Victor Klemperer, 1942–45*, abridged and translated by Martin Chalmers, Weidenfeld & Nicolson, 1999, p. 294.
4 Sheridan Morley, *A Talent to Amuse*, Heinemann, 1969, p. 78.
5 'The Talk of the Town', *New Yorker*, 26 September 1925.
6 Ernest Hemingway, *A Moveable Feast*, Jonathan Cape, 1964, p. 158.
7 Carlos Baker, 'The Sun Rose Differently', *New York Times*, 18 March 1979.
8 Anthony Powell, *Messengers of Day*, Heinemann, 1978, p. 2.
9 Anthony Powell, *A Question of Upbringing*, Heinemann, 1951, p. 203.
10 Alec Waugh, *My Brother Evelyn and Other Profiles*, Cassell & Co., 1967, pp. 257, 258.
11 Cecil Beaton, *The Glass of Fashion*, Weidenfeld & Nicolson, 1954, p. 153.
12 Morley, *A Talent to Amuse*, p. 77.
13 Ibid., p. 81.
14 Eric Maschwitz, *No Chip on My Shoulder*, Herbert Jenkins, 1957, p. 36.
15 Alec Waugh, *My Brother Evelyn and Other Profiles*, pp. 255, 256.
16 E. M. Forster, *Abinger Harvest*, Edward Arnold, 1936, p. 3.
17 Roald Dahl, *Boy: Tales of Childhood*, Puffin Books, 2008 edition, p. 158.
18 Alec Waugh, *The Loom of Youth*, Grant Richards, 1917. It became a bestseller but resulted in his expulsion from the Old Shirburnian Society. He went on to become a successful novelist though overshadowed by his younger brother, Evelyn.
19 Simon Leys, *The Hall of Uselessness*, New York Review of Books, 2013, p. 192.
20 W. F. Deedes, *At War with Waugh*, Macmillan, 2003. Deedes was a Cabinet minister in the governments of Harold Macmillan and Sir Alec Douglas-Home in the early 1960s and editor of the *Daily Telegraph* from 1974 to 1985.

21 Selina Hastings, *Evelyn Waugh: A Biography*, Sinclair-Stevenson, 1994, p. 492.
22 For an account of Waugh's drinking and its effects on his character see Philip Eade, *Evelyn Waugh: A Life Revisited*, Weidenfeld & Nicolson, 2016.
23 *The Diaries of Evelyn Waugh*, ed. Michael Davie, Weidenfeld & Nicolson, 1976.
24 Philip Snow, *Stranger and Brother: A Portrait of C. P. Snow*, Macmillan, 1982, p. 117.
25 'A new means of destruction', editorial by C. P. Snow in *Discovery*, September 1939. Reproduced in C. P. Snow, *The Physicists*, Macmillan, 1981, pp. 176, 177.
26 Charles Ritchie, *The Siren Years: Undiplomatic Diaries*, Macmillan, 1974, p. 101.
27 *Spectator*, 22 September 1955.
28 'Two Cultures? The Significance of C. P. Snow by F. R. Leavis', Richmond Lecture, 1962. Published, with an essay on Sir Charles Snow's Rede Lecture, by Michael Yudkin, Chatto & Windus, 1962.
29 Anthony Burgess, *Ninety-Nine Novels: The Best in English Since 1939*, Allison & Busby, 1984, p. 31.
30 *New York Review of Books*, 11 May 2017.
31 See, for instance, Stephen Pinker, *Enlightenment Now: The Case for Reason, Science, Humanism and Progress*, Viking, 2018.
32 Roger Williams, *Lunch with Elizabeth David*, Abacus, 2000.
33 Artemis Cooper, *Writing at the Kitchen Table*, Michael Joseph, 1999, p. 67.
34 Ibid., p. 139.
35 *New York Times*, 28 May 1992.

Conclusion

1 Robert Skidelsky, *John Maynard Keynes*, Vol. 2, *The Economist as Saviour, 1920–1937*, Macmillan, 1992.
2 Robert Skidelsky, *John Maynard Keynes*, Vol. 1, *Hopes Betrayed, 1883–1920*, Macmillan, 1983, p. 384.
3 Skidelsky, *John Maynard Keynes*, Vol. 2, pp. 520, 521.
4 Giuseppe Tomasi di Lampedusa, *The Leopard*, translated from the Italian by Archibald Colquhoun, Collins Harvill, 1960.
5 Skidelsky, *John Maynard Keynes*, Vol. 2, p. 573.
6 Ibid.
7 D. J. Taylor, *Orwell*, Chatto & Windus, 2003, p. 328.
8 Noel Annan, *Our Age: Portrait of a Generation*, Weidenfeld & Nicolson, 1990.
9 Taylor, *Orwell*, p. 356.
10 Fredric Warburg's Report on *Nineteen Eighty-Four*, typewritten on 13 December 1948. Published in *The Annotated Edition of Nineteen Eighty-Four*, Penguin Books, 2013.
11 Taylor, *Orwell*, p. 402.

Index

BRETT

BRETT

From Bloomsbury to New Mexico

A Biography

SEAN HIGNETT

HODDER AND STOUGHTON
LONDON SYDNEY AUCKLAND TORONTO

British Library Cataloguing in Publication Data

Hignett, Sean
Brett
1. Brett, Dorothy
I. Title
759.2 ND497.B/

ISBN 0-340-22973-X

 Printed in Great Britain for Hodder and Stoughton Limited, Mill Road, Dunton Green, Sevenoaks, Kent by St Edmundsbury Press, Bury St Edmunds, Suffolk. Photoset by Rowland Phototypesetting Limited, Bury St Edmunds, Suffolk. Hodder and Stoughton Editorial Office: 47 Bedford Square, London WC1B 3DP.

Contents

Chapter headings are intended only as a rough guide to time, place or persons.

Illustrations

John Manchester
neighbour of Brett's

1 John Manchester
2 The Tate Gallery, London
3 Mrs Julian Vinogradoff
4 Radio Times
5 Harwood Foundation, University of New Mexico
6 Mme M. Lacroix
7 The author
8 Humanities Research Centre, University of Texas.

1

1883–1910: Orchard Lea

In 1961 a team from CBS Television went to Taos, New Mexico, to make a programme on D. H. Lawrence. Dorothy Brett was at first reluctant to have any part of it, particularly when she heard that she was to be interviewed with the Lawrence scholar Harry T. Moore. Brett* had always taken exception to Moore's treatment of her in his biography of Lawrence, *The Priest of Love.*[1] But eventually she agreed to cooperate and was, in the end, pleased with the outcome. At a reception afterwards she was congratulated by one of her Taos friends. "Everyone says you were magnificent." "I should like," said Brett flatly, "to rub my father's nose in it."

Dorothy Brett's father was Reginald Baliol Brett, 2nd Viscount Esher, who had died thirty-one years earlier in 1930, the same year as D. H. Lawrence. Lawrence, inevitably and inexorably, as the Ph.D. industry grew on American campuses, remained with Dorothy Brett for the rest of her life. A constant stream of scholars, writers and Ph.D. students visited Taos to interview her, but hundreds of others also trekked across the sage-blown desert of northern New Mexico to the small adobe house by the flashing yellow light marking the crossroads that lead to Taos Ski Valley, seeking some contact with the past, some kind of touchstone, some belief that the glory that had been reflected on Dorothy Brett would be transferred to them: to have been in the same room as someone who was in the same room as D. H. Lawrence. A thin contact with immortality. Brett painted Lawrence, wrote about him, and occasionally quoted him, the quotation usually managing to reflect well upon herself and ill upon Frieda Lawrence. And yet until the end of her life Brett kept pet dogs called after her father, first Baliol, and later more than one mongrel named Reggie. She signed her letters "Brett and Little Reggie" and distinguished academics, trying to enter into the spirit of things, wrote back to Brett – and Little Reggie. And, to the end of her life, Brett had recurrent nightmares, bad dreams, about her father.

* After she entered the Slade in 1910, Dorothy Brett used only her surname.

Rather more than was readily apparent of Brett's life, particularly in later years, was tied into a personal mysticism, into myth and fantasy, even as to her family origins, so one ought perhaps to start a little further back than her father, Reginald Brett. Dorothy Brett's grandfather, the first Baron and Viscount, William Baliol Brett, was Solicitor General in the Conservative government of 1868, and became Lord Justice in 1876. He was made a Baron by Lord Salisbury in 1885, two years after the birth of his grand-daughter, Dorothy Eugenie Brett, became subsequently Master of the Rolls and a Privy Counsellor and was created a Viscount by Salisbury in 1897, two years before his death in 1899. In a footnote *Debrett* says of William Brett "on the bench, a sound and competent lawyer but uniformly lacked grace and sometimes courtesy". Elsewhere he is "distinguished for his confidence in the manly good sense of juries and some judgements that were considered reactionary".[2]

Dorothy Brett's grandmother, Eugenie, from whom she took her middle name, had a romanticised, rather more Bohemian background. Family myth – in which Dorothy strongly believed – held Eugenie to be a foundling on the field of battle after Waterloo. In her unpublished autobiography Brett wrote: "A prodigious hunt took place for the mother and eventually she was found, a very beautiful woman but of somewhat strange habits."

What the strange habits were, other than hanging around an otherwise undistinguished Flemish village during a ferocious battle, Dorothy Brett does not relate, but she became convinced that this camp follower was a mistress of Napoleon and that the Emperor himself may have been her great-grandfather. Despite the Napoleonic mementoes gathered by Reginald, this is almost certainly a family fancy. Eugenie is more authentically provided with a conventional birth in Lyons, as daughter of Louis Meyer or Mayer, an Alsatian. Meyer's wife later married Colonel Gurwood, aide-de-camp to the Duke of Wellington. Eugenie therefore became Gurwood's step-daughter and was brought up in literary and artistic circles in Paris. In London, she gravitated naturally to the salon of Countess Blessington, a milieu shunned by respectable society because of the disrepute of Lady Blessington's lover, Count D'Orsay, but which had become a centre for émigré writers and artists. D'Orsay himself drew Eugenie Meyer for Heath's *Book of Beauty*, an annual of Victorian times. Dorothy Brett saw her grandmother in later life as "a true martinet. She had black dyed hair, a partial wig, slightly askew. She would ask us all kinds of questions in French and expect us to answer back which we were terrified to do." Eugenie Brett was advised not to curtsey to Queen Victoria because she was so old she might not manage to rise again.

"She went [to court] dressed in a long train, feathers in her hair, curtsied and then down she went with a flop and could not get up."

Dorothy Brett's father, Reginald, the 2nd Viscount Esher, was born to William and Eugenie Brett in 1852. He was educated at Eton where he came strongly under the influence of William Johnson, a controversial figure and an expert on military history. Johnson formed very close and emotional relationships with his favourites, and resigned from Eton under something of a cloud in 1872, thereafter going entirely under the name William Cory. On Cory's death Esher published some of his letters from his former tutor in a memoir, *Cloud Capp'd Towers.*

From Eton, Reginald Brett proceeded to Trinity, Cambridge, where he was given rooms that were under the patronage of William Harcourt, then Professor of International Law and a leading Liberal. Reginald had become a close friend of Harcourt's son, Lewis (Loulou) Harcourt, at Eton, a friendship that was to have a deep and bitter effect upon Dorothy Brett as a young woman.

In 1879, at the age of twenty-seven, Reginald Brett married Eleanor van de Weyer, the seventeen-year-old daughter of Sylvain van de Weyer, the Belgian Ambassador to the court of St. James. Van de Weyer had been one of the founders of the new Belgian nation and was a protégé and collaborator of the *éminence grise* behind the Belgian throne, Baron Christian Stockmar. Stockmar was rumoured to have arranged the marriage of Victoria and Albert and, arriving in England as an emissary from Leopold of Belgium shortly before Victoria succeeded to the throne, rapidly became political mentor to the young Queen and her Prince Consort. Through his association with Stockmar, Van de Weyer too became a close friend of the royal family and Reginald Brett's marriage to his daughter made Reginald in turn an unofficial but intimate member of the Queen's circle.

Reginald and Eleanor (Nellie) Brett had four children in rapid time: Oliver, born in 1881, after a first child had died at birth; Maurice ("Moll"), 1882; Dorothy Eugenie, 1883; and Sylvia (Syv), 1885. Oliver Brett, who succeeded his father in 1930 as 3rd Viscount Esher, became President of the British Drama League and a trustee of the National Theatre and died in 1963. The standard contract of Equity, the actors' union, was formulated by a committee headed by Oliver Brett and is still known in the business as the "Esher contract". Maurice Brett married Zena Dare, the actress who was to appear on the stage for more than half a century, from Edwardian times to *My Fair Lady*. Maurice died relatively young in 1934, four years after the death of his father to whom he was extraordinarily close, often to the exclusion of the other children. The daughters led rather more unconventional lives than the two boys, despite a childhood that extended well into their twenties and was restrictive and secluded even by Victorian standards. Sylvia married Vyner Brooke, the last White Raja of Sarawak, after a long courtship that was thoroughly disapproved of by the Brett family. Encouraged by J. M. Barrie and George Bernard Shaw, she became a writer, later publishing two autobiographies, *Sylvia of Sarawak* and *Queen of the Headhunters*, as well as a number of romantic novels.

At the time of Dorothy Brett's birth in November 1883, at the family's London and, at that time, only home, in Tilney Street, just off Park Lane, Reginald Brett was MP for Penryn and Falmouth. Rejecting the family's Conservative tradition, he had taken this seat for the Liberals in 1879 and held it until 1885 when, moving his candidature to Plymouth, he was defeated. In the meantime, he built a country house, Orchard Lea, close to the Van de Weyers' home, New Lodge, and within easy reach of Windsor Castle where Queen Victoria held court.*

Ostensibly, on his defeat in 1885, Reggie Brett retired from politics and moved his family life out of London to Orchard Lea where he bred racehorses. In fact, he remained unceasingly active behind the political scenes, close to Rosebery, whom he had known at Eton. In 1886 he was offered the editorship of the *Daily News* and in 1887 the editorship of the *New Review*, both of which he refused. Through his in-laws, Reggie Brett rapidly became a member of the Queen's private circle. Victoria visited Orchard Lea often and the Bretts were frequent guests at the Castle. The ground was being prepared for Reginald Brett to progress to what was to become his image in the popular mind, the *éminence grise* behind the thrones of Victoria, Edward VII and George V throughout the following two and a half decades.

For the daughters, particularly, childhood was a cloistered affair, comfortable compared to the conditions in which the majority of children grew up in those days, and yet harsh. Both Dorothy and Syv have recalled that their parents were almost strangers to them and that they might see their father, if he was at home and that was infrequently, only to say goodnight to him in his smoking room before dinner – the parents' dinner, of course, for the children had little need to leave the nursery. Dorothy tells an almost certainly apocryphal story of being wheeled in a double pram with Syv in Hyde Park by their nurse and, on crossing the path of their father who was promenading with a friend,

* After Victoria's death, it was Esher who, as Secretary of the Office of Works, managed the moving of the court from Windsor back to Buckingham Palace during the early years of Edward VII's reign.

being told to wave. Reggie Brett, Dorothy would have us believe, wondered to his friend who were those children waving to them. Predictably the friend is supposed to have replied, "Perhaps they are yours." The story, like many of Dorothy's, is probably not quite true but certainly sums up the flavour of the lives of Dorothy and Syv.

Reggie was nevertheless a powerful influence on his daughters. "Being a child of the brilliant Reginald," Sylvia later wrote, "was like being related to the *Encyclopaedia Britannica.* In my mother's heart there was no one greater than Reginald Baliol Brett, except God . . . Our parents were too preoccupied – he with affairs of state and she with her wifely adoration. So we quarrelled and fought . . . our way through the toddling age into the bewilderments of adolescence."[3]

Sylvia used her childhood memories as material for at least two novels. *Toys*, described as "an allegory of the rise and fall of woman", centres on two girls, Deborah and Susannah, orphans, significantly, and their relationship with Osmund, a draper's son, and Matthew, a gardener's son. The children's initials are those of the Brett children and much of the story is a fictionalising of Sylvia's view of the childhood and rivalries of herself and her sister. "Deborah" is everything "Susannah" would like to have been, self-possessed, extraordinarily pretty, slender, erect, with large brown eyes, cold in expression but with red lips soft and full and skin like pink fruit. Whether that is an accurate description of young Dorothy Brett is difficult to say. Dorothy herself never denied that she was a comely child, developing only after adolescence the prominent teeth and distinctly unprominent chin that so characterised her features later. She, in her turn, described Sylvia simply, uncompromisingly, and with all the deliberate understatement of the American expression, as "homely".

In another of Sylvia's novels, *The Darlingtons*, the girls are no longer orphaned, Susannah is now Susan and wildly jealous of the more attractive Henrietta. The book is set in White Orchard Manor, that is, Orchard Lea, and the descriptions are those of the Bretts' Windsor home. The details of childhood also tally closely with the events described in Sylvia's autobiographies and with Dorothy Brett's own memories. Papa is something of a philanderer, loitering in Hyde Park "to wind his watch". The centre of the novel is the rivalry between Susan and Henrietta for the hand of an eligible young man who is staying nearby, an episode that matches Vyner Brooke's courtship of Sylvia in the early years of the century.

Inevitably a good deal of the Brett children's lives were spent with the servants. "Butlers, footmen, and maids buzzed around like ornamental but somewhat inefficient flies. They always wore white cotton gloves and I could never make up my mind whether it was they who were supposed to contaminate us or we them."

Dorothy Brett's own recollections of early childhood depict, like Sylvia's, the servants as friends and her parents as strangers, but the relationship between child and servant, master and footman appears to have been far from simple and straightforward. At times the intricacies of mental and physical violence were of Laingian dimensions. Nanny, a particular bogy, was fond of the bottle and her response when discovered by the Brett children was to encourage them to tipple. When Eleanor Brett heard of this, surprisingly, she did not dismiss Nanny but simply prohibited her from offering drink to the children. If the children offended, Nanny might lock them in a dark cupboard or produce one of her two ornamental walking canes, each with a handle carved in the shape of a dog's head, one a spaniel, the other a greyhound. The spaniel was for everyday, run of the mill, beatings while the greyhound, sharper in the nose, was reserved for especially severe punishment. On one occasion Nanny used this stick to beat to death Oliver Brett's pet bullfinch. It was not surprising that, responding to such savagery, young Oliver should pursue Nanny around the kitchen with a carving knife. Despite all, Nanny was never dismissed. In the end she dismissed herself in a fit of pique when the children were sent off on a seaside holiday and Nanny was not sent with them. Nanny is enshrined in Syv's fiction, dog's head handled canes and all.

The butler, who was known as "Pussy", frequently managed to irritate Reggie Brett during dinner by prematurely pulling the bell-cord, linked by an intricate Victorian system of springs and wires with the kitchen. The bell was the signal for the next course to be served and this invariably arrived before the dinner guests had finished what was already on their plates. Pussy was perhaps attempting to hurry things along and shorten the inordinate length of his Victorian working day. Reggie Brett's solution was to cut the bell-rope almost through so that, when next pulled, it came away in poor Pussy's hand to the delighted guffaws of the well-primed company. Pussy left in a huff. Then there was the governess appointed to look after the education of Doll and Syv while the boys were away at boarding school. Governesses did not fit easily into the servant-master hierarchy of the Victorian family and the lady was allowed to eat with the family, the only time of the day when she came face to face with Reginald Brett. Unfortunately for the poor lady, her nose twitched during dinner and eventually Reggie could stand it no longer. He dismissed her and handed the girls' education into the sole charge of their mother, Eleanor.

Incidents such as this were remembered by Doll with little more than anecdotal interest, although it did cross her mind later to question the difference in condition between herself and the boot-boy, Alfie Peters, who hauled buckets of coal throughout the house to keep the numerous fireplaces replenished with fuel. Whether Doll noticed the difference in life-style at the time is another matter.

Memories of childhood are episodic and incidental and rarely have a narrative line. One can attach continuity only by pegging things to external events. Orchard Lea, the Bretts' country house was built in 1885 when Doll was under two years old and the children spent most of their time there rather than in Tilney Street. Both Doll and Syv recall Maurice as being particularly nasty to his sisters as a boy but this may well only reflect their jealousy of the very intimate relationship which "Moll" shared with his father. Oliver, despite his violent reaction to the death of his bullfinch, was an imaginative and creative child and invented a game all four played in the garden of Orchard Lea, the basis of which was that the children believed themselves to be invisible to everyone except each other. Later in life Doll attached a great deal of significance to a couple of slight encounters with American Indians during a visit to the circus and, at the age of four, to Buffalo Bill's Wild West Show at Earl's Court in 1887. She spoke and wrote frequently of these two occasions, seeing a mystic significance in the looks that passed between Chief Sitting Bull and the golden haired English upper-class child, an event she tied in to her later fascination with the American Indian and his ceremonies in her paintings. There is, though, a memory, unlikely to have been embroidered by the intervening years, that gives a hint of her later interest and again there may be some selection and exaggeration but at least it is clear which incidents Doll selected for such processes. It was a very simple thing – a Christmas tree at her grandfather's house was seen during Christmas dinner by Doll alone to be radiating a strange light. Dorothy Brett was not short of such visions as her years advanced, although even her most intimate friends were unaware of this side of her nature. And, quite simply, just as she remembered Sitting Bull from the age of four, this is a memory she singled out in her unpublished memoirs. It hardly matters whether it was real or imagined, then or later.

Another event we can locate precisely, from a rare reference to his daughters in Reggie Brett's journals, is dated November 21st, 1892, shortly after Dorothy Brett's ninth birthday. "Dorothy and Sylvia go to dancing lessons with Princess Beatrice's children at the Castle. The Queen sat all through their dance on Friday."[4]

The dancing lessons for the Battenberg children, of the family known nowadays as the Mountbattens, occurred weekly and were often supervised by the ageing Queen. The excursion to Windsor Castle was looked forward keenly to by the Brett sisters as, with Oliver and Maurice away at preparatory school, they rarely came into contact with other children. The lessons took place in the Red Drawing Room of the Castle and were taken by a Mrs. Wordsworth whom the children believed, simply because she was lame and short of temper, to have both a glass eye and a wooden leg. Queen Victoria appeared "unceremoniously with about as homely a touch as a lion arriving in our midst. Sometimes she was accompanied to our delight by the Duchess of Teck, an enormously fat old woman, completely round like a cottage loaf, no waistline, topped by a tiny head and no visible neck," Dorothy Brett recalled.

Despite the break the dancing lessons provided in the monotonous lives of Dorothy and Sylvia, little pleasure seems to have been attached to them. The lessons began and ended with a grand march past the seated Queen by the terrified children, a reluctant Prince Leopold being dragged around by the hobbling Mrs. Wordsworth. The Queen froze into "an icicle of disgust and outrage" as Mrs. Wordsworth limped up and shouted out the misdemeanours of Prince Alexander and Prince Leopold into her "frightful face". Then Prince Alexander would refuse to dance and stood pulling faces at the Queen who, in her turn, wagged her cane furiously at him until, bristling with anger, she would stalk out of the room. If this were accounted pleasure, then the lives of Doll and Sylvia must indeed have been lonely and empty.

During the dancing lessons, Doll became friendly with the two daughters of the librarian at the Castle.

> . . . I remarked on their bracelets which had dingle dangles hanging on them. The following week their mother, a dragon with a thin hard face like a disagreeable horse pulled me behind the Queen's sofa into a long window recess and said she did not like the way I made personal remarks about the girls, criticising their bracelets and clothes, that if I ever did it again, she would tell the Queen and the Queen would cut off my head. I screamed and screamed at the top of my voice. The Queen wanted to know whose child was screaming and why. At last I screamed myself into exhaustion, but that night my mother wheedled it out of me and my father told the Queen. She was furious and the librarian's wife was not invited to any more parties.

Sylvia's memories are less indulgent of the Queen and more indulgent of her estimation of her own good looks, although she can have been little more than seven at the time. Queen Victoria "was a very aggressive, terrifying old woman . . . She sat in the middle of the dance floor with a big stick, thumping on the ground, screaming at us . . . she had me out in the front row because I had good legs."[5]

Sylvia also confirmed that these were the only other children she and Dorothy ever met. Thus, despite the unpleasantness and even terror of the dancing classes, they were the only social occasions the two girls had to look forward to each week. This contact between the Castle and Orchard Lea forwarded, not unwittingly, one suspects, Reggie Brett's interests. Reggie and Nellie were now frequent dinner guests of Victoria, who herself often visited Orchard Lea – informally, for a special entrance had been built for the Queen's sole use, an entrance later to be much utilised by her son, the Prince of Wales, the future Edward VII. At the time Reggie was writing a series of studies on the Prime Ministers of Victoria's reign, and it seems certain he had access to the Queen's diaries (he later edited her letters and journals). Rosebery, a contemporary of Reggie Brett's at Eton, was also a frequent guest at Windsor. On becoming Prime Minister, some of his ministerial appointments, including that of Brett, were thought frivolous. Brett had expected to be made Secretary for Woods and Forests and his appointment by Rosebery to the Office of Works was described by the Liberal Chief Whip as "execrable . . . a man with about £6000 a year with five houses in town and country who has always left his party in the lurch".[6] Brett was aware of the party's hostility but accepted Rosebery's decision and determined to make a success of his Secretaryship in an office that required him to deal with royal residences, state collections, museums, monuments, ceremonies of state and all questions of precedent.

The appointment to the Office of Works came early in 1895. Reggie Brett had already been much in the headlines late the previous autumn when the Tilney Street house had suffered a bomb attack. The bomb was not intended for the Bretts but for their neighbour, Justice Hawkins, who had, a little earlier, passed a severe and controversial sentence on an anarchist group known as the Walsall Dynamiters. Reggie and Eleanor Brett had been at the theatre, Eleanor returning home by carriage while Reggie decided to walk. Eleanor stepped over the bomb and was thrown from the hallway into the kitchen by the force of the blast which a correspondent to *The Times* a couple of days later confirmed could be heard from as far away as Camden Square. Dorothy and Sylvia at Orchard Lea heard the story from their governess – the lady who was soon to be dismissed for twitching her nose.

Around this time is another of the rare references to his daughters in Reginald Brett's journals. "January 13th, 1895: The snow very deep. In the afternoon we walked over to Quaker. A charming walk down the white road. Back in a fly to dinner. Then the tableaux vivants. They were good. Maurice as Cupid, Sylvia as the Alabama Coon and Dorothy as St. Elizabeth were the most admired."[7]

The following year, 1896, Dorothy Brett's great-aunt, Louise van de Weyer, died. She had been fond of Doll, who recalled her home, opposite Monkey Island on the Thames, as being always full of artists and musicians. In a copy of a will dated that year, Aunt Louise Maria Augusta van de Weyer left Dorothy £20,000 in trust via her mother. Aunt Lou had been crippled by a stroke some years before, was paralysed from the waist down and, it seems from Dorothy's description, aphasic. "She could not coordinate her speech or her handwriting. She wrote vertically from the bottom of the page upward and invariably asked for the wrong thing. If she wanted a pen she asked for a sponge . . . it terrified us small children."*

The legacy of Aunt Louise gave Dorothy Brett a small income for the rest of her life, though whether the full amount of £20,000 was ever settled upon her is not clear. The smallness of the sum it generated always irritated and puzzled Doll and she remained convinced that her father had at some time found a means of rifling the fund. Reginald Brett was himself left a Stradivarius violin which he promptly sold, the proceeds being used to extend Orchard Lea with a very large room that became known as the Gallery. According to Doll, "The problem with such a large room was that someone might be hidden in an armchair at the far end and hear everything one said without one realising it."

In the same year Reginald Brett also purchased The Roman Camp, a small estate on the edge of Callander, the gateway to the Scottish Highlands. The Roman Camp, known to the family as "Pinkie" because of its pink-washed walls, was used for holidays and as a shooting lodge for Reginald and his guests. Some of Doll's happiest memories were of Pinkie: walks on the mountains and moorland, bicycling trips as far as Oban and fishing expeditions to the River Stank that flows into Loch Lubnaig. It was at Pinkie that, some years later, she first began to take a serious interest in drawing and painting and where her sister Sylvia, by then a budding writer, had her own little piece of

* Other great-aunts, on the father's side of the family, terrified and intrigued the sheltered Brett daughters. Aunt Adele was plain and vain and overweight and had a very large and long nose with a perpetual drip at the end of it. "She would make us come in in the morning to pull up the strings of her stays but instead she had laced them up with wire as she was a very heavily built woman. When dressed, she would stand in front of the mirror and say to us, 'Am I not beautiful?' "

Adele's sister, Great-Aunt Zumala also suffered from a weight problem. On one occasion she entered a hansom cab and the belly-band of the horse broke, allowing the cab to tilt backwards, so that it lay with its shafts in the air and with the horse dangling by its traces. Aunt Zumala was so grossly heavy and fat that she was imprisoned in the cab for some time.

peace and quiet in a summerhouse on a small mound in the garden known as the Tump. Doll herself became an expert fisherman on the River Teith that flows by the bottom of the garden and carried the skill profitably and addictively with her to New Mexico where she fished until she was well into her eighties.

Reginald Brett's first opportunity to display his talent for ceremonial came with the Diamond Jubilee celebrations of 1897. That part of the arrangements for which he was responsible went smoothly enough, although there was notable chaos at functions under the charge of the College of Heralds. Even where he was not responsible, he could be relied upon for quick and sometimes drastic action. At one garden party in Buckingham Palace, over-dressed guests were fainting from the heat in a marquee. Reggie, wearing, as was proper for the occasion, full court dress complete with ceremonial sword, slashed great slits in the sides of the tent to provide rapid ventilation, much to the consternation and indeed danger of the surprised guests standing outside, immediately adjacent to the canvas walls.

In Jubilee year Dorothy Brett's grandfather, William Baliol Brett, retired from the bench as Master of the Rolls and was raised by Lord Salisbury from Baron to Viscount. Dorothy remembered the year for an occasion when she was forced into correspondence with the Queen. Doll was alone with Sylvia and the servants while her parents were in London, when a trooper arrived at Orchard Lea on horseback, bearing an invitation to Reginald and Eleanor to dine with the Queen. Dorothy sat him in the kitchen, to the delight of the maids and kitchen staff, while she pondered what to do, no doubt influenced by the awesome memory of those dancing classes punctuated by the thumping stick. Eventually she managed to word a cable to her parents in London and to compose a letter for the trooper to take back to Her Majesty. Reginald Brett, in another rare reference to his daughter in his journal, records the incident briefly on November 24th, 1897, in a mixture of pride and amusement.

> Dined with the Queen at Windsor. Invitation came while we were in London. Dorothy replied by the orderly of the Blues: THE LORD STEWARD, I HEAR FROM MY MOTHER, THE HON. MRS BRETT, THAT SHE WILL OBEY THE QUEEN'S COMMANDS. YOURS SINCERELY. DOROTHY BRETT.[8]

Since Miss Harvey had been dismissed for twitching her nose and the boys, Oliver and Maurice, were boarders at nearby Eton, the education of the girls was now entirely in the hands of their mother. According to both Dorothy and Sylvia it was not a great success. It consisted principally of a great deal of rote learning that had to be presented to Mumsy* while she was having her hair combed by her maid before dinner. Sylvia used to hide a crib in her handkerchief and the maid, privy to the deceit, always contrived to stand between Sylvia and her mother so that Mumsy would remain unaware of what was going on.

Dorothy, for her part, had so far shown little sign of any artistic talent. She had been encouraged to draw by a Miss Barnard, a water colourist who came to paint her portrait when she was barely six years old, but to judge by a letter written to her father early in 1899 her sights were set rather more in the direction of the stage.

Dear Pupsy,

I think the king in the play your [sic] writing ought to have a favourite page, as they always had them in those days. It would have to be a part like the midshipman in the Geisha, the sort of part I should love to do, in fact I don't see that I should not do it, I look very well in boys clothes, and I should have nothing very difficult to say, and I would do it for nothing, if you have to pay, don't you have to pay when the play is put on the stage by you.

I am writing because I can never get at you alone: I don't think its a bad plan, I should watch other people act and see how they did it and have nothing to do myself but walk in backward before the king.

And it would be much more amusing for you to come and watch.

I would take another name and no one would be any the wiser because I could not possibly be recognised in a long curly wig.

I shall never believe acting a nasty life unless I see for myself. It would interfere with nothing as there are only matinees on Saturday, and other days in the evening. I could live all alone in Tilney Street (rather dull) or have a season ticket and miss the last train every night (not much fun) I could come down for Sunday and go up late Monday.

Don't tell anyone but Mumsy or they'll all go against it, especially not Teddy. We'll tell him when it's settled.

Yrs,

Dorothy.

There are two afterthoughts, one written across the top of the page at the beginning of the letter: "This plan occurred to me in bed last

* Reginald Brett had decided that he did not like being called Papa or Daddy and settled on the name "Pupsy". Eleanor "Nellie" Brett, in consequence became "Mumsy".

night." And the other across the top of the last page: "You can tell Letty, I don't think she would mind having me for a page."[9]

Teddy was Teddy Seymour, a family friend, and Letty Lind a musical comedy actress. Dorothy wrote in her memoirs:

> About this time I developed a tremendous crush on Letty Lind, who was a great friend of my father's. So, she would come down [to Orchard Lea] very often and bring with her the most beautiful little boy with black curly hair, Jackie [Harrington]. Of course we did not understand; he played with us and we loved him too. But Letty I simply went head over heels for. I wanted to do splits, I wanted to go on the stage, and learned word for word all her parts in the plays I saw her in. Pupsy could hardly believe his ears when he discovered I knew practically every line of her parts. I think she was rather a simple little thing but this crush lasted until Pupsy and Mumsy with their usual protectiveness did not dare ask her down [any more]. They were afraid I might run off and go on the stage. [They] also discovered at the same time that I kept a complete boy's suit and a wig under my bed for the purpose of running away.

Two things are striking about Doll's letter to her father: it is not particularly mature for a girl of fifteen and a half years old, even granted the change in maturation that the intervening eighty years has produced. And a psychoanalyst would not find it hard to discern significance in its content – Dorothy wanting to walk backwards before the King as a favourite page, looking well in boy's clothes – given the daughters' jealousy of their father's attachment to their brother Maurice and the feeling iterated by both Syv and Doll of loneliness and rejection.

In May 1899 Dorothy Brett's grandfather, William Baliol Brett, died, and Reginald Brett inherited his title. Dorothy liked to believe that her father would have preferred to remain plain "Reggie Brett", the well-known and influential commoner, but there is nothing to suggest that the new Viscount Esher was in any way a reluctant peer. His post as Secretary of the Office of Works was, technically, that of a civil servant and precedent demanded that he should resign the post now that he was eligible to sit in the House of Lords. But he had by now made himself indispensable to both the Queen and the Prince of Wales, the future Edward VII, and both pressed that he retain his position.

Nevertheless, Esher was an obvious candidate for a more overtly political appointment. Within a few years, after Edward's succession, he was offered the War Office by the Unionist government and, despite being called to Balmoral by the King in an effort to persuade him to accept, Esher declined the post. A little later, with a Liberal government in power, Esher was offered the Viceroyship of India. He turned this down as well. The reality of the situation was that he already possessed a good deal more power and influence than either of these posts would have provided. During the Boer War the Queen had become the focus for every sort of submission and complaint from her subjects and at the time no intermediary between the War Office and the sovereign existed. Esher had therefore moved readily into the gap and made his position one of great power and little responsibility. The fact was not unrecognised by himself or his family. After his death in 1930, his journals were edited by his younger son, Maurice, and on Maurice's death in 1934, the task was taken over by Oliver, 3rd Viscount Esher. The fourth volume of the Esher journals, edited by Oliver Esher, is dedicated with a quotation from Lord Beaconsfield: "The most powerful men are not public men. The public man is responsible and a responsible man is a slave. It is private life that governs the world."

Privately, Esher, advising the Queen, exercised a strong influence on War Office matters, with the great advantage, not enjoyed by a politician, that there was no need to be consistent in his ideas and attitudes. It was largely for his activities in this sphere that, at the end of 1900, he was created a Knight of the Victorian Order. The letter confirming the honour was written by the Duke of Connaught, Sylvia Brett has recorded, "in the Queen's name, saying she was ill and tired or would have written herself".[10] It was one of the declining Queen's last official acts. Less than a month later, on January 22nd, 1901, Victoria died.

Dorothy and Sylvia had been preparing with great intensity and often fearfulness for their presentation at court. Constantly supervised by their mother as though they were unreliable infants, they were in terror of the slightest slip during the court ceremony: tripping on one's train – of a prescribed length and character – stumbling while curtseying, lingering too long before the Queen, all these possible accidents were impressed upon the sheltered daughters as more than mere peccadilloes and likely to bring the family shame and disrepute for generations to come. The Queen's failing health had caused the occasion to be continually delayed since the previous autumn and the coming out of the Esher daughters had now to be postponed more conclusively until after the funeral of Victoria and the coronation of the new King, Edward VII.

It had been a very long time since anyone had buried a Queen or crowned a King and there were few alive with any memory of such occasions. Nor had any preparation been made for Edward's succession. Esher threw himself into the task of researching procedures, resurrecting old records and ancient peers, such as the aging Duke of Cambridge who was old enough to have attended two previous royal funerals and coronations. The funeral arrangements at Windsor were entirely Esher's responsibility and he himself accounted his activities a "brilliant success", "perfectly arranged from start to finish".[11] He added, without any attempt at modesty, in one of his many letters to his son Maurice, "Keep always in your heart the memory of the Queen whom your immediate forefathers served so closely and faithfully and well."[12]

Dorothy and Sylvia attended the funeral, driving with their mother in a carriage from Orchard Lea. Despite the Queen's request that there be no black, they were swathed in such heavy crepe veils that within St. George's Chapel, in the dim light of the deep mid-winter, they had to grope their way to their seats.

The date set for Edward's coronation was the following year, June 1902, partly because of his tender health and partly in the hope that the Boer War would by then be over. The preparations for Victoria's funeral had given Esher intimate access to the Queen's papers. Thus when the idea of a biography of Her Late Majesty was mooted, the choice of a biographer fell upon Esher, who proposed instead that a selection of her letters be edited for publication.

Esher began also to set about the various rearrangements required by the new king, moving the court from Windsor to Buckingham Palace and ejecting enormous hoards of accumulated bric-à-brac. Esher was the broom of the new King sweeping clean. Edward was undoubtedly impressed and, as well as urging him to remain at the Office of Works, asked him if he would be prepared to arrange all of the late Queen's papers. Esher accepted the task but still wished to resign the Office and asked that he be given instead the position of Lieutenant and Deputy Governor of Windsor Castle in order that he should, instead of remaining a civil servant, have some status in the royal household. The new post gave Esher complete control of the royal archives, enabling him to restrict the access of historians and leaving with him the last word on matters of constitution and precedence. "His position as a political *éminence grise* to Edward VII and George V in successive crises involving the powers and prerogatives of the Sovereign rested on this basis."[13]

Meantime he set about organising the coronation, careful not to invade the territory of the Duke of Norfolk, to whom this right and duty fell as Earl Marshal and Senior Peer. Preparations were well in hand when in March 1902, Dorothy Brett fell ill. "I can remember the agony of it. [Pain] would come and go in great sweeping waves. Each time I thought I couldn't stand it any more." For some time her parents remained unaware of Doll's illness, Esher busy with the arrangements for the coronation and Eleanor her usual remote self. Finally they brought a nurse from Windsor.

> She was horrified at the sight of me, my tummy swollen up and in such pain that there was nothing she could do. She told my parents that if nothing more was to be done, then she must leave as she refused to be responsible for my death. Up to that time our country doctor had been taking care of me. He had a son who was also a doctor who tried to persuade his father to send for someone to operate but the old man had been obstinate. The nurse's announcement finally frightened him, and my father sent for our London doctor.

Dorothy's illness caused Esher to cancel a meeting with the King who was at Newmarket for the races. Edward sent Esher a telegram: "Grieved to hear of your daughter's illness. Pray send at once for Sir F. Treves. Trust to receive better accounts tomorrow. Edward R."

Sir Frederick Treves was the King's personal physician and Esher's footman was despatched from Orchard Lea to London where he found Sir Frederick, on his doorstep, about to depart for a weekend in the country. Treves examined Dorothy and diagnosed a severe case of appendicitis. He decided that there was no time to move her into hospital and that she must be operated upon immediately, in the house itself. A room was scrubbed out, a dining table brought in and the next morning Treves brought the necessary equipment down from London on an early train to perform the operation. It was, at the time, something of a rarity and a number of local doctors gathered to witness the event. Treves had only performed the operation two or three times himself and was by no means sure of a successful outcome. His own daughter had died following an appendectomy.

> Treves never hesitated [Esher wrote to Maurice Brett on March 16th]. After seeing Doll, he came down and explained that left alone she must die, and that the operation alone could save her. Even that was 10 per cent risk. It was all well managed and I think he was fairly satisfied. It was a difficult operation as there was a complication. There is danger for 48 hours of course; great danger. One can only hope for the best.[14]

Dorothy Brett herself recalls that the illness had progressed so far without a proper examination that her appendix had already burst before Treves was brought in.

> I can vaguely remember coming out of the anaesthetic but no one was allowed to see me for a while. Then I did not want to see my mother. Whether it was the antagonism that had already grown up between us for no reason that I could make out or whether I blamed her for this, I don't know. My father came to my bed and pulled my ears and talked to me in a very low, quiet voice.

Esher did not remain at the bedside for long. The King, while sympathetic, was anxious to have him back in harness. His secretary, Sir Francis Knollys, wrote to Esher on March 20th from Marlborough House.

> The King and Queen desire me to say how very glad they are to hear your most satisfactory report about your daughter and trust that everything will now go on well. The King wishes to know whether, when your daughter is able to be moved, Lady Esher would like to take her to Barton's Cottage, Osborne, for a little change, as if so, he will be very glad to lend it to you. He hopes you will go with him to Cowes on Thursday next for a day or two, living on board the Royal Yacht, as he proposes while he is there going over Osborne and settling various things in connection with it.[15]

Whether the offer of Barton's Cottage was accepted or not is unclear, but Esher felt it his duty to fulfil the King's hopes. He wrote home a few days later, March 28th, from the Royal Yacht, asking to be remembered to Nurse. Dorothy seems however to have spent most of her long period of convalescence at Orchard Lea, where the young local doctor attended to dress her wound. Sheltered and immature, seldom having met a man outside the family circle, she fell for him.

> I could hardly wait for his visits. One morning before he was to arrive, I asked for a large blue ribbon which I wound around my bandages and tied into a bow on top of my tummy . . . I thought I was in love . . . How dreadful at eighteen to be no older than perhaps ten years. Innocence and childishness do not appeal to me and why they appealed to my mother I don't know, because she was mostly responsible for this. My father was always so wrapped up in himself, I don't think he really noticed to any extent what was happening to us. Yet in a way he must have known what was the state of our lives. Can

> you imagine children of twelve and thirteen still playing with dolls, large stuffed toys that we would cuddle and coax? When my father found out, he ordered that they be burnt. One moment we were playing with dolls, the next moment the dolls were burned. But our immaturity remained and it was that immaturity that our mother seemed to nurture in us. Could it be that I had been making a doll of myself (tying myself with blue ribbon), hoping that someone would love me, cuddle me?

Dorothy recovered only slowly from the complications caused by the burst appendix and her convalescence lasted well into the summer. She spent some of this time taking the sea air at Folkestone, still in a wheelchair and unable to walk, accompanied by her nurse and by Sylvia, with the young doctor from Orchard Lea, "The Jungling", in occasional attendance. She wrote gossipy letters to her father, full of the trivia of seaside life. On June 4th, 1902, she described the major excitement of the previous day – a young man having a fit on the esplanade while the band were playing. Summers were apparently little better in that Edwardian golden age than today, for it had poured with rain and Dorothy had been kept awake by the noise of motors with their wooden wheels and by the marching fife and drum bands of the military volunteers. "If I had been walking I should have tried to get some lessons as the place is swarming with bands and tommies." Surprisingly, considering her sheltered existence, before her illness Doll had been learning to play the drums. "A huge Life Guardsman from the barracks at Windsor came to teach me. I was a perpetual shock to him, I was so young for my age."

She sketched from her bedroom window and was, she says, "fairly successful" but her principal news was of a courting couple in the hotel opposite.

> . . . they walk about arm in arm and she slapped him yesterday and stamped her feet on the ground and he helps her up the steps and squeezes her hand, they are the vulgarest couple I've ever had the misfortune to watch through my field glasses*, they are perfectly easy to see without. The father disapproves of the match and won't speak to either of them, the sister is tactful and the mother is dull.

* Years later, Dorothy Brett fell out with D. H. Lawrence's biographer, Harry T. Moore, who described her as keeping an eye on Frieda Lawrence's house through field glasses so she would know whether Frieda had any visitors worth meeting. Brett hotly denied this and yet, according to her companion and colleague, John Manchester, she always kept an unexplained pair of field glasses on the window ledge.

A few days later on June 9th, Dorothy blamed her poor handwriting from her wheelchair on the pier on Sylvia and Nurse rocking her in time to the music.

> The first violinist is the beau of Folkestone, mockum isn't the word for him . . . I have an air balloon on my wound now, it took Doctor C. all the afternoon to make and is fastened by long strings of tape.[16]

The slowness of Doll's recovery made it clear that she would have to miss the Coronation ceremony, the preparations for which were busily involving her father. The night he returned from London from the final rehearsal, Esher was spent, weary and dispirited. "He sat down by my sofa and broke the news that the Coronation was off. They feared the King had appendicitis."

So little was known at the time of the illness that Doll was under a cloud in the Esher family, for it was thought that her father had carried some germ from his daughter to the King. Sir Frederick Treves again operated, this time with greater success. The King recovered rapidly and the ceremony was now rearranged for August 9th but much shortened in view of the King's general poor state of health. Dorothy was selfishly grateful for the delay, for by August she had progressed sufficiently to claim the seat in Westminster Abbey to which she was entitled as the elder daughter of a peer.

She recorded her impressions of the ceremony in an article for *The New Yorker*, published in May 1953 and commissioned to mark the coronation of Elizabeth II. The completion of the article was complicated by the financial involvement of another writer but it is doubtful whether she actually remembered much of what she offered as reminiscence. She expressed her misgivings a number of times in letters to her brother Oliver, claiming that she remembered nothing and Oliver came to her assistance with the loan of books and newspaper clippings from the family library.

One of her father's bizarre inspirations she certainly recalled – the construction of an annexe at the west door of Westminster Abbey.

> As far as building and decoration were concerned it was a masterpiece. It was built of lath and plaster, so cleverly constructed that it was impossible to tell it from the Abbey itself. The merger was perfect. Outside there were niches for statues and gargoyles peered from the cornices. As some wit wrote, "After the Coronation is over and everything is being dismantled, that annexe is worth a visit to see. One does not know which is Abbey and which is annexe, the

imitation is so close and clever. I hope that when the time comes to remove it, the men don't take away the Abbey by mistake."

The ceremony was not without its mishaps. The Archbishop of Canterbury's sight and strength were failing and everything had to be copied in large type on a series of scrolls. At one point he had to be lifted from his knees by a couple of bishops. The anointing oil dripped on to the Queen's nose and only her self-control saved the occasion; the Duchess of Devonshire attempted to force her way out immediately the King and Queen left the Abbey and fell flat on her back, her coronet flying off in another direction.

It was an unofficial act that remained strongest in Dorothy Brett's memory. Esher's secretary, Stanley Quick, had managed to smuggle a government despatch box into the crypt below the Abbey. In it were sandwiches of chicken, tongue and ham and several bottles of champagne which were covered in napkins to muffle the sound of popping corks. The months of tension for Esher and the months of convalescence for Dorothy were over and the party became high-spirited.

> We laughed and talked unthinkingly. Suddenly there was a loud rapping on the door. My father called out "Come in" as if it were his own living room. The door was flung open and there was the Duke of Norfolk, several policemen and a group of Guardsmen armed to the teeth. The Duke stared at us in complete amazement. My father rose and with a charming smile said, "My dear Duke, won't you join us?"

The following year Dorothy's much delayed presentation at court took place. Dorothy recalled that she and Sylvia were debutantes in the same season, although Sylvia's autobiography suggests that she came out several years after her sister. Whatever the case the ceremony took place without mishap, that is to say, their father did not feel disgraced. According to Sylvia, "In fact he felt somewhat proud of us, even though he would have been much prouder if we had been beautiful."[17]

Not everyone glided so smoothly through the occasion.

> I can remember one very fat woman in a dress so extravagantly decorated that a titter ran all round the room as she literally bounced along. Just as she curtseyed the big drum gave a loud "boom". The dreadful hope for the ludicrous which filled everyone, the longing for someone to fall down, for their train to come off, to relieve the insuperable boredom of watching these women and girls take that awful walk was satisfied by that "Boom!" on the drum.

As debutantes, Dorothy and Sylvia followed the prescribed round of parties and balls that constituted the season, success being accounted as wearing an engagement ring by the end of the winter. Neither Doll nor Syv were successful or, for that matter, had the first inkling of how to go about it, thrust so suddenly into an adult world. Dorothy recalls her first ball, given by Lady Warwick for her daughters who had come out at the same time. At dinner she was seated next to Winston Churchill and was "scared to death. He expected me as a child of my father to be intelligent, witty and brilliant. I was shy, dumb and shrinking . . . petrified. After dinner there was some kind of mix-up and no guests arrived for the dance. The evening sort of snoofled out." It was an occasion that, despite all, was to be magnified in later American magazine articles: "*Her first date was with Winston Churchill!*" Churchill does not seem to have remembered the occasion. When Dorothy wrote to him during the Second World War with one of the hare-brained ideas she had from time to time on how to beat the Boche or the Russians or the Japanese or end rationing and save the economy, the reply came from his secretary and was addressed to Mr. Brett.

The high points of the season were the State Balls, where, when the King and Queen entered, the guests would respectfully back away from them. On one occasion Dorothy Brett was in front of a fireplace at this crucial moment in the festivities.

> The people backed and backed then someone pushed against me and I fell with a clatter into the fireplace among all the fire irons. The officials immediately thought the King had had a heart attack. At the time he was suffering from a heart condition and bottles of oxygen were usually held in readiness.

At another State Ball, one of the lady dinner guests with a head-dress of feathers leaned too near the candle flames and caught fire.

> The man next to her grabbed her and crushed out the fire on his chest. His gloves were ruined and his uniform covered with black soot. The room smelled of burnt feathers and burnt hair yet the woman remained calmly eating, the forlorn feather stumps sticking out all around her head.

Significantly the dance that remained strongest in Dorothy's mind was the occasion when Pupsy, her father, "elegant, debonaire", danced with her.

> My pride was immense. I could hardly contain myself because I knew I was the envy of all the women in the room. I never knew why he asked me unless he wanted to spite some woman who had been spiteful to him.

Despite the strenuous efforts of her mother in the marriage market that season, Doll failed to make a catch. According to Sylvia, while outwardly intensely feminine, Doll scorned the ritual of matchmaking and snubbed her escorts. Doll admits she was both fearful of and hostile towards men. The fear was understandable. She had been supposedly transformed in an instant from a socially retarded pre-adolescent into a mature marriage prospect, by means only of a new hairstyle and a thrusting-out into the adult world of dances and dinners. Her own mother, Eleanor, had been forced to cope with such a transformation herself and married Reggie when she was only seventeen. In an unpublished article entitled *Adolescence*, written many years later when she had followed D. H. Lawrence to Rananim in New Mexico, Doll traced her hostility to men to her brothers' treatment of her.

But it was not only her brothers Maurice and Oliver who had made her fearful of men. She had already had her first sexual experience, which had been traumatic indeed. The occasion is difficult to date exactly but it seems likely to have occurred shortly before the end of the century, when Doll was perhaps fourteen or fifteen years old.

> I was kept away from all contact with real life. My white rats and their increasing stream of infants left me unenlightened. I never questioned, never asked . . . and then my father had a friend – I will call him H. – a contemporary of his and old Eton friend, a very tall man, well over six feet. I had known him since I was two, he was part of the household for weeks at a time. One day my father asked me to fetch some books from the farm house across the one acre field. H. suggested coming to help me. We walked along the path through the little wood that led to the farm and when we got inside H. started looking at the pictures of racehorses that hung round the room while I collected the books. It was a dampish day so he had on a Burberry – the kind with false pockets. He took hold of my hand and pulled it through the false pocket. I suddenly felt something burning hot and soft. I can remember to this moment my stunned horror – I knew, how I knew I don't know, but I knew and I was horribly afraid. I stood stock still in an agony of surprise and fear – then I tore my hand away and turned to run. I was not quick enough. He was on me, he caught hold of me from behind and held me in a grip of iron, and

> began kissing the back of my neck. Wild terror broke out in me and I kicked and kicked and kicked myself free and rushed out of the house. That was my first realisation of sex and my body was stunned by it. I would let no man come near me and all I dared to say was that I would never be left alone with H. But the harm was done. For years I would never let a man come near me.

Years later, after Sylvia's marriage in 1911, Doll was at a Christmas party at Sylvia's and Vyner Brooke, Sylvia's husband, encouraged a man friend to kiss Doll under the mistletoe.

> He came up quietly behind me, caught hold of me and tried to kiss me. The old fear seized me and like a maniac I kicked that unfortunate man black and blue until, bewildered, he let me go, looking very apologetic, while I felt shaken and ashamed.

H. was Lewis Harcourt, later Lord Harcourt, known as "Loulou". Harcourt's father had been Professor of International Law at Cambridge during Esher's undergraduate days and had given the young Reggie a set of rooms that were in his gift. It was not Loulou's only venture into pederasty. Some years later, he made a homosexual approach to the twelve-year-old Edward James who told his mother and whose mother told the world. Not long afterwards, Harcourt died following an overdose of a sleeping draught. Edward James, oddly enough, turned up in 1940 in Taos, New Mexico, where Doll had by then settled and, to Doll's delight, began buying her paintings.

Esher, in fact, seems to have been rather unfortunate in the choice of friends and employees he introduced to the family circle and, of course, to his wide-eyed and naive daughters. Doll paints a picture of Sylvia as a precocious young lady in her early teens, for ever "ogling" young Guards officers. Sylvia, for her part, describes an experience exactly like Doll's at the hands of one of her father's male secretaries.

> My father's secretary kissed me in the dark, pressing his pale inadequate moustache into my mouth and exploring my twelve-year-old body with his secret searching hands. Thereby was laid the foundation of a wall of horror against all the male sex which took me many years to overcome.[18]

Doll recalls the same young man inventing a game with the Brett daughters to occupy idle hours while their parents were away in London. The game consisted largely of paying Sylvia a penny for a kiss. But then the role of the young male secretaries in the Esher household was always rather odd.

> [My father] was such a charming person . . . remarkable and very good looking. But he was not really interested in girls. You see, he was ambidextrous, he liked boys . . . he always had a young man in the family. He would bring them home. I never knew of a young man not being in the family. He was very discreet of course . . . He used to say, "The only thing in life is not to be found out." I have no idea what my mother thought of all this. I have often wondered if she enjoyed having all these boys about. She never did anything. Nothing.

It was hardly surprising that Doll's first serious emotional encounter should be a tempestuous adolescent crush directed towards an older woman. Educated by a governess and later somewhat ineffectually by Mumsy, she had had no geography mistress or hockey teacher upon whom to sublimate her unformed emotions. The affair began innocently enough. Margaret Brooke, Ranee of Sarawak and wife of the second White Raja,* had taken a house at Windsor, only four miles from the Eshers' Orchard Lea. She wrote to Eleanor Esher introducing herself and asking whether she might invite Dorothy and Sylvia to join a small amateur orchestra that she proposed to form.

Esher, true to form, objected strongly to his daughters accepting the invitation but his wife for once over-ruled him and Sylvia and Doll cycled over to Grey Friars House to become members of the band. Their first task was to rehearse for a charity performance of *His Excellency the Governor* in which the Ranee's youngest son, Harry, a talented amateur actor, was to take the leading role. The Grey Friars Orchestra, an all-female ensemble, "all of us extremely bad" according to Sylvia, composed of the pick of the eligible young ladies of the neighbourhood, was, it soon became clear, not such an innocent endeavour. With the Ranee and Harry in Windsor were her other two sons, Vyner and Bertram, and all three young men were unmarried. Margaret Brooke, Ranee of the head-hunting Dyaks, was indulging in a little head-hunting herself.

Sylvia, claiming no special talent, chose to play the bass drum, cymbals and triangle in the orchestra. Doll, already a keen drummer, anxious to improve her roll, was the obvious choice for the side and kettle drums. The orchestra's rehearsals rapidly became the highlight

* James Brooke, an English merchant adventurer, born in Benares and brought up in the East, became the first White Raja of Sarawak after assisting the local ruler to put down a rebellion among the head-hunting Dyak tribesmen in 1841. Margaret was the estranged wife of the second White Raja, James Brooke's nephew, Charles Brooke. According to Sylvia, she told the Esher girls that she finally left her husband when he had her four and twenty pet doves baked in a pie.

of the week for the Esher girls. Both Doll and Sylvia felt they were entering an entirely new and grown-up world for the first time, despite having completed the "season" that was intended to mark their entry into adulthood. Over tea after rehearsals, the Ranee held them spell-bound with, according to Syv, tales of the mystic orient and, according to Doll, talk of the arts and letters.

For whatever reason, Syv enthralled, Doll uplifted, they cycled back to Orchard Lea after the weekly rehearsals guilt-stricken that they had enjoyed their encounter with the outside world so much. Their parents remained unaware of the Ranee's plot to ensnare eligible young ladies as wives for her sons, so when Vyner Brooke, the eldest son and later the third White Raja of Sarawak, began sending small gifts and billets doux to Sylvia, there was uproar in the household. Sylvia was sent packing up to Scotland, to Roman Camp.

Sylvia had not been the initial object of Vyner's interest. At the Ranee's instigation, Vyner had first turned his attention to Doll but, whereas Syv was coyly accomplished in the Edwardian skills of flirting, Doll's distancing from the opposite sex had increased sharply since her encounter with Loulou Harcourt and with the brash young men who had been on the social list during her season as a debutante. One wet afternoon Doll was lingering in the music room at Grey Friars, tuning her kettle drums while waiting for the rain to stop, before cycling back to Orchard Lea. The Ranee sent Vyner Brooke in to her with a blue enamel necklace and orders to give it to Doll and ask for her hand in marriage. Vyner's courage failed him at the last moment, and he stuck the gift in Doll's hands and stumbled out without a word of explanation, leaving Doll confused and bewildered.

Vyner then turned his attention to Sylvia and over the succeeding years the couple made several half-hearted attempts at elopement that fizzled out when one or the other, usually Vyner, lost heart at the last moment. Doll, still unaware that Vyner ever had an interest in herself, took great delight in assisting in these escapades, delivering Sylvia, complete with a trousseau of disguises and often a rope ladder, to one or other of the inns of Windsor from which Vyner had already fled.

In later years Sylvia recalled the events of the period a little differently. She wrote to Doll in the early 1970s suggesting that Doll had never forgiven her for "stealing Vyner away". Doll, not unaccus-tomed by then to embroidering and fantasising on her role in various sexual encounters, for her part believed Sylvia to have inherited vast fortunes from Vyner Brooke, who had ceded Sarawak to the British Crown after the Second World War. She did not understand why some of these fortunes should not be used to support the visual arts – in the shape of Doll herself who was by then living under strained economic circumstances as a painter in New Mexico. Sylvia, to give her her due, had, in fact, funded Doll from time to time over the years, one such occasion being when Doll was building her house north of Taos in the mid-1940s.

Sylvia eventually married Vyner in 1911, despite continuing family opposition. Doll, in the meantime, had developed an immense crush on Vyner's mother, the Ranee, Margaret Brooke, that ran almost the length of the Edwardian decade. In the face of strong parental disapproval, Doll cycled over to Grey Friars or, less energetically, harnessed the Shetland ponies to a small trap and drove through the country lanes of Windsor to the Ranee's, the minute the Eshers had disappeared to London or Scotland, leaving Doll in temporary control of the household at Orchard Lea. Her few extant letters to her father at this time show how much the relationship occupied her mind and how greatly at odds she was with her parents over it.

(undated – first page missing)
. . . the Ranee abused, it is not right and on the other hand to answer back is not much better but I have not recovered yet from Mumsy's behaviour when I first knew the Ranee and I don't suppose I ever shall. When one is fond of someone, it is almost impossible to forgive disgusting insults said of them and Mumsy said things I would not be heard saying to a tramp . . . (P.S.) If you pay no attention to anything anyone tells you about me, you will find it more satisfactory.

(undated – 1905)
I don't want to go to any theatres, the Ranee is my friend and I must be loyal to her, if you do not care to ask her here, I don't care to go to London – I can't forget all her kindness to me and I know that circumstances and not inclination are at the bottom of all this. She is the greatest friend I have and I hold her my friend . . . in spite of everything and everyone.

January 4th, 1906
She is everything to me . . . I will never give up trying [to win her back].

October 30th, 1906
I don't know how angry she is but you know how impossible it is to enjoy oneself when one is really fond of someone and they are seriously annoyed with one and after not seeing her for 3 months it is rather hard.[19]

Doll was a few days short of twenty-three years of age when the last of this series of letters to her father was written and yet they remind one of scribbled notes confiscated in the classroom on long hot summer afternoons, written with all the manner and agitation of an adolescent. The reason for her parents' disapproval of the friendship, Doll discovered from her brother Oliver, many years after her father's death, was their belief that Margaret Brooke was a lesbian. Early on in their acquaintance, long before Sylvia and Vyner became involved with each other, the Eshers had invited the Ranee to lunch and were very rude to her, Esher in particular behaving as though the notion of a White Raja was some kind of Gilbertian joke. Some time later, Margaret Brooke was invited to lunch again. Doll, then over twenty years old, was locked by Esher in her second-floor room for the occasion while brother Maurice, her father's favourite, stood on the lawn below taunting and jeering at her. The immediate result of the meal was that Dorothy was banned from seeing the Ranee ever again and Sylvia was banished to the grouse moors of Perthshire. Doll reacted violently, cycling as madly as Edwardian dress would allow over to Grey Friars, hoisting herself into the locked house through a dining-room window, wriggling through the dumb waiter into the kitchen and then pursuing an alarmed and frightened Margaret Brooke, around the house with a carving knife.

Between times, Doll looked to the Ranee to save her from the suffocating influence of her family. The Ranee, protesting bewilderment at her adulation, wrote to Esher, "Doll turns up everywhere. I never know where I shall find her. The other day when I opened the little trap that leads from the kitchen to the dining room to find a nice leg of lamb, there, smug and smiling was your daughter Doll."[20]

The two incidents were probably the same, played down by Margaret Brooke, comically embellished by Sylvia, who quotes the letter, or dressed up in her memory by Doll. But in addition to the immense crush on the Ranee, the years of sneaking away from Orchard Lea to Grey Friars were for Doll a period of much delayed adolescent development when she was introduced at last to the world of music, books, and, most importantly, of painting, a world that her parents had never thought necessary or suitable for a young lady of aristocratic upbringing.

The visits to the Ranee were not all carving knives and kettle drums. Margaret Brooke had her "Wednesdays", a weekly tea-time salon at which a frequent guest was W. H. Hudson, the writer and naturalist with whom the Ranee was having, or rather, attempting to have, an affair. Hudson, "tall and thin, with a big hooked nose and greying hair . . . withstood the Ranee's advances by ignoring them". Doll believed

Hudson, who was born near Buenos Aires and was the son of American immigrants to Argentina, to be half South American Indian. "Only when I saw Navajos, did I understand his walk – he walked like an Indian," she recalled much later in New Mexico. Were it not for the error over Hudson's origins, it would not be an entirely romantic suggestion. There *is* something distinctive about the movement of the American Indian, though whether this is genetic or not, is another matter.

With Doll acting as a kind of foil or junior chaperone, all three went on long cycle rides through the Wiltshire and Hampshire countryside, through the downland villages described in Hudson's *A Shepherd's Life*. Occasionally there were just two cycling companions, Doll and Hudson, Doll "frightened of Hudson – frightened of anyone intellectual", Hudson encouraging Doll to attempt to identify the birds in the hedgerows, Doll tongue-tied and abashed.

From The Roman Camp, Doll wrote offering to send Hudson some of the season's grouse, shot by her father and brothers, and fish, caught by herself in Loch Lubnaig and the River Teith. Hudson, the lover of wild-life, if not of the Ranee, replied that while he would certainly not refuse the gifts should they arrive, he preferred his birds and speckled trout alive and in their natural surroundings.

Predictably Doll, in all her unworldly innocence, was at last suspected by the Ranee of trying to steal Hudson from her. The matter reached a head one evening when the Ranee, in a fit of temper, hurled a silver statue of St. Christopher at Doll and ordered her out of the house. The friendship and crush that had lasted almost a decade came to an abrupt and messy end and, although they must have met at Sylvia's wedding to Vyner Brooke in 1911, Doll never saw the Ranee again. "When I think about it, I do not like it at all. When I got out of the house and began to study at the Slade School, I never once went back to see her . . . odd, very odd."

Getting out of the house and studying art at the Slade was not something Doll had considered previously or aimed for in any way. One of Esher's military colleagues (Esher was by now Chairman of the Committee of Imperial Defence) was General Sir Ian Hamilton. ". . . swashbuckling, handsome, artistic and intelligent . . . he tried in vain to teach me how to flirt," she recalled. "He got mad and gave up finally. God knows what was wrong with me. I just didn't seem to understand or know what to do."

They met again when he and his wife were invited to tea at Roman Camp, only a short distance from their house at Doune. Doll showed the general some of her drawings and watercolours and Sir Ian was sufficiently impressed to persuade her that she ought to enter the Slade

School of Art that autumn. She had not seriously thought of entering an art school and she assumed, rightly as it turned out, that her father would put his foot down. But, for whatever motives, she now had a protagonist in Sir Ian who somehow persuaded Esher to allow her to enroll at the Slade in the autumn of 1910.

2

1910–1915: The Slade

In September, 1910, Doll, with no formal qualifications, indeed with no formal education, took her portfolio of drawings and watercolours to the Slade School of Art. Despite her parents' continued misgivings, General Sir Ian Hamilton had arranged an interview for Doll with Professor Frederick Brown. Brown asked Doll, who was "scared blue", why she wanted to enter the Slade. "I want to paint," she replied. Brown was not sure whether to believe her. Fashionable art schools were and still are used as a kind of substitute finishing school for upper-class young ladies who show little talent or inclination in any more formal direction. "We don't like people from your class," said Brown, according to Doll. "They usually come only for amusement or because they are bored at home. They take the place of a girl or boy who needs a scholarship." Somehow Professor Brown forced himself to look at her drawings. He admitted reluctantly that she might have some talent and agreed to allow her to enter the school for a six-month trial period, at the end of which a decision would be made as to whether she could remain for the full four-year course.

It is hard to believe that Brown, "a severe looking old man with grey hair and a goatee", would be quite so rude and straightforward to a young lady whose aristocratic father was a power in the land, and whose interview had been arranged by a titled army commander with some influence in the school. Doll became very intimate with Brown during her years at the Slade and her memory more than likely attributed to him attitudes that she discovered only later in the course of their acquaintance. But Brown was certainly determined that poverty should be no barrier to anyone of talent. Mark Gertler, already in his third year at the school, was the son of Polish immigrant parents and lived in "grinding poverty" in the East End of London, while David Bomberg, acknowledged by his contemporaries as the school's most talented student, had his fees paid by Brown himself. Of the same period as Gertler at the Slade, from 1908 to 1912, were C. R. W. Nevinson, Edward Wadsworth and Stanley Spencer, described by Doll as "a tiny little man who came in from Cookham every morning and so got the name of 'Cookham'". Half a century later, when her subjects were the Indians of New Mexico, it is not difficult to discern in Dorothy Brett's painting the style of that period of English art.

Although Spencer was known by the name of his home village on the Berkshire Thames, the tradition of the Slade called for students and staff, male or female, to be known only by their surname and thereafter the Honourable Dorothy Eugenie Brett, "Doll" to her family, became simply Brett.

The style suited her. What amounted to a new name confirmed her new identity as an art student and the beginning of at least a little independence from her family. Barbara Bagenal, who joined the Slade as a student in 1913, confirms that by then Brett resisted strongly any attempt to call her by her title, and for the rest of her life, except to her immediate family and to Frieda Lawrence, she was known simply by her surname.*

Brett began her six-month trial period drawing from the antique, that is, drawing from plaster casts of classical sculpture and parts of the body in the cast room. Here she met Dora Carrington, who had also entered the school that term. Brett, nearing twenty-seven years old, and Carrington, a slip of a girl of seventeen, rapidly became close friends and formed, with two other young ladies, Barlow and Humphries, the school's "wild group". For the first time in her life Brett was close to people younger than herself, art students of every social class and background. Carrington soon became involved with Mark Gertler who pursued her throughout her Slade career and after, with Brett acting, as the occasion demanded, as mother figure, father confessor, go-between and favourite aunt, depending on whether she was attending to Gertler's love-lorn self-pity or Carrington's indecisive "will-she, won't-she" to-ing and fro-ing.

In common with the other first-year students, Brett had to remain in the cast room until she produced a drawing of sufficient merit to be

* Frieda Lawrence called her "The Brett", a christening that suggests a note of hostility – as though she regarded Brett, who was by the time of their acquaintance severely deaf, as some kind of inanimate object. But, in German, "Der Brett", a phrase used by both Lawrence and Frieda in postcards home to Frieda's family in Germany when Brett was with the Lawrences in New Mexico, is, I gather, neither an uncommon nor a derogatory usage. So Frieda may not have been being as unkind as has been suggested.

On the other hand . . . I recently gave a copy of a picture postcard, sent by Lawrence to his German mother-in-law, to a German scholar to translate. The phrase "*Der Brett ist selig*", literally "Brett is happy", came out as "The plank is all right". Perhaps Frieda was quietly amusing herself for some forty years with a pun on the German "*Brett*" – a board or a plank, regarding Brett as "deaf as a . . ." She had a sense of humour after all.

signed by the professor in charge with a recommendation that she be promoted to the life class, although each afternoon, for the last hour of the school day, the beginners were allowed into the life class to make quick sketches of the model. Within a few weeks Brett's work was satisfactory enough for her to be recommended for life drawing and, to her surprise and delight, at the end of the six-month trial period imposed by Professor Brown, she was accepted for the full four-year course. There is no doubt that the probationary period was real and earnest. Noel Carrington, Carrington's younger brother, recalls Gertler confirming that Brett was initially regarded as little more than a debutante filling her time and a little later as some kind of "sport", that is, in the botanical sense, as a freak or oddity – "she only became an artist through sheer persistence and was only gradually accepted by her contemporaries at the Slade who held a continuing suspicion of her background."[1]

Brett herself was not unaware of her freakishness. She wrote to her father in the autumn of 1911, the beginning of her second year at the Slade, that it was "beginning to dawn on them I am a bit of a lunatic". The letter heading is 8 Cadogan Gardens, where Sylvia was living at the time. One of the difficulties in pinpointing Brett's movements is that she used whatever notepaper she could pick up. Thus, though many of her letters right up to 1920 or so are imprinted "Tilney Street", this does not mean that she was living in the family house full time but rather using, or as her parents came to believe, abusing it: for meals prepared by the Eshers' cook ("Brett went to Tilney Street to get a square meal" – Noel Carrington), for baths and laundry and for notepaper. In the same letter to her father, on October 21st, 1911, Brett tells him that she had been with her Slade friends to a boxing match. "Jack Johnson, the black boxer, is the most beautiful man I have ever seen."

In 1911 Brett was, however, still resident in Tilney Street with, most of the time, only the servants for company. Her father and mother were spending more and more of their time at The Roman Camp, Maurice had become engaged to Zena Dare, Oliver was in New York and about to announce his engagement and in February, 1911, Sylvia at last married Vyner Brooke.

Sylvia's wedding followed an exceptionally brief period of formal engagement. King George V and Queen Mary, though unable to attend, sent her a blue enamel diamond and pearl brooch with a royal cipher; J. M. Barrie, who had encouraged Syv a good deal in her writing and who based Wendy in *Peter Pan* upon her,* sent a necklace; and, after the honeymoon trip, George Bernard Shaw sent her a poem:

* Pauline Chase was the first Peter Pan. Brett's sister-in-law Zena was the second.

Ride a cock horse
To Sarawak Cross
To see a young Ranee consumed with remorse
She'll have bells on her fingers
And rings through her nose
And won't be permitted to wear any clothes.[2]

Vyner's father, James Brooke, the second Raja, suspicious of an Esher plot to take over Sarawak, put in a rare appearance at the wedding, but became thoroughly bored at the reception that followed at Orchard Lea. He turned to the nearest person and demanded "How the hell do I get out of this damned house?" The person was Esher himself whom the Raja had totally failed to recognise and the bemused Viscount, without uttering a word, showed Brooke the door.

Sylvia wrote: "Now all of us were settled except my sister, the bravely independent girl in her boyish attire and short haircut who was incapable of doing anything, in the eyes of our mother, that was either dutiful or right."[3]

In fact it was not for another year or two that Brett cut her hair short and she had not immediately on entering the Slade taken to wearing the trousers that were to characterise her later appearance. She was not, on the other hand, dressed in the height of fashion. Mumsy had made it a rule that her daughters should live simply and severely in order the better to enjoy life's comforts when they were safely matched to a husband of standing and income. Sylvia's reaction on at last cutting the apron strings was to become one of the most extravagantly dressed women of the age. Brett, perversely, went in exactly the opposite direction. Writing to her over fifty years later, Zena Dare recalled her astonishment that, in their very grand houses, Sylvia and Brett were so very badly dressed and that years later, seeing Brett naked in the bath in Scotland, she was struck by her beautiful figure.

> I thought to myself, "She doesn't look a bit like that in her clothes – they don't seem to fit anywhere" . . . but then you see I was dressed in sable stoles from head to foot at the age of 19, which was also going a bit far.[4]

Brett's attitude to her appearance was not entirely discouraged by her father. Shortly after Sylvia's wedding, which must have cost the Esher family a tidy sum, Esher found himself engaged in an acrimonious correspondence with Caleys Ltd., "Court Dressmakers, Mantle Makers, Milliners, Ladies' Tailors, Silk Mercers and Linen Drapers; House Furnishers & Upholsterers; Funeral Furnishers; 19 and 25

High Street, Windsor", on the subject of an account for a little over £13 that Doll had allowed to mount up over the previous nine years.

> We are sorry to trouble your Lordship about the account for the Hon. Miss Brett, but it is not only very old indeed, but our repeated applications requesting a settlement have all been ignored, and we are therefore making an appeal to Your Lordship to ask if you will either settle it or inform us through what channel we can obtain its settlement . . . and we hope Your Lordship will understand that although our request may have a note of being peremptory, at the same time it is not unreasonable, considering the extreme credit that has been given it.

Esher replied the following day, referring to Doll, who had run up the small account between the ages of twenty-one and twenty-five and was now over twenty-seven, as "a young girl not of age . . . youthful and irresponsible".

> I have received your letter enclosing an account rendered for goods apparently supplied to the Honble. Dorothy Brett between the years 1904 and 1908.
>
> There is no statement from you showing the nature of this account, nor do you give any reasons why you allowed a young girl not of age to become indebted to your firm.
>
> You had no authority from me or from Lady Esher to supply these goods and it is little short of a scandal that tradesmen in your position should encourage transactions of this sort.
>
> You are simply gambling upon the reluctance of parents not to fulfil obligations entered into by their children.
>
> It is high time that proceedings of this kind were exposed and that a stop was put to a practice which is more dishonest in the tradesmen than in youthful and irresponsible girls who incur obligations which without assistance they are unable to fulfil.
>
> You are at liberty to publish this letter in the local papers if you think fit.
>
> Perhaps you will be good enough to send me full particulars of this account, I will then consider the course I am prepared to take.

At the same time Esher took detailed legal advice.

> Points arising on Caley Correspondence.
>
> *Infants* . . . But if a tradesman were to collude with an infant, and furnish him with clothes or other articles to an extravagant degree,

then, without any question, he would certainly be unable to recover any demand for payment he might make of the father. (Extravagance must be proved. Collusion also).[5]

Brett was clearly not an infant, nor had she been unduly extravagant. As the detailed account then forwarded by Caleys showed, the most expensive item on it was a white net evening gown, purchased for £4.14.6 in the winter of 1903 when she had been doing her "season". Only two other items cost more than a pound. Collusion too was unlikely and Caleys, unbowed by the threat of an onslaught from one of the most powerful members of the nobility, wrote again, calling Esher's blustering bluff, and, for their part, threatening legal action.

Esher's fury was unabated but, rather than see Doll in the County Court, he paid up, flinging a final abusive letter at Messrs. Caleys.

From your letter of the 6th of April it is obvious that you do not understand the tenour of my remarks. I have no intention of disputing your account and I have given instructions that it shall be paid forthwith.

It is not a fact that Lady Esher was ever aware of this account until the 5th of January last and it is obvious that you only gave this long credit because Miss Brett is what you, in vulgar phrase, call "a young lady of position" and because you believed that in the event of her not being able to meet her liabilities she had behind her the security of others. There is nothing in your letter which justifies the system of giving to young and irresponsible persons long credit for petty sums which, in the aggregate, if left to accumulate together with interest, may amount to considerable ones. It is your system of doing this which in my opinion is a scandal and inconsistent with honest trading. It is a form of money lending to young persons and on the whole is as deserving of censure as the universally condemned transactions which are occasionally brought to light between young men and professional money lenders.

A firm of your standing should be above transactions of this kind. Transactions which can only serve to induce girls and women to incur liabilities beyond their means. Three times during the last four years I have been called upon to assist in extricating families of the working classes from overwhelming difficulties brought upon them by having been allowed to incur debts to Windsor tradesmen which they were unable to pay. In these cases also credit was given mainly because the persons involved were connected by their employment with those to whom an appeal could be made for financial assistance. The only effective protest which those holding strict views of honest

> and legitimate trading can make is to refuse to deal with firms who employ the system of prolonged credit deliberately given with the intention of luring young persons to spend more than they can afford. It is with the hope of stimulating the conscience of the public in this matter that I fully accord you permission to publish this correspondence if you desire to do so.

Still unbowed, Caleys managed to have the last written word.

> Do you seriously suggest that when a Peer's daughter, of apparently full age, enters our Shop and buys goods to the value of £5 in one instance, and mostly of only a few shillings, that we, before sending the goods, are to enquire of her parents whether we are justified in allowing credit, as if so, we are sure you would be the first to resent the insult both to her and yourself.
>
> Does your Lordship suggest that an account of £13 spread over a period of several years was beyond the means of the Hon. Dorothy Brett? and to suggest that the charging of 5% interest on an account that is years overdue, is parallel with the methods of professional moneylenders, is absurd.
>
> Your remarks about other Windsor Tradesmen are beside the question, we do not do business with servants or the working classes, and so do not give credit to them. To our mind the direction in which the public mind should be stimulated, is in checking the system, whereby persons of position (we repeat the vulgar phrase) impose upon Tradesmen by taking inordinately long credit, ignoring their periodical requests for payments which are due to them, and without which they are unable properly to carry on their business, and then finally only paying under threat of legal proceedings.[6]

Doll suffered rather more than thirteen pounds' worth of castigation when next she saw her father, and the debt was docked from her monthly allowance.

Although there was by now no frequent or close contact between Brett and her mother, Esher himself kept in close touch with his maverick daughter. More often than not, the encounter amounted to a confrontation over Brett's abuse of the facilities at Tilney Street, her insolvency or her mishandling of money matters – she complained to her dying day that she had never been taught to look after money or to cook. Of the former, her family, down to the second and third generation would testify. Of the latter, her friends and visitors had experience at first hand. Angelo Ravagli, Frieda Lawrence's third husband, when invited to dinner at Brett's in New Mexico, crept quietly into the kitchen, tipped a seething week-old stew out of the window, and suggested that they all go out to eat. Julian Vinogradoff, Ottoline Morrell's daughter, recalls being shown a solitary tin of Spam on the larder shelf when she visited Brett in New Mexico and learning that it represented dinner for the week.

Nevertheless, and despite Brett's later memories, her father was the only member of her immediate family who took any real interest in her new life and her views on the world of art she had now entered. He supported her in other ways too. Brett had the use of Esher's permanent box at the opera when, as was now frequently the case, he was not in town and had not promised it elsewhere. There she entertained her Slade friends, often after a dinner of extravagant and, for Gertler, unaccustomed splendour.*

> Dined with Brett and Syv at the Savoy. The richness of the place embarrassed me very much. I did not feel at all at ease. There was a lot of footmen in grey plush coats and stockings. They all looked at me suspiciously. The dinner was excellent and with that at least I felt at home. I had pea soup, oysters, lamb and potatoes and then a baba with rum and coffee. When I came to my cigarette, I had completely forgotten my worldly troubles. I don't suppose that the waiter there had any idea I hadn't a penny in the world! After dinner we went to see a play.[8]

Towards the end of 1911, with Brett successfully into her second year at the Slade, Esher found her a studio in Linden Gardens, Kensington, close to Notting Hill Gate. At Christmas he wrote from The Roman Camp, asking whether she had yet found out about a drawing she'd asked for as a Christmas present, sending an art book to be going on with, hoping her studio would be a great success and, perhaps more importantly, wondering how she was going to keep it warm. Brett had been spending Christmas commuting from relative to relative, decorating the Christmas tree for Syv and Vyner, and dining where she could. She wrote to her father:

> I got the thimble out of Aunt Violet's plum pudding and a baby out of Zena's. I feel embarrassed about it. My studio is a success, my painting a failure as yet. I have written to some models to turn up for my inspection.[9]

* "During an Interval, a strange man suddenly barged into the box, stared hard at Gertler, said "I wanted to see if he was a boy or a girl," and dashed out again . . ."[7]

Esher replied promising Brett "a good deal of loot from *your* room at Orchard Lea and lots of brilliant stuffs and a screen. Altogether you ought to make your permanent studio, when you get it, quite smart. It is easier to make a good studio than a good picture, I imagine."

The Eshers had now ceased entirely to live at Orchard Lea, much preferring the Scottish house, Roman Camp. With the moving of the court back to London and now, with George V on the throne, Esher's influence on affairs of state was diminishing and the house was not so useful as it had been. It remained a thorn in his side for the remainder of the decade. Oliver lived there for a brief period with his wife Antoinette. Then Syv and Vyner took a lease, having persuaded Esher that they would make Orchard Lea their permanent home in England. Esher, for his part, settled the house upon Syv in his will but made the clause "revocable"; Syv and Vyner tired of Orchard Lea after a few years and broke their lease.

The Linden Gardens studio did not last long. Brett found it too big and gloomy and hated it. But it was a beginning and she wanted to show it off as evidence of her seriousness as an artist. She sent W. H. Hudson a silk scarf that Christmas and invited him to visit her there to demonstrate that she was not "just a fluffy nonentity" but she neglected to tell Hudson when she would be there or even the number of the studio. Hudson replied that in any case his wife was so ill that he was unable to leave her for other than a hurried walk nor could he receive any visitors. The silk scarf arrived anonymously, and he wondered who could have imagined that a wild man of the woods could want such luxuries, but forgave "my dear Dolly" when he learnt it was Brett and promised for her sake to wear it.

Brett's Christmas letter to her father contained other news:

> I saw John in the street. You never saw such an apparition – just like Taffy out of Trilby. Tall and big and such "swank" as they say at the Slade . . . patent leather boots and a large homburg hat . . .

And, more significantly: "A wave of popularity seems to be passing over my head since the 'Nuts' at the Slade suddenly realised my existence."[10]

John was Augustus John. Although Gertler had known him for some time, it was not until the end of 1912 that he was introduced to Brett and Carrington. But the "Nuts" that Christmas was very much present in Brett's life.

"Nuts" or "Nutty" was the nickname of Professor Frederick Brown, who had been so suspicious of the motives of the Honourable Dorothy Eugenie Brett in wishing to enrol as a student of fine art. Now that the aristocratic young lady had survived his six-month trial period and, "born again" as plain "Brett", was successfully into her second year at the college, the "Nuts" had rather more than realised her existence. For the first time in her twenty-eight years Brett found herself the object of a crush. Barbara Bagenal, a Slade contemporary, confirms that it was Nutty who pursued Brett and not vice-versa. The relationship, too innocent to be legitimately termed an affair, continued in all its less than full and fervent ardour until the end of 1914, although Brett and Nutty would thereafter coincide as guests of Ottoline Morrell at Garsington. There was a slight hiccup at the end of 1912 when the crush was just a year old. Syv wrote to her father (October 16, 1912): "Doll is sunk in gloom over her man. It appears he is now suffering from a nervous breakdown." A little later, Brett herself wrote to Esher, "My affair is over and I'd rather not talk about it. It has been very painful." Brett reacted to love's little difficulties in the most feminine of ways. In a letter written on December 31st, 1912, she sent her father a drawing of how she proposed to enter the New Year with one of the first short crops of the post-Edwardian age. "I have cut my hair off. I am blessed if I am going to allow myself to settle down into a haggard scarecrow, yearning after men." Mumsy was horrified but she and Esher were, as usual, at Roman Camp for the holiday season and it was left to Brett's brother Maurice to report. Maurice did not think much of his shorn sister. "Doll came to lunch and tea", he wrote to his father a few days later on January 13th, 1913. "Front view of her hair is not so bad but profile and back, it is weird. She is frightened of it herself, I think."[11] The haircut, in that style peculiar to Slade students that caused Virginia Woolf to call them "cropheads", did not frighten Professor Brown. When term recommenced, he and Brett were back together and, for a while became what Brett called "semi-engaged".

At the end of her second Slade year, in the summer of 1912, Brett gained her Certificate in Drawing and Certificate in Painting. The following term, the autumn of 1912, she shared the Still Life Prize of £5 with another student. Brett wrote proudly to her father, telling him that Slade tradition demanded that on the proceeds she throw a party in her studio. She had by then moved to a studio in Fitzroy Street, much closer to the college. Zena and Maurice visited her there in October and Zena reported back to Esher:

> We went to tea at Doll's studio. The street is quite possible. The house is run on the lines of a tenement, every lodger having their own key. There is no one responsible for the place. I mean no landlady and caretaker to clean the stairs and light the hall and passage, it looks very dingy and ill-kept. If Doll wants a fire she must do the

whole thing herself. Doll seems very happy but of course, if you want to see it yourself, I am sure you would have a shock at her surroundings. Morally she is quite safe as there are always two together and generally more.[12]

Fitzroy Street did not appeal to Esher and he lost no time in finding Brett a studio more to his liking – in Logan Place, off the Earls Court Road. Her father's help was not totally disinterested. He had continued to receive complaints from the servants at Tilney Street of Brett entertaining her Slade friends and the new studio, with a balcony and its own kitchen, bedroom and bathroom, might encourage her to make less use of the Eshers' town house. To add to the encouragement, Esher bought Brett a new easel for Christmas 1912 – "I shall be disappointed if it is not *perfect*" – and suggested she try to loot Orchard Lea of some of the furniture that Syv and Vyner, who had now taken over the Windsor house, were rejecting.

. . . the big sofa – the dog kennel* – has been chucked out of the Gallery. Molly [Maurice] and Zena went down and found it gone and a sort of "Cosy Corner" (ugh!) in its place. Why don't you try to get it for your studio?[13]

Esher, when he visited Brett at Logan Place thought the house "charming". Mark Gertler, too, appreciated it, particularly the bathing facilities, for although he had finished at the Slade in 1912, he had received little recognition as an artist and continued to live in the East End with his parents who had no bathroom. At Logan Place Brett hung two of his drawings that she bought, without telling him, from an exhibition in June, 1913, knowing that the £5 paid would smooth his continual state of poverty for a while. "I find you have bought two of my drawings," Gertler wrote. "I have sold two others, so I have a few pounds still." A few weeks later he was broke again.

I am getting very poor now. I cannot even afford models or outings in the evenings, and there is no hope of selling anything more, as my work is getting more and more personal and less and less understood. You see the curse is that even the most cultured buyer looks for a little prettiness. Oh, he must have a little bit of it, else how can he hang it on his dainty wall! How could his white and scented wife look at it! How could one possibly go on eating asparagus in the same

* It was called "the dog kennel" because, sitting in front of the fireplace in the long Gallery, it was always commandeered by the Esher family's tribe of dogs.

> room! . . . those cousins* who don't like the types John paints are idiots![14]

Gertler had introduced Carrington and Brett to Augustus John shortly after leaving the Slade and, for Brett, "the crowning event was when John would come and take us out on a pub crawl or down Whitechapel to the gypsies". Brett took a kind of terrified delight in her encounters with John, waiting for a suitable moment to sneak out from his parties before they became too rough. When a Slade student was helping her slip away one evening, John stopped them and threw the poor youth across the room. Brett recalled: "The violence frightened me. I only knew by hearsay of the kind of orgies that took place after I had gone."

Later, at Garsington, John "would sit with me on the sofa and the wandering hand would begin. I would take hold of it and he would turn to me with a smile and say, 'You don't like it, do you?' 'No, I don't,' I would reply." Brett felt safer taking tea with the wild man of the gypsies.

> Dear Brett,
>
> Tuesday will do – I'll show up at tea-time . . . my sympathy in your troubles – I'm stone deaf myself lately besides having a weak knee and defective teeth, and moral paralysis. And last time you came to tea I was in an uncomfortable psychological condition, feeling much as did, I imagine, that Peri who stood at the gate of Paradise, disconsolate . . .[15]

Augustus John's letter has no date. It was probably written some time during 1915. Brett's troubles with her hearing, to which he alludes not very sympathetically, had begun some years earlier, although it is difficult to determine when or how severe the loss was. It seems likely that some impairment began as early as 1902 at the time of her operation for appendicitis with its subsequent complications and the extended period of convalescence. But there is little indication of any hearing loss in the small amount of correspondence that survives from the Edwardian decade and, where it is mentioned, much to suggest that her hearing did not present any serious problem. She was, after all, a prominent member of the Ranee's Grey Friars Young Ladies Orchestra, although admittedly on the noisiest of instruments. Barbara Bagenal, who entered the Slade in 1913, does not recall Brett having anything wrong with her hearing at that time and says that she did not

* Not just the cousins: Esher wrote to Brett, "I quite realise John . . . his drawings reveal him. Obscene *old* age and voluptuous youth."

use an ear trumpet or any sort of hearing aid. Noel Carrington, who first met Brett just a little later, remembers a fabric ear trumpet. And, in a letter to her father, dated October 21st, 1913, Brett writes, "I am going to see my aurist to suggest trying a radium cure – according to the *Daily Mail* marvellous cures have been effected."[16]

Lawrence and Middleton Murry both rather cruelly interpreted Brett's deafness as psychosomatic, an attempt to shut out the "boring conversation of her aristocratic family". Brett herself may have offered this as a reason – it sounds much more romantic, after all, than appendicitis. There are other suggestions, too, from the Slade and Garsington years, that Brett could switch her hearing on and off at will, much as in later years, with an electrical hearing aid, she would do so if the conversation bored her. Brett recalled a ticking off she received from the Provost of University College, of which the Slade is a part, for eating her lunch with Carrington and Humphries on the grass outside. When the Provost had finished, she said, "I'm sorry, I'm deaf, I haven't been able to hear a word you said." Yet she could later report the incident in detail.

Whenever and however her deafness started, by 1915 – the beginning of her friendship with Ottoline Morrell – it was a serious problem. Brett's memoirs recall:

> The weekends with Ottoline and her crowd delighted and terrified me. My deafness grew worse and I felt I was becoming cut off from life. I think it began with the desire to shut out the criticism and bullying of my brothers. My younger brother, Maurice, bullied me in a very nasty and cruel way, and the elder brother, Oliver, bullied me in very clever and amusing ways. All this gradually did something to me psychologically and physiologically. I simply organised my life to exclude the outside world. Friends have suggested that I "imposed" deafness whenever I met an intense intellectual type. It may very well be true. My deafness began at the time when I did begin to meet the engagingly frightening intellectuals who made up the world of painting and literature. In effect, I was between two worlds: the world of my own inner insecurity and longing for friends and the outer world of involvement with these amazing people: Gertler, Carrington, Ottoline, Huxley, Mansfield, Murry, Virginia Woolf, Bertrand Russell, and, of course, Lawrence and Frieda. The most frightening one for me was Bertrand Russell. I never seemed to be adequate enough for him. I would say some thing quite simple, *quite simple*, and he would turn on me and say, "Why did you say that? What do you mean?" Well, I had not meant anything by it, I was so frightened. He would get quite upset and angry if I got up and went

to bed at the precise moment he would want to read out loud to the group of us . . . he would make me come and sit close to him with my ear trumpet, Toby, practically in his book so that I could hear every word . . . I must confess that much of the time I felt utterly terrified of the life around me and the life that at the same time I was loving to lead.

Brett wrote at length of her deafness to Russell when he was in prison as a conscientious objector, shortly before the end of the First World War.

Garsington,
Aug 26th, 1918

Dear Bertie,

. . . I feel prison must in some ways be curiously like the life I lead. I rather wonder which is the worst – prison, I think, because with an effort I can be included in a small way in human life – you are more cut off. But can you imagine what it means to see life revolving round you – see people talking and laughing, quite *meaninglessly*! Like looking through a shop window or a restaurant window. It is all so hideous I sometimes wonder how I can go on. I think if it were not for my painting I would end it all. Of what use is it to go among human beings – of what use to have friends – I am just the shadow of a human being. What a strangely horrible existence it is. You can realise what devastating attacks of depression I get – and what touch and go it is when my painting goes wrong. The pressure of one's personality on oneself is so appalling.[17]

In an explanatory note to his archivists, Russell wrote:

The writer of the following letter was a daughter of Lord Esher, but was known to everyone simply as "Brett". She was a painter. She and another female painter, named Carrington, practically lived with Ottoline at Garsington. Carrington, later on, married a man with whom Lytton Strachey was in love; she was in love with Lytton, who permitted her the privilege of mending his socks. When he died she committed suicide. Carrington and Brett both come in Aldous Huxley's novels. Brett attached herself to D. H. Lawrence and went out to New Mexico. The last time I saw her was in Los Angeles in 1939. In spite of incredible adventures she still *seemed* just the sort of person one would expect to meet at a country vicarage.

Russell wrote back a couple of days later, half sympathy, half sermon.

> I think prison, if it lasted, would be worse than your fate, but as mine is so brief it is nothing like as bad as what you have to endure. I do realise how terrible it is. But I believe there are things you could do that would make it less trying, small things mostly. To begin with a *big* thing: practise the mental discipline of not thinking how great a misfortune it is; when your mind begins to run in that direction, stop it violently by reciting a poem to yourself or thinking of the multiplication-table or some such plan. For smaller things: try, as far as possible, not to sit about with people who are having a general conversation; get in a corner with a tête-à-tête; make yourself interesting in the first place by being interested in whoever you are talking with, until things become easy and natural. I suppose you have practised lip-reading? Take care of your inner attitude to people: let it not be satirical or aloof, set yourself to try and get inside their skins and feel the passions that move them and the seriousness of things that matter to them. Don't judge people morally: however just one's judgement, that is a barren attitude. Most people have a key, fairly simple: if you can find it, you can unlock their hearts. Your deafness need not prevent this, if you make a point of tête-à-tête. It has always seemed to me fearfully trying for you at Garsington to spend so much of your time in the middle of talk and laughter that you cannot understand. Don't do more of that than you must. You *can* be "included in human life". But it wants effort, and it wants that you should *give* something that people will value. Though your deafness may make that harder, it doesn't make it impossible. Please don't think all this very impertinent. I have only written it because I can't bear to think how you suffer . . . I hope I shall see you when you return from destroying your fellow creatures in Scotland. I sympathise with the Chinese philosopher who fished without bait, because he liked fishing but did not like catching fish. When the Emperor found him so employed, he made him Prime Minister. But I fear that won't happen to me.*

Brett never lost her hearing entirely and her speech, which might have suffered in consequence of total deafness, remained crisp and precise throughout her life. In absolute terms, with the advent of more and more sophisticated electrical hearing aids, her hearing gradually improved, physically if not physiologically, but the nature of her hearing

* There is a note in pencil on this letter, written by Elizabeth Trevelyan: "In 1923 these letters fell out of a book lent to B.R. when he was in prison in 1918." In the other letter, dated Friday, August 30th, 1918, Russell wrote to Ottoline Morrell: "I wonder whether you quite get Brett. I am sure her deafness is the main cause of all that you regret in her. She wrote a terrible account of what it means to her . . ."

loss was such that she was never suited to the kind of tiny electronic hearing aid that can be disguised as an ear-ring or hidden behind the ear. When I met her in 1970, she was still using a large piece of equipment that much resembled a scaled-down 1930s radio and this she would hang around her neck or place on the table between herself and whoever she was talking to. The equipment seemed to have a mind of its own and would emit, despite constant tuning, quite arbitrarily, loud hums and whines.

There can be no doubt, though, that throughout her years at the Slade, at Garsington and for many years thereafter, in the days of tortoiseshell curlicues like rams' horns, worn like a tiara, of ear trumpets of brass and of fabric, and of straws eagerly grasped, such as the radium cure, injections in the behind, even the possibility of the clean air and tropic heat of a trip to Sarawak with Syv "clearing her ears", Brett's hearing loss caused her immense personal and social hardship. Deafness is, of all ailments, that which least attracts sympathy and causes the greatest amount of amusement. It says much for Brett's spirit that, although she may never have conquered her deafness, it never conquered her.

Brett removed as usual to Roman Camp with her family for the summer of 1913 and invited Carrington and Humphries to stay. They arrived early in August and were "amazed at the scenery". Carrington painted the cabbages in the vegetable garden, Brett reported, deadpan. She herself, accustomed to the scenery and less than overwhelmed by the cabbages, spent the summer struggling with a painting of *The Seven Ages of Man*, that year's Slade School prize subject. The painting failed to satisfy her and, when she returned to the college in the autumn for the last year of her course, she did not submit it for judging. "I'm glad I didn't," she wrote to her father, who was still at Roman Camp, "the others are so appalling". It was not just her painting she was dissatisfied with that autumn. After initial enthusiasm for the studio in Logan Place, she had grown tired of it. "It is as dirty as Fitzroy Street," she wrote to Esher in October, 1913, ". . . like a cheap boarding house and utterly depressing." But, although claiming that she intended looking for a better place, she did nothing about it until the following spring, when she prompted Sylvia to write to Esher.

Sylvia, whose husband, Vyner, was away in Sarawak at the time, had been seeing a good deal of Brett. Brett, in her turn, was spending much of her time acting as mother-confessor to Mark Gertler, who was then at the height of his maudlin self-indulgence over his unrequited longing to relieve Carrington of all that a young lady held dear. Gertler had written to Carrington early in the year, "Apart from Brett, I see nobody." Gertler was painting Brett's portrait, taking tea with her, walking in the park and taking advantage of Esher's box at the theatre. On April 6th, Gertler went with Brett to Sylvia's house at Wimbledon for tea. A couple of days later, he dined with Brett and Sylvia at the Savoy and all three went on afterwards to the theatre (the occasion referred to in Gertler's letter to Carrington quoted above, p. 45). It seems more than likely that Brett and Sylvia, as thick as thieves at this time, plotted together the idea that Sylvia proposed to their father a few days later.

> I have had a brilliant idea about Tilney Street. If you are going to shut it up all except Doll's bedroom and live in Paris, or go to a Hotel every time you are in London, why don't you let Doll live entirely in Tilney Street and get rid of her studio which is very expensive. In that way you are rid of the idea of her living away from you all, and she is comfortably housed bedroom and studio in Tilney Street, costing you practically nothing with just a cook-caretaker. I think it is the idea of the season.[18]

Esher didn't. He lost no time in letting Brett know once more how charming he thought her studio in Logan Place and told her to choose a linoleum for the hall – "and send the bill to me!" In the end Brett remained in Logan Place until the summer of 1916 but she continued, her parents being increasingly absent on war duties in Paris, to bathe and board at Tilney Street and persisted in her endeavours to take over the whole house. She wrote to Esher, early in 1915: "I've seen so many studios for £50 that are mere cat runs, incapable of holding a canvas more than 3 feet long and Fitzroy Street is a dream to some of them . . ."

Although she did not reveal the fact to her father, Brett had not been seeking a studio for herself but had been helping Mark Gertler look for one, knocking at doors and inspecting possible premises, "her little startled face quite white with exhaustion". When a suitable studio was eventually found in Hampstead at 13 Rudall Crescent, Brett helped Gertler to move in.

> She dusted all the books and did many things which I shouldn't have thought of myself. She is altogether a wonderful help. I really don't know how I should get on without her. However unhappy or unnerved I am she always brings peace and happiness to me with her presence – she has simply grown a part of me.[19]

Brett needed a decent studio, she stressed, because:

> I'm a woman and therefore I've got to force myself on people – a young man is watched by collectors to see if he is a clever student. Then he makes a sensation and sells his work. Then he is dropped for a bit and they watch for his next move. By that time Society women are on the lookout for him and get him in tow if they can and buy a few works and keep him alive until the collectors return to him. None of this happens to a girl. One gets weary with the rottenness of it all. (Certain people are already beginning to watch me, the right ones too, at least according to my views.)[20]

Esher was unmoved, despite the fact that he now had little use for the Tilney Street house. Sylvia too had withdrawn her support for Brett's scheme, perhaps because of accusations from Eleanor Esher that, while Vyner was in Sarawak, she had taken as a lover a young army captain, and was herself making use of the house to consummate the affair. Whatever the reason, the "idea of the season" was disavowed by Sylvia, and she and Vyner supported the Eshers in rejecting it. Vyner wrote to Esher in April 1915:

> I am glad to hear that Doll's Tilney Street scheme has been squashed. We gave her a good jawing about it the other night. No. 2 would have been converted into a pigsty if Doll had had her way, full day and night of unkempt and unwashed second rate artists and artistes – Doll would have tired of No. 2 in six months and would be seeking another studio . . . [she] is suffering from swelled head. From what reason I know not.[21]

Despite her dislike of Logan Place as a studio, Brett's disenchantment with her work diminished, so that at the end of her fourth year at the Slade, in July 1914, she was awarded the first prize for Figure Painting. The subject, set by Professor Tonks, was "I am the Rose of Sharon and the Lilies of the Field" and Brett painted a young lady holding a dove in her hand. Tonks pointed out that, while the painting was charming and delicate enough, it was perhaps too virginal and not sufficiently earthy. Brett's inability to achieve sufficient earthiness in figure painting is significant in view of the character of her London work over the next few years and of her American painting later. Tonks had a high reputation as a teacher through several generations – his influence can be detected, for example, in Augustus John's work and in the work of Mark Gertler. Of Brett's contemporaries, the still adolescent Carrington, despite the difference in years, was perhaps nearest to her in artistic temperament but Carrington came closer to the physical in her art. A later painting of Carrington's with the sun shining from behind a cloud over a green hill patterned with a diamond field, is just the kind of conjunction in nature that Brett would have noticed and the magnificent, formalised water-colour of trees on a hill at Ham is also the kind of subject Brett might have chosen and treated similarly. The two also shared an interest, perhaps founded in English folk art, in painting on glass and in using its translucence in their works. Brett carried this to New Mexico where, early on, she decorated the windows of the Luhan hacienda. Later, many of her paintings of the thirties and forties glitter with tinsel and bits of coloured glass – "sparklers" she called these works. But, in her Slade years, thirty years old, deaf, afraid of the physical, and perhaps for much more of the rest of her life as well, Brett was confronting in her work her childhood background and inhibitions. Tonks' criticism of Brett's treatment of the figure painting subject, "I am the Rose of Sharon and the Lilies of the Field", a theme which, even in later years, might have been interpreted by Brett primarily in terms of its ethereal and floral character, was sharply to the point and could have been applied to her work at any period. "Painting is a love affair with the world around you," she wrote to her great-nephew, Simon Brett, in 1969. "I was thrilled to find that in *Last Temptation* (Nikos Kazantzakis) when Christ steps off the Cross, he steps into a field of flowers, masses of flowers, just like my painting. The Crown of Thorns flowering, the wound in His side a red rose, the wounds in his hands red roses. The feet do not show – they are in flowers. The Cross is flowering – the painting is called 'I walk in beauty, it is I'."[22] Despite his criticism, Tonks awarded Brett the first prize of £4 which she promptly gave away to a couple of impecunious fellow students before proceeding up to The Roman Camp once more for the summer. This time she had in tow Professor Frederick Brown – Nutty – with whom she was continuing her desultory relationship and whom her father had not yet met. Esher, caught up in the turmoil that marked the end of peace and the beginning of the First World War (declared rather inconveniently before the grouse season had even started), hastened back to London early. He wrote to Brett, still in Scotland, with unusual affection and with great care not to let it seem that he was disapproving of any possible match between Brett and Nutty from Brett's point of view.

Dearest Doll,

. . . I liked the Pro. and he talked very sensibly. There is no doubt that marriage would be most imprudent and wrong from *his* point of view until he can see his way after this infernal war. He is very delightful to you. I hope he will do lots of sketches. He can stay just as long as ever he likes . . .[23]

Doubts had already been cast in Brett's mind by her father's reaction on first seeing Nutty. "My God! He's as old as I am!" she recalled her father exclaiming. The simple truth she had been unwilling to face was driven home. Nutty was not only of her father's generation in age but also in attitude and belief and just as remote and distant from Brett's new-found life-style as a leading member of the Slade's "wild group".

The affair continued its halting progress throughout that first summer of the war but when they returned to London in the autumn Nutty, in a moment of stress, turned on Brett and said he was beginning to wonder whether she knew the facts of life. She looked at him horrified.

> He realised from my expression that I didn't and asked me to meet him in Hyde Park after dark as he would be too embarrassed to explain in daylight. We met and he told me the facts of life, what marriage involved, what it would be almost impossible for him to achieve at his age. To do me credit, I actually understood. What was even more surprising, it completely killed the whole affair. I gave him a gold cigarette case engraved with the lines: "I dreamed as I wandered by the way that winter was changed to spring" and we gradually drifted apart.

The drifting in fact took a considerable time. Nine months later, in June 1915, Brett spent a weekend in the country with Mark Gertler, staying with the novelist Gilbert Cannan and his wife Mary. Gertler wrote to Carrington, "[Brett] told me a very little tiny bit more about her relations with the old Prof! Brett has a great deal in her that she doesn't reveal."

Later, in 1916, there is a hint in a note to Ottoline Morrell that she is in love with Nutty and at the end of October, 1916, "when all other tales fail us, I will tell you of Nutty . . . My part is so unexciting – so strangely *unemotional*, *unlived*." A couple of weeks later on November 11th:

> I believe you when you are nice about Nutty but I have teased you about marrying him and made you uneasy. Nutty and I can be intimate friends without marriage. And if I married him, his very devotion to me would imprison me . . . Even at these moments when I long to rush out and seize a man, I do not and have not seized Nutty.[24]

So the drifting apart, recalled by Brett as initiated by her father in the summer of 1914 and almost complete by the time of their return to

London that autumn, in fact continued for at least another two years. But it was more satisfying perhaps, to pin the end of the affair on her father, and place it at the beginning of the First World War.

Esher wrote to her shortly after the war started from Paris, where she had written to him asking him to use his influence in finding a safe niche for Gertler and suggesting that she herself might be employed as a chauffeur.

> Gertler had better enlist in the R.A.M.C. He will be quite safe and will have some physical exercise that will do him good. Then he will not be molested. Will not Carrington enlist? She would make a famous Tommy. You select odd trades for yourself. A chauffeur! How are your poor ears ever going to hear the motor horns behind? You will have to have trumpets sticking out behind the motor.[25]

Brett's deafness never attracted much sympathy or gentleness from her father. When Esher's advice was relayed, Gertler was hysterical at the idea. "*Don't* ask me to enlist! Do you want my spirit broken forever?! . . . I shall go to the country to rot away – all my plans over, what I wanted to paint over . . ."

In a P.S. he added "thanks for your money". Brett, perpetually broke, had once more been subsidising Gertler, for ever broker, or perhaps simply seeming to Brett more deserving than herself.

Gertler did not of course rush off to the country, that is, not yet. The country, in the shape of Garsington Manor, was not in operation until the following year. Garsington had recently been purchased and was being made ready for occupation by Philip Morrell, the Liberal M.P., and his wife, Lady Ottoline Morrell. Both were convinced pacifists and the manor house, close to Oxford, became a haven for fellow pacifists and conscientious objectors who could be employed, if only in name, as agricultural workers on the manorial lands. Brett recalled:

> . . . Clive Bell and Aldous Huxley were working as conscientious objectors. Curiously enough, Clive Bell was immensely popular with the farm hands and farmers. He was jolly, never did a lick of work, but kept them laughing and gave birthday cakes to their wives and children. Aldous Huxley, with his bad sight, could do very little work.

Gertler had met Ottoline earlier in 1914 when he and Carrington were her guests at a performance of *The Magic Flute*. Later he and Brett became, as Bertrand Russell recalled, almost permanent residents at Garsington, along with weekending "Bloomsberries", precocious Oxford undergraduates and penniless painters. But in 1914 Ottoline's salon was the Morrells' Bedford Square house – her "Thursdays" were instituted in November of that year.

> A great many people came [Ottoline wrote] though none of course of the fashionable set – they avoided us as pacifists, or as they liked to say, "Pro-German" . . . Those who came often dressed themselves up in gay Persian, Turkish or other Oriental clothes, of which I had a store. Philip played tunes of all kinds on the pianola which was a new toy . . . these would inspire us to dance gaily, wildly, and often beautifully, following the rhythm as the spirit moved us.[26]

Before long the spirit moved Brett to dance in, providing her own exotic costume, and Gertler warned Carrington in advance.

> We are having an exciting time here in London just now. Last night we danced again at Brett's studio. There were Barbara [Barbara Bagenal], her friend [Faith Hiles], and Brett and myself. Barbara was in fancy dress – trousers – she looked quite well. She is awfully good to dance with. I must confess I enjoy these hilarious evenings. We are trying to arrange to all suddenly appear tomorrow at Lady Ottoline's with masks and fancy dress. I don't know whether it will come off. It'll be rather awful if we come upon them when they are rather in a quiet mood![27]

Gertler wrote again a few days later.

> At Lady Ottoline's things went off rather badly. Fortunately I myself was not in fancy dress. Brett ran away abashed at once. But I've never seen Brett look as well as she did that night . . . we couldn't altogether have been a failure . . .*

The girls were masked, with short haircuts in the Slade style, "which was why Virginia Woolf called them cropheads" and were introduced as "mysterious strangers", Ottoline recalled.

> Mark Gertler would bring with him some of his Slade friends . . . girls in corduroy trousers, coloured shirts, short hair . . . Carrington with whom Mark was passionately in love, and Dorothy Brett, their constant companion and "virgin aunt" . . . [who was] in years a good deal older, but for some reason looked hardly more than a girl of

* S. J. Darroch, *Ottoline*, p. 146. Both Darroch and Ottoline seem to be incorrect in including Carrington with Brett on Brett's first appearance at Bedford Square.

> seventeen, with her peach-like complexion, retrousse, Joe Chamberlain nose, small open rabbit mouth and very tiny childish hands.[28]

Elsewhere Ottoline adds to the rabbit mouth

> and no chin. She was of the squirrel type and, poor thing, very deaf. I liked her and felt sorry for her, as her deafness made it difficult for her to be friends with people, and I knew her family were not very kind or sympathetic to her. I felt she was a sort of Cinderella, and that I had to help her find new friends, and have her stay as much as possible.[29]

Ottoline's not entirely complimentary description was written some time after the two had fallen out with each other. Brett herself, many years later, used to describe Ottoline as "a very strange woman with a heart of gold and a yen for men", but initially the two were fascinated with each other and the fascination grew into a strong attachment over the course of the next two or three years. Ottoline's response to Brett's debut at Bedford Square was to invite her and her companions to dinner the following Thursday. Brett replied characteristically.

> Dear Lady Ottoline
>
> I was so afraid you would think my running away rude the other evening but I had awful indigestion and had spent most of the evening standing on my head to cure it – with very little success – I'm also very glad you liked my trousers. They are very agitating to wear as one never knows the exact moment they are going to slip off – I have no control over mine whatsoever –[30]

Two weeks later, Brett was invited to dine, this time without Gertler and Barbara Bagenal and, her reply suggests, not this time in trousers.

> Dear Lady Ottoline
>
> I shall be delighted to come & dine on Thursday [February 11th, 1915] & will be a perfect Lady – I have misgivings about my clothes, but will put on the best I have – but I have no evening clothes, only rather grubby things, I fear – these drawings are rather like me.
>
> Yrs. v. sincy
> D. E. Brett[31]

The letter is written around a couple of head and shoulder drawings of Brett, presumably before and after – the first in a buttoned jumper, the second décolleté. In both Brett has managed to represent herself as a

2, TILNEY STREET,
MAY FAIR.
W.

Sunday 7th 1/14

Dear Lady Ottoline

I shall be delighted to come & dine on Thursday = & will be a perfect Lady = I have misgivings about my clothes, but will put on the best I have = but I have no evening clothes, only gently things, I fear drawings rather

rather these are like me

yrs v. sincerely
D. E. Brett

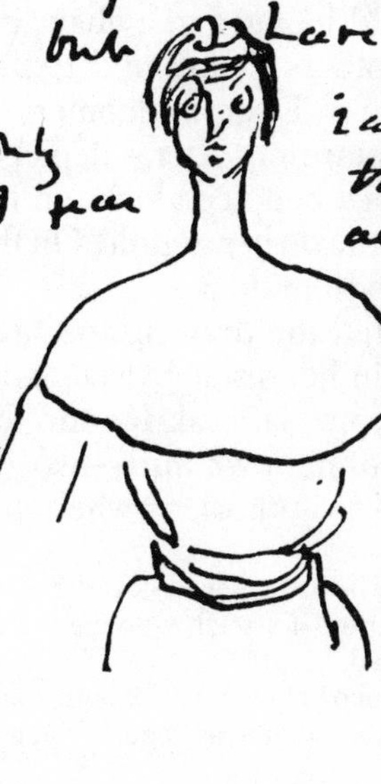

rather scruffy, unkempt schoolgirl. On the envelope Ottoline has written in pencil a note to Duncan Grant, the painter, who later became a close friend of Barbara Bagenal and married Vanessa Bell, Virginia Woolf's sister: "Duncan dear, do come and meet this person!"

Dinner was a success. Brett and Ottoline swept immediately into a constant correspondence, still, in salutation, of strict formality – Ottoline is "Dear Lady Ottoline", Brett signs herself always "Yrs v. sincy. D. E. Brett". Ottoline, looking back, was puzzled as to why her "Thursdays" were so successful. ". . . All who came were people who felt the war intensely and were certainly neither careless nor heartless about it . . . the pressure of unhappiness was so great that any diversion once a week was welcome, especially in the company of those who were sympathetic." By the middle of February, 1915, the pressure blew the lid off the vessel. Gertler wrote to Carrington: "Last Thursday was the wildest of all nights!! I smashed Dodgen's glasses, kicked Miss Strachey so that her foot bled, and made a Belgian girl's arm black and blue!!!* John was there. Lady Ottoline is stopping her Thursdays."

Brett was there too. She sent Ottoline a couple of drawings, one of the Thursday night, the other of the morning after. "Gertler has been ill, very bad headaches & touch of flu and has gone to the country for a few days." The drawing inscribed "Thursday" does indeed reveal Gertler, seen through a doorway, flaked out on a divan, one hand to his head, the other trailing in a debris of glasses and fallen flower vases. Before him, in the foreground, Augustus John, in an enormous hat, has his hand round Barbara Bagenal – firmly planted on her breast – while Enid Bagnold lounges in a chair, contemplated by the mirror-image Strachey brothers, James and Lytton. Brett herself, dressed like the other women in Eastern bloomers, shelters coyly behind John. "Friday" – the morning after – depicts just Brett, stretched out on a brass-knobbed bed, ice blocks on her head and under her feet, and a hot water bottle on her middle. On the wall the bedroom clock stands at twenty-five past midday.

Brett posted the drawing to Ottoline from Wimbledon where she was staying in her sister Sylvia's house. Syv, now mother and author, was home from Sarawak for the duration and Brett cited her as an explanation of her own thirty-two-year-old unmarried state. "[Sylvia] writes [i.e. as an author] =† when she isn't bulging with babies = which

* Maria Nys, who had come to stay with the Morrells for the duration of the hostilities in her own country. Through Ottoline she met Aldous Huxley at Garsington and the two later married.

† Brett developed her own style of punctuation. Full stops initially and, later, full stops and commas, were written as "equals" signs, thus : =

Brett (left), Barbara Bagenal, Augustus John, the Strachey brothers, Enid Bagnold and Mark Gertler.

Thursday at Ottoline's and . . .

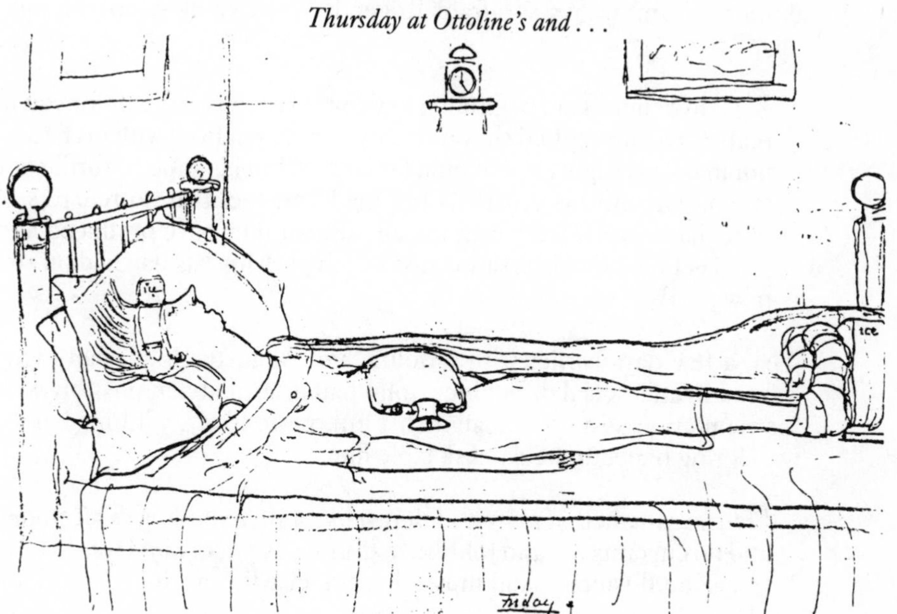

. . . the morning after.

has rather helped me toward spinsterhood more than the lack of offers, so to speak = one can't paint pictures and have babies ="[32]

Ottoline did not immediately suspend her "Thursdays" as she had threatened, for, in a letter that is undated but appears to have been written early in March, Brett turned down a further invitation.

> Alas on the 11th again I shall be cleaving to my hot water bottle = but I could come on the 18th = life is intolerable to me when I have a pash in my tummy = unlike most women I cannot fight against it = I hate everything and everybody =

In the same letter Brett reflected upon her deafness.

> . . . just as life began to unroll itself before me and I had struggled up through my environment to meet it, nature should deprive one of my full enjoyment of it = but still, perhaps in paint I may give something to the world = meanwhile I am going to make enquiries about instruments for general conversation because even then if brilliancy fails me, I can always lay blame on the instrument!! . . .[33]

A couple of weeks later Brett again wrote to Ottoline, on Friday March 5th, thanking her for dinner the previous evening, a longer letter now that the friendship was blossoming. At the top, scribbled sideways, is a note suggesting that Roger Fry, the art critic, had also been a guest at dinner. "I am always so afraid Roger Fry will swallow one by mistake."

> . . . I do believe I am beginning to thaw at last, it is difficult for you to realise my mummified condition as you have not lived with my father, not that I am frightened of him, far from it, but his superior brilliancy compared with his offshoots has made me feel that no remarks of mine have ever been worth the awful frost they have produced and so, alas I am no conversationalist which perhaps has dawned on you now . . .[34]

Tea, a few days earlier with Ottoline and Augustus John, had highlighted Brett's social difficulties. John had disarmed her, possibly with his reputation as a conversationalist but, more likely, with his hands, wandering beneath the damask table linen.

> I felt so ashamed of myself I felt just like a suet pudding = all stodge and no currants . . . and John!!!! at the mere sight of him I was in forty thousand flusters = and thus I do apologise for my dullness = I am

dull – dull – dull = & I sit alone in my little studio and weep over my dullness =

Acting on your suggestion I asked John to dinner here & treated him in a very motherly way, a manner I have always adopted towards him (which hasn't quite dawned on him yet) not that I am quite sure he wants a mother, but no matter = & we all spent a most enjoyable evening, except that I must add to the legs of my table as it was somewhat of a problem to know where to put John's legs, at least it was to me as the anxious hostess =

Meanwhile I am starting a new picture, and am like unto a broody hen with but half the egg hatched, one side of the egg has hatched nicely the other won't hatch at all = I wonder if John or Duncan Grant suffer in this way = All this is to pave the way to asking you to tea next Tuesday or Friday if you can face a quiet dull tea in my studio = 4 Logan Place = Earls Court Road = anytime from 4.30 onwards = I have scratched out Thursday, although it would be alright for me it is a bad day for you isn't it?

Yrs vy. sincy D. E. Brett[35]

Gertler, temporarily rejected by Ottoline, joined John at Brett's: "Last night was another exciting Thursday. Brett had John, Iris Tree, Barbara and myself to supper in her studio! John arrived with two large bottles of wine. Of course we got drunk . . ."[36]

Gertler had been working, on and off, on a portrait of Brett, begun, early in the winter, from sittings. He continued, now that Brett had discovered Ottoline's gay social whirl, from sketches, and wrote to Carrington in April:

> Early on Wednesday afternoon, just as I was busy painting, I heard a knock at my door. I went to see who it was and there stood Brett herself!!! I must say I was pleased to see her funny face again. We had tea and went for a walk on the heath.[37]

The completed portrait was shown in the New English Art Club exhibition in May, 1915. The critics too thought Brett's face "funny". *The Westminster Gazette* wrote:

> [Gertler's] power and surprising technical mastery are here again, but instead of sympathy has crept in an element of caricature. The comprehension has taken the form of cold, even cruel, dissection, rather than of sympathetic intuition. It is a remarkable portrait, perhaps the most remarkable in the exhibition (not excluding Mr. Augustus John's portrait of George Bernard Shaw) but a distasteful

> one. Along this road Mr. Gertler cannot advance; to sneer at humanity is to close the very gates of knowledge . . . this strong flood will be lost in the deserts of cynicism and unfruitful formalism.[38]

The *Observer* noted "the horrible distortion of the features" which "merely suggests the twisted mirrors in a hall of laughter". Mark Gertler, the *Observer*'s critic said, "worshipped at the shrine of ugliness". So, apparently, did Professor Brown, "Nutty", who bought Gertler's picture for £20.

Brett herself was in France when the exhibition opened and so avoided the scathing remarks of the critics. Since the outbreak of hostilities, her father, as Chairman of the Imperial Defence Committee, had been based in Paris. Lady Esher was with him and Brett's sister-in-law, Zena, wife of Maurice, now a Captain in the Allied forces, was also in Paris, working with the Red Cross. "[Brett] with that terrible woman Zena in Paris. How can she endure being with people like that," Gertler wrote to Carrington in May, 1915.

Despite Brett's new-found criticism of her family to Ottoline, she remained herself a staunch patriot, smugly self-important at being on the "inside" of the war, learning at first-hand from her father what was happening across the Channel. Esher delighted in her interest and the opportunity for some common ground. "You are an excellent correspondent," he had written shortly after he had arrived in France, "I love your war-like spirit. You ought to be a terrier*."[39]

Carrington too shared Brett's "war-like spirit" and, in January 1915, she wrote "THE TALE AND DOINGS OF THE MOST WONDROUS AND VALIANT BRETT: a Young Girl's Premier Poem". Seventeen verses, in limerick form and in Carrington's idiosyncratic spelling, all decorated with drawings, show Brett setting out with horse and lance, to conquer the Kaiser and the German armies. All are overwhelmed by her love and saintliness, the Kaiser falls for her, and, the war over, Brett returns successful to her Logan Place studio to share sultana cake with her poor friends – Carrington, Gertler and Barbara Bagenal are pictured – and to paint. The drawing for Verse XV shows how Brett's studio must have looked. Brett, perched on a high stool before an easel, is working on a still life of apples. Behind her a single gas ring burns on the floor and in a corner is a day-bed with a single cushion, adjacent to an open staircase rising to a small gallery or landing.

Brett's opportunity to visit France, rather more conventionally, arose at the end of April when her father's orderly and manservant, Taylor, was in London briefly and Esher suggested that Brett accompany

* A member of the Territorial Army.

XIII

But for medals & honours she cared naught
SHE had another kind of victory sought,
Not one, which Kings and generals seek
For SHE gained a triumph for the meek,
And righted the wrongs of the weak.

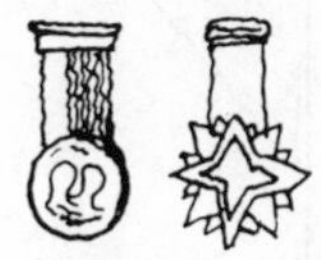

XIV

But feeling hungry she did take
As a reward a sultana cake
She asked her friends in who were poor
And divided the cake up in to four
Which they ate upon her studio floor.

Illustration from "The Most Wondrous and Valiant Brett" – Dora Carrington.

Illustration from "The Most Wondrous and Valiant Brett" – Dora Carrington.

Taylor back to Paris. "After the war," Brett later recalled, "Taylor became our butler. He knew a little of conjuring and would suddenly, while handing a distinguished guest, take a half-crown out of the man's hair, but Pupsie never saw what he didn't want to see." Brett took the train to Dover with Taylor.

> I travelled first-class. In the compartment were two women. They looked me up and down. I asked politely if they minded the window open. They barely replied. On the luggage of one of the women was "The Speaker of the House of Commons". I tried to talk to them. I got nowhere, so I gave up. On the boat I saw nothing of them, nor in the French train. But at the Gare de Lion [sic.] Pupsie met me in full uniform with all the porters bowing and rushing around to help him.

> I then saw the two women. They were both staring at me with their mouths open. I went off in a blaze of glory while they could not get a porter or a taxi. I felt for once I had scored over snobbery.

A victory of privilege over snobbery. Brett visited a devastated village close to the Front with Esher and her mother and accompanied Zena to the Paris hospital where she worked in daunting conditions. "The only time she fainted was when she was put to work in a ward full of faceless men. She just fainted dead away." With Taylor for company, Brett explored Montmartre and, when a combination of misunderstandings left her waiting in vain for Maurice to collect her to join her parents for lunch with a collector and painter who lived outside Paris, she and the conjuring butler ended up instead in the Quartier Latin. "Wonderful art shops, full of tempting brushes and paints, some of them full of very pornographic paintings. Taylor's face . . . was crimson with embarrassment and agitation," Brett wrote to Ottoline. But she regretted that she had missed the lunch.

> I would have given anything to see the early Picassos. And the silly old man with his piles of Cezannes – I am really peagreen with vexation . . . (but) I enclose a little picture of myself and the valet (Taylor) = not a typical knight errant but nevertheless most amusing =

The drawing, entitled "The Return from the Quartier Latin," shows Taylor in civilian clothes puffing contentedly at his pipe, while Brett, who appears to be clutching a couple of bottles, gives him a worried sideways glance.

A few days later she again wrote to Ottoline, wondering whether the two could begin to address each other less formally and suggesting that Ottoline should call her "Dorothy" if she found using "Brett" difficult.

> I should suggest you call me by my somewhat boring Christian name as to call me "Brett" might embarrass you if ever we met in other than artistic circles . . . Did you really want to know me? There is still time but you won't have to dig deep, I'm afraid = there is not much of me.[40]

"Other than artistic circles" is, of course, a delicate way of reminding Ottoline that, unlike Gertler, Carrington, Virginia Woolf, Aldous Huxley and Lytton Strachey, she and Brett were members of the aristocracy, the advantages of which Brett was always ready to capitalise upon.

Brett's most important news in her letter from Paris of early May was of a shop that sold workman's corduroy breeches. "I have discovered a marvellous shop where *les pantalons d'ouvriers* hang up by the thousand = I bought a pair promptly, dark brown, but can find no green ones for John."

She did find a pair for Carrington and, on Brett's return to England, the two "cropheads" drew themselves in their new French workingman's attire – "Brett in her breeks by herself = . . . Carrington in her breeks by herself – say mister one button undone!" "I am going to wheedle Nutty into paying for the whole blooming lot . . ." Brett told Ottoline.

By now Ottoline had transferred her salon to Garsington and in early June invited Brett for the weekend. Brett declined and Ottoline asked

Say mister
one button undone!
Brett in her Breeks
by herself =

her again in July. Brett had once more to decline. "I am on the verge of going to Paris again. When I return from France I go to Scotland."

This second visit to Paris did not, in the end, take place. Brett claimed later that her mother, shocked at her visits to Montmartre and the Left Bank with Taylor, had deliberately hidden her passport so that she could not travel abroad. She did go to Scotland, however, to Roman Camp, and stayed throughout the summer and early autumn, painting and fishing. After the brief Parisian truce in life's long battle with her father, encouraged by their facing a common enemy in Kaiser Wilhelm, Brett returned once more to the written attack. She complained in August of the difficulty she was having in obtaining the furniture she felt entitled to from Orchard Lea for her studio in Logan Place. For good measure, she threw in a short diatribe on social injustice, of which she always considered herself a victim. "All you people who live comfortably and have all and more than necessary to make life comfortable, never seem to care or have any idea of the discomfort of others." Esher, with more important things to think about in Paris, ignored the jibes.

Brett's first visit to Garsington finally took place at the beginning of October, 1915. She warned Ottoline that she had "terrible habits".

> I shall come armed with hot water bottles and night lights as I am always cold and always frightened in the dark and I go to bed at 10.30 at the latest . . . three months of [the country] make me feel I want to rush away and get roaring drunk.[41]

After her first Garsington weekend, Brett advised "My Dear Ottoline",

> May I at any rate postpone until the 20th? (of November) First and most important of all on the 13th I shall be suffering from the usual complaint which renders me not only incapable but also amazingly disagreeable.

So Brett visited Garsington in 1915 for one more weekend, that of November 21st, before joining Philip and Ottoline Morrell and their guests for a longer stay – the first of many – on December 19th, 1915, for Christmas.

That year, in October, Brett had for the first time been introduced by Gertler to D. H. Lawrence and his wife Frieda. Gertler and the Lawrences had encountered each other the previous autumn when Gertler "who had worn himself out with overwork and excessive sociability",[42] was on an extended stay with Gilbert and Mary Cannan in their windmill at Cholesbury in Buckinghamshire. Lawrence and Frieda were renting a cottage at Chesham nearby and saw a good deal of the Cannans and of Gertler, on whom Lawrence later based Loerke in *Women in Love*. Lawrence spent most of his time at Chesham being ill, a condition he invariably traced to his surroundings. Lawrence's ill-health finally led Frieda and him to move out and into Viola Meynell's cottage at Greatham in Sussex in January, 1915, but not before they had spent a claustrophobic Christmas with the Cannans. Amongst the Cannans' other guests for Christmas, 1914, were Katherine Mansfield and John Middleton Murry who, like Lawrence and Frieda, were living in a cottage nearby; Koteliansky – "Kot" – the Russian émigré Lawrence had met earlier in the year while walking in the Lake District and who later became a close friend and confidant of Brett's; and Gertler, the perennial house-guest.

The only excitement of a dull country Christmas appears to have arisen during one of the playlets written and performed to while away the monotony of over-eating and over-drinking. Murry and Katherine Mansfield acted out their intended separation but the psychodrama descended into farce when Miss Mansfield insisted on departing from the agreed plot and, refusing to be reconciled with Murry, clung instead to Gertler, who had been enrolled as the third corner of the triangle. Lawrence, absorbing all for later use in *Women in Love*, could at this point restrain himself no longer and leapt on to the improvised stage to try to get the play back on track, storming at Murry for "exposing himself". One wonders why Lawrence felt himself so threatened by the charade and whether the Murry–Mansfield–Gertler triangle may not, after all, have been the base of a pyramid.

At the time all three, as well as Koteliansky, were being urged by Lawrence to join him in founding a utopian community in Florida to be known as "Rananim" – a title apparently chosen from the first line of a Hebrew dirge moaned mournfully by Koteliansky. When Ottoline Morrell, to whom Lawrence had recently been introduced, came down, velvet-clad, to the cottage at Greatham at the beginning of February, Lawrence, hearing of her plans for Garsington, adjusted his reach somewhat. Garsington, handier and less alien than Florida, would be the home of the "new community which shall start a new life amongst us". Rananim, in early 1915, received little support and much mockery from the chosen disciples. Lawrence was forced to salt away the notion until 1924 when only Brett, of all the chosen, put her money where her mouth was and followed Lawrence and Frieda to the 9,000-foot high ranch in the Sangre de Cristo Mountains north of Taos, the final venue for Rananim where Utopia had a brief and bickering existence, anticipating by half a century the communes that were to sprout, peyote-like, in the northern New Mexican desert in the early 1970s.

Lawrence spent most of that winter in the country. Despite the fact that both he and Brett had discovered, or had been discovered by, Ottoline and were in constant touch with her, Brett and Lawrence did not coincide at Ottoline's Thursdays or elsewhere, although, with so many mutual friends and acquaintances, the two must have been aware of each other. They did not meet until the Lawrences had moved back to London to a flat in Hampstead's Vale of Health at the end of the summer. Even then it took much persuasion on the part of Gertler before Brett would accompany him to tea with the Lawrences.

> [Gertler] plagued and plagued me . . . insisting that I meet you [and] overcome my shyness and brought your invitation to tea. So we come to your tiny box of a house in the Vale of Health. It is dark and poky; there is a large woman, Frieda, and a man who scuttles out as we come in, Murry, and you . . . dark-looking in that dark house.
>
> A bright fire burns in the tiny sitting-room. Gertler, you and I sit in a row in front of the fire discussing O. [Ottoline] our mutual friend and enemy. I, terribly shy, in agonies of nervousness; you gentle, gently coaxing me out of my shyness. You sit very upright with your hands tucked under your thighs. We sit drinking tea, tearing poor O. [Ottoline] to pieces. We pull her feathers out in handfuls until I stop, aghast, and try to be merciful, saying, "We shall leave her just one draggled feather in her tail, the poor plucked hen!" Then it is arranged I give you a farewell party in my studio, as you are shortly leaving for abroad . . . and that is all I remember.*

That Brett remembered the occasion in quite such detail some seventeen years later is in itself surprising. At this time of her life, apart from a brief period at the beginning of the 1920s, Brett never kept any form of diary or journal. It is quite possible that the dissection of Ottoline may have taken place, not in October, but later in the year, in early December, for on December 12th, 1915, after Brett had visited for tea without Gertler, Lawrence wrote to Ottoline:

> Don't trust Brett very much; I think she doesn't quite tell the truth about herself to you. She is very satisfied as she is, really very

* *Lawrence and Brett: A Friendship* was written by Brett after Lawrence's death and published in 1933. The style – that of a monologue addressed to the dead Lawrence – was not new, in 1933, to her. It can be seen much earlier in a diary Brett kept in the form of a series of letters to Katherine Mansfield shortly after the latter's death in 1923.

> satisfied. She is one of the sisters of this life, her role is always to be a sister.[43]

All of which sounds very like Lawrence trying to make sure he gets his oar in before Brett, accusing her of being bitchy about Ottoline before Brett had any chance of persuading Ottoline that it was Lawrence who had been pulling the feathers from Ottoline's gaudy plumage.

Throughout the autumn of 1915, Lawrence still toyed with the idea of going to Florida to found Rananim and he and Frieda even booked a passage to America for November 24th, but this departure was cancelled when, early in the month, the police seized copies of Lawrence's novel, *The Rainbow*, from the publishers and took the book to trial for obscenity on November 13th. Nevertheless, their departure seemed sufficiently certain for Brett to offer her new found friends what she later recalled as a farewell party, although that, as a purpose for the celebration, may well have been coincidental, secondary or added to her memoirs with benefit of hindsight.

> Gertler and Koteliansky are the first to arrive; Koteliansky so broad-shouldered that he looks short, his black hair brushed straight up "en brosse", his dark eyes set perhaps a trifle too close to his nose, the nose a delicate, well-made arch, gold eye-glasses pinched onto it . . .
>
> A little later Katherine Mansfield and Murry appear. Katherine small, her sleek dark hair brushed close to her head, her fringe sleeked down over her white forehead; she dresses nearly always in black with a touch of white or scarlet or a rich, deep purple. Her movements are quaintly restricted; controlled, small, reserved gestures. The dark eyes glance about like a birds, the pale face is a quiet mask, full of hidden laughter, wit and gaiety . . . Middleton Murry rolls in with the gait of a sailor, his dark curly hair is getting a bit thin on top. He is nervous, shy, a small man. The eyes are large and hazel with a strange unseeing look; the nose is curved one side and perfectly straight the other, due to its having been broken . . .
>
> Carrington['s] . . . heavy bobbed hair falls around her face like a curtain; . . . she is dressed like an Augustus John girl, in a brick-red material. She sidles in, rather than walks . . .
>
> We have supper on the balcony round the small, square table. Afterwards we start playing charades. . . . In the midst of an engrossing bandit scene . . . twenty-two drunken people stagger in. From where? The news that I am giving a studio rag brings them, most of them strangers to me; and all have bottles in their pockets. They push in and take possession. Our quiet gay party is ruined.[44]

It does, again, seem extraordinary that, almost twenty years later, when she was writing *Lawrence and Brett*, Brett should remember precisely what Katherine Mansfield wore and that there were exactly twenty-two gatecrashers.*

> I can see someone carrying a woman I did not know across the room; of you [Lawrence] I have little recollection, except hearing you talk Italian to Iris Tree. K. is sitting on the sofa clasped in some man's arms; Koteliansky is singing on the balcony; Gertler and Carrington are squabbling as usual. While I, distraught, play the pianola fast and furiously, watching the party reflected in the bright woodwork of the piano. Some are dancing, some talking, all are more or less drunk.[45]

Among the gatecrashers was Lytton Strachey, of whom Carrington, "standing speechless next to a large silent dog"[46], later became so hopelessly enamoured.

> Some [of the guests/gatecrashers] seemed strangely vulgar, dreadful women on divans trying to persuade dreadful men to kiss them, in foreign accents, (apparently put on for the occasion).[47]

Iris Tree and Lawrence, perhaps, talking Italian to each other? Strachey wrote of Lawrence to David Garnett, a couple of days later on November 10th, 1915:

> There were a great many people I didn't know at all and others I knew only by repute, among the latter, the Lawrences, to whom I didn't venture to have myself introduced. I was surprised to find that I liked her looks very much – she actually seemed (there's no other word for it) a lady; as for him, I've rarely seen anyone so pathetic, miserable, ill, and obviously devoured by internal distresses. He behaved to everyone with the greatest cordiality, but I noticed for a second a look of intense disgust and hatred flash into his face . . . caused by – ah! – whom? Katherine Mansfield was also there and took my fancy a good deal.[48]

Strachey left Brett's Earls Court studio with Iris Tree, now in his party despite her "foreign accent put on for the occasion", "whistling with her fingers in her mouth for taxis, rushing in front of them, leaping on to the footboard and whirling off . . . It was a wild scene."

* Brett's great-nephew, Simon Brett, suggests that, for a deaf visual artist, this kind of visuo-numerical memory is not so odd. Perhaps.

For Brett the party was by then spoilt.

> At last it ends in the early hours of the morning; they are gone and we are propping a very amiable, completely drunk Murry up against the wall, and every time he falls down again. He is carried away, somehow, and we arrange that I give another farewell party, secretly, and we all pray fervently to be left in peace.[49]

The second party took place a couple of days later, this time without gatecrashers.

> We play charades . . . You [Lawrence] trotting round the room riding an imaginary bicycle, ringing the bell, crying in a high falsetto voice, "Ting-a-ling-a-ling!" and running over us all. I, too shy to act as well, choose as often as possible to be in the audience . . . The very next day you leave for abroad; I never see you again until 1923.[50]

Brett's memory is very much at odds with the facts here. Lawrence and Frieda left, but not the next day and not for Florida. A couple of days later, Lawrence departed, on his own, for a long mid-week at the rather more convenient potential Rananim of Garsington. He returned to London on Thursday, November 11th, 1915, bearing gifts from Ottoline of money towards the Florida trip, a pair of Hessian boots – handy for the mangrove swamps – and a bunch of flowers to assuage Frieda, plus the promise of a piece of tapestry to hang on the wall. And then, in all likelihood, Brett had tea with the Lawrences in early December before the couple left for Cornwall, where they stayed for almost the whole of the following year. It was not quite "abroad" but perhaps far enough away for Brett to regard it as so. What is clear is that the few brief encounters of 1915 can only have been on the most casual of levels, for there is no evidence of any further meeting between the two, and little mention in any correspondence, until Lawrence's return to Britain from the United States and Mexico in late 1923.

3

1916: Ottoline

After a Christmas and New Year amid the bright intellectual lights of Garsington, with Brett sheltering behind her ear trumpet to avoid having to take any active part in the dissension, discussion and inevitable charades, she returned to London and Logan Place feeling more than usually inadequate. She wrote to her father in January, 1916:

> The older I get, the more I see of people, the more I regret that when I was young you did not talk to me like you did to Noll and Molly [Oliver and Maurice] = they got all from you and because I was a girl I got nothing = I think this is the only grievance I have against you =[1]

The only grievance in *that* letter.

By June, Brett had completed her first picture of any importance, *War Widows*. The painting was shown at the New English Art Club exhibition and, as Carrington reported excitedly to Lytton Strachey a month later, characteristically misnaming the painting "*Black Widows*", it was bought by Lady Hamilton (the wife of Sir Ian Hamilton who had, five years earlier, been responsible for encouraging Brett to enter the Slade). The painting depicts a sewing group, dressed in black and all very pregnant – a fact that led one critic to re-title it "Out at the Front". In the foreground five seated women frame the standing figure of a woman who is gesturing downwards with a pair of scissors, set off by the bright yellow of a sheet being folded by two women behind her. A ninth woman faces out of the picture on the right, leaning against the green background wall. The whole composition anticipates in its sweeping forms and bright colours the style of Brett's later paintings of New Mexican Indians.

The painting was "lost" on the death of Sir Ian Hamilton but, in the late 1940s, it turned up in a London gallery and was spotted, quite by chance, by Brett's brother Oliver, then the 3rd Viscount Esher, who promptly bought it. It remains in the possession of his second daughter, Lady Shuckburgh.

Brett also worked throughout the year on a portrait of Ottoline, and in January, Brett wrote, addressing Ottoline as "dearest and most beloved": "I am painting you today and every day until you are finished ="

The portrait started as a head and shoulders, but at a later stage Brett decided it should be full-length. Unfortunately, the existing canvas was not large enough so, rather than begin afresh, Brett stuck an extra piece on the bottom. Then, finding it impossible to reach Ottoline's head, she had to use a step-ladder. Ottoline recalled sitting for the portrait in August 1916, in an orange dress and Turkish trousers – "bizarre but comfortable" – while Brett, perhaps struck by the unlikely colour combination, climbed up and down the ladder muttering "Marmalade".

Brett also began work that summer on another painting, a group of guests at Garsington – Lytton Strachey, John Middleton Murry, Katherine Mansfield, Gertler, Aldous Huxley, Brett herself, and Julian Morrell, Ottoline's daughter – gathered under a number of coloured parasols. She called the painting *Umbrellas*. In consequence, with eight other likenesses to paint, the portrait of Ottoline alone made slow progress. Brett wrote to Bertrand Russell on September 15th, 1916:

> I have been in a great state of mental agitation over my picture of Ottoline, and I have had to nail cardboard over it and take it away and hide it in Nutty's house, for safety – as I might have battered it to bits. I don't know what it is, whether it is very wonderful or very awful or a bit of both = but I do know that it haunts me, and peers over my shoulder suddenly if I try to forget it. I will tell you someday why I have such a horror of it. I am going to work at it again when I am installed in the Ark*, . . . and I am contemplating making it full length, 9 ft by 4 or 5 ft. Do you think this is too large and cumbersome?[2]

It was not until December that Brett resumed work on the portrait. She wrote to Ottoline on December 9th, 1916:

> Ottoline darling,
>
> I missed you so much that I drew out my picture of you and suddenly painted you all in until I could no longer bear your eyes = = those devilish eyes = they follow every movement I make and all

* Brett moved from her studio at Logan Place, Earls Court, towards the end of September 1916, and rented, with Carrington, Katherine Mansfield and John Middleton Murry, J. M. Keynes' house at 3 Gower Street. The menage became known as The Ark.

> the time they are saying something = = asking, mocking, seeking one = = mayhaps I shall be found raving mad in front of it = = It is an impossible picture to have = = at least for *you* to have = = I have you now sitting in a chair = = in a dark tight fitting velvet dress, with the lines and modelling of your legs showing through — lovely = I shall and *must* do some drawings for it next time I come = = The strange thing is that in spite of a nine foot canvas, I can only just fit you in *sitting down*! I seem to see you so enormous = = The background will be green like the drawing room — yellow and orange blinds and yellow chair = = and if I am not raving in a month I shall be very much surprised = = I can only work about 2 hours as yet on it = = by that time I am worn out mentally and physically and maddened by those eyes = =[3]

So Ottoline, now purple instead of orange, is once again sitting rather than standing. Even then, with Ottoline wearing a hat with a tall ostrich feather climbing straight out of the front, almost as though implanted in her forehead, Brett had difficulty fitting her into the canvas. "Appalling," Brett wrote to her father early in 1917. "I am tired out after two hours scrambling up and down it . . . when I first showed it [to Ottoline] she was so horror struck she nearly cried! That was just the head only – she has not seen it since with a body."[4]

A couple of weeks later Brett tried to reassure Ottoline and, at the same time, made excuses for not offering her the portrait, when completed.

> Your portrait is progressing beautifully . . . other artists are staggered when I say I am putting £1000 on it . . . I would have given it to you if I thought for one minute it would be a welcome or even a convenient gift but where would you put it! . . . Do you think you could collect your mingy brothers and make one of them buy it!!![5]

When Clive Bell saw the finished portrait, which Brett had, after months up and down the step-ladder, nicknamed "The Colossus", he thought it "not a success . . . a caricature 'au Lawrence'". Julian Morrell, then ten years old, told Brett, "It's no good your painting Mummy, you can't ever make her as beautiful as she is", and Ottoline herself thought Brett had made her look like a prostitute. Brett, in full crush over Ottoline, was downcast.

> I am really miserable at having hurt you over the portrait = it is chiefly a want of understanding of my idea of you and the difficulties

> and limitations of portrait painting = I have *not* made a prostitute of you = I swear I haven't . . .[6]

Brett's initial reaction to Ottoline's rejection of the painting she had toiled on for the previous year and a half was to want to destroy it, but she thought better of it and in fact, the full nine feet canvas remained in her studio until 1918 when Brett decided that Ottoline's face was, in her opinion at least, worth saving. Before burning the body of "The Colossus", Brett decapitated it, head and shoulders, with an open razor. Then in April, 1919, two years after she had first completed the original, Brett asked Ottoline for some more sittings so that she could finish to her satisfaction the much diminished portrait that remained. She painted out the hat with its soaring ostrich plume, leaving Ottoline simply but not unstrikingly bare-headed. Even in this final form the portrait was rejected by the London Group when submitted for their summer exhibition, a fact which doubtless influenced Brett's opinion of the paintings the group did select – she thought them "vile".

Lady Juliette Huxley* who, as Juliette Baillot, was governess to Ottoline's daughter Julian and consequently known to Garsington as Ma'amselle, was one of the few who did not share the contemporary view of Brett's Ottoline portrait. She wrote to Brett in 1972: "You once painted a wonderful strange imaginary portrait of Ottoline – with turquoise eyes and hair that flamed like a comet. I wish I had that portrait – it was so fabulous."[7]

The portrait seems unfortunately to have disappeared, although Brett retained a photograph of it. She abandoned all idea of asking £1,000 for it after its rejection by the London Group. She instead at last gave it to Ottoline who was less distressed by this head and shoulder version than she had been by the full-length Colossus. But she was never sufficiently fond of it to hang it at Garsington and gave it in her turn, Brett believed, to her brother, Henry Bentinck.

Brett wrote to her father in May 1916:

> We all bathe in the pond, the children run about nude, looking too lovely and afterwards we all go up to the roof and take off our bathing dresses and dry in the sun = the men in one corner – as the roof has a square tower which makes a screen.[8]

* Juliette married Julian (later Sir Julian) Huxley, whom she met at Garsington. Aldous Huxley, who had met his wife, Maria Nys, at Garsington, wrote to Ottoline: "What a clean sweep the Huxley family has made of Garsington – all but Brett; and who will sweep her? She will require a 40 horsepower vacuum cleaner."

Although she never learned to swim – "I have learnt to float", she wrote to her father, three years later in 1919 – Brett took to Garsington like a duck to water. "From July 1916," wrote Ottoline, "she came to stay on a visit that lasted 3 years."[9] It is easy to see why. In June, 1916, Brett finally finished with the Slade and had no longer any commitment tying her to London during the week; the Slade over, her relationship with Professor Brown was allowed to die away; not unimportantly, living at Garsington was very much cheaper than fending for herself in London and less trouble than battling with her parents over the use and misuse of Tilney Street; and, with the bread and dreams, there was love: she fell, in her adolescent way, for Ottoline. By the end of 1916, Ottoline was "My dear and wonderful Ottoline". Brett signed herself "your very very devoted Brettie" and "your very devoted villain". At the peak of their relationship, when not at Garsington, Brett wrote to Ottoline almost daily. Indeed, even when at Garsington, Brett continued to write, partly because her deafness cut her off from so much of the conversation of her hostess and the weekending Bloomsberries, and partly because she felt less inhibited writing than conversing face to face. "I so long to talk to you instead of writing = as I have never dared venture to talk to you of things I seem able to write to you about."[10]

As the salutation became less formal, so the contents of the letters escalated emotionally. By October, Brett could write:

> Three times I have written to you and burnt the letter in despair. I love you so much that I turn to stone or else babble weakly . . . you like the passionate burning flame and I like a sheathed sword in a drab coloured scabbard.[11]

Although none of the correspondence from Ottoline to Brett remains, the sentiments were initially reciprocated by Ottoline. Three weeks after the letter above, Brett wrote:

> Your letter . . . whirled me away from prosaic life = Am I really so much to you, do I really mean all this in your life = . . . I haven't told Carrington that you have stolen me from under her very nose yet = but I shall . . . I love you I love you, for the song you Sing, for your own Courageous self = and the joy and the Happiness of having you to race through life with and challenge the World = yes, we are indomitable, you and I, and we will sweep Katherine [Mansfield] along with us = and that poor delightful puppy Carrington.[12]

Two letters and four days later:

> My dear and wonderful Ottoline,
> . . . your last letter broke me = I cannot answer anything so wonderful I will make no further attempt until I see you = and when will that be? and yet I can't keep away from that letter of yours = I don't think I can possibly strike more sparks in you than you do in me = I think we are like flint and steel! and the harder we knock against each other the more wonderful sparks will come =[13]

Then after a week's interval: "I love you dearest Ottoline more than I can ever say and I long to perch on the end of your bed or you to perch on mine and tell you so and talk ourselves silly."[14]

Again, a further ten days on, acknowledging a gift from Ottoline in a letter gushing like a burst pipe in a spring thaw: ". . . on receiving the Amber Beads . . . I draw out from my dull scabbard the quivering steel of my hidden sword."[15]

Despite the highly-coloured language and Brett's frequent references to an armoury that her generation was beginning to know as Freudian, it is unlikely that there was any physical relationship between the two. Brett's "shining, hidden sword" represented her belief that, as an artist and as a person, she possessed great gifts and hidden talents, which, trodden under by her family and hidden in the dull scabbard of her plain body, could be revealed only to the chosen few, the few who demonstrated their own genius by recognising hers. The constant protestations of love and undying affection were those of an adolescent schoolgirl. For Brett Ottoline represented a striking centre of attraction, leading a wild, precocious life, conducting a series of brief and tempestuous affairs with Brett, the less attractive prop and butt, admiring and idolising Ottoline, wishing she could be her, fantasising that she was and bathing in the reflected glory and gossip of Ottoline's affairs. And Ottoline, of course, provided the useful excuse of a female companion should the possibility of a close encounter with the opposite sex occur.

For Brett, accustomed throughout her Slade days to the outpourings of Gertler and the protestations of Carrington, as the former conducted his constant inept and whingeing attacks on the latter's teasingly preserved virginity, access to the intimate details of Ottoline's all too real liaisons was both an eye-opener and a challenge. Alongside the metaphorical "shining sword" of latent genius, Brett felt compelled to invent almost uncontrollable sexual urges in herself and to hint continually of her own dark sexual secrets. When Maria Nys confided in Brett that she was considering eloping with Aldous Huxley, Brett, pretending the wisdom of many affairs and a thousand elopements, told her to go ahead without telling anyone and then wrote to Ottoline:

> I feel so horrid when Maria murmurs bashfully how much she hates men and their doings = ought I to know or not to know = as a maiden aunt I must ignore such knowledge = but in my present horrid glee I long to startle her with a vivid description of it all = even with you I dare not say how much I know . . .

A few days later she wrote again:

> You are quite wrong in thinking that I am unsexy! I hardly dare confess to you that I am rather the other way . . . how much I suffer at intervals from being a spinster! In fact I want to confess to you as I hate myself for my lapses and it will take all your arts and crafts to worm it out of me =[16]

Ottoline appears to have remained unconvinced that Brett was quite as worldly-wise in sexual matters as she kept hinting and, contrarily, made every attempt to educate her and Carrington, who wrote to Lytton Strachey from Garsington, "Ottoline insists on trying to get my state of virginity reduced . . .! And Poor Brett got sent out 4 times in one morning with Bertie [Russell] for long walks across remote fields by her Ladyship."[17]

From Ottoline's point of view, Brett was the first intimate friend of the same sex that she felt she could treat as an equal, at least as far as matters other than sex were concerned. "She is highly tense and nervous," Ottoline recorded in her journal some time after their friendship began.

> So nervous that it is difficult to get in touch with her, partly from her deafness and partly from the effect of her family. She is like a shy squirrel and it needs time and tenderness to win her confidence. She seems to hide her thoughts as a squirrel hides a nut and is very secretive, but I believe she has an immense power of devotion and love and understanding.
>
> Her deafness gives her an instinctive power of knowing one's thoughts. I love her and feel that she is one of the few people I have met lately that I could be intimate with, and who could take a part in my life. I usually feel as if I were an eternal elder sister but with her I feel more on a level and that is a relief.
>
> She is very comic in her observations and witty in what she says about people and we have great fun together. I enjoy her companionship very much. It is a relief to have someone to talk to about everyday things, and to laugh and talk about the people who come

> here. Philip is always so busy in his mind and occupied with politics and the farm.[18]

The relationship was inevitably magnified by Brett, for being "on a level" with Ottoline was so much closer than the daughter-mother relationship she had had with the Ranee and the maiden-aunt role she had pretended to with Carrington. Brett wrote to Ottoline shortly before her Christmas visit to Garsington in 1918:

> The old Ranee said she heard I was having the same *affair*! with you as I had with her = Thank God you and I had it out and are away and beyond such things == and I can laugh now, perhaps a little bitterly = = of course she is only jealous and possibly hurt but she never loved me as you do = = . . . how many people, I wonder, cherish this charming notion of me![19]

The pair must, indeed, have seemed a classic lesbian duo to any number of people, Ottoline in her customary velvet and pearls, Brett in her constant corduroy breeches.

For Brett and other Garsingtonians, Ottoline *was* "pearls and velvet". Brett wrote:

> You will get a terrible hymn of hate from me if you break your promise and ever sell the big ones [pearls] . . . you without pearls would be almost as bad as you wearing a Burberry = [Brett, of course, constantly wore a Burberry] . . . a sacrilege = Pearls are so like you = hard, round . . . but soft and luminous = you must never sell them . . .[20]

Brett was similarly boots and breeches to everyone, and proud of it.

> I went to a tailor [in 1916, an exclusively male domain] and ordered some corduroy Breeches! and was measured very seriously by a solemn man in most strange places = without a smile he rummaged up my skirt and measured my legs, I hoped I was a normal size, I sat looking very innocent, as if tailors constantly measure my bustle. I believe the trying on requires even more dignity =[21]

The breeches became whole suits and the following Easter Brett wrote to her father from Garsington: ". . . I have some very comic corduroy suits like this . . ." – a sketch intervenes – "which I wear down here and sometimes in London = when very cold = they are everlasting!!!!"[22] Later that year, Virginia Woolf noted after her first visit to Garsington in October 1917: "People were strewn about in a sealing wax coloured room . . . Brett in trousers, Philip tremendously encased in the best leather; Ottoline, as usual, velvet and pearls; 2 pug dogs."[23] Even the dogs must have added to the misinterpretation of the relationship between Brett and Ottoline.

Early in 1917 the gossip of Garsington and Bloomsbury at last filtered its way down the funnel of Brett's ear trumpet. She protested to Ottoline that she had no physical feelings for her other than the "intense enjoyment a beautifully shaped head and beautiful form give to anyone who loves forms and shapes. I have no real perversion: My love for you is as clean and clear as Crystal and fresh as the Wind."[24] Nevertheless, Brett's devotion was encouraged by a sense of practicality and her stay at Garsington that first summer of 1916, was doubtless extended by her growing dislike for Logan Place, her London studio. In the course of that summer, one of Ottoline's guests was J. M. Keynes, the economist. Clive Bell, as a conscientious objector with a commitment to till the soil was, like Brett, almost a permanent guest at Garsington, and his house in Gordon Square was more or less permanently empty. Keynes was living in a large house in Gower Street, close to Bedford Square, with his friend John Tressider Sheppard and the two decided that Bell's smaller house would suit them better. Keynes offered Brett the Gower Street house and by the beginning of September 1916 the matter had been decided. Keynes wrote to Brett, noting that the total outgoings on the house were £144.10 per annum; and again, a few days later: "I don't think we need a legal agreement . . . I would like one third of the rent, that is £27.10s on September 29th and ditto on December 25th and March 29th . . . who exactly is to live in the house?" It was a pertinent question. Brett was already calling 3 Gower Street "The Ark". John Middleton Murry and Katherine Mansfield, with whom she had become close that summer at Garsington, and who were staying temporarily at Logan Place, were to live on the first floor, Brett herself on the second and Carrington in the attic. Carrington wrote excitedly to Lytton Strachey, *her* Garsington discovery of the summer: 'My rent will be only nine pounds a year!!! . . . I shall like living with Katherine I am sure . . ."

Carrington's euphoria was short-lived. Within a few days of the Ark getting afloat, Brett wrote to Ottoline, "Carrington doesn't like Katherine!! . . . at least she suspects her of being double faced!" One of the reasons rapidly became clear – Katherine was waylaying everyone who came to call and enticing them into her first-floor rooms. ". . . To our chagrin, *no one* gets further than Katherine!" Brett wrote to Ottoline at the end of October. "Bertie, Lytton, etc. all disappear like magic . . . I have my little instrument trained on the cracks in the floor!"

The Ark had been established only a month when Brett was writing to Ottoline that it might be better if Katherine were to leave.

> "I think she is in *Love*, some man has arisen like the dawn on her horizon, like they will all her life = = . . . she is torn, I believe = = pity for the shy, gentle, clinging man she lives with [Murry] and the passionate desire for freedom . . . behind her, if she goes, a knife left buried in Murry's heart, the loss (possibly) of valued friends = = . . . could you, if she ever tells you of her trouble just drop a hint that her flight into the unknown from the Ark would not offend *me* = = a consideration I doubt ever entering her mind as I know her so little yet?[25]

Notably, there is no suggestion in Brett's letter that Murry should leave the Ark. She had already written to Ottoline a couple of weeks earlier "Murry has been here this evening, making love to me all evening!" and although the verb did not have the meaning one would attach to it in the present day, the grounds for a liaison between the two were evidently being laid as early as this and were strengthened during Christmas at Garsington when Murry left a Christmas Eve note on Brett's pillow, saying that she was a darling and hoping they would spend every Christmas together and every Christmas Eve kissing.

John Manchester, Brett's companion of later years, believes the note was taken a good deal more seriously by Brett than was intended by Murry. Katherine Mansfield was, that Christmas, off on one of her little affairs, this time with Bertrand Russell, and Murry, aware of the rapid rate at which gossip travelled at Garsington, may well have intended the contents of the note to reach Katherine as much as to impress Brett. Nevertheless, the pretended secrecy, the adolescent note-passing and vicarious sexuality of it all, struck a chord in the thirty-three-year-old spinster, but the affair did not immediately blossom.

"Katherine," Brett recalled, "played with emotions to see what would happen." On Christmas day, "after dinner", Carrington wrote to her brother, Noel:

> A most extraordinary game instituted by Katherine M. Everyone wrote to someone present in the room, a short anonymous letter addressed only to the person, not signed – They were then read and the public left to wonder who wrote them and what was the meaning – if any . . . it became almost too exciting – and personal – even libellous sometimes.

Ottoline later recorded in her journal:

> Katherine Mansfield left [the Ark] soon and went to Chelsea because she did not like the atmosphere . . . she had been made uncomfortable by Carrington who spied on her, who went in, who came out, who visited her. Carrington made up fantastic tales: Katherine Mansfield (Carrington said) used to disguise herself and go out at night, seeking adventures, she acted for cinemas, had mysterious visitors and so on . . .[26]

Katherine's departure was not unexpected. When she moved out of the Ark towards the middle of February, 1917, she told Murry she needed freedom to concentrate on her writing and their relationship must take second place to that. Murry himself remained a little longer but he too moved out eventually, to Redcliffe Road, having overstayed his welcome in the Gower Street menage. "We can't get rid of Murry," Brett wrote to Ottoline shortly after Katherine's departure.

Brett herself did not stay in the Ark any longer than the lease required, even though in later years she remembered the nine months in Gower Street as a time of great joy and friendship. She wrote to her father as early as January, "I am not taking the Ark again: the servant I have is intolerable: cooks the books and can't cook the dinner. I had one meal their [sic] and nearly died = Since then I do my own cooking under her flaming red nose =" Carrington too, at close quarters, was getting under Brett's feet.

> I don't want to set up a menage again of the Gower Street sort [Brett wrote to her father from Garsington at Easter], I don't want to hurt Carrington's feelings but I just want to glide away quietly. She is really very nice but unfortunately certain bad qualities or uncongenial ones to me . . . her mode of life is too untidy, too much of a turmoil . . . it disturbs me to have it splashing over me . . .[27]

By the time the Ark foundered at the end of June, all the original residents had abandoned ship. Lord and Lady Esher were still in Paris and Brett was following her customary pattern of using the family home in Tilney Street as a weekday hotel and Garsington as a weekend residence. She offered her father's house to Ottoline as a kind of quid pro quo. "Come any day to Tilney Street," Brett wrote from Gower Street. "You won't mind a less magnificent room, will you? The advantages are a hot bath* night and morning = and scrumptious

* "There was no hot water at Garsington and my mother used to go up to London to Brett's to have a bath." – Julian Morrell (personal communication)

coffee = and a latchkey so that you can frisk to your heart's content all alone."

Esher was not entirely enchanted with his daughter's largesse, and wondered to the housekeeper why his bills were always so much higher when he was away than when he and Eleanor Esher were at home. The housekeeper blamed the costs on "Miss Doll's goings on" and threatened to give notice. Esher's reaction was to order her to take up all the carpets, take down the curtains, remove the mattresses, cover everything else in dust-sheets and lock the door to Brett. "Dearest Doll," he wrote, "I must ask you not to make use of Tilney Street in any way while we are away . . . needless to say, delighted you should do so when we are here."

Brett fared no better with Keynes. He wrote on June 7th, 1917, pointing out that no rent had been paid since December, that £44.13.1d. was owing for sundry items and that he had a bill "for £36 for the damage alleged done to the contents of the house . . . since you took occupation of Gower Street, the house has cost me £142, against which I have had from you so far £53.3s.6d, so even when you have paid up the above, it shall still have cost me nearly £50 plus what I have to pay for the house to be redecorated . . . it's a beastly business having to do with houses."[28]

Ever righteous, Brett, in turn, blamed Carrington, whose friendship had not stood the strain of life at close quarters with her "maiden-aunt". Brett complained to her father:

> Maynard Keynes and I are both rather annoyed over a damages bill which I have sent to Carrington as the damage is to the furniture and I had my own!! It will teach Carrington a lesson but I don't know what they will do as Carrington has no money = but it's time she discovered that other people's furniture is more of a nuisance than one's own.[29]

4

1917–1919: Garsington and Hampstead

The winter of 1917 had been hard – Brett and Carrington had skated a good deal on the frozen lake in Regents Park. Brett had planned to escape to Sarawak with her sister, Sylvia, who was now Ranee, on the succession of her husband, Vyner, to the Raja's throne. Brett wrote to Esher, "I hope to return with my deafness cured . . . because really I don't see much use in being alive and stone deaf."[1] Sylvia fell ill, however, the trip was postponed and, in the end, never made. By June, having abandoned the strange belief that the tropical airs of Borneo might improve her hearing, Brett was having "injections in my behind. I hope to hear marvellously afterwards."[2] Doctor Foster's Miracle Cure was presumably less dangerous than having her affliction attended to by Dyak head-hunters.

During Sylvia's illness, Brett moved into Syv's Paddington home to look after her young nieces. Then, when Syv came out of hospital, Brett took her to Garsington for a weekend.

"Lady Ottoline's entourage appals me," Syv wrote to Esher in August:

> The C.O.'s [conscientious objectors] are so awful – flabby cowards – over-sexed – under-sexed – never normal – The conversation consists of depraved and curious conditions in life so that you long for an ordinary couple to come in and say "Well, we live an ordinary life, do ordinary things in the ordinary way and have ordinary children."*
>
> At breakfast with your bacon and eggs you get a minute and detailed description of life *à la* Oscar Wilde – by dinner time the tales become more lurid – Eleanor Glyn's *Three Weeks* would pale before one day in the life of Mark Gertler or Clive Bell – Doll [Brett]

* One of Sylvia's own three daughters married Harry Roy, a popular dance-band leader of the Thirties, another an all-in wrestler.

> sits smiling, hearing nothing but with an expression on her face as much as to say "These are *real talkers*, real brains – away with your great wars and your great politicians and your great soldiers – *these* at Garsington are men of 'Kultur'" – Oh it made me feel very sick inside – Clive Bell, who Doll is always quoting as if he is Jesus Christ, is a fat greasy looking creature with long *Henna* coloured hair – he has a trick, most embarrassing, of fiddling with himself – all day and all the time – Doll wanted *me* to tell him not to – Oh, I tell you I had to have a mental bath when I got home, as well as a bodily one.[3]

It seems to have been a long bath. According to the Garsington guest book, Sylvia's visit was in early April – the letter is dated mid-August. Another visitor to Garsington that year was Virginia Woolf who found

> endless young men from Oxford, and Brett and Lytton and Aldous Huxley who talks too much about his prose romances for my taste and falls into deep glooms, when, according to Ottoline, he is thinking of Maria . . . Brett is a queer imp. She took me to her studio and is evidently very proud of a great picture full of blue umbrellas, which seems to console her for being deaf.[4]

The "horror of the Garsington situation" did not deter Virginia Woolf from paying a further visit the following July when, she confided to her diary, she was "further paralysed by the task of describing a weekend at Garsington . . . I was taken to Gertler's studio and shown his solid 'unrelenting' teapot (to use Brett's word)."[5] There follows a bitchy description of Ottoline and a eulogy for bed ("like layer upon layer of springy turf") and building ("almost melodramatically perfect"). To Ottoline she wrote, with perfect ambiguity, "to describe my pleasure during the weekend is very difficult", but she did praise the bed and the view "and that is to say nothing about the human beings, who were all wonderfully interesting, I thought".[6]

Brett's painting "full of blue umbrellas" was, indeed, *Umbrellas – a Conversation Piece on Garsington Lawn*. The large painting, six feet by six feet, has been lost but a photograph remains. In it, Ottoline sits in a tall brimmed hat, bound with a scarf, between Brett and Lytton Strachey who has been reading aloud to the company. Aldous Huxley is sitting on the ground before them, Julian Morrell standing behind him with her hands on his shoulders. Behind them are four multi-coloured parasols and to the right, under a further two parasols, sit Katherine

Mansfield and John Middleton Murry, oblivious of the others, while to the left, almost lost under his own sunshade, is Mark Gertler.

Brett worked on *Umbrellas* during the whole of the summer at Garsington, padlocking the door of her studio, an outbuilding known as the Monastery, and allowing the painting to be seen only by invitation. Murry was one of those invited and Katherine Mansfield wrote to Brett that wet summer, telling her of Murry's enthusiasm for the painting, especially its treatment of Ottoline.[7] Murry must have had some doubts as to Ottoline's reaction for, the same day, he wrote himself to Ottoline, who had not yet been allowed to see the work. He enclosed, confidentially, a letter Brett had sent him which, he felt, held some truths about Ottoline that she would more easily understand when she was allowed to see the picture and he urged her to like it, adding that it was due to Ottoline's encouragement that Brett had produced her first real painting.[8]

Brett herself was enthusiastic and wrote to her father, "This new picture is a distinct advance on my *Widows* = in fact I have realised some wonderful moments of Ecstasy!! and acknowledgement for the first time from other artists . . ."[9]

In the same letter, she reported that Loulou Harcourt and his wife, May, had popped over to Garsington. ". . . it is so tiresome that Loulou is such an old roue = he is as bad with boys as with girls, so returning their call is fraught with anxiety. He is simply a 'sex maniac', it isn't that he is in love = it is just ungovernable Sex desire for both sexes."

Esher replied to his wayward daughter, a long and sympathetic letter from Sentes in France, "a dear little place. There are forests all round and the sound of guns ever, flashes all night but birds and wild flowers and broken villages and soldiers' graves . . . I have no doubts about your talents. I never have had since I saw the *Widows* . . . I am very proud to be related to you in blood as well as sympathy."[10]

Indeed, all Esher's letters to Brett around this time, despite the ill-feeling over Tilney Street, show a sympathy for her life-style and encouragement for her chosen career that is lacking in the correspondence of other members of her family. In one, he talks of a "curious deft insight that may spell genius"[11] which makes it all the more remarkable that, both at the time and in retrospect, Brett blamed, of that family, her father so much.

Brett's reply of September 28th warned her father not to be disappointed over how little she had achieved on canvas.

> I never seem to have much to show, chiefly because I paint over things so much = the failures of which I seem to have heaps, I cover

up = and so paint about four things on a canvas, one after another . . . Gertler* has been here two months and has left today.[12]

Esher, replying to Brett's September 28th letter, dissuaded her from thinking once again of travelling to Sarawak with Syv. Brett's answer contains a note, significant in view of her later emigration to New Mexico. "I don't know about Borneo = I think after the War it would be a great thing to have a tremendous change . . ."

From Paris Esher sent a book on Cezanne and Brett wrote long in reply. The air raids on London were at their peak and Brett, who, at the beginning of the war, had kept a map with pins in it to show the Allied advances, had by now, under the influence of the conscientious objectors at Garsington, wearied of the battles.

> I would like to put Lloyd George = Kaiser Bill and his War Party = the French Government and all the Fighting Countries governments into a Pillbox and fire heavy guns at it = throw bombs at it and then drive a Tank slowly over them = and in the Future *hang* immediately any government with Warlike tendencies = but the "People" are so stupid = they believe all the bunkum of Patriotism and the glory of War = tell (Mumsy) that I am glad and proud I am not still sticking pins in a map . . . Oxford is a mass of legless–armless men = and processions of men in long bathchairs = they don't complain but there is a never-again kind of feeling about them . . .[14]

Brett's pacifism evaporated a little during the following spring's offensive of the dying war. She sent Esher in April, 1918, an elaborate plan that she believed would have solved the Allied defence problems.

> Why didn't we build a deep wide ditch 30 ft. deep and 30 ft. wide. I've drawn it badly . . . The Germans would have fallen into the Ditch and could only cross by walking over their own men when the ditch was full up. Why do we never have our defence really capable of defence![15]

The air raids on London had in part helped keep Brett at Garsington, now she had given up the tenancy of the Ark and the studio in Earls Court. But there were other reasons, as she explained to Esher.

* A month later, on November 4th, Gertler wrote to Brett from London:

> On the 9th I am 26 and you are now a prosperous artist, I am poor, lonely and cold. So will you please get me a woollen waistcoat? not too bright and not too big. About Murry's size would fit me.[13]

> First of all, because I like Lady Ottoline – secondly because I have so many of my belongings here – I couldn't move if I wanted to = and thirdly if I have to divide myself up = Syv and Zena are two and I don't make much difference up there [Roman Camp] and then the immense expense of getting to Scotland now = if I had to come back, I should be broke = Also I should always be fishing! I miss it terribly = I simply long for it. I am very happy here and very *free* = I have the Monastery to myself = except for the milk cows below = [16]

Wintering at Garsington for the first time, Brett pressed on with *Umbrellas*. She added Lytton Strachey to her fans. Carrington wrote to him: "I am glad you thought Brett's picture so good. From the photograph I thought the Aldous part of the composition looked a bit feeble. But it was hard to tell."[17] Brett entered *Umbrellas* for the New English Art Club exhibition in January (1918). It was rejected, which Gertler thought a good sign. "I really don't think one ought to send there at all. I don't think I shall ever send again."[18] In April, however, Gertler reported to Ottoline that *Umbrellas* had got into the London Group exhibition and looked "bright and gay".

At the beginning of 1918, Brett agreed to illustrate Aldous Huxley's *Leda and the Swan*, but, by the end of the Garsington summer, no drawings had been produced. Huxley wrote to Juliette Baillot who, now that Julian Morrell was at school, had become governess to Sylvia's children and moved with them to the Roman Camp for the season. Huxley, Brett, Ottoline and Julian Morrell and Gertler had had "a great evening of it", he told her, at the Ballet Russe, where they met, backstage, André Gide, looking like "a baboon with the voice, manners and education of Bloomsbury in French",[19] and Diaghilev, "like a great white fat pig trying to woo Gertler"[20]. "Brett is coming north fairly soon," Huxley wrote. "She seems to have become much odder and Brettier than ever: no development, but an accentuation of eccentricities . . . she was painting a very good picture . . . she is going to do some illustrations for my *Leda* poem."[21]

As soon as Brett arrived at Roman Camp, Huxley wrote to her. "I picture you stumping out in macintosh breeks to fish and in the intervals tearing the clothes off Mademoiselle's back and drawing her. At least, that's what I hope you are doing . . . I am most excited to see the Swans begun and the Leda illustrations too." Brett failed to answer so Huxley wrote to Juliette again, asking her to tell Brett, "I am just approaching the crucial moment of *Leda* . . . tell Brett also to remember to vote and to vote Labour, our only hope."[22]

When Brett did reply, it was Huxley's turn to plead difficulties with the poem. "I have only succeeded in writing very little more of *Leda* . . .

to the point when the Swan approaches and does his worst. When that episode is finished, I will send you the whole thing as far as it has gone."[23]

It took another month before what he'd written could be sent up to Scotland, where Brett had remained right through the Christmas season, "for you to read and select the indecent passages for illustrations . . ." By this time she had managed to produce a couple of sample drawings for the book. "Thanks very much for the blue drawing. It is very lovely, the figures particularly though I'm not sure that the tree isn't almost better in the first version. I long to see your drawing of the actual swan scene . . ."[24] There Brett's employment as Huxley's illustrator seems to have died. Her only further artistic endeavour on his behalf was to help him paint his sitting room when he married Maria Nys the following August.

Huxley used Brett as the basis for "Jenny Mullion" in his "Garsington" novel, *Crome Yellow*, published in 1921.

> [Jenny] was perhaps thirty, had a tilted nose and a pink-and-white complexion, and wore her brown hair plaited and coiled in two lateral buns over her ears. In the secret tower of her deafness, she sat apart, looking down at the world through sharply piercing eyes . . . In her enigmatic remoteness, Jenny was a little disquieting. Even now some interior joke seemed to be amusing her for she was smiling to herself, and her brown eyes were like very bright round marbles.

Huxley is not beyond squeezing some humour from Jenny's deafness.

> "I hope you slept well," he said.
>
> "Yes, isn't it lovely?" Jenny replied, giving two rapid little nods. "But we had such awful thunderstorms last week."

And when volunteers are called for to "do something" at the village fair:

> She frowned thoughtfully for a moment; then her face brightened and she smiled. "When I was young," she said, "I learnt to play the drums."
>
> "The drums?"
>
> Jenny nodded and, in proof of her assertion, agitated her knife and fork, like a pair of drumsticks, over her plate. "If there's any opportunity of playing the drums . . ." she began.
>
> "But of course . . . there's any amount of opportunity. We'll put you down definitely for the drums."

Only one passage of any length is devoted particularly to Jenny in the book. Denis, the hero, discovers a notebook in which he has seen her scribbling and, in the style of Garsington, where steaming open other people's letters occasionally helped pass the time, Denis sneaks a look.

> "Private. Not to be opened," was written in capital letters on the cover. He raised his eyebrows. It was the sort of thing one wrote in one's Latin Grammar while one was still at one's preparatory school . . . It was curiously childish, he thought and smiled to himself. He opened the book. What he saw made him wince as though he had been struck.
>
> Denis was his own severest critic; so at least he had always believed. He liked to think of himself as a merciless vivisector probing into the palpitating entrails of his own soul; . . . his weaknesses, his absurdities – no one knew them better than he did. Indeed he imagined that nobody beside himself was aware of them at all . . . In his own eyes he had defects, but to see them was a privilege reserved to him alone. For the rest of the world he was surely an image of flawless crystal. On opening the red notebook, that crystal image of himself crashed to the ground . . . he was not his own severest critic after all . . .
>
> The fruit of Jenny's unobtrusive scribbling lay before him. A caricature of himself, reading (the book was upside-down). In the background a dancing couple, recognizable as Gombauld and Anne [Gertler and Maria Nys] Beneath, the legend: "Fable of the Wallflower and the Sour Grapes". Fascinated and horrified, Denis pored over the drawing. It was masterful . . . in every one of those cruelly clear lines . . . the expression of the face . . . the attitude of the body and the limbs . . . the turned-in feet – these things were terrible. And more terrible still was the magisterial certainty with which his physical peculiarities were all recorded and subtly exaggerated.
>
> Denis looked deeper into the book. There were more caricatures of other people . . . he scarcely glanced at them. A fearful desire to know the worst about himself possessed him. He turned over the leaves, lingering at nothing that was not his own image. Seven full pages were devoted to him.
>
> "Private. Not to be opened." He had disobeyed the injunction; he had only got what he deserved . . . this, he reflected, was how Jenny employed the leisure hours in her ivory tower apart. And he had thought her a simple-minded, uncritical creature! It was he, it seemed, who was the fool.[25]

Dorothy Brett aged five. Portrait by Katherine Barnard.

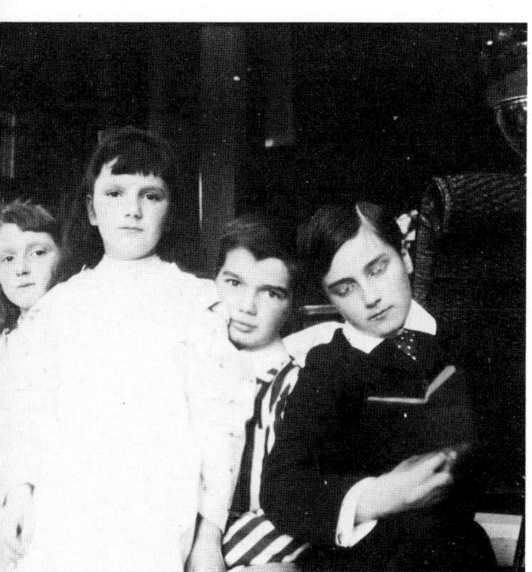

Doll, Syv, Moll and Knoll – Dorothy, Sylvia, Maurice and Oliver Brett, *c.* 1895.

Lewis ('Loulou') Harcourt.

Slade College of Art, 1912. Front row from the left: Carrington, unknown, Nevinson, Mark Gertler, unknown, Adrian Allison, Stanley Spencer, unknown. Dorothy Brett is seated behind Gertler and Nevinson; Isaac Rosenberg is crouching on one knee on the left of the second row; Professor Frederick Brown ('Nutty') is third from the right in the back row.

Slade 'cropheads': Carrington, Doris Humphries with Brett on the right. Brett, 'sunk in gloom' over her crush on Professor Brown, cut her hair off on New Year's Eve, 1912. 'I am blessed if I am going to settle down into a haggard scarecrow, yearning after men.' Maurice, her brother, wrote a fortnight later, 'Front view of her hair is not so bad, but profile and back, it is weird. She is frightened of it herself, I think.'

Umbrellas, Garsington – Brett, 1917. Front, left to right: Julian Morrell, Aldous Huxley, Brett, Ottoline, Lytton Strachey. John Middleton Murry and Katherine Mansfield in the background.

'Oh, if only the Bloomsberries could see what you have up your sleeve': Katherine Mansfield.

'I'm glad you thought Brett's picture so good. From the photograph I thought the Aldous part looked a bit feeble. But it was hard to tell': Carrington to Lytton Strachey.

Lady Ottoline Morrell – Brett, 1918.

'You once painted a wonderful strange imaginary portrait of Ottoline – turquoise eyes and hair that flamed like a comet. I wish I had that portrait – it was so fabulous': Lady Juliette Huxley.

GARS

Brett and Clive Bell, hoe in hand, in conversation. 'Bell and Aldous Huxley were working [on the farm] as conscientious objectors . . . He was jolly, never did a lick of work but kept [the farm-hands] laughing.'

A weekend group. Seated: Brett, Bertrand Russell, Julian Morrell. On the step
Augustine Birrell, Tony Birrell, Aldous Huxley, Lytton Strachey, J. T. Shephe

N, 1916

Aldous Huxley, Brett and Mark Gertler.

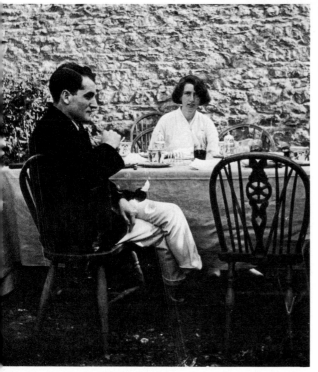

n Middleton Murry and Brett.

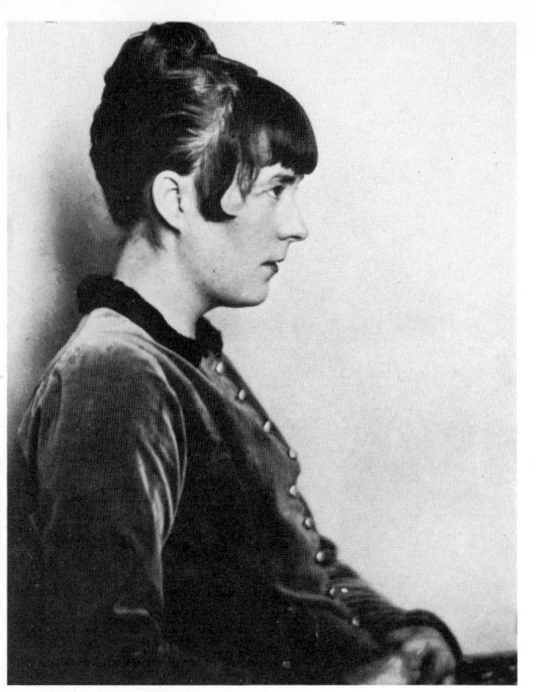

ABOVE LEFT: Katherine Mansfield. 'Her polished black hair rolled on top of her head in a sort of fan shape. The fringe brushed down over a forehead that bulged at the top, then straightening down to the dark eyebrows': Brett. ABOVE RIGHT: John Middleton Murry: pencil drawing, Brett, 1923 – too soft and gentle and not the Murry she knew, Katherine Mansfield told Brett.

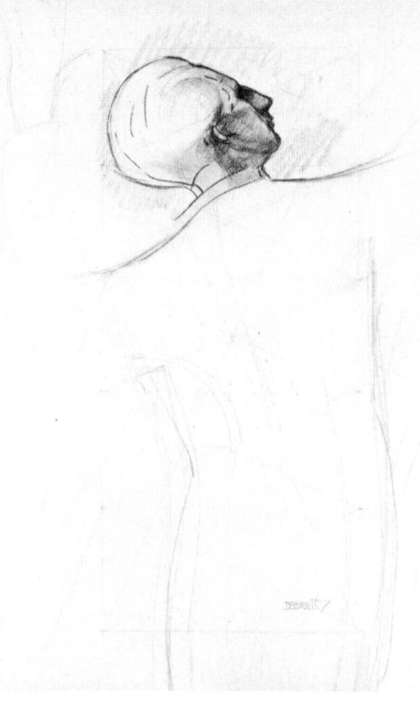

ABOVE LEFT: D. H. Lawrence in Oaxaca, Mexico, December, 1924: photograph by Brett. ABOVE RIGHT: Leopold Stokowski: pencil drawing, Brett, 1933. 'The most difficult thing of all is his NOSE. I've had a God-Almighty struggle with that . . . damn his nose!'

ABOVE LEFT: Brett and 'Toby' – her ear trumpet. 'Do you think I liked it when I saw that brass dipper swallowing up Lorenzo's talk to me? It was worse than Frieda's restraining influence': Mabel Luhan. ABOVE RIGHT: A pack trip in the Sangre de Cristos, 1926. Betty Cottam, Spud Johnson, Bobby DuBarry and Brett, laid low with a broken rib after being thrown from her horse.

The Three Fates of Taos: Mabel Luhan, Frieda Lawrence and Brett on the porch of the Lawrence ranch.

The Tower Beyond Tragedy, 1932.

Brett: self-portrait, pencil, at Taos Indian Pueblo, 1924.

Brett in western gear at the garden doorway of the Mabel Luhan hacienda, 1924. 'By this time Brett had evolved a costume for the West, consisting of a very wide-brimmed sombrero on the back of her pin-head, high boots with a pair of men's corduroy trousers tucked into them and, in her right leg, a long stiletto . . . it seemed to give her great satisfaction for she had secret fantasies about assault': Mabel Luhan.

Huxley's Jenny resembles remarkably Brett's own view of herself as having a secret and hidden inner being, the shining sword in the dull scabbard, of her correspondence wtih Ottoline. By mid-1918, however, for Ottoline, the shine was beginning to wear off. Gertler had given up his almost permanent residence at Garsington and wrote to Ottoline that he felt out of place anywhere else. "I really fear becoming too attached to it like Brett!"[26] Ottoline noted in her journal for August 1918, "I had it out with Brett about staying at Garsington forever", but, after a brief skip to London, and a hop up to Roman Camp, Brett returned to Garsington once more. The reconciliation was strained. Ottoline felt that Brett was becoming too dependent upon her and the creature comforts provided by Garsington, a view separately shared by both Katherine Mansfield and Mark Gertler.[27]

Garsington was, in any case, like all fashions, beginning to fade. The war over, the conscientious objectors needed no longer to pursue the myth of agricultural employment on Philip Morrell's farm; the air raids ended, Brett needed no longer to fear being forced to hide in the Tube or under the Arches on the Embankment in London. During the winter, she had found a house and studio for herself at 28 Thurlow Road, Hampstead, and, while waiting to move in, began to make use of Tilney Street once more, along with Sylvia whose husband had returned to Sarawak and whose children were still up at Roman Camp. The domestic staff were quick to report to the Eshers what were delicately described as "goings on" – Captain Gifford, a male friend of Sylvia, had been invited for dinner and allowed to stay overnight. The correspondence between Roman Camp and Tilney Street, Esher and Nellie, Brett and Sylvia, flew thick and furious.

Dear Pupsy,

I got your rather unnecessary letter this morning. Up till now Tilney Street has had that apparently meaningless word Home applied to it . . . the great mistake is ever thinking that after the age of twenty it is possible or advisable to live in other people's homes . . . when I am settled into my rooms, I shall be far happier and so will you = . . . I have a definite purpose in life – a difficult ladder to climb = and everything I do is directed towards eliminating or adding such things as make the road a little easier . . . perhaps in centuries to come when one has faded out of existence, one's voice will still be heard as others are heard . . . but there is nothing but faith and belief in oneself to hold one to the task.

Yrs Doll[28]

Both parents replied, first Eleanor:

My dear Doll,

. . . Tilney Street is and always was open to you to use as a home . . . you could have entertained there freely in our absence and had a studio for day work as well . . . but entertaining your friends and using the house as a furnished hotel are not the same thing, as is shown by the gossiping of all your's and Syv's friends and relations and the giving warning of our servants who wished to leave owing to the "goings on" of our daughters.

The moment the servants revolt against trickery and attempts to hoodwink, it creates an impossible position . . .

Yours E.E.[29]

Then Esher:

Dearest Doll,

I understand your aspirations and disappointments well. Everything you say is perfectly sound and to the point. I have no grievances only feelings – like you and the rest of the world. We cannot eliminate the clash of interests and ideas from the world's order.

It is because of this fatal weakness in the hearts of men that conventions exist.

I have only one criticism and that is of a phrase. "Tilney Street" has never been a "home". It is a perch. If we have a home, it is the hearthstone here and here you are always welcome [Roman Camp] But let us not argue.

I love and admire you. So lead your life in your own way . . . but there are orbits in which different lives cannot move without friction, therefore let us all be free in action and thought . . . Interchange of the latter is always pleasant to me.[30]

Next Sylvia took up the cudgels.

Dearest Pupsy,

. . . I will not set foot in or approach the door of Tilney Street . . . should you not desire it. Nor will I ring up or in any way interfere, or shock, or create "Goings On", whatever they may be . . . one has rather believed in the milk of human kindness which in this case seems to have turned a little sour – there have been no goings on in your house and neither Doll nor I are *living* with any man . . . Doll and I aren't prostitutes, tho' we do unconventional things . . .

Yours ever,
Syv[31]

After spending Easter at Garsington, Brett moved into Thurlow Road.

> The colours will be beautiful = my studio lemon colour = the little bedroom pink = the billiard room cream = the basement passage blue = the kitchen sea-green – or duck's egg = the bedroom lemon yellow – the bathroom pink = the painters are getting slightly confused . . . I sold a small drawing at the Friday Club . . . a man called Schrift bought it – brother to the Schrift who was done to death by a miner = a nasty man = his brother was nicer, I believe but the miner's daughter was the cause of the trouble . . . everything is getting more difficult = I honestly believe a bloody revolution and sudden death would be the best . . . have you ever heard of a man called Gray who was tutor to some members of the Royal Family years ago and is now an amazing tramp = I met him in Fitzroy Street . . .[32]*

By June, the house was decorated, if disordered and not yet furnished, and Brett threw a party. Katherine Mansfield and John Middleton Murry, who were about to move into a house nearby in Portland Villas, known as "The Elephant" because of its size, were among the guests. Murry upset Brett, telling her Katherine was frightened of Brett's house, a remark Brett took quite literally, forcing Katherine to explain that it was simply the amount that would need doing to the house that overwhelmed her and the feeling that its sheer size might dominate Brett's life.[33] Brett, who already had a lodger living in the basement that Gertler was shortly to move into, responded by suggesting the setting up of a second "Ark", conveniently forgetting all the problems of the first. Katherine was chary of the idea of living "in company" once more, of Gertler gossiping or a drunken Chili (the Chilean painter, Alvaro Guevara) blundering in, she told Brett. She also wrote to Ottoline the same day, adding Brett herself, the state of her clothing and her lack of dental hygiene to the list of reasons why she felt unable to join the menage in Thurlow Road. She admitted it was vile of her to write in such a manner but she felt it strongly.[34]

* Amongst Brett's papers is a curious letter, dated February 20th, 1920 and headed 28, Thurlow Road, N.W.3:

> Dear Mr Gray,
>
> I forbid you either to come to this house or to speak to me. I give you warning that if you come to this house or attempt to speak to me, I shall summon the police. I also desire that you do not write to me or attempt in any way to communicate with me.
>
> Yours truly,
>
> Dorothy Brett

Whether this is a rough copy of a letter that was never sent is impossible to say but it does seem to refer to the amazing tramp of Fitzroy Street.

For her new house Brett was promised furniture from Orchard Lea. Eleanor Esher insisted that, although that house was empty, Brett should wait until Vyner's lease ended officially and the contents were put up for auction. A bitter correspondence ensued between Brett and her parents that summer about that and, as usual, about money. In the absence of the Orchard Lea furniture, Brett bought the odd piece here and there, in Heal's, in Maples, and in the Caledonian Market, sending her father the bills – with a promise that he would be repaid when she sold a painting.

Matters came to a head when Brett appeared at Roman Camp in September and on her return to London, she was talked to, at her father's suggestion, by a family friend, Teddy Seymour. Seymour offered Esher his suggestions:

> She [Brett] requires
> 1. an allowance of £400 a year
> 2. furniture and general setting up of her house
> 3. that you should continue to pay her rent
>
> . . . I think everything sent there should be useful and not valuable . . . supposing that all the above is done, I feel that you and Nellie would then be in a position to know that you had behaved in such a way that under no conceivable conditions could she ever ask or expect anything more.
>
> This would be the final act of renunciation – . . . if I have erred and made a mess of things, I am sorry.
>
> Doll is a curiosity – but being as she is, I do not think she can live decently on a smaller scale than I have outlined.[35]

The plan disturbed Eleanor Esher, so Seymour expanded on his ideas.

> I think Doll is a very hopeless character – I do not believe she will ever reform.
>
> Under the old arrangement I think her regular payment was on the small side . . . I think the irregular payments were far too large.
>
> I should like to see this settlement of her affairs made absolutely final – under no circumstances might she be given one penny more . . . if you and Reg decide to follow the suggestions I have made, then I feel that you both must be as hard as granite from that moment. No more concessions – no more help in money or kind . . . only in this way will you and Reg be able to free yourselves from what has become an intolerable nuisance. To be honest, I feel that she is a very hopeless character; I think therefore that it is wisest and cheapest to

> be generous *and to cut adrift*. . . I am very sorry for you as I think she is a terribly difficult proposition.[36]

The financial arrangements do not seem to have unduly disturbed Brett but the Orchard Lea furniture, when it arrived, did. She told Ottoline, "rumour has it after six months waiting they have given me a servant's suite for the State Apartment".[37]

To her mother she wrote:

> The furniture arrived. The black carpet is very lovely and looks well in my yellow room = and the round table with its strange feet is quite large enough for all the entertaining I'll ever do = the rest of the furniture is not the kind one wants to live with so I have hidden most of it in the basement . . . after so long a wait, I had hoped for something rather more beautiful . . . it must be so much better to be quite indifferent and oblivious to shapes and forms.[38]

Esher stood aside while the correspondence between Brett and her mother became increasingly acrimonious. He had written shortly after her departure from Roman Camp:

> I think the picture (from a photo) excellent and perhaps the best thing you have ever done. But as you do not value my opinion on any subject at a pin's fee, I cannot imagine why you care to know what I think.[39]

Brett replied:

> You are really quite wrong = I always have appreciated your opinion on most things – I regret very much you did not say more about the picture. I feel somehow that the family torch has been handed on to me = I have inherited that something that drove Grandpa upwards and you and now me = the others have lost the thread . . . you may think this conceited of me but it is not meant to be = it is just a fact really = tho I would not want the others to know = a fact better kept to ourselves.[40]

Brett had been, since the completion of *Umbrellas*, engaged first on still lifes and then portraits. The painting Esher so approved of may have been a portrait of Julian Morrell that Brett was working on that autumn. Brett had taken charge of Julian while Ottoline was in Ireland and Ottoline not only disliked the portrait intensely but objected strongly to

Brett's "mothering" of Julian, a quality Julian acknowledges[41] she received more from Brett than from her mother. One or other matter came to a head in a cable Brett despatched to Ottoline in mid-September: "So sorry to have hurt you. Quite a mistake. Much Love. Please don't be unhappy."[42] Gertler tried to smooth matters a couple of days later, advising Ottoline to dismiss the irritating part of Brett from her mind.

There was another cause for strained relations. Early in the year Brett had become attached to "Toronto", the Canadian poet Frank Prewett, but the affair fizzled out when Brett learnt of Prewett's involvement with Ottoline. She wrote to Ottoline in October:

> I often wonder how much Toronto did like me = . . . I fear love affairs more than Bombs = they tear one to bits, destroy one's capacity for work = burn one up and leave one utterly forlorn = Nothing lasts = least of all love = it dies as soon as it has flowered = but why tell you this who pursue the shadow so persistently =[43]

Brett remained in London that Christmas, refusing an invitation to Garsington "because of the cost". She and Ottoline saw each other occasionally during the following year, and in 1921, when Brett joined Ottoline "with her troupe" in October, gatecrashing a party H. G. Wells was giving for Charlie Chaplin. Chaplin had not yet arrived and Virginia Woolf describes Ottoline, second-hand via Koteliansky, as taking up a commanding position in the middle of the room in sealing-wax green crinoline silk, white feathers in her hair and an early Victorian white silk umbrella with tassels: "Her influence is said to have struck people dumb, even on the balcony . . . at last Ottoline, meeting him [Chaplin] in the hall, opened her umbrella in his face."[44]

But Brett's long affair was coming to an end. The last straw, so far as Ottoline was concerned, was Brett's sending Julian Morrell, now at a convent school at Roehampton, a tuck hamper containing a rope ladder, a plan of an escape route and advice that she would be waiting outside in a car, all of which was discovered and forestalled by the nuns. Brett had earlier prompted a similar rebellion in Maria Nys who absconded from Newnham College to be nearer Aldous Huxley in London, and Ottoline had then insisted that Brett accept her responsibility in the matter and put Maria up in the Ark. Brett's last letter to Ottoline is dated October 10th, 1921.

> You seem to have the strangest ideas of friendship. Anyhow, I post your letters regularly = I've no doubt it's something to be useful! But I feel a line or two at the same time thanking one for one's small

services might be more polite or even friendly. I had thought of suggesting myself for a weekend but think perhaps it would be better for me to wait for you to ask me.

Yours,

Brett.[45]

A cold, formal note, after the years of "your devoted Brettie". The "affair" with Ottoline was over.

5

1920: Katherine 1

When I think of Ottoline and my feelings for her, it was more compassion, compassion for this woman who fell in love so ardently and so unwisely. I felt impatient at times, impatient with her greed. She was a greedy lover. She was also a very sick woman: her terrible headaches, the emotional agony she went through. However sympathetic I felt for her, it is also true that I was bored with it all. I tried to make her see how she frightened men. Then it finally got to the point that I was getting involved with the problems of her husband, Philip. I made the mistake of telling her of Philip's affair with her maid . . . that and the endeavour to help Julian, who was miserable in a Catholic school, broke up our friendship.

Time discoloured Brett's memory of Ottoline, much as it enhanced her recollection of her relationship with Katherine Mansfield. Although, in her own book, Brett recalls Katherine and John Middleton being at her 1915 party for Lawrence and Frieda, Brett later wrote of meeting Katherine Mansfield for the first time on a Garsington weekend. She recalled in her unpublished memoirs:

Because of a sort of stage fright that I had of very intellectual people I refused again and again to meet her. Her reputation of brilliancy, of a sort of ironic ruthlessness toward small minds and less agile brains, terrified me. Yet apparently one can not escape one's fate, and while I was staying at Garsington, Ottoline told me she had invited Katherine down for the weekend. Already in imagination I was suffering all the humiliation I expected from her.

Saturday morning after the dog cart had gone to the station to meet her, I waited in apprehension in the gay scarlet pannelled dining room . . . The sound of the door opening and Ottoline's soft voice purring out a welcome made me turn around. A small woman came in, strangely dark in her black and white clothes. Could this little bit of a thing be the woman I so much feared? But I had no time to think, only to hold forever this picture of her stillness against the bright background, of the black and whiteness, and aliveness of her against the scarlet, yellow and orange of that Elizabethan room.

After the other guests arrived, young men from Oxford on bicycles, Lytton Strachey, Duncan Grant, Vanessa and Clive Bell, I can't remember how many; Bertrand Russell was among them. Why Ottoline placed me next to Katherine at the lunch table, I don't know. Her long refectory table brought the people opposite very close while the two ends receded into voids. But here I was sitting next to the small quiet woman I had so much dreaded. We never spoke a word. I sat in agonies of shyness, she sat watchful, cold, withdrawn into herself. Conversation roared up and down the table, Bertrand Russell's horse-like laugh, exploding at intervals, while Ottoline glowered at me, from her seat bang opposite, for my silence. There was nothing that I could do, nothing that Katherine could do. Suddenly I noticed that the pocket of the yellow jumper she had put on over her frock for lunch was bulging. Into this pocket I began surreptitiously to drop small pellets of bread. All through the interminable lunch I kept dropping them in her pocket.

How guarded she was during that first weekend of hers at Garsington. We walked in the afternoon, all of us, in a long procession, two by two or in threes and fours. It is the most uncomfortable form of walking I know, and I hated it . . .

That evening after much persuasion, Katherine consented to sing. She fetched her guitar and sang quaint old folk songs, Negro spirituals, ballads of all kinds. She sang in a low whispering voice, all caution momentarily forgotten, her quick expressive face rippled with light and fun, her humour bubbling over. Then suddenly she felt something or thought she felt an antagonistic criticism and abruptly stopped. Everyone tried to get her to sing again but nothing would induce her, the guard was up, the face became a mask, the eyes watchful, and a sort of discomfort fell upon us all.

I stole off to bed. My deafness which allowed me to hear so little brought on an excessive tiredness after so long watching people's mouths continually opening and shutting. Later that night Katherine came into my room. Sitting on the edge of my bed, she told me that while walking in the garden in the afternoon she had discovered the breadcrumbs in her pocket. It was then she realised she had one friend in the house. She asked me to be her friend. We made a secret pact of friendship which was never broken for the rest of her life. The following day with the pact a secret between us, I watched Katherine, holding her own with the Bloomsburies . . . the knowledge that Katherine was as frightened of them as I was, encouraged me . . .

Later on in the manuscript Brett recalls:

That same day . . . she begged me to show her the painting I was doing in the Monastery . . . with dreadful misgivings, I took her up secretly. I was then painting a group of Ottoline's weekenders . . . Ottoline, Strachey, Murry, Katherine, Gertler, Aldous Huxley, Julian . . . sitting on the lawn under coloured umbrellas. That painting is now lost. She stood astonished, looking at it. Then, in her wicked, mischievous way, she said, "Oh, if only the Bloomsburies could see what you have up your Monastic sleeve" . . .

It is difficult to describe Katherine . . . When I knew her, she was slim and about half a head shorter than I am. Not petite by any means. Her features were small and delicate, the eyes dark in a pale, clear skin, beautiful even white teeth, and her polished black hair rolled on top of her head in a sort of fan shape. The fringe brushed smoothly down over a forehead that bulged at the top, then straightening down to the dark eyebrows. Her hands were thin and sensitive, restricted, almost precious in their movements. She hardly ever wore anything but black, her favourite colour being violet or purple, but I never saw her in anything but black and white. Her changes of mood were rapid and disconcerting, a laughing joyous moment would suddenly turn through some inadequate remark into biting anger; how biting that anger could be, only those who experienced it know. Katherine had a tongue like a knife, she could cut the very heart out of one with it, and repent of her brilliant cruelty the next moment. She could be cruel. She had no tolerance of the stupid or the slow. Her mind was so quick, so clear, so ahead of the thoughts and conversation of others, that if they lagged behind she became impatient, bored and finally angry, I was an object of affectionate compassion with her for many years, because to her I did not seem to adventure out to life as she did. Katherine would take jobs – strange jobs – just for the experience. She would have strange relationships with people for the same purpose. Her great delight was a game she played of being someone else. She would act the part completely, until she even got herself mixed up as to who and what she was. She would tell me that the acting became so real to her that she didn't always know which was her real self. She gave me encouragement I needed badly. Katherine really started me doing some serious painting in England.

The two extracts are from separate drafts of the same manuscript. The second extract has been deleted in the later version but there is no evidence that Brett was bothered by the inconsistency of describing her first meeting with Katherine and then, *the following day*, taking her up to the Monastery to show her *Umbrellas*, in which Katherine herself is portrayed as a regular Garsington weekender. In the first draft, Brett stuffs breadcrumbs into the pocket of a "tightly waisted black jacket", in the second, in the pocket of a "yellow jumper put on over her frock for lunch". All of this indicates how loose Brett could be with her recollections, adding and subtracting events and emotions to suit her later attitudes and doubts. The long passionate affair with Ottoline she could dismiss in a few lines, while the less certain, though no less involved, relationship with Katherine becomes, in retrospect, a time of wine and roses. The strong adolescent streak in Brett is clear – well into her thirties, she is swearing a secret pact of friendship with Katherine, like characters in a girls' school romance. Lawrence, though not at the time in contact with Brett, would, with his enthusiasm for "blood brotherhood", have understood.

It was Brett's later entanglement with John Middleton Murry that distorted her memory of the early part of her relationship with Katherine Mansfield. Murry and Mansfield were, in 1917, not yet married. Towards the end of May, Katherine poured out her bitterness and anger to Brett at the rumour that Murry and Ottoline had become involved while Katherine and Murry were staying at the Ark. Murry had a more one-sided explanation. He was utterly miserable, he said, because the most dreadful thing had happened . . . Ottoline had fallen head over heels in love with him. Katherine, despite the fact that she and Murry were, for the while, living apart, wrote to her Ladyship complaining bitterly. Murry was now, she claimed, suffering physically. Brett leapt promptly to Ottoline's defence and Katherine replied at once, pointing out that if Ottoline was upset by her letter, then the converse was equally true. A day later Katherine swallowed her pride and anger and, despite her belief that Murry's illness had been caused by Ottoline, beseeched her to let Murry convalesce in the cottage at Garsington.

Ottoline accepted Murry uncomfortably. "A thick veil has come between us since he accused me to Katherine of being in love with him . . . I went for a walk with him and Brett. How I hated it! But when I could, I walked alone and left Murry and Brett to talk together and those moments were so happy – as if I were floating through space."

Katherine followed Murry to Garsington the next week but, after developing a severe cold, stayed only for the weekend. As Murry recovered, Katherine's health worsened. Her doctor diagnosed a spot on the lung and refused to allow her to travel to Garsington for Christmas. But Brett was there and so was the lad, being hugged by Brett perhaps, without doubt putting on the mysterious enemy Flesh in the aftermath of the Christmas turkey (or as the Garsington gossip rumoured – the Christmas peacock, for a peacock was missing, presumed dead, and some of the guests came down with food poisoning), and busying himself with writing out his Christmas presents, for he had neglected to buy any. Brett's was "*The Wakened Dryad*: a Poem written for D.B. by J.M.M." In it, Brett, the Dryad, wakened from her forest sleep runs frightened to the town where the only person to understand her and greet her with sympathy is the local poet.

The whole thing rambles on for some 120 lines of turgid sub-Keatsian allegory and Brett may well have read more into it than Murry intended. For him it was simply what it claimed to be – his Christmas gift and a hoped-for exchange – a poem for a picture. Seven months later the picture had not arrived and he wrote complaining and hoping that it would be his by mid-August when he and Katherine were planning to move into "The Elephant", their new home at Portland Villas.[1]

By then Murry was in better health, reconciled with Katherine and the two had married. Brett, with J. D. Fergusson, another painter friend of the Murrys, was one of the two witnesses at their wedding in May. The ceremony was originally planned for the end of April and Katherine wrote to Brett on April 20th, asking her to collect Murry the following Thursday at one and bring him to the Kensington Registry Office, but there were problems over the completion of Katherine's divorce from her first husband and the ceremony had to be postponed until Saturday May 3rd, 1918.

When Murry came to write his autobiography, *Between Two Worlds*, the single mention of Brett was as witness at the wedding – nothing more. In 1918 things were different. Brett was undergoing a process of deep soul-searching as a painter, "wondering", she wrote to Ottoline, "whether I shall leave a footprint". She turned to Murry for support and he replied with a long letter on art as the perfection of Life and what he thought it meant to be an artist. The letter meant a great deal to Brett and she carried a copy of it wherever she went for the rest of her life, copying it and re-copying it and presenting it to those friends and acquaintances she thought merited the gift.[2]

Katherine was then in Looe where she had travelled shortly after the wedding. When, in the autumn of the following year, 1919, she was advised by her physician, Dr. Sorapure, to spend the winter in a warmer clime, she left England for Italy, later crossing the border to

Menton in the south of France. From there she wrote asking Brett to look after "the little lad". "Well, I did," Brett later recalled in a straight-faced understatement of what then ensued. To the "little lad" Katherine wrote, suggesting that, when she returned to health, they adopt a child, for she couldn't bear the thought of a future alone. She added that she would ask Brett to promise to be the child's guardian if her health did not improve.

Katherine could, simultaneously, present several faces to different correspondents. She told Richard Middleton Murry, John's brother who had been staying at Garsington, "learning to farm", that she thought Brett pathetic and that she would never make a true painter, only a reflector. But to Brett herself she wrote fulsomely in March 1920, from the Villa Isola Bella at Menton, marvelling at Brett's ideas for the present and intentions for the future but chiding her for attributing her shortcomings to the influence and attitudes of her parents. Everyone, she said, had that cross to bear and there could be no progress until one had overcome the desire to blame them for both good and ill.[3]

Murry had spent Christmas with Katherine before returning to London and his editorship of the *Athenaeum* on January 2nd. He went to Garsington for the weekend of February 19th and must have travelled to Menton to see Katherine soon after for, by March 8th, he was back in London and writing to Brett from Portland Villas. Brett had been at Garsington that weekend in February and may have experienced the "Revelations" of which she hinted to Katherine. Brett could never resist hinting, to Ottoline, to Katherine, to whoever, of the secret gifts she carried deep inside, the hidden depths she might one day reveal to the favoured and the mysteries that only her correspondent had been chosen to share. And, more often than not, she seems to have had a masochistic urge to drop her hints before and tempt with revelations those whom she might, were she rational, least want to know.

For there had been that winter the beginnings of a liaison between Brett and Murry. Murry, when he wrote to Brett immediately on his return from that quick March visit to Katherine, presented an essay in rationalisation, justifying the affair with Brett as benefiting his marriage with Katherine at the same time as leading Brett to happiness and fulfilment – having his cake and simultaneously eating it.[4]

Some time during the early spring of 1920, Brett and Murry at last abandoned words for at least a little tentative action. Stricken with remorse and high-mindedness, both promptly confessed to Katherine, each attempting to forestall the other and neither in full. Murry wrote telling her of a "country expedition" with Brett and, pressed for details, elaborated on his noble self-sacrifice. Katherine had begun to have had enough.

She told Murry she wanted to hear no more of the business until she returned home and, to Brett's plea for forgiveness, she replied that the boot was on the other foot, that it was she herself, Katherine, who should seek forgiveness for having exposed Brett to hurt and anger in an earlier letter that she begged Brett to seek out and destroy. Although the letter is missing, in view of the fact that Brett kept and treasured every other letter from Katherine, it seems unlikely that she followed Katherine's request. It may possibly have been kept by Murry, after Katherine's death, when he borrowed the correspondence to select and edit for publication.

Brett wrote back almost immediately, asking Katherine to "put her in the dust-bin" and Katherine tried, on the face of it, to reassure Brett with verbal hugs and kisses. But, a week later, Katherine revived one of her favourite epithets, telling Murry she'd had another letter from Brett – "pathetic".

Murry tried to keep his head down in all this. At the end of April he replied to a short note from Brett by quoting in its entirety Shakespeare's 116th sonnet, "Let me not to the marriage of true minds admit impediments".

How far the relationship between Murry and Brett had really progressed one can only guess. Not, it seems likely, in view of later events, so far as what is nowadays called "making love". However, during 1920, Brett kept a journal for the first time in her life. Although the entries in the leather-bound diary with a brass lock – broken, she recalled, by herself when she lent the journal to Murry some years later – begin on January 1st, 1920, and run through to the end of March, the page dates are unconnected with the entries. She simply used the diary as a relatively secure notebook. Above the printed date "Feb 8th", for example, reference to an event that can be verified elsewhere suggests that the journal was commenced in the late summer and continued through to the end of the year, with the last entry being added some months later, in 1921, when Murry returned briefly from France.

The journal begins:

> I am writing these notes down because directly you come in to the room I am so shy every idea goes out of my head = I wonder if I will ever learn to talk =
>
> I could not tell you at first in what way I felt your telling me you loved me = I had crashed so badly the tide had gone so far out and

> left so much dry sand between me and Love that all I knew was that the tide had turned and was slowly sweeping back again.[5]

Brett addresses herself throughout to Murry, the only exception being a short passage directed towards Katherine, whose name has been crossed out where it first appears and who thereafter is referred to as "T", the initial of Katherine's pet name, "Tig". Katherine's name is covered over with curlicues, in a style Brett used elsewhere in her correspondence when she wished to strike something out though, in this instance, it left the underlying word clearly discernible. But, elsewhere in the diary, passages have been completely and heavily obliterated so that they are impossible to read. Brett claimed that these heavy deletions were the work of Murry and the location of the passages suggests that they may have elucidated just how far Murry succeeded at this period in his advances to Brett. That he made advances is clear, for Brett continually reproaches herself for refusing him, referring to Murry's oft-repeated thesis that the sex act is unimportant except insofar as *not* carrying it out acts as a barrier between them as eternal friends.

When Katherine returned to Portland Villas at the beginning of May, 1920, "she started in accusing me of having an affair with Murry. I was appalled! It had never entered my head . . . she upset the boiling water from the tea kettle onto her legs. She was crying and miserable. I did all I could, but I don't think I convinced her."

Despite protestations, Murry had gone a considerable distance beyond holding hands and expressing brotherly love and devotion. And, in the same breath, he was busy assuring Brett that, if she agreed to the act in full, it would not harm or damage Katherine in any way and might even enhance the Murry marriage. Brett, he suggested, would be doing everyone a service by allowing Murry to make love to her. The onslaught fed Brett's neurosis and she tried to assuage her anxiety by means of a constant correspondence with Katherine and by more material endeavours – she sent Katherine a stove and a bunch of yellow roses to welcome her back to Portland Villas.

Murry and Brett continued to commune and Brett built her plans for the summer around him, though pretending that what concerned her was being close to Katherine. She wrote to her father, thanking him for a cheque she had used to pay her coal bill:

> My idea, as you know, was to come up [to Roman Camp] this month – but owing to Murry and his friends all having their holidays in August, I shifted mine – as I wanted to keep the house open for them to come and play bowls = then Murry's wife returns to France

> in September = and I want to see as much of her as possible before she goes = and also I am one of the few people that Murry feels easy with and when his wife goes he will feel terribly lonely and dreary for a bit . . . (It is important to see Mrs. Murry before she goes = because she is not returning to England next summer and I may not see her again for years, unless I go out to her) . . .[6]

Having paid the coal bill and bought Katherine a stove, Brett decided that Murry too needed something more than her love to keep him warm. She sent him a sweater and he invited her to some "real games" – tennis on a court behind Hampstead Library.[7]

Between keeping her house open for "Murry and his friends" – which added up simply to Murry – to come and play bowls, and playing some "real games" of tennis, Brett and Murry were still seeing far too much of each other for Katherine's liking. Matters reached a climax when Murry received the sweater and Katherine stormed over by taxi to Brett's house in Thurlow Road. Brett and Murry, Drake-like before the Mansfield Armada, continued to play bowls. Katherine, according to Brett, "cold, remote, furious . . . drove off, looking straight before her like a stone image", and, back at "the Elephant", went straight to her private journal:

> 9–viii–20
> I should like to have a secret code to put on record what I feel today. If I forget, may my right hand forget its cunning . . . and the lifted curtain . . . the hand at the fire with the ring and stretched fingers – no, it's snowing – the telegram to say he's not – just the words arrived 8:31. But if I say more, I'll give myself away.
>
> *I wrote this because there's a great danger of forgetting that kind of intensity, and it won't do.
>
> No, there is no danger of forgetting.*

Three days later Katherine intercepted or was given to read – it is not clear which – a letter from Brett to Murry in which Brett described how she wanted to run amid the corn and have Murry smack her hard until she cried all over him and soaked him with tears. Brett, Katherine decided, thirty-seven years old with the shadow of her upbringing looming large over her, was unhinged and hysterical. "Her face is entirely changed: the mouth hangs open, the eyes are very wide: there is something silly and meaning in her smile which makes me cold. And

* The passage asterisked was inserted four months later on December 8th, 1920.

then the bitten nails – the dirty neck – the film on the teeth! . . . the truth is she flattered him and got him!"[8]

A week later Murry revealed that he was thinking of lodging with Brett that winter and Katherine pressed him to say whether their relationship was more than platonic. Murry confessed that Brett and he held hands and kissed and were on the brink of something deeper and more hazardous. He added that, in any case, Gertler lodged at Thurlow Road. Gertler, Katherine noted, never had anything like a kissing and cuddling relationship with Brett and Murry, unabashed, implored her to be nice to Brett.[9] An entry in Brett's journal seems to fit this same August date, offering the curious image of the two Hampstead ladies furiously scribing their innermost thoughts, almost within shouting distance of each other, while Murry practised his tennis between:

> You [Murry] must not ask me to live with you because I regard you in a way that makes it impossible for me to have a close relationship with you . . . your letter has changed the face of the universe = I must do away with pretence = Of what good am I to you as a friend if I do not give you everything I have to give? Is this physical relationship so great a thing that it should be withheld and prevent a free intercourse of mind and affection = How can I take you by the hand when I know I am holding back what is almost necessary to you? it is an insult to your exquisite delicacy to keep back what is so small a thing to give = . . . I had two reasons for my reticence = I did not want to seduce you and I am a coward = the first was due to a reluctance to run the risk of hurting her [The word "Katherine" is scratched out] . . . then I am a coward = My fear of physical pain is abnormal = and even now with every wish to give you what you want, I cannot tell what I would do = I might collapse from fright or I might find it less fearful than I have been led to believe = I have been told and seen too much = . . . I would rather not hide anything from T, ["Katherine" scratched out] I would prefer to face her with the truth and let her judge me = I know I could prove my honesty towards her = . . . I have not kissed you, not taken you by the hand because my fear is so great that you might think I wished to seduce you . . . so I deny myself = If I hold my Love for you too precious it is because you are too delicate, too fine an instrument to soil =

Then, a few lines to Katherine: ". . . I have stolen nothing from you T. dear = I have been faithful = in my thoughts I may have been treacherous but never in my deeds ="[10]

The day she discovered Murry's plans to take rooms at Thurlow

Road, Katherine wrote to Brett, asking her in the name of friendship to return all of her letters so that she might destroy any that she felt ought not to have been written.[11] Brett's answer was to send Katherine a copy of her sister Sylvia's novel *Toys*. Katherine replied sharpish, telling Brett she'd rather not say what she thought of it in case it hurt her too deeply.

The emotional upheaval was now affecting Brett physically, as Gertler observed when in late September he returned from France to Thurlow Road. He told Ottoline:

> . . . Brett seemed so distant and deaf. I couldn't think of anything to say. She seems so lonely and reduced. I am sorry for her and yet unable to help. She is dried and shrivelled in some way; . . . this afternoon she goes to play tennis with Murry. Yesterday she asked with a catch in her voice if I have read Murry's poem on Tolstoy. In order to avoid a row, I made some evasive answer . . .[12]

But Brett was exercising her pen as well as her racket arm and Katherine complained to Murry that she was sick of hearing about their tennis parties and Gertler's ill-health. Gertler, she said, had plenty of rich friends to turn to while she, Katherine, knew more about ill-health than Brett, despite her deafness, could ever imagine.[13]

Brett saw Murry's tennis-playing through rather more hero-worshipping rose-tinted glasses: "Playing tennis you are like a reed in the wind = and I have rarely seen anyone so graceful, such harmony of action, such delightful running = . . ."[14], but she realised the change that Gertler had noticed.

> I have become old at last. That strange look of youth has gone = I can see it in the glass and in the eyes of my friends also, the suffering of those summer months. The suffering of T., my own suffering, yours, have broken me. I have gone grey almost in a night and what a night. My dear friend, write me no more letters of that kind. There is no need. To haunt my life with a fear of your hatred was too cruel a blow for one of your sweetness of nature and gentleness to deal one. Small wonder that I am old and grey. Only the intensity of your suffering has helped me through. I burnt the letter because I could not bear it even locked away. Heaven help T. if she ever discovers the pain she has given through her pain. There was my first shock and shall I ever forget my visit to her. T. with the tears trembling down her lashes and in a low voice she denied your love for her. My protestations were useless. She would not believe . . . when she said "I know that

> he loves you" I should have pulled her up and asked her what she meant, instead of putting it aside as too foolish to take seriously =[15]

The page, printed February 8th, 1920, has the date "October 1920" written in by Brett. By then Katherine had returned to Menton for the winter. Two or three entries later, Brett writes:

> I knew so well the feeling you [Murry] had for me – you clung to me as a child to its Nurse or Mother or Sister = for sheer relief and then other things crept up and swamped us = But that you should turn to T. was as it should be = no other thought was in my mind – but that I should retain a passionate Love for you was inevitable = Remember it was the first time any man had dared Love me[16]

The lines immediately following, i.e. October – November 1920, are completely obliterated – not just written over or scratched out but inked thoroughly and completely – but it seems unlikely that loving meant making love in the full sense. That was to come later.

Since the beginning of 1919, when his job as Chief Censor* at the War Office ended, Murry had been editing *The Athenaeum* – and from time to time, employing Katherine as a book reviewer. He now decided that it was time to allow the magazine to be taken over by *The Nation*, leaving him free to pursue his own writing full-time and, without a job to tie him to London, free to do that writing in the south of France with Katherine. To Brett, he seemed post-amorously cool and evasive, offering overwork and an excess of dinner engagements as reasons why he would be unlikely to be able to see her before he left for France.[17]

The truth was Murry had spent the latter part of November spreading his amorous energy a little thin. In the space of five days he had, on Saturday, quite unexpectedly, kissed both his hostess and a guest at dinner; on Monday, picked up a prostitute in Leicester Square and entertained her to dinner and conversation and, he claimed, nothing else; on Tuesday, phoned Brett late in the evening and gone round to Thurlow Road for a kiss and a cuddle; and on Wednesday, again quite unexpectedly, made a pass at Margot Asquith's daughter, Princess Elizabeth Bibesco, whom he had just met for the first time at dinner, when they shared a taxi home. Sunday appears to be the only day without any recorded sexual endeavour. Princess Bibesco fell hook, line and tiara and it is difficult not to believe that Murry encouraged her, for the affair pursued him, by letter, into France and into the spring of 1921.[18]

* Experience he later made great use of.

Unaware of the growing number of her rivals for Murry's exquisite delicacy, Brett hoped to follow him to France. A legacy was due from the estate of a relative, so she wrote to her father, trying to hurry the settlement and laying the ground for the notion that a trip to France was, for an artist, a necessity rather than a luxury.

> Is it possible for you or someone to help me get Howdie's money = it isn't that I am ghoulish about it = only I had the bath and the hot water put in on the strength of it . . . and Maples are getting restive = I enclose the bill to show you it is true . . . Merry Christmas to everyone.[19]

Esher left the reply to his wife.

> My dear Doll,
>
> You will of course get your money; but only when the executors can pay it. You had no right to anticipate it and you must tell Maple & Co, that you will pay when you can. If you are civil to them, then they will be civil to you . . . you have chosen to [look after your affairs yourself] just as you have chosen a life which suits you, and a house without hot water . . . I hope you will have a happy Christmas with some of the family. They will all have beanos I imagine.
>
> Yours,
> Eleanor[20]

Brett pressed her father again.

> You don't understand or deliberately ignore the fact that I am an artist and like artists from all ages choose the least comfortable road = it has to be so = why artists rouse such antipathy God only knows = . . . Painting to me is not merely sitting down and painting just what I see = I have the whole history of art behind me, the effect of modern life on art to grapple with = many modern methods to explore and explode. I am considered a freak because I have not been to the Louvre = and there are French painters of 30 years ago I have hardly seen = . . . I could not come up last summer as I had hoped for two reasons = first I had a friend, who cannot return again probably to this country for two or three years = & unless I go out to her I shall not see her = secondly, I had a very important experiment to make, which I had to make without interruption or criticism = it was touch and go as to the result but the result is in my favour = I succeeded = . . . I had thought of coming up in May but if you are feeling so unsympathetic, it may do my painting more harm than good = that if you want to know is my fear = of the harm an

unsympathetic, highly critical outlook will do me . . . the clash of ideas, the seemingly unbridgeable division . . . I don't care a damn about money . . . I had no one to help me as how to manage . . . I've found a man now = a Russian Jew [Koteliansky] who will help me = not with money = but with advice = I had no grievance = I simply wanted help = . . . I am going to all the beanos tho I have not been asked = . . . I am simply walking in to Antoinette's = I am sending two paintings to the New English = they will probably be thrown out =[21]

Esher's Christmas letter was very short on comfort and joy:

Dear Doll,

We are not so dull as you think, and you are not the first artist we have known, although you appear to think so. There are, however, other things in the world beside self-absorption and self-glorification.

If society – i.e. human intercourse – is to issue from the barbaric stage, there must be give and take. Your idea of an artist is that he should take everything and give nothing.

We have always been ready to give you "sympathy" and appreciation but when have you shown that you asked for either?

By your own free choice you have looked further afield for companionship than your family. No one complains. You have perfect liberty of choice. But you cannot have it both ways. I suppose the artistic temperament does not realise so elementary a proposition.

I am glad you find a Russian Jew more helpful than your brothers and relatives. It used to be the fashion for young men to go to the Jews when they got into scrapes. I fully realise both the equality and similarity of the sexes in these days.

When you wish to come here you are always welcome, as you know. Perhaps, after the next European war, we shall see you.

Till then,

yours ever,

E[22]

It must have seemed to Brett a very unkind and thoughtless greeting and it took her an uncommon six days to cope with a reply:

. . . perhaps if you had become deaf at my age and realised that nearly all contact with the outside world was slowly receding from you = that you were practically dead among the living, you would understand the horror and the despair of such an existence and how in a desperate endeavour to remain sane you, even, might cling to your art as the only salvation, but those things for the unafflicted are hard to realise = just when life began to open out for me, the greater half was snatched away = and I am as solitary, as isolated, as the criminal in his cell = . . . I try to keep hold of something, and just those friends who are interested in me as a painter, and are interested in my painting in regard to real painting = just those few, are the people who keep me alive, and give me strength to survive the monstrous cruelty of my deafness = . . .[23]

6

1921–1922: Katherine 2

Murry returned to London for a brief visit on January 11th, 1921, principally to try and hasten the coalition of *The Athenaeum* with *The Nation* but setting aside time to ensure that affairs of a different nature were kept warm, if not over-heated, encouraging Princess Bibesco's head to rotate a little further over her heels.

He found little time for Brett on that visit. They met for long enough for Brett to keep him up-to-date on the news and gossip and little else. Murry returned suddenly – the word is Katherine's to Ottoline – to France and, from there, asked Brett to let him have the address of the lung specialist that she'd told him Gertler had been consulting. Katherine, he told her, was very ill. The address was to be sent not to Menton but to Portland Villas, where he could collect it when he came back once more in February. Murry spent a little over a week in England on that next visit, arranging for "The Elephant" to be packed up for good and making a quick trip up to Oxford, where he stayed with Ottoline, to confirm arrangements for the lectures he had agreed to give in Trinity term. He suggested that Brett come to tea with him at Portland Villas on his way back through London. Brett received his note too late and missed Murry entirely. He was, in any case, saving his spare moments for Princess Bibesco.

A couple of weeks later, in the middle of March, "LM", Ida Baker, the close friend Katherine described as "my wife", who had become the "mistress" of the Murry household, arrived in London to finish clearing up Portland Villas and to dispose of the furnishings and possessions that remained. Although they detested each other, Brett assisted "The Mountain", as Ida Baker was also known, to clear out The Elephant and, in the process, bought some of the household goods for Thurlow Road. Katherine later protested she paid too much for them.

The rift between Brett and Katherine was beginning to heal and Katherine's ill-will was now directed towards Princess Bibesco, whose fires Murry was still stoking to such effect that Katherine wrote "ordering" her to stop writing love letters to her husband. So far as Brett was concerned, Murry was trying to keep her coolly at arm's length and she, for her part, guilty about Katherine and wanting to mend their friendship, suggested going down to Menton to be with Katherine when Murry came to Oxford. Murry responded stiffly, work, he said, getting in the way of a more adequate reply. Menton would be a bad idea as Katherine was planning to be away while he was in England. He wished Brett well with her "Thursdays" though – they, he thought, *were* a good idea.

Brett's "Thursdays" had just started, partly in an attempt to round up the company she had forsaken over the previous year and partly to make up for the disenchantment between her and Ottoline and the consequent lack of welcome at Garsington. Perhaps too there was a gesture of defiance in her choice of that weekday, the regular day for Ottoline's pre-Garsington soirées in Bedford Square. Apart from Brett, the company was usually entirely male and not always to everyone's taste. Gertler, back from Paris to his lodgings with Brett, wrote to Ottoline: "Last Thursday there came Sullivan, Waterloo and Milne – the atmosphere they sat in and their 'Intellectual' conversation was so hot and stuffy I crept to bed at 9-30."[1] Murry was staying with Ottoline at the time. He had come back from France on May 4th and gone straight up to Oxford to give his promised lectures on style. This time Brett managed to see him. She made the last entry in the diary she had kept through the previous year's hullabaloo:

> And so you have returned after four months = I have not seen you looking so well in body and mind, since you first settled into your house = you are leading so right a life for you = In fact seeing you I felt a great elation, which lasted several days = I was happy that all I hoped should happen had happened = that your nerves and body were rested, that you were happy = I longed to take you in my arms, to kiss you, to tell you how glad I was and how much I loved you still = But I couldn't, I could only tell you of the little trifles that had been happening to me = I hid behind the trivialities, I could not hurt myself = and I was not sure I wanted you to know or to be too aware of my feelings = While you have been over here I have been filled with a longing, a great longing for you.[2]

Something then went wrong, seriously wrong, for Murry wrote in haste to Brett the day before he was due to return to France, totally confused, he said, by some news she had given him and taking back everything that he had said in an earlier letter, written, he claimed, when he was in a state of complete shock. He asked her to try to meet him the next morning on the platform at Victoria where he would be catching the 9.15 a.m. boat train.[3]

Brett wrote the same day to Koteliansky, one of her "Thursday" circle and fast becoming her latest confidant.

> . . . one of the worst things that has ever happened to me, happened the day before yesterday. It knocked my Paris trip on the head, but suddenly today it is all cleared away and I am off tomorrow on the ten o'clock train from Victoria. The cards are amazing. Some day perhaps I will tell you the whole story – but not yet – it is too complicated, too tragic, and not entirely my own.[4]

What "the worst thing that has ever happened" was, it is difficult to say. There *is* a letter from Katherine telling Brett, quite straightforwardly and with few frills, that she does not want her to carry on to Switzerland – where she had now moved – from her planned visit to Paris and suggesting that she delay her trip until the following year, 1922. It is not a gracious letter but it does no more than tell Brett that Katherine is busy, "working against time". And it is dated June 4th so it could hardly have reached Brett by June 6th – the "day before yesterday". As for Murry, he did not write again until after Christmas and then only to thank Brett for her present of a diary and to excuse himself for not having written for so long. Or rather, not to excuse it – simply to say that he found it impossible to write to anyone except in the way of business. And, as usual, to rationalise his own failure to send other than a few words as his own Christmas gift.

Katherine, however, wrote constantly to Brett, her lengthy letters usually no more than a fortnight apart, no longer, that is, than the interval required for her letter to reach Hampstead from Switzerland and for Brett's reply by the following mail to return. Brett told Katherine of the gulf between herself and her family – she spent the remainder of the summer at Roman Camp – of her painting, of her Thursdays, eager to re-establish herself after the long ice-age.

Katherine wrote back, telling Brett to be cold and brutal with any man who bothered her about sex. It was impossible to hurt men's feelings, Katherine said – if they had any, they would recognise distaste, anger and even boredom in the woman. Stand up for our sex, she urged Brett, make men realise how impertinent they were.[5]

At Roman Camp Brett was fishing – "I caught eleven trout and the whole village was staggered . . . [they] have been flogging the river since March and caught nothing!"[6] – and painting, both with equal determination. She came away in September with a number of family portraits to complete in London over the winter and several still lifes – of flowers from the Roman Camp garden and of the playthings of Sylvia's children – but not without having a "scene in the summer-house" with her father.

> As for my past, I developed late and slowly [she wrote to him as soon as she was back in Hampstead]. I owe to Loulou [Harcourt] an irreparable injury, which was perhaps the chief cause of my seeming waywardness = such things happen and it is natures like mine, the most unaware and innocent that become the most suspicious and so I had to find my own way in everything . . .[7]

To Katherine she sent photographs of her Roman Camp paintings, to which Katherine replied at great length with praise, advice, doubts and detailed criticism. She had some misgivings about a group portrait of Brett's brother Maurice's children but thought one of them amazingly well painted, she disliked the portrait of Ottoline who she thought Brett had represented as some kind of giantess and she enthused over a portrait of Maurice's daughter, Marie-Louise, on her own. Best of all, Katherine said, she liked Brett's flower paintings, of asters and of white gloxinias. Colour, she thought, was what Brett's art depended upon. She added that it was just as well that she could not attend Brett's "Thursdays" for she might destroy the seriousness of the occasion with party games.

Virginia Woolf did attend one of the Thursdays. "Brett's salon need give no one the gooseflesh," she told her journal, after a dinner with Brett and Gertler in Thurlow Road:

> I thought to myself, as I sat in my black dress by the anthracite stove in the studio that if Sydney, Kot, Gertler, Brett, Milne and Sullivan with one voice denounced me, I should sleep the sounder. It is a group without teeth or claws. For one thing they have no faith in each other. In my day groups were formidable because they coalesced (but not this group) The hours wore rather thin . . . I don't believe Gertler can paint a picture though his pertinacity would bore holes in granite, if *that* helped . . . Brett is soft, docile and small. She danced before Queen Victoria (held by the renowned Mrs. Wordsworth).[8]

Katherine's New Year letter to Brett wondered on January 4th, 1922, whether she minded shopping for her. Brett, from the remoteness of Switzerland, had been asked, in the course of the year, to buy wool, cardigans, shoes, books and any number of odds and ends to be sent without delay to the Swiss mountains. For New Year, Katherine fearing she had become round-shouldered from lying in bed, wanted a pair of shoulder straps. Gamages, she suggested, would be the place to find them.

Katherine had decided at last to consult Manoukhin, the "specialist" whose address Murry had asked Brett to get from Gertler, and who offered a misguided X-ray treatment to the spleen that he claimed would cure tuberculosis. Katherine's initial intention was to visit Paris for a few days in mid-January and, if Manoukhin agreed to treat her, to return in the spring, find a flat and spend some months there. But, too ill to get out of bed – she had been confined for six weeks, she told Brett on January 21st, 1922 – she put the trip off for a couple of weeks and arrived in Paris at the beginning of February. The news agitated Brett:

> I can hardly sit still – I figit and figit and am in such a temper all because of your trip to Paris – I can't paint, I can't do anything but think of you, follow you into the train, to your hotel in Paris and leave you on the doorstep of Manoukhin's and walk up and down outside until I know = the exact day he begins the cure = I hope he will begin immediately =[9]

Manoukhin did decide to begin immediately, so Katherine found a hotel and stayed in Paris. Murry had argued once again with Katherine and had not travelled to Paris with her. When Brett heard the news, along with the information that Murry was refusing to offer any help in paying Manoukhin's large bills, she was furious.

She offered to send money to Katherine – despite the fact that she was again engaged in an acrimonious correspondence with her father over the way she had been over-spending her allowance – and threatened to thrash Murry. Katherine replied in haste, telling Brett never to send money and to drop all thought of thrashing – she understood perfectly Murry's attitude. By then Katherine had had her first treatment from Manoukhin and she felt that it had gone so well that in a few weeks' time she would be up and about and Brett could come and visit her. But, till then, she insisted, she did not want to think of her illness at all – Brett must fill her next letter only with herself.

Brett did fill her next letter with herself, writing about the small still life she was working on at the time and Katherine noted in her journal:

> Feb. 6th, 1922. Letters from Brett and Murry. Brett's letter was the most beautiful I have ever received. It gave me a strange shock to realise Murry never even asked how things were going . . .

The pity is that there appears to be no trace of that letter of Brett's. Indeed the only letter *from* Brett *to* Katherine available is that quoted above for January 29th. Nothing else. The rest may, like much else, have been "edited" by Murry on Katherine's death.

Katherine tried to deter Murry from leaving Sierre for Paris, but the effect was to bring Murry to Paris in rapid time. Brett should still come for Easter and, clutching at the all-purpose straw, she, too was to approach Manoukhin and see if his treatment might be as effective for her ears as he claimed it was going to be for Katherine's tubes. At the time Brett was preparing to move from Thurlow Road to a house not far away, at 6 Pond Street, next door to Boris Anrep, the sculptor. While waiting for the house to be painted, plastered, connected to the gas, electricity and telephone and generally prettified, she moved in with her former Nanny who lived in Paddington. Once more she pressed her father for money. Esher lost all patience with her.

> You write me insolent letters and then proceed to try and borrow money: I suppose these are the accredited methods in the world in which you have chosen to live. Here is my answer: If you go down to the London Museum and produce any urgent bills up to £50, Maurice [Brett's brother was Deputy Keeper of the Museum] will pay them. I shall recover the £50 from your allowance. As I told you before, I refuse to give you more than £500 per annum: As for your pictures you should sell them (if you can) for what they will fetch and to anyone who will buy them.[10]

It took Brett more than a month to respond to that, telling her father once more that she had chosen the stony and self-sacrificing road of freedom and the arts but that she could not expect her philistine family to see any value in that. She had taken the precaution, between times, of obtaining the full £50 loan via Maurice and the house in Pond Street was almost ready for her to move in. But she ignored her father's advice about selling her paintings and not subsidising her friends and had sent Katherine the still life of pink cyclamen she had promised early in February, followed later by an enormous and very expensive Easter egg that Katherine guessed had cost "a fearful sum". As for the painting, Katherine promised to hang it in her room wherever she was. "One day I shall pay you back with a story. And even then, I'll still be in your debt."

Brett had also been subsidising Gertler – letting him lodge at Thurlow Road without expense, funding him from time to time, making his bed and heating his water and fetching and carrying constantly. Katherine was shocked that Gertler was behaving in such an uncivilised way and told Brett not to pander to him. Then, realising Brett would find it difficult to act on her advice, Katherine wrote to Koteliansky asking him to put a flea in Gertler's ear – if necessary in the guise of a good solid parable.

The Easter egg arrived instead of Brett. Although Katherine had pressed her several times and Brett had promised to arrive on April 18th – the Tuesday after Easter – because of being in the process of moving from Thurlow Road to Pond Street, she did not. On reflection, Katherine decided it was a good thing on the whole, for Manoukhin's ill-conceived all-purpose X-ray treatment was not causing the slightest improvement in her condition and she was once again stuck in bed.

The latest plan was for Brett to arrive in Paris at the end of May. Katherine, who had been enormously impressed by a man she'd met in a cafe who had left Croydon at 11.30 a.m. and was in Paris for lunch, tried to encourage Brett to take one of the new passenger flights. "Flying seems so clean – like cutting one's way with a pair of sharp scissors."[11] Brett hinted again to Katherine that she was still hesitating because of the house move. It was not quite the whole story. The truth was she had been refused any further overdraft by her bank and was once more pressing her father, first for the overdraft to be paid off and £20 added to get her on her way, then, that failing, she suggested that the "best thing" would be for Esher to give her £100, in return for which she would give a written guarantee to live within her means and not bother him financially for two years, by which time, she wildly believed, she would be in a position to pay him back. Esher had already laid down conditions for any increase in his financial support that included *not* going extravagantly abroad while Roman Camp was available for holidays and ceasing to have men lodgers – that is, Gertler and, from time to time, Murry's brother, Richard. Brett's reaction was to attempt to overdraw at her bank once more, claiming that her father would guarantee her up to £50. When that failed, she high-tailed it to Paris on the £20 she had remaining, leaving a string of post-dated cheques behind her and an instruction to Eva, her maid, to sell the silver drums that remained from her days in the Ranee's orchestra. Even then, she wrote from Paris, this time to her mother, saying that she had hurt her back picking up her paintbox, which was the explanation of her ill-tempered letter to her father and asking her mother to send a cheque so that she could pay her newly run-up French bills and buy some more paints.

She had reached Paris on May 29th and found Murry waiting at the hotel in case she "arrived early" but in fact, to ensure that he talked to Brett before she had a chance to meet Katherine. "I confirmed certain things of which I was more or less convinced beforehand," Brett wrote to Koteliansky, without detailing any further. Undoubtedly Murry waylaid Brett to let her know, before she saw Katherine, that Manoukhin's expensive treatment was not working and that she probably had not a great deal longer to live. And, perhaps, too, to try to ascertain from Brett how things stood between them and let her know how they stood between him and Katherine.

> Then the telephone rang to say Katherine was downstairs and the lift wasn't working = so we went down and there she was standing at the foot of the stairs = small, fragile and wonderfully beautiful. She had to creep up five flights of those damn stairs and I went with her. Murry hurried on ahead and then we talked . . . in that first talk she revealed herself = the feeling I had was one of intoxication. I was drunk with relief, with her gentleness to me – her own radiant beauty. It's no good Kot = Katherine is so lovable there can be no half measures.[12]

Brett had hardly arrived in Paris when Katherine and Murry left for Switzerland. Manoukhin had decided that Katherine should rest until the autumn and then return for a further eighteen sessions. "I am infinitely better," she told an unconvinced Brett. "As long as the sun shines," she added, as unconvinced herself. The trip to Switzerland was a nightmare. It was Whit Sunday, the station was crowded, there were no couchettes and no porters, Murry left things in the luggage rack, gave a 500 franc note instead of a fifty and lost the registered baggage tickets. Even the parting from Brett at the hotel had not gone well.

"Every single thing went wrong," Katherine wrote to Ida Baker, who had returned to London when Murry joined Katherine in Paris. "The laundry didn't come back in time. We were off late. Brett was laden with large parcels which we could not pack and which she promised to store for us – until when?"[13] And, in the rush, she and Brett had got into a shouting match.

Shortly after Katherine and Murry's departure, Gertler, an old Paris hand, joined Brett. He was impressed with the way she'd fallen into the life of the city, strutting about with "her toes well out, and as if she had never lived anywhere else in the whole of her life". Gertler brought Brett ill tidings – her servant, Eva, had given notice. Gertler told Brett the reason was that Eva did not want to remain alone in the empty house and that she disliked cooking but Brett was convinced that Eva was resigning from her employment because of some other event:

> whether Gertler has been inconsiderate = or whether his coming in drunk one night = or if he and Valentine have been indiscrete [sic] = or if it's Sullivan who I gather has been there . . . whatever it is, one has to balance one's life against one's servant. I felt annoyed at first = I felt they had overworked her and so on = now I realise one's attitude (to one's friends) is more important. To become a slave to one's servant is impossible.[14]

Brett followed Murry and Katherine to Switzerland on June 29th, despite a suggestion from her mother, who was funding her in Paris, that the trip was an extravagance. "I am only going to Switzerland," Brett protested, "1st class with a sleeper it only costs £4." Now that the visit was imminent, Katherine began to have qualms about life with Brett at close quarters, particularly as she knew that Ida Baker, the Mountain, who was once again looking after her, did not get on at all with Brett. Katherine warned Brett that she too would be poor company as she was working every day, Sunday included, every morning and every evening and would only have the afternoons to spare, to feel free and not guilty.

As anticipated, Brett and the Mountain did not get on, each believing herself to be Katherine's true and only protector. The Mountain claimed Brett was wearing Katherine out, sitting up late and chattering, causing Katherine to shout down her ear trumpet so she could hear, while Brett regarded the Mountain as a lumpen usurper. Katherine was, initially at least, uneasy and sent a note to Murry who had taken himself off down the mountain, the real mountain, to the Hotel Angleterre to be free of the women. Brett, Katherine said, had been visited upon her by God as a trial – she would fail it and it would serve Him right. The trial lasted the better part of a month before Brett returned to England.

The day before Brett's departure Katherine wrote to Koteliansky. She felt like "Campbelling" or gossiping about Brett – the verb derived from Beatrice Campbell, Lady Glenavy, who was exceptionally skilled in that art. Katherine thought Brett was frightening evidence for the damage that background and upbringing could cause and she had, so far, not encountered anything strong enough to counteract the ill effects. Nor did Katherine think Brett ever would, for she was like an ivy that gained no sustenance from the soil but depended upon clinging to some living tree. It might be possible for someone with sufficient strength and determination to make her overcome the disastrous results of her childhood but only by means of constant endeavour, forever soothing her fears and suspicions and, in her art, taking her by hand through each and every painting she produced. Brett, Katherine was convinced, had been born a slave and no slave could be cured of that, even though in him or her was the seed of freedom. Brett might be good and kind and feeling and Katherine loved her and wanted to help in return, but slave Brett would remain.[15]

It was, on the surface, a harsh and unforgiving picture but, nevertheless, peculiarly perceptive of Brett. Immediately following Brett's departure from Sierre, Katherine wrote to Ottoline, a shorter note, made perhaps more cruel by its conciseness, describing Brett as pitiful, with only one saving grace, her will to work. Katherine was unsure whether she really had even that but the clear evidence of Brett's later life, right into great old age, is that Brett had that will in plenty.

Katherine seems somehow to have survived the visit successfully for, before Brett's departure, she completed *The Canary*, the gift she'd promised Brett in exchange for the cyclamen painting and the last story she was to write. She seems also, while Brett was in Sierre, to have discussed, without Murry's knowledge, plans to visit England and consult Dr. Sorapure who had been her medical adviser while she and Murry were in Portland Villas. Quite suddenly, Katherine made up her mind, cabling Brett on August 10th. Brett's reply returned only four hours later, confirming that the sitting room she'd mentally decorated with Katherine in mind, even before she herself had moved into the house, was ready. Katherine then wrote that she couldn't arrive before Thursday, as there were no sleepers available. "Let us go and see Charlie Chaplin . . . on the fillums, of course, I mean . . . Murry has taken up golf. I've always wondered when this would happen . . ." But sleepers there were and Katherine wired again to say that she would now be arriving on Wednesday. The following letter added:

> I've been horribly ill since you left. I must see Sorapure with as little delay as possible. Please don't tell anyone I'm coming, not even Koteliansky . . . there's only one thing. If you can put me in a bedroom rather than the sitting room . . . No, I take that back. That's nonsense. If you knew how those orange curtains are waving in my mind at this moment . . .[16]

The immediate problem with Katherine's request was that Gertler normally lodged in Brett's spare bedroom in Pond Street, and was due back at any moment from the Pyrenees, where he'd travelled on to from Paris. Brett wrote and told him to stay away until the end of September or find somewhere else in London temporarily should he return before then. "God only knows what it is all about," Gertler complained to Ottoline, "the only thing I can think of is that perhaps Murry may be in London and wants to be put up."[17] By the time of Gertler's letter,

Katherine was already established in his rooms in Pond Street and Murry was lodging next door at Boris Anrep's. And, on the day Gertler wrote to Ottoline, only four days after her arrival in London and with Murry out of the way for the day, Katherine was called upon by Orage, an old friend and editor of *The New Age*. Orage's visit had no literary purpose. He had taken up the ideas of the Russian mystic Gurdjeff and was introducing to Katherine the notion that here might lie her salvation.

> I can't remember when she first got the Gurdjeff idea [Brett wrote in her unpublished memoirs]. It was Orage who told her about it and Katherine was full of it. This was going to be her salvation. This would cure her. This was the real Gate of Heaven at last. Orage came to Pond Street to see her. Murry was out of the way and I was told to keep to my room upstairs. I remember leaning out of my top window and seeing the back of Orage's head and not liking it.

The reality was that Katherine's health was rapidly deteriorating. "She would come up to my room on the top floor to feed and clean my canary. She did it twice. The stairs were too much for her and she would sit and gasp for ten minutes before she could open the cage." She had seen Sorapure as soon as she arrived and, when he offered no magic wand, rapidly summoned Orage to Pond Street. Further visits and discussions with Orage and Ouspensky, Gurdjeff's lieutenant and publicist, followed, always in Murry's absence. When, in early September, Murry left Pond Street to go and stay at East Grinstead for the duration, abandoning Katherine to her illness and her own devices, she made her mind up. After consulting Sorapure once more, she attended a lecture by Ouspensky on September 18th. The theories expounded – of fulfilling one's many selves – were hardly revolutionary, but Katherine, having been told by Sorapure that she was dying, needed "a Gate of Heaven". She hurried back to Paris, ostensibly to continue the X-ray treatment with Manoukhin, the further eighteen sessions, but in fact to arrange to enter the Gurdjeff Institute at Fontainebleau. Orage and Ouspensky knew of this; she had told Brett and hinted to Koteliansky; but no one else, not Murry who was writing in Sussex.

Brett saw Katherine and Ida Baker off at Victoria Station on October 2nd and Katherine wrote immediately, upset at the chaos of their departure. Brett had had to rush up and down stairs with their baggage and then the carriage window had jammed and they had been unable to say proper farewells. To cap it all, they had had difficulty in finding a decent hotel in Paris, ending up first in a terrible one and then in one that was only moderately awful. But they would holiday together soon,

Katherine promised, as soon as she finished her book and Brett completed her series of portraits. But, at the same time, Katherine wrote to Koteliansky, illustrating once again her ambivalence towards Brett who, she said, was bombarding her with letters but who, deep down, did not like Katherine whom she accused of not taking her seriously enough, of mocking Brett when she lapsed into a fit of tearfulness. Brett, Katherine thought, was desperate for romance, but romance of a story-book nature, all unrequited longing and no fulfilment. She was like some awful seaweed, permanently underwater, struggling against nothing at all forever. Massive and forceful, yes, but still just weed.

Manoukhin's treatment started immediately but with little better effect than earlier in the year and by the time Orage arrived in Paris in preparation for Katherine's visit to Fontainebleau, she was openly disillusioned and felt she was right back where she started and just pretending that she was better. Murry meantime remained in Sussex from where he wrote to Brett occasionally, asking her to run small errands for him – to send a copy of Tchekhov's *Love and other Stories* to Katherine, to pick up some boiled shirts, buy pianola rolls, pass messages to his brother Richard and put him, Murry, up for dinner and breakfast when he came to London at the beginning of December, when, he promised, he would pose for Brett – he liked Brett's self-portrait, he said and would be proud to sit for his own. Brett, between the errands, took a short autumn trip to Roman Camp where her father delivered an ultimatum – she must stop "living" with Gertler: "Not that they ever lived," Virginia Woolf wrote to Vanessa Bell[18] "save in the sense of sharing the same saucepan. So he lodges two doors off", that is to say in Anrep's house, from where he continued to attend Brett's Thursdays, of which Virginia Woolf was even more scathing than she had been earlier in the year.

> We have been elected to that horrid muling, puling society that meets on Thursday – Murry, Sydney, Brett, Gertler and Koteliansky. The absurd creatures model themselves, I gather, upon the Apostles: first you are looked at, then voted for. Sydney's wife was blackballed, so it is a great compliment. But what I say is, if you can't be clever, isn't it better to be beautiful?

Katherine wrote to Brett twice more in 1922, the last of more than forty letters she had written to her that one year and the last she was to write before her death in the following January. On December 15th, from Fontainebleau, she apologised for the month-long gap in their correspondence and thanked Brett for hitting on the idea of sending her some decent tea. The final letter was written on New Year's Eve, 1922, cheerful, chatty arguing about art, asking Brett to buy her some velvet and brocade shoes from John Lewis in Oxford Street and an evening jacket to wear at a party at the Institute, and thanking her for her Christmas gifts of a beaver muff and two drawings of Murry. The drawings, she confessed, she did not like for they were too soft and gentle and did not show the Murry Katherine knew. Brett's Murry, Katherine said, was too much dove and lamb, too little serpent and lion.[19]

A curt note from Murry reached Brett by the same post, to tell her that he planned to travel to France on the night-boat the following Monday, travelling direct to Newhaven from Ditchling, just north of Brighton, where he had rented a cottage just before Christmas. The implication was that Murry would not be passing through London on his way to Paris and would therefore have no opportunity to exchange New Year greetings with Brett. He asked Brett to send him the shoes she had bought for Katherine in Oxford Street and anything else she wanted taken to Fontainebleau. As Katherine had written, Murry's intention was to spend a week at the Gurdjeff Institute and return to England on January 15th. He arrived at the Institute on the afternoon of Tuesday, January 9th, having stopped in Paris to collect some of Katherine's things from the Hotel Select. That evening at 11 p.m., Brett noted in her diary for 1923, "Katherine died at the early age of 33 of haemorrhage of the lung."

Koteliansky brought the news to Brett, crying, the following day, and on the Thursday she left for Fontainebleau. Brett recalled:

> I was full of hatred for the place. I felt they had killed Katherine which was quite wrong. I met two women walking in the grounds who told me I was trespassing. I was still more furious – they were the usual scrawny, forlorn-looking females that those places attract. I went to the theatre, a huge aerodrome. The windows were stained, the floors covered with priceless carpets. Murry took me up to a man sitting on the floor, a powerful handsome man in a black astrakhan cap and a heavy moustache: Gurdjeff. That evening the dances and exercises were given. Without understanding, I was seeing a great exhibition of control – control over the body. I can understand some of Gurdjeff's ideas better now . . . and understand just what Katherine found in them . . .

Looking back, forty years later, Brett recalled Katherine's funeral as "a dismal event". Closer to the occasion, she thought differently.

. . . my thoughts go back to the Theatre, to the Stables, to the cold church = the Spanish shawl draped over you with the flowers while I walked up in a dream and placed my little basket of Lillies of the Valley with its large pink bow just above your head . . . if only you know – ah – but you did – no one but you could have made your death and burial so simple or so lovely = in the dusk with the light slowly falling you were lowered into your grave and that old French clergyman . . . his white hair shining in the dim light gave you his final blessing . . .[20]

7

1923: Murry

After the funeral, Brett joined Murry at his cottage in Ditchling. Murry's neighbours, Miller Dunning and his clairvoyant wife Bill, were close friends – Murry later wrote of "loving" Dunning – but at this point it was the red-haired Irish Bill who pressed herself upon him. At the exact moment of the funeral, she claimed, Katherine, though dead and across the Channel, had manifested herself to Bill and had described in great and accurate detail the service and the mourners. Bill now believed that Katherine's soul had become united with her own and that her destiny was to assume Katherine's place in life, including her role as wife to Murry. Bill *was*, she believed, to all intents and purposes, Katherine. Dunning apparently had no objection to the notion of Murry and himself sharing two women in a single body and one has the impression from Murry's later letters to Brett that Murry may himself have encouraged Bill to take Katherine's place, at least as bed-companion. The notion of a permanent Bill–Katherine, though, was more than he could suffer in the cause of sexual satisfaction and he fled with Brett to London where he stayed in the Pond Street rooms Brett had put aside for Katherine the previous summer and which, still containing many of Katherine's possessions, he referred to as "Katherine's rooms". By the end of the month – now fleeing Brett – he had moved once more to East Grinstead – not a million miles from Ditchling – although he continued to use Pond Street from time to time, as a pied-à-terre, when business brought him to London.

On St. Valentine's Day, 1923, Brett began to keep a diary in a leather-bound, brass-locked volume given her for Christmas by Ottoline. Unlike the earlier journal, the entries are specifically dated and were now addressed, not in the form of letters to Murry, but to the dead Katherine. Despite that, Brett managed to record day to day events in these letters and an entry for late July shows that, back in January, Murry had begun to press his attentions upon Brett once more, immediately upon his retreat from "Bill–Katherine" and within a very short time of Katherine's funeral. "Tig darling," the entry for July 21st reads, "when J.M.M. fled from Ditchling and came to me I refused to sleep with him, I couldn't allow him to do in haste an act that had no truth, no real impulse behind it except fear. I knew our friendship would be hurt by it . . ."

Murry baited his advances with the possibility of marriage but quickly had second thoughts. He wrote to Brett from East Grinstead on January 31st that he wanted to remain alone – "for some time. It is good for me." The letter crossed with one from Brett, not available, but, one surmises, asking Murry to name the date. Murry replied immediately, asking Brett to forget everything he had said about the possibility of their marrying, to forgive him and try to understand the state he had been in.

Brett did not understand so, when Murry decided to come to London the following weekend to look through some of Katherine's belongings which he had arranged to be sent to Pond Street from France, he asked her to invite him to lunch on Sunday, saying that he would be staying with his mother and not, he stressed, available.

Brett reacted in two directions. First, she vented her ill-feeling on Ida Baker who was helping Murry organise Katherine's effects and sort through her manuscripts and correspondence, activities that brought her constantly to Pond Street. The two had never got on as rivals for the living Katherine's affection and, with Katherine dead, there was no longer any need to hide their feelings. Brett wrote to Kot, upon whom she was increasingly leaning, "Her outlook is so limited that I feel a large cushion is being pressed down on me."[1] A month later, when Brett and Ida Baker coincided on a weekend with Murry in East Grinstead, Murry attacked Brett sharply for claiming that Katherine had been "tortured" by the Mountain. Brett and even himself, he said, had been just as much guilty of that.[2]

Brett's other reaction was an escape into the spirit world. Taking a leaf from Bill Dunning's book, she began to "see" Katherine. "March 31st: Dearest Tig = How early you came this morning = Had you been sitting on the stairs? . . ." "April 1st: I found you yesterday on the stairs and you came up later to my studio – today you have been more fleeting." When Virginia Woolf wrote, sympathising with Brett on the loss of Katherine, "all I could say seems futile; but that does not mean my feeling is. I am glad to find how many of her letters I have. So don't let us become strangers and believe how I have thought of your sorrow",[3] Brett hurried round to assure Mrs. Woolf of Katherine's continued "presence".

> Poor Katherine has taken to revisiting the earth; she has been seen at Brett's by the charwoman. I feel this somehow a kind of judgement

on her for writing the kind of thing she did. Brett told me the story the other day and seemed so bare and rasped that I could not have taken this comfort from her had I wished. Nor do I wish seriously to obstruct any decent investigations of brain and nerves, seeing how much I've suffered that way myself. But then Brett is not scientific, she at once takes the old fables seriously and repeats jargon learnt of Dunning but no doubt diluted in transit, about day and night, birth and therefore death, all being beautiful. She feels the "contact" she says; and has had revelations; and there she sits deaf, injured, solitary, brooding over death, and hearing voices, which will soon become, I expect, entirely fabulous; and even now talking to her has a good deal robbed the image of KM of its distinction. For it came back distinctly when I read her letters. And I saw her wink when poor Brett's note was handed in, and she said that little person can wait, or something like that. Now Brett idolises her, and invests her with every quality of mind and soul. Do people always get what they deserve, and did KM do something to deserve this cheap posthumous life? and am I jealous even now?

No, I think I can be honest at my age.[4]

With the spring, Murry's fancy once more returned to Brett. She confided in her diary:

Tig, My Beautiful little friend,

I have felt you so close to me these last few days – only you do not come so often now or so clearly = dearest, I've been worried – what am I to do with your little lad – I hear you still saying – "Look after the little lad for me, Brett, oh do look after him" – and then I remember all my looking after led to . . .[5]

A couple of nights later Brett looked after the little lad the way he'd been pressing her to for the past two years or more.

Dearest Tig,

For the first time in my life I slept with a man and that man was yours = I found you on the stairs – quite early in the evening – were you hurt? = were you angry or only sad that we could find no other way out = Tig – since that night – (I am writing this two days later) I feel that our bodies have a life of their own = and they compel us not to ignore it.[6]

Brett was in her fortieth year and Murry had opened her eyes at last to sex. "What a strange beauty lies in physical love," she told "Katherine" at the end of that week, "I have heard many men – and some women – speak openly of it – and yet they have never given me quite the impression of that faint lingering beauty that can surround it." Murry wrote, assuring her that if she had lost her terror of sex then he had at least taught her something worthwhile.[7] He added an odd postscript that reads like the Middleton Murry equivalent of a nine-mile run and cold shower to help Brett take her mind off her newly-discovered interest, suggesting that she take a long holiday in the countryside and then re-organise her life completely, get a woman in to clean, dine on bread, cheese and apples and so on.[8]

Within a day or two there came the post-coital falter. "After another night together, I failed = at least he failed this time = and now it is finished, perhaps it is a really genuine loyalty to you – I hope so – perhaps it is the other women – he has many – all eager to live with him."[9] But it wasn't finished. "I'm a queer mixture, Tig; my fear was mixed with audacity = at one and the same time as I was doing all that was possible to shield myself, I also felt I ought to be doing some of the tricks I learned from the Arabian Nights."[10] What the tricks were we shall never know for the following sentence has been heavily deleted by Murry.

Brett took at least part of Murry's advice on good living and went down to the country, choosing, despite all omens and auras, to visit the Dunnings at Ditchling. Bill was still convinced that she was inhabited by Katherine – "her very voice makes one shiver", Brett told Koteliansky.[11] It was too much for her and she returned to London the following day.

A fortnight later, with continued attention from Murry – "each time I bring something new to it" – Brett thought she was pregnant. It might answer Murry's unspoken prayer, she confided to "Katherine". "If it is so, I am utterly alone. J.M.M. will be frightened = he will forsee in a panic his liberty impinged = he will fear the danger of new shackles = and yet if I had my own money such fears would be groundless = I would face the world with my little baby on my own."[12] There was no need to. Another fortnight "of suspense and anxiety and then relief = all is well = I am getting back to my painting – some ox-eyed daisies and sunflowers ="

Murry had begun to collect together, from their recipients, Katherine Mansfield's letters for later publication. Assisted by Ida Baker, he was using "Katherine's rooms" at Pond Street for storage of the correspondence and manuscripts and Brett had already complained to Koteliansky that she disliked Ida's attitude – "she puts a handkerchief over Katherine's letters and papers when I come into the room . . ." Now, spurred on by a hint from Koteliansky* that Katherine had not always been charitable in her opinion of Brett in her correspondence with others, Brett found an opportunity to go through Katherine's letters while Ida was out of the way. Brett was horrified at what she found: "Was I that rotten mushy kind of female? = and am I still?"[13]

> Reading those letters has reopened an old wound = what I hoped was a private matter between us, is common property = it explains much of JMM's attitude towards me = that queer indifference . . . I can't help even now being astonished and once more horrified that you could have loved me as you did and yet written of me like that = hardly once have you said of me to your other friends a kind word . . . I am not a yearning female = I am not forlorn = . . . if I love, I give, why count the change or the cost =[14]

Brett wrote to Murry at once, leaving out the essential information that she'd been reading Katherine's letters. He, hiding away in a cottage near Chichester, was mystified and suggested that she come down and see him the following weekend on her new motor-bike. Murry had bought a motor-bike too and they could go for a few rides together, he wrote, adding that he'd read her letter three times and couldn't work out what the fuss was about. What had become "common property"?

The weekend with Murry wasn't entirely a success. His brother Richard was staying in the tiny cottage as well and "rather got in the way". "But good has come out of it – I feel we are drawing nearer together . . . sometimes I think he is foolish not to marry me = and then I have a glimpse of some gay little woman who might be better for him = . . . all the time I long for a real friendship . . ."[15]

From her weekend with Murry, Brett went on to one of her now rare visits to Ottoline at Garsington, while Murry went to stay with Walter de la Mare on his farm in Pembrokeshire. He wrote warning Brett of the enormous amount of work he would have to get through in September but offering that he might have time for "a little tour" with Brett at the end of the month. Murry did indeed go on a little tour at the end of September. His companion was not Brett, but, back alone from the New World, and without her husband, Frieda Lawrence.

Frieda arrived back in Britain at the beginning of September, her return signalled a month earlier by Lawrence in letters to Murry and Koteliansky. "I wish you'd look after her a bit," Lawrence wrote to

* See above pp. 127–8 and p. 130. Koteliansky may well have shown Brett these letters himself.

Murry, "would it be a nuisance? She will be alone. I ought to come but I can't . . . F. wants to see her children. And you know, wrong or not, I can't stomach the chasing of those Weekley children."[16]

Murry told Brett of Frieda's impending return and the probability that Lawrence himself would follow, using the possibility of a "blood friendship" with Lawrence as yet another reason for postponing any permanent commitment.[17] Brett, ever helpful, arranged rooms for Frieda in the same house as Gertler, who wrote to Ottoline:

> Something very dreadfully [unexpected] has happened to me! When I got to my rooms I found to my horror that Frieda Lawrence had taken for three whole weeks a room in my house!!! She starts today! Brett's doings! I immediately got a splitting headache and am now in full expectation of a complete nervous breakdown![18]

A few days later, Gertler managed to drop his exclamation marks.

> It has all worked out much simpler and less tiresome than I anticipated. There is no question of her sharing my sitting room or meals. She is at the top of the house where she has a bed-sitting room, where she sleeps and god knows what else. Since she has come I have seen her only three times. She is quite alright only somehow very uncomfortable to be with and also somewhat of a bore. She is worse than she might be because she apes Lawrence and his ideas coming out of her large German body sound silly and vulgar. Both her plans and Lawrence's are very vague for the time being, so I don't know how long she intends to stay in the house, but Koteliansky is trying to persuade her to go to Germany to see her people and wait *there* for Lawrence's plans to materialise – a good idea . . .[19]

Although Gertler had seen Frieda only two or three times, Murry was a constant visitor to the bed-sitting room where she slept and "god knows what else". When Frieda left for Germany to visit her parents at the end of September, Murry conveniently decided to tour, not with Brett, but to Switzerland, to Sierre, to clear up, he said, what remained of Katherine's belongings there. That Murry and Frieda consolidated their affair by coinciding on the Continent seems certain – for one thing, Brett's letters to Murry at Sierre failed to reach him. Brett, however, did not at this stage put two and two together to make a couple, although she began to build up an antipathy to Frieda that was to wax and wane for the next forty years. To "Katherine" she wrote:

> I want to tell you, dear, of Frieda = of the appalling indecency of her to me and JMM. Oh, why are people so indelicate = Here is this great porpoise of a woman shouting out "why don't we marry" and talking of me in an exasperated sentimental way that makes me writhe = I am proof more or less against such things, but I feel JMM must feel angry and sick . . . I feel as though a bucket of dirty water has been thrown over me = I must clear away the muck that woman throws off . . . I feel singularly disgusted, Tig, . . . I think of how you would have shrunk from Frieda's vulgarity.[20]

Murry's thoughts from abroad failed to remedy Brett's ill humour for he told her that he had decided to move out of her house on his return, partly, he said, because he was unable to work in Katherine's old room but, more importantly, because he felt it unwise for him and Brett to live in the same house for the moment. If he were to remain in Pond Street, he claimed, his feelings for Brett would inevitably sour as he did not think he was capable of having a straightforward sexual relationship with her with no strings attached – he was too fond of her for that.[21]

It was the kind of letter at which Murry was expert, suggesting that his love for Brett might be diminished by making love, that it was something in him with respect to all women that made this so and yet . . . and yet . . . perhaps with some other woman this might not be the case – all leaving it open for his affair with Frieda to continue when he returned to England without *that* coming into conflict with his carefully stated principles so far as Brett was concerned. In Murry's favour it ought to be said that Brett's record was of heart-over-head crushes and immense possessiveness, of spending for today and wishful thinking for tomorrow; and that Katherine, however imperfect their relationship may have been, was not long dead, and Murry was in no state to seek a permanent companion and had every reason to seek solace and comfort in another's bed. And he was, perhaps, by today's standards, averagely promiscuous, the only pity being that he seems not to have been able to accept this but to need to keep running and playing every fish ever hooked on his line.

His following letter, two days later, was more of the same. His integrity and their friendship, he said, would be destroyed unless he could give himself as a whole. Anything less would betray Brett and be untrue to himself. It might be possible to give himself wholly one day but for the present they could not continue to be lovers.[22]

This was more to Brett's liking. "A very much better letter," she wrote to Koteliansky, "in fact a very good one indeed . . . I think we shall come to a much clearer understanding and I shall be able to help him over this . . . will you let me know directly you hear the day of

JMM's return?"[23] Murry in fact returned within a day or two and, with Brett assuring him of understanding his attitude, felt safe to enter her bed for a few more nights before moving out, as forewarned. Despite her cheerful note to Kot, Brett was desperately depressed and wrote to "Katherine":

> I have been through a bad time = ever since JMM wrote telling me of his decision to leave my little house and move into his flat, I have felt chilled = he is right in his way = it is difficult for us to live so intimately together unless we go further and marry = and so the crack is widening = I understand him perfectly but it does not lessen the regret = I would have liked a deeper relationship but I do not now think that it will ever be for me = For the first time since early youth he feels free = there are young women = and to man they are eternally exciting, mysterious and perhaps desirable = Oh, Tig, of what use to torment oneself = I lack those things men really need = I cannot pander to men's vanity enough – I cannot dress myself or concern myself enough to attract or distract them = I have not the habit and what is stranger still I seem not to have the instinct = I never think of men in relation to myself = I never have = . . . those last nights together were perhaps the last = I shall no more hold him in my arms = no more feel the physical love surging up = no more run my hands down his warm body = [the following six lines have been very carefully and heavily deleted by Murry] No, I don't think I ever shall – I have loved this man too much = and the other – the tenderness, the intimacy, the life together – all must go = I have torn it out of myself = these last few days have been hell = I feel tired, oh, tired beyond words . . .[24]

The depression deepened when, a month later, Brett again suspected she might be pregnant. The only person she felt she could turn to was Koteliansky.

> The return of Lawrence is great news – only it is overshadowed for me with the fear that I have a baby coming. I have tried not to burden anyone with this, but I can't bear it alone any longer and it's useless to tell Murry until I know for certain. I am afraid. I have struggled through a terrible time of depression. I go to Sorapure on Friday. The worry, the fear exhausts me. With Lawrence coming and Murry's having to face the reality of Lawrence, his judgement almost, it will be difficult to keep the secret of our relationship. I feel, as I suppose every woman feels, that the burden is all left to me. Murry can turn from one woman to another while I have to face the

> beastliness of an illegal operation = or the long strain of carrying a child and perhaps death = not that I mind the last = it might be the best way out if I am not strong enough to stand alone . . .[25]

Brett arranged to see Sorapure, the doctor in whom Katherine had placed such trust, the following Friday morning and then met Koteliansky for lunch. By then she had confronted Murry with the possibility that she might be pregnant. Murry reacted violently and insisted that she arrange for an abortion. As a first stage he would consult a doctor friend about "some stuff to take and whether [Brett could] get rid of it by any safe means . . ." "Getting straighter with Murry freed me from him," Brett told Koteliansky. "I think I can stand alone and act alone now = it would be a relief if it is anything but a baby . . . I only hope that if I have to go through with this he will not try and break me . . ." Throughout lunch Kot tried to defend Murry and Brett exploded in anger. Immediately afterwards she wrote to Kot apologising.

> I really did myself an injustice today = I bear no grudge against Murry. I am really at heart most anxious for my sake and for his to get rid of this baby . . . and the fear lurks that I can't . . . I don't want to force anything on Murry. And he is so sensitive really that if the baby came he would feel as angry at not marrying me as he would at marrying me = and it would take more skill than I possess to save our friendship . . . I explode to you lots of things I know in my heart aren't true or important because through you I get my balance again. Believe me, I am very gentle and tender with Murry . . . I haven't reproached him with anything . . . what he has given me has been good and genuine. I pound all the bad things out of myself against you and it does me good . . . because I know you will never let me down and pretend bad thoughts and feelings are good ones in me. But I don't think I want to burden Murry or myself with a false position. I am far too fond of him . . . I spoil him dreadfully.[26]

A week later the panic subsided. Murry's physician friend, the Dr. Young who had been at the Gurdjeff Institute with Katherine, made out a prescription for Brett and arranged for her to see a colleague who would be prepared to carry out the illegal operation. The consultation proved to be unnecessary. Either Dr. Young's pills performed their required trick or Brett's pregnancy was, like that earlier in the year, a false alarm. She and Murry had a long talk over breakfast, ending up "closer to each other than ever".[27]

That, of course, failed to please Frieda Lawrence. Frieda had just heard from Lawrence, who was still in Mexico, in terms that suggested that he was thinking that he and Frieda should formalise their separation and make it permanent and that he would settle the financial details of this on his return to England shortly. That, for Frieda, meant that for the moment it ought to be *she* and Murry who were "closer to each other than ever" and, although she may have been unaware of the precise nature of the event that had brought Murry back into residence in Pond Street, she saw her affair with him collapsing. She stalked over to Brett's "breathing fire and brimstone . . . angry with Murry and hostile to me."[28] A day later, Lawrence embarked at Vera Cruz on a boat for Plymouth and Frieda decided to turn her attention back to her husband for, when the news arrived, she burst into Gertler's studio shouting, "Prepare yourself – Lorenzo's coming!"

Brett seems not to have realised that an affair had developed between Frieda and Murry. She attributed Frieda's ill-will towards her as something entirely general to Frieda's nature: "she would wear out a Hercules = she wears me out = she is heading for disaster." In the same diary entry she complains to "Katherine" that Murry is using her.

> He would sleep with me . . . I like it very much = But is it worth the fatigue, the energy, the amount of thought required to keep on exciting it? Do I not cease to be myself? Under those conditions I become a game, a relaxation for a man? a nothing in myself = all that I really am he passes by = that definite human being vanishes = we become a sham = the real HE and She, the blending of a male and female, of real separate beings, ceases – we become the hunter and the hunted = Because I have liked physical love, it has been taken from me = it was doing me harm . . . but I wish we were lovers still = it seems to me a more perfect friendship.[29]

The last entry in that diary addressed to "Katherine", apart from a brief note written the following February, 1924, is dated December 3rd, 1923. Brett and Murry were then, she wrote, "very deep friends" but no longer lovers – "he may really be trying to lead a completely chaste life". That Murry was completely chaste is unlikely. A few days later, when Lawrence arrived in England, he was met by Murry, Koteliansky and Frieda at Waterloo Station. Murry thought Lawrence looked ill and had "a greenish pallor". Almost the first words Lawrence spoke were "I can't bear it." Lawrence's turning green, however, was interpreted rather differently by Catherine Carswell, with whose brother Frieda was lodging. "Murry and Frieda so chummily together was enough to turn him greenish pale all over" – the green, that is, of jealousy and distaste – which puts a rather different complexion on

Lawrence's first words than the notion that they expressed some generality of feeling about England.

What was keeping Murry from Brett's bed, then, was his over-interest in Frieda's and not any sudden attack of chastity, for which he had no previous track record. Now Lawrence was back, there was an obvious dilemma. Murry had been anticipating his return so that he might pass to him the editorship of *The Adelphi* in which role Murry had been deputising. For Lawrence, though, there was no question of Murry deputising in so far as Frieda was concerned and all thought of a permanent separation from his wife seems to have flown out of the carriage window of the boat train the moment it was pulled down at Waterloo, to reveal Murry and Frieda's "chumminess" together. The truth was probably that Lawrence had some inkling already that Frieda had taken up with Murry, possibly from Frieda herself in the belief that her marriage was at an end.

With Lawrence's return, however physically inadequate, to the scene, Murry was forced to keep his distance from Frieda for the time being. To Brett's naive and unquestioning delight, he abandoned his quite singular chasteness towards her and was once more in her Pond Street bed. To Koteliansky, she wrote on Boxing Day, 1923, "In spite of all our troubles, Murry and I are closer than ever before . . . we are lovers still, Kot. I never refuse him." Murry and Brett's "chumminess" now upset Frieda. She and Lawrence, along with Koteliansky, Murry and Richard Middleton Murry, had been entertained to Christmas dinner in Brett's basement dining room and a postscript to Brett's letter to Koteliansky adds: "Murry and I were disgusted with Frieda last night. I am sure she tried to spoil the party."[30]

It was events at another party, however, which had taken place soon after Lawrence's return from Mexico that were to play an important part in Brett's life: Lawrence's now infamous "Last Supper" at the Cafe Royal.

According to her account of the Lawrence years, *Lawrence and Brett, a friendship*, written by Brett a decade later, after Lawrence's death in 1930, Brett was "not allowed" to meet him at the station with Murry, Frieda and Koteliansky on his return at the beginning of December. The truth is probably less severe than that, for, apart from that much earlier party in 1915, given in Brett's Earls Court studio, Brett hardly knew Lawrence at the time. In the intervening years there are a bare three or four mentions of Lawrence in her letters to Ottoline and not very sympathetic mentions at that, advising Ottoline to use ridicule as a response to Lawrence's portrayal of her in *Women in Love* and "hooraying" at the rejection of a Lawrence manuscript by his publishers. Later, however, an undated letter from Pond Street to her father, probably written in 1923, supports Lawrence, in tandem with Murry: "*The Adelphi* . . . is the green tree in the Wilderness = Murry and Lawrence may be the leaders of the new generation."

But that is all – Brett had no proper reason to be a part of the welcoming party at Waterloo, except as one of the contenders for the position of mistress of Murry. "Not allowed" means simply that there was no point in a relative stranger being at the station. "I see and hear nothing for a couple of days," Brett continues, "until you phone me that I am invited to the dinner that is being given you at the Cafe Royal."[31]

The other dinner guests were the Carswells, Donald and Catherine, Mary Cannan, Gertler, Koteliansky, Murry and of course Frieda and most of them have at one time or another written their account of the proceedings. What all agreed on was that after a very great deal of wine had been drunk, Koteliansky stood up and began to make a speech, in praise of Lawrence and of not much else, smashing a wine glass between each sentence, having prudently emptied it first, and declaiming, "No woman here or anywhere else can understand the greatness of Lawrence." Inspired perhaps by Koteliansky's dismissal of the female sex – he had carefully excepted Frieda – Murry then rose and kissed Lawrence fervently, claiming, "Women can't understand this, this is an affair between men," to which Catherine Carswell replied, "Maybe, but it wasn't a woman who betrayed Jesus with a kiss." Murry then embraced Lawrence again and exclaimed, "I love you, Lorenzo, but I won't promise not to betray you."

At some point in all this Lawrence asked for recruits for Rananim, the utopian colony he had tried to promote all those years before, the new home for which was to be not Florida nor Garsington but New Mexico. Only Mary Cannan said no – the rest, whether from drunkenness or evasion, said yes, Murry with a great deal of further effusion. Brett, perhaps missing half of what was going on in her deafness and encouraged by Murry's seeming acceptance, also agreed to join the colony.

A little later, Lawrence ordered port, knowing it did not agree with him, collapsed sick and vomiting, and was carried back to Hampstead where Catherine Carswell's brother claimed next morning to have seen clearly "St. John and St. Peter (or maybe St. Thomas) bearing between them the limp figure of their Master." Koteliansky and Middleton Murry had at last joined the Apostles.

In the cold and sober light of the December dawn, the enthusiasm of the Cafe Royal's recruits for a utopian Rananim high above the New Mexican desert, evaporated, leaving only Murry and, one guesses because of him rather than out of any direct enthusiasm at that stage,

Brett. Lawrence, hungover and suffering a gastric aftermath, the port having put his stomach in a storm, stayed in bed for several days, "sitting up in a knitted red shawl, looking very pale and ill and hurt", and writing to Mabel Luhan who would be their hostess in Taos, "We seriously think of New Mexico in the early spring: and Middleton Murry wants to come along – also, probably, Dorothy Brett, who paints, is deaf, forty, very nice, and a daughter of Viscount Esher."[32]

Lawrence – the working-class aristocrat – was careful always to let his friends and correspondents know of Brett's titled background. A letter of Ivy Litvinov records: "Lawrence was an incorrigible snob: his first letter to me was on crested paper. 'Don't mind the paper. My wife's father's a baron and we have to use up the old stuff' – in three letters, one after the other."[33]

Brett then, according to Catherine Carswell, became "as constant a visitor as Murry to the Lawrences' rooms" where modelling small figures in plasticine became a pre-Christmas craze.

> We are doing, amidst shouts of laughter, an Adam and Eve . . . we look at Adam . . . Murry and I look at each other, then at you.
>
> "Lawrence, you just can't leave Adam like that."
>
> "Do you good, Brett," you say tartly; but we will not allow you to leave him so indecent, so with ironical glee, you snip off his indecence, and then mourn for his loss.[34]

Brett was beginning to know what life with the Lawrences could be like – Murry had already experienced it in Cornwall with Katherine some years before.

> You suddenly seize the poker and, in a white heat of rage, you emphasise your words by breaking the cups and saucers. It becomes terrible to watch . . .
>
> "Beware, Frieda! If ever you talk to me like that again, it will not be the tea things I smash but your head" . . . Later . . . Murry and I put on our coats. You come down the stairs with us . . . Our departing footsteps echo on the frosty air. I turn and look back. You are standing on the steps in the bright moonlight . . . straight and . . . faunlike.[35]

The departure of Murry and Brett into the frosty Hampstead night was used almost exactly by Lawrence for the opening of his short story, *The Last Laugh*, in which Miss James is a deaf spinster painter, complete with hearing aid, while the despised Marchbanks, killed off in fiction by Lawrence, is Murry. The story was written early in 1924, when Murry, now that Rananim had been reduced from a golden circle of friends to little more than the possibility of a small number of permutations upon the eternal triangle, was beginning to vacillate in his determination to go to New Mexico. His first doubts were expressed towards Brett, who took them to mean that he did not want her to go with him. Within a day or two, he retracted – "apparently it was all a false alarm . . . Murry has much the same feeling as I have about Mexico and Lawrence too, about my going", Brett wrote to Koteliansky.[36]

If the presence of both Frieda and Brett in the caravan was not encouraging Murry to go West, neither, wholeheartedly was Lawrence. To Murry he wrote: "I don't know if you really want to go to Taos . . . but if you really want to go with Frieda and me and Brett – *encore bien*!",[37] while to Koteliansky he directed, "If Murry talks to you about America at all, dissuade him from going, at least with me."[38]

By then Murry had in any case decided that, while the arrival might be pleasant, the travelling itself might not be all that it was made out to be. He wrote to Lawrence, pleading absurd sartorial obstacles to his journey and telling him he would rather follow him to New Mexico in April than join him on the boat in March. Lawrence replied snappily to Brett:

> Your and Murry's letter this evening. Tell him not to bother to buy a new dark suit. And if he is not coming until the first week in April, why bother with a new overcoat?
>
> . . . You must decide whether you will come with us or with Murry at the end of the month. Perhaps better with us . . . you can arrange a visit with your millionaire relatives in the interim of waiting for Murry . . . perhaps better if Jack makes that little trip on the ocean alone. He *wants* to be alone for a bit.[39]

It was an imperative "wants", for Lawrence had, by now, realised the full complications of Murry's relationship with the two women and was prescribing a period of isolation for Murry. Then Koteliansky blundered into the act, forcing Brett to face up to the relationship between Murry and Frieda and at the same time suggesting that Brett's motive in travelling was not to cement her affair with Murry but to initiate one with the latest in her long line of crushes – Lawrence himself. Brett wrote angrily to Kot:

> This kind of thing makes me ill = you accuse me, owing to an ill-timed, vulgar jest = born of some vulgarity of Frieda's, of a behaviour towards Lawrence in thought and action which revolts me, which to me is indecent, and of which I am utterly incapable =

There are two outstanding reasons against my behaving or even thinking in such ways = First, it is against my beliefs = For to pour such dirty muck over a man like Lawrence – over any man – would necessitate destroying myself =

Secondly, I have been Murry's mistress. I shall never be his wife = but to me that makes no difference = I have given myself – that is final – not casually, but out of a real love. He is free but I am not = I keep myself clean = I am not ashamed = but I do not change =

. . . I have made mistakes, so has he = we have hurt each other = but even that I understand and I am his friend . . . I made no conditions = I will never be his mistress again because he must keep faith with Lawrence . . . I spoke of what you said to me = I was shocked at the time and I ought to have made sure what I was hearing = I could not reconcile you with it = there has been a mistake = I misheard = but I have not invented = nor am I spiteful = if you break our friendship, I shall never believe in your friendship again =[40]

But broken the friendship was. Brett never saw Koteliansky again and it took the occasion of Lawrence's death in 1930 for her to write to him just once more. A note from Frieda, written from Vence in 1932, following the publication of Lawrence's letters, throws a little light on the rift. Frieda was furious with Kot, she wrote, for having refused Aldous Huxley access to Kot's Lawrence correspondence. "How Lawrence would have hated him for practically putting it into your head that Lawrence might marry you and I Murry – and then *hating you* for his tricks!"[41]

Lawrence himself may have been partially responsible for the notion of some liaison with Brett at this time. He had been preparing *The Boy in the Bush* for publication from a manuscript written by the Australian, Mollie Skinner. Miss Skinner later credited Lawrence with writing the whole of the last two chapters and much of the preceding one. In these closing chapters, Lawrence introduced a new character, Miss Blessington, whose description corresponds closely with that of Miss James, the character in *The Last Laugh* that he had based on Brett. "There was something slightly uncanny about her, her quick, rabbit-like alertness and her quick open defiance, like some unyielding animal . . ." and later:

Slowly he formed an idea of her precise life, with a rather tyrannous father who was fond of her in the wrong way, and brothers who had bullied her and jeered at her for her odd ways and appearance, and her slight deafness. The governess who had mis-educated her, the loneliness of life in London, the aristocratic but rather vindictive society in England, which had persecuted her in a small way . . .

Miss Blessington is to be Jack's "second wife". Lawrence wrote to Mollie Skinner two days before leaving with Brett and Frieda for America, "You may quarrel a bit with the last two chapters. But after all, if a man has really cared, and cares, for two women, why should he suddenly shelve either of them? It seems to me more immoral to drop all connections with one of them, than to wish to have the two."[42]

By the date set for departure, Brett realised that Murry would not be following, despite his continuing insistence that he would do so. She made her last diary entry to "Katherine":

> I'm off to Mexico* = I am leaving JMM = It's been fearfully hard to do – but I feel it is right = I've loved him, cherished him . . . but I am going because it is best for him to be alone for a little while = I've done all I can – and lately I've been held back, because I felt the need in him of being free = I have given no outward sign of affection = it's been difficult to restrain myself – but it is right = he must have freedom when he needs it =
>
> So I go = Lawrence, Frieda and I =[43]

Brett called on Gertler to say her farewells on Sunday, March 2nd, 1924 and a note from Gertler to Ottoline suggests that the fiction that Murry would follow on was still being maintained. Carrington had carried her farewells to Pond Street the day before and found there:

> . . . this dreadful collection of Adelphites . . . Lawrence and his fat German spouse and the great decaying mushroom Middleton Murry and an attendant toadstool called Dr. Young . . . Lawrence was very rude to me of course and held forth as if he was a lecturer to minor university students. Apparently he came back this winter expecting to be greeted as the new Messiah. Unfortunately very few saw his divination . . . a few critics called him a genius but that wasn't enough. "England is rotten, its inhabitants corrupt." Mexico is the only country where prophets and great writers are appreciated. So tomorrow Lawrence and Frieda and Brett set off in an ocean liner for Mexico . . . the decayed Murry sat on the sofa and said nothing; he swayed backwards and forwards like a mandarin, with toothless

* Almost all of Lawrence's insular friends, encouraged by Lawrence, referred to Mexico rather than New Mexico. The friends in ignorance, Lawrence perhaps in the desire to associate his Rananim with the wilder country of the blood to the south of the United States of America.

> gums, a vacant smile and watery eyes. Only once he spoke. "Say, Brett, your butter's bad." It is reported he has given up the *Adelphi* and is, in a few months, going to follow the Messiah, Frau Messiah, and Brett to Mexico.[44]

Lawrence, Frieda and Brett left on the *Aquitania* on March 5th, 1924, for New York. Murry came to Waterloo to see them off. They cannot have been surprised that he failed to follow them to Rananim but were certainly so when, within a couple of months of their departure, he announced his marriage to Violet le Maistre, a young and hitherto unheard of twenty-two year-old contributor of poetry to his magazine. Brett, when she heard the news, touched "lightly but scornfully" on the subject in a letter to Gertler, "putting it all down to Kot who she says 'Betrayed' her".[45] "Most of the letter is about Bessie and Nellie," Gertler told Ottoline, adding a postscript: "P.S. I must explain that Bessie and Nellie are horses."

8

1924–1925: Rananim

Lawrence, Frieda and Brett arrived in a windy, snow-driven New York on the afternoon of March 11th, 1924, after a voyage that had started calm and pleasant but had ended in rough seas, enjoyed by Brett and Lawrence but upsetting for Frieda, who spent the last couple of days sheltering in her cabin. Brett had problems first with her passport – the immigration authorities could not understand why her surname was entered as "Brett" and that of her father as "Esher" – and then with the customs, who wanted her to pay duty on her "paints, artist's materials and banjolette". Lawrence's irritation at the delays turned to fury at both Brett and the authorities. Still under the impression that Murry was to follow them to the United States, he warned him, "when you come, don't declare anything on your customs paper – put 'Personal Effects and Clothing' – no more".

After a week in New York, they set off west, via Chicago across the great flat prairies and section-land of middle America, to New Mexico. The party was met at Lamy, the rail-head for Santa Fe, by Wytter Bynner and Spud Johnson, writers whom Lawrence had met on his earlier visit and who had shared his Mexican trip the year before. Lawrence was, as always, careful to make it clear that Brett was of "the quality" – "an English viscountess or something", Bynner wrote to his mother that evening, "deaf but likeable".

Bynner's adobe home in Santa Fe had become something of a staging post for travellers on their way to Taos, which is seventy miles further on, up the valley of the Rio Grande, and Bynner was a regular greeter at Lamy Station. He had put up the Lawrences for the night when they were first on their way to Taos a couple of years earlier and then, a decade later, offered shelter to Lawrence's ashes when his mortal remains went to Taos for the last time. In 1924, with Brett along, Lawrence decided that Bynner's house would be too crowded and the threesome took rooms at the Fonda Hotel, joining Bynner and Johnson – his secretary in the Somerset Maugham sense – for dinner. Brett wrote that, after dinner, "a restlessness seizes you, and you begin to enquire about the stage to Taos, of the road. Can the stage run? It can, so you take places and next day we start".[1]

Lawrence's initial reaction to New Mexico on his first visit a couple of years earlier but recorded later, has been much quoted: "The moment I saw the brilliant, proud morning sun shine high over the deserts of Santa Fe, something stood still in my soul, and I started to attend." Elsewhere he wrote that New Mexico was "the greatest experience from the outside world that I have ever had".

On that journey, in 1922, Lawrence and Frieda had arrived from the West Coast, by rail from San Francisco to Albuquerque and up through the middle of central New Mexico to Santa Fe, then by road, an unpaved dirt road, to Taos in the north of the state. In the south and centre of New Mexico, the great river, Rio Grande to Americans, Rio Bravo del Norte to Mexicans, flows wide and shallow, its banks irrigated and cultivated. As one travels north from the Mexican border, on either side the orange-brown plain ripples away to a rising horizon of stark mountains. Forty miles in either direction one looks and there the mountains rise, red, yellow, curved and convoluted, jagged and flat topped, their strata on edge like the marbling at the back of a book. Harsh and, but for their own curiosities, unadorned. By Albuquerque the land, already high, has begun to rise further into the beginnings of the Rocky Mountains. The river level is 5,000 feet and the great flat valley is bounded on the west by a low rock mesa and on the east by the Sandia Mountains, mountains which, now that one is further north and higher, are more temperate in the heights and treed with pine and scrub oak. Then, pressing north again to Santa Fe, the state capital, a spreading adobe town built around the old Spanish plaza, one travels through a desert – but not the stretching sands of the Middle East: a desert polka-dotted with piñons and slashed with dry washes that run deep with flash floods in the electric storms of summer – one "sees" more weather in a week of New Mexican summer than in a lifetime elsewhere. A storm, thunder, lightning, a black wall of rain cutting the sky, not here but there, elsewhere, forty, fifty miles away, the heavens split with forked lightning, but here one can sit, in the shade of a pine and watch it all, far away, through the sunshine.

Here and there centuries of erosion have produced mini-Monument Valleys. North of Santa Fe a distant mesa has been carved by the wind into a series of what look like apartment blocks, rock Brasilias. Elsewhere by the road one finds a rock that is almost in the shape of a camel, another backed like a weasel or very like a whale. To eyes conditioned by John Ford and John Wayne, it is a landscape easier to categorise and accommodate than it can have been in Lawrence's day. My own first sight of the United States was New Mexico. By plane from

Britain with a change in Chicago airport, through the electrical storms of a hot Kansas night to Albuquerque in the neon dark and then, jet-lagged in the bright New Mexican morning, thrust into a hired car in this alien landscape for the drive north through the state to Taos. But, though hardly believable in its scale and sense of distance, its harsh reality, I had been there before in a thousand second features and could always say, "My God, it's just like the movies."

The Lawrences and Brett, in 1924, did not have that background, that history, those categories in which to load the visual fireworks. And what must have been a surprise to Brett at least – for Lawrence's first arrival had been in a September: the expected desert was under snow north of Santa Fe. South, except in the hills, the snow rarely lies long or deepens – the wide sun of day removes it as soon as it arrives and the desert is rarely more than frosted like angel cake. But beyond Santa Fe, the snow can deepen. Today, despite Highway Patrols and crack-of-dawn snow-ploughs on two, three and five lane roads, one can still spend the night stuck by the roadside in a drift. In 1924, none of that. A dirt road and no snow-ploughs. Something better than driving across bare desert but not much.

North of Santa Fe, immediately north, the rock-cream hills roll gently up and then down, advance warning of the Rockies, hinting at the Sangre de Cristos to come. The Conquistadores saw them, these mountains, snow capped in a setting sun, dripping crimson, and named them for the blood of Christ. Then one descends to what might pass for a plain once more, at Espanola where the road moves ever closer to the river, just above the fruit orchards – apple and pear, melon and peach – and irrigated fields – pepper, chili and salad – that hug the banks. Here then, at that time, the stage from Santa Fe going north met the stage from Taos going south and swapped passengers, as though, almost as though, only a decade or two since motor cars had first made the trip, they had to be renewed like horses on the way, at staging posts for cars.

Brett had already seen her first Indians – a couple had been offering woven baskets on the station platform at Lamy and there may have been more, selling silver and turquoise Navajo jewellery outside the seventeenth-century Palace of the Governors in Santa Fe. Now her first cowboy rode in, driving the stage from Taos: John Dunn, tall and gangling, a walrus moustache drooping down, what was left, perhaps, of the Mountain Men and trappers who had descended on Taos annually during the last century for the spring "rendezvous", to sell their furs and spend the proceeds on "Taos Lightning", an infamous local liquor, now deceased. John Dunn is deceased, too, but not before his exploits, real and invented, had, literally, become sufficient to fill a book.

Lawrence, Frieda and Brett transferred their baggage from the Santa Fe stage to John Dunn's rig and pressed on from the orchards north of Espanola into the gap in the mountains that marks the entrance to the canyon of the Rio Grande. Here the dirt road kept close to the river as it cut and twisted between the high rock walls and the car skidded and slipped on the bends in the thick snow on "the narrow ledge that is called a road", on one occasion forcing a horse-drawn wagon coming in the opposite direction half-off and almost into the swirling river beneath.

"Coming out of the canyon," Lawrence later wrote, "is an unforgettable experience with all the deep mountains sitting mysteriously around and so much sky." It is. Even when one's senses have been dulled by an eight-hour jet lag, a night kept awake by the hum of the air-conditioning and a day in a hot car made drowsy by the lack of it, the view is breathtaking. One is quite abruptly released from the confined space of the river's deep gorge and there stretching ahead fifty miles to Colorado, is the great mesa, flatter than anything one has passed through to reach it, 7,000 feet high and sitting in a circle of mountains that rise a further 6,000 feet around, the Sangre de Cristos to the east and the splintering backbone of the Rockies and the Continental divide to the west, the mesa interrupted only by the strange triple-peaked outcrop of Tres Orejas and marked only by the thin dark crack of the Rio Grande, invisible now in its gorge a hundred feet below. In the south-east corner sit the three towns of Taos. First, Ranchos de Taos, with its old adobe mission church of the Conquistadores; San Fernando de Taos, that is, Taos itself, an adobe town built Spanish-style round a central plaza; and beyond, perfectly hidden from sight no matter from which direction one approaches, San Geronimo de Taos, the 500-year old Indian pueblo, brown wedding cake apartment buildings of adobe piled on adobe, the upper floors reachable only by external ladders.

From the canyon's exit one can just make out in the distance, forty miles away along the shoulder of the Sangre de Cristos, a small clear patch in the pine forest, a field on the ranch 9,500 feet up where the Lawrences and Brett were to spend the summer of that year and the next, together and apart.

The immediate destination, though, was the Taos home of Mabel Evans-Stern-Dodge-Luhan, recently married for the fourth time to Tony Luhan, a Pueblo Indian. It was Mabel who had originally invited Lawrence to Taos, "willed" him to come, to write about the mysteries of the Pueblo Indians. Taos was already an artist community. It had been "discovered" in 1896 by a couple of itinerant painters who had trundled a broken wagon wheel into town for repair and had stayed.

Others followed so that nowadays every second shop is, or has some pretensions towards being, an art gallery, every third Taoseno an artist or writer and even the bank has as its coat of arms a paint palette rampant, while alongside run a coterie of patrons, rich or pretending to be, eccentric and otherwise, the latest of whom in 1924 was Mabel.

Mabel's home is today much as it was when Lawrence, Frieda and Brett arrived in 1924. It sits on the eastern edge of Taos, bordering the lands of the Pueblo and unlikely therefore to be affected by any building development ever. One can approach from this direction, driving north through town towards the Pueblo and turning off where Taos ends along a dirt track through scrub and sage. The better route is east from the galleries and coffee shops of the plaza and then through what appears to be a rundown collection of fenced off plots and tumbledown adobe dwellings. The adobe of New Mexico is illusory – inside can often be, quite literally, an Aladdin's cave of delights. Most Taosenos are collectors of one sort or another who stuff their homes with treasures, while adobe is a gentle and plastic material, so that the rounded and curved interiors do, indeed, seem troglodytic. "Mabel-town", as Lawrence called it, is as much a community as a house, reminding one, with its high surrounding wall, heavy solid wooden gates and pillared walkway along the rambling length of the main building, of a western cavalry fort in miniature. The effect is accentuated by the fact that, as in many dwellings in the west, guests are accommodated not in integral guest rooms but in detached and semi-detached "guest houses", some budding off from the spine of the main house, others scattered about the grounds and across a field, separated from the main concourse by a stream that runs down from the pueblo.

Mabel and Tony were not at home when the party arrived. Both had been spending the winter on the Pacific coast from where they returned the following day. Mabel had, on Lawrence's earlier visit, built up a strong resentment towards Frieda, whom she regarded simply as a rival for possession of Lawrence. The resentment was now transferred to Brett. Mabel, in *Lorenzo in Taos*, described their first meeting:

> A tall, oldish girl came into the room. She had pretty, pink round cheeks and a childish expression. Her long thin shanks ended in large feet that turned out abruptly like the kind that children draw. She was an amusing and attractive grotesque, and her eyes were both hostile and questioning as she came slowly up to me, examining me, curious, arrogant and English . . . Brett had stuck a brass ear-trumpet in her ear and was turning it in all directions to pick up scraps of conversation. It had a bland-looking, flat dipper end to it

> that seemed to suck into itself all it could from the air . . . inhibiting all one's spontaneity . . . it was an eavesdropper . . . a spy on any influence near Lorenzo. Inquisitive, pertinacious and solitary, it was forever between Lawrence and the world . . . Do you think I liked it when I saw that brass dipper swallowing up Lorenzo's talk to me? It was worse than Frieda's restraining influence.[2]

The trio stayed in Mabeltown throughout April, visiting the pueblo dances with Mabel and Tony, bathing in the hot springs down in the Rio Grande gorge and introducing a little of Garsington to Taos in the charades they played in the evenings. Brett, surprisingly, in view of the fact that her father had at one time kept a stud and bred racehorses, had never ridden. To her delight, Lawrence, himself a newcomer to horseback, decided to give her lessons, introducing the Lawrentian notion of "feeling the flow" between the horse and herself. Brett, according to Rachel Hawk, who lived on the Del Monte Ranch up in the mountains, immediately below the ranch on which Lawrence, Frieda and Brett were shortly to settle, never overcame a fear of heights and, when a picnic ride took them up one of the canyons that cut into the Sangre de Cristos, had to be "pushed" to the top of the mountain. But, under Lawrence's tuition, expert in his own opinion at least, and out on the flat desert mesa, away from the mountain gullies, Brett progressed rapidly, spurred on by the fact that she had Lawrence all to herself, as she did on their joint painting expeditions in and around Taos. She had already decided that she must look the part and early on adopted a cowboy style of dress. "It was very odd, even by western standards. Pants, boots with a knife stuck in the side, an ankle-length coat, a Mexican hat, and a pocket-book on a long strap . . . I said to her 'I suppose you dress like that to get yourself looked at?' "[3]

Certainly to get herself noticed, was Mabel's opinion:

> By this time Brett had evolved a costume for the West, consisting of a very wide-brimmed sombrero on the back of her pin-head, high boots, with a pair of man's corduroy trousers tucked into them, and, in the right leg, a long stiletto! I suppose this was somehow reminiscent of a Scottish dirk for her. It seemed to give her great satisfaction, for she had secret fancies about assault. As a matter of fact, the natives were all afraid of *her*, and one old Mexican refused to drive her up to the ranch.
>
> "Senorita with dagger very dangerous!" he told Tony.[4]

Frieda, for the moment, could afford to be amused at Brett's metamorphosis into a passing likeness for Belle Starr, for, with a new rival for Lawrence's attention, Mabel's jealousy was no longer aimed in her direction. While Frieda lit her cigarettes and looked on, Mabel became increasingly annoyed.

> I cannot describe my increasing irritation at Brett's ridiculous ways. She had an annoying habit of employing the diminutive for anything she could; . . . and she talked incessantly, thinking out loud, naming everything: her feelings, her wishes, or the names of the little blocks with which mah jongg* was played. With little shrieks she would exclaim: "Oh! a li-ittle flower pot!" until I was rolling my eyes and finally imitating her, *sotto voce*, which amused Frieda and made Lawrence sore.[5]

When Mabel hinted one evening that Lawrence might give her a haircut as she hated barbers so much, Brett, to Mabel's annoyance, leapt in with the scissors, claiming, according to Mabel, that she had served an apprenticeship on Katherine Mansfield's locks. Brett's version is that the haircut was at Mabel's suggestion despite the fact that she had just seen Brett make an amateurish mess of Lawrence's head. Whatever the case, the coiffing had to stop when Brett snipped the top off Mabel's ear. Brett said the amputation was an accident. Mabel decided it was deliberate and reacted with a mixture of amazement and admiration for Brett's sheer gall, looking for Freudian explanations of the event. "I couldn't get over it. She hated me, and she was deaf, and she tried to mutilate my ear! That seemed so interesting I forgot to be indignant."[6]

A month of Mabeltown and mah-jongg, piquet and pique, was enough for Lawrence who was anxious to move on from Taos and spend the summer at the ranch above San Cristobal in the Sangre de Cristos where Frieda and he had spent much of their time on their previous visit. Mabel had wanted to give the ranch to Lawrence but Lawrence had been, for once, doubtful of accepting too many favours and perhaps bonding himself too much in her debt, so a kind of compromise had been reached. Lawrence suggested to Mabel that she give the ranch to Frieda and suggested to Frieda that she give the manuscript of *Sons and Lovers* to Mabel, not in payment – rather as an exchange of gifts.

* Mabel had imported the game from San Francisco and the four played it in the evenings when not performing charades and when Brett was not monopolising Lawrence with piquet.

Flying Heart Ranch was not, in fact, at the time, Mabel's to give for she had already given it to her son, John Evans. She now assuaged him, almost as an afterthought, with a buffalo skin robe and $400 cash, an odd transaction which very much suggests that the initiative in transferring the ranch came from Lawrence or Frieda, rather than Mabel herself. Much has been made of the notion that Mabel got the better part of the bargain here and then abused Lawrence's generosity by passing the *Sons and Lovers* manuscript on to A. A. Brill, the psychoanalyst, to pay for the treatment of a friend. But, at the time, Lawrence appears to have attached little value to his manuscripts and the market-place even less. When Lawrence came to put a price on the ranch just four years later – careful to make it clear that his concern was not for himself but for Frieda's assets – his estimate was $5,000. It is hard to believe the manuscript of *Sons and Lovers* was worth anywhere near that sum in 1924. If anyone got the better of the bargain it was probably Lawrence or, technically, Frieda. In any case, none of the parties ever complained – the carping came from later Lawrentians. Better perhaps to view the whole transaction as a late-spring, Rocky Mountain Christmas, where presents were swapped beneath the tree without obligation but with unexpressed evaluation.

On May 5th, exactly two months after the Rananim seekers had left England, the caravan set off for the ranch, now re-named Lobo Ranch by Lawrence, after the mountain behind it. "Dates," noted Brett, "seem important to you." Names, too. A little while later the name of the ranch was altered once again, this time to Kiowa Ranch, perhaps in an attempt by Lawrence to persuade his wandering soul that even while staying still, a change of address would keep him on the move. A wagon, driven by two Indians and carrying the trunks and stores, led the way, followed by three saddle horses, provided by Mabel for the new settlers and led by Trinidad, a Pueblo Indian who remained a close friend of Brett throughout her life. Taking up the rear, Brett, Lawrence, Frieda and Mabel packed into Tony Luhan's car for the twenty-mile journey.

Kiowa Ranch and its lands had been owned until some eight years previously by a goat-herd. Lawrence used it as the setting for *St. Mawr*, which he wrote there that summer, and the short story gives an accurate description and a near-enough history of the ranch at the time. When the party arrived, the dung of 500 goats still lay, sweetly rotting, in the corral and the log-and-adobe buildings were semi-derelict. "One house has been a cowshed for years, by the look of it: it is full of dung. The second is better, and with cleaning could be made fit to live in. The third house is so tiny we wonder if it is possible to get a bed in it. The view is magnificent."[7]

The view was, and is, indeed magnificent. From the porch of what became Lawrence and Frieda's cabin, one looks, across the small garden with its huge pine tree, south-west over a sloping clearing in the pine forest to the ring of mountains that closes off the southern end of the mesa, 2,500 feet below. Behind rises the southern tail of the Rockies, the snows of a winter passing only ever just disappearing before early autumn caps the peaks once again. To the west, better seen from the small chapel up the steep slope behind the cabin that now holds Lawrence's ashes in an immovable block of concrete, the mesa stretches away towards Arizona, neatly pock-marked with piñons and cut by the black, wrinkled crack of the gorge of the Rio Grande hidden below. And all around, as Lawrence wrote, so much sky. But rarely a clear and empty blue, almost always holding great towers of cumulus, thundering up dramatically.

Beyond the two fields that slope away from the cabin and form a pasture for the horses, is the pine forest through which an irrigation ditch brings water from Gallina Canyon a couple of miles away. The Conquistadores recognised this kind of landscape from their own Iberia and knew how to channel and protect the water, so that to this day each house and piece of land carries with it water rights that are jealously guarded and preserved. It is hard to grasp that one has driven such a short distance – five miles only but most of it upwards – from the scrub and sage desert below. Trails lead through the pine forest along which Brett and Lawrence, guided by the Hawks from nearby Del Monte Ranch, rode on picnics, trails along which, in the sudden September snows that mark the end of summer, one can see the spoor of possum and bear, porcupine and raccoon. Bright blue jays and humming birds inhabit the pines and then, a few feet higher up Lobo, the thickly scented conifers whose sticky pollen in spring can paint a car yellow for ever, give way to silver-thin, ever-quivering aspens till eventually the trees end in the harsh tops of the Rockies. It is, indeed, a magnificent view. Living there one can pass whole days in thrall to it, just sitting and looking, intrigued by the slightest inconsistency in the desert below, and aided in one's indolence by the fact that it is also, quite literally, breathtaking – the shortest walk up the slope from the cabin to play at water babies in the irrigation ditch leaves one gasping for oxygen at this altitude.

The party set about cleaning the most habitable of the cabins at once. Over the course of the summer, guided and assisted by a changing group of Indians, who camped up the hill in a tepee, and by a chicano carpenter, who from time to time took over the smallest cabin for a two-day drunk and a three-day recovery and was eventually sacked by Lawrence for calling Frieda "*chiquita*", which may have been a misjudgment but was hardly an insult, they succeeded in renovating the larger cabin for Lawrence and Frieda and the smallest cabin, hardly bigger than a bed and a cupboard, for Brett. Those two cabins still stand, little changed since 1924, and are known as the Lawrence cabin and the Brett cabin. The third cabin, between the two, known then as the Indian cabin, was replaced in the 1930s with a larger and much more comfortable house by Frieda's third husband, Angelo Ravagli. The building, destroying her memories as it did, was always referred to by Brett as "Angie's Swiss chalet", although it merits the description hardly at all.

Shortly after their arrival at the ranch, Brett heard from Murry, his first letter since their parting at Waterloo Station. In it he told her he was about to marry Violet le Maistre and that it would be better than wild-goose-chasing in another continent. Brett passed the news on to Lawrence who wrote coolly in congratulation and then one or other destroyed Murry's letter, one must presume, for it is the only letter from Murry to Brett that she did not preserve and cherish. In any case, Brett's never-ending round of crushes had found a new object – Lawrence himself. When this had annoyed Mabel, it had amused Frieda, but now that Mabel was twenty miles away, down the mountain, in Taos, it was Frieda's turn to be irritated.

> Brett was always with us. I liked her in many ways; she was so much her own self.
>
> I said to her: "Brett, I'll give you half a crown if you contradict Lawrence," but she never did. Her blind adoration for him, her hero-worship for him was touching, but naturally it was balanced by a preconceived critical attitude towards me. He was perfect and I was always wrong, in her eyes.
>
> When Brett came with us, Lawrence said to me: "You know, it will be good for us to have the Brett with us, she will stand between us and people and the world." I did not really want her with us, and had a suspicion that she might not want to stand between us and the world but between him and me. But, no, I thought, I won't be so narrow-gutted, one of Lawrence's words, I will try.
>
> So I looked after Brett and was grateful for her actual help. She did her share of the work. I yelled down her ear-trumpet, her Toby, when people were there, that she should not feel out of it. But as time went on she seemed always to be there, my privacy that I cherished so much was gone. Like the eye of the Lord, she was; when I washed, when I lay under a bush with a book, her eyes seemed to be there, only I hope the eye of the Lord looks on me more kindly. Then I detested her, poor Brett, when she seemed deaf and dumb and blind to everything quick and alive. Her adoration for Lawrence seemed a

> silly old habit. "Brett," I said, "I detest your adoration for Lawrence, only one thing I would detest more, and that is if you adored me."[8]

The sole recruit for Rananim had, indeed, turned out a willing disciple and Lawrence and Brett were spending a good deal of their time in joint activity. Brett joined Lawrence in the hard labour of moving logs for the cabin walls, laying stones for the foundations and making adobes for the chimney-piece, enjoying what amounted to the first physical activity in her life. Even Frieda was reluctantly impressed: "Brett, straight from her studio life, was amazing for the hard work she would do," but, once more, found the explanation in fanaticism – "She adored Lawrence and would slave for him." Frieda meantime cooked and laundered for the trio and, when that was done, lay on her cot smoking – an activity that was in those days regarded as a kind of sport for which one wore a uniform and set aside a time. When Brett and Lawrence rode together, Frieda, who disliked riding, followed where she could in Mabel's car. Brett and Lawrence painted together, often literally so, contributing bits and pieces to the same work, while Frieda threw away her amateurish efforts in disgust. And Brett was acquiring a new skill, one at which she never became quite perfect. That summer Lawrence wrote not only the novella *St. Mawr*, but the short stories, *The Princess*, the heroine of which he modelled on Brett, and *The Woman Who Rode Away*, perhaps based on Mabel. As he completed each hand-written page, he passed it on to Brett who laboriously copied it out on a typewriter borrowed from Mabel.

By mid-June with the renovations more or less complete, the ranch was habitable but Lawrence was already making plans to move on for the winter to Mexico, partly because he wanted to be away from the snow and cold of the Rockies and partly in order to finish his Mexican novel, *The Plumed Serpent*. He refers to his plans to go south throughout his correspondence that summer and by October, the group were ready to board up the ranch for the winter. Lawrence wrote to Murry on October 3rd, 1924:

> We are leaving here next week. There was a flurry of wild snow in the air yesterday, and the nights are icy. But now, at ten o'clock in the morning, to look across the desert at the mountains you'd think the June morning was shining. Frieda is washing the porch. Brett is probably stalking a rabbit with a 22-gun. I am looking out of the kitchen door at the far blue mountains, and the gap, the tiny gate that leads down into the canyon and away to Santa Fe . . . The country here is very lovely at the moment. Aspens high on the mountain like a

fleece of gold. The scrub oak is dark red, and the wild birds are coming down to the desert.[9]

To Catherine Carswell four days later he wrote:

> We shall go down to Taos on Saturday, stay a day or two, then go down to Mexico City . . . Brett will go down with us. But if we take a house, she must take a little place of her own. Not be too close. Here she has a little one-room cabin to herself . . . It's so much easier that way. The house is half dismantled; we are fastening the place up and leaving it. The snow is dripping wet off the pine trees, the desert seems to be decomposing in the distance – ugh! I must catch Aaron, my black horse, and ride down in the slush under these snow-dripping trees. Ugh![10]

Although the life together was beginning to strain their relationship, Lawrence agreed that Brett should not be left on her own to fend for herself in the hostile mountain winter, so, with just a very little of the Rananimistic spirit remaining, all three set off for Mexico.

Frieda's patience was tested early in the trip, in the Mexican Consulate at El Paso, the Texas town that shares the Rio Grande border with Ciudad Juarez.

> . . . (the official) looks up and makes a gesture towards me [Brett].
>
> "You wife?" he asks . . . I pretend to hear nothing; I hide behind the baffling wall of deafness.
>
> "No," you reply.
>
> "Your sister, then?"
>
> "No," you reply, impatiently. "A friend."
>
> The man says nothing, but fumbles among the papers. Then, suddenly, pointing at Frieda:
>
> "Your mother?" he asks with an engaging smile. I feel Frieda tauten and begin to bristle.
>
> "No," you reply abruptly, "my wife."
>
> "You wife?" he repeats, weakly.[11]

From Juarez they took the train, via Chihuahua, through a country still in post-revolutionary turmoil, to Mexico City. Immediately behind the engine was an armoured wagon packed with soldiers. Other soldiers lay along the roofs of the carriages, heavily armed. They spent two weeks in Mexico where Lawrence, equipped in advance with the introductions and invitations the travelling writer is careful to erect in his path, was wined and dined and gave lectures in order that he could later write of how much he detested it all. Through the British Vice-Consul in Mexico City, Lawrence obtained a further onward introduction, to the diplomat's brother who was a priest in Oaxaca and had a house available to let. So, on November 8th, the three set off once again, further south to that pleasant Zapotecan town, close to the Mixtec sites of Monte Alban and Mitla and not a great distance from the Guatemalan border.

Somewhere along the way, between the station at Oaxaca and the Hotel Francia, or in the hotel itself, Brett's ear trumpet, her "Toby", disappeared. It was probably stolen by the enterprising thieves of Oaxaca who, according to Brett, had developed a technique of "fishing" for valuables by sticking long poles with bent nails on the end through the hotel windows.

> The town is now plastered with notices about my stolen Toby, but Senora Monros [the hotelier] shakes her head.
>
> "They will be too frightened to bring it back. My daughter will take you to a tinsmith to see if he can make you one."
>
> The tinsmith is a very intelligent Indian. I make a drawing in his shop, and in a few hours he has made an ear-trumpet that serves me well until another comes from London.[12]

"Much excitement among the natives when she uses it," Lawrence wrote to Bill Hawk of Del Monte Ranch, who was harbouring their belongings for the winter. "Her machine* also works very fitfully, so that her ears are out of luck."[13]

As he had indicated in his correspondence that summer, Lawrence was wary of Brett remaining at too close quarters. He and Frieda moved into Padre Rickard's house on the Avenida Pino Suarez, at that time almost on the outskirts of Oaxaca, near the road to the ruins of Monte Alban and south of the teeming market where the Zapotec Indians display the highly engraved daggers of the region and the intricately woven sandals, tanned with urine and, nowadays, soled with truck tyres and practically indestructible. The house was of ample size, "cool and spacious", and Brett, having laboured, as at the ranch, to prepare it, expected to stay there as well. But, at the last moment, Frieda "blurted out" that she didn't think there was enough room for all three, so in the Hotel Francia, on the Zocalo in the town centre, Brett remained. But to Frieda's mounting fury, Brett and Lawrence continued their joint activities, exploring the town and, later, the surrounding countryside, despite warnings from the local gringos of

* Brett also had a battery-powered hearing aid: "her machine".

lawlessness and banditry outside the city walls. Lawrence was frequently sharp-tongued, even petulant, with Brett but she, in her adulation, appears hardly to have noticed. Dead-pan, she relates:

> We have seen nearly all of the churches . . . we are haunted by the intense *santos* – the agonised Christs and Saints.
>
> "Look, Lawrence," I say of one, "look at the eye in the middle of the forehead!"
>
> "Good gracious, Brett," you answer angrily, "have you never heard of the third eye?" And you disappear up a small, corkscrew staircase in a turret.[14]

On their expeditions into the countryside, Brett drew and painted while Lawrence found himself some cactus shade and worked on *The Plumed Serpent*, and, from time to time, added a touch or two to Brett's paintings, again with a certain lack of grace.

> I hold up my painting, proudly. "Oh, Brett," you say, testily, "do look at the mountain. It has great bare toes, where it joins the desert. Here, let me have a try." Down you sit, and with delicate finger-touches, you proceed to give the mountain its toes. You roughen the fir-trees on the mountain and darken the blue of the sky. "You are dumb, Brett; you don't look at things; you have no eyes" . . . "What about tomorrow?" I ask, as we reach the door. You hesitate. "I don't know," you reply. "You had better come up and see. I don't think Frieda likes it."[15]

Frieda didn't like it but she was in bed with a cold which, by the evening, Lawrence had caught. He, in turn, took to his bed. The confrontation was put in cold storage for the time being and Brett busied herself doing the shopping for the housebound duo, and continuing to type out Lawrence's manuscript of *The Plumed Serpent*.

It was then approaching Christmas and the time of the Fiesta de Rabanos, the Feast of the Radishes, a Zapotecan celebration during which a young man might declare his love for a young lady by presenting her with a phallicly carved and decorated radish. Unaware of the implications, Brett bought "a fairly modest, unexaggerated radish" to present to Lawrence, who was still in bed, but recovering. The phallic radish was hung on the Christmas tree by Lawrence, where it produced broad grins from the Indian servants who were finally persuaded to reveal its connotations – none of which added to Frieda's amusement. A couple of years later Brett used the Radish Festival as the subject of a painting which she then gave to Lawrence. The painting, like many of her earlier works, was unsigned. After Lawrence's death it was sold as one of his own.

Brett spent Christmas Day playing tennis in the morning and in the late afternoon called at the Avenida Pino Suarez with her Christmas present for Lawrence, a typical Oaxacan knife with an eagle's head surmounting the carved bone handle and the blade etched to carry the maker's name on one side and a proverb on the other. Brett's gift for Lawrence, though, was special, for instead of the maker's name, it bore his own. Lawrence, like Murry with his hastily penned Christmas poems, had the writer's disinclination for the bourgeois business of gift-giving, although he was not, of course, averse to gift-receiving. Still in bed recovering from his cold, he gave Brett a penny from among his things on the bedside table. "I am not such a knify person as you, but I must give you a penny, so as not to cut our friendship."

By now Frieda had had enough. Shortly after Christmas, Brett and Lawrence went out into the country where they talked and walked and walked and talked, leaving Frieda, once more stricken with a cold, in the house.

> We are excited, happy, exhilarated . . . we return joyously. Frieda is sitting smoking in a rocking chair – she looks at us. Our joyousness radiates out . . . Frieda's mouth tightens but she says nothing to me.[16]

She said a good deal, however, to Lawrence, whose first reaction was to withdraw totally from the confrontation. "I see you sitting on a bench in the Zocalo . . . pale, remote, your eyes unseeing, your whole figure withdrawn, untouchable . . . I am appalled at the feeling of hate that pours out of you." And again: "I see you, walking along the street . . . looking as if you were seeing nothing, hearing nothing."[17]

A few days later, early in the New Year, Lawrence sent a note to Brett, via the Indian servant, Rosalino:

> The simplest thing perhaps is to write, as one can't shout everything.
>
> You, Frieda and I don't make a happy combination now. The best is that we should prepare to separate: that you should go your own way. I am not angry: except that I hate "situations", and feel humiliated by them. We can all remain decent and friendly, and go the simplest, quietest way about the parting, without stirring up a lot of emotions that only do harm. Stirred up emotions lead to hate.
>
> The thing to do is to think out quickly and simply, the best steps. But believe me, there will be no more ease between the three of us.

> Better you take your own way in life. Not this closeness, which causes a strain.
>
> I am grateful for the things you have done for me. But we must stand apart.[18]

Brett thought the letter fierce and cruel. The opening sentence, emphasising her deafness, is all of that. She could not produce a reply for the servant to carry back to Lawrence so at tea-time she went up to the Avenida Pino Suarez to collect the day's manuscript for typing.

> As usual, we say nothing. Frieda is hintingly hostile; her eyes are hard, her mouth a line. The tea-table is balanced on a volcano . . . I return to the hotel. As I am sitting typing in my window, you appear: excited, stormy, despairing.
>
> "Frieda . . . made such a scene that I can no longer stand it. The only thing I could think of was to come down and ask you not to come up again to the house."
>
> ". . . well," I say, "the simple easy way out is for me to go. I will go back to Del Monte for a while."
>
> Thus we arrange it. I decide to go the following Monday . . .
>
> "I will go and tell Frieda," you say. And your step is more springy as you go out of the room.[19]

Frieda herself wasted no words in her description of the Oaxacan interlude:

> The Brett came every day and I thought she was becoming too much a part of our lives and I resented it. So I told Lawrence: "I want the Brett to go away," and he raved at me, said I was a jealous fool. But I insisted and so Brett went up to Mexico City.[20]

Before Brett left Oaxaca, Frieda tried, in a hamfisted way, to clear the air.

> She says she cannot bear that I think it is her fault any longer. She has with her a letter which she has written, explaining it all. I take it and read it in amazement. In it, she accuses us, Lawrence and myself, of being like a curate and a spinster; she resents the fact that we don't make love to each other . . .[21]

Brett's stern aristocratic breeding came to her help:

> "But Frieda," I say, "how can I make love to Lawrence when I am your guest; would that not be rather indecent?" "Lawrence says he could not possibly be in love with a woman like you – an asparagus stick!" . . .
>
> . . . [But] in some mysterious fashion we end amicably; Frieda leaves me in a state of complete bewilderment. Are we friends or are we not? And what is the correct behaviour in a triangle?[22]

What, indeed? As for the asparagus stick, that can only have been in contrast to Frieda's rotundity for none of Brett's photographs suggest that she was by any means wraith-like.

A couple of days later, on January 19th, Brett left Oaxaca for Mexico City. Lawrence and Frieda just made it to the station to see her off, with a handshake from Lawrence and, much to Frieda's surprise, a kiss for her from Brett – "she is astonished; so am I".[23]

After the quiet backwater of Oaxaca, where, as late as the 1970s it was still possible to see ox-carts with huge medieval wooden discs for wheels just as was pictured by Brett in *The Road to Mitla*, the painting Lawrence dabbled his fingers in, Brett found Mexico City "unpleasant". Despite that, she lingered a fortnight, perhaps waiting for Lawrence to forward a new hearing aid that was being shipped via Vera Cruz to Oaxaca. For her part she sent on to Lawrence a letter from Murry that was waiting at the Consulate. Lawrence was in bed again, now with "malaria", although the truth was that tuberculosis was by now showing its firm grip. He wrote a nasty note to Murry and sent a lecture to Brett.

> . . . Your letter with Murry's enclosed this morning. They make me sick in the pit of my stomach: the cold, cold, insect-like ugliness of it.
>
> If Mexico City is so unpleasant we shall probably stay here an extra week or fortnight, and go straight to Vera Cruz. I don't like the sound of it.
>
> And a word about friendship. Friendship between a man and a woman, as a thing of first importance to either, is impossible: and I know it. We are creatures of two halves, spiritual and sensual – and each half is as important as the other. Any relation based on the one half – say the delicate spiritual half alone – *inevitably* brings revulsion and betrayal. It is halfness or partness, which causes Judas. Your friendship for Murry was spiritual – you dragged sex in – and he hated you. He'd have hated you anyhow. The halfness of your friendship I also hate. And between you and me there is no sensual correspondence.
>
> You make the horrid mistake of trying to put your sex into a

spiritual relation. Old nuns & saints used to do it, but it soon caused rottenness. Now it is half-rotten to start with.

When Maruca likes a man and marries him, she is not so wrong. Love is chiefly bunk: an over-exaggeration of the spiritual and individualistic and analytic side. If she likes the man, and he is a man, then better than if she loved him. Each will leave aside some of that hateful *personal* insistence on imaginary perfect satisfaction, which is part of the inevitable bunk of love, and if they meet as mere male and female, *kindly*, in their marriage, they will make roots, not weedy flowers of a love-match. If ever you can marry a man feeling *kindly* towards him, & knowing he feels kindly to you, do it, and throw love after Murry. If you can marry in a spirit of kindliness, with the criticism & the ecstasy both sunk into abeyance, do it . . . Why do you jeer? You're not superior to sex, & you never will be. Only too often you are inferior to it. You like the excitation of sex in the eye, sex in the head. It is an evil and destructive thing. Know . . . that a bit of warm flame of life is worth all the spiritualness and delicacy and Christlikeness on this miserable globe. No Brett, I do *not* want your friendship, till you have a full relation somewhere, a *kindly* relation of both halves, not in *part*, as all your friendships have been. That which is in part is in itself a betrayal. Your "friendship" for me betrays the essential man and male that I am, and makes me ill – Yes, you make me ill, by dragging at one half at the expense of the other half. I am so much better now you have gone. I refuse any more of this "delicate friendship" business, because it damages one's wholeness.

Nevertheless, I don't feel unkindly to you. In your one half you are loyal enough. But the very halfness makes your loyalty fatal.

Know, know that this "delicate" halfness *makes* evil. Put away all that virginal stuff. Don't still go looking for men with strange eyes, who know life from A to Z. Maybe they do, missing out all the rest of the letters, like the meat from the empty egg-shell. Look for a little flame of warm kindness. It's more than the Alpha and the Omega. And respect the bit of warm kindliness there is in people. And try & be *whole*, not that unreal half thing your brothers hated you for, and that all men hate you for, even I. Try and recover your wholeness, that is all. *Then* friendship is possible, in the kindliness of one's heart.[24]

Lawrence added a pencilled P.S.: "Remember I think Christ was profoundly, disastrously wrong."

One wonders why. It cannot all have been simply to pacify Frieda or because Brett was trying to smother Lawrence in friendship. Perhaps somewhere along that road to Mitla, attempting to explore the other half of Brett, Lawrence had made some kind of pass which she, in her timidity and not knowing how to behave in a triangle, had refused.

Almost from his arrival in Oaxaca, Lawrence had written saying how much he detested the place, and Mexico, and America, and how determined he was to return once more to Europe in the spring but without wasting time in London or even England – "last time was once too many" he had told Murry. Lawrence asked Brett to look up steamship timetables from Vera Cruz while she was in Mexico City and he and Frieda made firm plans to leave Mexico by sea on February 20th but the "malaria", in reality tuberculosis, laid him low. The most he and Frieda could cope with was a move from the priest's house down into town to the Hotel Francia. The house on the Avenida Pino Suarez was close to a military hospital and it was from there, Frieda believed, that the malaria microbes "like tarantulas that eat all the red corpuscles out of the blood", had surged over the walls in battalions to attack Lawrence. That, and an earth tremor which shook the beams in the walls while Lawrence lay helpless in bed, determined them once more to set out on their way.

Frieda wrote to Brett, who by now had reached Taos, on February 20th – "the day we should have sailed" – telling her that the new plan was to travel up to Mexico City on the 24th and take the first available ship from Vera Cruz to Europe. She added a long postscript:

> And Brett, this I will tell you: live at the ranch, if you like, but I *do not* want you to have your little house as a permanency nor that you have a *right* there – It may be *you* were happy, *I* wasn't – You only saw Lawrence, jeered at me, at the Azul [Frieda's horse], were glad when I didn't ride and told me from time to time how infinitely inferior I was to Lawrence – I don't quite see where I was the gainer in that relationship – I will never again share my life with a third person except servants and guests – And I can't treat you as a guest because you say: "I am here by *rights*." You know I wish you well, but my life is my own and I don't want you to boss either my life or my ranch – and you would soon do both as your will is stronger than mine – This is how I feel, I shall be glad to see you from time to time but live with you as a kind of marriage, I can't.[25]

Brett had not in fact gone up to the ranch yet, preferring to remain lower down the mountain with the Hawk family at Del Monte until the snows cleared a little. Within a week of writing, Frieda and Lawrence struggled from Oaxaca to Mexico City where Lawrence collapsed once more. The "malaria" was diagnosed, realistically at last, as tuberculosis and, although Lawrence shied from the word, Frieda learnt clearly how ill her husband was. All notion of a prompt return to Europe was abandoned. Lawrence wrote to Brett from his sick bed:

> The doctor says I must *not* go to England nor take a sea voyage at present, but the ranch is where we ought to be – we hope to arrive by 21st or 23rd. And let us pray to the gods to keep us all quiet and kindly to one another, *all* of us. We *can* do it, if we will.[26]

Frieda didn't want to take too much chance on that. She wrote to Brett a few days later:

> It would be better if you will stay at the Danes' Cottage*, I think it would be a strain if you came to our ranch, both for L. and me . . . you see, both to Lawr and me you *are* a guest and a friend, anything else was just your idea – but never a *fact* . . . there is a strangled self in you that does all sorts of things you never know . . . I always felt you waiting and watching and I hated it – let us be simple friends and release all that other soul stuff – and it isn't that I want myself the adoration you give to Lawrence, it would stifle me – it makes everything tight around me and Lawr feels the same – and surely that silly, poky little house can't in itself mean much to you – anyhow I couldn't have you there again – You will hate me for this, but I also have my own life to live . . .[27]

Lawrence and Frieda finally arrived back at the ranch, or, to be precise, at Del Monte Ranch below, on April 1st. Later in the summer, Frieda accused Brett of not having bothered to make any preparations for their arrival. "When we came from Mexico, I only know that I was disappointed, that there was no cottage, there would have been no food, hadn't we brought it." Brett must have been confused. Frieda had herself insisted that Brett stay in the cottage on the Hawks' Del Monte Ranch while Lawrence had written from Mexico City asking Brett to tell the Hawks to get that cottage ready for them, the Lawrences. To confound matters further, Lawrence and Frieda arrived before his letter:

> No sound has come from you for a week or so. I decide to ride to the Hondo, [the river, flowing from what is now Taos Ski Valley, through the village of Arroyo Hondo, to the Rio Grande – in 1924 on the direct route, a dirt road, from Taos to the ranch] then miles to

* The cabin at Del Monte occupied by two Danish painters on the Lawrences' first visit.

> the post office, to inquire if there is any news. I have bought a new horse, a golden sorrel called Prince . . . when I get there . . . the news is that you have passed through the town on your way to Del Monte . . .[28]

Lawrence had been confined to his bed a further week in Mexico City and then spent two days fighting his way past US immigration officials at El Paso, hence the delay. After resting a few days at Del Monte, they moved up the mountain to Kiowa Ranch where the snow still lay on the ground and the clouds threatened to dump more Rocky Mountain spring powder. But the log fire was warm, well supplied with wood by Trinidad, the young Indian who was working for Lawrence full-time, the cabin made comforting by Trinidad's wife, Ruffina, and Frieda sang as she arranged her Mexican souvenirs on the kitchen shelves. Although she had greeted Brett warmly down at Del Monte, the warmth still did not extend to welcoming her up to Kiowa. The restriction was first on an ad hoc basis.

> No, don't come this afternoon, Lawrence is not fit for explanations – And there aren't any – I offered you being a distant friend but you want to be an intimate one – you and I have never been friends what *I* call friends – no we never could be and I am mad, when you bully me here on my own ground, where surely I may have or not have people as I choose – Your attitude towards me I have always resented – I wish you no ill, but don't want you in my life.[29]

Frieda's irritation extended not just to Brett but to almost anyone who intruded upon her territory in any permanent way. Before long some minor disagreement with Ruffina, still only a teenage girl, caused Frieda to blow up and Ruffina to pack her belongings in a bundle and set off, sobbing loudly, on the long walk back to the Pueblo. All attempts by Lawrence, Brett and Trinidad to persuade her to return failed. Finally, as she trailed wailing through the forest, Lawrence gave her an ultimatum – "if she goes, she is not to come back". It was to no avail. Trinidad decided that where his wife went, so followed he, and the hapless pair were driven back to Taos pueblo in Lawrence's newly acquired buggy, Brett and Lawrence in front, Ruffina and Trinidad behind. "We drive on with the low sobbing behind us and the low singing of the perplexed Indian boy. He sings softly all the seventeen miles back to the Pueblo."[30]

Frieda squabbled constantly with Lawrence as well, perhaps stimulated by the conflict in both that Lawrence's unusual attitude of permanency produced. For now he was recovering his health, he was throwing himself into turning the ranch into a working farm as though he intended never again to wander. With the aid of a farmer from the village below and of Trinidad, before his abrupt departure, the irrigation ditch had been repaired, huge iron pipes, originally chimney stacks rescued from an abandoned timber mill at Tres Orejas down on the mesa, had been dragged up the mountain by pack-horses to carry the water across deep gullies and a new dam had been dug in Gallina Canyon to hold the melting snows. At the ranch, the newly-dug vegetable garden and the two clearings could now be irrigated, one as a pasture, the other to grow alfalfa as winter feed for the horses and for Susan the cow, whose idiosyncrasies caused as much cursing and ill-temper as any of the domestic squabbles.

The rows were not always initiated by Frieda. Lawrence could be just as violent and arbitrary. One evening the Hawks, Bill and Rachel, were invited to dinner with Brett tagging along. When Frieda took a chicken from the oven for Lawrence to carve, it was very under-done.

> You poke about. No good. Raw everywhere. Then you burst out in a fury at Frieda.
>
> "It's no good," you storm, "unless I do everything myself, it is always wrong, always."
>
> Frieda shouts back . . . to and fro the battle goes . . .[31]

Rachel Hawk tells the same tale and also recalls another occasion when Lawrence took some bottles of milk from his horse's saddlebags and placed them on the ground, where the horse stood on them. "He flew into a rage and blamed Frieda."[32]

By now, although Brett was semi-employed as Lawrence's typist and general carrier, her visits to the ranch had been reduced by Frieda to three a week and restricted to a precise timetable.

> We don't want you to come every day – It's too much – Come on Monday + Wednesday and Saturday – Sunday I want for myself – Friedel [Frieda's nephew who was visiting the Lawrences] likes to ride for the mail but if one of those three days you will bring the letters + stay for tea, I will be glad – But I want my life here to be clear and unmixed with yours, it's my show that I am responsible for and I can't have it messed up and mixed up.[33]

Brett told Lawrence she intended to pay no attention to what she regarded as tantrums on Frieda's part. "If Frieda starts her spinster and curate and asparagus nonsense again, I will rope her to a tree and hit her on the nose until she really has something to yell about. You stare at me flabbergasted."[34] Well Lawrence might. Clearly the rip-roaring spirit of the old mountain-men of Taos had already sunk deep into Brett. She broke the curfew immediately, using as an excuse the recalcitrant Susan who was constantly escaping through the broken fence and being herded back to Kiowa by Brett.

> We find her in the same nest of scrub oak and drive her back. As we reach the barn, Frieda appears. She is white with fury, almost unrecognisable. She strides up to me and says in a choking voice,
>
> "I won't have you up here every day. I won't have you on the place. You are a mischief-maker. I hate you, hate you!" I stare at her amazed.
>
> "Oh, go to hell!" I say, airily, "I won't be bossed by you!" She, then, is amazed.[35]

Frieda slammed the door in Brett's face, refusing to invite her into the cabin. Lawrence followed Frieda in to try to make the peace while the farmer from San Cristobal who had been laying the waterpipes for Lawrence and had just helped him and Brett catch Susan looked on in astonishment. "I see you go into your bedroom and write a little note. Then you come out and I ask what has happened. You say you will come down and tell me in the morning."

Lawrence was unable to face Brett with the result of his deliberations with Frieda. Next morning he sent the note down to Del Monte.

> There's not much to say – & it's no good saying much. I don't believe Frieda would ever feel friendly towards you, again – ever. And that means friction and nothing else.
>
> You are, you know, a born separator. Even without knowing that you do it, you set people against one another. It is instinctive with you. If you are friendly with one, you make that one unfriendly to the others: no matter who it is. It's just a natural process with you – But it usually turns everybody into an enemy at last.
>
> It's no use talking about friendship. I know you have done many things for us like making the dandy beer and bringing eggs. On that side, your friendship is good. But the spirit, the flow, is always towards separating. Most of us, myself included, are a good deal that way. But it's useless in the end. Among three people, always two against one.
>
> It's no good our trying to get on together – it won't happen. Myself, I have lost all desire for intense or intimate friendship. Acquaintance is enough. It will be best when we go our separate ways – A life in common is an illusion, when the instinct is always to

> divide, to separate individuals and set them one against the other. And this seems to be the ruling instinct, unacknowledged. Unite with the one against the other. And it's no good.[36]

So much for Rananim and all the heady notions of that evening at the Cafe Royal. Lawrence had rediscovered high on Mount Lobo what he had learnt countless times already – that he could not stand company at close quarters for long, particularly – as had been the case when he and Frieda had lived with Katherine Mansfield and Middleton Murry in Cornwall – when rural isolation forced that company upon each other night and day. Cornwall had been difficult enough but escape to London and a wider circle of enemies was not impossible. Here in the Sangre de Cristos there was nowhere for Brett – or Lawrence, or Frieda – to go. Ride a horse up the canyon or climb to one of the rocky outcrops of Mount Lobo to cool off but what then? Sooner or later one has to descend for dinner, cooled off or not, with no nearby neighbours to bury oneself in. Letters might pass up and down the mountain but life is very much face to face. And home, for Brett in 1925, was still in reality 5,000 miles away – one does not settle down on the northern New Mexican mesa in ten minutes flat. Rananim was over, had never even reached Waterloo Station, but Brett, exasperating as she might be – her close friends and relatives throughout her life confirm at least that – and despite Frieda's constant antipathy, could not be abandoned or even ignored. And she *had* worked hard the previous summer to help turn Kiowa from a ruin to a ranch. She felt on that basis and the forgotten promises of Rananim, that she had earned at least a right to the poky little cabin on the hillside. Lawrence's feelings were less constant than Frieda's. "You are always gentle and friendly after your angry letters. How tiresome it all is! . . . another note from Frieda, telling me to get up and go . . . the breaker up of happy homes." Frieda's note read:

> That I *owe* you something is cool – I looked after your physical well-being for about a year you thought *nothing* of that, but only the high falute with L – I cooked for you and you flourished, no you ought to be grateful I should say the balance is considerably on my side! You did things for Lawrence but *never* for me – you just thought me an inferior fool – I *do* know enough of Katherine and you to judge – If you were so fond of Murry and yet always let Katherine think you adored her, no I can't swallow it – I believe that Carrington & Gertler might perhaps have brought it off, but for you – I believe that any woman with some go in her you try to *down*, – look at Ottoline – I *know* that your motives are wicked – I am not coming,

> what for? You want to get round me and I hate it – I feel what I feel, right or wrong – It's all very simple, we *want* to be *alone*, we *don't* want you except as a distant friend, you insist on intimacy and when we came from Mexico I only know that I was disappointed, that there was no cottage, there would have been no food, hadn't we brought it – Were you an angel we would still want to be alone – I have no feeling for you not even of hate but want to be rid of you so does Lawrence – You must accept it, so it is – your little will wont alter it –[37]

Brett wrote a reply to that letter – "no bitterness, just ironical and amusing – sarcastic" – and persuaded Lawrence who, in spite of all, continued to drop in on his way up and down the mountain, to take it up to Frieda. The next morning Lawrence was back at Del Monte with an invitation from Frieda for Brett to come to tea.

> I ride up . . . Frieda runs out. Her greeting is fulsome, nervous, a little uncertain . . . I feel more at ease, until I ride off – when I see Frieda give you a dig in the ribs . . . [she] has the air of a child asking if it has not played up well. And I feel disturbed.[38]

Not a little of the antipathy between the two may be explained by the different reactions to Brett and Frieda of the casual visitor to the ranch, reactions that Frieda cannot have failed to notice. Sometime during the summer, Lawrence was interviewed for a magazine by Kyle Crichton, a journalist then living in Albuquerque. Crichton, nearly thirty years later, cooperated with Brett on an article for the *New Yorker* on Queen Elizabeth II's coronation. Writing around the time of his 1925 visit to Lawrence, he spent only a single line describing Frieda: "She was a large handsome woman and spoke with a decided German accent." Of Brett he offered a complete family background and potted biography, a eulogy and a detailed description.

> She turned out to be a wonderful person. She was wearing a man's woollen shirt, riding boots, and a man's breeches, and she was quite deaf. She was about twenty-five years old, had a long nose, a marvellous English complexion and used a long flat horn-like instrument for hearing.[39]

Frieda, on the other hand, was simply large, handsome, and German, and can only have been further irritated by the judgment of her visitor that Brett was "about twenty-five years old". Brett was, at the time, forty-two and Frieda just four years older. One suspects that it was

Brett's manner more than her appearance that belied her age. She had, after all, been treated as a child by her parents until she was well into her twenties – "She never learnt to tie her shoes till she was twelve years old"[40] – and that may well have had a slowing down effect upon the maturation process.

Soon after Crichton's visit, Frieda relented yet again and lifted Brett's three-day-a-week curfew. The new plan was that, whenever Brett approached Kiowa, on foot or on horseback, whether helpfully herding the wandering Susan back into the fold or bearing gifts of twenty-seven trout, fresh caught in the Rio Hondo with skills transplanted from the River Teith at Callander, she was to blow on a whistle. Then Lawrence would emerge to tell her whether she was welcome or not. Brett heralded soon became just as tedious for Frieda as Brett unannounced and, before the summer was over, the three-day curfew was once again imposed.

Lawrence, however, remained a constant visitor to Del Monte, calling by when he rode down to pick up the mail or the milk, interfering in Brett's painting, insulting her the while, and taking lessons in shooting from her.

> My big picture of the desert with all our ranch life going on is progressing. We are all working on it. You and I do most of it – most of the squabbling about it, too. You insist that landscape without figures is dull . . .
>
> "Why do all the painters have to sit in front of what they paint?" you inquire irritably.
>
> "Quien sabe," I reply.
>
> "It's because," you continue, "they feel nothing inside them, so they must have it all before their eyes. It's all wrong and stupid: it should all be brought from inside oneself."
>
> And you spit neatly past the picture onto the grass.[41]

Lawrence had other habits of his time and upbringing. Brett offered one explanation of why practically no correspondence *to* Lawrence remains. Not only was he careless of preserving it, he would clear his nose and throat each morning on the day's post. Lest the timid protest, let me say that there was nothing at all uncommon about that in the pre-Kleenex Twenties and Thirties. My own father, on catarrh-ridden Merseyside, used to use the *Liverpool Echo*, principally, I imagine, because working class families received very few letters apart from the Littlewoods coupon. The *Echo* had other toiletry uses too, as I have no doubt did the *Nottingham Post*, and, a little later, the *Taos News*.

As for the shooting lessons:

> I take my gun. "Come on and try," I say to you.
>
> "But I can't. I have never fired a gun in my life and I hate killing things."
>
> "It will take you some time to kill anything with this gun. Try at a target." You look around. "I will shoot at the doorknob on the toilet door," you say. I give you the little .22 and show you how it works. You hold it so awkwardly; I have a misgiving that I may get shot. You put it up to your shoulder and squint down the barrel, shutting the wrong eye.
>
> "The other eye," I say briskly.
>
> "Why?" you ask; and bang! – you have hit the red tin side of the toilet. You are terribly pleased with yourself. "I must hit the knob," you say, as the toilet is becoming riddled with holes, "I'll try kneeling down." So down you kneel, while I suggest your shutting the right eye. There is a long pause of adjustment, then a bang. The knob is still intact, but the lock close to it is smashed to smithereens – and never can the toilet door be locked again.
>
> "There!" you exclaim, triumphantly. "What do you think of that?"[42]

A day or two later, full of his new accomplishment at having shot the lock off the privy door, Lawrence killed a porcupine that had frightened Frieda and was threatening the trees. It took three shots. "You are immensely proud of yourself in one way, and full of regrets in another."

Lawrence had been, as early as April, laying plans to go back to Europe in the autumn and now, perhaps with the notion of a draughty winter ahead, he pressed Brett to consider returning. She was wary of the idea.

> I cannot imagine what I am going to do. To go back to the old life in London seems impossible. And to travel with my deafness . . . "Look here," you say. "All this about deafness is bunk, sheer bunk. You have plenty of money, you are free. Have you ever been to Italy? You ought to, everyone who can ought to see Italy. I may be there this winter. Why don't you go to Capri?"[43]

9

1925–1926: Europe

Lawrence and Frieda left the ranch on September 10th, 1925, travelling north from Taos this time, via Denver, instead of south through Santa Fe. Before he left, Lawrence gave Brett half a dozen manuscripts to be typed – a commission that was to cause ill-feeling between them later, not on account of Brett's errant typing but when Lawrence and, in particular, Frieda wanted to retrieve the hand-written copies for sale. Ominously for Brett, she discovered that the kitchen mirror at the ranch had broken – seven years' bad luck – and that Lawrence "because of [her] superstitious nature" had hidden the fact from her. "You did not want me to know . . . you are still a bit mixed in your feelings about going. You have but a few days, now."[1]

Susan the cow resented their departure too, for it meant fresh fields and pastures new for her as well.

> It is awful. We have ropes tied round her head and neck. I hold one rope, you another, and Frieda is to walk behind. But she doesn't: she just goes home.
>
> We are being dragged along by Susan. You are on your back, now, on the ground. Susan is running hard. You are covered in leaves and dirt, but you hold on tight. I let go; I can't hold on to her and the horses any longer. But once through the gate, we untie her. I have the horse, so we mount and drive her easily the rest of the way.[2]

The chickens followed Susan down to the Hawk ranch, in cardboard boxes, on a wagon that also carried the ranch perishables – that is to say, those household goods such as mattresses that were likely to be devoured by the invading pack rats as soon as the buildings were empty. Finally the shutters went up, with all the mishaps of a Buster Keaton comedy.

> You and I have struggled with them all this morning. You end by dropping the largest one on my head. When it is finished, you look at the cabinets sadly.
>
> "Their eyes are shut," you say. "How dismal they look!"[3]

The trio, "depressed and tired", walked down behind the clucking wagon, to the Hawk ranch, leaving the horses behind, in the big field that slopes away below the ranch, "indifferently munching". The following morning, just after dawn, Lawrence and Frieda left, Lawrence for the last time. "The car gathers speed. You peer round the hood for one final wave to me. Then I sit down against a pine tree. You are gone."[4]

Brett followed a week or two later. It had been at Frieda's insistence after the Mexican disaster that Brett was not allowed to leave with the Lawrences. Brett's supposed plan, in any case, promoted by Lawrence during the course of the summer, was to travel direct from America to Italy. Lawrence wrote constantly. A postcard from Denver advised Brett against taking that route – he and Frieda had waited three hours at night in snow for a connection. From New York Lawrence wrote:

> If I were you, I wouldn't stay long here. I'll ask about Italian ships and let you know, so you can plan your departure. New York is useless . . . perhaps the simplest way for you to carry money to Italy would be for you to take $100 worth of travellers' cheques from the American Express Co., . . .[5]

A postscript said there was no sign of Brett's "machine", that is, her hearing aid, that had been sent to New York for repair. With the letter were pages of sailing times ripped from a newspaper. A couple of days later the advice continued, with more details of sailing schedules direct to the Mediterranean and, as always, an outburst against wherever Lawrence happened to be at the time – the grass just left or that not reached was always greener. "Bah! it's much better to stay on the ranch, and not even try these cities. I hate it here really."[6] Before they left New York, Lawrence sent another note – Brett's ear machine was mended, there was $25 to pay – "at least you'll have ears again in New York". From the Atlantic the barrage of advice continued to roll in: "*Don't* go second class on a small boat – be sure you get enough promenade room, it becomes unbearable after a few days when there isn't enough room to walk about."[7]

Frieda wrote too, friendly and concerned now that Brett was out of reach and in permanent curfew, thanking Brett for the shawl she had been lent to keep her warm on the crowded deck. Shortly after docking,

Lawrence wrote yet again, pressing on Brett once more the desirability of travelling straight to Italy:

> You were quite right not to come to England; it's much worse than when I was last here, almost gruesome. Gertler is in a sanatorium in Norfolk. Kot, I've heard nothing of. Catherine Carswell is buried alive in a horrid little cottage in damp and dismal Bucks . . . Murry wants us to go down to Dorset. But he's got the Dunnings next door. And he's got Jesus badly and nastily . . . There's no *life* in anybody. And at the same time, London is so expensive, it makes one's hair stand on end . . . Compton Mackenzie and his wife, Faith, were here to lunch. Faith is going to Capri for the winter. She says she will look for you and help you all she can. She seems reliable and nice – so you won't feel lonely.[8]

At the back of Lawrence's mind was the idea that, now that there was half America and the whole of the Atlantic between them, Brett might ignore his continued pressure to give England a miss. She had never herself been over-enthusiastic about the idea that she should travel directly to Italy. At the ranch, ever unwilling to contradict Lorenzo and win the wagered half-crown from Frieda, she had nodded compliance all summer, particularly when she realised that part of Lawrence's plan was to leave Frieda with her children and carry on himself alone to Capri or thereabouts. Now that Lawrence was in London, Brett was able to make up her own mind. She decided that there was really no reason why she should not follow the same travel itinerary and suffer the catalogue of woes – dreary cities, awful people – too. At the end of October, she set sail from New York for Southampton with the concocted excuse that some fault in her passport prevented her travelling straight to Italy. As soon as she arrived in Britain, she cabled Lawrence, who replied briskly:

> We leave tomorrow for Baden-Baden – it was all fixed up when we got your cable. But what can have made you come to England? – Your passport was all right . . . shall you go to Capri? . . . we may stay on the Italian Riviera for a while . . . Better I think for you to go to Capri.[9]

Lawrence reiterated his disbelief in Brett's passport difficulties from Baden-Baden, surprised that she was "back in the old milieu". "I can't imagine *what* was wrong with your passport. It seemed to me all right." Once more he offered his travel agent service, a new habit dying hard: "The Brewsters and Faith Mackenzie are expecting you in Capri . . .

train will probably be cheaper than boat to Naples. Go to Thomas Cook and Son in Ludgate Circus" as well as a postscript of advice on how to treat her deafness, less dismissive of it as a psychosomatic fake than usual:

> It is just possible that you might be cured by hypnosis but it's risky. If you like, you can ask Dr. Eder, 2 Harley Place, Marylebone Road. He knows all about those things and is a friend of mine, a *nice* man, not a liar. He's poor – pay him a little fee; but he'll do you for nothing if you tell him it's from me.[10]

Having missed Lawrence so narrowly, there was little to hold Brett in London. She was hardly back in her "old milieu". Indeed, she found it so hard to find any of her old friends still in town that she stayed with her brother Oliver in his house in Mayfair. From there she wrote to Frieda that she was dressing respectably but, despite her attempts at conformity, was regarded by Oliver and his wife, Antoinette, as more eccentric than ever, with all her cowboy ways. Oliver, to her dismay, presented her with a bill he had taken care of as guarantor of a rental agreement, for a pianola that she had managed to reduce to a shambles in Pond Street before leaving for America. Brett, of course, argued the toss and blamed Carrington who was not there to defend herself and had been a rare visitor to Pond Street anyway, but Oliver pursued the issue by letter to Capri in time for Christmas: "You will see that your liability is now reduced to 10 guineas, a fairly reasonable sum which you can pay at any convenient moment."[11]

Brett did manage to see Murry, who kept a strict and formal distance, and Gertler, who wrote excitedly to Ottoline, "Do you know Brett is in London!"[12] By then Brett was on the point of departure for Italy and she did not meet her ladyship, either at Garsington or in town. Nor did she bother to contact Koteliansky, with whom she was still not on speaking terms. It was left to Gertler again to tell him of her visit and to realise that Lawrence, far from trying to escape Brett, had promoted her Italian trip in the full knowledge that he too would be in Italy for the winter.

> Brett is going to Capri . . . I do not believe Lawrence is trying to get away from her . . . he seems always to prefer hurling himself back into relationships with people, even when they have long since been rotten . . .[13]

By the time Gertler wrote that, Brett was gone, cabling Lawrence once more of her movements. The brief stop-over in London was a failure in so far as the revival of former friendships was concerned. Even Gertler, apart from Murry the one friend she did see, felt they no longer had much to offer each other. A little later he wrote to Ottoline: "The Lawrences and Brett are in Capri at this moment" – the Lawrences were, of course, in Spotorno, but it was all Italy to Gertler – "Brett writes to me but I cannot answer her – I tried today but tore up my effort – what is the good. I do not care for her now."[14]

Lawrence and Frieda had arrived in Spotorno from Germany just before Brett left London for Capri and, after a couple of days in a hotel, rented the Villa Bernarda from "a nice little Bersaglieri officer". "I am thrilled at his cockfeathers," Frieda wrote, with more Freudian undertones than she may at the time have realised. "He is almost as nice as the feathers!"[15] The Teniente de Bersaglieri was Angelo Ravagli who was to become, after Lawrence's death, Frieda's third husband, legitimising, partly for the sake of the US immigration authorities, the affair with Frieda that began the following spring when Lawrence left Frieda in a huff and himself travelled further south to the Bay of Naples to conduct a poor excuse of an affair with Brett.

Brett took a stinking cold with her from London to Capri and, despite introductions to Lawrence's friends, Earl and Achsah Brewster who were renting the Villa Quattro Venti for the season and to Faith Compton Mackenzie, her spirits flagged. She wrote "dismally" to Lawrence and Murry. From Murry, too obsessed with his own problems, she got little sympathy. His whole family were suffering from the same colds on top of which, he said, he was chronically overworked and deeply unpopular with the literary world.[16]

Lawrence too told Brett, "The cold in the head is universal. We were motoring in Switzerland – hated it – and got colds in the head, to stop a clock."[17] A week later he offered a little more sympathy – "You've got the real doldrums. But one always feels bad the first few days when one comes to Italy,"[18] and the consolation that his American publishers, Knopf, were going to use Brett's cover design for *The Plumed Serpent* and would pay £50. With the letter came a couple of manuscripts for typing – Brett had his typewriter with her in Capri – "count the thousands and I'll pay the current rate – 1/– per 1000, 3d. per carbon". Frieda offered her own advice: "You will like Capri when the ranch has gone out of your bones a little." New Mexico and the ranch, though, would not go away. Faith Compton Mackenzie recalled:

> Brett used to come to my little parties and dance with Italians and Russians to my noisy gramophone in her red Mexican coat and hair flopping wildly. In her heart was a world of which we knew nothing, a world where mountains shook, Indians danced, and a horse could be

> your best friend. When she went back . . . it [became] her whole life and full one.[19]

On the promise that spring would bring Lawrence south, Brett settled in to Capri, began to paint, continued to type the manuscripts Lawrence sent, and kept in constant touch. She sent Lawrence and Frieda early Christmas presents, brought with her from London: "The 'ledgers' are most [word indistinct] and imposing. I feel nothing could go in them but scandalous stories"[20] . . . "Frieda is still charmed with her clothes. You should see her in the black step-downstairs coat and the bowler riding hat! I am swathed in the blue scarf, which if I were a chippy [chipmunk] I wouldn't be, only my own stripes." The riding hat had arrived accidentally to go with the coat from Brett. Lawrence had left "a nice new felt hat" in London, asked the hotel to forward it to Spotorno and had received instead a lady's black bowler riding hat – "very chic!! Frieda fancies herself in it. I'll get you one if you're envious." Promises, promises. Like Murry, Lawrence found it difficult to organise himself into the bourgeois chore of seeking out Christmas presents. On Christmas Eve he sent Brett "2 quid for a little wine . . . nothing to buy here . . . try a bottle of Strega", along with the usual Compleat Traveller's advice: "to keep your innards going, drink plenty of cold water at bed time." Frieda thought of sending Brett a camel* they'd seen in a travelling menagerie but fell back on handkerchiefs. Brett, in a second round of Christmas giving, simultaneously packed off handkerchiefs for Lawrence and Frieda. A good deal of postage seems to have been wasted but perhaps Brett was tempted by that odd little shop in Sorrento, stocked full of hand-made lace handkerchiefs and called simply, in English, not Italian, "Handkerchiefs". As late as 1978, "Handkerchiefs" was still offering elegant, if impractical, lace and also linen, too expensive and beautifully made ever to be used other than as decoration and keeping a visitors' book for its more important customers.

Brett seems to have become slightly more reconciled to her father during her London visit, having hardly been in touch with him at all since she first left London for America. His Christmas gift was a pair of field glasses. "I rushed out and tried them and they were splendid and will be wonderful when I get back to New Mexico." Forty years later the use to which it was claimed Brett was putting the field glasses in New Mexico – spying on Frieda – caused a permanent rift between her and the Lawrence biographer, Harry T. Moore. Brett was painting, she told Esher:

* Mrs. Gandhi, later Prime Minister of India, visited Brett in Taos in the 1950s and promised to send her an elephant. She told Brett that New Mexico was just like India.

a picture of the Crucifixion and it's a lovely colour = it isn't finished yet = but I get so badgered by people wanting to see it – I took it up for a day to the Brewsters, but today I am bringing it back again = & I shall finish it slowly = It's a very gay picture, which is unusual for a crucifixion, and the Christ is Primrose colour =

In the same letter Brett offered a cameo of Capri in 1926:

The place abounds in writers and painters, mostly painters and the little shops teem with horrible paintings: all Reckitt's blue! until the sea looks faded . . . there is the usual idiot led about on a much disgusted donkey – one can't seem to get away from them = and the usual mixture of arty women in handkerchiefs and smart women in tight skirts and immense legs – men in Bavarian shorts or German student caps and so on = Is there nothing strange on this earth now – or should I say new – the strangeness is there all right only we are accustomed to it! luckily! [that, from Brett in her cowboy finery, must have seemed odd] There is a fierce looking Russian woman who comes and massages my ear, she is determined to make me hear better = I buzz less – I only pay her 10 lire a time, so it's fearfully cheap, and worth I suppose trying =[21]

Brett had written to Lawrence of the crucifixion painting. Frieda replied, "To be crucified only once seems comparatively little, we have done that several times."[22] And Lawrence: "I am surprised at your adding one more to the list of Crucifixions . . . whom are you popping on the Cross?"[23] Later, in Capri, when the picture was nearly finished, Lawrence asked her again. "Your primrose Christ? . . . I am longing to see what kind of a Christ you have made. Not my idea of a Christ, I bet." Whether it was, in truth, Lawrence's idea of a Christ is open to opinion for whom Brett was popping on the Cross this time, as well as below and beside it, was Lawrence himself.

You look at it in astonishment . . .

"It's a good idea, but it's much too like me – much too like."

"I know," I reply, "But I took the heads half from you and half from John the Baptist."

"It's too like me," you repeat abruptly. "You will have to change it . . . but wherever did you get the idea from?"

"I don't know . . . it seemed to come from you, to be you."

The picture is of a Crucifixion. The pale yellow Christ hangs on the Cross, against an orange sunset. With the final spurt of strength before death, he is staring at the vision of the figure in front of him.

His eyes are visionary, his figure tense and aware. Before him, straddled across a rock, is the figure of Pan, holding up a bunch of grapes to the dying Christ; a dark, reddish figure with horns and hoofs. The heads of Pan and Christ are both your head. Behind lies the sea. A deep curve of rocks brings the sea-line low in the middle of the picture; and below Pan's rock is just visible the tower of the Quattro Venti. Alas, that the laughter and criticism of others made me cut the picture up in a rage! I have only the heads that I rescued. But some day I will paint it again.

"It is you," I say.

"Perhaps," you answer grimly.[24]

Crucified or not, Lawrence began to feel he was being sacrificed at the Villa Bernarda. Unrealistically ignoring all his recent experience of shared premises, he had invited Murry and his family down for the winter. Had Murry arrived, the menage would have proved a disaster. When he refused, Lawrence attacked him bitterly, directly and in letters to Brett. The wrath extended all round. One of the reasons he and Frieda had settled on Spotorno – apart from a recommendation by Martin Secker, the publisher, that it was off the beaten track, a track which, to Lawrence's annoyance, Secker then beat – had been that Frieda wanted to spend some time with her children. Barby, the eldest, recently graduated from the Slade and engaged to be married – much to Lawrence's disapproval – was staying nearby at Alassio. "[She] has unfortunately got some art talk", Lawrence complained to Brett before Christmas.[25] And after Christmas: "The Slade took all the life out of her work . . . that Slade is a criminal institution and gets worse," knowing full well that he was denigrating Brett's revered Alma Mater. (Barby, in all this, gained the impression from Lawrence that Brett had taught him to paint. The Slade cannot have been all bad.) Brett was later to suggest that the tensions ran deeper than disagreement over the value of a Slade education and hinted at a Freudian fracas.[26] Her version of events is almost certainly fantasy out of gossip by wishful thinking, and Frieda's version is, not surprisingly, quite different:

I had not waited in vain for so many years and longed for these children. But Lawrence did not share my joy. One day at our evening meal came the outburst: "Don't imagine your mother loves you," he said to Barby; "she doesn't love anybody, look at her false face." And he flung half a glass of red wine in my face. Barby, who beside my mother and myself was the only one not to be scared of him, sprang up. "My mother is too good for you," she blazed at him, "much too good; it's like pearls thrown to the swine." Then we both began to cry. I went to my room offended.

"What happened after I went?" I asked Barby later on.

"I said to him: 'Do you care for her?'" "It's indecent to ask," he answered; "haven't I just helped her with her rotten painting?"

Which again puzzled me because he would gladly help anybody. It did not seem a sign of love to me.[27]

With the possibility that Frieda was already showing more than a passing interest in her later lover and husband, Angelo Ravagli, there is the makings of a maelstrom. Conventional accounts skate over all of this and have matters coming to a head with the arrival of Frieda's other daughter, Else, on the one hand, and of Lawrence's sister Ada and a friend, on the other, at a time when Lawrence was stricken low with flu.

There were two hostile camps . . . in Lawrence's room with the balcony, I could hear him complaining to [Ada] about me. I could not hear the words but by the tone of their voices I knew.

His sister Ada felt he belonged to her and the past, the past with all its sad memories. Of course, it had been necessary for him to get out of his past and I had, of equal necessity, to fight that past, though I liked Ada for herself.

Lawrence was ill with all this hostility. I was grieved for him. So one evening I went up to his room and he was so glad I came. I thought all was well between us. In the morning Ada and I had bitter words. "I hate you from the bottom of my heart," she told me. So another night I went up to Lawrence's room and found it locked and Ada had the key. It was the only time he had really hurt me; so I was quite still. "Now I don't care," I said to myself. He went away with Ada and her friend, hoping at the least I would say some kind word, but I could not. [Then] Lawrence went to Capri to stay with the Brewsters.[28]

Brett was waiting patiently and expectantly in Capri. Lawrence had persuaded her to winter there in the first place, baiting the suggestion with the possibility that he might visit her alone. Throughout his correspondence that winter were hints that he might arrive, with or without Frieda, and fantasies of a Mediterranean Odyssey aboard some sailing craft, "*our* yacht", "*our* lugger", provided and vittled by the Brewsters, Brett's Capri neighbours, by Brett's rich family, by whoever might be persuaded. Brett's fires were fuelled by fiction as well as fantasy. Before the end of 1925, Lawrence sent her for typing the manuscript of *Glad Ghosts*. "Tell me what impression it makes on you. I am curious to know."

Glad Ghosts was written originally for Cynthia Asquith to include in her *Ghost Book*, which, in the end, included instead *The Rocking Horse Winner*. In the story Lawrence himself appears as the gifted – both naturally and supernaturally – Mark Morier who, while a guest of Carlotta Fell and her husband, Lord Lathkill, is visited in the night by a woman ghost. "The following autumn" the "very dark" Lord Lathkill writes to Morier that Carlotta has unexpectedly given him a son and heir. "He has yellow hair, like a little crocus, and one of the young plum-trees in the orchard has come out of all season into blossom."

Richard Aldington, in an introduction to *Glad Ghosts*, described it as "a piece of reckless impudence" for, in the end, Carlotta and Lathkill seem remarkably similar to the Asquiths themselves. But, in the beginning, the description of Carlotta Fell and her family background is that of Brett and the Eshers.

> I knew Carlotta Fell in the early days before the war. Then she was escaping into art, and was just "Fell". That was at our famous but uninspired school of art, the Thwaite, where I myself was diligently murdering my talent. At the Thwaite they always gave Carlotta the Still-life prizes. She accepted them calmly, as one of our conquerors, but the rest of the students felt vicious about it. They called it buttering the laurels, because Carlotta was Hon., and her father a well-known peer.
>
> She was by way of being a beauty, too . . . She had come into five hundred a year of her own, when she was eighteen; and that to us, was an enormity. Then she appeared in the fashionable papers, affecting to be wistful, with pearls, slanting her eyes. Then she went and did another of her beastly still-lifes, a cactus-in-a-pot . . .
>
> She and I were "friends" in a bare, stark but real sense. I was poor, but I didn't really care. She didn't really care either . . . she didn't know what I was after. Yet she could feel that I was It, and, being an aristocrat of the Kingdom of It, as well as the realm of Great Britain, she was loyal – loyal to me because of It, the quick body which I imagined within the dead . . . she was always a bit sad when we were together . . .
>
> She and I had a curious understanding in common: an inkling, perhaps, of the unborn body of life hidden within the body of this half-death which we call life; and hence a tacit hostility to the commonplace world, its inert laws. We were rather like two soldiers on a secret mission to an enemy country. Life, and people, was an enemy country to us both . . . She depended on me morally . . . we

had then a curious abstract intimacy, that went very deep, yet showed no obvious contact. Perhaps I was the only person in the world with whom she felt, in her uneasy self, at home, at peace. And to me, she was always of my own *intrinsic* sort, of my own species. Most people are just another species to me. They might as well be turkeys.[29]

It cannot have been difficult for Lawrence to imagine the impression *Glad Ghosts* would make upon Brett. She felt he was wooing her in fiction and did not find it difficult to ignore the change in character that moves Carlotta Fell from Dorothy Brett to Cynthia Asquith by the end of the story. For Lady Asquith, a description at the beginning of the story far from herself and readily identifiable as Brett, might be sufficient to allay suspicion that she herself was being written about. For Brett, the beginning wooed her on paper and thereafter she would pay little attention to the fact that the character ultimately little resembled her.

There were one or two worries before Morier/Lawrence finally arrived in Capri to lay the ghost, gladly or otherwise. First Lawrence asked Brett to post back his typewriter so that Frieda's daughter Else could type a German translation of the play *David*. Brett jumped to the conclusion that he might be severing the ostensible reason for so much correspondence between them. Then Lawrence wrote "a chapter of dismalness":

I doubt if we shall ever see comfortable days together. Frieda declares an implacable intention of never seeing you again and never speaking to you if she does see you – and I say nothing. Don't you say anything either, it only makes scenes: which is ridiculous. As for plans, I feel it's the Flood, the only thing is to build an Ark.[30]

The Ark was not for Frieda. The hostility between her and Lawrence's sister Ada was so great that the villa split into two camps, Frieda and daughters on one side, Lawrence and sister on the other. A few days later, continuing the nautical metaphor, Lawrence wrote that Frieda had "abandoned ship and stays down in the little hotel with her two daughters, pro tem". Lawrence then accompanied Ada and her friend to Monte Carlo, when the two ladies set off for Britain on February 25th, telling Brett that he might stay in the South of France for the rest of the winter. He did not linger. As soon as Ada left, he cabled Brett on the 26th: "Coming to Capri now", and again, on the 27th, from Rome: "Arriving this evening". Brett and the Brewsters' daughter, Harwood, met Lawrence at the Marina off the electric boat from Naples and carried his bags up the "many, many steps to the Quattro Venti", where he was to stay.

Brett, at long last, had Lawrence to herself. Or almost, for there was strong competition for his attention from Mary Cannan who was also wintering in Capri and whose constant streams of conversation caused Brett to nickname her "The Gadfly".

> The Gadfly is chattering, chattering. Even the sandwiches can't quell her garrulousness. You listen patiently and answer "yes" and "no" and giggle occasionally. I get stonier and stonier. Our days are ruined: we always have to trail her along with us. I sit and throw stones at the nearest tree-trunk. The olives are just as silvery as ever, as feathery in the wind, the sea as deep a blue; but the peace and silence has gone – it has vanished in this constant babble.[31]

Despite "The Gadfly", Brett somehow managed to walk the island with Lawrence and to dream once more hopeless dreams of the lugger – "to be free of everything for a while". Lawrence listening for once, Brett told him of her early years, in particular, of the encounter with Loulou Harcourt.

> You turn on me, angrily; you are indignant, hurt; something in your manhood flames angrily, fiercely outraged. I stand for a moment, helpless, at a loss what to say. You turn away with a heavy sigh.
>
> "It's not fair, Brett," you say. "You have never had any luck – never a decent chance!" . . .
>
> "Look, Lawrence!" I cry, "Look! Our lugger!" . . . But you are fast asleep . . . I sit and watch you. The sun pours down relentlessly on your head; a heavy lock of hair falls over your face; your beard glitters red in the sun. As I watch you, the meaningless modern suit seems to drop away. A leopard skin, a mass of flowers and leaves wrap themselves round you. Out of your thick hair, two small horns poke their sharp points; the slender cloven hoofs lie entangled in weeds. I stare at you in a kind of trance. Your eyes open suddenly, a gleam of blue. Nothing moves, nothing stirs; but your eyes are looking at me, looking at me . . .[32]

That evening they dressed up for dinner, Lawrence as a schoolmaster, hair powdered, eyelids blackened and hair parted in the middle, and Brett as what sounds like a tart but which she believed was a woman of the world.

> I powder my face a dead white, sleek back my hair with water, paint my eyebrows a deep black, blue my eyes and paint my lips the brightest scarlet I can find . . . after dinner we act charades. I become, somehow or other, your daughter, I flirt outrageously. You are the brutal father but your brutality fades before my bewildering onslaught. Never have you seen me act like this before, and never have I acted like that since. What with the wine, the disguise of paint, the presence of the Gadfly – the grotesque old child of five – [Mary Cannan had dressed as a five-year-old infant with bare knees and a large bow] I am drawn out of my usual shyness and self-consciousness vanishes. I charm you into embarrassment. The austere father turns into responsible male.[33]

When Lawrence reminisced about life on the ranch, Brett seized the opportunity to press him to return with her, for she had already applied for immigrant status, for "the Quota". Lawrence hedged, complaining that his lack of strength following the bout of flu in Spotorno would make it impossible for him to deal with Consuls and public health inspectors. Brett changed her tack, suggesting that, if Lawrence could not come with her to America, then she should stay with him in Europe.

> "I would be nearer at hand, in case of trouble. I would feel uneasy in my mind, if I went so far. What do you think?" I say.
>
> "Yes," you reply, with so much weariness mixed with boredom, that I feel nothing on earth matters very much to you. "It would be best. I don't know what to do. We must wait and see."[34]

A decision could not be delayed for long. The Brewsters were about to move on to India and throughout Lawrence's stay at the Quattro Venti, the household was being slowly dismantled and packed away around him. The charades had taken place in a library emptied of books and, as part of his performance, Lawrence adapted the schoolmaster as a shoe salesman, stacking the empty shelves with every shoe that could be found in the villa. A fortnight after Lawrence's arrival in Capri, the Brewsters were ready to leave. "Lawrence stayed on to the end, closing the garden gate as we drove down to the boat in the harbour." Later the same day, Lawrence and Brett took the steamer to Sorrento and Amalfi where Lawrence was hoping to run into some English friends, Millicent Beveridge and Mabel Harrison.

After checking the hotel in Amalfi where the two ladies were expected to be, Lawrence and Brett drove on to Ravello, passing "masses and masses of macaroni, laid out over wires or strings stretched from posts" to dry. Every hotel in Ravello was full but

Lawrence persuaded the proprietress of the Hotel Palumbo to let a nearby cottage, not part of the hotel proper. That done, they at last discovered the Misses Beveridge and Harrison and had tea with them. "They didn't like me," Brett admitted later, although at the time and in writing *Lawrence and Brett* in the early Thirties, she said nothing.

Of what followed at Ravello, Brett gave more than one account. There is no record from Lawrence. Indeed, between arriving in Capri at the end of February and returning to Frieda in Spotorno at the beginning of April, Lawrence wrote what was by his prolific standards a remarkably small number of letters. Brett's original account, published in 1933 in *Lawrence and Brett*, one of the spate of memoirs that followed Lawrence's death, was, without doubt, incomplete, censored by herself and possibly on the advice of others. Half a century later, in the late 1960s and early 1970s, she wrote at least two further versions that differed from each other only in detail but gave radically different accounts of the time spent with Lawrence in Ravello than that published in 1933. There is little reason to doubt the veracity of the later versions, despite their being written so long after the event, for in neither of them is there a hint of self-glorification, nor do they show Brett – or Lawrence, for that matter – in a particularly favourable light. One of these accounts, sealed in an envelope labelled "For John Manchester after I am in Outer Space" and deposited to be opened only after her death, is dated December 1970. Just a few months earlier, in the summer of that year, I met Brett for the first time when she was refusing to travel up from Taos to the ranch to take part in the Festival that was being held there to mark the fortieth anniversary of Lawrence's death. "All those Lawrence scholars want to know is whether I slept with Lawrence and I'm afraid that's my business."[35] Her business or not, by the end of that year she had written a short account and deposited it with her lawyer. She later sent a copy or possibly another version to Enid Hilton in California, with instructions that it should be opened only after her death but this, unfortunately, appears now to be lost. Then, perhaps not very much later, Brett prepared a further, extended account for her companion, John Manchester, which formed the basis of an Epilogue Manchester provided for a reprint of *Lawrence and Brett*, published in Santa Fe in 1974. What follows is based principally on Brett's own typescript version of this latter account but it is worth noting the brief description of events that Brett provided in 1933.

> "I wonder," you say, "if I can find my way to the cottage" . . . you haul an immense old iron key out of your pocket. It is at least eight inches long; a huge mediaeval key . . . We come to the old wooden

> door in the stone archway. You fit the key in the lock and turn and twist. Only a rusty squeaking. You turn and twist more angrily, swearing and cursing. Suddenly, for no apparent reason, the lock turns. We push the heavy door open, feel our way in, relock the door, and climb up the pitch-dark stone staircase. You turn into your room with a cheery goodnight. I fumble my way into mine, find the matches and tallow candle, and jump into the hard, relentless bed.[36]

Brett and Lawrence spent a couple of days exploring Ravello, wandering down to Amalfi with the Misses Beveridge and Harrison and painting together in the gardens of the Villa Cimbrone, Brett using a blue pigment given to her by Miss Beveridge, "a marvellous blue – a blue I have longed for ever since and never traced". "I like the way you have done the trees," she told Lawrence. "So do I," he replied, "I think mine is so much the better!"

> As always you do think so, I never argue. The only remark I venture is that I like my blue the best.
>
> "Colour is not everything," you reply tartly . . . We sit and watch the sea and the sailing ships.
>
> "We are the only two left," you say sadly to me. "Only you and I. Everyone else has gone over to the enemy."[37]

The rooms in the hotel's cottage, "clean but a bit austere", adjoined each other. That evening, Lawrence walked in to Brett's chamber in his dressing gown, saying, "I do not believe in a relationship unless there is a physical relationship as well," although, curiously, no woman other than Brett has ever reported that Lawrence made this a condition of their friendship.

> I was frightened as well as excited. He got into my bed, he turned and kissed me. I can still feel the softness of his beard, still feel the tension, the overwhelming desire to be adequate, I was passionately eager to be successful, but I had no idea what to do, nothing happened. Suddenly, Lawrence got up, said "It's no good", and stalked out of the room. I was devastated, helpless, bewildered. All the next day Lawrence was a bit glum. Nothing was said, I was too tense and nervous to say anything, if I had known what to say. Then that night he walked into my room and said, "Let's try again." So again he got into my bed. So there we lay. I felt desperate; all the love I had for him, all the closeness to him spiritually, the passionate desire to give what I felt I should be giving, was frustrated by fear and not knowing what to do. I tried to be warm and loving and female, he

> was I think struggling to be successfully male; it was a horrible failure. Nothing happened until he got up and stalked out of the room turning on me and saying, "Your pubes are wrong", which left me ashamed, bewildered, miserable. After hours of self-torment, misery, I slept.[38]

Early next morning, only a little after dawn, Brett found Lawrence in a towering rage, packing his bags, exclaiming that he could not now possibly stay on in Ravello. Brett pointed out that Miss Beveridge and Miss Harrison had laid their travelling plans around him and that he could not now abandon them. The only solution would be for Brett herself to leave, under the pretext of having to go to Naples to see the U.S. Consul about her Quota number. This calmed Lawrence and, without the slightest delay, he went out to the hotel and ordered a carriage to take Brett to Amalfi while she now packed her bags. "You know I don't believe in love or friendship," he told her. "Cut out the ecstasy. Oh, I know; I know the ecstasy. Cut it out, Brett. Cut it out."

The two drove miserably down to Amalfi, Brett hoping all the way that Lawrence would change his mind, that they would turn the carriage around in the early morning and go back to Ravello but Lawrence was adamant. Brett should return to Capri until her Quota number arrived and, if he was still in Ravello then, he might want her to come back to him there. Or perhaps they might meet in Florence where he planned to be a little later and, who knows, it was quite possible that he might himself return to the ranch quite soon – "I never know how I am going to feel." At Amalfi, they discovered that the direct steamer to Capri did not leave until after lunch, so they killed the morning strolling restlessly through the town, fidgeting over lunch "under the constant glances in the dining room", then sitting disconsolately on the terrace until the boat was about to leave. Throughout it all, Brett tried to persuade Lawrence to allow her to stay but without success.

> I stood in my white overcoat on the deck. Lawrence returned to the carriage. As he drove away up to Ravello, he waved and waved to me, and I waved back. I can see myself even now, standing on the deck, in that white coat, waving to him until he vanished around a bend. I never saw him again, and I have never cared to wear anything white since. He was gone, I was alone – tortured, desolate, miserable. I went back to the hotel in Capri. The chambermaid took one look at me and said, "He has been cruel to you."[39]

Brett's departure from Ravello took place in such haste that her washing was left behind. Lawrence sent it on to Capri with a postcard, telling her that Frieda had written to him and was much milder.[40] He followed the postcard with a letter, justifying himself, lecturing Brett, telling her Capri was better for her than "mooning in an unknown place".

> One just has to forget and to accept what is good. We can't help being more or less damaged. What we have to do is to stick to the good of ourselves and of each other, and continue an understanding on that. I don't see that we shouldn't be *better* friends instead of worse. But we must not try to force anything.
>
> Frieda writes more quietly and humanly – she says we must live more with other people: which I think is true. It's no use trying to be exclusive. There is a good *bit* in a lot of people. If we are to live, we must make the most of that, and not try to cut ourselves off . . . I'll let you know my plans as soon as I make any. Just be quiet and leave things to the Lord.[41]

To Mabel Luhan he wrote the same day, "we are all changing drastically, even Brett", and then, in response to a plea from Brett, sent a note to Capri via an English girl and her father who had watched the two playing bezique one evening in Ravello.

> Don't you mope and lie around, it's infra dig. The greatest virtue in life is real courage, that knows how to face facts and live beyond them. Don't be Murryish, pitying yourself and caving in. It's despicable. I should have thought, after a dose of that fellow, you'd have had too much desire to be different from him, to follow his sloppy self-indulgent melancholics, absolutely despicable. Rouse up and make a decent thing of your days, no matter what's happened. I do loathe cowardice and sloppy emotion. My God, did you learn *nothing* from Murry, of how not to behave! Even you write the sort of letters he writes! Oh basta! Cut it out! Be something different from that, even to yourself.[42]

All that was missing was a recommendation to learn a language or take evening classes in petit-point, to twist the knife in Brett's open wound. A couple of days later Lawrence left Capri with the Misses Beveridge and Harrison and travelled slowly north via Rome and Perugia to Florence, keeping Brett informed of his progress by postcard and letter. On the 30th of the month, he wrote to Brett that he was going on to Ravenna but by then, in despair, Brett had chased to Florence after him. She booked into the Pension Lucchesi where she knew that Lawrence normally stayed. On this occasion, with the Misses Beveridge and Harrison in tow, he was staying elsewhere.

> I went looking round every corner, everywhere hoping to see Lawrence, sitting on stone steps hoping he might go by. I never saw a sign of him, perhaps the old women spotted me and would not let him meet me. I remember the amazement and wonder of the Botticellis, then I went to the Palace of the Medici. I walked into the small stone room, there on the wall was the marvellous painting of Lorenzo de Medici, on horseback, leading the procession, the man with the beard. I sat down and burst into tears. For the first time the whole misery, torment, of the failure in Ravello, the parting, the humiliation swept over me. I sat and wept the whole misery out of me. I never saw him, never again . . .[43]

When Lawrence at last returned to Spotorno and Frieda, a letter from Brett was waiting. "Brett can't stand Capri any more," he told the Brewsters, "and I can't stand it when she clings too tight."[44] A quick postcard to Brett was followed by a letter, each explaining that he had no idea she was in Florence and that everyone – that is, Frieda and her daughters – in Spotorno was now as nice to him as possible: "Quite different* . . . I think we should find Frieda much more tolerant."[45] He added that he might be going down to Perugia again, at which Brett wrote suggesting a meeting. Lawrence was in no mood for that. "We should only be upset," he wrote. "Better to get a fresh start on all round: we need it badly," and adding, "Frieda will write to you nice and amicably."[46]

Frieda indeed wrote to Brett but was nice and amicable only by the standards of their well-established antagonism. She suggested that Brett go to America, to the ranch and do as she like there "and don't think that we hate each other only I am so impatient of any will that's put over me."[47]

Still hoping that Lawrence would arrive in Perugia as he had suggested, before the end of the month, Brett decided to move on from Florence, cabling Lawrence of her intention. He was unmoved and unmoving. "You'll like it," he responded, "I might come down . . . at present [though] I don't feel like making any effort."[48] At last Brett gave up her pursuit and, on April 15th, returned to Capri and began to pack her belongings. In the course of her mainland Odyssey, she had collected her immigrant Quota number from the US Consul and could now arrange to travel back to New Mexico. She booked a passage from Naples for the beginning of May and tried, without much success, to get a decision from Lawrence on his own return to the United States. "I really don't want to go to America", he wrote to the Brewsters,[49] and to

* Perhaps because she had, in Lawrence's absence, begun her affair with Angelo Ravagli.

Koteliansky in London, "every week alienates my soul further", but to Brett he stalled, promising that the following spring might see him at the ranch in the Rockies and, back on his old form, sending her a long travel-agent lecture on negotiating the sea passage, landing in the US alone as a proper immigrant, arranging finances, travelling to New Mexico and irrigating the ranch. It can have offered little comfort to Brett that the letter was written from the Pension Lucchesi in Florence where she had hoped and waited for Lawrence four weeks before.

Brett arrived in New York on May 16th and was thrilled by it, she wrote to Lawrence, who reported her arrival to Mabel, adding, "I don't even want to be thrilled." By the second week in June she was back at the ranch and Lawrence was writing, promising that next spring he would return, "before the leaves come on the aspen trees, and the snow is gone", writing joyfully, spiritedly, now there was an ocean and a continent between them.

> Is the messiness of the old corral passing away?
> Are there very many flowers?
> Will there be raspberries?
> Were there still humming birds round the squawberry bushes or had they gone?
> Does the ditch run a nice stream?
> Oh, by the way, tell me how much money you paid for cleaning the ditch, and for Azul, and all those things. Because I will pay for them. You'll have no money. *Don't forget!*
> Has the old tree down at the well, the old fallen aspen, still put out leaves? I often think of it.
> And has the big greasewood bush grown over the track of the well, so that it pushes your bucket aside . . . *how* is the big picture?[50]

"What a bore the rats had done so much chewing," the letter began.

10

1926–1930: The Ranch

"How are you for money? Let me know. I like the seal to your letter. Where did you find the bird? Does Aaron still have a running eye? And Azul's jaw? The poor creatures! Is Prince mild as a lamb with you?"[1] Thus Lawrence, from Scandicci in July, 1926. Over the next few years, Lawrence intermittently showed an interest in Brett's finances, more often than not wanting to know how much the horses' feed cost, occasionally offering direct assistance. This time Brett replied that she was "a bit stumped". Her letter was intercepted by Frieda to whom Brett also wrote and who reacted sharply:

> You are a humbug. You say, my friendship is there for you, and wherever I go you have said nasty things about me and tried to belittle me – I have never hated you, vitally you have never existed for me – And the lecturing, superior tone you take to me in your letters amuses me – You used to irritate me, now it's just funny – Your great love for Lawrence is just bunk.[2]

That, more or less, established the pattern for the next four years, until Lawrence's death in 1930: Brett writing to Lawrence, telling him how hard she was working to look after *his* ranch and offering a thousand different reasons why he should hurry across the Atlantic to her – with, invariably, no mention of Frieda; Lawrence reminding her that the ranch belonged technically to Frieda and not to himself, while, his health declining, ever shilly-shallying over returning to America; and between times, Brett and Frieda exchanging letters, long and short, that rarely stepped outside the boundaries of the vitriolic and the abusive. Despite her apparent shortage of cash, by September Brett had acquired a car, a Chevrolet, the idea and even the make of which irritated Lawrence, ready, as ever, with headmasterly advice and pontification:

> How rash you are! You'll go bankrupt, you'll go over the edge of the Hondo Canyon, you'll run over Mexican babies, you'll – God knows what you won't do! And however will you hear when anything is tooting behind you? I'm sure they weren't your friends who urged you to buy the Chevrolet. For the Lord's sake, go gingerly, in every respect.[3]

A month later, with the snows of late autumn already falling at the ranch, Brett drove the new car down to Taos to stay with Mabel till the spring – "a grand test if you can pull off a winter successfully with Mabel," wrote Lawrence.[4] In Mabeltown, she made her first attempt at writing, trying to rationalise her crush on Lawrence in a short article she called *Adolescence.* She sent him a copy. Lawrence was unimpressed and told Mabel so.

> I have Brett's *Adolescence.* Most people experience *something* the same. The worst is, the body, *the blood* are practically unbreakable: they don't yield at all to the mind, but remain underneath like a rock substratum. The mind and spirit may play their own game, on top: but it never passes through the rock bed. But I'm glad you're friendly.[5]

"Today is a day when I can imagine Taos," he added, dithering again over whether to return to New Mexico. Just a fortnight later, his mood ever volatile, he offered Brett the thought that he might get rid of the ranch for ever, a possibility that nagged at her for years. "I'd sell the ranch if it were mine . . . You say you'd buy it – but my dear Brett, what with?"[6]

By the end of the month, Lawrence was again in Ravello. It was almost exactly a year since he and Brett had been there together. He wrote, perhaps callously, certainly thoughtlessly, a joint letter with the Brewsters and their daughter, an after-dinner jest to which each contributed a line at a time. Lawrence's opening contribution must have particularly hurt Brett: "The irises are out in the garden and my blue Venus – you remember – is as blue as ever, poor dear!"[7] While he was at Ravello, Lawrence suggested to the Brewsters that they should join Brett at the ranch – "we'd come too. But our difficulty is Frieda won't go near Brett again, and is doubtful of Mabel." To Brett he wrote at the same time, tantalising her once more with the thought of owning the ranch, into the upkeep of which she was putting much time and effort: "Why struggle with the ranch anyway? – unless you'd really like to buy it. Would you? I guess Frieda would sell it to you. You ask her."[8] What Lawrence well knew was that Brett was the last person to whom

Frieda would sell the ranch but he persisted in the fiction of disinterest in its future, at the same time, too, teasing Brett with the possibility of his return this year, next year, sometime, to New Mexico.

The summer passed in attending to the ranch, successfully negotiating the dirt roads in the Chevrolet, less successfully riding horseback – she suffered one severe fall early in the season – and settling down once more to her painting. She held a running exhibition in the old La Fonda Hotel on the Taos plaza, on the same walls now occupied by the paintings Lawrence was working on during exactly the same period. Brett's paintings caused a "furore" in Taos, Lawrence wrote to Kot, adding that Brett too was furious "because we don't go out there – but really these wonderful women begin to scare my soul". "The way she writes now," he told the Brewsters, "seems to me cheek. 'You come over here and keep me amused –' – and then wraps it up in 'acts of faith'."[9]

Once more, in the autumn, Brett shut up the ranch and moved down to stay with Mabel. The two soon got on each other's nerves, a situation partly aggravated by the fact that Brett decided to have all her teeth out in a single fell swoop ("Do you really think it was necessary to have them *all* out? . . . I'm afraid you'll hate false teeth. I've got five, and I've always hated them," Headmaster Lawrence chided,[10] and that Mabel was charging her a small rent when she was, as always, in her words, "flat broke". She was, in fact, desperate enough to write in February to a wealthy Mr. Montagne, a comparative stranger she had met through Mabel and whom Mabel was then visiting in the warmth of California, asking him to lend her $1,000 and promising faithfully to pay it all back by a year to the day later. "I'm really in a fix," Brett wrote and, to lessen the cheek, recommended Mr. Montagne a "good murder story = 'The Man they couldn't arrest' . . . there are others only I forget the names."[11] When Mabel returned from the West Coast, notes flew between her and Brett. Mabel complained testily:

> You often talk of sharing and community ideals and never once contribute any share! I waited for you to bring in the choccies in your turn like a good "guest" but never once! Then when I was tired and wanted one badly after the trip – who had consumed them all? . . . broke the camel's back!"

Brett responded threateningly: "Next time you drive through the town above the speed limit, I go straight to the sheriff."[12]

When Brett moved away from Taos and up once more to the ranch in the spring, matters improved sufficiently between the two for Mabel to write to Alfred Stieglitz, the photographer, who had opened a gallery in

New York, "The American Place", known also to its intimates as "The Room". Stieglitz, whether through politeness or an interest in Mabel as a rich patroness of the arts, responded favourably enough for Brett herself to write to him, telling him that no one seemed to have had the inspiration to let him know that she had only six pictures in all – could she send them to him to look at? She wrote at the same time to Lawrence to try once again to tempt him to return to America, the bait this time being the possibility of a joint exhibition, but without success – Lawrence was already committed to a show at the Warren Gallery in London.

Encouraged by Stieglitz's reply, Brett promised to send the pictures to him in November and, at the same time, took the opportunity to let him know of her close friendship with Lawrence, as an excuse seeking his support should Lawrence's new book, *Lady Chatterley*, have any problems on publication. She made sure, too, that Stieglitz was aware of her financial circumstances as well as her dedication to art.

> I am financially in a small way independent – I have $2,000 a year – it sounds a lot and yet somehow it isn't – but down here I can keep a car and horses and paint = I would like my pictures to sell – especially just now because I have got into debt keeping the Indians = You see in the Summer I move 17 miles up the mountain-side & look after D. H. Lawrence's little Ranch for him = For the last two summers I have had Indians to look after me – now I have gone broke and so I am alone . . . I have five horses and three colts & a Police dog pup to look after . . .[13]

By October she had finished a further painting and was working on another, all Pueblo Indian subjects, some of them of religious ceremonies, the so-called *Ceremonials* for which she was later to become best known. While, naturally, using her art to record life and times at the ranch from the moment she arrived, she seems, early on, also to have taken up whole-heartedly the Pueblo-dwelling New Mexican Indian as a subject. She had brought with her to New Mexico a style of painting – swooping arcs, formalised and centrally focused design, bright primary colours – and a belief that painting was an "inward spiritual beauty" that she was able immediately to project upon the impassive Indian. A number of Indians became her friends over the years – not an everyday phenomenon even in present-day Taos – and Trinidad a particularly close friend. He guided Brett in her painting of the religious ceremonies, at times providing detail, at times holding her back from too great an intrusion, always a discreet mediator and protector in her dealings with the Pueblo. It was – and theoretically is, though the restriction is often nowadays overlooked or abused – forbidden to record ceremonies and dances and, from time to time, cameras have been smashed and sketchbooks confiscated. Brett herself liked to recall that, soon after her establishment in Taos, the Pueblo elders heard of her work and, unannounced and uninvited, a group of Indians walked into her house, contemplated her paintings silently for a long time and then left. A few days later a second blanket-wrapped delegation walked in and, once again, stared long at the paintings, one of which was an attempt to record the most important date in their religious calendar, the annual ceremony at Blue Lake, a sacred place hidden high in the mountains behind the Pueblo. By then Brett was genuinely frightened. When, at last, they turned to leave, one of them indicated the Blue Lake painting and spoke – just two words: "Never again".

She sent Stieglitz a list of her works with wildly optimistic suggested prices:

Rabbit Hunt	$2,000
Indian Love Song	$2,000
Indian Ecstasy	$1,000
The Eternal Mother	$1,000
Benito (property of Mabel Luhan)	–
Preparing for the Dance of The Ripening Corn	$ 500
Women at Race Meeting	$ 500
The Apaches have come to Taos	$ 500

Brett now decided to appear in New York herself, bringing the last of the paintings with her. She travelled with Mabel, arriving in the city in the first week of November.

Stieglitz had opened "The Room" to promote contemporary American art and in particular, that of Georgia O'Keefe, his young wife. O'Keefe was later invited by Brett and Mabel to visit New Mexico where she eventually settled and where, as was always the case with Brett's female friends, the two fell in and out with each other with monotonous regularity. On her first visit, the following spring, however, Brett doted on her, writing fulsome letters back to Stieglitz in New York, describing at length O'Keefe's efforts at learning to ride on Brett's horses up at the ranch and going more than overboard in praise of her painting. Between the lines, one can read Brett's somewhat naive efforts to capitalise on the friendship in an attempt to persuade Stieglitz to show Brett's own paintings at "The Room" but, in the end, this never happened. So far as "The Room" was concerned, O'Keefe had made it clear to Stieglitz that there was room for only one woman artist and that, without question, was herself. Brett was compelled to try her artistic luck elsewhere. On November 24th, 1928, she wrote to Spud Johnson:

> Up in our tiny room on the 27th floor of the Shelton [in New York] my seven pictures were brought = & spread themselves about – some in the bedroom too = & then O'Keefe came down from her 30th floor = & seemed somewhat stunned by them = later that evening Stieglitz came down & brushed past me as if I were a chair & went straight to the pictures = I was in a sweat – cold and hot alternately = at last (I had sat on my bed in agony) Stieglitz having stared hard at my picture with the moon, I ventured to ask him what he thought = & he said they were "very fine indeed" = I nearly hugged him = then the question was what to do = what indeed = as Stieglitz so obviously was too frail to heave those huge heavy pictures about = so it was decided to get hold of Rehr = so next evening there was another seance = & Rehr and his wife came = Rehr just fell for my pictures & gobbled the whole seven up = Hook, line & sinker – and there I am, an artist of note = my pictures all at Rehr's gallery = what an enormous feather in my cap = & now a critic called Brinton has fallen for them & his enthusiasm is great & he wants to get up an exhibition of them immediately = you see, coming like a bolt from the blue – Rehr is jammed up with pictures – he tried to get rid of a man last week but couldn't wriggle out = meanwhile I've got such a swelled head that if I sell a picture it will burst.[14]

A few days later Brett wrote to Stieglitz:

> I still have it on my conscious [sic] that you lifted that heavy photograph box. Heaven knows what a bore our bodies are. It's the same with my deafness. There comes a time when I feel I must explain how much DEAFNESS slows me up. The whole mechanism seems to creak around like a rusty wheel. Basta! Do you know I think of The Room a great deal. It's like an oasis in a desert or a quiet pool sheltered by rocks from a turbulent sea. It's queer, isn't it, that the real forces of life make no noise . . . the bear comes out of her hole with her cubs. The little Mexican boy who helps me in winter with my horses, comes running to my door and says "Your colt is here!" All so quietly the eggs lie in the nests. Even the heavy sea makes no sound until lashed by the wind. So with The Room. One comes in and there is the soil under one's feet and the invisible stir of life around one. I have explained this to Lorenzo. I want him to know The Room . . . when I go back to New Mexico, to Taos or to

the little Ranch, The Room will be there too. That's what it means to me.[15]

While in New York, Brett, following her usual winter pattern, fell out with Mabel, who was having trouble anyway with her psychiatrist. As a result, Brett was forced to move out of Mabel's swank apartment at No. 1, Fifth Avenue and back into the Shelton Hotel. To cap it all, she sold not a single picture, a pill that was all the more bitter for she had been fantasising that her autumn in New York would bring a big overnight success and provide funds to buy the ranch at last – Lawrence was now dropping heavy hints that he had had cash offers from other quarters and was quite ready to sell elsewhere. "I'm flat broke," Brett wrote to Spud Johnson, just before Christmas. Johnson replied offering Brett his studio in Taos for the winter but that lasted only till the end of January – the studio, too, was part of Mabel's domain, and she laid down the ground-rules: "No rent only there would be a goodwill situation. Not park your car so it would be in the way. Not have the dog. Keep the place clean and attractive. Not throw your things in the little front patio, etc, etc. *You* know." Brett, of course, failed to keep them and was booted out as soon as Mabel herself returned from New York. She moved into a room at the northern edge of Taos, close to the pueblo road. The room was on top of an adobe house belonging to the Chaplines, a Taos couple, and could only be reached, Pueblo-Indian style, by an outside ladder. Her winter address for some years thereafter became "The Chapline Roof".

As usual, Brett and Mabel were quickly reconciled, or as far so as their possessiveness over Lawrence and Taos jealousies would allow, and, when Brett moved up to the ranch that spring, she bubbled: "The fairies are here! Isn't that lovely! They came when Ella Young was here. And again two nights ago. I put out milk for them. I have seen one. So lovely. In fact I've seen two."

Equally as usual, the reconciliation quickly evaporated and, more serious than fairies at the bottom of the alfalfa field, what relationship remained between Brett and Lawrence began to founder when hints and suggestions from Mabel produced the suspicion in Lawrence's mind that Brett was selling off his manuscripts to cover her permanent state of insolvency. The episode began innocently enough with a letter from Lawrence at the beginning of March:

> I worry sometimes a bit about the ranch. Do you think we ought to deposit the MSS. in some safe place? They are getting valuable now, they may come in so handy some rainy day. And so many have already been stolen from me. All the early ones are gone for good.

> Sometimes I think it would be best to sell the ranch. You said we ought to offer it to you: and I agree. But you'd never be able to pay anything to Frieda, would you now? The bank at Taos wrote last year offering $2,000 but surely it's worth more than that. We don't really want to sell it but if we can never get back, it seems useless to hang on.[16]

Lawrence wrote at the same time to Mabel, enquiring casually what she thought he ought to do about his manuscripts. Mabel replied so strongly that Lawrence later told Brewster, "Brett has had some kind of ructions with Mabel",[17] while to Frieda he reported, "Mabel has got your 'rabies' about Brett". Frieda herself had just broken her ankle in Majorca and was in a mood to urge Mabel on: "You expressed so thoroughly well how I feel. I loathe Brett"[18] and again: "Brett is so godforsakenly fixed and widdershins," she told Mabel, "a poor thing & a 'case' . . . not a Dostoievsky idiot but an English one." But Mabel had put a flea in Lawrence's ear and he wrote to Brett again, on the surface once more an innocent enquiry: "Somebody said you were trying to sell some of the MSS., but I expect you were only dangling bait, to see what sort of fish would rise."[19]

Brett had indeed sold a manuscript, to a Mrs. Hare, to cover her winter in New York. But, she claimed, it was one of six that Lawrence had given to her, in return for typing. Frieda was furious.

> Lawr says *he never gave her any* [she wrote to Mabel], but when she typed for him she may have kept some small thing or other . . . I feel she must have sold a big one to Mrs Hare, we wondered how she got enough money to stay at the Shelton so long – She *must* give them to you to put in the bank & tell us what there is, she had no right to break into that little wooden cupboard that L had made, where he kept his manuscripts – And sell the ranch for us, be an angel . . . both L & I want to have done with her . . . I don't want her rent . . . Brett is a sore spot on the face of the earth . . . Yesterday L's picture show was opened . . . I shall be relieved when the ranch is gone & you have the MSS.![20]

Lawrence meanwhile persisted in maintaining the fiction that, in the unlikely event that Brett should be able to raise the cash, Frieda would sell *her* the ranch. "If you still want the ranch, can you raise the money? You see Younghunter would pay on the nail."[21] The postscript asked her once more whether she had gathered up the manuscripts and deposited them in the Taos bank. Brett, for reasons known only to herself, stalled again, later telling Stieglitz that, in her opinion, the bank was no place for Lawrence's works but that she would herself transport them to his agents in New York at the first opportunity – "the little wooden cupboard Lawrence had made", was, contrary to Frieda's belief, entirely ramshackle and without any form of lock. A month later, the time had come for Lawrence to write at length, single-mindedly and by registered post:

> I want to write to you just about my manuscripts. You know I keep them as a sort of nest egg. One day I shall need them, so I depend on them for my reserve. For this reason I don't sell them. I've only sold one manuscript in my life and that is the complete version of *Sun* which Harry Crosby printed unexpurgated in Paris, and he gave me a hundred gold dollars. Beyond that nothing. Yet I am always hearing of MSS. for sale in dealers' catalogues – things that have been sneaked from me by various people – friends and otherwise. And it's very unpleasant.
>
> So now I want you to get straight for me the MSS. I left at the ranch. Will you please make me a list of them, and let Mabel and Mr. Read, of the Taos bank, check [cheque deleted] the list: then take a safe deposit *in my name* in the Taos bank, put the manuscripts in it, and give the key to Mr. Read to hold for me. – At the same time will you give the deeds of the ranch, all the papers connected with the property which we left in the iron trunk, to Mr. Frayne, the lawyer – I suppose he is still there – for him to see if the holding is properly recorded in Court; and then give the papers to Mr. Read to put in the safe deposit with the rest.
>
> I trust you to do this faithfully, and as soon as possible after you receive this letter.
>
> Then I want you to tell me exactly what manuscripts I gave to you: and which exactly you sold to Mrs. Hare: and how much she paid – Also if you have sold any others elsewhere. You will see that I need to keep track of my manuscripts, sold or unsold, and I need to know the price they went at, in fairness to any possible future purchaser. So please answer me quite plainly and definitely, or I shan't know what to think . . .
>
> I wonder what is happening about the sale of the ranch. I think almost certainly we shall come over this autumn to settle up – or if I don't come, then Frieda will come alone. We must get it wound up now, it's no use dragging on.
>
> I shall trust you loyally to do the things I ask you to do in this letter.[22]

So far as the ranch was concerned, Brett was trying to consolidate her position. She had taken a couple of young men as lodgers at $5 a day and, at the same time, steadfastly refused access to other prospective buyers. "I heard from Younghunter," Lawrence wrote, "he said you didn't even let him come to the ranch for a day." Meanwhile, she proposed various optimistic financial schemes to Lawrence, offering either $5,000 for a half share with Frieda or $2,000 in back rent plus $500 a year for the next ten years. Again she protested her innocence of any attempt to dispose of Lawrence's manuscripts. "Who are the people who spread this calumny?" she complained to Stieglitz.[23]

By now, she was on speaking – or at least, note-exchanging – terms with Mabel once more, although she suspected that Mabel may have been behind her troubles with Lawrence. She didn't like the Younghunters, she told Mabel in mid-July, because they were snobbish, which, coming from Brett, must have sounded odd in the extreme.[24] There is a curious footnote to the letter, which gives something of the flavour of Taos then and indeed now: a well-known Taoseno called Manby, who owned the hot springs down by the Rio Grande, and after whom the springs, a favourite excursion for Lawrence during his days on the ranch, are still named, had been found dead with his head chewed off by his two pet dogs. The probable explanation was that he had died in his bed of a heart attack while the dogs were locked in the room with him and, after several days of starvation, they had begun to devour the by now decomposing body. But that was too simple a story for Taos, the land of Geronimo and Kit Carson, of mountain men who married fat Indian wives before setting out on their winter trapping expeditions and came back in the spring well-fed and spouseless. Local rumour had it that Manby, up to his eyes in debt, had secretly exhumed a recently buried body, dressed it in his own clothes and then cut off the head which he fed to the dogs, so that it would be unrecognisable as belonging to its previous owner. Manby himself, the gossip went, had been seen alive and well and passing through Juarez en route to a new life in Mexico.

A slightly less bizarre picture of life on the northern New Mexico mesa in mid-1929 was drawn by John Marin, the painter and friend of Stieglitz, who was invited west by Mabel that summer. To Stieglitz he wrote:

> The horse still exists here, here the Indian and Mexican, they can ride. They at Taos have a movie. *Tom Mix* is here a *hero. Brett* came away down from the ranch to see *Tom Mix*, a curious combination *Brett*, of timidity and sheer grit. She goes about in a colorful garb, a

big sombrero stuck jauntily *atop* with a *dirk* stuck in her boot top and her tin trumpet in hand.

My – how these women who prowl the earth compliment the men (their not taking advantage) or is it that they despise them *not being men*. With all their air and a keeping up a jollity of spirits, there is a seeming to miss something . . . astanding here you can see six or seven thunderstorms going on at the same time.[25]

Lawrence wrote again about his manuscripts at the end of July. He was in a low mood. His health was failing rapidly and his pictures had been seized by the police from the exhibition at the Warren Gallery on grounds of obscenity. "So wearisome this nagging," he complained to Brett. By now Frieda had decided to make a direct entry into the fray, making up for the effort lost in complaining indirectly to Mabel. Frieda wrote twice to Brett on the same day:

It was a final blow to Lawr, Brett, you selling his manuscripts. I never thought much of you or your "love" for anybody, but to do that is more than I expected you to do – You have got away with it in the past with all the mean things you have done, people were so jolly glad to be rid of you – You are a poor failure of a thing & try to high-falute, one feels sorry for you, not very, because you look after yourself hard enough & that's all – all the pretence of caring for others is to serve the hon Dorothy – What did you sell of the MSS.? do you not know how *dishonest* that was without telling Lawr – criminal, you know, did nobody ever teach you honesty? Put those MSS. into the bank *at once* send a list of the MSS. in that little cupboard of L's or it will be put into the hands of Curtis Brown's lawyers, you don't want that humiliation, I hope – I don't want to sell the ranch – You can "look after it", you can't do it much harm –, But mind what you do Lawr has completely & forever done with you & it was a grief to him that you are quite such a soulless, selfish Brett – Not that you are capable of any shame, but as far as I can help it, you shall not swindle us, I will go to any length – I don't want any money from you for the ranch, but put those MSS. in the bank at once. If you haven't done so inside of 2 months that I hear, it will be nasty for you – Frieda

Pull yourself together, someday we shall come back & things will go badly for you – You needn't be as horrid as you are, there is not a person in England has a good word for you, not one – how will you end?

And again:

> Two letters to L from you, Brett, just as I had send the other – You talk of "faith" in you, how could I have faith in you, after all the things you have *said* & *done* against me, do you think I didn't mind, when I had approached you frankly & in a friendly human spirit? Is your soul as split that somewhere you serenely float in a beatic [sic] vision of a beautifully souled Brett & underneath you are so horrid and diabolical? You cost Lawr a lot of his faith & it can never be restored, I mind that most, because *I* never cared for you, I always thought you & your love a swindle, an unconscious one perhaps, but that makes it *worse* in effect – Lawr is so terribly busy nowadays and can't be bothered about the ranch & how can you say when he is dead I shall be provided for? Don't bother about me – In that we agree: *I don't want to sell the ranch*, Lawr does, because he wants to have done with you. But you can stay at the ranch and do as you like with it & I don't want any money that you may make on it, keep it to pay your debts – but tell me *what* manuscripts there are & leave Lawr alone, it only irritates him & he tries to think of you as well as he can & I want him to for his sake, *not* for yours – If you have an atom of real regard for him, leave him alone – he has his work to do – he wants to left [sic] alone – The ranch was too high for him – the sea suits him best, but if he gets stronger we'll come back – I don't worry about myself and the future & the money, we have enough for the present – And anyhow Lawr didn't want any of his manuscripts sold – But if you wanted anything you would sell your friends' bodies to get it – So there you are – I don't want the ranch at present, but I don't want to sell it, you can do what you like on it . . .
> *What* a chance you had to be L's & my friend & how you abused it![26]

And, for good measure and to save tramping up and down to the post office, she wrote to Mabel as well, now retracting her plea to Mabel to get rid of the ranch for her:

> I *don't really want to sell the ranch*, I think Lawr wants to that he can have done with the Brett . . . she doesn't say what MSS. there are nor puts them in the bank . . . she is one of God's misfits . . . she ruins ones nerves with her robotness and her sweetness is a trick.[27]

"Two terrible letters from Frieda," Brett told Stieglitz, "so crude – so vulgar – & so insane. Did you hear that 13 of Lawrence's paintings have been seized – that Dorothy Warren made 500 pounds in shillings gate money – that 12,000 people went to see them & Lawrence has made next to nothing."[28] A couple of weeks later, a further terrible letter from Frieda arrived:

> Do stop your monkey tricks about the ranch, the manuscripts & all the rest – We don't really care, you know – But please send me a list of the manuscripts, we want to know all about them, & give them all to Curtis Brown that they are together – We are not short of money, *I don't want to sell the ranch* I like to feel that we have a foothold in America = you can live at the ranch for nothing, unless you won't hand over the manuscripts and any other things we want – We can turn you out, you know, lock stock & barrel quite ignominiously – *I* don't care – And your tricks are a dreadful bore – Mortgages! why, a mortgage, you are *dotty*, Brett, no, you only *want* to be *important* & you never will be – *That's* your disease & all your would be wickedness – You don't really affect anybody – your only line to make you happy is to be humble, really humble, then you won't be a bore! I think your life of tricks must be *such* a bore!
>
> F
>
> You ask for trust, Brett, yes, indeed I trust you to play all the silly, ugly tricks in the world! But you see nobody cares anymore! And be *thankful* that you may be at the ranch on your own, you haven't really deserved such generosity from me, after all your mean games – We have enough mony [sic] & don't be a humbug looking after me! I had some, thank you![29]

To Mabel, Frieda wrote: "I'll find some way of turning her out and I'd enjoy it," but, by now reeling under the abuse from Frieda and the heavy hints from Lawrence, Brett had made a list of the manuscripts she had found in the cupboard at the ranch, and it was already on its way. It confirmed Lawrence's fears:

> It is as I felt – there must be some missing. There were two complete MSS. of *The Plumed Serpent*, I think in four complete books. These I remember in the little cupboard – and they are not on the list. They are of course much the most valuable MS. I left, & worth the whole ranch itself. Don't you remember them too? And I have always said: I hope those *Plumed Serpent* MSS. are safe! I suppose someone just stole them. Or, more probably, stole the final & complete MS. But if it is gone, we can always put the police on it if it appears for sale.
>
> That MS. of *Sea & Sardinia* in New York can only be a typescript or a forgery, as I destroyed the original with my own hands.
>
> I am not short of money, Lady C. made me over $1000 last year – so there is not that worry. And don't imagine that I believe for

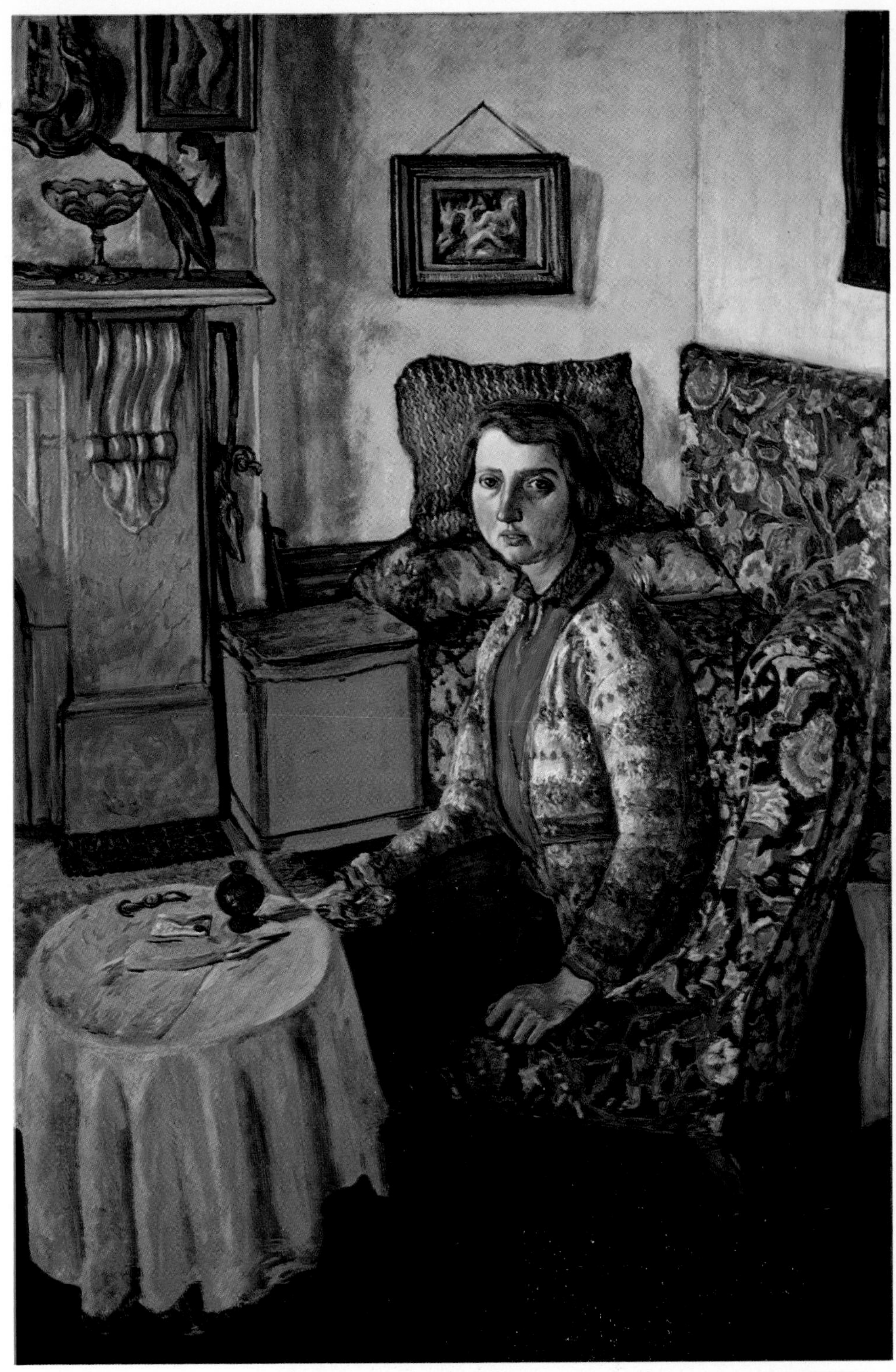

The Hon Dorothy Brett by Alvaro Guevara, 1920–21

War Widows, Brett, 1916.

Aldous Huxley at Garsington, Brett, 1919.

The Road to Mitla: Mexican landscape near Oaxaca, Brett, 1924–25.

'Oh, Brett, do look at the mountain. It has great bare toes, where it joins the desert . . . you don't look at things; you have no eyes': D. H. Lawrence.

The Man Who Died, double portrait of D. H. Lawrence, Brett, 1963, a reworking of the Capri crucifixion of 1926. The original was partially destroyed by Brett.

Lawrence's Three Fates (Mabel Luhan, Frieda Lawrence and Brett), Brett, 1958.

The Lawrence cabin, September 1970.

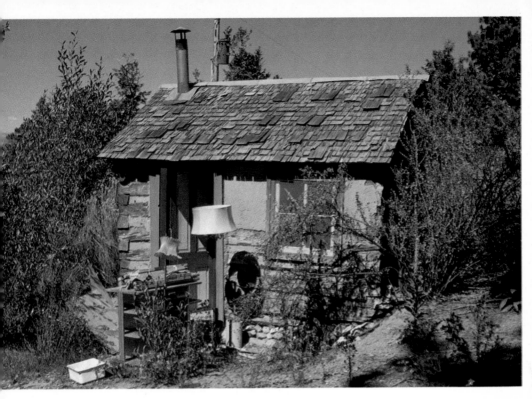

Brett's cabin, September 1970, still much as it was in 1924.

'Coming out of the canyon is an unforgettable experience with all the deep mountains sitting mysteriously around and so much sky': D. H. Lawrence.

Brett in her El Prado studio, 1956: Lawrence above the fireplace, a WWII 'bomber' painting high on the left and a second, just visible on the right.

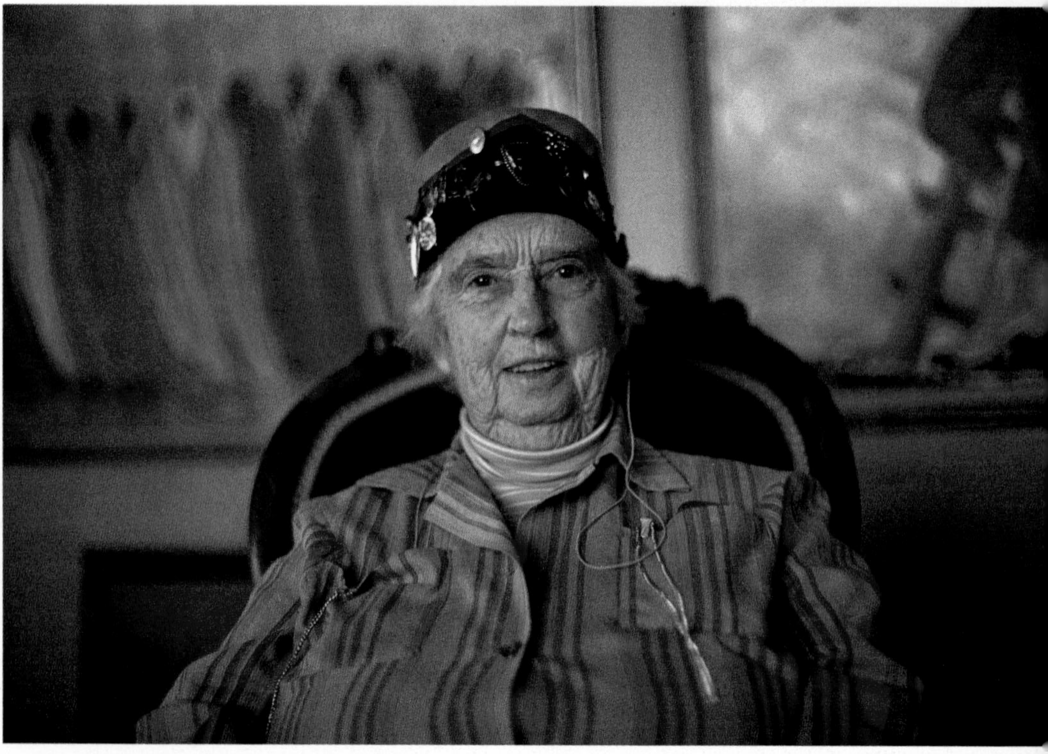

Brett in September 1970, aged 86.

Sundown Dance: Taos Pueblo, Brett, 1967–68.

Indian Corn Dance, Brett, undated.

a moment in lurid suggestions of my manuscripts sold from the ranch, etc, etc. I'm afraid, since it hasn't showed up on your list, that the real & complete MS. of *Plumed Serpent* has been stolen – and a beautiful MS. But if so, then I'm sure some American "admirer" has sneaked it. But perhaps it will turn up . . . meanwhile I hope you'll live peacefully & pleasantly, in Taos & the ranch.[30]

Quite clearly, Lawrence *did* believe the lurid suggestions. Within three days he wrote again, at length, accusing Brett of hiding something from him and claiming that, if she had stolen some manuscripts, he was not one to break his heart but had she not spoken so much of loyalty?

I have been looking down your list again, and am amazed to see that nearly all the hand-written manuscripts must have disappeared. All those you give as typewritten manuscripts, *Love*, *Taos*, *Life* – the Dance essays – and all the essays from the Porcupine book – all these should be there in handwritten manuscript, in various books. Why, I can *see* some of the books still, in that cupboard – the grey ones with perforated sheets, the black ones – I can see them there. Then the whole MS. of *David*. Then stories, *The Last Laugh*, *Jimmy and the Desperate Woman* – these were all left in that cupboard in handwritten manuscript. Then the three or four complete books of *The Plumed Serpent*. Why, Brett, wherever are they all? They can't all have been stolen, without you ever noticing. It means that at least half of the whole cupboard-ful is gone – & surely that couldn't happen without your seeing. No, there is something wrong somewhere – and I wish you'd tell me . . . If you think the MSS. you typed should all be yours – surely, it's going a bit far. Those you've got must be worth towards a thousand dollars, and did you do so much typing?

I wish all this business was settled up. I feel that things aren't straight – and I hate to feel it . . . somehow I feel depressed about it all.[31]

A week later, a brief postcard arrived from Lawrence, on his way, he said, to the South of France and written in haste. "Had a list from London of MSS. in the New York office of CB – & find that several things are there, which I thought were still at the ranch – so glad – will write fully."[32] When he did, there was, after months of accusations and recrimination, only the merest hint of an apology.

You will have had my letters and the one where I suddenly got a slump, feeling that there was a great loss of MSS. Fortunately came that list from Curtis Brown, showing most of those which I remem-

> bered at the ranch, are now in New York. I was very relieved. It's not so much the loss as the sense of being robbed, which one minds. That little cupboard was utterly unsafe. And even when I was at the ranch myself, my books were stolen from the shelves. – Of course I knew quite well you would not sell my MSS., in spite of what anybody said. But your visitors are another matter: same as anybody's visitors. – And the MSS. I gave you, of course you do as you like with, only I wish you'd tell me. – By the way, is my copy of *The Rainbow* still there? – bound in blue, the first edition . . .[33]

One could have expected Brett to have now reacted with the I-told-you-so that would have been so in character. She had every ground to. The "stolen manuscripts" story remained current in Taos gossip and has not entirely disappeared from biographies of Lawrence to this day. Instead Brett, still idolising Lawrence, was convinced that Lawrence's final conversion was due to blind faith and a mystic bond between them that no one else could match or understand, rather than the simple facts. She wrote to Stieglitz telling him that when she received Lawrence's brief and ungracious postcard, she felt "that innermost light that lies in that quiet pool between us flash into a clear flame."[34]

A month later, Brett was contemplating the possibility of producing "that innermost light" by an entirely different and very New Mexican means. A Professor Prinzhoene was staying with Mabel and had been experimenting with peiote, a drug used by some of the Pueblo Indians in connection with religious ceremonies. It "intensifies sight and hearing," Brett told Stieglitz. "I am going to take it – the first chance I get."[35]

The same autumn Brett heard for the first time in years from Murry whose marriage was foundering on the chronic illness of his wife Violet. The effort of looking after her, he said, had become so great that he had been on the point of telegraphing Brett and asking her to return to England and him but he had thought better of it. He went on to describe a trip to Le Touquet in August, paid for by a rich friend, during which he had spent the night with a prostitute, "a simple soul . . . we parted good friends". Were the prostitute in London, he said, he would visit her often but if Brett were to return and Violet still be ill, Brett would become his mistress. Not, one imagines, an invitation entirely likely to flatter and seduce even Brett at her most doting. For good measure Murry's postscript asked Brett to write back but not to his home address.

Before Christmas, Brett and Mabel were in New York once more, Brett to arrange another exhibition – a little more successfully this time for, by New Year, her paintings were beginning to sell – and Mabel to see her psychiatrist. "The turtle doves are in New York," Frieda commented, "being psyched – Gurdjeffing" – this last referring to the fact that Katherine Mansfield's last mentor was in town for the winter season and was being lionised. Brett did not now think much of the master. "A Bald-headed Bandit," she called him. "Black magic – something has turned his powers to evil." In Europe, Lawrence was fast declining. "I hardly walk a stride," he wrote[36] and assured Brett that he was now quite seriously making plans to return to New Mexico in March or April. "I believe we must all fit together and make a life. I have always said Frieda's hate was at least half illusory . . . I don't believe there'd be any squabbling with a bit of patience."[37] Brett greeted the news enthusiastically. "If Lorenzo comes, I must be clear in myself and then I can handle anything that happens," she wrote to Mabel,[38] and, Gurdjeffing despite herself, she consulted what she called the Chinese sticks – presumably the I-Ching: "Maintain a firm correctness" they told her, "and there will be no error – there will be good fortune".[39]

But neither winter nor spring brought the promised good fortune, spiritual or otherwise. Brett's father, Esher, died at the end of January and Lawrence, reading the news in the paper, wrote immediately, a touch of bitterness at his own physical suffering over-riding the sympathy he may have wished to express: "I saw your father died – apparently it was easy for him – and 78. I hope he has left you better off – if not, never mind."[40]

Esher hadn't. Brett's mother wrote the same day to tell her there was nothing in the will for Brett but, after all, "Aunt Lou's £500 left you well provided for".[41] Sympathy came instead from a surprising quarter:

> Your letter gave me real pleasure – We saw your father's death in the paper . . . he looks so like *Weekley* (my husband) [Frieda Lawrence's first husband] . . . of course neither of us care a damn about what the *social* world has to give – success and all that bunk – But this is really to tell you that Lorenzo is *very*, very ill – I am almost despairing – Damn this sanatorium . . . He suffers much – I feel that the few who are fond of him should be with him to buck him up – *now!* Could you come over Do you remember how we got him better at the Hawks? And then at the ranch? He must get better again.[42]

In later years, Brett recalled Frieda's letter as a cable but no cable ever existed – simply the letter that, travelling by sea and directed initially to Taos, did not reach Brett in New York until March 4th. It was too late. Lawrence had died two days earlier in Vence. Brett had, in fact, written to Mabel, on March 3rd, when, unknown to her, Lawrence was already dead, trying to persuade herself that newspaper reports of Lawrence's terminal illness were "just an exaggeration = some reporter with a write up".[43] Nevertheless, she warned Mabél that she had no intention of returning to Taos for the time being and must remain in New York, "near the ships", in order that she could sail at a moment's notice should Frieda need help in bringing Lawrence back to New Mexico. "Has he paid with his life for our squabbles?" she added. Before the letter was posted, Brett knew. "Lawrence is dead," a scrawled post-script reads, "what does anything matter now." The next day she wrote to Kot, breaking the silence of a decade: "Long solitary summers have matured me . . . The death of my father was as it should be. A quick end at a good age. But the death of Lawrence is a far reaching disaster . . ."[44] and later sent a cable to Frieda in Vence: "Deepest sympathy. Life is conditioned. We cannot alter it."[45] Her Daily Reminder for 1930, a record of day-to-day expenditure in New York, shows: "SUNDAY MARCH 2ND: Lawrence died. It does not matter to him now but it will matter to me forever," and "WED. MARCH 5TH: Brett, will you never learn to accept."

1930 was a year for bereavement. Towards the end of it, on December 2nd, Brett's dog Reggie, one of a succession of mongrels she named after one or other of her father's Christian names, died too.

11

1930–1935: The Tower Beyond Tragedy

Brett was forty-seven years old when Lawrence died, exactly half way through her life. Already New Mexico had fostered in her a forthrightness and self-confidence she had so chronically lacked in England and her later role as community elder and holy terror, village eccentric and tourist attraction, began to take shape. The characteristics that enabled her to move into the second half of her life with a vigour that she retained to the end, were her genuinely continuing hard graft as a painter and her lively and often bizarre sense of humour and the ridiculous that enabled her to engage actively in local scandal, backbiting and slanging matches with the enthusiasm of a born meddler in other people's affairs, an enthusiasm for the large part now unencumbered by any genuine emotional or physical involvement of her own. Brett had known Lawrence closely for only three years and it had been four years since she had last seen him. She was quite unashamed of capitalising for the rest of her life upon this brief acquaintance and the niche it gave her in literary history but, despite that, her stature in the American south-west – as a painter rather than a figurehead – was her own achievement.

The day she heard of Lawrence's death, Brett was about to leave on a short visit to Philadelphia and the art foundation of the self-willed collector and connoisseur, Alfred Barnes. They had already exchanged missives or perhaps missiles. Barnes wrote:

> Your letter is sheer vituperation and boasting. Only extreme courage or ignorance of my reputation as an assassin in that line could have made you write that way . . . your epithet "art school" – I invited you to join these cripples because many have recovered and are doing their own living and painting. If we are an art school then you are a fat scrub woman . . . You say you want to see our collection. All right, come over, even if your letters do indicate that you lack the intelligence to appreciate them.[1]

Brett's visit sufficiently mollified Barnes for him to offer her a scholarship in Philadelphia but Brett, uncertain as to Frieda's intentions with regard to the ranch, was anxious to return to Taos. Borrowing $100 from Mabel, she was back in New Mexico by the beginning of April. For Barnes, Brett had grander financial arrangements in mind than the loan of a rail fare. She wrote to Mabel:

> . . . my hat I would like to paint a picture to hang in that collection = in memory of Lorenzo . . . I am thinking of seeing if Barnes would perhaps loan me a large sum of money – and hold in trust for it Lorenzo's letters – a fair bargain . . . I want so passionately now to buy the ranch . . . Maybe he would buy the little head of Lorenzo and the combined picture of the ranch – say for 10,000 dollars or 20,000 because after all they are unique – almost the only portrait of Lorenzo and the only one of his life at the ranch in existence = curse this money problem – only my $2,000 a year has prevented its killing me.[2]

Unfortunately, in Taos, a letter from Frieda was waiting that seems finally to have removed any lingering hope Brett may have harboured that she might purchase the ranch. Frieda was not only planning to return herself, accompanied by her daughter Barby, but wanted to bring Lawrence, or at least his remains, with her.

> . . . what would console me would be to build him a little temple there ourselves – I know the place at the Ranch, high up beyond the spring . . . Don't tell about the temple please to anybody – only Mabel – send her this letter . . . I want to take Lawrence to the Ranch & build him a place there . . . where we looked towards Colorado.[3]

Mabel was horrified:

> Can you *picture* the *kind* of people, most hated of *all* by Lorenzo – who make picnics at Temple sites? Curiosity-impelled trippers! Good Lord! . . . I forsee you and Frieda living together in mutual uncongeniality, taking care of a Temple on the ranch and – Oh *Lord!*[4]

If the idea of a temple wasn't enough, whether by coincidence or cussedness, the spot where they had "looked towards Colorado" was precisely the spot that Brett – "I don't want to complicate life for Frieda and her daughter" – having given up the idea of owning the whole ranch, had marked down for building a new cabin for herself. It took a great deal of persuasion on the part of Mabel, Tony Luhan, the Indians working at the ranch, old Uncle Spud Johnson and all, to prevent her from going ahead and driving in her lodge pole. Mabel wrote, "Tony says you mustn't build anything on Frieda's land without permission. Legally it will be hers. Nuff said!"

With unusual flexibility, Brett rapidly pitched her aim a little lower down the hillside. She arranged with the Hawks to dismantle an existing log cabin in their orchard, to which she'd from time to time been banished by Frieda, and move it to a spot beneath a pine tree a little way up the old trail that led circuitously to Frieda's property and down which Lawrence used to ride for the milk and mail. "Only five minutes from the ranch by a new trail I am making," Brett wrote to Mabel down in Taos, appending a drawing of the cabin, which she was extending with huge windows inserted in each wall and enlarging with an upper-storey studio built almost entirely of glass. The Tower Beyond Tragedy, she called it, taking a line from a verse by Robinson Jeffers that, hammered out on tin, is affixed to the door to this day. The reconstruction was completed by the end of June and the Tower Beyond Tragedy became Brett's home for more than a decade.

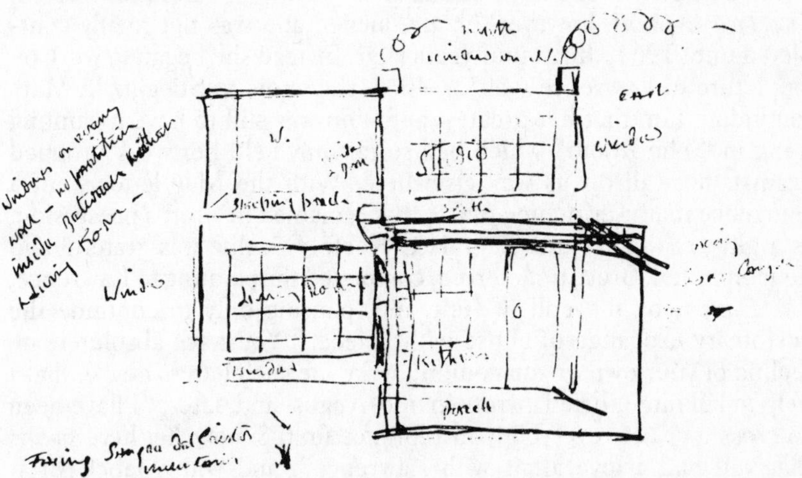

Frieda meantime was bombarding Brett and Taos with frantic cables in an attempt to uncover a valid will to Lawrence's estate. "The town is being ransacked for it," Brett told Stieglitz in April and, later, "Another cable from Frieda: WILL IMPORTANT! LOOK! – I've a hunch Lorenzo never made it."[5] The will was never found and it was two years before Frieda's claim reached a settlement in the courts. The clinching evidence was offered by Murry who testified that he and Lawrence had witnessed each other's wills back in 1914, Murry's in favour of Katherine Mansfield, Lawrence's in favour of Frieda. The relationship between Murry and Frieda had been following a switchback course in the thirty months between Lawrence's death and Murry's court appearance. June 1930 found Murry hurrying to Vence to Lawrence's graveside and taking Frieda as mistress once more. But a year later, when Murry published his Lawrence memoir, *Son of Man*, Frieda set fire to her presentation copy and posted the ashes back to the author.

Murry's book was only the first of the rash of Lawrence memoirs and biographies that were being penned by his contemporaries and pursued by publishers with the corpse hardly cold in the grave. Brett was approached within a month of Lawrence's death and had, in the search for Lawrence's will, re-discovered diaries she had written in Mexico and during her early American years. "I found my diaries," she wrote to Stieglitz, "I have a tin box of letters, I have snapshots of the ranch & Old Mexico & to my horror that publisher Lippincott is coming."[6]

It was October before Brett began work on *Lawrence and Brett* for, in her new studio, atop the Tower Beyond Tragedy, she started painting again. The picture she was working on at the time of Lawrence's death, *The Two Koshani*, however, lay untouched and was not finally completed until 1964, thirty-four years later. Instead she began to work on "a picture to Lawrence – 60″ × 40″", she wrote to Stieglitz in May[7] reminding him that her greatest ambition was still to have a painting hung in "The Room" which had so far only held her work propped against the wall on its way elsewhere. With the May letter went a Lawrence manuscript, one of five that remained in Brett's possession, as a gift to Stieglitz and Georgia O'Keefe. Stieglitz was grateful and noncommittal. Brett, undeterred, completed the painting to Lawrence, *The Dancer*, by the end of June and, pausing only to continue the customary exchange of abuse with Frieda ("You have absolutely no feeling of your own or you couldn't write me such letters now & that I help to kill him", Frieda wrote in mid-August and, later, "I have been so cross, because everybody in Florence first, & now *Kot* here *swears* that you had a love affair with Lawrence") and with Mabel (Brett claimed that she had given all her decent clothes to the Indians and so had been forced to attend dinner with Mabel dressed in cowboy pants, at which Mabel had Tony check round the pueblo to find out exactly what clothes of Brett's his relatives were wearing and then responded, "I did hate you putting it off on the Indians that you can't be clean"), pressed on, painting "better than ever", she claimed. In the late autumn as winter returned to the Sangre de Cristos, she hit the post-Lawrentian blues once more and recalled to Stieglitz that "I spent one whole summer sitting with a loaded revolver in my lap, wondering whether to go or to stay and finally decided to give myself another chance."[8] By December she was in New York for the winter again, having sent eleven paintings ahead of her, ten of her own, the eleventh, the joint painting of life at the ranch, by herself and Lawrence.

Mindful now of mortality, Brett drew up her first will that winter in New York on the last unleaping day of February 1931, distributing her possessions with great care and discrimination and accompanying the intended bequests with recommendations as to their utilisation. Her horses were to go to William Hawk; to Rachel, her saddle, silver bridle and painting materials "it being my wish that she give such painting material to any artist she may consider in need of the same". To her sister Syv's daughters, Brett bequeathed her Indian blankets, one each, Leonora to get her silver belt, Elizabeth her bead-work gloves and Valerie her Indian bead belt. Spud Johnson was to receive her Stieglitz photographs and, in the other direction, Stieglitz and Georgia O'Keefe the diaries, letters and manuscripts, both Lawrence's and her own. Her paintings were to go to Barbara Cottam, a niece of the Hawks, "to be sold to pay for her education" and her Mexican horn-handled knife and revolver to the Hawks' son, Walton. Two years later, Brett added a codicil: "If I die I want Mrs. L. L. Chapline to have my pup Baliol. Eithne Golden [daughter of a neighbour], to have my typewriter. Rachel Hawk to have the Royalties from my book *Lawrence and Brett*, the American, the English and any foreign Royalties."[9]

Brett returned from New York in the spring without having found a single "furcoat", her current term for a wealthy buyer, to discover that Frieda was at last returning to New Mexico and bringing with her the "Capitano", Angelo Ravagli. It only then penetrated the egocentricity of Brett and Mabel that what had kept Frieda away since Lawrence's death was not fear of the terrible two in Taos but the fact that Angie was "chained to the garrison".[10] As Frieda had still not realised her claim to Lawrence's estate, Brett could not see how she would be able to maintain her Angelino. "With the gold!" she wrote to Stieglitz, after spending three weeks scrubbing the floors at the ranch in preparation for Frieda's return. "Maybe if their [sic] is really enough they are digging now but usually here the gold found is hardly enough to fill a teaspoon." When Brett saw Angelino with Frieda, she could hardly believe it. Mabel wrote to Una Jeffers, the wife of the poet: "Brett's eyes are rolling and she is knocked speechless! She says she just realises she has made the great mistake all her life of being romantic."[11] What Brett meant, of course, was that, in her eyes, the liaison of Frieda and the Capitano provided yet more evidence that it was only Frieda's connivings that had hindered the course of real love and kept Brett and

Lawrence from their true romantic destinies. She wrote to Stieglitz at the beginning of June:

> The lifelong struggle to keep Frieda from what he [Lawrence] called "pulling up her skirts at every man" ends in a lusty Roman and I feel chilled to the bone . . . I feel I am more truly his widow than Frieda. That one week of intense living, the nights of tragedy, have given him the only widow he is likely to have . . . I will make mine [her memoir] slowly, not a chatty tale of squabbles, but just myself and Lawrence . . . to see that man (quite a nice man, too) in Lorenzo's blue shirt, his white trousers, that won't button on him, gives me a pain. The sacred mountain is hurt, the big tree is hurt, the Indians are outraged as he treats them like soldiers and Trinidad saw Lorenzo standing by the fence . . . and into this apparently Murry is coming, if her Italian leaves her . . . ye gods what a climax . . . Lawrence could not, I know, sexually satisfy a woman like Frieda, he had not the physical strength, this lusty Italian keeps her nerves quiet, keeps her satisfied but Lawrence couldn't fulfil his excitement . . . and whenever she forced him to it, he beat her up afterwards.[12]

There were few dull moments up the mountain. A month later Brett wrote to Una Jeffers:

> An awful boy of eighteen forced himself on Frieda as a guest and thought he was a reincarnation of Lawrence. He and the Capitano hated each other, the boy resented Frieda's affair with the Italian and his manner of showing it was strange, one day the Capitano put on white flannel trousers and a silk shirt, so the boy immediately took off all his clothes and came to lunch without even a fig leaf!! and kept doing this at intervals . . . we are all of us puffing over our various memoirs.[13]

At that point, Brett was thinking of calling *her* memoir "D. H. Lawrence and One Friend". "I rather wanted to call it Lui et Elle – which is what he used to write when we played Bezique but Frieda was suddenly jealous," she wrote to Stieglitz.[14]

Throughout that winter and the rest of 1932, Brett remained in Taos "puffing" over the book. She wrote to Una Jeffers:

> I have done nothing all summer but whack this damn machine. Ella [Ella Young, an Irish visitor from California whom Brett had installed first in a wigwam, then in a minute cabin in a small clearing a little way up the mountain from the Tower Beyond Tragedy]

> listened patiently, corrected my awful grammer and encouraged me . . . my dumb diaries helped . . . Knopf are already after me . . . I think of Frieda singing all night long to Lawrence as he lay dead, that almost redeemed her crimes to him while he was alive.[15]

When Frieda wrote asking to see the manuscript, Brett procrastinated. "Why did you get the wind up when I just asked?" Frieda complained, adding, in response to Brett's claim that the spirit of the dead Lawrence was writing the book for her, "My dear, we all write our own books." When, at last, Brett reluctantly allowed Frieda a sight of the manuscript, she suggested replacing various passages with asterisks. "Frieda at work through the stars" was how Brett described the idea.[16] But Brett had already acted as her own censor. "There is no word of lovemaking," she told Stieglitz, "no sign of any act, nothing but the emotion, the pictures of him in Italy, the same feeling intensified by the Italian scene".[17] Knopf's pursuit failed for, by December, 1932, Lippincott had confirmed their deathbed interest with a contract and promised the book would head the forthcoming spring list.

Lawrence and Brett: A Friendship appeared the following April. "My book looks very nice but they have made a bad mistake with the dedication – it should read simply – 'To the Potential Lover'," Brett wrote from Santa Fe* to Una Jeffers,[18] adding later that the French rights had been sold and that Secker had given her $50 down for the English edition. Mabel, also writing to Una Jeffers, who for a time, despite her location in California, must have acted as a clearing house for Taos gossip, picked up on the incorrect dedication: "Very gay! 'Written for the Potential Lover!' My dear! [It's all] one long and consistent creation – all pure fantasy. But quite convincing."[19] A little later, Mabel added Frieda's reaction:

> Frieda says Brett's book is pathetic and that she is deaf in her soul . . . Brett didn't hear right and put a spider and a curate (instead of a spinster). She says Brett used to come in regular as a clock every day at 3 o'clock just in Frieda's one hour of the day when she tried to rest on her bed and so of course she always saw her lying in the bed smoking cigarettes![20]

* Brett was passing through Santa Fe on her way back from a trip with Mabel to the Jeffers in Carmel, California, and stopped off to do more early feminist shopping. In the same letter she told Una Jeffers: "I have bought a new pair of pants!! A new pair of cowboy boots!! The flag of liberty is waving strongly . . . Ramakrishna's mother said to him 'Put not the written word between yourself and life' – I say 'Put not the silk stocking between yourself and life.'"

The book was not, at the time, in the welter of Lawrence biographies, well received.

> About my book, I have felt a bit depressed, review after review, if one calls the cheap kind of newspaper criticisms that have been coming in reviews, all saying the same thing, that it is sentimental slush, some have gone so far as to say it is unreadable and the worst book of the month.[21]

But the book did not do too badly. By the end of 1933, sales in America had failed by only $80 to reach the $500 advance paid by Lippincott and a further $159 arrived from the English edition. Nevertheless Brett complained: "Books are not selling at all." Nor apparently, in those depression years, were pictures. In the spring the University of Nebraska had asked how *little* Brett would take for her painting of an Indian Madonna and then decided they could not afford the picture at all. Stieglitz, to whom Brett wrote of this, provided little sympathy, saying simply that her pictures were not yet right for showing.

One of Mabel's guests in Taos in the summer of 1932, when Brett was pounding the typewriter keys up the mountain, had been the conductor Leopold Stokowski. Brett, true to form, developed an enormous crush and, when Stokowski wrote her "two very lovely letters", she decided to follow the "very lovely man" to New York and Philadelphia, at the earliest opportunity, the ostensible reason being to hear him conduct. Soon after Stokowski's departure, she wrote to Stieglitz of "the best painting I have done since the little one Stokowski has = the one I hid in his baggage when he left"[22] and then, "I do not know whether my budding friendship with Stokowski will survive or fade. My Western roughness is hard for so civilised a man = I feel his politeness, his perfect manners, revolting at my western slanginess."[23]

In the excitement of publishing *Lawrence and Brett*, the pilgrimage of discovery had to be postponed until the end of 1933. Borrowing a wardrobe in Taos*, Brett again travelled east, this time in pursuit of the perfect portrait whose subject was to be – naturally – Stokowski. "New York is a puzzle to me," she wrote to Mabel, "starvation and bigger and better cars seem to go hand in hand . . . the faces frighten me."[25] Brett described her solution to both her own and the country's economic problems in a letter a few days later to Eithne Golden, the young girl in Taos to whom she had bequeathed her typewriter:

* "She pulled the clothes on over her cowboy pants to see what she looked like and, when the tradesmen wanted her to pay up her bills before leaving, she told them 'Don't be tiresome.'"[24]

> Last night I dined with Evangeline Stokowski . . . very very rich . . . I came away with a FUR COAT . . . A DARK BLUE LINEN FROCK . . . a SCARLET SILK HEAD HANDKERCHIEF . . . a PAIR OF MARVELLOUS PAJAMAS . . . and feel THERE IS YET MORE TO COME . . . I intend to write to Roosevelt to suggest the unemployed should build COMFORT STATIONS at every tenth street as this town is devoid of any means of TOI-ing [toileting] . . . it is perfectly harassing.[26]

The whole of December and most of January, Brett spent either listening to Stokowski's concerts on the radio in New York, or travelling to Philadelphia where she spent mornings and afternoons watching her new hero in rehearsal and matinée through a part-open door at the back of the concert platform, sketching Stokowski and filling a notebook with a mixture of intimate diary, gushing love letters to the maestro, and notes for her paintings.

> I've got tracings of his hands by putting them flat on paper and drawing round them . . . the most difficult thing of all is his NOSE. I've had a God-Almighty struggle with that. It is the most difficult of all combinations, a very big nose and a very delicate nose too.

The evenings she dedicated to attending the concerts "in the Royal Box", she and Stokowski "bowing to each other like Queen Victoria" before each performance.[27] "After sitting for a solid month, listening in to the concerts and watching Stokowski . . . the portrait suddenly manifested itself . . . of course I have yet to bring it about on canvas."[28] By the time the concert series ended, Brett had decided that a single portrait would not suffice. There would be a whole symphony of likenesses.

> Stokowski goes for a five week trip while I sit and ponder his nose = damn his nose . . . I have had the most astounding time = My privileges, my being permitted to sit back-stage, has annoyed Philadelphia considerably = apparently all Stokowski's admirers have begged for years to be given this privilege = and he has flatly refused = then behold = the audience catch glimpses of me = they meet me at parties = it leaks out through the gossiping orchestra men that I am sitting smugly in the Holy of Holies = presumably painting a portrait that nobody sees (it isn't there to see) . . . finally a badgered man tries desperately to find me a better corner to hide me in = with the result the cellos get such a draught down their necks from the slit I peep through that they all strike = so I threaten to sit at the harp and play it = upon which Stokowski throws up the sponge and says sit

> where you like but if you open a squeaky door while the music is going on, The Lord help you . . . Lord, what an experience = I feel I belong to the orchestra = like the goat of the regiment I am its MASCOT = but what of the portraits? Well, I have some sort of a face to go on with = but whether it's his face I don't know = now I have five weeks to play about in . . . Also I have found what I have been seeking = the AIR BRUSH = no, I'm not dropping my aitches = it's a marvellous thing = but in deep disrepute, chiefly because it is used mainly for Commercial Art and is considered too perfect for what people call easel pictures (what a horrid description of painting) no = "easel pictures must not be too perfect, easel pictures must have the charm of imperfection" = the doddering donkeys.[29]

Brett worked on the series of paintings throughout the summer of 1934 in Taos and, by December, *The Stokowski Symphony* of a dozen portraits was ready for exhibition at the Boyer Galleries in Philadelphia, along with a portrait of Lawrence and a couple of paintings of Indian ceremonies. The *Philadelphia Record* wrote,[30] in a review matched only by Brett's diary of her Stokowski watching:

> . . . an intense interpretation of musical moments that vibrate about the person and from the fingertips of a great conductor . . . from the "Invocation", a recognizable impression of Stokowski as he first stands before his orchestra, to "Liebestod", the abstract conception of that same figure, the series of studies, wavering between the abstract and the real, exerts a mysterious, mystical power over the reactions of its audience, giving in terms of paint what Stokowski himself gives in terms of music. Even in the most abstract of the compositions one feels the Stokowski presence. "Liebestod" rises from black calyx to white lily form, with white hand shapes falling at each side as the movement of the central form shoots upward. The compositions vibrate with a quiet intensity that marks the mystical and creative bond existing between individuals emotionally akin.*

* The Stokowski paintings were exhibited as a set again ten years later in the Santa Fe Museum in 1944. Wrote *Time* magazine, less fulsomely:

> Most of the eleven Brett Stokowskis are luminous, elongated impressions in which Conductor Stokowski seems to be swooning under water. In "Leopold Stokowski Conducting Parsifal" there is only a Stokowski like manifestation, a sickle moon, blank planes of periwinkle blue and a cometlike effulgence . . . crop-haired Brett confesses complete indifference to criticism of her work for which she asks prices up to $10,000.[31]

Stieglitz, who, to Brett's disappointment, failed to make the journey to Philadelphia to view the exhibition, was more phlegmatic and as non-committal as ever. "I didn't write about your paintings as I never say anything from photographs . . . the photographs interested me but they were in the main pretty much what I imagined they might look like."[32] When the exhibition closed, a month later, Brett had sold only two paintings and "traded" one. Mabel suggested moving the Symphony on to New York: "Won't Stieglitz exhibit them? I bet if he won't, there is some connexion with Georgia for she won't let him show another woman's pictures I feel." Brett wrote to Stieglitz:

> Financially I am a wreck. Boyer [the gallery owner] antagonises people by holding a pistol at their heads – he will not show [the paintings] unless they intend to buy . . . I don't quite know what is going to happen – perhaps I will struggle to New York with them . . . but you know that when it comes to New York my dream is to be found worthy of the Room . . . I await that moment.[33]

Stieglitz knew Boyer, he said, and knew Brett's dream: "*His* [Boyer's] struggle for existence comes first with him. I really wonder what you will do with your paintings. I know your wish, your hope about the Place [i.e., "The Room"] and your work."[34] However, as Mabel had guessed, he had no wish to fulfil Brett's dream. Boyer only released the paintings when "the bought ones" were paid for – he was morally, Brett complained, so deficient as to be frightening. The paintings went back to Taos where Brett worked on them occasionally until the following October (1935) when she tried again to interest Stieglitz. The whole Symphony was crated and once more despatched to Stieglitz who, objecting to the use of the airbrush, left them unexhibited in their crate until the spring of 1936 when "the Sarcophagus . . . so huge I thought Stokowski himself was in it",[35] was returned to Brett in Taos.

During Brett's stay in Philadelphia, Murry turned up on a lecture tour. He had written to her the previous summer, a week after his forty-fifth birthday. Murry was preparing his autobiography and had been re-reading Brett's diary of their affair, the diary she had sent him when he was editing Katherine Mansfield's letters. Very few people, he said, could understand that a man could love two women at the same time. Not only that – some men needed a second woman to gain the strength to love the first properly.[36] One imagines that rather more people than Murry expected to understand that line had, at least, encountered it on life's journey through seduction. The diaries, in which Murry had blacked out heavily all references to himself, were returned to Brett by Murry's brother, Richard, only after Murry's death. When Brett and Murry met in Philadelphia that winter of 1935, "after ten years, he thought I was *older* – I am . . ."

The previous year, relations between Frieda, Mabel and Brett had so improved that, by August 1934, Frieda was able to write to Una Jeffers, "Isn't it strange how Mabel and Brett and I are at peace with each other with a genuine bond between us nowadays." The fragile peace began to shatter when Frieda determined to press on with her plan of bringing Lawrence back to New Mexico and building him a temple on the hillside behind the ranch. By the end of 1934, it was settled that Angie Ravagli would go to France to arrange the export of Lawrence's remains. Originally, Frieda planned to travel with him. "I bet Angie intends to charge admission," Mabel wrote to Una Jeffers, "however, Brett and I think he will not come back but will leave her there with the coffin!"[37] In the event, Angie travelled alone and, on March 13th, 1935, supervised the exhumation and cremation in Vence of Lawrence's remains. It took a further fortnight before Ravagli managed to obtain the U.S. Consular documents that deal with the transportation of the ashes of dead writers. He faced further difficulties with Customs and Immigration in New York but an unusually helpful Stieglitz had been alerted by Brett.

> . . . it was I who accompanied Angelo to the Custom House. It is quite an amazing story how we chased about the city up and down owing to the mistakes of officials and the endless red tape. So you can see even I finally met Lawrence. His ashes were at the door of 509 [The Room]. Should I introduce him to the Place or not? I left them go their natural way. Some day I'll tell you the story. Nothing quite like it has ever happened. Angelo really has no idea of what did happen.[38]

What Stieglitz was hinting at in New York has never been revealed but, by the 1970s, the saga of Lawrence's ashes in New Mexico had been embroidered to epic and farcical proportions. Lawrence, I was solemnly assured by Taosenos, had been first abandoned by Angie Ravagli on the station platform at Lamy, the railhead for Santa Fe. Then Lawrence's writer friend Wytter Bynner had inadvertently emptied the urn over a Mexican dinner in the La Fonda Hotel in Santa Fe and quietly refilled it from the fireplace. Next Mabel, unsuspecting, had secretly cast those ashes to the winds on the Indian reservation behind her house, replacing them with ashes from her own fireplace, and finally Brett, unaware of the two previous substitutions, had scattered those ashes at the ranch and refilled the urn once more, this time with ashes from her stove. Thus Taos creativity, although one does wonder quite why Brett specifically decreed that her own ashes should be scattered on the so-called Red Rocks that lie between the Tower Beyond Tragedy and the Lawrence ranch. Closer to the time, Brett's account to Stieglitz was probably near the truth but only a little less farcical:

> Did I tell you of the arrival of the Ashes . . . Frieda meeting Angelino in Santa Fe – a tea party with the ashes on the table and Frieda pointing giggling to them and saying "Here is Lawrence" and how even hard-boiled Santa Fe was shocked. Most of the tea party was a bit drunk too. And then the drive up with the ashes resting on Mrs. Fechen's feet and Angelino leaning over from the front seat and saying "This is Lawrence" to scandalised friends. And their finally forgetting them for a whole week at Mrs. Fechen's house – she being Russian – emotional – made a little altar for them under an Icon and put candles round them and she says a great peace came from them, a great radiance, and she says from those ashes for the first time she really knew Lawrence. Meanwhile Angelino has built this horrid chapel, this ghastly Villa d'Este affair of grass steps and fir trees and huge poles with a flame on top, with a cattle guard. It is so vulgar everyone is disgusted and laughing, then on top of it all, a visitors' book. I was up there two days ago and I told her frankly there were two ways of paying homage to Lawrence. One was to bury the ashes quietly under the great pine tree he loved and make the pine tree the altar. The other was to put in the ugly cold desolate chapel of firebricks something so astoundingly beautiful that one's breath was taken away . . . I am writing to Brancusi to see if he would make a fitting and beautiful piece of sculpture of a phoenix for Lawrence and how little he would charge – as they don't want to spend money on Lawrence other than firebricks . . . there is still a third way out – shall I steal the ashes and place them in a tree where they will never be found . . . to exploit that lovely man . . . to have a vulgar showplace . . . a visitors' book . . . perhaps it will be a greater punishment for her finally for everyone to know her vulgarity . . . and Angelino is simply common and I suspect at last of being only after her money. That's the situation here and I have told Angelino frankly he is not fit to make a monument even to a monkey . . . and that I hope to live to bury his ashes in a drainpipe.[39]

To Una Jeffers, Brett had already written:

> To be the adoring widow of a great man – how easy that is. To be the wife of a great man – how difficult. But even an adoring widow might at least realise the ashes need respect, remembrance, tenderness, that a tea-table is hardly respectful and forgetting them altogether in the house of a friend, in fact leaving them behind is hardly tender . . . and is a Mausoleum looking like a station toilet a fitting resting place? That old four-poster of a woman – a four-poster is all she needs or ever has needed – you will say I am green-eyed, that a bit more four-postering on my part would have done me good . . . oh Basta![40]

The fact that all three women, Brett, Mabel and Frieda, believed they were alone in confiding in Una Jeffers was only one of the complications of that farcical summer. Another was the visit of Barby, Frieda's daughter, and her husband, Stuart, and the consequent enlargement of the circle of intrigue, for Barby and Stuart began to suspect Angelo Ravagli of a plot to strip Frieda of her moderate wealth. Neither were discouraged in this belief by Mabel or Brett who, initially, welcomed the couple as allies against Frieda. Brett reported gleefully to Stieglitz:

> Barby is here with her husband . . . they dislike Angelino, they suspect him of simply skinning Frieda . . . things came to a head this week when Angelino induced Frieda to sign a document making him her partner in everything. She has signed over half her royalties, half her movie gains and his second boy inherits the ranch . . . my attitude is this – if a woman wants a man, likes a man, and doesn't care whether he skins her or not – well, what of it?*
>
> . . . One cannot rescue people, especially a silly old woman like that. And my word, she is silly.
>
> Later:
>
> Lord what a *mess*. I went up to see Frieda and she told me Barby attacked Angelino and accused him of being a chiseler and demanded proofs of his honesty . . . (Oh, here comes Barby on horseback)
>
> Later still:
>
> Well Barby threw a glass at him whereupon he slapped her! . . . He told Barby and her husband that he did not love Frieda, that *SHE* loved him and it gave him a living!![41]

Brett was surrounded on all sides by family feuds. If the bickering up the hill were not enough, down below, at the Hawk Ranch, was further

* An interesting attitude, in view of the antagonism of many of her later friends to the menage in which she ended her days.

fracas. The letter to Stieglitz continued, "... Now there is a situation on the ranch here between the two brothers Bill and Harold Hawk – for more than a year they have not spoken." "Ye gods," Stieglitz replied, "what a mess Taos seems to be in".[42]

Unfortunately for Brett and Mabel, Barby and her husband were unreliable allies. Brett's idle notion that she and Mabel should steal the ashes had been taken seriously enough by Mabel for her to enroll a friend, Daniel Crispin, to stand by to do the dirty work. Mabel, however, let her tongue run away with her, and she revealed the plot to Barby while she was cutting Barby's hair at the Luhan ranch. When Barby told Frieda all this and more, the fat was in the fire. Mabel wrote to Una Jeffers, who, unknown to her and Brett, was an additional source of revelation for Frieda.

> Barby and Stuart made a last desperate attempt last week to [influence Frieda]. It consisted in their going to her and making a confession. Their confession was that they had said many mean things but that Brett and Mabel had said the following ... followed all about the ashes project! Only saying it was my idea and Danny had agreed to carry it out to please me! Horrors! I racked and racked my brains and could not *recall* telling Barby but I think I must have. You know Tony always says "You talk too much". If I did tell Barby this, it was the day I cut her hair upstairs ... she has turned out such a snake ... Frieda sent insulting letters to us all. She ... had Brett for three hours and used third degree and police methods, trying to get her to admit the thing but true to British diplomatic tradition, she denied everything. She [Brett] said [she was] called ... a swine and a liar and she sat in her cabin for 3 days, afraid that [someone] was coming to burn it down.[43]

Mabel herself did not manage to retain such an aristocratic stiff upper lip. Una Jeffers, once again, learnt from Brett, "Mabel came rushing up here and in her excitement drove straight into the ditch out of which I had to haul her with my car."[44] Mabel then, in order to protect her friend Crispin, by carefully avoiding naming any names, managed to place the blame for the whole episode squarely upon the unfortunate Brett. Angie, for his part, had now hit on a way to prevent all further tampering with the ashes, accidental or otherwise*. What was left of Lawrence was combined with sand and cement to form a massive, solid concrete block, the altar of the Lawrence temple-cum-shrine, immovable for ever. Brett, unaware of Mabel's manoeuvrings, innocently

* And, according to the most recent addition to the ashes saga, possibly to ensure that his own misdeeds were buried for ever. *See* p. 269.

assumed that Mabel would be the principal target of Frieda's venom. She wrote to Stieglitz:

> The Tomb opening or shutting is tomorrow – a notice in the paper in Santa Fe, a sort of open invitation . . . a Mexican band singing hoop-la songs. The Indians have refused to sing – they will never forgive Angelino for his treatment of them that first summer. I don't know what will be the outcome of all this but I foresee trouble for Mabel.[45]

Brett and Mabel, as well as the Indians, boycotted the ceremony,* with the result that the record of the Hawk brothers in non-communication was thereafter easily broken by Brett and Frieda. Two years later, when Aldous Huxley visited New Mexico, the two were still not speaking.

* There is, however, a slightly different version of events. According to Marianna Howes, Brett arrived at the Goldens' ranch on the Rio Chiquito, agog with news of a plot with Mabel to blow the chapel up completely. She also recalled that, while Mabel sent flowers to the ceremony but was afraid to attend in person, Brett hovered wraith-like on the outskirts. Marianna Howes claimed to have been aware of the plot to steal the ashes but not to have been involved in it in any active way. A letter of Frieda's to Mabel suggests that in fact it was originally Miss Howes who agreed to carry out the actual theft. Oh, Taos!

12

1936–1943: The Chapline Roof and Mabeltown

> If you prefer to remain a British subject, by all means, go East next Sunday whether you have filed your petition or not [a Taos judge wrote to Brett in 1935]. If you go on, before you file the petition, you may have the life-long pleasure of complaining of officials at Taos, Denver, El Paso and Washington.
>
> If, on the contrary, you actually desire to become an American Citizen, then let nothing keep you from filing your petition before you go. Make it now or never. Do your own part now, or just forget the subject, please.[1]

Brett obtained her American citizenship on June 29th, 1936. When Aldous Huxley arrived the following May to spend the summer of 1937 at the ranch, he not only found her still not speaking to Frieda but "odder than ever in a Mexican 10 gallon hat with a turkey's feather stuck in it, sky blue breeks, top boots and a strong American accent".[2] Huxley's ear must have been tuned to the finely-fluted tones of Garsington and Bloomsbury for, thirty years later, Brett's accent, if not her vocabulary and excluding the American "a", was still that of pre-war, upper-class England.

The hat was a gift from Mabel following a trip to Mexico:

> I at last secured you a tan coloured felt hat embroidered with gold flowers . . . an "antigua" [antique] but in perfect condition . . . the outer edge of the brim is of a slightly darker shade of tan and there is a handsome gold cord put four times around it and this has nubbins at the end. You may not find it resembles your heart's desire and will therefore hate me for bringing it but one must take these risks. It is not too exaggerated or conspicuous to *wear*.[3]

It is difficult to imagine anything too exaggerated or conspicuous for Brett to wear. In fact the "antigua" hat remained a carefully preserved part of her varied headgear for the rest of her life. However, with Frieda still mute on the mountain – the two did not start speaking to each other again until the end of 1937 – and the relationship between her and Brett at least steady, Brett and Mabel had to look to each other for emotional variety. They found it within weeks of Mabel's return from south of the border with the Mexican hat, when Mabel suggested that Brett remove a painting from the Don Fernando Inn in Taos. The picture was of an Indian and had been based by Brett upon Tony Luhan. "Tourists ask if it is a man or a woman. Frieda says why don't I confiscate it."[4] Brett replied:

> It happens to be considered by everyone one of the finest and best interpretations of the Indian . . . I have sat many times in the tavern and I HAVE NEVER SEEN ANYONE LAUGH AT IT . . . AS FOR INDIAN MEN BEING MISTAKEN FOR WOMEN this happens not only in paintings but in REAL life as you know perfectly well – the confusion of long hair and blankets makes it inevitable and leaves me stone cold = As for Tony he showed no dislike for that painting when it hung for months in the TAVERN without his EVER giving it a glance – but as you know the Indians do not really understand our art so it seems a pity to confuse Tony in regard to a painting . . . I have never hurt his RACE or him in my painting and that is too well known to be discredited = If he says anything to me about it I shall tell him this = I think tho he ought to know the law = that the painting is *my personal property* any confiscating or damage or so on would entail another lawsuit – & marvellous publicity for me!! but I certainly don't see why I can't derive my paintings from my friends if you can write about them . . . anyway I will soon be returning to Hollywood & that may be all for the best.[5]

Brett had driven to Hollywood earlier that year to stay with Syv who was acting as adviser on the set of *The Great White Rajah*, a film that was being made, based on the history of the Brooke family in Sarawak. The two sisters had not seen each other for twelve years and, in Syv, Brett found her match for sartorial eccentricity. "My sister tells me she never wears anything now except Native dress which means Malay costume . . . heavens, how embarrassing," Brett wrote to Una Jeffers.[6] One of the attractions of Hollywood was the presence of Stokowski, who provided introductions to the movie industry. Brett returned to Taos brimming with excitement at her discovery of the techniques of film animation and determined to buy a "seven speed" movie camera for use in conjunction with her airbrush in making a new kind of moving picture. A year later she wrote to Mabel:

> I have rediscovered my Mickey Mouse films – as one leaves (the studios) they present one with a souvenir – which consists of a little bunch of coloured films and would you believe it this is going to help me with my Moving painting – I can see how they move them! – and it is not so slight a movement after all . . . it will be a complete resume of Indian life – all turning and returning to the Circle Dance – it's a pity you haven't my exasperating imagination – I know it's exasperating to others.[7]

Brett did, a little later, at the beginning of 1939, lay out $40 on a movie camera and there are constant references in her letters of the time to using movies in and as an inspiration for her painting as well as, conversely, painting for the movies, hoping, she told Mabel, that the Disney Studio would one day have a "research department for such as myself". However, in 1937, the experiments were destined to wait, for the reunion with Syv seems to have inspired Brett to renew contact with the rest of her family. She dropped her plans to return to Hollywood and, now that her US citizenship was secure and she was sure of re-entry, travelled instead to England on January 14th, 1938.

Absence had made the hearts grow, at least initially, fonder. Brett stayed with Syv's husband, Vyner Brooke. "For the first time I am enjoying my family," Brett told Mabel,[8] although she did have a set-to with one of brother Oliver's daughters "who announced that she thought starving was a good incentive to make an artist work"[9] and found to her dismay that she was referred to, not as Western cowboy "Brett" but as safe and sure, middle-aged "Auntie Doll". "Auntie Doll!!!" she complained, "Damn!!!" To her other regular correspondent, Una Jeffers, she wrote, "I was in a minor accident when a two deck bus sideswiped the car I was in – five policemen – four busmen & *all* the unemployed gathered round . . . Kot wont speak to me nor will Ottoline!! Grievances of some sort for all these years."[10] Meanwhile, back at the ranch, Frieda was revelling in the relative tranquillity. "With Mabel and Brett away, the place seems cleaner."[11]

It did not take more than a few weeks for Brett to resume her old financial finanglings, claiming, despite the correspondence course she had had from headmaster-cum-travel-agent Lawrence in the matter, total naivete regarding the transfer of funds between one country and another. Oliver, now Lord Esher, was not taken in: "The way to pay for things in England is the way I pay for things in America. You ask your Taos bank to give you a draft in sterling."[12] But when Brett left Britain at the end of June, after a six-month stay – "Lord how I hate the *Queen Mary*. She is a snob from her head to her tail and rolls like a pig"[13] – she did not leave empty-handed. She had had new kilts made in the family tartan, a garb that became in later years as famous in the south-west as her Mexican hat and had filled her trunks with family hand-me-downs. "I have really a trousseau of *female* clothes which will last me until my Bathchair finale," she told Mabel, a fact that Mabel must have taken with a covered wagon full of salt, for she continued to find it necessary thereafter to chastise Brett for her appearance at elegant dinner parties at the Luhan spread dressed, as ever, in whatever fell off the end of the bed.

In Taos, a frosty letter from Murry was waiting. Knopf, Katherine Mansfield's American publishers, had heard a rumour that Brett was arranging to publish Katherine's letters to her and were worried that their interests might be infringed. The copyright, Murry pointed out, belonged to him and Brett could not publish anything of Katherine's without his permission. That, he said firmly, he was not prepared to give.[14]*

The truth of the matter was that Brett had been pursued some years earlier by a young man from Harvard who wanted to photocopy the Lawrence letters, but not those of Katherine Mansfield, for publication as part of a research thesis. The Lawrence letters were, in fact, in a tin box in Stieglitz's keeping in New York where Brett had taken them, along with her Lawrence manuscripts, when Stieglitz had asked if he could read them. She warned Stieglitz not to allow the Harvard student any access and then, later, in the summer of 1936, twice asked Stieglitz to return the letters to her in New Mexico but, for some reason, Stieglitz ignored her request and held on to them. It was not, in fact, until after the death of Stieglitz in 1946 that the Lawrence letters and manuscripts were finally returned to Brett by Georgia O'Keefe. Katherine's letters were, however, in 1938, safe in Taos. The rumour Murry had heard arose because Brett had written again to Stieglitz asking him to try to find a buyer for both Lawrence's and Katherine's letters, the proceeds of which, she said, she wanted to use to educate Rachel Hawk's children.[15] The best offer Brett managed to obtain then for Lawrence's letters was $100 and so they remained in her possession until 1951 when, with the assistance of Stephen Spender, she sold them, along with those of Murry and Virginia Woolf, to the University of Cincinnati for a larger but by no means excessive sum that helped her complete the purchase of her final Taos residence, the studio on the Arroyo Seco road. Katherine's letters she sold for $2,250 in 1942 "to a woman who adores her and all connected with her, which is a huge relief to my mind, as they will be safe and well cared for".[16]

* Plus ça change . . .

Early in 1939, Brett finally made some sort of peace with Frieda, although they were to continue to snipe at each other for ever after.

> The Frieda business is over – what a blessing – we are now friends again. When we buried the hatchet I gave her the painting she always wanted of the ranch with all the work going on in different corners. Also her own copy of *The Rainbow* which I have kept for her – she has had most other things pried off her or stolen. And now I have his fountain pen to give her to put in the Chapel. His typewriter is there!!! Because Angelino wishing to use it and discovering it was all sticky and dirty and that it would cost $12 to have it cleaned by a firm, took it and BOILED it. When he took it out of the boiling water there was practically nothing left – all the keys being rubber had come off!!! The roller was plain wood . . . and the whole thing had more or less jelled!! And was he mad. It just can't be mentioned. Now it reposes as an historic relic in the chapel.[17]

Since her visit to London, Brett had resumed correspondence with her family. Brett's income from Aunt Lou's trust fund amounted to $585 quarterly on which, she claimed, she was never able to manage, so her letters were often thinly disguised begging letters, which usually failed to deceive their recipients: "If I send you those last 2 volumes", Oliver replied to one, "you will have to pay duty. They have been published by Scribner in New York and you had better order them from there."[18] Undeterred, Brett offered a description of her industrious and frugal day, which may or may not have impressed her brother:

> Up at 5.30. Light fire. Back in bed till 6.00 or dawn. Exercises. Dress. Breakfast, etc., 8.30. Paint till lunch, paint a bit after lunch. Supper 6.30. Bed with a book 8.30–9.30.[19]

Brett followed a relatively strict regime of this nature till very late in her life, rising early so that a full day's work at the easel could be accomplished before most of the Taos artist tribe had even risen. By lunchtime she had time to spare for local affairs which, in Taos, meant gossip. The afternoons were less strictly organised and were varied with fishing trips – she was a lifelong addict – and visits to the Indian ceremonies. Since sketching or taking photographs or notes was prohibited, Brett attended regularly, observing the same dances year after year and building a prodigious visual memory. Each of the pueblo villages up and down the Rio Grande has its own calendar of dances, some tied to the seasons of growing and harvesting, others celebrating the feasts of Christian saints with the pagan dances of the Indians' natural religion. The ceremonies can occasionally be tatty and tired, sullied in the name of tourism and commerce, but they often develop a deep psychic intensity, building up through the long, sunbaked day, through hours of nonstop rhythmic shuffling and swaying, low, throat-throbbing chanting and the continual rapid pounding of drums. The dance grows until, quite suddenly, it stops and one *feels* the silence – the Indians call it "drum sickness".

When war was declared in England, emergency regulations put a temporary block on Brett's receiving the income from her trust fund each quarter. Within a month or so, through Oliver's influence in arranging a Treasury permit, the allowance was restored. Brett sent a loud "Hooray" to her brother and, having failed in 1917 to convince her father and the Imperial Defence Committee of the excellence of her ideas for winning the First World War, now offered Oliver the first of her endless schemes as to how the Second might be ended in the shortest of time:

> Why doesn't Sir Nevill Henderson go to those meetings with Hitler with his waistcoat lined with bombs and suddenly press a button and blow Hitler and himself to smithereens . . . I am writing to Anthony Eden to suggest it.[20]

Brett later sent her war-winning ideas direct to Winston Churchill – "LOOK OUT . . . BEWARE – his [Hitler's] delayed invasion may mean that he is tunnelling under the Channel"[21] – reminding Oliver at the same time that the Prime Minister had been her partner at her first dinner dance, prior to the First World War. Churchill clearly had no recollection of this important encounter – a formal acknowledgment by way of reply came to Brett from his secretary and began "Dear Sir . . .".[22]

Although the transmission of Brett's allowance from Britain was thereafter only occasionally delayed or interrupted, the war brought a reduction in the income generated by the trust fund, at one point bringing it down to as little as $40 a quarter.[23] Her moderately straitened circumstances provided Brett with an excellent opportunity to persuade Mabel, who felt the war was making Brett nervous and jittery, to give her a free room on the Luhan hacienda. Brett gave up her tenancy of the Chapline roof and moved into a studio across the patio from Mabel's "two-storey house". She had occupied the studio from time to time before and she now converted it into modest living quarters. She failed to persuade Mabel to build a bedroom on the studio roof and so make that building two-storey too but did add, at her own expense and in lieu of rent, she claimed, a bathroom and toilet, "the last in Taos before FDR froze them – such a joy, no going outside in the cold or wet."

Brett had hardly installed herself once more under Mabel's roof when a tenant arrived for another of Mabel's houses: Edward James. Brett wrote excitedly to her brother: "Could be Evie James son. If you know anything about him, do tell me!! My ears will be flapping on my head".[24] Oliver replied tersely, "Edward James is the boy who complained to Evie about Loulou . . . I understand he is an effeminate fellow and people don't like him".[25] Brett, with more intimate and less sympathetic memories of Loulou Harcourt than her brother, took to James at once.

> I must say I like Edward James, he is amusing, clever, but of course as you say very effeminate, but what of it. We heard that he is the illegitimate son of Edward VII. Now is that true or not? Our ears are fairly waggling. I can well believe that about old Loulou. I owed Loulou a perpetual grudge, nasty old bird he was, in spite of his soft voice and outer niceness, he was an old stink inside. So he destroyed everything for so little. He should have been castrated, that would have been easier for him.[26]

Closer contact with Edward caused Brett to moderate her enthusiasm for the Last Great Eccentric a little: "Edward James is a queer fellow, mad as a hatter, now gone to Hollywood, having led everybody a somewhat irritating life. No sense of time, no sense of quiet, yet one can't help liking him, at the same time one wants to smack him."[27] And: "He is nice in many ways but so timeless and tiresome too. Always rushing in to read his poems out loud, always getting into fights with Mexicans and Sheriffs. His tales are amusing but somewhat straying from the path of truth."[28]

A tale that does seem to embroider the truth a little is quoted by Philip Purser in his biography of Edward James, *Where is He Now?* as evidence of James' skill as a raconteur. It concerns, coincidentally, Brett. Claiming Brett as a cousin, James proceeds:

> [She] lives in a shack in New Mexico and weaves her own clothing and, burned by the sun, does look rather like an Indian. While minding the local store to oblige the storekeeper one day, she dozed off and found herself being studied by four earnest travellers. "Excuse me," said one of them, "we were wondering whether you were a Navajo, Cherokee or Pueblo squaw." Cousin Dorothy replied, "I'm just an impoverished English gentlewoman."[29]

It is difficult to believe that, despite her artistic skills, Brett ever wove her own clothing or that anyone, however Texas-tourist,* should

* A New Mexican term of abuse.

mistake her profile for that of an American Indian; equally hard to imagine any down-home Taos trader leaving Brett to mind the store. She did, however, occasionally stand in for Spud Johnson at the Heptagon, a cooperative art-gallery-cum-souvenir-shop that Johnson usually looked after. "I am not much good as a salesman but as they mostly come out of curiosity, buying nothing but a postcard, I don't imagine my lack of salesmanship will matter much. Five have already been in and that means 50 cents. We charge a dime entrance and that pays most of our expenses."[30]

Despite Brett's conclusion that Edward James was "a queer man . . . hard to have for long in the house. Does odd things at odd moments", the two became close friends. When James reappeared out of the blue a couple of years later, he bought a number of Brett's paintings.

> He believes in me . . . he collects me and Dali!!! . . . he bought a largish painting of a Santo Domingo Indian, a small one of the pueblo here and has commissioned a copy of some Indian Angels I did for Frieda. It totals up to $580!"[31]

Although Brett's paintings were selling moderately well in numbers in those early war years, the financial returns were not great. She reported selling nine at one blow in March, 1941, but six of these went for only $5 each and the other three from $25 to $100. She had, however, never been one for cutting her coat to suit her cloth and, only two months earlier, she had "plunged off the deep end [and] bought a simply beautiful Pontiac Station Wagon, a dream of loveliness and I just adore it".[32] When, by the autumn, she was having difficulty in keeping up the payments, she followed her usual ploy of dropping heavy hints in Oliver's direction and then asking him direct for $100 to tide her over. Oliver had, in the three years since their reunion, become wise to Brett's methods. A suggestion a year earlier that it might be possible to contribute to "my only extravagance" – the latest in combined hearing aids and portable radios – had brought a delayed reply pointing out that he was down to a single servant and was paying income tax at 15/– in the pound. This time, Oliver had the law on his side:

> I thought your large and expensive car would get you into trouble. We are reduced here to an 8 horse-power two-seater and an amount of petrol per month that would last you a day. As I also was left nothing at all by either of my parents, I share your surprise that they did not appreciate our obvious merits . . . as far as I can see it is quite possible, if you are not very careful about your expenditure, that I

> may one day be saying, "poor Doll, her pittance gave out & she just died of starvation". For I must make it *quite clear* to you that until the end of the war – possibly ten years – no money can pass from a British subject to your account, except what you receive from your trust fund. It is absolutely illegal for me to send you $100 as you suggest, nor can any American income of mine be transferred to you. The position of vastly rich Oriental potentates may be different, & that mean creature your sister might, if she were made differently, transfer you something from that furnace on the Equator in which she lives.* But we here can do nothing, & the hard heart of the Treasury will not be moved however much you starve . . . for the moment you can count on your £95 a quarter from the Trust Fund.[35]

Brett and her brother were not alone in the wartime battle to keep the wolf from the entrance gates. Murry wrote that he was trying to sell Katherine's manuscripts in the USA and that he had noticed in *The Times* that Philip Morrell was selling the Garsington estate. "So we pass into oblivion," he added,[36] and later, "in order to keep going at all, I have had to set up as a beekeeper".[37]

While Murry was a convinced pacifist, Brett was now patriotic, if not downright warlike. "I carry the Union Jack and the Stars and Stripes on the front window of my car," she wrote to Oliver, and by 1943, she had found her own means of assisting the war effort and a new theme – aeroplanes – for her art. "I paint in the mornings and in the afternoon I fold bandages: my day is divided between war and peace."[38] In between, lunch was not exactly a gourmet meal:

> I have put my lunch in the ash pan in the stove which I use as an oven, works very well if no ashes fall in, I have creamed potatoes with grated cheese . . . I am painting BOMBERS, beautiful B 24's, I just love the Flying Fortresses and B 24's and P 38's . . . I buy all the mags full of flying and planes and that does it.[39]

* Oliver's affection for his sister Syv had diminished radically when, on the death of his father, he went through the bound volumes of family correspondence. ". . . you cannot conceive the beastly things she said about G."[33] Syv retained her capacity for bitterness about fellow members of the family. She wrote to Brett on the occasion of their mother's death in 1943:

> I am amazed at what you say about Pupsy. I never thought you liked him. I didn't and he disliked ME intensely . . . Mumsy WAS jealous . . . NOT of you or any other woman but of M. and of T.S. and the many others that he fancied. I feel very bitterly about him. He ruined my childhood and I don't think he helped you either. He never realised that he had a good artist in his midst and an appreciably good writer. He clung round the feeble flights of his sons' imaginations – we just didn't count.[34]

That more than did it. Not content with fantasising over the aeroplane magazines, Brett, now nearing her sixtieth birthday, wanted a more direct share of the action. She wrote again to Oliver a few months later:

> Would it be possible to wangle a job for me . . . my dream is to go up in a Flying Fortress and here I am the wrong sex, the wrong age, and I am damned mad . . . I am going to write to Lord Halifax, he must remember Pupsy, and get him to speak up for me . . . I am scared blue of bombs but I would lump even bombs to get over the Pacific in a bomber, I would paint things in a way that most of the dumb-bells never dream of painting . . . nurses are sent out, so why not I? Can you get me into the Royal Navy or RAF by proxy, an honorary member like one of the Royal Family* In memory of Pupsy they might at least do that. I could then paint for Britain. How's that for an idea? (P.S.) Tell Winston C. I sat next to him at my first dinner party – seventeen years old and petrified with fright. I drew him again for my partner for another dinner – tell him to get me into the RAF or NAVY – & I'll paint some lovely paintings for him.[40]

* The urge to enroll in the RAF appears to be a not uncommon phenomenon in old ladies of elegance and breeding. George Melly, raconteur, blues singer, wit and, like Philip Purser, biographer of Edward James, recounts how his mother, Maud Melly, turned ninety and in a nursing home in Surrey, could be found each day blacking out with great diligence each separate word in *The Guardian*, oblivious of meaning and typographical peculiarities. One day, while down there on a visit, George observed that, in an otherwise totally blacked-out newspaper, one item had been left unsullied and therefore legible: a recruiting advertisement for the RAF. "I have decided what I want to do," said Maud. "What?" enquired George. "I'm going to join the RAF." "But, mother," George explained, "it says 'between 18 and 24'." "Oh, I'm sure they'll overlook a little thing like that," Maud replied.

13

1943–1956: The El Prado Studio

As the war continued, life at close quarters with Brett began to tell on Mabel. Mabel's ideas of good housekeeping were rather more orthodox than those of Brett who when not warming up potatoes and cheese in the ash pan, was proselytising the virtues of an everlasting stew to the younger and more impressionable. To Eithne Golden she wrote:

> Eithne dear –
> The secret of the stew is to *boil it every day* = I advise you to boil it when you make your breakfast – but gently – not so that it boils like this /\/\/\/\/ but like this ~~~~~ then you can reheat it for lunch – but *boil it must* or it will sour –
> Courage – Eithne dear.[1]

Tiny irritations – Brett's dog, her tidiness or lack of it, the fitful operation of her hearing aid – after a year or two of communal living, had Mabel, like the stew, boiling. Brett wrote:

> We have had a series of blow ups, and the latest went off with a bang two nights ago. I went over to supper and of course there is always the washing up project afterwards, well, she had been nagging me beyond endurance because I don't barge about like she does, rushing around like a baby elephant . . . she began again, nag, nag, nag, I exploded and flung the bowl I was drying on the floor and it smashed into a million pieces. I felt just fine but she is tearing mad.[2]

It was not in Brett's nature to apologise or seek a compromise with her landlady/hostess. Instead she bombarded Mabel with a mixture of abuse and sermonising, pulling aristocratic rank and old-world savoir-faire at every opportunity and brazening it out when Mabel suggested that, if Brett could not help with the dishes and keep her quarters clean, she had better start paying some rent.

> I don't think breaking bowls is a particularly praiseworthy occupation, on the other hand I don't think nagging and tormenting those who try to help is any more praiseworthy . . . my attitude about houses and dust is different to yours, I'll admit. I don't like dust. On the other hand I don't approve of taking too much out of another's life or my own to fuss over a spot of dust . . . you don't think I polish and dust enough, well I don't, but I do what I can and my place is moderately clean. I have to conserve my energies for the things I like doing and I try to keep a balance.[3]

Four or five more letters followed, pages long, machine-gunning out of Brett's typewriter at break-neck speed, making up for what she was missing in the gun-turret of a Flying Fortress over Okinawa. All followed the same theme – that Brett had no objection to Mabel following a mundane everyday existence but, for her part, she was cut out for finer things. And as for paying rent . . .

> I don't think that is advisable, in the first place I can't afford it. I can trade with the helping but when it comes to paying for meals I don't like the idea, nor do I think for one moment it would work. You would be dissatisfied with the amount I paid and the amount I eat, it would mean more criticism and right now with the war and money difficulties, I just don't feel up to it . . . Our approaches to life and living are different. All my training with painting and with Scots ghillies has been one of method and slowness. The rushing, stomping around attitude appears on the surface more energetic but I fancy it has been proven over and over again not to be any swifter, any surer than the steady even pace . . . any Indian will tell you this . . . there is not a single soul in this town who doesn't know how to dry plates, as far as I can make out . . . it is not a craft.
>
> This is not a complaint, merely a marshalling of facts, to show that insulting people over matters over which they have not complete control is unfortunate. The Highlander and the Indian are more nearly akin in their ways than the Indian and the American. And believe me the Highlander will outlast any American on a hike. Just as the Indian will.
>
> So, hoping this airing of our racial differences will not disturb our happy relationship, but cooperation has to be on both sides . . . to be a slave to a piece of dust is all "Much ado about nothing".[4]

And so on, until Mabel was buried under Brett's paper bombardment and began to feel that it was easier to wash and break the dishes herself. But her pen, at least, did not lie idle. "I like to be on friendly terms but I want to say one thing frankly: I can't *stand* having you take books & things from here & never bring them back."[5] And, "I don't like lending you books. They come back soiled, rubbed by your car or the dog or something and are no longer attractive."[6] Fortunately for Mabel's blood-pressure, Brett moved, as usual, up the mountain to the Tower Beyond Tragedy for the summer, although even here she had been beginning to feel that she was outstaying her welcome. The situation was undoubtedly aggravated by Brett overplaying her new-found jingoism, "England standing alone against the alien horde", and ever trumpeting her "Highland" superiority.

> I don't know whether I will go up much to the Cabin this summer, it's such a chore moving everything, lovely as it is up there, and people [are against] England and the English, which was one of those shocks that the war produced, I never dreamed of it, and it makes me so uncomfortable, I can't believe in a friendship if you hate the race and country the friend belongs to.[7]

Though she did spend that summer on the mountain, things failed to improve and the following year, 1943, Brett stayed in her Tower only intermittently. "I am contemplating giving up my cabin as S—— is still kicking me in the face everytime I go up there," Brett wrote with typical exaggeration to Spud Johnson, "so wearisome and boring I just can't face it any more."[8] A month later she wrote to Spud again, telling him she had, after thirteen years, given up the Tower Beyond Tragedy. No sooner was Brett back down in Taos, than she was irritating Mabel once more. Mabel's theme was not unfamiliar.

> I try & keep the house in order & bright & gay, & have nice dinners & have the maids always clean and neat. Then, when I work all day, it is refreshing to wash & change & be a part of the picture of order and pleasure . . . and if you just come in & have the same old shirt and sweater & your trousers like you've had them lately, it doesn't fit the picture & besides it's bad for one to be slack and soft – and it makes other people laugh . . . you have loads of clothes – knitted dresses & all sorts – why shouldn't you change into one at night like even the least of the shopkeepers' wives over town do, as a concession to another hour of living and being after work is over?[9]

Finally, it all became too much for Mabel. She decided that the time had come to give Brett her marching orders.

> Brett, you are not *convenient* . . . I want the studio in 4 months time . . . as for friendship, it is not friendship you want but care, attention, the right to take liberties. You are not entitled to food and the usual needs of a fourteen year old . . . you will be better off some place where you can indulge yourself.[10]

For Frieda, enjoying it all quietly from her side of Taos' eternal triangle, Mabel's ultimatum was too good an opportunity to miss. She was comfortably off now, with a steady income from Lawrence's royalties and was living less at the ranch. Winters she spent with Angie in Port Isabel on the Texas coast of the Gulf of Mexico and, for the rest of the year, she and Angie had built a more modern Taos home "on the rim", as Taos mountain dwellers refer to the mesa below. She had some land to spare and so she offered it to Brett as a site for a house and studio. Brett, again in the market for funds, wrote to Oliver:

> I want to be independent . . . Frieda Lawrence will give me a patch on her property so that I can live an independent life, not be open to the tantrums of friends . . . I lost my cabin like that and now for a month Mabel has not spoken to me and goes past with a frozen face, and its just a BORE. I have written Syv to ask her if she will lend me $4,000 to build a house . . . the house will consist of a living room, kitchen, garage and upstairs, because I love Towers, a studio, bedroom and bathroom. A well will be drilled and an electric pump . . . I will be near Frieda, and three or four miles out of town on the desert with a view all round the world . . . I will have an automatic heater for the bath and gadgets. Why people have to slave I don't know with all the wonderful gadgets invented by men like Bendix.[11]

Syv's initial response was a cheque for $400, whether by chance or calculation, exactly a tenth of what Brett had asked for. When Oliver failed to jump immediately at Brett's hints, she wrote again, "I am having the trees cut down this week, (i.e. forest trees to act as beams or 'vigas' for the construction of the house) then I make the adobes . . . if you have any ideas about the money side, let me know."[12] Days later, sending airmail letters out like prayers to the pueblo's Magic Mountain, she hinted again, her financial sights already significantly lowered:

> $2000, that's all I need . . . directly you need money, people melt into thin air . . . I am beginning to get desperate . . . I need 6000 adobes, they will take about a week to make. (P.S.) as the poor relation I have kept going fairly well, its only when a crisis arises I begin to seek help . . . Syv could have helped, out of £6,000, $2000 would not have

> been such an effort. Do you realise all I got from Mumsy & Pupsy were two wrist watches!!! Ironical isn't it![13]

Once more Oliver explained wearily that there were Treasury restrictions on the transfer of funds from Britain but, fortunately, his wife, Antoinette, Lady Esher, whose family were American, had $1,000 due from a trust fund in New York and she and Oliver managed to transfer that to Brett. Money ran out again when problems were encountered with the water table and the well had to be drilled 154 feet deep. Frieda, still with an eye to one-upping Mabel – "I am glad you get good meals at Mabel's," she added tartly to her note – offered to help Brett out with the $135 a month owing to the well driller. Syv, too, despite Brett's lack of gratitude, sent a further $1,000 and, in the summer of 1946, Brett at last moved into the first home that was clearly her own. It was her last move. She lived there for the rest of her life without making too much fuss so far as the household chores were concerned. A couple of years later "a huge wind" blew a letter of her next-door-neighbour from the trash heap to her feet.

> Before I realised it, I saw my name and read what he said!!! And what he said was this: "I don't understand Brett's house, it seems it needs a psychiatrist or a street cleaner, preferably a street cleaner"!!! Well, I was hopping mad. He could not have built his house without all my tools, he used everything I possessed, broke some of them, lost others, had the key of my house, used the bathtub, I gravelled their road, gave them extra land and dammit, all that is all that I get!!![14]

Brett's floor gradually became a mass of what Taos came to call "dinosaur bones", the stock-bones from many an eternal stew, which ended up as food and playthings for Brett's succession of dogs, while Taos legend has a group of very proper ladies visiting Brett for tea and being offered a teacup containing a mouse-nest complete with mouse. While they screamed and stood on their chairs, Brett marvelled at the creature's tiny eyes peeping out. Simon Brett, her great-nephew who stayed and painted with her in the mid-1960s, recalls bookshelves being covered in chicken wire to keep the dog, Little Reggie, off. Reggie made himself useful, though, to his deaf mistress. Explaining the gaping holes in the ankles of her socks, Brett would point at the dog: "That was Reggie – telling me that the phone was ringing." In 1973 a reporter from the *Chicago Tribune* described the "decor" as "Late Squalor".

"No one can push me around any more, only the Lord can push me out in a coffin, what a blessing," Brett wrote to Una Jeffers in July.[15]

After a life-time of seasonal migration from one dwelling to another, never in the previous twenty years a place she could call her own, the importance of the house at the crossroads to Brett was inestimable. She produced here an enormous quantity of work, ranging from the large "ceremonials" to small "pot-boilers" that sold more readily and brought in a small but steady income. Some of her best work is, in fact, to be found in these "pot-boilers" where she felt free to paint simply and realistically. Frequently in the "ceremonials" the Indian is a stylised being, slim and graceful, his physique strikingly unlike the typical thick-set stature of the mature Pueblo Indian. Brett herself was aware of this contradiction and told Simon Brett, "If my paintings of the Indian, as he thinks and feels about himself and life are not apparent to you, then you do not understand the Indian."[16]

In gratitude for the assistance given in purchasing her final home, Brett sent a US Government CARE parcel of rice and cheese to Oliver and Antoinette, whom she imagined to be suffering untold deprivation in post-war Britain:

> Did you know the turtles in Texas march like on armies on the rice fields – they put up electrified fences but the turtles clamber up on each other's backs and get over like that!! Tell Antoinette if she wants nylon stockings, I can send things over bit by bit.[17]

Murry's nourishment, too, concerned Brett, her first lover mattering more than cheese and rice to her. For Murry it was caviare but the jar seems to have spent a long time crossing the Atlantic and by the time it reached Murry, it was well beyond its best. He fed it to his chickens who, he said, greeted it as a great treat when mixed with their mash.[18]

Mabel, having managed to get Brett off her premises, reacted predictably to Brett's Frieda-sponsored independence. "Mabel has got her hooks into me and I have been trampled and spat upon," Brett complained, hyperbolic as ever. Frieda, continuing in her new-found role of benefactor, as a 1947 Christmas gift, waived what Brett still owed her for the land. At the same time, she chided Brett for her own generosity with Christmas presents "for all the neighbours",[19] for Brett's painting sales were moving slowly. She sold only a single $25 work that winter to Edward James who was again back in town and offered a way out of her financial straits with a free apartment and studio at West Dean Park, his estate in Sussex that later became an arts and crafts centre, but Brett, nearing seventy, felt it would be difficult to start a new life in England. However, later that year, a patron appeared on the horizon, in the shape of Millicent Rogers, a heiress to the Standard Oil fortune and a recently arrived Taos resident.

Brett had, in fact, already benefited from Millicent's patronage a year earlier, when she wrote to Oliver, "Yesterday a woman called Mrs. Rogers came to see my studio and bought a painting for $300 right off the wall, isn't that wonderful?"[20] Now, in the autumn of 1948, Brett had, surprisingly, forgotten that earlier encounter and was impressed all over again by Millicent's wealth, about which she wrote breathlessly to everyone. Millicent bought more of Brett's paintings and Brett, glimpsing fame and, more importantly, fortune at last, immediately decided to raise the price of her *Ceremonials* from $3,000 to $5,000, reasoning, somewhat illogically in view of her past experience, that the more expensive her paintings were, the more likely people were to buy them.

In less time than it takes to prime a canvas, Brett had a new crush, founded on cupboard love, and she and Millicent became bosom companions. "Millicent Rogers will look after me," she wrote to Oliver, adding that Mabel and Frieda were hopping mad and not speaking to her.[21] Mabel sent letter after letter complaining of Brett's "back-biting" while Frieda, wise to Brett's ways, raised old ghosts. "I think it is the pattern of your soul to have these enthusiasms – now you have it for Millicent"[22] and "Friends are good things to have, that's why you should watch it and not be so disagreeable".[23]

Brett was unperturbed – "Mabel and Frieda have both got me in their dog-kennels. Mabel is simply jealous of Millicent and Frieda too I suspect. The seventy year olds are certainly acting up"[24] – for Millicent had invited her to spend the winter in Jamaica, and was busy buying Brett the clothes and luggage she would need. When Millicent fell ill and the trip had to be delayed, Frieda, who was, as usual, on the Texas coast for the winter, and Brett filled the January hours re-playing by mail the same old arguments that had been going on for thirty-five years.

> It would have been so simple if you had only said: Frieda I am sorry I hurt your feelings. But your friendship, your wonderful gift of Friendship, was not strong enough to do so – at the ranch I felt, my goodness what is this! Because it was the same as with Lawrence! You feel the same possessiveness that you felt for Lawrence for Millicent. You were horrid. And your interest in Mabel diminished with the advent of Millicent. She sent me your letter where you say Frieda went haywire. But I did not go haywire for nothing.[25]

> Well Brett here comes another of your gentle lovesongs, you tough old bird! Have you not written hundreds of "stinkers" to people, dont they know you? You ran around attacking me but many come

> delighted that I protested and told me how you had trodden on their toes! . . . I want to put salt on the tail of that lovebird that you think you are – it's a make-up! You artful dodger! This is the last I say no more![26]

It was February before Millicent had recovered from her illness sufficiently for the trip to proceed. She and Brett took with them to Jamaica Benito, Millicent's Indian chauffeur/companion, and Trinidad. While she was in Jamaica, Brett's first New York one-man show of any importance opened at the American British Art Gallery. The works shown were almost entirely *Ceremonials*, several of which had already been bought by Millicent. Largely as a result of this exhibition, one of Brett's paintings, *The Blessing of the Mares*, was selected for "American Painting Today", the winter show at the Metropolitan Museum that opened in December 1950.

By then, the relationship between Brett and Millicent was beginning to run into familiar difficulties:

> I have a hunch Millicent was really scared of that powerful feeling you have for her. She doesn't understand it. I believe you dont understand yourself how powerful your nature is. You must get over this chapter in your life. You waste yourself. *You* aren't what she wants.[27]

Frieda worried too about Brett's health and her ability to pay for medical treatment, should a small cyst on her neck prove, as was suspected, cancerous. She wrote to Mabel:

> Brett says she is broke, her nest egg gone. We have known her so long, Mabel, & I am disturbed. Should she be really ill, what could she do? I have my responsibilities as you know and if you take more responsibility than you *can*, you get into a mess. I told her it was bad for her to live with Millicent, she wants to live lavishly like Millicent. She has $100 a month. You could live on that with a house. She wont learn to be poor, she told me she wont try . . . she says: "I am so glad I never took any money from Millicent." Maybe she had no hard cash from Millicent but Millicent must have spent a few thousand on her.[28]

Though the cancer scare turned out to be unfounded, life at Millicent's standards had made inroads into Brett's finances. In August, 1951, Brett sold her correspondence with Frieda and Mabel to Yale for $250, but that failed to stem the tide of debt. "Bills surround one like a deep

deep sea," she wrote a few months later.[29] When Millicent Rogers, whose health had been poor throughout her friendship with Brett, died at the beginning of 1953, Brett's sense of loss was not unmixed with great expectations. The expectations were not realised. Brett's lawyer told her, "If Millicent made a gift to you, that is one thing; but if the gift was never consummated prior to her death, there is nothing we can do about it."

Brett reluctantly decided that she must now try to sell her letters from Lawrence. She wrote first to Harvard, pitching her price and deserving high. "No matter how battered your finances, we do not have anything like $5000 for the purchase of Lawrence's letters," Harvard replied unmoved.[30] Brett next tried Yale who stalled, seeking details of the contents of the letters, of who owned the copyright and publication rights and so on, before they would make an offer.[31] In the end the University of Cincinnati was persuaded by Stephen Spender, a visiting fellow at the time, to buy the correspondence, along with letters from Frieda, John Middleton Murry, Augustus John, J. M. Barrie, J. M. Keynes, Siegfried Sassoon and Virginia Woolf. Brett received $700, no doubt the market value at the time. A few years later that sum would hardly have bought a single letter.

The $700 did little more than provide a temporary respite. "If it weren't for the tradespeople* here, I should be starving," Brett wrote in March.[33]

Eventually Oliver realised that Brett was no longer crying "wolf" and that her financial situation was genuinely difficult. In April Brett sent Oliver, in order to satisfy Treasury regulations, a notarised statement of her day-to-day expenditure. The outgoings came to far more than the $100 monthly income that her trust fund was then producing. As a result Brett's fund was reorganised and her monthly income raised to a slightly more useful level.

The same spring another crock of gold turned out to be less crammed with doubloons than Brett had fantasised. Kyle Crichton, a journalist Brett had first met nearly forty years earlier when he interviewed Lawrence at the ranch, had written to her suggesting that

* Despite deploring the notion of a ruling class in correspondence with her viscount brother, Brett's attitude to "tradespeople" was, to say the least, ambiguous.

> The man who runs the hardware store here is taking a trip including England and he asked me if I would give him an introduction to you, as he and his wife want so much to meet you. Well, short of howling "snob" I said of course . . . quite simple people, a bit out of our swim, so to speak. But I feel a discreet tea would solve the problem so he can return and talk around that he has met you and so on. Do you mind? It kind of put me in a hole.[32]

she write an article on Edward VII's coronation to be published to coincide with the coronation of Queen Elizabeth. Crichton told her he was going to ask $10,000 for the article but made it clear that this sum was simply an opening gambit so that they might make a worthwhile lower deal, adding that, for his editorial assistance, he would require half of whatever was paid. Brett insisted that she should have two-thirds and, initially, accepted that the figure of $10,000 was no more than a bargaining ploy. "Short of a flight in a flying saucer, I could not imagine anything bringing such a sum," she wrote to Oliver, whom she asked to send books and diaries from the family library for, fifty years after the event, she could remember hardly a single detail. Brett's mind was, of course, fully occupied at the time with surviving on a day-to-day basis and there followed letter after letter from Crichton, trying to get her moving with the article. When it was completed, Crichton was understandably disturbed at the small amount of true reminiscence the article contained, guessing rightly that most of it had been culled from the material provided by Oliver.[34] Brett, in turn, was furious to discover that Crichton proposed to edit the article heavily, and asked a New York lawyer friend to intervene. "Would you accept a small painting for this," she wrote, "I am BUSTED." The lawyer, pleading lack of time, wisely kept out of that hornets' nest and the piece finally appeared in the *New Yorker* in May, 1953. The $10,000, a figure Brett had conveniently forgotten was notional and had begun to look upon as her right, turned out to be pie in the sky, for the *New Yorker* paid only $410 which, after the deduction of an agent's ten per cent and Crichton's one-third, left Brett with only $246. Nevertheless, if Edward's coronation turned out not to realise the fortune she had hoped for, writing, she decided, might and thereafter she bombarded the New York literary agency with pieces on Queen Victoria's funeral, Queen Victoria's Jubilee, Queen Victoria and Dancing Classes at Windsor, Stokowski, Katherine Mansfield and anyone and anything else she thought might be worth the price of an honest painting. When that failed to bring in more than $35 – for a reprint in a collection of her *New Yorker* article – the idea of barter now occurred to Brett, despite the fact that her offer to swap a small painting for legal advice had been given short shrift. She was, after all, as an artist, accustomed to being on the receiving end of such propositions – "Dear Lady Brett, Would you swap a painting for drapes, vegetables, a hat and suit, anything," one letter dated 1963 reads. Unfortunately, the value of the art she was offering appears to have been unappreciated by those she wished to make her partners in the proposed transactions. When her car began to show signs of age, she addressed herself directly to Henry Ford Jr:

I am writing to ask you whether you can do something for me, while at the same time I do something for you. Will you accept a painting of mine in exchange for a new Station Wagon? My present Station Wagon, a 1951, is beginning to crack up. For years now I have been painting the Indians. I have painted their beautiful Ceremonial Dances, in order to make a record of them as they do not allow them to be photographed or any drawings made of them. I have done this to preserve a record in case in course of time the American way of life entirely absorbs the Indians and they cease to dance. I have to memorise the dances and paint them entirely from memory. They take months to paint. They are records of a way of life and of a culture.

I enclose some photographs to show you the kind of work I do. I put a high price on the Ceremonials because of the risks I run (of offending the Indians), the length of time it takes to paint them. Will you exchange a Station Wagon for a Ceremonial?[35]

14

1956–1969: Mink Coats and Baked Beans

Early in 1956, pressed by Frieda, Brett revealed that, since shortly after Millicent Rogers' death in 1953, she had been cultivating a "secret" friendship with a woman in Santa Fe. "My friend is what is called a 'Healer'. I have followed her teaching for three years . . . the only reason I have been secretive is to avoid argument."[1] The woman was Ruby Corput, who called herself "Tiny Rimpoche" or, in her healing role, simply "Tiny Mother". Brett was already seventy years old at the time of their first meeting. Her deafness had not improved with age, although the hearing aids she used had advanced a little on "Toby", the tin ear trumpet of Garsington days, and, though she tried still to keep physically active, her body often rebelled. She wrote of a planned fishing trip with Angie Ravagli:

> I want to get a big one, one of the old gang not a fish hatchery one. All the same, fish or no fish, I love prowling the rivers. I squeak and creak in every limb but am gradually limbering up."[2]

Brett's financial situation remained as precarious as ever and, while her eyesight still allowed her to paint without difficulty, selling her work successfully was an absolute necessity if she were, in her own phrase, to keep her chin above water. And, as a letter written to Oliver a few years earlier shows, she was, naturally, as much concerned with the certainty of death as with the possibilities of life.

> As one gets older, there seems to be no future – one speculates on life all one's life, then suddenly one realises that all one has to speculate about is DEATH and that carries one into a void, there is no visual picture, there are no boundaries, so when one plans about life, one plans a phantasy!! That is what I suppose drives old people to dwelling on the past, there is the past like the tail of a kite streaming out behind one, but in front of one there is just a huge uncharted SPACE . . . I feel hustled, I want to paint so many things before I take that leap into the Unknown.[3]

The beliefs provided by Tiny Mother were tailor-made for Brett. They offered a kind of cargo cult to which was added the reassurance of direct communication with that "uncharted space", with what Brett learnt to call "the Other Side". On the Other Side were, on the one hand, "the Boys", that is to say, Lawrence and Murry and, when the occasion demanded, her father, to provide emotional and romantic succour; and, on the other, Brett's personal spirit guide, Father Flaminthorius, to whom she turned for advice on day-to-day problems and decisions and who was responsible for her everyday material needs. Father Flaminthorius dispensed in accordance with a primitive post-hoc determinism – if he gave to you, you'd been good, if he didn't, you hadn't. Father Flaminthorius would assess Brett's need and deserving and provide either a "supply" – with a certain delicacy the word "money" was never referred to – or a "load".

> Dearest Tiny Rimpoche,
> . . . you say it is NOT YOU THAT GIVES OUT THE LOADS BUT OUR HOUSE . . . You said on the phone that if it was you that gave the loads, you would give me much more than I was getting. Now that kind of upset me, because I feel I have lately carried quite a heavy load and considerable pain for weeks . . . I am waiting to get the green light from Father Flaminthorius to have the cyst taken out of my shoulder.[4]

Thus, from the mid-1950s onwards, unknown to even close friends, Brett followed Father Flaminthorius. Each morning, waking with the dawn or before, while still in bed, she took her daily trip to "the Other Side". There she and the Boys – there were no female rivals – often decked like ancient Romans in togas of cloth of gold, communed mystically with each other. Returning, Brett lay in bed with her dog, Little Reggie, and composed her daily letter to Father Flaminthorius. Often pages long, each began with the same salutation, "I am to be with Thee and Thou art to be with me," taught to her by Tiny Mother. Each, except when she was seeking the most mundane advice – "Should I go to Sante Fe on Thursday or Monday" – was on very much the same theme: "When is the Supply coming?" If a "supply" had recently arrived, in the shape of a painting sold or an allowance received, unabashed and more ambitiously, Brett would ask, "When is the Big Supply coming?" By the time her eyesight began to fail in the early 1970s, Brett had filled several large tin trunks with these handwritten and carefully filed daily outpourings. Brett's relationship with Tiny Rimpoche, to whom for many years, she sent small monthly sums[5] and the escapist fantasy the beliefs provided, became an important part of her life and was yet known perhaps only to her later partner, John Manchester, who, like many Taosenos, Indian or Anglo,* was not averse to a touch of mysticism himself. For down-to-earth Frieda, once she satisfied her curiosity and her not-unexpected jealousy over Brett's secret new friend, the simple religious water-wings of "the Brett", "the Holy Russian Idiot", had little appeal, even though by 1956 Frieda was seriously ill. Frieda died in August, on her seventy-seventh birthday, in her home a few yards from Brett's, and, according to Brett's account, remained an earth-mother to the very last.

Brett's title to the land given her by Frieda for her house had never been properly documented. When she asked Angelo Ravagli to verify her ownership, Angie, writing in an Italian accent that had defied his twenty-five-year residence in the Rocky Mountains, demanded a quid pro quo.

> Talking about houses, you remember that girl called Niki? Well, in the spere of the moment, I let have my appartment for half of the rent. She gave me a check for $35. Later on I cash it and it came beck, was no good . . . somebody did broke in my appartment, so I checked that olso, they try to bracke but nothing was stollen . . . in caming to California, I had the same trouble you had in the car. My not only did not warmed the heater but the radiator was boiling badly. I had to stop and find the wrong. They finded a water pump liking and after washing the pump thoroly, averthing is O.K.
>
> The picture I would like to have in exchange for the abstract of the clear title of your land, is the one like you did for Sebastian. Of course, the abstract I shall give to you only if the deal with Mrs Mex goes trought. O.K.?[6]

Some modest recognition came Brett's way in April, 1957, when, with Oliver's assistance, a portrait of Lawrence was sold to the National Portrait Gallery for $300. Encouraged by the sale and perhaps hoping to see her two former lovers, the Boys from the Other Side, face to face with each other in Trafalgar Square, Brett offered to donate to the gallery a portrait of John Middleton Murry, who had died in 1957. The gallery was compelled to refuse the gift because of a rule requiring its subjects to have been dead at least ten years. Brett also asked Oliver to try to trace the missing Garsington conversation piece, *Umbrellas*, again with the intention of donating it to the National Portrait Gallery. Oliver's inquiries revealed that in 1939 *Umbrellas* had been acquired by the Contemporary Art Society who intended to exhibit it at Platt Hall,

* White residents of New Mexico who are of neither Indian nor Spanish origin.

Manchester, but did not do so because of the outbreak of war. Thereafter, all record of the work had been lost. Brett's "revealing little painting"[7] of Lawrence was hung in the National Portrait Gallery the following December (1957), alongside a "genial" drawing of Lawrence by Edmond Kapp. The heady prospect of a belated recognition led Brett to visit London the following year for the first time since 1938. Brett was, of course, short of funds for the trip and Taos held a party for her, a kind of bridal "shower". At the centre of the room an out-of-season Christmas tree was placed, and each guest was invited to hang on it a $1 note. When the party ended, Brett counted the donations and was appalled to discover a Russellian problem in one-to-one correspondence – the number of notes amounted to one less than the number of people. In the aftermath, she got rather more than a dollar's worth of vindictive pleasure, speculating on which of her so-called friends could have been so mean. Brett then sailed to Southampton on the *Queen Mary* in October, 1958, attended the State Opening of Parliament, went to see her sister-in-law, Zena Dare, as Mrs. Higgins in the long-running *My Fair Lady* and, in all the excitement, was persuaded that it would be a great honour to be allowed to give a work to the Tate Gallery, the painting to be forwarded from New Mexico on her return. "In the face of your own generosity," the Tate wrote, "it does seem petty to mention the question of costs . . . [could the painting be] rolled and sent by the least expensive route?"[8]

One of the myths that faced Brett in Taos, principally due to the belief that a member of the British aristocracy could not possibly be poor, was that, somewhere or other, probably under the ramshackle bed in her studio, was a secret hoard and that her apparent poverty was simply artistic eccentricity. Brett was rarely able to refuse an outstretched hand – and there were many, not only from impecunious Taosenos but, also, dressed up in bonhomie and jest, from passing academics and scholars. One such, to whom she had given free the right to reproduce passages from *Lawrence and Brett*, wrote "jolly" letters at regular intervals, mentioning, by-the-by, that "the place on the wall was ready" for one of her paintings, and "when I'm rich, the first thing I'm going to do is buy one", and so on. Fortunately, there is no evidence that Brett ever fell for it, for although she managed, from time to time, to make a gift of everything from a car to a cotton handkerchief, her own work was a different matter.

She was very well aware of the attitude that the work on the studio wall has no value until someone *else* has bought it, and that there is something quite special about fulsome praise for a painting that makes one deserve it as a gift. Brett rarely gave her work away though she might distribute the proceeds the minute a painting was sold, and she did, as every artist must, encounter a good number of india-rubber cheques in the course of her career, including one from a much-respected poet. Institutions were often little better behaved. When she sold her remaining correspondence, 2,000 letters in a tin trunk for $2,700, it took six months of reminders for the cheque to arrive. When it did, it was accompanied by somewhat ungracious exhortations for the old lady to "get to work on the Hawks". Later, most of her photographs and negatives, the value of which was, at the time admittedly, unclear, were removed from her at little or no cost by the big collecting institutions.

In 1962 Mabel died. She had been physically unwell and mentally a little unstable for some time. One of her natural urges was to reduce the number of her possessions as she grew older. Brett recalled that this could go so far that Mabel had often to be restrained from throwing her false teeth away through the car window. The following year Brett's brother Oliver died. The two had discovered in recent years a much greater affinity than had been apparent during Brett's rebellious and Oliver's relatively orthodox youth, in particular in their attitude to their father and the psychological damage they felt had been caused to them by the double standards of morality he had adopted. Oliver's mantle, so far as Brett's welfare was concerned, was quietly and efficiently assumed by her nephew, Lionel and his wife Christian, the present Lord and Lady Esher, who became the sounding boards for Brett's plans and fears and the target of her undiminishing supply of tangled financial problems. In Taos, with Frieda and now Mabel on the Other Side, Brett felt for a time alone but, in the spring of 1963, a new neighbour, John Manchester, moved into the house next door. Within a very short time Brett, now eighty years old, and Manchester, in his late-forties, had become close friends, not least because Brett felt that, in this disciple of Carl Jung, she might have someone who would understand her secret life with Father Flaminthorius. "We have a mutual outlook on God and Guardians," Brett wrote to Lionel. But Brett, the living remnant of Lawrence, was as much a touchstone and totem for the Anglos of Taos as was the Blue Lake for the Indians of the pueblo or the desert morada for the Spanish Penitentes, and when the friendship of Brett and Manchester turned first into a business relationship and later into a partnership, domestic and financial, Taos was suspicious to say the least.

The first venture of the MBB Corporation – the initials stood for Manchester, Brett, and a third, unidentified individual – was to convert a house in Taos into an art gallery. The house was bought on mortgage, as Manchester had been unable to sell his former home in Santa Fe, a building that was also mortgaged. In their new gallery, opened in the summer of 1964, Manchester, taking a standard agent's commission, exhibited Brett's work and that of just one or two others, fixing the price of Brett's paintings at a much higher level than had ever previously been asked.

Manchester, in contrast with some of the galleries that had formerly shown Brett's work, galleries that may have been handling twenty or more other artists and at the same time have been run by an artist or artist-manque, as much interested in promoting his or her own work as anyone else's, made every effort to see that, at this higher price, Brett's paintings sold. And sell, at last, they did, so that, in 1965, with painting sales of $8,000 in the previous twelve months, much more than she had ever sold in a single year before, Brett proudly crowed that, for the first time in her life, she had made enough money to pay income tax.

Relief was short lived for, by the following year, the financial pressures were as great as ever, principally because of a complex series of mortgages and loan agreements that Manchester or the MBB Corporation, into which Brett had paid all the proceeds from her painting sales, had entered into. Taos jealousies now became venomous but there is not the slightest evidence from Brett's correspondence that she was not completely aware what she was up to financially. Tomorrow had never been a day that she had lived for and a close friend and neighbour was beyond price. "I will be eighty-two next birthday," she wrote to Lionel, "dead money piled up in a Bank doesn't seem decent. If with some of what I make I can help others, O.K. Money should be alive and moving. All one needs is enough to bury oneself with!"[9] What bothered the First State Bank of Taos was whether there might be enough even for that. Brett's liabilities amounted to her share of the mortgage on the new gallery, plus a separate mortgage on the house next door which had been bought at the same time but was let and thus produced an income to cover its outgoings; her half-share of the liability for interest and capital charges on a loan of $2,750, made by the bank to her and Manchester jointly; and a separate loan, for which she alone was liable, of $1,150. In addition to that there were mortgages on Manchester's house and the house in Santa Fe that he had still failed to sell and, although Brett was clear that these had nothing to do with her, nevertheless the relationship between the two was now sufficiently strong for Brett to feel a responsibility. The first and most positive result of this financial entanglement was the decision to sell off the gallery premises and house in the centre of Taos and move the gallery into Manchester's own home, next door to Brett's, a plan that Brett welcomed, as it meant that she did not have to leave home when it was her turn to look after the shop, but could do it from her studio window.[10] Brett then had the interesting notion of asking the bank whether she might pay off debts by mortgaging her paintings in the same way that one might mortgage a house, repayment to take place when the paintings were eventually sold. Not surprisingly, it was an idea that failed to excite the Taos bank, despite the palette rampant upon its coat of arms.[11] The bank suggested that Brett seek support from her family, for the new generation of Bretts she had encountered on her London trip of 1958 were much more fascinated by and indeed, proud of their "Aunt Doll" than the generation she'd grown up with which had become accustomed to her pleas of insolvency. When Lionel, who was already regularly supplementing her allowance, was approached, Brett had again to convince the Treasury of her penury, before he was allowed to transfer funds. Brett produced a detailed account of her finances but the Bank of England took almost a year to approve the transfer, looking carefully into every last detail. Brett complained to her Taos bank manager:

> You and I have told them before, that I have no Income except what my nephew sends me and my Social Security Check of $65 a month. That's all that is secure and regular. The selling of paintings is a hazardous profession, it can be a Mink Coat or baked beans. Mostly baked beans, as you know. That's all there is to it.[12]

At the time, Brett's great nephew, her brother Maurice's grandson, Simon Brett, also a painter, was staying in Taos on an extended visit and he, less involved in the hothouse Taos atmosphere of slight and counter-slight, provided Lionel Esher with what was perhaps the fairest summary of the relationship between Brett and Manchester as it stood in 1966.

> There are a couple of payments to Mr Manchester apart from gallery commission, nothing that is not quite justified by their intimacy. She has been buying groceries for him during the past year, but now the situation is reversed . . . the financial relationship of Doll and John Manchester as artist and dealer and as friend and friend, seems to be entirely above board. For this and that she perhaps gave him $150 in 1966 – quite reasonable. What John "gets out" of Doll is rather her name and prestige, the opportunity to be known as her protector and the closest companion of her declining years . . .[13]

John Manchester, it might be added, acknowledged himself as a diagnosed schizophrenic and had made several attempts on his own life. Brett was clearly fascinated by the whole business and wrote obsessively of it to Lionel and Christian Esher and of a miracle cure with vitamin pills that had apparently worked wonders in Manchester's case.[14] Brett seems also to have been able to regard the condition with a certain amount of humour and detachment. She wrote to Lionel in the poor summer of 1967: "We have had an unusual amount of rain, most of the town suffers from Arthritis that doesn't suffer from Alcoholism and Schizophrenia."[15]

But Manchester, although he was now taking a fifty per cent commission on Brett's paintings, showed that he could promote her work and sell it. It may have been possible for Brett to retain sixty-six per cent of the proceeds in another gallery but, as she noted in a letter to Lionel, an extra sixteen per cent is of little value if the painting is not sold at all.

> Pat me on the head! At 83 I am having as much fun as I have ever had and my paintings are being recognised . . . A PATRON BOUGHT SEVEN OF MY PAINTINGS – TWENTY TWO THOUSAND DOLLARS!!!!! *WHAT* do you think of that? John has raised and raised my prices in the face of squawks from the Collectors, he has taken a great deal of abuse and now here we are repaid.[16]

Brett was aware that the sale would raise her prices, that she was acquiring, as she grew older, a certain scarcity value, and that her rapidly diminishing life expectancy might cause the collectors to hurry over. The following year, 1968, she broke even the 1967 record and in September sold just a couple of paintings for $24,000 – one for $18,000, the other for $6,000. For even such small fortune and for the fame reflected from Lawrence, there was, of course, a toll . . .

> Dear Madam . . . you see I know the real Lawrence . . . not the Lawrence of Eastwood, but the former one, whose great-aunt once had an accouchement in Esher House . . . I would appreciate your thoughts regarding this one person I have in mind.[17]

* * *

> My name is Fritz. Can you find work for my girl friend in Taos as a cook?[18]

* * *

> My brother visited you about three or four summers ago and although he didn't purchase it, was most attracted by your painting of

an Apache(?) encampment . . . it has haunted us ever since. May my wife and I call on you on Sunday, after skiing?[19]

* * *

I am a young lawyer and aspiring novelist. Your [radio] talk has made me resolve to spend a week of vacation time in Taos. [Can you] or one of your friends provide me with some information as to where in Taos a man and his wife can stay cheaply and away from the tourist bustle? I would deeply appreciate a reply from you. However, as one who values his own privacy to an extent bordering upon paranoia, I will fully understand if you prefer not to respond.[20]

* * *

A Christmas card from a young man who was in the gallery last summer: "you know, the one with the beard."[21]

* * *

Was Frieda Lawrence left-handed?[22]

* * *

Did Lawrence ever discuss with you the ideas of Schopenhauer and Nietsche. What was his general attitude towards them? Did he ever mention any particular debt to them?[23]

* * *

Dear Dorothy . . . I do not know you and you dont know me . . . I am a photographer . . . I want to have some pictures of indians and I feel like coming up, unfortunatly I am a poor photographer but good so good sometime I impress myself. Unfortunatly I have to ask you if you can put me up while I am up there and what would be the cheepest I can live on on my journey.[24]

* * *

You may recall that in 1950 my husband and I were honeymooning in Taos. I have learned that you have written a book – I would like to buy two . . . would you write an inscription in each one: one "To

Jack . . ." and one "To Helen . . ." . . . when we were in Taos, my husband was using his real name . . .[25]

* * *

I am a Burbank police officer and as my hobbies I collect law badges and autographs. I would consider it an honour if you would be kind enough to send me your autograph. If you ever paint a portrait or a painting of a policeman, please be kind enough to advise me as I would love to display it with my collection.[26]

* * *

25 years ago you visited Ojo Caliente with Tony Luhan . . .[27]

* * *

You may remember me: I was the one visiting you last August and my friend had a camera.[28]

15

1970–1977: Ceremonials and Pot-boilers

> There is a dreadful Lawrence Festival in September, got up by some local females, I was put down unasked to lecture on Lawrence, I have flatly refused. I am not a lecturer, I dont like the idea of talking about a close friend, in public, its kind of indecent.[1]

> Brett had refused to take part in the conference, whose sponsors would not pay the exorbitant fee she demanded.[2]

> All they want to know is whether I slept with Lawrence and that, I'm afraid, is my business.[3]

Most of the Taos money was on the belief that John Manchester put Brett up to it. As Manchester was on an extended visit to New York when Brett first refused to be co-opted as a delegate to the Lawrence conference, the probability is that the decision was Brett's own and that the idea of asking a large fee occurred to her only as a means of refusal. But she did not *ask* for it – the story arose following an interview with *Women's Wear Daily*, where, after explaining her attitude, Brett flung in a joking aside: "They offered me $200. If it had been $2,000 I might have crept out and said something. Probably something a little indecent."[4]

Brett could have done with the money. 1968, when a single afternoon's sales had brought in $24,000 for just two paintings, turned out to have been the financial peak of her artistic career. In 1970 hardly a painting was sold, the following year the same. For one thing, there were very few paintings to sell. Although at eighty-three, and at eighty-four, eighty-five and eighty-six, Brett was having "as much fun as ever", sheer age and failing eyesight were making it difficult for her to produce any quantity of finished work. She was managing to complete only two or three paintings in the course of a year and these were no longer, on the one hand, the large and expensive "Ceremonials" nor, on the other, the small and easily sold "pot-boilers", Brett's own term for the rapidly-produced works that had represented the backbone of her painting income. The complex "Ceremonials" had become physically too taxing, the pot-boilers she quite perversely refused to paint – the large sales of the late 1960s had convinced Brett that she was now above that kind of painting. The fact was that she had, in reality, been living on capital rather than income. Many of the paintings sold in those few halcyon summers were not recent works but were from stock, large works that because of their price, had hung fire on the gallery walls. Little was being produced to replace them.

But, despite her age, her correspondence that year, although a little repetitive, shows her to be still lively and active. At the end of 1969, she had been given a new two-year driving licence. She later suggested that the clerk, concerned that she might fail it, had skimmed over the eyesight requirements of the test. Announcing the news in a New Year letter to Lionel Esher, she wrote "for the moment, everything is hunky dory . . . when I am old, I would like to find someone to live with me".[5] She was eighty-six.

A year later, she wrote more realistically, "I wish I could find a companion" and, by the end of 1971, Brett's eyesight had so far declined that a further renewal of her driving licence was refused. It was not an unjust decision as her letters of the time had begun to show. Typed in all directions on the page, often one line on top of another, the correspondence is only decipherable when one examines the possible mis-hits and near-misses of the typewriter keyboard. Brett, stubborn to the last, blamed the typewriter rather than her failing vision and many of those letters ask for $100 to replace the machine. Gossip later accused John Manchester of withholding Brett's correspondence. On the one hand, she could not have read any incoming mail without assistance. On the other, Manchester wisely failed to post the almost unintelligible letters that could not have failed to have given distress to their intended recipients. The loss of the driving licence hit Brett severely, coinciding as it did with the news of the death of her sister, Syv, who, apart from Zena, who died in 1975, represented to Brett the only surviving member of her generation. News of Brett from Taos was second-hand and conflicting. One life-long friend, with no axe to grind, reported Brett in the spring of 1972 as being well cared for and in very good shape. Other friends of long-standing, equally concerned, were disturbed that she had given power of attorney over all her affairs, financial and otherwise, to her partner, John Manchester. Matters came to a boil early in 1973 when a group of Taosenos cabled Lord Esher in London, asking him to travel to Taos at once for they feared for Brett's safety. So far as Manchester was concerned, Brett, at nearly ninety years of age, was decaying rapidly and needed a very great deal of looking after. He had, indeed, been doing just that for the whole of the previous decade, as companion more than neighbour to an old lady who, even in her younger days, had never been notoriously concerned about herself or her surroundings. To the well-intentioned group of Brett's friends, Brett appeared to need more care and attention than she was receiving. Even at the time and on the spot, it would have been difficult to disentangle myth and reality, for Taos is a place of bitter and often arbitrary jealousies. Manchester had never been wholly accepted or liked in Taos. For ten years he had monopolised a lady regarded more as a monument and historical institution than as a living and frequently very idiosyncratic human being – there is no lack of evidence from Frieda and Mabel that Brett was not the easiest of people to live with or even near. Faced with conflicting cables, letters, round-robins and petitions, Lionel Esher was forced by the doubt and anxiety to make a flying visit to Taos in the late summer of 1973. The situation seems to have been soothed, if not resolved, by the finding and employment of a living-in companion and housekeeper for Brett, a lady called Muriel Holle, the funds for whom were provided by the Brett family as a whole. Holle seems to have been a much needed model of cleanliness and efficiency but, needless to say, in less than no time, Brett hated having someone in her house all the time and would refuse to speak to Holle for days on end.

Brett's fifty years in New Mexico were marked in 1974 with retrospective exhibitions in both Taos and Santa Fe and by the re-publication of her book, *Lawrence and Brett*, but her painting days were, by then, to all intents and purposes over. When Manchester, after many false starts and changes of mind, left Taos and Brett for Las Vegas in 1977, he wrote:

> I don't know what keeps her alive, except that she now has a great fear of dying – and hangs on to life (and to me) with great voraciousness. That is one reason I have to get out of here. She would completely consume me otherwise. She *wants* me to die when she does so she won't have to go alone – so I'm (psychologically) fleeing for my life.[6]

Brett survived Manchester's departure by only a month or so. She was admitted to hospital on August 24th, 1977, with congestion of the lungs and died three days later, a couple of months short of her ninety-fourth birthday.

And the ashes? In Brett's will, she directed that she be cremated and that "the urn which will contain my ashes shall be taken and deposited at the Pink Rocks of the Del Monte Ranch", a spot where she hinted that she had scattered some of Lawrence's remains in 1935. Del Monte is the home of Rachel Hawk who, quite reasonably, did not welcome the possibility of her ranch becoming a new tourist mecca. Nor was Mrs. Hawk a great friend of John Manchester. In consequence Brett's request could not be carried out with any expediency and the urn containing the ashes was taken by Manchester to Las Vegas after the cremation ceremony. A casual inquiry as to the whereabouts of the ashes a few months later, revealed that they were in the garage of his new home. Manchester's house on a suburban development in Las Vegas is by no means spacious and, at the time, most of his belongings were still in packing cases in the garage, itself an integral part of the single-storey building and, in effect, an annexe to the dining room. His answer seemed, therefore, neither odd nor disrespectful. He was, he said, waiting for the fuss to die down before seeking a means of carrying out Brett's wish. When, a little later, over lunch in Taos, I received a similar inquiry, I passed on the information without a thought. Within days it had returned to me: "Do you know what that guy has done with Brett's ashes? Put them in his goddam garage!" Brett's remains must have been vibrating wickedly in her urn.

Epilogue

When Frieda Lawrence died in 1956, she left the Ranch to the University of New Mexico. Over the years it developed into a conference centre and a faculty weekend facility, breeze block and quonset huts hidden in the pines. A caretaker lives in the house built by Frieda and Angie but, behind it, the original small cabin remains, housing each summer a fellow appointed by the university. In 1970 I was that fellow, living with my family in the log and adobe cabin, tending the hat, jacket, suitcase and typewriter left by Lawrence and sitting on the porch in the chair supposedly made by him, looking out past the great pine in the yard down the slopes to Taos in the distance.

At that time, Rananims were springing up like psilocybe mushrooms in the rarefied New Mexican air for there had been a great immigration of hippies from California when the flower children had discovered the San Andreas fault. The influx had brought problems. The Chicano population had reacted strongly to the all-you-need-is-peace-and-love generation who had, despite their philosophy, bought up every spare acre from the Anglo realtors, acres that the Chicanos had been coveting all their hard-working lives, and then messed up the ancient Spanish water rights. Some of the burger stalls carried recommendations about good ways of keeping America beautiful and most of the gas stations reserved the right to refuse the use of their rest-rooms to persons suspected of endangering the social health of the community – translated that meant, "long hair and bright clothes, you better go piss in the desert". The net result was that it was open season on long-hairs. Communes had been burnt and their inhabitants attacked and raped and the long-hairs responded by forming a security force – two-way radios in the front of the car, baseball bats in the back.

To complicate matters Dennis Hopper, the Easy Rider himself, on the crest of his film success, had moved into Mabel Luhan's ranch and no one seemed sure whether he was an Anglo, a compadre or a long-hair. The local radio station tried to sort things out one morning when it asked compadres to try to distinguish between those newcomers who wore strange clothes and had long hair and were a menace to the social health of the community and those newcomers who wore strange clothes and long hair and were our beautiful friends from Hollywood. It was clearly a difficult distinction to make and one afternoon a little while later, Hopper was involved in a hassle with some Chicano kids while asking the way to the cave Lawrence was supposed to have used in *The Woman Who Rode Away*. Hopper tried to make a citizen's arrest with a little help from his friends but a few days later found that he himself was up on an assault charge. There was even talk of a gang of angels descending from the coast to protect their new-found hero so we all left town one weekend expecting a holocaust. Meanwhile, the Luhan ranch began to resemble a cavalry fort waiting for Geronimo with bit-players in cowboy dudes stalking the flat adobe roof, toting carbines and shotguns.

One afternoon, in the midst of all this, I had managed for the umpteenth time to trek down from the mountains to find the bank closed and a flash-flood threatening – I never did work out the banking hours but I did see a great deal of thunder and lightning – so I ducked into the Manchester Gallery to kill an hour or two and hide from the weather. Manchester showed me around and invited me to return for dinner to meet Brett. A couple of weeks later I was sitting with Brett on the porch, while Manchester busied himself with the cooking. Brett would not have looked out of place in one of the nearby communes. Round her head she had wrapped a long flowing scarf and over it she wore a small hat covered in badges and signs of the Zodiac. While we were talking, her Art Deco hearing aid tuned to my wavelength and crackling on the table between us, the phone rang and Manchester suddenly announced that, quite on the spur of the moment, we had all been invited to dinner elsewhere. There would be no problem – we would take what he had prepared with us and we would have a slap-up meal. It transpired that what he had prepared was not a lot – some salad and some pissole. I still don't know what pissole is but I do recall that it didn't seem much for three people but, at the time, it didn't cross my mind that the venue for dinner might have been pre-arranged.

We piled into Manchester's car, leaving mine at the gallery, and crossed town, striking off the main road and into a warren of dirt roads and adobe. A lady in a long white shroud with feathers standing upright in her hair and one of those handsome tanned faces ridged with deep firm furrows like a map of trench warfare, was waiting to greet us. "Sean!" she acclaimed. "We know each other already!" I suppose I looked legitimately puzzled at this from a complete stranger, so she went on, "We have met in a thousand previous incarnations!" That didn't help very much either but nor did it surprise me – Taos has always been heavily into that brand of mysticism.

So we had pot roast and pissole and whisky and choke-cherry wine while the sun gave us a great old set out across the high New Mexican plateau. I don't remember much of the conversation except that Brett's hearing aid fizzed and hummed between the lighted candles and the batteries appeared to be running out and causing her difficulty. Brett bent over attentively, continually twiddling the knobs but there seemed to be some peculiar kind of time delay so that she would enter the conversation around three sentences too late, adding some remark to a topic we had finished discussing a paragraph earlier. Eventually the batteries ran out altogether and Brett started to nod off so that Manchester decided it was time he drove this very old lady home. But, he insisted, I should stay for dessert and then phone him to return and pick me up. My car, you will recall, was back at his place on the other side of town.

That did not seem too problematic. America in those days impressed me as a place where cars grew, like abandoned refrigerators, on backlots and there was always one around to be borrowed. So Manchester departed, with my sweater still on the back seat of his car and Brett still trying to get some sense out of her hearing aid. I returned to the table and my hostess excused herself, leaving me in the candlelight to my strawberries and choke-cherry wine.

At this point recollection becomes blurred. It was a long room, low-beamed and irregular, just growed, as adobe dwellings do, with limbs going off in all directions. We had been dining at one end, near the kitchen and the Metro-Goldwyn window where we had watched the sun giving its late night performance over Tres Pechugas. Up at the other end was some kind of complex of bathrooms – where I figured my hostess had gone – staircases, libraries, all twisting about beneath the thick oak vigas and slender aspen latillas. There, between the beams, appeared a naked lady, shrouded only in the light of the candle she was holding. A large naked lady, advancing on me like the spirit of Christmas coming. My hostess. She, it transpired, had decided, or the stars had foretold, or Jung had predicted, or the Sacred Blue Lake had sent the message down or the vibes had turned her on to the idea, depending on which of the current local philosophies was on line at the moment, that she ought to conceive a leprechaun and, with a name like mine, she was sure I could turn that particular trick.

Well, I started humming and crackling like Brett's deaf aid about getting back to the ranch and she started saying it would be a terrible thing to phone Manchester now it was one in the morning and ask him to come and pick me up, so I said I'd borrow her car and she said her car was her right arm, so I said why didn't she get some clothes on and drive me and she said she was too drunk and besides what was the hurry. Well, I said, it's late. And I'm tired. And . . . flash . . . flash . . . flash . . . idea . . . thinks . . . and next morning, ahem, next morning . . . it was like this: sitting up there on the Lawrence ranch, I'd been longing to climb Mount Lobo right behind and it was something I couldn't do on my own and . . . and . . . by an incredible coincidence, at last I'd found an experienced guide and the only day he could do it was tomorrow, that is today, starting at six in the morning because we'd need all day. I was very sorry but that was it, I'd been waiting all summer to do it. But, she replied, she'd been waiting months and years to do it, for the chance to conceive a leprechaun and we could get an alarm call for five a.m. and then she'd be sober enough to drive me back to my car.

Climb Mount Lobo after a five a.m. alarm call and a night spent conceiving leprechauns with a Jungian with a feather in her hair who was drunk on choke-cherry wine? A last straw floated across and I clutched at it. "I'll walk," I said. "You'll walk!" she cried. "People don't walk!" "I do and what's more, I am," all the time moving towards the door until I stumbled through the fly-screens into the yard, cursed her silent car and searched a way through broken-down fences and adobe abodes to the road.

Down at the road, outside a supermarket masquerading as a trading post, was a pay-phone. Now, in the whole of my time in Taos, before and indeed after, I never saw hide nor limb of a taxi but, at one-thirty a.m. on that hot August night, I thought "Taxi!" as though I were standing in Piccadilly in the rush-hour. Firstly, the glass in the booth had been smashed. Then, there was blood all over the handset and flies were buzzing around like vultures over Mexican offal. And, if that weren't enough, there was no listing under "Taxi!" and I didn't have a dime piece in my pocket anyway. So I started to walk.

I had driven that road a good many times. Straight as a guardsman's crease, spotted between drifts of desert by gas stations, Taco Bells and Tastee Freeze. In the thin daylight air, seeing the town as near as that, it seemed no distance at all. But, on foot, at night, four straight miles was endless. I guess I was about half way when I saw a pair of headlights, high-off-the-road-pickup-truck headlights, coming towards me out of town. The lights slowed down as they neared, went on, pulled a sharp circle round an all-night gas station and came back and slowed down.

Well, something about the way it slowed down told me all was not too well so I moved a pace or two down the flood ditch, up the other side and sheltered behind a small bush on the Indian reservation. The pickup stopped for a minute or two, shouting indecipherable compliments across at me and then drove off again into town. I suppose I had gone another quarter mile when more lights appeared in the distance, this time two sets of headlights and I figured somehow it was the same guys plus friends and that there must be something special about those friends, so, without waiting to see, I took off into the reservation, lowered myself down the bank of an arroyo and peered back over the top. Sure enough, the two trucks careered round the gas station and screamed to a rapid halt just where I'd left the road. I couldn't understand what they were shouting but I wasn't about to go looking for an interpreter, for the next thing I knew, they were shooting at me. Or rather at anything out there in the desert that they thought might be me-shaped. I slid my strange clothes and long hair down into the arroyo again and prayed. To Jung, the Sacred Blue Lake, Father Flaminthorius and the Holy Mother, figuring that ought to cover all the local possibilities. After an eternity, the wheels screeched again and I peeped out of the arroyo.

The trucks had gone and with them any courage I had, so I started to zig-zag from lot to lot, running from one side of the road to the other in an attempt to dodge any light that was filtering about, turning the four miles into six or eight. For a while I hid and rested in the foundations of a new bank that was being built for a community solid and respectable enough to deserve two banks and, while I sheltered in the mock adobe, a huge car-transporter tore past, empty and rattling wildly. I sneaked out from the unfinished bank and walked on. When I reached the built-up zone, the truck had pulled up outside the local Safeway and its driver was checking the rattles with a wrench the size of a Turkish wrestler's upper arm. As I approached, he turned and held the wrench in the port-arms position and said, "Wanna ride?"

At the same time, across the road, a prowl car had stopped prowling and I figured if I refused the ride, they'd want to know what the hell I was doing walking. After all, just ahead, at the town's only traffic lights was a sign flashing in the night "DON'T WALK" and for all I knew there was a local ordinance against pedestrians. So I said, "Right," and climbed into the high cab. Inside, the trucker placed the wrench carefully between us and I got the message: I was obviously some kind of character and he was taking no chances.

Apart from the fact that he had been hoping I would keep him awake as far as Denver, that was that. I climbed down four miles further on at the flashing yellow lights and cut across Brett's yard to the gallery to pick up my car. The dog Reggie, I remember, barked but I took off without saying howdy neighbour back to the ranch in the quiet pines where the greatest danger came from the racoons racketing in the trashcans.

Late in 1973, the year of the round-robins, I was back in Taos and called on the old lady again. She fumbled with the intricate locks and latches that kept Reggie from wandering in the desert and I stepped over the chicken wire that fenced the doorway for the same reason and into the studio. We talked for a while about my last visit and about Scotland where I now lived and which she hadn't seen since the days of horse carriages. As she reminisced about Callander and Roman Camp, the phone rang. Brett held it to her mouth to boom "Hello" into the mouthpiece and then lowered it to the deaf aid that was hanging like an amulet from her neck to listen to the reply. She repeated this several times – "Hello" into the mouthpiece, lower it to the chest to listen for an answer – till eventually she raised it for the last time and boomed down it, "Oh, do go away, whoever you are!" and rammed the receiver back down on its hooks.

As I left I noticed a card pinned inside the back door. It read: "Remember to offer guests a drink." Whether it was an admonition to Holle, who had just moved in as Brett's housekeeper, or a reminder to herself, I never found out for they both forgot. Outside the Sangre de Cristos were sprinkled with the first snow of winter and the grey rock clearing on Mount Lobo that sometimes resembled a face, seemed to be smiling slightly. I never did make it up that mountain and I suppose I'm unlikely now to do so as I am to have lunch with Pedro. But I did have dinner with Brett.

* * *

April, 1984

The ashes, neither Lawrence's nor Brett's, agree to lie down. When this biography had reached page-proof stage, I received a call from Emil Delavenay, a Lawrence scholar who lives, appropriately enough, in Vence. Professor Delavenay had recently been in correspondence with, and later interviewed, Baron Prosper de Haulleville, a Belgian petroleum engineer. Baron de Haulleville is related by marriage to Aldous Huxley but has no interest in Taos rivalries and loyalties and certainly no axe to grind. Of his veracity, there is no reason to doubt. Shortly after Frieda's death and immediately prior to Angelo Ravagli's return to his first wife in Italy, the Baron, who was working temporarily in New Mexico, visited Ravagli in Taos. Angelo, the Baron discovered, was "a miser to an incredible degree . . . when we stayed at his place, we had to bring our own food otherwise we would have died of starvation" and "he indulged in the pleasure of drinking spirits – as long as he had nothing to pay". The Baron, therefore, brought Angelo a gift of several bottles of Bourbon which, in the course of two evenings, Angelo drank. As he did so, he "confessed", the "trois petits tours", he said, of a *bersaglieri* before dying or, in Angie's case before returning to mother church, mother country and his first wife. The substance of the confession was that Lawrence's ashes *never* left France at all but that Ravagli, in order to pocket for himself most of the expenses given him by Frieda, and believing erroneously that very large customs duties were applied to the transport of human remains, jettisoned Lawrence's ashes in Vence and then went through the rigmarole of accompanying an *empty* funeral urn from the South of France to New York, where he filled it with American ashes collected on the spot. Whether Stieglitz's remark (p. 224) claiming that even Angie really had no idea of what did happen in New York, supports this bizarre story or not seems impossible to say. Which leaves the ashes . . . where?

As for Brett's remains, they are now, I am assured, scattered where she wished them to be, on the Red Rocks below Mount Lobo. But the mountain was not happy about it. When the scatterer returned to his car, all four tyres had mysteriously gone flat.

And Brett's studio by the flashing yellow light marking the junction that leads to Taos Ski Valley is now, the billboard proclaims, Whitey's – a restaurant.

* * *

"Poor old D. H. Lawrence. He never
knew who he was working for . . ."

Angelo Ravagli on his succeeding to fifty per cent of Lawrence's literary estate on the death of Frieda Lawrence in 1956.

—Saki Karavas

Acknowledgments

The Epilogue of this book is based on an article written for the *Guardian* in 1974 to mark Dorothy Brett's fiftieth year in New Mexico. The article prompted Brett's great-nephew, Julian Shuckburgh, to suggest that I write her biography and, through him, I received the support of Brett's family in England. Lionel and Christian Esher gave me freely of their time, loaded me with parcels of letters from "Aunt Doll", and allowed me generous access to the family archives at Watlington. Simon Brett, another of Brett's great-nephews and himself a painter, who lived in Taos during the 1960s, was able to offer me an artist's insight into Brett's painting and invaluable comments upon the manuscript as it proceeded. I am grateful also to Mrs Leonora Tompkins and Sidgwick & Jackson for permission to quote from the autobiographies and correspondence of Brett's sister, Sylvia Brooke, and to Mrs Angela Thornton for permission to quote from the correspondence of Brett's sister-in-law, Zena Dare.

The biography would have made scant progress without the cooperation of Brett's business partner, companion and literary executor, John Manchester, who gave me complete access to Brett's diaries, journals, notebooks, unpublished manuscripts, unposted letters, scribblings and menu jottings, and to the two large tin trunks which acted as a cross between filing cabinets and wastepaper baskets for her correspondence. Once she realised there was gold in them thar ephemera, she was urged by collecting institutions to throw away nothing.

I also mined John Manchester's memory for the intimate detail of Brett's life he had accumulated over the years of their partnership, information freely given despite its not always reflecting well upon their relationship.

Julian Vinogradoff has given me generous permission to quote from the writings, published and unpublished, of her mother, Lady Ottoline Morrell, and has provided several of the photographs used to illustrate this book. Noel Carrington gave me memories of his sister, Dora Carrington, and of Mark Gertler and directed me to Barbara Bagenal in Sussex – she too I must thank for her hospitality and her memories of the Slade years. I have to thank Noel Carrington for permission to reproduce some of the photographs in this book and Frances Partridge for permission to quote from the letters of Dora Carrington. Luke Gertler has given me permission to quote from Mark Gertler's letters and kindly sent me copies of some of Brett's recollections of his father. Lady Juliette Huxley also gave me of her time and permission to quote from her correspondence with Brett.

Research visits to the United States were carried out partially with the assistance of a travel grant from the Scottish Arts Council and principally by imposing on American friends, some new and unused, others well-worn, for bed and board and borrowed cars. Jess and Emma Walters put me up in Austin and gave me a night at the opera while I was working at the Humanities Research Centre of the University of Texas; Phil and Lilian Gerard in New York offered their country accommodation so that I could research in the Beinecke Library at Yale; and Jan Joines in California allowed me to use her house and car for visits to Stanford University, UCLA at Berkeley, and up-state through the wine country to Ukiah to talk in what must be the smallest house in the United States with Enid Hilton, the tough and resilient old lady who once helped D. H. Lawrence smuggle copies of *Lady Chatterley's Lover* into England in her knickers.

Joe Zavadil and Ernest Tedlock of the English Faculty of the University of New Mexico were prime movers in offering me the Fellowship that took me to Taos and the Lawrence Ranch in the first place. On visits to New Mexico since I have parked myself on Norma Weaver in Albuquerque, used her as a taxi service and purloined her gas-guzzling Dodge Ramcharger pick-up truck for the high-riding, four-wheel drive up to Taos and the Sangre de Cristos. In Taos, Saki Karavas has been ever hospitable, as he was to Brett in her lifetime, and filled me with tales of Brett, Frieda, Mabel and Angelo over Mexican dinners in Cal Loving's Cocina (the whole enchilada), sometimes joined by Barbara Chavez, who has given me permission to quote from her correspondence with and memories of Brett. She and her father, Louis Cottam, generously provided some of the photographs used in this book. Marianna Howes and Arturo and Jacquie Peralta Ramos also gave me their time and recollections.

Up on the mountain, Rachel Hawk, despite long years of Lawrentians, scholars and the merely curious picking at her memory, welcomed me warmly to Del Monte Ranch and the Tower Beyond Tragedy and told me of her times with Brett, while at the Lawrence Ranch, Al Bearce, the tough-talking and hard-living custodian, regaled me with news, slanders, burritos and tacos. More often than not, through the hospitality of Ernie Blake and Jean Mayer at Taos Ski

Valley, I was able to combine work with considerable pleasure skiing the afternoons on Taos' fearsome slopes and talking Brett down in town in the evenings. My research visits to New Mexico were usually subsidised by commissions to write travel articles and I am particularly grateful to TWA for providing travel facilities in connection with these articles.

I am grateful to Gerald Pollinger, Laurence Pollinger Ltd and the Estate of the late Mrs Frieda Lawrence Ravagli for permission to quote from the works and correspondence of D. H. Lawrence, Frieda Lawrence and Angelo Ravagli; to Peter Fraser and Hart-Davis, MacGibbon for permission to quote from *Lord Esher: a Political Biography*; to Donald Gallup and the staff of the Beinecke Rare Book and Manuscript Library of Yale University for their assistance in obtaining copyright permissions in respect of the correspondence and works of Mabel Luhan and the letters of Alfred Stieglitz and Dorothy Norman and for permission to quote from letters in their possession by Brett and by Frieda Lawrence; to Mrs Laura Huxley and Chatto & Windus Ltd. for permission to quote from Aldous Huxley's *Crome Yellow* and from his correspondence; to Michael Holroyd, the Strachey Trust and William Heinemann for permission to quote from *Lytton Strachey: a Biography*; to George Allen & Unwin for permission to quote from *The Autobiography of Bertrand Russell*; to the author's literary estate and the Hogarth Press for permission to quote from the letters and journals of Virginia Woolf; to Jeffers Literary Properties for permission to quote from the poems of Robinson Jeffers and from the letters of Brett and Mabel Luhan to Una Jeffers; to the University of Wisconsin Press for permission to quote from Edward Nehls' *D. H. Lawrence: A Composite Biography*; to the staff of the Humanities Research Centre, University of Texas at Austin, for their assistance and for permission to quote from a variety of correspondence in their collection, including that of Ottoline Morrell, Mark Gertler and Spud Johnson; to the Bancroft Library of the University of California, Berkeley, for permission to quote from the correspondence of Mabel Luhan, Frieda Lawrence and Brett in their collection; to the Special Collections Department, Stanford University Library for permission to quote from letters from Katherine Mansfield to Ottoline Morrell, although it has not, unfortunately, proved possible for me to act upon that permission; and to Alice M. Vestal and the Archives and Rare Books Department of the University of Cincinnati Library for providing microfilm of their "Brett" collection and for permission to quote from the letters of D. H. Lawrence, Frieda Lawrence, Virginia Woolf, Augustus John and J. M. Keynes in that collection – they granted permission also for extensive quotation from the letters of John Middleton Murry to Dorothy Brett but, again, other interests made it impossible tomake use of that permission.

The staff of the National Library of Scotland has been ever helpful and patient of my demands and the staff of Moray House College Library, especially David Fairgrieve and Hazel Robertson, have worked hard on my behalf to obtain books from other libraries and to provide facilities to read microfilmed copies of correspondence. I am grateful also for technical assistance to Janet Queripal, Billy Gibbs and Frank Williamson. Muriel McAughtrie clean-typed the earlier sections of the manuscript until the microchip rendered her redundant. In that context I am grateful to Peter Barker and the staff of the Moray House Computer Department for educating me in the intricacies and ease of word processors.

On my first research visit to the United States, I was on my way through New York after a trip that had taken me from Las Vegas to Texas, back to the West Coast and slowly east again via New Mexico, Oklahoma, Cincinnati, Harvard and Yale. I had interviewed people for their Brett memories for hours on end, often adjusting my role to that of therapist, counsellor or drinking partner rather than biographer, more often than not coming away from an encounter with a note that read simply "Brett was a real nice/crazy/wonderful person." In Taos so many people had taken Brett out to lunch at least once a week that I began to wonder at the number of lunch hours in the New Mexican calendar. I had one more possible contact, L., on my New York list and it was a toss-up whether I arrange a meeting or take the next plane out. I decided to call it a day and phoned L. but she persuaded me that a taxi to Kennedy Airport would pass by her apartment and I might as well drop in. It was a fortunate detour. L. had known Brett since her childhood. When Brett sold her letters from Katherine Mansfield in the 1940s, she had been given the chore of typing out readable copies for the purchaser. By chance L. had stuck a carbon into the typewriter and made and kept copies of more than 100 letters from Katherine Mansfield to Brett. I had already tried to trace these letters and failed, so coming across this hoard of carbon copies was a heartening stroke of luck. Over the weeks that followed airmail packages of photocopies arrived from New York. Many of the letters had never been published and those that had were, in most cases, heavily censored. Unfortunately, late in the day, I was refused permission to quote anything of Katherine Mansfield or John Middleton Murry. Such quotations have therefore either been excised completely or summarised for their information only. I am grateful to L. both for her foresight in making the carbons and for spending so much time over the Xerox machine. I only hope that she does not consider that time wasted.

Sean Hignett, October, 1983

Notes

Unless otherwise stated, all extracts by Dorothy Brett are from *My Long and Beautiful Journey*, her unpublished memoirs.

References to surnames refer to books listed in the Select Bibliography.

The following abbreviations have been used:

AH – Aldous Huxley
Alpers – see bibliography
AS – Alfred Stieglitz
AUS – University of Texas, Austin, Texas
BERK – University of California (Berkeley)
BM – British Museum
Brett – see bibliography
Brooke – see bibliography
CINN – University of Cincinnati, Ohio
Carrington – see bibliography
DC – Dora Carrington
DEB – Dorothy E. Brett
DHL – D. H. Lawrence
E – Reginald, 2nd Viscount Esher
EG – Eithne Golden
FDHL – Frieda Lawrence
Fraser – see bibliography
Gertler – see bibliography
Holroyd – see bibliography
Huxley – see bibliography
JM – John Manchester
JMM – John Middleton Murry
KM – Katherine Mansfield
KOT – Koteliansky
LE – Lionel, 4th Viscount Esher
Luhan – see bibliography
MDL – Mabel Luhan
MG – Mark Gertler
Moore – see bibliography, Penguin ed.
Morrell – see bibliography

Nehls – see bibliography
OE – Oliver, 3rd Viscount Esher
OM – Ottoline Morrell
Purser – see bibliography
STAN – Stanford University, California
UJ – Una Jeffers
VW – Virginia Woolf (see bibliography)
WAT – Esher family archives, Watlington, Oxford
Woodeson – see bibliography
YALE – Yale University, New Haven, Connecticut

ONE. 1883–1910: ORCHARD LEA. p1–p37

1. Moore
2. Fraser
3. Brooke (*Headhunters*)
4. E, unpublished journals, Nov. 21st, 1892
5. Sylvia Brooke, *The Listener*, April 27th, 1972
6. Fraser
7. E, unpublished journals, Jan. 13th, 1895
8. E, unpublished journals, Nov. 24th, 1897
9. DEB – E, 1899: WAT
10. Brooke (*Sarawak*)
11. E, unpublished journals, Feb. 4th, 1901
12. E – Maurice Brett, 1901: WAT
13. Fraser
14. E – Maurice Brett, March 16th, 1901: WAT
15. Sir Francis Knollys – E, March 20th, 1901: WAT
16. DEB – E, June 9th, 1901: WAT
17. Brooke (*Sarawak*)
18. Brooke (*Sarawak*)
19. DEB – E, 1905, Jan. 4th, 1906, Oct. 30th, 1906: WAT
20. Brooke (*Sarawak*)

TWO. 1910–15: THE SLADE. p38–p77

1. Noel Carrington, private communication
2. Brooke
3. Brooke (*Headhunters*)
4. Zena Dare – DEB, 1970
5. Correspondence between Caleys Ltd. of Windsor and E, April, 1911: WAT
6. Points arising from Caley correspondence: WAT
7. DEB – Luke Gertler, July 11th, 1968

8. Woodeson, p. 140
9. DEB – E, Dec. 26th, 1911: WAT
10. DEB – E, Dec. 26th, 1911: WAT
11. Maurice Brett – E, Jan. 12th, 1913: WAT
12. Zena Dare – E, Oct. 12th, 1912: WAT
13. E – DEB, Dec. 1912: WAT
14. MG – DEB, June 1913
15. Augustus John – DEB, undated: CINN
16. DEB – E, Oct. 21st, 1913: WAT
17. Bertrand Russell Archives, McMaster University Library, Canada
18. Sylvia Brooke – E, April 14th, 1914: WAT
19. Gertler
20. DEB – E, Jan. 10th, 1915: WAT
21. Vyner Brooke – E, April 20th, 1915: WAT
22. DEB – Simon Brett, June 3rd, 1969
23. E – DEB, August 1914: WAT
24. DEB – OM, Nov. 11th, 1916: AUS
25. E – DEB, 1914: AUS
26. Morrell
27. MG – DC, Jan. 20th, 1915, Gertler
28. Morrell
29. OM, AUS
30. DEB – OM, Jan. 27th, 1916: AUS
31. DEB – OM, Feb. 7th, 1914 (1915): AUS
32. DEB – OM: AUS
33. DEB – OM, undated 1915: AUS
34. DEB – OM, March 5th, 1915: AUS
35. DEB – OM, March 1915: AUS
36. Gertler
37. Gertler
38. *Westminster Gazette*, May 1915
39. E – DEB, Aug. 29th, 1914: AUS
40. DEB – OM, May 1915: AUS
41. DEB – OM, Oct. 1915: AUS
42. Moore, p. 264
43. DHL – OM, Dec. 12th, 1915: AUS
44. Brett
45. Brett
46. Holroyd
47. Lytton Strachey – James Strachey, Nov. 8th, 1915, Holroyd
48. Holroyd
49. Brett
50. Brett

THREE. 1916: OTTOLINE, p78–p89

1. DEB – E, Jan. 20th, 1916: WAT
2. DEB – Bertrand Russell, Sept. 15th, 1916: Bertrand Russell Archives
3. DEB – OM, Dec. 9th, 1916: AUS
4. DEB – E, Jan. 1917: WAT
5. DEB – OM, 1917: AUS
6. DEB – OM, (April?) 8th, 1917: AUS
7. Juliette Huxley – DEB, 1972
8. DEB – E, May 22nd, 1916: WAT
9. Morrell
10. DEB – OM, Oct. 25th, 1916: AUS
11. DEB – OM, Oct. 1st, 1916: AUS
12. DEB – OM, Oct. 25th, 1916: AUS
13. DEB – OM, Nov. 1st, 1916: AUS
14. DEB – OM, Nov. 10th, 1916: AUS
15. DEB – OM, Nov. 10th, 1916: AUS
16. DEB – OM, Nov. 1st, 1916: AUS
17. Carrington
18. Morrell
19. DEB – OM, Dec., 1918: AUS
20. DEB – OM, Oct. 25th, 1916: AUS
21. DEB – OM, Oct. 21st, 1916: AUS
22. DEB – E, Easter Sunday, 1917: WAT
23. Virginia Woolf, *Diary*, vol. 1, p. 78
24. DEB – OM, undated: AUS
25. DEB – OM, Dec. 1918: AUS
26. Morrell
27. DEB – E, Easter Sunday, 1917: WAT
28. J. M. Keynes – DEB, June 7th, 1917: CINN
29. DEB – E, July 14th, 1917: WAT

FOUR: 1917–19: GARSINGTON AND HAMPSTEAD, p90–p103

1. DEB – E, pre-Easter, 1917: WAT
2. DEB – E, June 8th, 1917: WAT
3. Sylvia Brooke – E, Aug. 11th, 1917: WAT
4. VW – Vanessa Bell, Nov. 27th, 1917: Woolf, *Letters*, vol II
5. Virginia Woolf, *Diary*, vol. 1, July 29th, 1918
6. VW – OM, Aug. 1st, 1918: *Letters*, vol. II
7. KM – DEB, Aug. 1st, 1917: private source
8. JMM – OM, Aug. 1st, 1917: AUS
9. DEB – E, Aug., 1917: WAT
10. E – DEB, Sept. 10th, 1917: AUS

11. E – DEB, Dec. 7th, 1917: AUS
12. DEB – E, Sept. 28th, 1917: WAT
13. MG – DEB, Nov. 4th, 1917: AUS
14. DEB – E, April, 1918: WAT
15. DEB – E, undated: WAT
16. DEB – E, Nov. 29th, 1917: WAT
17. DC – Lytton Strachey, Nov. 22nd, 1917, Carrington
18. Woodeson, p. 257
19. AH – Juliette Baillot, Sept. 14th, 1918: Huxley Letters
20. DEB – unpublished letters
21. AH – Juliette Baillot, Sept. 14th, 1918: Huxley Letters
22. AH – Juliette Baillot, Nov. 25th, 1918: Huxley Letters
23. AH – DEB, Dec. 1st, 1918: AUS
24. AH – DEB, Jan. 17th, 1919: AUS
25. Huxley, *Crome Yellow*, ch. XXIV, 1921
26. MG – OM, mid-1918: AUS
27. KM – OM, Dec. 4th, 1918: AUS
28. DEB – E, undated: WAT
29. Eleanor Esher – DEB, April 11th, 1919: WAT
30. E – DEB, April 12th, 1919: AUS
31. Sylvia Brooke – E, April 13th, 1919: WAT
32. DEB – E, April 1919: WAT
33. KM – DEB, June 7th, 1919: private source
34. KM – OM, June 10th, 1919: STAN
35. Teddy Seymour – E, Oct. 6th, 1919: WAT
36. Teddy Seymour – Eleanor Esher, Oct. 13th, 1919: WAT
37. DEB – OM, Oct. 20th, 1919: AUS
38. DEB – Eleanor Esher, undated: WAT
39. E – DEB, Sept. 26th, 1919: AUS
40. DEB – E, Nov. 25th, 1919: WAT
41. Private communication
42. DEB – OM, Sept. 15th, 1919: AUS
43. DEB – OM, Oct. 10th, 1919: AUS
44. VW – Vanessa Bell, Oct. 24th, 1921
45. DEB – OM, Oct. 10th, 1921: AUS

FIVE. 1920: KATHERINE 1. p104–p118

1. JMM – DEB, July 18th, 1918: CINN
2. JMM – DEB, June 1918: CINN
3. KM – DEB, March 1st, 1920: private source
4. JMM – DEB, March 8th, 1920: CINN
5. DEB Diary, 1920
6. DEB – E, July 6th, 1920: WAT

7. JMM – DEB, Aug. 5th, 1920: CINN
8. KM Journal: Reems Collection: AUS
9. KM Journal, Aug. 19th, 1920
10. DEB Diary, 1920
11. KM – DEB, Aug. 19th, 1920: private source
12. MG – OM, Sept. 23rd, 1920: AUS
13. KM – JMM, Sept. 25th, 1920: Mansfield, 1951
14. DEB Diary, 1920, page Feb. 22nd
15. DEB Diary, 1920, page Feb. 8th
16. DEB Diary, 1920, page Feb. 17th
17. JMM – DEB, Dec. 7th, 1920: CINN
18. Alpers
19. DEB – E, Dec. 14th, 1920: WAT
20. Eleanor Esher – DEB, Dec. 17th, 1920: WAT
21. DEB – E, Dec. 19th, 1920: WAT
22. E – DEB, Dec.23rd, 1920: WAT
23. DEB – E, Dec. 29th, 1920: WAT

SIX. 1921–2: KATHERINE 2. p119–p132

1. MG – OM, May 7th, 1921: AUS
2. DEB Diary, 1920
3. JMM – DEB, June 8th, 1921: CINN
4. DEB – KOT, June 8th, 1921: private source
5. KM – DEB, Aug. 8th, 1921: private source
6. DEB – KOT, Aug. 3rd, 1921: private source
7. DEB – E, Sept. 7th, 1921: WAT
8. Virginia Woolf, *Diary*, vol. II
9. DEB – KM, Jan. 29th, 1922: AUS
10. E – DEB, April 1921: WAT
11. KM – DEB, May 1st, 1922: private source
12. DEB – KOT, 1922: private source
13. Alpers
14. DEB – KOT, June 10th, 1922: private source
15. KM – KOT, Aug. 2nd, 1922: BM
16. KM – DEB, Aug. 1922: private source
17. MG – OM, Aug. 22nd, 1922: AUS
18. VW – Vanessa Bell, Dec. 22nd, 1922: Woolf, *Letters*, vol. II
19. KM – DEB, Dec. 31st, 1922: private source
20. DEB Diary, 1923, page Feb. 14th and 20th

SEVEN. 1923: MURRY. p133–p149

1. DEB – KOT, March 3rd, 1923: private source
2. JMM – DEB, April 4th, 1923: CINN

3. VW – DEB, Feb. 24th, 1923: CINN
4. Virginia Woolf, *Diary*, vol. II, March 6th, 1923
5. DEB Diary, April 18th, 1923
6. DEB Diary, April 22nd, 1923
7. JMM – DEB, May 5th, 1923: CINN
8. JMM – DEB, May 5th, 1923: CINN
9. DEB Diary, May 8th, 1923
10. DEB Diary, May 8th, 1923
11. DEB – KOT, June 3rd, 1923: private source
12. DEB Diary, June 18th, 1923
13. DEB Diary, July 21st, 1923
14. DEB Diary, July 22nd, 1923
15. DEB Diary, August 24th, 1923
16. DHL – JMM, Aug. 7th, 1923: Lawrence, 1962
17. JMM – DEB, Aug. 1923: CINN
18. MG – OM, Sept. 7th, 1923: AUS
19. MG – OM, Sept. 11th, 1923: AUS
20. DEB Diary, Sept. 30th, 1923
21. JMM – DEB, Wednesday (Oct. 3rd): CINN: although the letter is not dated, its contents and those of the following letter are referred to by Brett in a letter to Koteliansky of October 9th, 1923, which places them fairly accurately.
22. JMM – DEB, Friday (Oct. 5th), 1923: CINN (see note 21)
23. DEB – KOT, Oct. 9th, 1923: private source
24. DEB Diary, Oct. 26th, 1923
25. DEB – KOT, Nov. 11th, 1923: private source
26. DEB – KOT, Dec. 16th, 1923: private source
27. DEB – KOT, Dec. 21st, 1923: private source
28. DEB – KOT, u/d: private source
29. DEB Diary, Nov. 22nd, 1923
30. DEB – KOT, Dec. 26th, 1923: private source
31. Brett
32. DHL – MDL, Dec. 19th, 1923: Lawrence, 1962
33. BERK. 71/93C: copy of a letter from Ivy Litvinov sent by Mabel Luhan to Una Jeffers.
34. Brett, pp. 29–30
35. Brett, p. 32
36. DEB – KOT, Feb. 5th, 1924: private source
37. DHL – JMM, 1924: Lawrence, 1962
38. DHL – KOT, Feb. 9th, 1924
39. DHL – DEB, Feb. 13th, 1924: CINN
40. DEB – KOT, Feb. 25th, 1924: private source
41. FDHL – DEB, May 14th, 1932: AUS

42. DHL – Mollie Skinner, March 3rd, 1924: Lawrence, 1962
43. DEB Diary, March 2nd, 1924
44. Carrington, March 3rd, 1924
45. MG – OM, July 9th, 1924: AUS

EIGHT. 1924–5: RANANIM p150–p176

1. Brett, p. 42
2. Luhan
3. Rachel Hawk, private communication
4. Luhan, p. 191
5. Luhan
6. Luhan
7. Brett
8. Lawrence, Frieda, pp. 143–4
9. DHL – JMM, Oct. 3rd, 1924
10. DHL – Catherine Carswell, Oct. 7th, 1924
11. Brett, p. 159
12. Brett, p. 172
13. DHL – W. Hawk, Nov. 14th, 1924
14. Brett, p. 176
15. Brett, pp. 193–4
16. Brett, p. 199
17. Brett
18. DHL – DEB, January 1925: CINN
19. Brett, p. 205
20. Lawrence, Frieda, p. 140
21. Brett, p. 207
22. Brett, p. 208
23. Brett, p. 209
24. DHL – DEB, Jan. 26th, 1925: AUS
25. FDHL – DEB, Feb. 20th, 1925: CINN
26. DHL – DEB, February 1925: CINN
27. FDHL – DEB, March 1925: CINN
28. Brett, p. 215
29. FDHL – DEB, undated: CINN
30. Brett
31. Brett, p. 229
32. Rachel Hawk, private communication
33. FDHL – DEB: CINN
34. Brett
35. Brett, p. 230
36. DHL – DEB: CINN
37. FDHL – DEB, 1925: CINN

38. Brett
39. Nehls, vol. II, p. 410
40. Rachel Hawk, private communication
41. Brett, p. 241
42. Brett, p. 243
43. Brett, p. 236

NINE. 1925–6: EUROPE p177–p195

1. Brett
2. Brett
3. Brett
4. Brett
5. DHL – DEB, Sept. 15th, 1925: CINN
6. DHL – DEB, Sept. 17th, 1925: CINN
7. DHL – DEB, Sept. 28th, 1925: CINN
8. DHL – DEB, Oct. 8th, 1925: CINN
9. DHL – DEB, Oct. 29th, 1925: CINN
10. DHL – DEB, Nov. 4th, 1925: CINN
11. OE – DEB, December 1925: WAT
12. MG – OM, Oct. 16th, 1925: AUS
13. MG – KOT, Nov. 20th, 1925: Gertler
14. MG – OM, Dec. 9th, 1925: AUS
15. FDHL: CINN
16. JMM – DEB, Dec. 9th, 1925: CINN
17. DHL – DEB, Nov. 19th, 1925: CINN
18. DHL – DEB, Nov. 26th, 1925: CINN
19. Nehls
20. DHL – DEB, Dec. 7th, 1925: CINN
21. DEB – E, Jan. 26th, 1926: WAT
22. FDHL – DEB, Dec. 11th, 1925: CINN
23. DHL – DEB, December 1925: CINN
24. Brett, pp. 287–8
25. DHL – DEB, Dec. 20th, 1925: CINN
26. Private communication
27. Lawrence, Frieda, pp. 167–8
28. Lawrence, Frieda, p. 168
29. DHL (*Glad Ghosts*)
30. DHL – DEB, Feb. 11th, 1926: CINN
31. Brett, p. 281
32. Brett, p. 286
33. Brett, p. 284
34. Brett, p. 287
35. Private communication

36. Brett, p. 292
37. Brett, pp. 292–3
38. Brett, MS 2
39. Brett, MS 2
40. DHL – DEB, March 17th, 1926: CINN
41. DHL – DEB, March 28th, 1926: CINN
42. DHL – DEB, March 20th, 1926: CINN
43. Brett, MS 2
44. DHL – E. and A. Brewster, April 11th, 1926
45. DHL – DEB, April 5th, 1926: CINN
46. DHL – DEB, April 8th, 1926: CINN
47. FDHL – DEB, undated 1926: CINN
48. DHL – DEB, April 12th, 1926: CINN
49. DHL – E. and A. Brewster, April 20th, 1926
50. DHL – DEB, April 23rd, 1926: CINN

TEN. 1926–30: THE RANCH p196–p212

1. DHL – DEB, July 1926: CINN
2. FDHL – DEB, Aug. 20th, 1926: CINN
3. DHL – DEB, October 1926: CINN
4. DHL – DEB, Nov. 24th, 1926: CINN
5. DHL – MDL, Feb. 21st, 1927: YALE
6. DHL – DEB, March 8th, 1926: CINN
7. DHL et al – DEB, March 24th, 1927: CINN
8. DHL – DEB, May 13th, 1925: CINN
9. DHL – E. and A. Brewster, 1927
10. DHL – DEB, Feb. 12th, 1928: CINN
11. DEB – Montagne, Feb. 24th, 1928: YALE
12. DEB – MDL, 1928: YALE
13. DEB – AS, Aug. 10th, 1928: YALE
14. DEB – Spud Johnson, Nov. 24th, 1928: AUS
15. DEB – AS, Nov. 28th, 1928: YALE
16. DHL – DEB, March 2nd, 1929: CINN
17. DHL – E. and A. Brewster, June 2nd, 1929
18. FDHL – MDL, Sept. 4th, 1929: YALE
19. DHL – DEB, April 27th, 1929: CINN
20. FDHL – MDL, May 15th, 1929: YALE
21. DHL – DEB, May 19th, 1929: CINN
22. DHL – DEB, June 23rd, 1929: CINN
23. DEB – AS, June 20th, 1929: YALE
24. DEB – MDL, July 15th, 1929: YALE
25. John Marin – AS, July 21st, 1929
26. FDHL – DEB, July 29th, 1929: CIN

27. FDHL – MDL, July 29th, 1929: YALE
28. DEB – AS, Aug. 10th, 1929: YALE
29. FDHL – DEB, Aug. 20th, 1929: CINN
30. DHL – DEB, Sept. 9th, 1929: CINN
31. DHL – DEB, Sept. 12th, 1929: CINN
32. DHL – DEB, Sept. 19th, 1929: CINN
33. DHL – DEB, Sept. 29th, 1929: CINN
34. DEB – AS, Oct. 5th, 1929: YALE
35. DEB – AS, Nov. 27th, 1929: YALE
36. DHL – DEB, Dec. 12th, 1929: CINN
37. DHL – DEB, Jan. 8th, 1930: CINN
38. DEB – MDL, Feb. 14th, 1930: YALE
39. DEB – MDL, Feb. 18th, 1930: YALE
40. DHL – DEB, Jan. 24th, 1930: CINN
41. Eleanor Esher – DEB, Jan. 25th, 1930: AUS
42. FDHL – DEB, Jan. 21st, 1930
43. DEB – MDL, March 3rd, 1930: YALE
44. DEB – KOT, March 4th, 1930
45. DEB – FDHL, March 3rd, 1930: BERK

ELEVEN. 1930–5: THE TOWER BEYOND TRAGEDY. p213–p228

1. Alfred Barnes – DEB, Feb. 13th, 1930: AUS
2. DEB – MDL, March 1930: YALE
3. FDHL – DEB, March 1930: CINN
4. MDL – DEB: AUS
5. DEB – AS, April 1930: YALE
6. DEB – AS, April 18th, 1930: YALE
7. DEB – AS, May 3rd 1930: YALE
8. DEB – AS, Oct. 26th, 1930: YALE
9. DEB, Will 2, Dec. 28th, 1932
10. MDL – UJ Aug. 2nd, 1931: BERK
11. MDL – UJ, June 3rd, 1931: BERK
12. DEB – AS, June 2nd, 1931: YALE
13. DEB – UJ, July 3rd, 1931: BERK
14. DEB – AS, Oct. 18th, 1941: YALE
15. DEB – UJ, 1932: BERK
16. DEB – AS, Feb. 1933: YALE
17. DEB – AS, Oct. 1st, 1932: YALE
18. DEB – UJ, April 24th, 1933: BERK
19. MDL – UJ, 1933: BERK
20. MDL – UJ, May 6th, 1933: BERK
21. DEB – AS, May 19th, 1933: YALE

22. DEB – AS, Nov. 19th, 1932: YALE
23. DEB – AS, Feb. 14th, 1933: YALE
24. Marianna Howes, private communication
25. DEB – MDL, Oct. 20th 1933: YALE
26. DEB – EG, Oct. 24th, 1933
27. DEB – EG, Nov. 12th, 1933
28. DEB – UJ, Dec. 10th, 1933: BERK
29. DEB – EG, Jan. 20th, 1934
30. *Philadelphia Record*, Dec. 16th, 1934
31. *Time Magazine*, May 8th, 1944
32. AS – DEB, Dec. 12th, 1934: YALE
33. DEB – AS, Jan. 10th, 1935: YALE
34. AS – DEB, Jan. 20th, 1935: YALE
35. DEB – AS, 1936: YALE
36. JMM – DEB, Aug. 13th, 1934: CINN
37. MDL – UJ, Oct. 12th, 1934: BERK
38. AS – DEB, June 28th, 1935: YALE
39. DEB – AS, July 19th, 1935: YALE
40. DEB – UJ, May 4th, 1935: BERK
41. DEB – AS, July 5th, 1935: YALE
42. AS – DEB, July 13th, 1923: YALE
43. MDL – UJ, Sept. 19th, 1935: BERK
44. DEB – UJ, Sept. 14th, 1935: BERK
45. DEB – AS, Sept. 14th, 1935: YALE

TWELVE. 1936–43: THE CHAPLINE ROOF AND MABELTOWN p229–p238

1. Kiker – DEB, Oct. 28th, 1935: YALE
2. AH – Julian Huxley, June 3rd, 1937
3. MDL – DEB, undated
4. MDL – DEB, 1937
5. DEB – MDL, Aug. 5th, 1937: YALE
6. DEB – UJ, March 4th, 1937: BERK
7. DEB – MDL, Nov. 24th, 1938: YALE
8. DEB – MDL, Jan. 27th, 1938: YALE
9. DEB – AS, Jan. 28th, 1938: YALE
10. DEB – UJ, Feb. 18th, 1938: BERK
11. FDHL – Angelo Ravagli, Feb. 16th, 1938: YALE
12. OE – DEB. Feb. 17th, 1938: AUS
13. DEB – OE, July 11th, 1938: WAT
14. JMM – DEB, July 3rd, 1938: CINN
15. DEB – AS, July 11th, 1938: YALE
16. DEB – Dorothy Norman, May 10th, 1942: YALE

17. DEB – AS, May 30th, 1939: YALE
18. OE – DEB, Feb. 3rd, 1939: AUS
19. DEB – OE, April 28th, 1939: WAT
20. DEB – OE, Oct. 19th, 1939: WAT
21. DEB – OE, July 29th, 1940: WAT
22. Aug. 30th, 1940: AUS
23. DEB – MDL, Oct. 12th, 1940
24. DEB – OE, May 26th, 1940: WAT
25. OE – DEB, July 2nd 1940: AUS
26. DEB – OE, July 29th, 1940 WAT
27. DEB – OE, October 12th, 1940: WAT
28. DEB – OE, Nov. 1st, 1940: WAT
29. Purser
30. DEB – OE, undated: WAT
31. DEB – OE, Jan. 24th, 1943: WAT
32. DEB – UJ, Jan. 5th, 1941: BERK
33. OE – DEB, March 11th, 1947: AUS
34. Sylvia Brooke – DEB, April 12th, 1943: AUS
35. OE – DEB, Oct. 21st, 1941: AUS
36. JMM – DEB, Aug. 29th, 1940: CINN
37. JMM – DEB, Dec. 6th, 1940: CINN
38. DEB – Dorothy Norman, March 10th, 1943: YALE
39 DEB – OE, March 3rd, 1943: WAT
40 DEB – OE, July 5th, 1943: WAT

THIRTEEN; 1943–56: THE EL PRADO STUDIO p239–p249

1. DEB – EG undated
2. DEB – Dorothy Norman, May 10th, 1942: YALE
3. DEB – MDL, May 1943: YALE
4. DEB – MDL, May 1942: YALE
5. MDL – DEB, 1942: YALE
6. MDL – DEB, 1942: YALE
7. DEB – Dorothy Norman, May 10th, 1942: YALE
8. DEB – Spud Johnson, July 30th, 1943: AUS
9. MDL – DEB, 1944: YALE
10. MDL – DEB, Aug. 3rd, 1945: YALE
11. DEB – OE, July 4th, 1945: WAT
12. DEB – OE, Aug. 10th, 1945: WAT
13. DEB – OE, Aug. 26th, 1945: WAT
14. DEB – B. Chavez, Oct. 16th, 1948
15. DEB – UJ, July 15th, 1946: BERK
16. DEB – Simon Brett, Jan. 26th, 1968
17. DEB – OE, Oct. 26th, 1947, WAT

18. JMM – DEB, Aug. 30th, 1948: CINN
19. FDHL – DEB, Jan. 4th, 1948: YALE
20. DEB – OE, Aug. 28th, 1947: WAT
21. DEB – OE, Sept. 28th, 1949: WAT
22. FDHL – DEB, Nov. 14th, 1949
23. FDHL – DEB, Dec. 28th, 1949
24. DEB – OE, Nov. 14th, 1949: WAT
25. FDHL – DEB, Jan. 6th, 1950: YALE
26. FDHL – DEB, Jan. 18th, 1950: YALE
27. FDHL – DEB, Dec. 7th, 1950: YALE
28. FDHL – MDL, Dec. 30th, 1950: YALE
29. DEB – B. Chavez, Dec. 7th, 1951
30. Feb. 5th, 1953: Harvard Library
31. March 13th, 1953: YALE
32. DEB – OE, Dec. 6th, 1949: WAT
33. DEB – Dorothy Norman, March 17th, 1953: YALE
34. OE – DEB, November 1952
35. DEB, Aug. 15th 1955

FOURTEEN: 1956–69: MINK COATS AND BAKED BEANS p250–p259

1. DEB – FDHL, Jan. 17th, 1956: AUS
2. DEB – B. Chavez, April 12th, 1951
3. DEB – OE, Feb. 14th, 1949: WAT
4. DEB – Tiny Rimpoche, Jan. 19th, 1956
5. See e.g. chequebook stubs for 1957
6. Angelo Ravagli – DEB, Dec. 9th, 1959: AUS
7. *The Times*, Dec. 24th, 1957
8. John Rothenstein – DEB, July 25th, 1959
9. DEB – LE, Oct. 23rd, 1965: WAT
10. DEB – LE, February 1966: WAT
11. DEB – J. Brandenberg (Taos Bank), June 15th, 1966
12. DEB – J. Brandenberg, Dec. 15th, 1966
13. Simon Brett – LE, Jan. 5th, 1967: WAT
14. DEB – LE, June 1966: WAT
15. DEB – LE, June 19th, 1967: WAT
16. DEB – LE, May 14th, 1967: WAT
17. Jan. 28th, 1964
18. March 1966
19. April 12th, 1966
20. April 20th, 1967
21. December 1967
22. Feb. 14th, 1968

23. March 21st, 1968
24. May 27th, 1969
25. Sept. 17th, 1969
26. Nov. 30th, 1969
27. October 1970
28. 1976

FIFTEEN: 1970–7: CEREMONIALS AND POT-BOILERS p260–p263

1. DEB – LE, July 18th, 1970: WAT
2. Moore
3. DEB – Author, Aug. 20th, 1970
4. *Women's Wear Daily*, July 17th, 1970
5. DEB – LE, Jan. 18th, 1970: WAT
6. John Manchester, June 29th, 1977

Select Bibliography

Alpers, Anthony. *Katherine Mansfield*, London: Jonathan Cape, 1954 and 1980

Brett, Dorothy. *Lawrence and Brett: a Friendship*, New York; Lippincott, 1933

Brooke, Sylvia. *Queen of the Headhunters*, London: Sidgwick & Jackson, 1970

Brooke, Sylvia. *Sylvia of Sarawak*, London: Hutchinson, 1936

Carrington, Dora. *Carrington: Letters and Extracts from her Diaries*, Chosen and with an Introduction by David Garnett. London: Jonathan Cape, 1970

Fraser, Peter. *Lord Esher: a Political Biography*, London: Hart-Davis, MacGibbon, 1973

Gertler, Mark. *Selected Letters*. Edited by Noel Carrington, and with an Introduction by Quentin Bell, London: Rupert Hart-Davis, 1965

Holroyd, Michael. *Lytton Strachey: a Biography* and *Lytton Strachey and the Bloomsbury Group*, London: William Heinemann, 1967 and 1968

Huxley, Aldous. *Crome Yellow*, London: Chatto & Windus, 1921

Huxley, Aldous. *Letters of Aldous Huxley*. Edited by Grover Smith, London: Chatto & Windus, 1969

Lawrence, D. H. *Collected Letters*. Edited by Harry T. Moore, London: Heinemann, 1962

Lawrence, Frieda. *Not I But the Wind*, London: Heinemann, 1935

Luhan, Mabel. *Lorenzo in Taos*, London: Secker, 1933

Mansfield, Katherine. *Letters from Katherine Mansfield*. Two volumes. Edited by John Middleton Murry, London: Constable, 1928 and *Journals of Katherine Mansfield*, London: Constable, 1927

Moore, Harry T. *The Priest of Love* (previously titled *The Intelligent Heart: the Story of D. H. Lawrence*) London: Heinemann, 1955, 1962, 1974 Penguin, 1976

Morrell, Ottoline. *Ottoline: The Early Memoirs of Lady Ottoline Morrell*. Edited by Robert Gathorne Hardy, London: Faber, 1963

Nehls, Edward. *D. H. Lawrence: a Composite Biography*. Three volumes, Madison, Wisconsin: University of Wisconsin Press, 1957–9

Purser, Philip. *Where is He Now?*, London: Quartet, 1978
Woodeson, John. *Mark Gertler*, London: Sidgwick & Jackson, 1982
Woolf, Virginia. *Diary*. Edited by Anne Olivier Bell. Four volumes, London: Hogarth Press, 1977–82
Letters. Edited by Nigel Nicolson & Joanne Trautmann. Six volumes, London: Hogarth, 1975–80

Index

Note: abbreviations used in the Index –

D.E.B Dorothy Brett
D.H.L. D. H. Lawrence
F.D.H.L. Frieda Lawrence
K.M. Katherine Mansfield
O.M. Lady Ottoline Morrell
J.M.M. John Middleton Murry

NOTTINGHAM
UNIVERSITY LIBRARY